DICTIONARY OF MEDIA AND COMMUNICATION STUDIES

DICTIONARY OF MEDIA AND COMMUNICATION STUDIES

James Watson and Anne Hill

7th Edition

Hodder Arnold

A MEMBER OF THE HODDER HEADLINE GROUP

First published in Great Britain in 1984
Second edition 1989
Third edition 1993
Fourth edition 1997
Fifth edition 2000
Sixth edition 2003
Seventh edition published in 2006 by
Hodder Education, a member of the Hodder Headline Group,
338 Euston Road, London NW1 3BH

www.hoddereducation.com

Distributed in the United States of America by
Oxford University Press Inc.
198 Madison Avenue, New York, NY 10016

British Library Cataloguing in Publication Data
A catalogue record for this book is available from the British Library

Library of Congress Cataloguing-in-Publication Data
A catalog record for this book is available from the Library of Congress

ISBN-10: 0 340 91338 X
ISBN-13: 978 0 340 91338 3

1 2 3 4 5 6 7 8 9 10

EG 35414

LEARNING C. √

302. 2303

WAT

Typeset in 8.5 on 11.5pt Baskerville BE by Phoenix Photosetting, Chatham, Kent
Printed and bound by Gutenberg Press, Malta

What do you think about this book? Or any other Hodder
Education title? Please send your comments to the feedback
section on www.hoddereducation.com.

PREFACE TO THE 7TH EDITION

It is an axiom in the study of communication that what is absent is generally as significant as what is present. At all levels, communication is about selecting in and selecting out; and the fascination of study is to investigate presences and omissions and the reasons for these. Compiling dictionaries is also all about selection: what qualifies for an entry; at what point has an entry ceased to be important enough to retain?

Obviously a lexicon of terms must reflect the ever-changing cultural landscapes in which it is produced and used. It owes a duty to the past as well as to the present, thus in all our editions of the *Dictionary of Media and Communication* the legacy of the radical journalism of the nineteenth century has been ring-fenced for posterity (see TAXES ON KNOWLEDGE and UNDERGROUND PRESS).

We keep faith, too, with the pioneers of the *study* of communication. While conceding that GATEKEEPING is an infinitely more complex process than is illustrated in WHITE'S GATEKEEPING MODEL, 1950, we acknowledge David White's lasting contribution to our understanding of the process of mass communication.

What is particularly evident in the study of mass communication is the speed at which new technologies have driven production of media and reception. The mobile phone is now a leisure centre. The massive expansion of INTERNET use has impacted on our lives in ways that would have amazed even Marshall McLuhan, the media prophet of the 1960s, and would have had him coining new phrases to slip eloquently off the tongue and spark off the page. Communicative power seems to be experiencing seismic shifts, though whether these shifts will progress or be reversed by the Usual Suspects as far as the exercise of control is concerned, it is hard to predict (see BLOGGING).

In their agenda-setting model of 1987 E.M. Rogers and J.W. Dearing refer to spectacular news events that impact on the nature and direction of communication. Existing patterns and trends are suddenly knocked sideways, or forced into touch by events that command the headlines so dramatically that nothing in life, at the personal, community, national or global level, is ever the same again. The terrorist attacks on New York and the US Pentagon on 11 September 2001 (9/11) were one of those spectacular events.

9/11 led to the 'war on terror'. As far as our dictionary is concerned, this produced a new batch of entries on the upsurge, particularly in the States and in Britain, of new legislation, new laws of censorship; and when war on terror became invasion, of Afghanistan and Iraq, the focus of attention inevitably turned to issues of war reporting, of the performance of media in times of war, of the relationship between governments and media, of the predicament faced by multiculturalism in a divided world (see the expanded entry, COMMUNICATION: INTERCULTURAL COMMUNICATION).

On to the lexical terrain now step EMBEDDED REPORTERS and NEWS MANAGEMENT IN TIMES OF WAR. In the UK, clashes between the New Labour government and the BBC prompted reports by Lords Hutton and Butler in 2004. The London bombings of 7 July 2005 (7/7) have prompted government measures aimed at defeating terrorism while at the same time being perceived as a threat to freedoms of speech and expression.

Readers will note in this 7th edition an expansion in coverage of public relations communication (see BERNSTEIN'S WHEEL; JOHNSON AND SCHOLES: STAKEHOLDER MAPPING; PUBLICS), and updated entries on broadcasting following the UK Communications Act of 2003 and the establishment of Ofcom, the Office of Communications, the UK's broadcasting regulatory body.

There has been much tidying up, some painful excisions and over 50 new entries, including one that really should have been there from the start: MEDIA THEORY: PURPOSE AND USES. Also a little tardily comes in DOWNLOADING and, on the theme of surveillance and information control, PODCASTING and PSYOPS bow in along with INDY MEDIA and JOURNALISM: CITIZEN JOURNALISM.

We are delighted to see that, at least in Europe, PUBLIC SERVICE BROADCASTING continues (more or less) to hold its own in the real world. As for the torrent of technological change, we confess to hanging on with our fingertips as the new is passé almost before it has reached the customer. However, whether they are consumers, citizens, listeners, viewers or interactors on the net, people respond to the pace of change according to their own needs and priorities; sometimes ahead of the game, sometimes resistant to the imperatives of technology.

They may be subjected to spin, but as the ACTIVE-AUDIENCE THESIS suggests, they are not necessarily *in* a spin. As for whether the population is becoming a nation of couch potatoes or whether the media that serve them have become dumbed down, we can only say – read on.

James Watson and Anne Hill

ABOUT THE AUTHORS

James Watson is now Visiting Lecturer in Media Studies on the BA in Media and Communication Studies offered by the University of Greenwich in partnership with West Kent College in Tonbridge. He is also author of *Media Communication: An Introduction to Theory and Process* (UK: Palgrave Macmillan, 2nd edition, 2003) and a number of books for young readers, including *Talking in Whispers.*

Anne Hill is now Principal Lecturer in Communication Studies at Southampton Solent University.

A CHECKLIST FOR USE

- Words in CAPITALS mean that there is a separate entry.

- Source references are included in the text of the relevant entry rather than presented in an end-of-dictionary bibliography.

- Use is made of an asterisk (*) at the end of some entries: here books of special interest or value for further reading on the topic are recommended.

- The traditional practice of referring to the city or town where a book was first published has been modified in this dictionary, reference being made to the country of origin (US or UK).

- Where *c.* is used it is an abbreviation for century.

- Communication models are listed using the name of the person(s) who conceived them (e.g. SHANNON AND WEAVER'S MODEL OF COMMUNICATION, 1949), and commissions/committees on the media are referred to by the name of the chairperson(s) (e.g. PILKINGTON COMMISSION REPORT ON BROADCASTING (UK), 1962).

ACKNOWLEDGEMENTS

The publishers and authors would like to thank the following for permission to include copyright material.

AEJMC for: 'White's gatekeeper model, 1950', page 307, from *Journalism Quarterly* 27 (1950); 'Wesley and MacLean's model of communication', page 305, from *Journalism Quarterly* 34 (1957); 'McNelly's model of news flow, 1959', page 165, from *Journalism Quarterly* 36 (1959); 'Bass's "double action" model, 1969', page 22, *Journalism Quarterly* 46 (1969).

Sage Publications Ltd for: 'Kepplinger and Habermeier's model of events', page 97, from *European Journal of Communication*, September 1995; 'Ball-Rokeach and DeFleur's dependency model of communication effects, 1976', page 19, from *Communication Research* 3 (1976); 'Rogers and Dearing's agenda-setting model, 1987', page 251, from *Communication Yearbook* 11; 'McQuail's accountability of media model', page 166, from *European Journal of Communication*, (1997); 'McQuail's audience analysis', page 15, from *Audience Analysis* by Denis McQuail, Sage (1997); 'Westerståhl and Johansson's model of news factors in foreign news, 1994', page 306, from *European Journal of Communication*, March 1994; 'Griswold's cultural diamond model, 1994', page 118, from *Cultures and Societies in a Changing World*, Pine Forge Press, 1994.

Harcourt Publishers for: 'Dance's helical model of communication', page 74, from *Human Communication Theory*, edited by Frank Dance, Rinehart & Winston (1967); 'Berlo's SMCR model of communication, 1960', page 25, from *The Process of Communication: An Introduction to Theory and Practice,* by David K. Berlo, Holt, Rinehart & Winston (1960).

HarperCollins Publishers for: 'Barnlund's transactional models of communication, 1970', pages 20–21, *Foundations of Communication Theory* edited by K.K. Sereno and C.D. Mortensen, Harper & Row (1970).

Perseus Books Group for: 'Riley and Riley's model of mass communication, 1959', page 250, from *Sociology Today: Problems and Prospects*, edited by Robert K. Merton, Leonard Broom and Leonard S. Cottrell, Jr, Basic Books (1959).

Sam Becker for: 'Becker's mosaic model of communication, 1968', page 24, from the University of Minnesota's Spring Symposium in Speech Communication (1968).

Hans-Bredow/Institut for: 'Maletzke's model of the mass communication process', page 157, from *The Psychology of Mass Communications*, Verlag Hans-Bredow-Institut (1963).

Palgrave Publishers for 'The news revolution model', page 8, from *News Revolution* by Mark D. Alleyne (1997).

International Communication Association for: 'Eisenberg's model of communication and identity, 2001', page 90, from 'Building a mystery: toward a new theory of communication and identity' by Eric A. Eisenberg, published in the *Journal of Communication*, September 2001.

Every effort has been made to trace and acknowledge ownership of copyright. The publishers will be glad to make suitable arrangements with any copyright holders whom it has not been possible to contact.

ABBREVIATIONS: A SELECTION

AA	Advertising Association
AAP	Australian Associated Press
ABA	Australian Broadcasting Authority
ABE	Association of British Editors
ABS	Association of Broadcasting & Allied Staffs
ACTT	Association of Cinematography, Television & Allied Technicians
ADP	Association of Directors & Producers; Automatic Data Processing
ADSL	Asymmetrical Digital Subscriber Line
AFDC	Australian Film Development Corporation
AFP	Agence France-Presse
AIJ	Association of Investigative Journalists
ALCS	Author's Lending & Copyright Society
AP	Associated Press
AR	Audience Research
ASA	Advertising Standards Authority
ATV	Associated Television (Associated Broadcasting Company)
BAFTA	British Academy of Film & TV Arts
BAPLA	British Association of Picture Libraries & Agencies
BARB	Broadcasters Audience Research Board
BBC	British Broadcasting Corporation
BBFC	British Board of Film Classification
BBS	Bulletin Board System
BCC	Broadcasting Complaints Commission
BFI	British Film Institute
bit	binary digit
BJA	Black Journalists' Association
BLT	Bright, Light and Trite
BMIG	British Media Industry Group
BMWA	Black Media Workers Association
bps	bits per second
BSB	British Satellite Broadcasting
BSC	British Society of Cinematography
BSC	Broadcasting Standards Council
BT	British Telecom
CACI	Campaign Against Censorship of the Internet
CAM	Communications Advertising & Marketing Educational Foundation
CAP	Code of Advertising Practice; Campaign Against Pornography
CAR	Computer Assisted Reporting
CARM	Campaign Against Racism in the Media
CATV	Cable Antenna Television System
CCCS	Centre for Contemporary Cultural Studies (University of Birmingham)
CCD	Charge-Coupled Device
CCN	Cable News Network
CD	Compact Disc
CDA	Critical Discourse Analysis

CDV	Compact Disc Video
CIPR	Chartered Institute of Public Relations
CMCS	Computer Mediated Communication Systems
CNNI	Cable News Network International
COI	Central Office of Information
CPBF	Campaign for Press & Broadcasting Freedom
CPJ	Committee to Protect Journalists (US)
CRA	Community Radio Association
CRIS	Communication Rights in the Information Society
CRT	Cathode Ray Tube
DAB	Digital Audio Broadcasting
DBS	Direct Broadcasting Satellite
DIT	Digital Imaging Technology
DOS	Disc Operating System
DP	Data Processing
DTP	Desk Top Publishing
DTT	Digital Terrestrial Television
DVD	Digital Video Disc; Digital Versatile Disc
EBU	European Broadcasting Union
EDP	Electronic Data Processing
EFF	Electronic Frontiers Foundation
ENG	Electronic News Gathering
ENS	Electronic Newsroom System
ESM	Experience Sampling Method
FAIR	Fairness and Accuracy in Reporting (US)
fax	facsimile
FFE	Fund for Free Expression (US)
FFE	Feminists for Free Expression
FM	Frequency Modulation
FOIA	Freedom of Information Act (US)
GAK	Government Access to Keys
GAMA	Global Alternative Media Association
GBNE	Guild of British Newspaper Editors
GCHQ	Government Communications Headquarters
GIGO	Garbage In, Garbage Out (computer operator's acronym)
GII	Global Information Infrastructure
GPS	Global Positioning System
HDTV	High-Definition Television
HDVS	High-Definition Video System
HF	High Frequency
HMD	Head Mounted Display
HMSO	Her Majesty's Stationery Office
IAD	Internet Addiction Disorder
IAMCR	International Association of Mass Communication Research
IARP	Independent Association of Radio Producers
IBA	Independent Broadcasting Authority (succeeded by the ITC in 1991)
IBM	International Business Machines

Abbreviations: a selection

IBT	International Broadcasting Trust
ICANN	Internet Corporation for Assigned Names and Numbers
ICF	Internet Crime Foundation
IFEX	International Freedom of Expression Exchange
IFFI	International Foundation for Freedom of Information
IFJ	International Federation of Journalists
IFVA	Independent Film & Video Makers Association
IGC	Institute for Global Communications
ILR	Independent Local Radio
INR	Independent National Radio
Intelsat	International Telecommunications Satellite (consortium)
IOJ	International Organization of Journalists
IPA	Institute of Practitioners in Advertising
IPA	International Publishers' Association
IPC	International Publishing Corporation
IPDC	International Programme for the Development of Communication
IPI	International Press Institute
Iras	Infra-red astronomy satellite
IRL	In Real Life
ISBN	International Standard Book Number
ISDN	Integrated Services Digital Networks
ISN	International Services Digital Networks
ISOC	Internet Society
ISP	Internet Service Provider
IT	Information Technology
ITC	Independent Television Commission
ITCA	Independent TV Companies Association
ITU	International Telecommunications Union
ITV	Independent Television
IV	Interactive Video
IWF	Internet Watch Foundation
IWMF	International Women's Media Foundation
IWPR	Institute for War and Peace Reporting
JICNAR	Joint Industrial Council for Newspaper Audience Research
JICPAR	Joint Industrial Council for Poster Audience Research
JICRAR	Joint Industrial Committee for Radio Audience Research (succeeded by RAJAR in 1992)
JICTAR	Joint Independent Committee for TV Advertising Research
LAN	Local Area Network
laser	light amplification by stimulated emission radiation
LED	Light Emitting Diode
LOP	Least Objectionable Programme
MBS	Mutual Broadcasting System
MDC	More Developed Country
MIS	Management Information System
MO	Mass Observation
modem	modulator-demodulator
MOMI	Museum of the Moving Image
MMX	Multi-Media Extensions
MPAA	Motion Picture Association of America

MR	Motivation Research
MUD	Multi-User Domain
NAHBO	National Association of Hospital Broadcasting Organizations
NANAP	Non-Aligned News Agencies Pool
NASB	National Association of Student Broadcasting
NBC	National Broadcasting Company (US)
NCIS	National Criminal Intelligence Service (UK)
NCU	National Communications Union
NFA	National Film Archive
NFT	National Film Theatre
NGO	Non-Government Agency
NIC	Newly Industrialized Country
NIIO	New International Information Order
NPA	Newspaper Publishers Association (UK)
NUJ	National Union of Journalists
NVLA	National Viewers & Listeners Association
NWICO	New World Information & Communication Order
OB	Outside Broadcast
OCR	Optical Character Recognition
Ofcom	Office of Communications (UK)
Oftel	Office of Telecommunications (UK)
PA	Press Association
PC	Politically Correct; Personal Computer
PCC	Press Complaints Commission
PEN	Poets/Playwrights/Editors/Essayists/Novelists: PEN International
PII	Public Interest Immunity
PKC	Public Key Cryptography
PLR	Public Lending Rights
PR	Public Relations
PRN	Public Relations News
PSI	Para-Social Interaction
PSN	Public Switched Network
RA	Radio Authority
RAJAR	Radio Joint Audience Research (succeeded JICRAR in 1992)
RDS	Radio Data System
RI	Reaction Index
RIPA	Regulation of Investigatory Powers Act (UK)
RMB	Radio Marketing Bureau
RP	Received Pronunciation
rpm	revolutions per minute
RSF	Reporters Sans Frontières
RSI	Repetitive Strain Injury
RTS	Royal Television Society
SCA	Speech Communication Association (US)
SEFT	Society for Education in Film & Television
SIGINT	Signals Intelligence
STV	Straight-To-Video
SYNCOM	Synchronous Communication Satellite

Abbreviations: a selection

TAM	Television Audience Measurement
T&SG	Television & Screen Writers Guild
TBDF	Trans-Border Data Flow
THESIS	*Times Higher Education Supplement* Internet Service
TNAUK	Talking Newspaper Association of the United Kingdom
TNC	Transnational Corporation
TTL	Through The Lens
UDHR	Universal Declaration of Human Rights
UHF	Ultra High Frequency
UNESCO	United Nations Educational Scientific and Cultural Organization
UPI	United Press International
USP	Unique Selling Point/Proposition
VDU	Visual Display Unit
VES	Video Encoding Standard
VHD	Video High Density
VHF	Very High Frequency
VHS	Video Home System
VLV	Voice of the Listener & Viewer
VR	Virtual Reality
WELL	Whole Earth Lectronic Link (US)
WPFC	World Press Freedom Committee
WSET	Writers & Scholars Educational Trust
WSIS	World Summit on the Information Society
WWW	World Wide Web

TOPIC GUIDE

Entries are summarized under the following topic headings:

ADVERTISING/MARKETING
AUDIENCES/CONSUMPTION & RECEPTION OF MEDIA
BROADCASTING
COMMISSIONS, COMMITTEES, LEGISLATION
COMMUNICATION MODELS
COMMUNICATION THEORY
CYBERCULTURE: THE NET, THE WEB
GENDER MATTERS
GLOBAL PERSPECTIVES
INTERPERSONAL COMMUNICATION
LANGUAGE/DISCOURSE/NARRATIVE
MEDIA ETHICS
MEDIA: FREEDOM, CENSORSHIP
MEDIA HISTORY
MEDIA INSTITUTIONS
MEDIA ISSUES & DEBATES
MEDIA: OWNERSHIP & CONTROL
MEDIA: POLITICS & ECONOMICS
MEDIA: POWER, EFFECTS, INFLUENCE
MEDIA: PROCESSES and PRODUCTION
MEDIA: TECHNOLOGIES
MEDIA: VALUES & IDEOLOGY
NEWS MEDIA
RESEARCH METHODS
REPRESENTATION
TEXTUAL ANALYSIS

ADVERTISING/MARKETING

Advertising; Advertising: ambient advertising; Advertising: pester power; Advertising Standards Authority (ASA); AIDA model; Alter-EU; Attention model of mass communication; Attitudes; Audience; Audience: active audience; Audience appreciation; Audience: fragmentation of; Audience differentiation; Audience measurement; Bernstein's wheel; Campaign; Class; Commercial *laissez-faire* model of (media) communication; Commercial radio; Conglomerates; Congruence theory; Connotation; Consumerization; Consumer sovereignty; Consumption behaviour; Content analysis; Cultural capital; Culture; Culture: consumer culture; Culture: globalization of; Culture: popular culture; Custom audience research; Decode; Deconstruction; Demographic analysis; Dissonance; Dominant, subordinate, radical; Effects of the mass media; Encode; Ethnographic (approach to audience measurement); Expectations, horizons of; Expectations; Focus groups; Franchises for Independent Television (UK); Franchises from 1993; Gantt chart; Gender; Grunig and Hunt model: four models of public relations practices, 1984; Hegemony; Hidden Needs; Identification; Idents; Ideology; Image; Image, rhetoric of; Infomercials; Information blizzards; Infotainment; Interpretant; Intertextuality; Intervening variables (IV); iSociety; JICNARS scale; Johnson and Scholes: stakeholder mapping; Latitudes of acceptance and rejection; Marketing; Market research; Maslow's hierarchy of needs; Media imperialism; Metonymy; Motivation; Motivation research (MR); News: public relations news (PR); Niche audience; Nielsen ratings; Object language; One-step, two-step, multi-step flow model of communication; Opinion leader; Passivity; Perception; PIE chart; Play theory of mass communication; Polysemy; Pressure groups; Product placement; PR: Public relations; Publics; Reading; Reception studies; Reflexivity; Reinforcement; Representation; Resistive reading; Resonance; Salience; Sampling; Selective exposure; Self-concept; Self-identity; Self-presentation; Semantic differential; Semiology/Semantics; Semiotic power; Sign; Signature files; Signification; Smiling professions; Socialization; Sponsorship; Sponsorship of broadcast programmes (UK); Stakeholders; Status; Stereotype; Structuralism; Subliminal; Surveillance society; SWOT; Tactics and strategies; Ten commandments for media consumers; Tertiary text; Text; Uses and Gratifications theory; VALS typology; Values.

AUDIENCES/CONSUMPTION & RECEPTION OF MEDIA
Accessed voices; Advertising: pester power; Attention model of mass communication; Audience; Audience: active audience; Audience appreciation; Audience: fragmentation of; Audience differentiation; Audience measurement; Blogging; Boomerang response; Button apathy; Catharsis; Commercial *laissez-faire* model of (media) communication; Compassion fatigue; Complicity of users; Consensus; Consistency; Constituency; Consumerization; Consumer sovereignty; Consumption behaviour; Cultivation differential; Cultural capital; Cultural, or citizen rights and the media; Culture; Culture: consumer culture; Culture: globalization of; Custom audience research; Decode; Dependency theory; Deregulation: five myths of; Disempowerment; Desensitization; Displacement effect; Dissonance; Dominant, subordinate, radical; Downloading; Effects of the mass media; Emancipatory uses of the media; Empowerment; Ethnographic (approach to audience measurement); Expectations, horizons of; Expectations; Extracted information; Focus groups; Frankfurt school of theorists; Global scrutiny; Gossip networks; Hegemony; Historical allusion; HICT Project; Hidden Needs; Homophily; Hyperdermic needle model of communication; Identification; Ideology of romance; Information blizzards; Information gaps; Interpretant; Intervening variables (IV); iSociety; J-Curve; JICNARS scale; Knowns, Unknowns; Kuleshov effect; Kuuki; Latitudes of acceptance and rejection; Maslow's hierarchy of needs; Misinformed society; Motivation; Mobilization; Motivation research (MR); Niche audience; News: audience evaluation, six dimensions of; Ofcom: Office of Communications (UK); One-step, two-step, multi-step flow model of communication; Opinion leader; Panopticon gaze; Parasocial interaction; Passivity; PEST; Play theory of mass communication; Pleasure: active and reactive; Polysemy; Public opinion; Publics; Prejudice; Reading; Realism; Reception studies; Reflexivity; Reinforcement; Resistive reading; Resonance; Right of reply; Salience; Selective exposure; Self-fulfilling prophecy; Self-identity; Semiotic power; Socialization; Surveillance society; SWOT; Tactics and strategies; Ten commandments for media consumers; Uses and Gratifications theory; VALS typology; Values.

BROADCASTING
Annan Commission Report on Broadcasting (UK), 1977; Balanced programming; BARB; BBC Digital; BBC, government white paper, 1994; BBC, origins; Beveridge Committee Report on Broadcasting (UK), 1950; British Media Industry Group (BMIG); Broadband; Broadcasting Act (UK), 1990; Broadcasting Act (UK), 1995; Broadcasting Act (UK), 1980; Broadcasting legislation; Cable television; Campaign for Press & Broadcasting Freedom; Campaign for Quality Television Report (UK), 1999; CCTV: closed-circuit television; Ceefax; Cellular radio; Channel 4; 'Clean-up TV Movement'; Colour TV; Commercial radio; Communications Act (UK), 2003; Community radio; Cross-media ownership; Digitization; Duopoly; Europe: cross-border TV channels; Fourteen-day rule (UK); Franchises for Independent Television (UK); Franchises from 1993; Hankey Committee Report on Television (UK), 1943; High-definition TV; Hunt Committee Report on Cable Expansion and Broadcasting Policy (UK), 1982; Hutton Report (UK), 2004; Interactive television; Internet: wireless Internet; KPFA Radio; Media-Most; Minority Report of Mr Selwyn Lloyd; Naturalistic illusion (of television); Ofcom: Office of Communications (UK); Paper Tiger TV; Pilkington Committee Report on Broadcasting (UK), 1962; Pirate radio; Podcasting; Programme flow; Public service broadcasting (PSB); Quotas; Radio broadcasting; Radio Northsea; RAJAR; Reality TV; Reflective-projective theory of broadcasting and mass communication; Reithian; Saniel Pedwar Cymru; Satellite transmission; Scheduling; Secondary viewing; Selsdon Committee Report on Television (UK), 1935; Sit-com; Soap opera; Social action broadcasting; Soundbite; Sound Broadcasting Act (UK), 1972; Sponsorship of broadcast programmes (UK); Telegenic; Teletext; Television: access television; Television broadcasting; Television drama; Television news; Time-shift viewing; Ullswater Committee Report on Broadcasting (UK),

1936; Universality; Video; 'War of the Worlds'; Westminster view; Wireless Telegraphy Act (UK), 1904; World Trade Organization (WTO) Telecommunications Agreement, 1997.

COMMISSIONS, COMMITTEES, LEGISLATION

Annan Committee Report on Broadcasting, 1977; Broadcasting Act, 1980; Broadcasting Act, 1990; Broadcasting Act, 1996; Broadcasting legislation; Butler Report (UK), 2004; Campaign for Quality Television Report (UK) 1999; Commissions/committees on the media; Communications Act (UK) 2003; Cross-media ownership; Communications Decency Act (US); Defamation; Fairness Doctrine (US); Franchises for Independent Television (UK); Franchises from 1993; Freedom of Information Act (UK), 2005; Human Rights Act (UK), 2000; Hunt Committee Report on Cable Expansion and Broadcasting Policy, 1982; Hutton Report (UK), 2004; Libel; Paperwork Reduction Act (US), 1980; Phillis Review of Government Communications (UK), 2004; Pirate Radio (UK); Prior Restraint; Regulation of Investigatory Powers Act (RIPA) (UK), 2000; SLAPPS; Sponsorship; Sponsorship of broadcast programmes (UK); Terrorism: Terrorism, Crime and Security Act (UK), 2001; Text: integrity of the text; Video Recording Act (UK), 1984; Wireless Telegraphy Act, 1904; World Trade Organization (WTO) Telecommunications Agreement, 1997

COMMUNICATION MODELS

Alleyne's news revolution model, 1997; Andersch, Staats and Bostrom's model of communication, 1969; Attention model of mass communication; Ball-Rokeach and DeFleur's dependency model of mass communication effects, 1976; Barnlund's transactional models of communication, 1970; Bass's double action model of internal news flow, 1969; Becker's mosaic model of communication, 1968; Commercial *laissez-faire* model of (media) communication; Dance's helical model of communication, 1967; Eisenberg's model of communication and identity, 2001; Galtung and Ruge's model of selective gatekeeping, 1965; Gerbner's model of communication, 1956; Grunig and Hunt: four models of public relations practices, 1984; Herman and Chomsky's propaganda model (see CONSENT, MANUFACTURE OF); Hypodermic needle model of communication; Jakobson's model of communication, 1958; Kepplinger and Habermeier's model of media events, 1995 (see EVENT); Lasswell's model of communication, 1948; Maletzke's model of the mass communication process, 1963; McCombs and Shaw's agenda-setting model of media effects, 1976; McLeod and Chaffey's 'kite' model, 1973; McNelly's model of news flow, 1959; McQuail's accountability of media model, 1997; McQuail's four stages of audience fragmentation (see AUDIENCE: FRAGMENTATION OF); Newcomb's ABX model of communication, 1953; Noelle-Neumann's spiral of silence model of public opinion, 1974; One-step, two-step, multi-step flow models of communication; Propaganda model (see CONSENT, MANUFACTURE OF); Riley and Riley's model of mass communication, 1959; Griswold's cultural diamond model, 1994; Schramm's models of communication, 1954; Rogers and Dearing's agenda-setting model, 1987; Shannon and Weaver's model of communication, 1949; S-IV-R model of communication; Tripolar model of competing agendas (see ROGERS AND DEARING'S AGENDA-SETTING MODEL, 1987); Wesley and MacLean's model of communication, 1957; Westerstähl and Johansson's model of news factors in foreign news, 1994; White's gatekeeper model, 1950.

These and other models not included in the Dictionary – such as Comstock's psychological model of television effects on individual behaviour, 1978, DeFleur's model of the American mass media system, 1979, and Gieber and Johnson's model of source-reporter relations, 1961 – may be read about in detail in *Communication Models for the Study of Mass Communications* (UK: Longman, 5th impression, 1998) by Denis McQuail and Sven Windahl.

COMMUNICATION THEORY

Allness attitude; Attribution theory; Audience; Codes; Codes of narrative; Communication; Communication: intercultural communication; Communication models; Communication, Non-verbal (NVC); Communicative rationality; Congruence theory; Convergence; Cultural capital; Culture; Culture: globalization of; Cybernetics; Cyberspace; Decode; Deconstruction; Dependency theory; Discourse; Discourse analysis; Disempowerment; Eisenberg's model of communication and identity, 2001; Encode; Ethnocentrism; Frankfurt school of theorists; Functionalist (mode of media analysis); Groups; Guard dog metaphor; Hegemony; Hot media, cold media; Hyperreality; Identification; Ideology; Interpersonal communication; Johari Window; Life positions; Linguistic determinism; Linguistics; Lookism; Market liberalism; Marxist (mode of media analysis) Maslow's hierarchy of needs; Meaning; Mediasphere; Media theory: purpose and uses; Medium; Message; Metamessage; Mobilization; M-time, P-time; Narrative; Narrative paradigm; Noise; Normative theories of mass media; Objectivity; Panopticon gaze; Paradigm (paradigmatic); Paradigms of the media; Play theory of mass communication; Postmodernism; Postulates of communication; Primacy, the law of; Proxemics; Queer theory; Realism; Reflective-projective theory of broadcasting and mass communication; Resonance; Roles; Sapir-Whorf linguistic relativity hypothesis; Scripts; Self-concept; Self-fulfilling prophecy; Self-identity; Semiology/Semiotics; Semiotic power; Sign; Social action (mode of media analysis); Structuralism; Stereotype; Supervening social necessity; Symbolic convergence theory; Symbolic interactionalism; Technique: Ellul's theory of technique; Technological determinism; Television news: inherent limitations; Texts; Transactional analysis; Uses and Gratifications theory; VALS typology.

CYBERCULTURE: THE NET, THE WEB
Blogging; Communications Decency Act (US); Convergence; Culture: copyrighting culture; Cybernetics; Cyberspace; Downloading; Globalization of media; Hacker, Hacktivist; Hyperreality; Indy media; Journalism: citizen journalism; Mobilization; N-Gen; New media; Podcasting; Pornography; Pretty Good Privacy; Regulation of Investigatory Powers Act (RIPA) (UK), 2000; Signature files; Teledemocracy; Text: integrity of the text; Transculturation; USA- Patriot Act, 2001; Virtual reality; Wiki, Wikipedia; Web: World Wide Web (www).

GENDER MATTERS
Empowerment; Expectations; Feminism; Film noir; Gender; Gender and media monitoring; Gendered genre; Genderlects; He/man language; Ideology of romance; Intimization; Male-as-norm; News: the 'maleness' of news; Patriarchy; Pleasure: active and reactive; Profane language; Queer theory; Report-talk rapport-talk; Representation; Semiotic power; Stereotype.

GLOBAL PERSPECTIVES
Al-Jazeera; Blogging; Commanders of the social order; Commoditization of information; Communication: intercultural communication; Consumerization; Convergence; Core nations, peripheral nations; Culture: copyrighting culture; Culture: globalization of; Cyberspace; Empowerment; Ethnocentrism; Europe: cross-border TV channels; Globalization of media; Globalization: three engines of; Global media system: the main players; Hybridization; Internet; Localization and transnational TV; M-time, P-time; MacBride Commission; McDonaldization; McWorld vs Jihad; Media imperialism; Misinformed society; Mobilization; MTV; Media moguls: four sources of concern; Murdoch effect; New media; News: globalization of; New World Information Order; News management in times of war; Organization cultures; Postmodernism; Press barons; Publics; Self-identity; Talloires Declaration, 1981; Teledemocracy; Transculturation; Universality; Yamousoukrou declaration; Wiki, Wikipedia; World Trade Organization (WTO) Telecommunications Agreement, 1997.

INTERNET, See CYBERCULTURE: THE NET, THE WEB; AND MEDIA: TECHNOLOGIES

INTERPERSONAL COMMUNICATION
Accent; Anti-language; Apache silence; Assertiveness training; Attitudes; Attribution theory; Bad language; Civil inattention; Closure; Cocktail party problem; Communication; Communication: intercultural communication; Communication, Non-verbal (NVC); Congruence theory; Confirmation/disconfirmation; Conversational styles; Defensive communication; Disqualifying communication; Dress; Eisenberg's model of communication and identity, 2001; Elaborated and restricted codes; Empathy; Eye contact; Facial expression; First impressions; Framing: Interpersonal; Gestural dance; Gender; Gesture; Gossip; Gossip networks; Groups; GSR; Guide signs; Halo effect; Head nods; Homophily; Identification; Impression management; Indicators; Influence; Insult signals; Integration; Interpersonal communication; Intervening variables (IV); Johari Window; Kineme; Kinesics; Latitudes of acceptance and rejection; Leadership; Life positions; Listening; Metamessage; Metasignals; M-time, P-time; Newcomb's ABX model of communication, 1953; Non-verbal behaviour: repertoire; Non-verbal vocalizations; Object language; Orientation; Other;

Overhearing; Perception; Personal idiom; Personal space; Postural echo; Posture; Projection; Proxemics; Queer theory; Report-talk-rapport-talk; Roles; Scripts; Self-concept; Self-disclosure; Self-fulfilling prophecy; Self-identity; Self-monitoring; Self-presentation; Shortfall signals; Silence; Situational properties; Strategy; Tag questions; Territoriality; Tie-signs; Touch; Transactional analysis; Values; Zones.

LANGUAGE/DISCOURSE/NARRATIVE

Accent; Anti-language; Arbitrariness; Assertiveness training; Bad language; Climax order; Codes; Codes of narrative; Cognitive (and affective); Common sense; Communication: intercultural communication; Communicative rationality; Connotation; Conversational styles; Corporate speech; Crime and the media; Crime: types of crime on screen; Cultural capital; Cultural memory; Cultural modes; Culture; Culture of deference; Deep structure; Determiner deletion; Diachronic linguistics; Dialect; Discourse; Discursive gap; Disqualifying communication; Dominant discourse; Eisenberg's model of communication and identity, 2001; Elaborated and restricted codes; Emotive language; Fiction values; Film noir; Flashback; Framing: media; Gendered genre; Genderlects; Gossip; Hedges; He/man language; Iconic; Ideational functions of language; Idiolect; Journalese; Kineme; LAD (Language Acquisition Device); Lame; Language pollution; Langue and parole; Lexis; Linguistic determinism; Linguistics; Machinery of representation; Male-as-norm; Metaphor; Metonomy; Modality; Morphology; Narration; Narrative; Narrative: kernel and satellite; Narrative paradigm; Newspeak; News: the 'maleness of news'; Object language; Onomatopoeia; Open, closed texts; Paradigm; Performatives; Personal idiom; Phatic language; Phoneme; Phonetics; Phonology; Polarization; Postmodernism; Profane language; Projection; Propp's people; Proxemics; Radio Death; Reading; Realism; Received pronunciation (RP); Redundancy; Reflexivity; Register; Report-talk, rapport-talk; Rhetoric; Sapir-Whorf linguistic relativity hypothesis; Semantics; Semiology/Semiotics; Sentence meaning, utterance meaning; Sign; Slang; Soaps; Style; Tag questions; Television drama (UK); Text; Text: integrity of text; Traditional transmission; Verbal devices in speech-making.

MEDIA ETHICS

Advertising: pester power; Alter-EU; Butler Report (UK), 2004; Commercial Confidentiality; Communications Decency Act (US); Cross-media ownership; Data protection; Democracy and the media; Flak; Human Rights Act (UK), 2000; Human Rights Watch; Index; Internet: monitoring of content; Journalism; McQuail's accountability of media model, 1997; Media: alternative (or radical) media; Media theory: purpose and uses; Normative theories of mass media; People's Communication Charter; Privacy; Radio Death; Reality TV; Reithian; Supervening social necessity; Taste; Television: access television; Ten commandments for media consumers; Universality.

MEDIA: FREEDOM, CENSORSHIP

'Areopagitica'; Article 19; Blogging; Butler Report (UK), 2004; Clipper chip; Commercial Confidentiality; Communications Decency Act (US); Conspiracy of silence; Data protection; Democracy and the media; Defamation; D-Notices; Echelon; Embedded reporters; Freedom of Information Act (UK), 2005; Gagging order; Hays Office; H-certificate; Historical allusion; HUAC: Hutton Report (UK), 2004; House Un-American Activities Committee; Human Rights Act (UK), 2000; Human Rights Watch; Index; Internet: monitoring of content; Lord Chamberlain; Media-Most; Milton's paradox; Music: censorship of music; Official Secrets Act (UK); Opera Omnia; Oz trial; New media; News management in times of war; Panopticon gaze; Paperwork Reduction Act (US), 1980; Phillis Review of Government Communications (UK), 2004; Pool system; Pretty Good Privacy (PGP); Prior restraint; Privacy; Psyops; Regulation of Investigatory Powers Act (RIPA) (UK), 2000; Re-regulation; SLAPPS, 'Somme, The Battle of the; Spycatcher case; Stamp Duty; Supervening social necessity; Surveillance society; Taste; Terrorism: Anti-Terrorism, Crime and Security Act (UK), 2001; USA – Patriot Act, 2001; Video nasties; War: four stages of war reporting; Wiki, Wikipedia; Williams Committee Report on Obscenity and Film Censorship, 1979; World Press Freedom Committee; World Trade Organization (WTO) telecommunications agreement, 1997; Zinoviev letter, 1924; Zircon affair.

MEDIA HISTORY

Agit-prop; Agora; Alexandra Palace; Animation; 'Areopagitica'; Audience measurement; BBC, origins; Beveridge Committee Report on Broadcasting, 1950; Bribery; British Board of Film Censors; British Film

Institute; Calotype; Camera; Celluloid; Cigarette cards; Cine-clubs; Cinema Legislation; Cinematography, origins; Cinéma Vérité; 'Clean up TV' movement; Colour TV; Comics; Commercial radio; Communications Act (UK), 2003; Convergence; Cylinder or rotary press; Daguerreotype; Digitization; Facsimile; Federal Communications Commission (FCC); Federal Radio Commission; Film noir; Fourteen-Day Rule (UK); Fourth estate; Franchises for Independent Television; Franchises for 1993; Global jukebox; Gramophone; Hays Office; H-certificate; HUAC: House Un-American Activities Committee; Kinetoscope; Linotype printing; Lithography; Lord Chamberlain; March of Time; Mass Observation; McGregor Commission Report on the Press (UK), 1977; Minority Report of Mr Selwyn Lloyd; Miracle of Fleet Street; Monotype printing; Morse Code; Musical – film musical; Newspapers, origins; Newsreel; Nickelodeon; Northcliffe revolution; 'Pencil of Nature'; Persistence of vision; Phonodisc; Photography, origins; Photogravure; Photo-journalism; Picture postcards; Pilkington Committee Report on Broadcasting (UK), 1962; Pirate radio (UK); Poor Man's Guardian; Posters; Press barons; Printing; Privacy; Press Complaints Commission Code of Practice, 1977; Projection of pictures; Public service broadcasting (PSB); Radio broad-casting; Radio drama; Reithian; Roll film; Satellite transmission; Selsdon Committee Report on Television (UK) 1935; Shawcross Commission Report on the Press, (UK) 1962; 'Somme, The Battle of the'; Sound Broadcasting Act (UK), 1972; Stamp Duty; Stereoscopy; Synchronous sound; Telegraphy; Telephone; Telerecording; Television broadcasting; Thaumatrope; Typewriter; Ullswater Committee Report on Broadcasting, (UK) 1936; V-discs; Victim funds; Video; Vitaphone; 'War of the Worlds'; Watergate; Wireless telegraphy; Yellow Kid; Zinoviev letter, 1924; Zoopraxography.

MEDIA INSTITUTIONS
Advertising Standards Authority (ASA); BBC, origins; British Board of Film Censors; British Film Institute; British Media Industry Group (BMIG); Casualization; Commanders of the Social Order; Commercial radio; Communications Act (UK), 2003; Conglomerates; Core nations, peripheral nations; Deregulation; Deregulation: five myths of; Diversification; Europe: cross-border TV channels; Globalization of media; Guard dog metaphor; Indy media; Institution; Media imperialism; Network; New media; News agencies; News: globalization of; News management in times of war; Newspapers, origins; Normative theories of mass media; Occupying powers; Ofcom: Office of Communications (UK); Organization cultures; Power; Press; Press barons; Press Complaints Commission; Public service broadcasting (PSB); Radio Broadcasting; Regulatory favours; Television; Underground Press; World Trade Organization (WTO) Telecommunications Agreement, 1997.

MEDIA ISSUES & DEBATES
Advertising; Audience: active audience; Butler Report (UK), 2004; Censorship; Commanders of the social order; Commoditization of information; Communications Act (UK), 2003; Computers in communication; Conglomerates; Consumerization; Core nations, peripheral nations; Crime and the media; Cultural or citizen rights and the media; Culture: globalization of; Cyberspace; Data protection; Dependency theory; Deregulation; Deregulation: five myths of; Disempowerment; Downloading; Effects of the mass media; Empowerment; Ethnocentrism; Feminism; Freedom of Information Act (UK), 2005; Gatekeeping; Globalization of media; Globalization: three engines of; Global media systems: the main players; Hegemony; Hutton Report (UK), 2004; Hyperreality; Ideological presumption; Ideological state apparatus-es; Ideology; Ideology of romance; Impartiality; Information gaps; Journalism; Journalism: citizen journalism; Journalism: celebrity journalism; Localization and transnational TV; McDonaldization; McQuail's accountability of media model, 1997; McWorld vs Jihad; Media: alternative (or radical) media; Media theory: purpose and uses; Mobilization; Murdoch effect; News aid?; News management in times of war; News: the 'maleness' of news; News values; New World Information Order; Objectivity; Other; People's Communication Charter; Phillis Review of Government Communications (UK), 2004; Pool System; Polysemy; Pornography; Power; Predatory pricing; Privacy; Privatization; Producer Choice; Psyops; Public opinion; Public service broadcasting (PSB); Public sphere; Queer theory; Reality TV; Racism; Regulatory favours; Representation; Right of Reply; Self-identity; Showbusiness, age of; SLAPPS; Sponsorship; Sponsorship of broadcast programmes (UK); Supervening social necessity; Surveillance society; Tabloid, tabloidese, tabloidization; Text, integrity of the text; Virtual reality; Wedom, Theydom; Web: World Wide Web (www); World Trade Organization (WTO) Telecommunications Agreement, 1997.

MEDIA: OWNERSHIP & CONTROL

Advertising; Advertising Standards Authority (ASA); Agenda-setting; Alter-EU; British Media Industry Group (BMIG); Berlusconi phenomenon; Casualization; Citizen Kane of the Global Village; Class; Commanders of the social order; Commercial confidentiality; Commoditization of information; Communications Act (UK), 2003; Cross-media ownership; Conglomerates; Consumerization; Convergence; Cultural apparatus; Culture: copyrighting of culture; Culture: globalization of; Deregulation; Diversification; Elite; Europe: cross-border TV channels; Frankfurt school of theorists; Functionalist (mode of media analysis); Globalization of media; Globalization: the engines of; Global media system: the main players; Guard dog metaphor; Hegemony; Ideological state apparatuses; Ideology, Indy media; Journalism; Journalism: citizen journalism; Leadership; Localization and transnational TV; Market liberalism; Marxist (mode of media analysis); McGregor Commission Report on the Press (UK), 1977; McLeod and Chaffee's 'kite' model, 1973; Media control; Media moguls: four sources of concern; Media-Most; Murdoch effect; New media; News: globalization of; News management in times of war; Northcliffe revolution; Occupying powers; Ofcom: Office of Communications (UK); Organization cultures; People's Communication Charter; Phillis Review of Government Communications (UK), 2004; Power; Power elite; Press barons; Privatization; Producer choice; Public service broadcasting (PSB); Publics; Public sphere; Regulatory favours; Social Action (mode of media analysis); Sponsorship; Sponsorship of broadcast programmes (UK); Synergy; World Trade Organization (WTO) Telecommunications Agreement, 1997.

MEDIA: POLITICS & ECONOMICS

Accusatory studies; Advertising; Accessed voices; Alleyne's news revolution model, 1977; Audience; Berlusconi phenomenon; Butler Report (UK), 2004; Commoditization of information; Consent, manufacture of; Conspiracy of silence; Core nations, peripheral nations; Class; Cultural apparatus; Cultural capital; Cultural or citizen rights and the media; Culture; Culture: globalization of; Democracy and the media; Deregulation, five myths of; Elite; Empowerment; Ethnocentrism; Fairness Doctrine (US); Fatwa; Feminism; Flak; Frankfurt school of theorists; Functionalist (mode of media analysis); Freedom of Information Act (UK), 2005; Gagging order; Guard dog metaphor; Hegemony; Human Rights Act (UK), 2000; Hutton Report (UK), 2004; Ideological state apparatus; Ideology; Intervention; Leaks; Lobby practice; Legitimation/delegitimation; Machinery of representation; Market liberalism; Marxist (mode of media analysis); Media: alternative (or radical) media; Media control; Media imperialism; Media moguls: four sources of concern; Media-Most; Mediasphere; Mediatization; Misinformed Society; New World Information Order; News management in times of war; Orientalism; Paradigms of media; Politics of accommodation; Polysemy; Power; Press barons; Privatization; Professionalization (of political communication); Public opinion; Public service broadcasting (PSB); Public sphere; Regulatory favours; Sponsorship; *Spycatcher* case; Surveillance society; Synergy; Television: access television; Terrorism as communication; Terrorism, Crime and Security Act (UK), 2001; USA – Patriot Act, 2001; World Trade Organization (WTO) Telecommunications Agreement, 1997; Zinoviev letter, 1924.

MEDIA: POWER, EFFECTS, INFLUENCE

Accessed voices; Agenda-setting; Anecdote; Anomie; Attitudes; Attribution theory; Audience; Ball-Rokeach and DeFleur's dependency model of communication effects, 1976; Bigotry; Butler Report (UK), 2004; Catalyst effect; Colonization; Commoditization of information; Compassion fatigue; Consensus; Consent, manufacture of; Consistency; Conspiracy theory; Consumerization; Contagion effect; 'Coups and earthquakes' syndrome; Crime and the media; Crisis (definition); Cultivation; Cultural or citizen rights and the media; Democracy and the media; Deviance amplification; Disempowerment; Displacement effect; Effects of the mass media; Extracted information; Frankfurt school of theorists; Global media system: the main players; Hutton Report (UK), 2003; Hypodermic needle model of communication; Ideological state apparatuses; Ideology; Information blizzards; Inheritance factor; Intervening variables (IV); Journalism; Kuleshov effect; Kuuki; Labelling process (and the media); Legitimation/delegitimation; Mainstreaming; McCombs and Shaw's agenda-setting model of media effects, 1976; Media imperialism; Media moguls: four sources of concern; Mediasphere; Mobilization; Moral panic; MTV; Multiplier effect; Narcotizing dysfunction; News management in times of war; Noelle-Neumann's spiral of silence model of public opinion, 1974; Other; Pornography; Power; Primacy, law of; Public opinion; Psyops; Radio Death; Resonance; Self-fulfilling prophecy; Showbusiness, age of; Significant spiral; Sleeper effect; Slow-drip; 'Somme, The Battle of the'; Survivors and the media; Television news: inherent limitations; VALS typology; Visions of order.

MEDIA: PROCESSES & PRODUCTION

Advertising; Agenda-setting; Anchorage; Attention model of mass communication; Attitudes; Blogging; Commoditization of information; Common sense; Compassion fatigue; Conglomerates; Convergence; 'Coups and earthquakes' syndrome; Culture; Culture: globalization of; Demonization; Determiner deletion; Diffusion; Digitization; Ethnocentrism; Fly on the wall; Folk devils; Framing: media; Gatekeeping; Gendered genre; Guard dog metaphor; Hammocking effect; Historical allusion; Hyphenized abridgement; Immediacy; Impartiality; Intensity; Intimization; Journalism; Journalism: citizen journalism; Label libel; Labelling process (and the media); Legitimation/delegitimation; Lookism; Loony leftism; Mainstreaming; Mediation; Mediatization; Mobilization; Multi-actuality; Myth; New media; News; News management in times of war; Structure of reassurance; One-step, two-step, multi-step models of communication; Other; Packaging; Performatives; Personalization; Personalizing Transformation; Power; Programme flow; Publics; Radio Death; Reality TV; Representation; Scheduling; Slow motion; Socialization; Special effects; Tabloid, tabloidese, tabloidization; Television news: inherent limitations; Voiceover; Vox popping; Wedom, Theydom; Wiki, Wikipedia.

MEDIA: TECHNOLOGIES

BBC Digital; Bookmark (electronic); Broadband; CCTV: closed-circuit television; Clipper chip; Colour TV; Computer graphics; Connectivity; Cyberspace; Cylinder or rotary press; Daguerreotype; Digitization; Digital retouching; Digital video disc (DVD); Downloading; Electronic newsgathering; Fibre-optic technology; Flat-screen technology; Gramophone; Hacker, hacktivist; High-speed photography; Holography; Interactive television; Internet; Internet: wireless Internet; Journalism: citizen journalism; Kinetoscope; Kuleshov effect; Linotype printing; Lithography; Mobilization; Newsroom, The; Omnimax; Photography, origins; Photomontage; Phototypesetting; Podcasting; Pretty Good Privacy; Printing; Projection of pictures; Satellite transmission; Speech-recognition technology; Stereoscopy; Supervening social necessity; Technique: Ellul's theory of technique; Technological determinism; Telegraphy; Telematics; Telephone; Telerecording; Television broadcasting; Typewriter; Video; Vitaphone; Web: World Wide Web; Wireless telegraphy; World Trade Organization (WTO) Telecommunications Agreement, 1977; Xerography; Zoetrope; Zoopraxography.

MEDIA: VALUES & IDEOLOGY

Accessed voices; Agenda-setting; Agenda-setting research; Audience; Balanced programming; Bias; Bigotry; British Board of Film Censors; Calcutt Committee Reports on Privacy and Related Matters, 1990 and 1993; Campaign for Press and Broadcasting Freedom; Censorship; Certification of films; Chapultepec, Declaration of, 1994; Chequebook journalism; 'Clean up TV' movement; Communications Decency Act (US); Conglomerates; Consensus; Consent, manufacture of; Conspiracy of silence; Conspiracy theory; Consumerization; Convergence; Counter-culture; Coups and earthquakes syndrome; Cultivation; Cultural apparatus; Culture: consumer culture; Culture: copyrighting culture; Culture: globalization of; Culture of deference; Culture: popular culture; Cyberspace; Defamation; Democracy and the media; Demonization; Deregulation, five myths of; Deviance; Deviance amplification; Discourse; Discourse analysis; Disempowerment; D-Notices; Dominant discourse; Effects of the mass media; Elite; Emancipatory use of the media; Emergent culture; Emotive language; Empowerment; Ethnocentrism; Exnomination; Feminism; Fiction values; Folk devils; Framing: media; Frankfurt school of theorists; Freedom of Information Act (UK), 2005; Functionalist (mode of media analysis); Gatekeeping; Gender; Glasgow University Media Group; Globalization of media; Global scrutiny; Guard dog metaphor; Gultang and Ruge's model of selective gatekeeping, 1965; Hegemony; HUAC: House Un-American Activities Committee; Human Rights Act (UK), 2000; Ideological presumption; Ideological state apparatuses; Ideology; Ideology of romance; Image, rhetoric of; Immediacy; Impartiality; Implication; Information gaps; Infotainment; Institution; Intensity; International Federation of Journalists (IFJ); Intimization; Invisibility; Issues; Jingoism; Journalism; Journalism: celebrity journalism; Journalism: 'postmodern journalism'; Knowns, Unknowns; Kuuki;

Labelling process (and the media); Legitimation/delegitimation; Lobby practice; MacBride Commission; Machinery of representation; Mainstreaming; Marginality; Market liberalism; Marxist (mode of media analysis); McCombs and Shaw's agenda-setting model of media effects, 1976; McQuail's accountability of media model, 1997; McWorld vs Jihad; Media: alternative (or radical) media; Media imperialism; Mediasphere; Moral entrepreneurs; Moral panic; Mr Gate; Myth; News; News Aid?; News frameworks; News: globalization of; News: the 'maleness' of news; News values; New World Information Order; Non-aligned News Pool; Normative theories of the mass media; Objectivity; Orientalism; Other; Paper Tiger TV; Partisan; People's Communication Charter; Personalization; Photo-journalism; Pornography; Postmodernism; Power; Preferred reading; Prejudice; Press barons; Press Complaints Commission (UK); Privacy; Privacy: Press Complaint's Commission Code of Practice, 1977; Propaganda; Public opinion; Public service broadcasting (PSB); Public sphere; Racism; Realism; Reinforcement; Reithian; Representation; Rogers and Dearing's agenda-setting model, 1987; Self-identity; Sexism; Signification spiral; Silence: strategic silence; Soap opera; Social action (mode of media analysis); Socialization; Sociometrics (and media analysis); 'Somme, The Battle of the'; Sponsorship; *Spycatcher* case; Status quo; Stereotype; Structuralism; Sub-culture; Surveillance society; Tabloid, tabloidese, tabloidization; Technique: Ellul's theory of technique; Teledemocracy; Ten commandments for media consumers; Underground press; Values; Video nasties; Violence and the media; Visions of order; Watchdogs; Watergate; Wedom, Theydom; Western; Westerståhl and Johansson's model of news factors in foreign news, 1994; Whistle-blowing; Wiki, Wikipedia; Youth culture; Zinoviev letter, 1924; Zircon affair.

NEWS MEDIA

Agenda-setting; Agenda-setting research; Alleyne's news revolution model, 1997; Al-Jazeera; Anchorage; Bass's 'double action' model of international news flow, 1969; Chronology; Compassion fatigue; Coups and earthquakes syndrome; Crimes of self-publicity; Critical news analysis; Determiner deletion; Embedded reporters; Event; Fiction values; Framing: media; Frequency; Gagging order; Galtung and Ruge's model of selective gatekeeping, 1965; Historical allusion; Horse-race story; Hyphenized abridgement; Ideological presumption; Immediacy; Impartiality; Implication; Indy media; Intensity; Intimization; J Curve; Journalism; Journalism: celebrity journalism; Journalism: citizen journalism; Journalism: 'postmodern journalism'; Journalism: Project for Excellence in Journalism (US), 1995; Knowns, unknowns; Kuuki; Marginality; McLeod and Chaffee's 'kite' model, 1973; McNelly's model of news flow, 1959; News; News agencies; News: audience evaluation, six dimensions of; News elements: breaking, explanatory, deep background; News: globalization of; News management in times of war; News: public relations news (PR); News: structure of reassurance; News: the 'maleness' of news; News values; Newsroom, The; One-step, two-step, multi-step flow models of communication; Performatives; Personalization; Photojournalism; Phillis Review of Government Communications (UK), 2004; Pool system; Psyops; Representation; Rogers and Dearing's agenda-setting model, 1987; Significant spiral; Silence: strategic silence; Spot news; Television news: inherent limitations; Visions of order; War: four stages of war reporting; Westerståhl and Johansson's model of news factors in foreign news, 1994; White's gatekeeper model, 1950.

RESEARCH METHODS

Agenda-setting research; Audience measurement; Children, young people and the changing media environment; Communicology; Consumption behaviour; Content analysis; Control group; Crime: types of crime on screen; Critical news analysis; Cultivation differential; Custom audience research; Deconstruction; Demographic analysis; Discourse analysis; Empirical; Ethnographic (approach to audience measurement); Experimental group; First impressions; Focus groups; Functionalist (mode of media analysis); Glasgow University Media Group; Groups; HICT Project; Interviews; JICNARS scale; Marxist (mode of media analysis); Mass observation; Mean world syndrome; Media theory: purpose and uses; Motivation research (MR); Narrative paradigm; Nielsen ratings; One-step, two-step, multi-step flow models of communication; Paradigms of media; Participant observation; People meter; Pleasure: active and reactive; Proxemics; Public opinion; Reception studies; Research centres (into the media); Sampling; Segmentation; Semantic differential; Sleeper effect; Social action (mode of media analysis); Sociometrics (and media analysis); Viewers: light, medium and heavy; Vox popping; Wiki, Wikipedia.

REPRESENTATION

Caricature; Chronology; Collective representations; Colonization; Coups and earthquakes syndrome; Crime and the media; Crime: types of crime on screen; Demonization; Determiner deletion; Deviance; Deviance amplification; Dominant, subordinate, radical; Ethnocentrism; Folk devils; Gender; Gender and media monitoring; Hegemony; Invisibility; Label libel; Labelling process (and the media); Machinery of representation; Narrative; News; News: the 'maleness' of news; Orientalism; Other; Paraproxemics; Pornography; Power; Primary, secondary definers; Propaganda; Public opinion; Publics; Queer theory; Racism; Realism; Reality TV; Representation; Self-fulfilling prophecy; Self-identity; Sign; Soap operas; 'Somme, The Battle of the'; Stereotype; Style; Visions of order.

TEXTUAL ANALYSIS

Aberrant decoding; Anchorage; Audience; Audience: active audience; Audience, fragmentation of; Bad language; Berlo's SMCR model of communication, 1960; Bowdlerize; Bricolage; Chronology; Codes; Codes of narrative; Communication, Non-verbal (NVC); Connotation; Content analysis; Conventions; Cultural metaphor; Culture; Culture: Consumer culture; Culture: copyrighting culture; Culture: globalization of; Culture: popular culture; Cyberspace; Decode; Deconstruction; Deep structure; Dialect; Discourse; Discourse analysis; Discursive gap; Dissolve; Dominant discourse; Dominant, subordinate, radical; Double exposure; Emotive language; Encode; Encrypt; Establishing shot; Ethnocentrism; Euphemism; Excorporation; Exnomination; Expectation, horizons of; Fade in; Film noir; Flashback; Framing: media; Frequency; Gendered genre; Genre; Hedges; Hegemony; He/man language; Hybridization; Hypertext; Iconic; Ideological state apparatuses; Ideology; Ideology of romance; Image; Image, rhetoric of; Insert shot; Interactive television; Interpretant; Intertextuality; Jargon; Journalese; Journalism: celebrity journalism; Jump-cut; Kineme; Kinesics; Kuleshov effect; Lexis; Linguistics; Lip-sync; Machinery of representation; Male-as-norm; McGuffin; Meaning; Mediation; Medium; Message; Metamessage; Metaphor; Metasignals; Metonymy; Mimetic/semiosic planes; Mix; Mixing; Monroe motivated sequence; Montage; Morphing; Morphology; Multi-actuality; Myth; Narration; Narrative; Narrative paradigm; Naturalistic illusion (of television); 'Niche' audience; Noise; Open, closed texts; Phoneme; Polysemy; Postmodernism; Post-synchronization; Preferred reading; Programme flow; Propp's people; Reaction shot; Realism; Referent; Representation; Resistive reading; Reterritorialization; Rhetoric; Segmentation; Semantic differential; Semantics; Semiology/Semiotics; Sender/receiver; Shot; Sign; Signal; Signification; Signification spiral; Slow motion; Sound-bite; Special effects; Stereotype; Storyboard; Storyness; Structuralism; Symbol; Synchronous sound; Syntactics; Syntagm; Syntax; Tabloid, tabloidese, tabloidization; Tactics and strategies; Tag questions; Technique: Ellul's theory of techniques; Technology of the media; Tertiary text; Text; Text: integrity of the text; Voiceover.

→ **A**

AA-certificate, A-certificate See CERTIFICATION OF FILMS.

Aberrant decoding See DECODE.

Abstraction, ladder of See NARRATIVE: LADDER OF ABSTRACTION.

ABX model of communication See NEWCOMB'S ABX MODEL OF COMMUNICATION.

Acceleration factor What results from the speed-up of forms of transportation, thus having far-reaching impact upon communities, nations and cultures. Marshall McLuhan preached that the combination of accelerated modes of transport communication and the rapid development of electric communication – telephone, TV – was having the effect of reducing the world to a 'global village'. 'All meaning,' says McLuhan in *Understanding Media* (UK: Routledge, latest edition 2001), 'alters with acceleration, because all patterns of personal and political interdependence change with any acceleration of information.' See MOBILIZATION.

Accent The entire pattern of pronunciation typical of a particular region or social group. Accent is a feature of dialect. The use of most languages is marked by differing dialects and their accompanying accents. In Britain a range of regional accents still survive and are important signs of regional identity and affiliation. Though received pronunciation (RP) may still be regarded as the prestige accent, more recently it has been argued that Estuary English, a slightly Cockneyfied accent, has made in-roads into the traditional social territory of RP. Many individuals can use a range of accents and switch from one to another depending on the social situation. Accent is also an aspect of non-verbal communication.

A number of experiments have shown that reactions to speakers can be influenced by the accents they use. For example, Howard Giles and Peter F. Powesland, in their study of responses to speakers using regional accents, *Speech Style and Social Evaluation* (UK: Academia Press, 1975), found that speakers with Scottish or Yorkshire accents tend to be rated more favourably than received pronunciation speakers for qualities like personal integrity, good humour and good-naturedness.

In an article entitled, 'It's not what you say, it's the way that you say it', in the UK *Independent* (15 October 1997), Emma Haughton identifies RP, Refined Scots, Welsh and Irish, Yorkshire and Estuary English as being favourably received, but Brummie, Belfast, Glaswegian and West Country accents as being viewed unfavourably. These findings are similar to those of Giles' and Peter Trudgill's study entitled 'Sociolinguistics and linguistic value judgments' in Trudgill's *On Dialect* (UK: Blackwell, 1983).

Judgements will vary, though; an individual with a Brummie accent may not share the general view. Further there is evidence that among certain groups within society, a covert prestige can be attached to accents generally viewed as not prestigious, especially when they are part of 'non-standard' speech. Such accents and 'non-standard' speech may also be used to convey an image of toughness and masculinity in certain situations, irrespective of the actual social status of the speaker. Differences in accents will often reflect differences in the social structure of a society, and in particular its patterns of social stratification.

Access provider Or INTERNET service provider (ISP); company selling Internet connections, such as CompuServe, Demon, EasyNet and AOL (America On Line).

Access television See TELEVISION: ACCESS TELEVISION.

Accessed voices Within any society, these are the people who have a ready and privileged access to the channels of mass communication: politicians, civil servants, industrialists, experts of various kinds, pundits, royals and celebrities; and it is their views and styles that are given voice in preference to the views of others in society. Roger Fowler in his *Language of News: Discourses and Ideology of the Press* (UK: Routledge, 1991) writes of this selectivity, 'The political effect of this division between the accessed and unaccessed hardly needs stating: an imbalance between the representation of the already privileged, on the one hand, and the already unprivileged, on the other, with the views of the official, the powerful and the rich being constantly invoked to legitimate the status quo.'

With the advances in communicative exchange brought about by the INTERNET, the public has more choice in terms of who and what they access. However, though there is less reliance on traditional channels of mass communication, the 'usual suspects' as listed by Fowler still dominate the press and national broadcasting.

Accommodation, politics of See POLITICS OF ACCOMMODATION (IN THE MEDIA).

Accountability of media See McQUAIL'S ACCOUNTABILITY OF MEDIA MODEL, 1997.

Acculturation, deculturation The process by which a society or an individual adapts to the need for cultural change. The conditions for such change occur, for example, when encounters with other cultures continue on a prolonged basis such as in colonization, emigration and immigration. In analysing the process by which individuals adapt to life in a new country, Young Yun Kim in 'Adapting to a new culture' in Larry Samovar and Richard Porter's *Intercultural Communication: A Reader* (US: Wadsworth, 1997) comments, 'They are challenged to learn at least some new ways of thinking, feeling, and acting – an activity commonly called acculturation ... At the same time, they go through the process of deculturation ... of unlearning some of their previously acquired cultural habits at least to the extent that new responses are adopted in situations that previously would have evoked old ones.'

Such a process produces stress and anxiety and it necessarily affects the communicative performance of those undergoing it. However, communication with those in the new culture is essential to adaptation. Interestingly Kim argues that the mass media can be a useful source of information for those trying to acclimatize to a new culture as the messages they carry 'explicitly or implicitly convey the world views, myths, beliefs, values, mores and norms of the culture'. See COMMUNICATION: INTERCULTURAL COMMUNICATION.

Accusatory studies Jib Fowles in *The Case for Television Violence* (US: Sage, 1999) uses this term to describe the research studies that have focused on the effects of screen violence. They are 'accusatory' in the sense that they purport to prove the connection between screen and real violence, the one likely to instigate the other, or to desensitize audiences in their response to real violence. Such studies, in Fowles' view, amplify the 'derogatory discourse' concerning violence in the cinema and on TV. See VIOLENCE ON TV: THE DEFENCE.

Action code See CODES OF NARRATIVE.

Action research Some social science research is motivated by the desire to alter and improve a social situation. Action research aims not only to collect and analyse information but also to bring about practical social change.

Active-audience thesis See AUDIENCE: ACTIVE AUDIENCE.

Active listening See LISTENING.

Active participation Occurs in situations where media interest in a news story becomes involvement, and the story takes on a media-induced direction. An appetite for stories of scandal and sensation, and the cutthroat competition for circulation, can lead newspapers into playing the role of agent provocateur, as handy with the chequebook as the reporter's notebook.

Actuality Material from real life – the presentation in a broadcast programme of real events and people to illustrate some current theme or practice. RADIO, in parallel with film documentary, pioneered actuality in the 1930s. Producers such as Olive Shapley and Harry Harding were early innovators in this field. The radio programme *Time to Spare*, made in 1934, documented unemployment, broadcasting the voices of the unemployed and their families, and creating an impact that was both moving and disturbing.

Actualization See MASLOW'S HIERARCHY OF NEEDS.

Adaptors See NON-VERBAL BEHAVIOUR: REPERTOIRE.

Advertising The extent of the *reliance* of all forms of mass media upon advertising can be gauged by glancing at any monthly edition of *Brad*, which comprises some 400–500 pages of information on where advertisements can be placed and how much they will cost. Everything is there – the national and local PRESS, TV and RADIO, CINEMA, POSTERS, bus shelters, parking meters, litter bins and transport advertising.

If advertising merely sold products, it would cause less critical concern than it does. But it also sells images, dreams, ideal ways of life, ideal images of self; it sells, then reinforces time and again, values – those of consumerism; and it trades in stereotypes. In *The Shocking History of Advertising* (UK: Penguin, revised edition, 1965), E.S. Turner states that 'Advertising is the whip which hustles humanity up the road to the Better Mousetrap.'

Advertising has speeded the introduction of useful inventions to a wide as distinct from a select circle of consumers; it has spread markets, reduced the price of goods, accelerated turnover and kept people in employment. For some analysts, advertising is a kind of magic. Raymond Williams in *Problems in Materialism and Culture* (UK: Verso, 1980) argues that it has the ability to 'associate consumption with human desires to which it has no real reference. The magic obscures the real sources of general satisfaction because their discovery would involve radical change in the whole common way of life.'

Judith Williamson in *Decoding Advertisements* (UK: Marion Boyars, 1978, 1998) shares a similar concern: 'Advertisements obscure and avoid the real issues of society, those relating to work, to jobs and wages and who works for whom. The basic issues in the present state of society which do concern money and how it is earned, are sublimated into "meanings", "images", "lifestyles", to be bought with products not money.' Further, the magic of advertising means that we may believe commodities can convey messages about ourselves; this leads to us being 'alienated from ourselves, since we have allowed objects to "speak" for us and have become identified with them'. Such alienation may well lead to feelings of fragmentation and discomfort within the self, feelings which may fuel a desire to seek solace in further consumption.

A number of critics point to the danger that advertising messages and the consumption they partly fuel may undermine and distort self-development. Anthony Giddens writes in *Modernity and Self-Identity* (UK: Polity Press, 1991) that 'The consumption of ever-novel goods becomes a substitute for the genuine development of self: appearance replaces essence.' Self-actualization is 'packaged and distributed according to market criteria. Mediated experience is centrally involved here. The mass media routinely present modes of life to which, it is implied, everyone should aspire.' For Don Slater in *Consumer Culture and Modernity* (UK: Polity Press, 1997), 'Consumer culture "technicizes" the project of self by treating all problems as solvable through various commodities.'

Not all would agree with such criticisms. Those subscribing to the doctrines of nineteenth-century Liberalism, for example, would argue that consumer culture, of which advertising is an integral element, liberates rather than oppresses, in providing the individual with many opportunities to rationally pursue his/her self-interest. The range of choices offered by consumer culture and post-traditional society is to be celebrated rather than seen as a cause for concern: to be able to choose being seen as the essence of being human. It should also be borne in mind that the messages of advertising have to compete with a range of other influences on behaviour in their battle for hearts, minds and identities.

The many modes of advertising may be categorized as follows: (1) *Commercial consumer* advertising, with its target the mass audience and its channel the mass media. Latterly, of course, the new frontier for commercial advertising has become the INTERNET. (2) *Trade and technical* advertising, such as ads in specialist magazines. (3) *Prestige* advertising, particularly that of big business and large institutions, generally selling image and good name rather than specific products (see PR: PUBLIC RELATIONS). (4) *Small ads*, directly informational, which are the bedrock support of local periodicals and are the basis of the many giveaway papers which have been published in recent years. (5) *Government* advertising – health warnings, for example. (6) *Charity* advertising, seeking donations for worthwhile causes at home and abroad. (7) Advertising through *sponsorship*, mainly of sports, leisure and the arts. This indirect form of advertising has been a major development; its danger has been to make recipients of sponsorship come to rely more and more heavily on commercial support. Sponsors want quick publicity and prestige for their money and their loyalties to recipients are very often short term.

The effect upon newspaper and broadcasting editorial and programme content is rarely overt; rather it is a process of media people 'internalizing' advertisers' demands. Ad-related newspaper features have grown enormously in the post-Second World War period, especially in the 'quality press', such as, in the UK, *The Times, Guardian, Independent* and *Daily Telegraph*, which derive over half their revenue from advertising. In press advertising, numbers count for less than the estimated purchasing power of the target readership. This explains why two major UK newspapers with big circulations – the *Daily Herald* (see MIRACLE OF FLEET STREET) and the *News Chronicle* – were closed down in the 1960s. They simply did not appeal to the advertisers.

Advertising has suffused our culture and our language, helping to form a consumer culture (see CULTURE: CONSUMER CULTURE). Its influence has been felt in modern art movements such as pop art; its snappy techniques as developed for TV have been widely adopted in the cinema. It has drawn into its service actors, celebrities, artists, photographers, writers, designers and film-makers. It is often said that on TV the adverts are better than the programmes; there is a grain of truth here as there is in the claim that it is because of the adverts, and the goals of those who commission and make them, that the programmes are not better, more original or more challenging. See ADVERTISING STANDARDS AUTHORITY (ASA); AIDA MODEL; HARMONIOUS INTERACTION; PRODUCT PLACEMENT; SPONSORSHIP; SPON-SORSHIP OF BROADCAST PROGRAMMES (UK); SUBLIMINAL.

* Gillian Dyer, *Advertising as Communication* (UK: Methuen, 1982); Robert Goldman, *Reading Ads Socially* (UK: Routledge, 1992, reprinted 1995); Ien Ang, *Living Room Wars: Re-thinking Media Audiences for a Postmodern World* (UK: Routledge, 1995); Sean Brierley, *The Advertising Handbook* (UK: Routledge, 1995); Jib Fowles, *Advertising and Popular Culture* (UK: Sage, 1996); Angela Goddard, *The Language of Advertising: Written Texts* (US/UK: Routledge, 1998); Anne M. Cronin, *Advertising and Consumer Citizenship: Gender, Images and Rights* (UK: Routledge, 2000); John Tullock, *Watching Television Audiences: Cultural Theories and Methods* (UK: Arnold, 2000); Peter N. Stearns, *Consumerism in World History: The Global Transformation of Desire* (UK: Routledge, 2001).

Advertising: ambient advertising Advertisements that feature in contexts other than the printed page, on film or in broadcasting, which we encounter in everyday life situations, designed to surround and to confront the prospective customer – in the street, on bus shelters, in underground stations and trains, in airports, public lava-tories and latterly in places of education; indeed wherever there is space for the advertiser to press home image and message. On London's underground trains in 1997, for example, hang-straps were embellished with anti-perspirant ads – in a hot summer the perfect ambient reminder to consider Vaseline Intensive Care.

An alternative term is *captive audience* advertising. David Bollier of the Annenburg School of Communications, in an article entitled 'The grotesque, smirking gargoyle: the commercialization of America's consciousness' published on the tom.paine.com website (8 August 2002), writes of advertising 'ambushing people as they use public restrooms, gas pumps, elevators ... By ones and twos, such actions gen-erally are inconsequential. In aggregate, however, the sheer pervasiveness of commercialism in public spaces and contemporary life has the malodorous whiff of a Corporate Big Brother.'

Bollier believes that the 'sheer ubiquity of marketing in hundreds of nooks and crannies of daily life has become a defining framework of cultural values'.

Advertising boycotts The reliance of the press and of commercial television upon advertising for revenue indicates the important influence advertisers and their clients can wield over the media. Where a newspaper may be deemed to be publishing material or expressing views which might be detrimental to consumerist interest, companies pull out their expensive advertisement – or threaten to do so, and thus exercise censor-ship. The financial consequences of such boycotts can be devastating.

Advertising Standards Authority (ASA) Independent body set up by the advertising industry to police rules incorporated in advertising codes. On 1 November 2004 the ASA became the regulatory authority for broadcasting advertising following the COMMUNICATIONS ACT (UK) 2003 and the creation of the Office of Communications (OFCOM). The Authority's mission is to 'apply the advertising codes and uphold standards in all media on behalf of consumers, business and society'. It offers a 'one-stop' approach to cus-tomer complaints, a 'single point of reference for consumers, advertisers and broadcasters, while respecting the different obligations inherent in broadcast and non-broadcast media – the one licensed, the other not'.

The Committee of Advertising Practice (CAP) revises and enforces the CAP Code, which is 'primarily concerned with the content of market communications'. The ASA endorses and administers the code, ensur-ing that the self-regulatory system works in the public interest. There are codes for non-broadcast media, radio and TV, and text services. The Non-Broadcasting Code covers topics such as Decency, Honesty, Truthfulness, Matters of Opinion, Fear and Distress and Safety.

For example, Section 11, on Violence and Anti-Social Behaviour, states 'Marketing communications should contain nothing that condones or is likely to provoke violence or anti-social behaviour', while Section 13, on Protection of Privacy, urges marketers 'to obtain written permission before referring to or portraying members of the public or their identifiable possessions'; however, 'the use of crowd scenes or general pub-lic locations may be acceptable without permission'.

The Broadcasting Committee of Advertising Practice (BCAP) is under contract from Ofcom to supervise advertising on radio and TV. Section 9 of the Radio Code deals with Good Taste, Decency and Offences to Public Feeling: 'Each station is expected to ... take into account the sensitivities of all sections of its audience when deciding on the acceptability or scheduling of advertisements.'

Under Section 11, on Children and Younger Listeners, the code states that 'Prices of products advertised to younger listeners must not be minimized by words such as "only" and "just"', nor should ads 'lead children to believe that unless they have or use the product advertised they will be inferior in some way to other children or liable to be held in contempt or ridicule'. Inviting children to ask mum or dad to buy an advertised product also breaks the rules. Section 13 of the Radio Code, on Racial Discrimination, declares that advertising 'must not include any material which might reasonably be construed by ethnic minorities to be hurtful or tasteless'.

The TV Code covers similar ground to the other codes. Section 4, on Political and Controversial Issues, states that no advertisement '(a) may be inserted by or on behalf of any body whose objects are wholly or mainly of a political nature (b) may be directed towards any political end (c) may have any relation to any industrial dispute' (with limited exceptions). Section 10, on Religion, Faith, Systems of Belief, forbids '(a) advertising by or on behalf of any organization or individual whose objectives are or appear to be wholly or mainly concerned with religion, faith or other philosophies or beliefs (b) any other advertising which appears to have a doctrinal objective (c) advertising for commercial products or services which reflect doctrine'.

While the TV Code seeks to 'prevent causing offence to viewers generally or to particular groups in society (for example, by causing significant distress, disgust or insult, by offending against widespread public feeling)', it recognizes legitimate differences of opinion on certain matters: 'The ASA and BCAP will not act … where advertising is simply criticized for not being in "good taste" unless the material also offends against generally accepted moral, social or cultural standards. Apart from freedom of speech considerations, there are often large and sometimes contradictory differences in views about what constitutes "bad taste" or what should be deplored.'

On matters of redress, the ASA states: 'The vast majority of advertisers, promoters and direct marketers comply [with the codes]. Those that do not may be subject to sanctions. Adverse publicity may result from the rulings published by the ASA weekly on its website. The media, contractors and service providers may withhold their services or deny access to space. Trading privileges (including direct mail discounts) and recognition may be revoked, withdrawn or temporarily withheld. Pre-vetting may be imposed and, in some cases, non-complying parties can be referred to the Office of Fair Trading for action, where appropriate, under the Control of Misleading Advertisements Regulations.'

The ASA publishes regular news and reports on its adjudications of high-profile ad campaigns and it carries on its website (www.a.s.a.org.uk) instructions on how the public can make complaints, including a complaint form with space for 1500 words of explanation. See SPONSORSHIP OF BROADCAST PROGRAMMES (UK).

Aesthetic code See CODES.

Affect displays See NON-VERBAL BEHAVIOUR; REPERTOIRE.

Affective See COGNITIVE (AND AFFECTIVE).

Agenda-setting Term used to describe the way the media set the order of importance of current issues, especially in the reportage of news. Closely linked with the process of gatekeeping, agenda-setting defines the context of transmission, and establishes the terms of reference and the limits of debate. In BROADCASTING the agenda is more assertive than in newspapers where the reader can ignore the order of priorities set by the paper's editorial team and turn straight to the small ads or the sports page. Broadcasting is linear – one item following after another – and its agenda unavoidable (except by switching off). Interviewers in broadcasting are in *control* of pre-set agendas. They initiate, formulate the questions to be asked and have the chairperson's power of excluding areas of discussion. Very rarely does an interviewee break free from this form of control and succeed in widening the context of debate beyond what is 'on the agenda'.

G. Ray Funkhouser and Eugene F. Shaw in 'How synthetic experience shapes social reality' in *Journal of Communication*, Spring 1990, subdivide agenda-setting into *micro-agenda-setting* and *macro-agenda-setting*. The first describes the way the mass media are able, through emphasis on content, to influence public perceptions of the relative importance of specific issues. The second they define as follows: 'The potential of electronic media to colour, distort, and perhaps even degrade an entire cultural world view, by presenting images of the world suited to the agenda of the media (in the US case, commercial interests), we might term "macro-agenda-setting".'

In recent years agenda-setting has been viewed as working from two levels, that of *subject* and that of *attribute*; the theory is that the media's attention to the attributes of a subject is met with a corresponding image in the mind of the public. Level 1 of agenda-setting concerns the central theme or object of a public issue/news story, Level 2 the salient characteristics of the theme or object as emphasized by the media.

In an article, 'Agenda-setting in the 1996 Spanish General Election', published in the *Journal of Communication*, Spring 2000, Maxwell McCombs, Esteban Lopez Escobar and Juan Pablo Llamas refer to 'agendas of attributes, those characteristics and traits that fill out the picture of each object'. Some attributes are emphasized, given prominence, others de-emphasized, 'while many are ignored'. McCombs and his colleagues explain: 'Just as objects vary in salience, so do the attributes of each object. Just as there is an agenda of public issues, political candidates, or some other set of objects, there is also an agenda of attributes for each object. Both the selection by journalists of objects for attention and the selection of attributes for detailing the pictures of these objects are powerful agenda-setting roles.'

The authors point out that 'although object and attribute salience are conceptually distinct, they are integral and simultaneously present aspects of the agenda-setting process'. In their research into public attitudes to candidates at the 1996 election in Spain, the following attributes of the major contenders were measured: ideology/issues position of rival candidates, biographical details, perceived qualifications and integrity. See McCOMBS AND SHAW'S AGENDA-SETTING MODEL OF MEDIA EFFECTS, 1976; ROGERS AND DEARING'S AGENDA-SETTING MODEL, 1987.

* Maxwell E. McCombs and Donald L. Shaw, 'The evolution of agenda-setting research: twenty-five years in the marketplace of ideas' in *Journal of Communication*, Spring 1993; James W. Dearing and Everett M. Rogers, *Agenda-Setting* (US/UK: Sage, 1996).

Agenda-setting research A key area of research into the relationship between mass communication and audience consumption of media, agenda-setting research generally takes two forms. James W. Dearing and Everett M. Rogers, in *Agenda-Setting* (UK: Sage, 1996) explain that research has traditionally taken a *hierarchical* form; this they describe as 'one-point-in-time correlation comparisons of media content with aggregated responses by the public to survey questions about issue salience' – that is, their perceived importance. More recently the research approach has been through *longitudinal* studies. Such investigations 'include over-time participant observation in media organizations' as well as the analysis of quantitative variables such as real world indicators'.

Longitudinal studies can detect trends and directions of influence; they can tease out whether media coverage prompts public awareness and interest or whether the media perch on the 'bandwagon' of public opinion. The over-time study can identify variants of events and issues and thus, as Dearing and Rogers put it, 'illuminate the nature of media effects with special clarity'.

A further focus of research into agenda-setting involves what Dearing and Rogers term 'trigger events'. These act as a 'cue-to-action that occurs at a point in time', each trigger event serving 'to crystallize attention and action'. A trigger event essentially 'simplifies the nature of a complex issue into a form that the public can more easily understand'.

Agitprop The Department of Agitation and Propaganda was created in 1920 as part of the Central Committee Secretariat of the Communist Party of the Soviet Union. Its responsibility was to use all available media – especially film – to disseminate information and ideas to the population of the world's first Communist state. The term agitprop has come to be used to describe any unashamedly political propagandizing.

Agora In the city states of Ancient Greece the agora was the place of assembly where the free citizens debated matters of public concern; where public *opinion* was formulated and asserted. Public spaces have long been surrendered to enclosure or to shopping malls, but the concept remains; its practice continues at second remove – the media speak for the people, purporting to articulate and defend public interest in their role as WATCHDOGS, guarding the public from the abuses of state. PUBLIC SERVICE BROADCASTING is perceived as an extension of the agora; hence the concern often expressed about the privatization of broadcast media, that it is turning the agora into a marketplace of commodities (including COMMODITIZATION OF INFORMATION and entertainment) rather than a marketplace of ideas and debate. However, it could be claimed that a modern, and expanding, form of the agora is the INTERNET. See INFORMATION COMMONS; MEDIASPHERE; PUBLIC OPINION; SALON DISCOURSE.

AIDA model Guide to the principal stages of advertising a product or service: A – create Awareness; I – create Interest; D – promote Desire; A – stimulate Action or response.

Alexandra Palace Birthplace of television in the United Kingdom. The first TV broadcasting took place from London's 'Ally Pally' on 2 November 1936. Initially the service reached only a few hundred privileged viewers in and around the capital. Some 400 TV sets, costing around £100 – the price of a small car – were in use. With the coming of the Second World War, TV broadcasts came to an abrupt end on 1 September 1939, by which time there were an estimated 20,000 TV sets in operation. The Alexandra Palace studios reopened for business on 7 June 1946 but had to briefly shut down transmission again in early 1947 because of the acute fuel crisis. The Alexandra Palace studios remained in service until 1955. See BROADCASTING; TELEVISION.

Alienation As a concept, derives largely from the work of Karl Marx (1818–83), who argued that the organization of industrial production robbed people of opportunities for meaningful and creative work, performed in cooperation with others and over which they had some control. Researchers have posed the question whether the mass character of the modern communications industry produces a sense of alienation in its own workers. Lewis Coser in *Men of Ideas* (US: Free Press, 1965) believes that the industrial mode of production within media organizations hamstrings the individual producer by denying his or her creativity in the quest for a mass culture and that this results in alienation.

The term has a wider application. Alienation is seen as a socio-psychological condition which affects certain individuals. William Kornhauser in *The Politics of Mass Society* (US: Free Press, 1959) argues that the breakdown and decline of community groups and the extended family in modern society produces feelings of isolation and increases the possibility that people will be influenced by the appeals of extremist political groups. Alienation might therefore be a significant variable in determining an individual's receptivity to certain types of communication. See ANOMIE; INTERVENING VARIABLES.

Alignment See FRAMING.

al-Jazeera Arab satellite TV channel, started up in 1996, which grabbed world headlines with its exclusive NEWS footage from Taliban-held areas during the war in Afghanistan, 2002, and the US pursuit of Osama bin Laden, thought to have masterminded the events of 11 September 2001. Translated as 'Peninsula', al-Jazeera scooped rival western channels with bin Laden's pre-recorded video messages. The channel's coverage of world affairs, including the Israeli–Palestinian conflict, the second Gulf War (2003) and the occupation of Iraq, has offered alternative perspectives and analysis, braving CENSORSHIP whenever it is threatened.

Often referred to as the Arab world's BBC, al-Jazeera is based in Qatar and is substantially funded by its liberalizing emir. It was through al-Jazeera that viewers were able to witness the destruction by the Taliban of the giant Bamiyan Buddhas. Noureddine Miladi, in 'Mapping the al-Jazeera phenomenon' in *War and the Media: Reporting Conflict 24/7* (UK/US: Sage, 2003), edited by Daya Kishan Thussu and Des Freedman, says that with a regular audience of 35 million and available to most of the world's 310 million Arabs, al-Jazeera 'has redefined Arab broadcasting': 'The weekly talk shows and discussion programmes often tackle crucial yet taboo subjects, like human rights, democracy and political corruption, women's freedom, banned political groups, polygamy, torture and rival interpretations of Islamic teachings', which other Arab channels 'would not even consider screening … The animated political discussions that were confined to private spaces in Arab countries have been brought into the open after decades of stagnation and state censorship, to be debated at a transnational level …'.

Unmediated by western media influences, al-Jazeera has incurred the wrath of both the West, the US in particular, and of Arab governments. In a UK *Guardian* article, 'Reality television' (21 April 2004), writing of his time as London correspondent for the website al-jazeera.net, Arthur Nelsen refers to al-Jazeera's 'track record of honest and accurate reporting', commending its 'principled pluralism in the face of brutal and authoritarian regimes within the region, and increasingly from those without'. This, in Nelsen's view, 'is why it has been vilified, criminalized and bombed. It is also why it should be defended by those who genuinely believe that successful societies depend upon an independent media'.

---

* Mohammed El-Nawawy and Adel Iskander, *Al Jazeera: The Story of the Network that is rattling Governments and Redefining Modern Journalism* (US: Westview, 2003); Mohamed Zayani, ed., *The Al-Jazeera Phenomenon: Critical Perspectives on New Arab Media* (UK: Pluto, 2005).

Alleyne's news revolution model, 1997 In *News Revolution: Political and Economic Decisions about Global Information* (UK: Macmillan, 1997), Mark D. Alleyne offers a model which 'is both a description of the international news system's political economy and a theory of the international relations of that system'. The Global News System located in the model's oval 'refers to the system of companies, organizations and people that produce the world's news'. Democratic necessity 'describes the body of reasons used to justify the existence of the news media' – the political justifications – and these Alleyne classifies as (1) watchdogs on government, (2) 'conduits for the two-way flow of information between people and their government', and (3) 'a source of information in the so-called marketplace of ideas'.

Along with political justification there is economic necessity: 'The press system and the economic system interact at a basic level whenever the media carry advertising. At a more sophisticated level, the media perform the information functions needed for trade, currency, equities, and bond markets to perform.' Not the least of the factors relating to economics is the capacity of the media to attract or deter capital: 'News of political instability scares away investors. More positive news attracts them.'

The model identifies a dynamic of interacting and sometimes conflicting claims which often operate in a process of exchange, what Alleyne terms a 'trade in claims'. Claims at the top of the model are what the media want from structures of power and authority, while those at the bottom of the model are what the structures deem critical in the nature of information and its flow.

Says Alleyne, 'Like the news media, these actors [states, companies, international organizations] like to manage what information the news media disseminate about them. They do this through censorship and propaganda. Like the news media, these actors seek self-preservation, and the actors operating in the marketplace are particularly concerned with getting information that will help them make efficient decisions.' Alleyne's own claim for his model is that it 'takes us from the stage of merely describing the wonders of new technologies and assuming positive political consequences from the so-called information revolution to a clear explanation and understanding of how the news media function in international relations'.

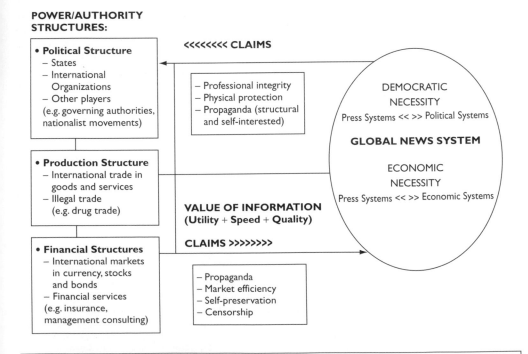

The news revolution model

Allness attitude Gail and Michele Myers in *The Dynamics of Human Communication* (US: McGraw-Hill, 1985) refer to what Alfred Korzybski termed 'allness', that is the attitude that you can know or say all there is about a person, group, issue and so on. As Myers and Myers point out, the allness attitude can constitute a considerable barrier in communication. It may mean that you communicate with certain people on the basis that you know all there is to know about them or the topic under discussion, and few people take kindly to such assumptions.

The attitude may also affect how you receive messages. For example, you may believe that you already know all that you are being told or you may reject a message which contradicts what you think you know. As Myers and Myers conclude, 'The allness attitude may do much to prevent you from developing satisfying relationships with others and from communicating effectively with them.'

Allusion See HISTORICAL ALLUSION.

Alter-EU Coalition formed in July 2005 to pressurize the European Union into vetting the multi-million-pound LOBBYING system, largely representing the interests of major corporations. The Alliance for Transparency and Ethics Regulation argues for mandatory disclosure of information about what Granville Williams in 'Alter-Net launched' (*Free Press*, July–August 2005) calls a 'powerful lobbyocracy in Brussels'. Over 140 organizations, including the European Federation of Journalists and the CAMPAIGN FOR PRESS AND BROADCASTING FREEDOM (UK), signed up in support of measures demanding disclosure and transparency. See EUROPEAN COMMISSION AND MEDIA: 'TELEVISION WITHOUT FRONTIERS'.

Alternative (radical) media See MEDIA: ALTERNATIVE (OR RADICAL MEDIA).

Amplitude See NEWS VALUES.

Analysis – modes of media analysis See DISCOURSE ANALYSIS; ETHNOGRAPHIC (APPROACH TO AUDIENCE MEASUREMENT); FUNCTIONALIST; MARXIST; SOCIAL ACTION (MODES OF MEDIA ANALYSIS).

Anarchist cinema Epitomized in the work of French film-maker Jean Vigo (1905–34) who was 12 when his anarchist father, known as Miguel Almereyda, was found strangled in a French police cell. In *A propos de Nice* (1930), Vigo expressed the anarchist's views on inequality, contrasting the luxurious, suntanned life of wealthy holidaymakers with the underfed, deformed bodies of slum children. In his comic masterpiece *Zéro de Conduite* (Nought for Conduct), produced in 1932, Vigo used anarchist friends as actors. His theme was the rebellion of schoolchildren against the rigidity of the school authorities. It was immediately banned by the French authorities. Vigo was a direct inspiration for the 'anarchistic' film of a modern, public school rebellion in Lindsay Anderson's *If*, made in 1968. (Anarchy: complete absence of law or government.)

Anchorage The part that captions play in helping to frame, or anchor, the meaning of photographic images, as reproduced in newspapers and magazines. French philosopher Roland Barthes used this term to describe the way captions help 'fix' or narrow down the choice of meanings of the published image. He defines the caption as a 'parasitic message designed to connote the image'.

Andersch, Staats and Bostrom's model of communication, 1969 Environmental or contextual factors are at the centre of the communication model devised by Elizabeth G. Andersch, Lorin C. Staats and Robert N. Bostrom and presented in *Communication in Everyday Use* (US: Holt, Rinehart & Winston). Like BARN-LUND'S TRANSACTIONAL MODEL, this one stresses the transactional nature of the communication process, in which messages and their meanings are structured and evaluated by the Sender and subjected to reconstruction and evaluation on the part of the Receiver, all the while interacting with factors (or stimuli) in the environment. See *TOPIC GUIDE* under COMMUNICATION MODELS.

Anecdote A short narrative, usually of a personal nature, used to illustrate a general issue. Anecdotes are often used in media coverage to heighten the emotional aspect of an issue. Colin Seymour-Ure in *The Political Impact of the Mass Media* (UK: Constable, 1974) recounts the use made of one such anecdote by the politician Enoch Powell in his efforts to bring the immigration issue to public attention during 1967 and 1968. Powell claimed to have received a letter from a correspondent in Northumberland expressing concern about an elderly widow in Wolverhampton who feared harassment by newly arrived immigrants in the area. This

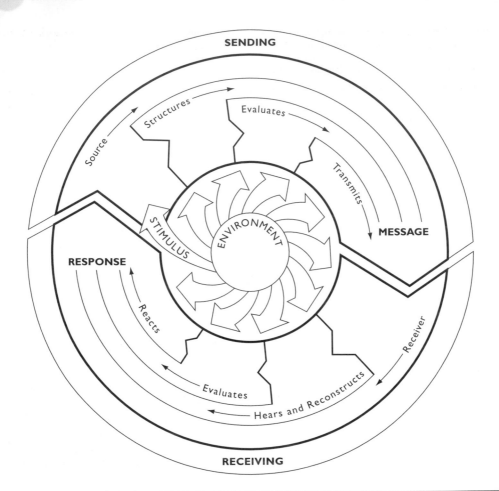

SENDING

Source — Structures — Evaluates — Transmits

MESSAGE

STIMULUS

ENVIRONMENT

RESPONSE

Reacts — Evaluates — Hears and Reconstructs — Receiver

RECEIVING

Andersch, Staats and Bostrom's model of communication, 1969

anecdote was widely reported by the press, yet, despite strenuous efforts, no trace of the elderly widow could be found. The story did, however, do much to fuel the emotive manner in which the immigration issue was discussed in the popular press. See LOONY LEFTISM.

Animatic Sequence of drawings representing the story of a television advertisement, prior to filming. Another term for STORYBOARD.

Animation The process of filming still drawings, puppets, etc. in sequence to give the illusion of movement; also the actual direct drawing and painting on to positive or negative stock or on to clear celluloid itself. Long before CINEMATOGRAPHY was invented devices were in use which gave drawings the illusion of movement. By 1882 Emile Reynauld had combined his Praxinoscope with a projector and a decade later opened the Théâtre Optique in the Musée Grevin in Paris.

Live-action cinema became all-important once the Lumière brothers had shown its possibilities in 1895, but animation soon captured interest, from 1908 onwards, with the work of J. Stuart Blackton in the US and Emile Cohl in France. *New York Herald* cartoonist Winsor McCay made *Gertie the Dinosaur* in 1909, and in 1919 the first animated feature, *The Sinking of the Lusitania*.

In November 1928 Walt Disney (1901–66) presented Mortimer, later Mickey, Mouse to the world using synchronous sound, in *Steamboat Willie*, along with his *Skeleton Dance* (1929) one of the true classics of animation film. The laboriousness of producing thousands of drawings for filming was dramatically altered in the 1980s by the introduction to animated film-making of computer graphics.

* Paul Wells, *Understanding Animation* (UK: Routledge, 1998).

Annan Commission Report on Broadcasting, 1977 Historian Lord Annan chaired the Royal Commission on the Future of Broadcasting whose main task was to decide what should happen to the BROADCAST-ING industry once the right to broadcast of the RADIO and TELEVISION companies lapsed at the end of July 1979. Also, the Annan Commission was asked to make recommendations on a fourth television channel.

Annan favoured the continuance of much of the existing broadcasting system, though the Report suggested that both the BBC and IBA should lose their local radio stations to a new Local Broadcasting Authority. Annan also proposed a broadcasting complaints commission, empowered to award costs if a complaint were upheld, and a Public Enquiry Board for Broadcasting. The task of the Board would be to hold seven-yearly public audits of the way each authority had met its responsibilities and to conduct hearings on specific issues, particularly the award of franchises. A further recommendation was for an Open Broadcasting Authority to operate the fourth channel 'more as a publisher of material provided by others'.

What Annan wanted above all was a shift from duopoly to a more diverse system of broadcasting in Britain: 'We want the broadcasting industry to grow. But we do not want more of the same ... What is needed now are programmes for the different minorities which add up to make the majority.' Annan also declared that there was 'a widely shared feeling that British broadcasting is run like a highly restricted club – managed exclusively by broadcasters according to their own criteria of what counts as good television and radio'.

The then Labour government published a white paper, *Broadcasting* (July 1978), in response to Annan, declaring itself against the Local Broadcasting Authority and the Public Enquiry Board but in favour of the Complaints Commission and the Open Broadcasting Authority. Before there was time for legislation, the Conservatives came to power in May 1979. The Queen's Speech promised the fourth channel to commercial television and the proposal for an Open Broadcasting Authority was rejected. See CHANNEL 4. See also *TOPIC GUIDE* under COMMISSIONS, COMMITTEES, LEGISLATION.

Anomie It was Emile Durkheim (1858–1917), a French sociologist, who first used this term to describe a state of 'normlessness' in which the individual feels that there are no effective social rules governing behaviour or that those rules and VALUES to which he/she is exposed are conflicting and therefore confusing. The anomic state is most likely to occur when contact with others is limited. Durkheim linked anomie with the disturbance caused by social change and upheaval and saw it as a temporary social phenomenon. Several contemporary observers consider it a more permanent feature of modern industrial society.

MASS SOCIETY theorists have tended to view those suffering from anomie as being particularly vulnerable to over-influence by mass communication. Observers have also found that some behaviour that was considered anomic was in fact sub-cultural. Another feature of anomie is that the individual may react to it by becoming ceaselessly ambitious and this in some cases can lead to severe agitation and discontent.

Dissatisfied ambition is a target for much advertising and is often seen as a desirable trait in modern capitalist societies – a perspective reinforced by some of the outpourings from the mass media. A question of concern is, then, the contribution of the mass media and in particular advertising to the condition of anomie. Anomie can lead to extensive personal as well as social breakdown, to suicide and mental illness as well as to crime, delinquency, drug addiction and alcoholism.

Anti-language Anti-languages, according to Martin Montgomery in *An Introduction to Language and Society* (UK: Methuen, 1986; Routledge, 1993), 'may be understood as extreme versions of social dialects'. Typically, anti-languages are developed by sub-cultures and groups that take an antagonistic stance towards mainstream society. This stance may be general or relate to a specific area of social activity. Further, the core activities of the group, those around which the anti-language often develops, may well be illegal.

The anti-language serves both to establish a boundary and a degree of separateness between the group and society and to make its activities more difficult for outsiders to detect and follow. By their nature anti-languages are difficult to study but Montgomery discusses several types including those developed in Polish prisons, by the Calcutta underworld and CB radio slang – a weak form of anti-language even when the use of CB radio was illegal, but one with which many outsiders are now familiar.

Anti-languages are created by a process of *relexicalization* – that is, the substitution of new vocabulary for old, usually those words that refer to the activities which mark the group off from the wider community. The grammar of the parent language is often preserved. So, for example, in CB radio slang, the phrase 'bear in the air' was used for a police helicopter. Making up new words happens frequently in anti-languages, thus making them even more difficult to penetrate. *Overlexicalization* is often also a feature of anti-languages. Here a variety of new words may refer to an activity and may be used interchangeably in order to mislead or confuse 'outsiders'.

Anti-Terrorism, Crime and Security Act (UK), 2001 See TERRORISM: ANTI-TERRORISM, CRIME AND SECURITY ACT.

Apache silence The complex meanings of silence, as observed by the North American Apache tribes, have been tabulated by K.H. Basso in 'To give up words: silence in western Apache culture' in P. Giglioli, ed., *Language and Social Context* (UK: Penguin, 1972). Basso describes Apache silence as 'a response to uncertainty and unpredictability in social relations'. Often baffling to the outsider, Apache silence was an important element in the courtship process; when meeting strangers; even when greeting children back from a long journey; and in the presence of other people's grief. See COMMUNICATION, NON-VERBAL.

* Adam Jaworski, *The Power of Silence: Social and Pragmatic Perspectives* (UK: Sage, 1993).

Apocryphal stories Those of doubtful origin, false or spurious. See DEMONIZATION; FOLK DEVILS; LOONY LEFTISM; MYTH; RUMOUR.

Arbitrariness One of the characteristic features of human LANGUAGE is that between an object described and the word that describes it there is a connection which is purely arbitrary, that is, the speech sound does not reflect features of the object denoted. For example, the word chair describes the object, chair, because the English have arbitrarily decided to name it thus as a matter of convention. In contrast, *onomatopoeic* expressions are representative rather than arbitrary in that they reflect properties of the nonlinguistic world (for example, clatter, buzz, flap – and snap, crackle and pop).

'Areopagitica' Title of a tract or pamphlet by the English poet John Milton (1608–74) in defence of the freedom of the press, published in 1644. Milton spoke out, with eloquence and courage, following the revival of censorship by parliamentary ordinance in 1643 (traditional press censorship had broken down with the Long Parliament's abolition of the Star Chamber in 1641). The title was taken from the Greek *Areopagus* – the hill of Ares or Mars in Athens, where the highest judicial court held its sittings; a 'behind closed doors' court.

Milton celebrated the power and influence of the printed word: books 'do preserve, as in a vial, the purest efficacy and extraction of that living intellect that bred them. I know they are as lively, and as vigorously productive, as those fabulous dragon's teeth; and being sown up and down, may chance to spring up armed men. And yet, on the other hand, unless wariness be used, as good almost kill a man as kill a good book: who kills a man kills a reasonable creature, God's image; but he who destroys a good book, kills reason itself, kills the image of God, as it were, in the eye.' See MILTON'S PARADOX.

Artefacts Things produced by human workmanship, for example a mobile phone, a CD or a television programme. Artefacts may be read as signs that reveal information about the society in which they are produced and used or about the individuals who possess them. Thus adornments such as jewellery and accessories can be taken to 'say something' about the wearer, as can the newspaper they read. See OBJECT LANGUAGE; SELF-IDENTITY; SEMIOTIC POWER; TACTICS AND STRATEGIES; TASTE.

Article 19 This clause in the European Convention for the Protection of Human Rights and Fundamental Freedom states: '(1) Everyone has the right to freedom of expression. This right shall include freedom to hold opinions and to receive and impart information and ideas without interference by public authority and regardless of frontiers. (2) The exercise of these freedoms, since it carries with it duties and responsibilities, may be subject to such formalities, conditions, restrictions or penalties as are prescribed by law and are necessary in a democratic society, in the interests of national security, territorial integrity or public safety ... for preventing the disclosure of information received in confidence, or for maintaining the authority and impartiality of the judiciary.'

The upholding of the Convention is the task of the European Court of Human Rights, based in Strasbourg. The article gave birth to a pressure group, Article 19, centred in London, using electronic media to monitor state censorship around the world. See CENSORSHIP and *TOPIC GUIDE* under MEDIA: FREEDOM, CENSORSHIP.

Assertiveness To be assertive is to be able to communicate one's thoughts, feelings, beliefs, ATTITUDES, positions and so on in a clear, confident, honest and direct manner; it is, in short, to be able to stand up for oneself whilst also taking into consideration the needs and rights of other people. Anne Dickson in *Women at Work* (UK: Kogan Page, 2000) argues, 'Being assertive ... springs from a fulcrum of equality. It springs from a balance between self and others ...'.

Being assertive differs from being aggressive in that aggressiveness involves a standing up for one's rights and needs at the expense of others. In recent years there has been much interest in assertiveness training – that is, in enabling people to develop techniques and strategies, verbal and non-verbal, for INTERPERSONAL COMMUNICATION which will encourage them to assert themselves in social situations. The ability to be assertive is linked to self-esteem and self-confidence and thus to a positive SELF-CONCEPT. Such training provides the opportunity for considerable exploration of the relationship between the self-concept and interpersonal behaviour.

Whilst assertiveness in communication may be encouraged in some individualistic cultures, such as those of the US or UK, collectivistic cultures, like that of Japan, tend to stress the importance of respect for others, tact, politeness and the maintenance of interpersonal harmony. In which case, assertiveness may be perceived as rudeness.

These different perspectives on assertiveness can be found within a culturally diverse society. Larry Samovar and Richard Porter in *Communication Between Cultures* (US: Wadsworth/Thomson Learning, 2001) provide the following example from the US: 'In yet another experiment Caucasian mothers tended to interpret as positive those aspects of their children's speech and behaviour that reflected assertiveness, excitement and interest. Navajo mothers who observed the same behaviour in their children reported them as being mischievous and lacking discipline. To the Navajo mothers, assertive speech and behaviour reflected discourtesy, restlessness, self-centredness, and lack of discipline ...'.

It would seem that assertiveness in communication is a potential barrier to successful intercultural communication. See COMMUNICATION: INTERCULTURAL COMMUNICATION; HIGH AND LOW CONTEXT COMMUNICATION.

* Sue Bishop, *Develop Your Assertiveness* (UK: Kogan Page, 2000).

Attention See PERCEPTION.

Attention model of mass communication Denis McQuail in *Mass Communication Theory: An Introduction* (UK: Sage, 1987; 5th edition, 2005) writes that 'the essence of any market is to bring goods and services to the attention of potential customers and keep their interest'. Thus, in mass media terms, the attention model is about stimulus to buy: communication is considered to have succeeded as soon as AUDIENCE attention has been won, regardless of how that attention was won. This paradigm contrasts with the TRANSMISSION MODEL OF MASS COMMUNICATION, which essentially relates to notions of PUBLIC SERVICE BROADCASTING; that is, the function of communication is to deliver *messages*, to transmit information, knowledge, education and enlightenment as well as to entertain. Hence public *service*. See *audience-as-public* and *audience-as-market* in the entry on AUDIENCE.

Attitudes We all hold a range of attitudes on a variety of topics and issues. An attitude, according to Milton Rokeach in 'The nature of attitudes', *Encyclopaedia of the Social Sciences* (UK: Collier-Macmillan, 1965), is '... a relatively enduring organization of beliefs around an object or situation predisposing one to respond in some preferential manner'.

Attitudes are learned from direct experience or through socialization and are capable of being changed. Attitudes may vary in their direction (that is, they may be positive, negative or neutral), in their intensity and in the degree of importance attached to them. It is possible to discern three component elements of an attitude: the *cognitive* component, that is the knowledge one has, true or false, about a particular subject which may have been gathered from a wide range of sources; the *affective* component, that is, one's emotional response or feelings towards a particular subject which will be linked to one's beliefs and VALUES; and the *behaviour* component, that is, how one reacts with respect to a certain subject.

Attitudes cannot be seen. Their existence can only be inferred from what people say or do. It is for this reason that accurate attitude measurement is considered to be highly problematic: people may not be that willing to communicate what they really think or feel. It is basically through communicating with others that one develops attitudes. Attitudes, once developed, influence the way in which we perceive other people and thus how we behave towards them. The mass media may shape, reinforce or challenge attitudes. For example, in conveying STEREOTYPES, mass media messages may shape people's attitudes towards GROUPS with which they have had little, if any, contact. CAMPAIGNS, such as ADVERTISING campaigns, may be designed to change people's attitudes towards a certain product.

Attribute dimensions of agenda-setting See AGENDA-SETTING.

Attribution theory Concerned with the psychological processes by which individuals attribute causes to behaviour. Such attribution can be *dispositional* – behaviour attributed to such factors as personality and attitude – or *situational* – behaviour attributed to factors in the situation. We may, for example, blame a person's failure to gain employment on his/her laziness (dispositional attribution) or on the state of the economy (situational attribution). We tend to overestimate the influence of dispositional factors in the behaviour of other people and underestimate the influence of situational factors. Dispositional attribution can be difficult to change as evidence suggests that we are unwilling to discard dispositional attributions even when they are discredited.

This may help explain the persistence of STEREOTYPES and PREJUDICE. Carole Wade and Carol Tavris in *Psychology* (US: HarperCollins, 1993) note, 'When it comes to explaining their own behaviour, most Westerners tend to choose attributes that are favourable to them ... This self-serving bias means that people like to take credit for their good actions and let the situation account for their bad ones.'

Several studies have, however, noted cross-cultural differences in the attribution process. For example, J.G. Miller conducted a study comparing subjects from the US with Hindus in India as regards the use of dispositional and situational attribution. In 'Culture and the development of everyday social explanation' in the *Journal of Personality and Social Psychology* 46 (1984) Miller reported his discovery that the subjects in the US were more likely than the Hindu subjects in India to employ dispositional rather than situational explanations for behaviour.

* William Gudykunst and Young Yun Kim, *Communicating with Strangers: An Approach to Intercultural Communication* (US: McGraw-Hill, 1997).

Audience Students of media communication recognize the term 'audience' as overarching all the reception processes of message sending. Thus there is the audience for theatre, TELEVISION and cinema; there is the RADIO listener; there is the audience for a pop concert or at a public meeting. Communicators shape their messages to fit the perceived needs of their audience: they calculate the level of receptiveness, the degree of readiness to accept the message and the mode of delivery. Audience is readership too and success in meeting audience/readership needs relies extensively on FEEDBACK, but perhaps more significantly of late, identification of what audience actually is. Does it in any meaningful sense actually exist, bearing in mind the inevitable fragmentation of the traditional audience for media as a result of the diversification of the modes and channels of mass communication on the one hand and the accelerating growth of network communication on the other? Denis McQuail in *Audience Analysis* (UK/US: Sage, 1997) writes of the 'audience problem', acknowledging that 'there is much room for differences of meaning, misunderstandings, and theoretical conflicts'. He goes on, 'The problems surrounding the concept [of audience] stem mainly from the fact that a single and simple word is being applied to an increasingly diverse and complex reality.'

McQuail's book addresses these problems in an interesting and illuminating manner. We know that audiences exist; the trouble is that without rigorous and sustained monitoring through research in one form or another, they are liable to 'escape' – that is, from agencies of control whether these are governments, institutions, advertisers or organizations that exist to place audiences under surveillance and produce the data on which decision-making is based.

McQuail does not go as far as agreeing with some commentators that the audience for mass media is verging on the extinct. In his chapter on 'The future of the audience concept' there is a subhead, 'The audience lives on', suggesting that the determination of communicators to hold on to mass audiences along with that of those who measure and monitor responses has been sufficiently successful to rescue audience from escape.

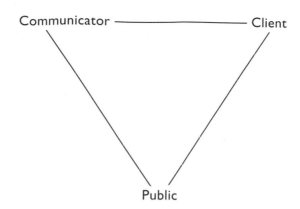

In other words, fragmentation has been checked, if not halted. Audiences are slower to switch allegiance – from public service broadcasting services, for example – than some have predicted; and a look at the popularity of many programmes offered in the UK by the BBC and independent television would give substance to that argument. We may still, as the words in the title of Ien Ang's 1991 publication, be *Desperately Seeking the Audience* (UK: Routledge & Kegan Paul), but research indicates, as McQuail points out, that the 'dispersion of [audience] attention among channels has been marked by moderation and gradualness'. The author concludes: 'We can no longer use the term without giving a clear indication of what we mean by it in a given instance, and any "measure" of audience will have to be understood in a specific way.' See *TOPIC GUIDE* under AUDIENCES/CONSUMPTION AND RECEPTION OF MEDIA.

* Pertti Alasuutari, ed., *Rethinking the Media Audience: The New Agenda* (UK: Sage, 1999); Will Brooker and Deborah Jermyn, eds, *The Audience Studies Reader* (UK: Routledge, 2003).

Audience: active audience An age-old media debate centres on the nature of audience reaction to media messages. The notion of the active audience considers audiences proactive and independent rather than docile and accepting. The active audience is seen to use the media rather than be used by it (see USES AND GRATIFICATIONS THEORY). This perception has come about substantially through findings of research which has observed members of audience consuming media in their own homes (see ETHNOGRAPHIC APPROACH TO AUDIENCE MEASUREMENT).

American media analyst Herbert Schiller takes issue with the optimistic view of the active or resistive audience. In *Culture Inc. The Corporate Takeover of Public Expression* (US: Oxford University Press, 1989), Schiller argues that transnational corporations have colonized culture and cultural expression, in the US and globally. He writes of 'corporate pillaging of the national information supply' and the 'proprietary control of information'. Such manifest power, he believes, calls into question the active-audience paradigm: 'A great emphasis is given to the "resistance", "subversion", and "empowerment" of the viewer. Where this resistance and subversion of the audience lead and what effects they have on the existing structure of power remain a mystery.'

Schiller goes on: 'It is not a matter of people being dupes, informational or cultural. It is that human beings are not equipped to deal with a pervasive disinformational system – administered from the command posts of social order – that assails the senses through all cultural forms and channels.'

In turn Schiller has been criticized for underestimating the potential resistance of audience to 'corporatization'. John B. Thompson in *The Media and Modernity: A Social Theory of Media* (UK: Polity, 1995) says that 'even if one sympathizes with Schiller's broad theoretical view and his critical perspectives, there are many respects in which the argument is deeply unsatisfactory'. In particular, Thompson counters Schiller's view that American cultural imperialism has wreaked havoc with indigenous cultures throughout the world, and that it is a seemingly unstoppable force. Thompson is of the opinion that 'Schiller … presents too uniform a view of American media culture … and of its global dominance'. See AUDIENCE: FRAGMENTATION OF; MEDIA IMPERIALISM; SELF-IDENTITY; SEMIOTIC POWER; TACTICS AND STRATEGIES.

Audience appreciation Term employed by RATINGS researchers, and to be differentiated from response measurement – to RADIO or TV programmes – concerned with numbers alone. Audience size, while being important, is considered by BBC radio as only one criterion for measurement; gauging audience interest (AI) and its judgement of quality is also crucial. In contrast, audience research into TV viewing focuses almost entirely on numbers watching. See BARB.

Audience: audience for news See NEWS: AUDIENCES FOR NEWS. See also *TOPIC GUIDE* under AUDIENCES/CONSUMPTION & RECEPTION OF MEDIA; MEDIA ISSUES & DEBATES; NEWS MEDIA.

Audience differentiation Like the 'mass', audiences – for RADIO, TELEVISION, the cinema or readers of the PRESS – are often simplistically regarded as a homogeneous lump. It is easier to make generalizations that way, but misleading. Audience differentiation works from the premise that analysis of audience response to media messages can be purposeful only if it recognizes that the mass is a complex of individuals, differentiated by gender, age, social class, profession, education and CULTURE. See ANALYSIS – MODES OF MEDIA ANALYSIS.

Audience: fragmentation of In *Audience Analysis* (UK: Sage, 1997), Denis McQuail publishes the following models, with acknowledgement to Jan van Cuilenburg, illustrating in four succeeding stages how audiences have become fragmented since the early years of TV. The Unitary Model 'implies a single audience that is more or less coextensive with the general public'. The texts of media – BROADCASTING in particular – were shared by all, and homogenous. With the expansion of provision and the increase in the number of channels, diversity is shown in the Pluralist Model, representing a 'pattern of limited internal diversification'. The Core–Periphery Model 'is one in which the multiplication of channels makes possible additional and competing alternatives outside this framework'.

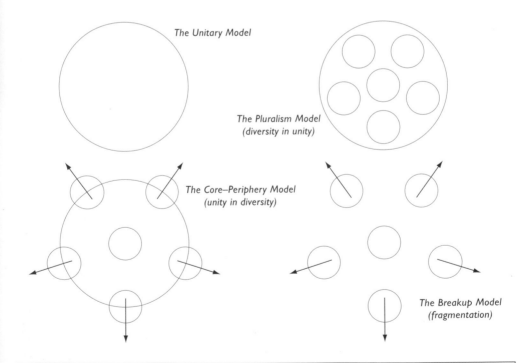

The Unitary Model

The Pluralism Model
(diversity in unity)

The Core–Periphery Model
(unity in diversity)

The Breakup Model
(fragmentation)

Models of audience fragmentation (McQuail, D., *Audience Analysis*, 1997, p. 138. Reproduced by permission of Sage Publications Inc.)

At this stage, says McQuail, 'it becomes possible to enjoy a television diet that differs significantly from the majority or mainstream'. The Breakup Model is characterized by 'extensive fragmentation and the disintegration of the central core. The audience is distributed over many different channels in no fixed pattern, and there is only sporadically shared audience experiences'.

McQuail says that currently and for the most part, the 'core' still dominates audience use of TV: 'The reasons lie primarily in the near-universal appeal of mainstream content and the advantages to media organizations of continuing with mass provision, plus the continuing habits and patterns of social life.' The author believes that 'media change is not enough on its own to disrupt established patterns of shared culture'. The breakup stage 'is certainly becoming more possible', but it is 'still a hypothetical pattern and has not been realized'. See DIGITIZATION.

Audience measurement Investigation of the size and constitution of mass media audiences has become one of the world's major service industries. Initially, audience measurement, or audience research (AR), is about number-crunching: How many readers? How many listeners or viewers? This data is then broken down along lines of class, gender, spending power, age, occupation, etc. There are two categories of measurement – quantitative and qualitative – with pressure always to translate the one into the other.

In the UK, audience measurement of one kind or another has operated since the beginning of BROADCASTING. Once the monopoly of the airwaves held by the BBC gave way to competition with the advent of commercial television, audience preferences became increasingly significant and audience measurement was quickly regarded as a duty and a lifeline for survival. In the UK the BBC and the ITCA (Independent TV Companies Association) share ownership of BARB (the Broadcasters' Audience Research Board) with Channel 5, BSkyB and the Institute of Practitioners in Advertising.

Two key terms (one might say dread terms, for programmes live or die by them) are *ratings* and *shares*. A rating is defined as the estimated percentage, in the case of television, of all the 'TV households' or of all the people within a demographic group who view a specific programme or station. A share refers to the percentage of the overall viewing figures which a particular programme commands. Such figures were traditionally obtained through telephone research, the use of viewing diaries and the set meter.

In 1983, a British firm, Audit of Great Britain (AGB), entered the US audience measurement field with the so-called people meter (introduced into Europe as early as 1978 by Irish Television Audience Measurement and in West Germany by Telescopie). The people meter is designed to combine the personal element of the diary with the electronic objectivity of the set meter. The premier US ratings company, ACNielsen, responsible for the immensely influential *Nielsen ratings*, answered AGB's challenge with the *Homeunit*.

Of course the problem with the people meter has turned out to be people: they forget to switch on or to switch off and this human trait plays havoc with the accuracy of viewing figures. Also, the people meter has not proved very popular with the networks because an unexpected outcome of its use has been the registration of lower viewing figures than those denoted by traditional modes of measurement.

As long ago as the 1980s, in *Inside Prime Time* (US: Pantheon, 1983), Todd Gitlin dubbed the obsession of the TV networks with ratings 'the fetish of immediate numerical gratification'. This fetish now extends to ways of measuring audience response using sensory devices that register viewing without buttons having to be pressed. The hunt for qualitative data arises essentially from the need of the sponsors and advertisers to have the question answered: Is TV helping us to sell our products? Current research in the States is focusing on 'single-source' measurement by linking the viewing habits of specific families to their actual purchasing habits. Households are provided with an electronic 'wand' connected to the TV's people meter. With this, the household shopping is checked in, using the universal product code stamped on most packaged goods.

A major problem that has come to further haunt the already hypersensitive minds of measurers of audience is the fragmentation of audience through cable, video, DVD, satellite, network communication and the multiple functions of hand-held devices, not to mention the difficulties facing measurement with the zapping and zipping that goes on, facilitated by the remote control pad. In *Desperately Seeking the Audience* (UK: Routledge, 1991), Ien Ang argues that the obsession with measurement is ultimately self-defeating: 'There is no way,' she writes, 'to foretell the ratings performance of a new programme.' There is equally no way that the networks, faced with the pressures upon them to prove that someone out there is taking notice, are going to heed Ang's conclusion: the audience must be conquered and controlled. See CUSTOM AUDIENCE

RESEARCH; DOWNLOADING; ETHNOGRAPHIC APPROACH TO AUDIENCE MEASUREMENT.

* Shaun Moores, *Interpreting Audiences: The Ethnography of Media Consumption* (UK: Sage, 1993); James S. Ettema and D. Charles Whitney, eds, *Audiencemaking: How Media Create the Audience* (US: Sage, 1994); Raymond Kent, ed., *Measuring Media Audiences* (UK: Routledge, 1994); Denis McQuail, *Audience Analysis* (UK: Sage, 1997).

Audience needs See USES AND GRATIFICATIONS THEORY; MASLOW'S HIERARCHY OF NEEDS. See also *TOPIC GUIDE* under AUDIENCES/CONSUMPTION & RECEPTION OF MEDIA; MEDIA: POWER, EFFECTS, INFLUENCE.

Autocue Or teleprompt. A device which uses angled mirrors to project the words of a script on to a screen just below the lens of the TV camera. This enables a presenter to 'read' a script without looking down.

Autonomy The capacity to be self-governing, self-controlling and able to act in an independent manner. The term can be applied to individuals, groups or institutions. Debate normally centres on the degree of autonomy a particular individual, group or institution has; an example here would be debate about the degree to which the BBC can act independently of the government of the day. See IMPARTIALITY.

Avant-garde The innovative, advance guard in any art form; usually assaulting tradition and boundaries of acceptability. The phrase was used as early as 1845 by Gabriel-Désiré Laverdant, and the anarchist Michael Bakunin named a periodical *L'Avant-garde* in 1878.

 B

Back region, front region See IMPRESSION MANAGEMENT.

Bad language Lars Gunnar Andersson and Peter Trudgill in *Bad Language* (UK: Penguin, 1990), whilst acknowledging that the term 'bad language' is far from clear and unambiguous, refer to it as 'all those things (sounds, words and phrases) that may be dangerous to use. Language contains explosive totems that should be handled with care'. The authors state that bad language can usefully be analysed by explaining the possible explosions which may be caused by certain words, pronunciations or use of grammar. They also argue that '"badness" is not found in the language itself but in people's views of the language', indicating the importance of examining the values, attitudes and ideologies within societies that underpin the evaluation of some language as 'bad'.

When ordinary people are asked, Andersson and Trudgill argue, '"What do you think of when you hear the phrase bad language?", most of them will certainly say "swearing"'. Whilst swearing seems to be for most people what 'bad' language is, Andersson and Trudgill point out that the term is also used to refer to the use of slang and jargon, the incorrect or misuse of words, certain accents and dialects and the use of 'non-standard' English. Several studies have shown that the evaluation of language as 'bad' in a particular instance will depend on a number of variables, which include the degree to which taboo words or words relating to taboo behaviour are used, the social context and the social roles, age and gender of the interactors.

The media also have to be mindful of the limits of acceptability as regards bad language or complaints will ensue. The Broadcasting Standards Council, for example, undertook a study in the early 1990s to explore perceptions of and attitudes towards bad language in response to the number of complaints received about its use, particularly on television. The results were published in a report edited by A. Millwood Hargrave entitled *A Matter of Manners? – The Limits of Broadcasting Language* (Broadcasting Standards Council, Research Monograph Series, 3, John Libbey, 1991).

The time of viewing and social context in which the programme was likely to be viewed, particularly the likelihood of children being around, were key variables affecting judgements regarding the acceptability of language used. Generally speaking the study found that the possibility that a word might offend others was an important factor in judging the acceptability of its use.

Bad or offensive language in UK broadcasting is dealt with in Section 1 of the Broadcasting Code of OFCOM, Protecting the Under-Eighteens.

Balanced programming The PILKINGTON REPORT, 1962, put forward three criteria for the creation of balance in TV programmes. Balance would be achieved, Pilkington stated, if channels provided the widest possible range of subject matter, if the fullest treatment was given to each subject within the range and if scheduling did not create imbalances by concentrating certain types of popular programmes at peak viewing times while relegating others, deemed less accessible, to inconvenient times.

Balance has a more controversial, political connotation when it is seen as a device to counter and control bias. More than any other medium public broadcasting aspires to *equilibrium*. Being fair to all sides can have paradoxical results: if one programme, for example, condemns the destruction of Amazon rainforests, must the balance be sustained by allowing a programme which defends that destruction? It is questionable whether fairness is actually achieved by giving airtime to ideas which flout the very principle of fairness.

Balance might ultimately mean always sitting on the fence; it may indicate a position which considers all standpoints to be tenable. Yet the balanced position – the fulcrum, as it were – from which other viewpoints are presented has to be decided by *someone* whose IMPARTIALITY in turn might be questioned by others.

Ball-Rokeach and DeFleur's dependency model of mass communication effects, 1976 (See also, DEPENDENCY THEORY.) Sandra Ball-Rokeach and Melvyn DeFleur's model poses the question, to what extent is contemporary society dependent, for information and for viewpoints, on the all-pervasive mass communication industry and, arising from this question, how far are we dependent on the media for our orientation towards the world beyond our immediate experience? In 'A dependency model of mass media effects' in *Communication Research*, 3 (1976), the authors argue that the nature and degree of dependency relate closely first to the extent to which society is subject to change, conflict or instability and second to the functions of information provision and attitude shaping of the mass media within those social structures.

The model emphasizes the essentially interactive nature of the processes of media effect. The societal and media systems interact and influence audience responses which in turn influence media and society. The

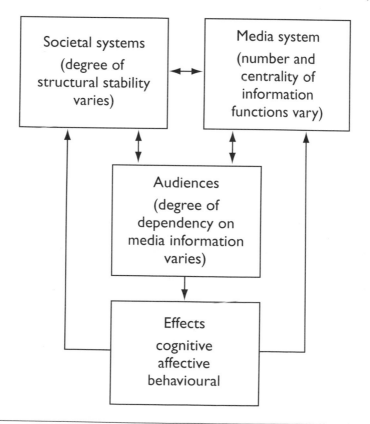

Ball-Rokeach and DeFleur's dependency model of communication effects, 1976

cognitive effect is that which relates to matters of the intellect and the affective to matters of emotion. In the cognitive area, the following areas of effect or influence are identified: creation and resolution of ambiguity; attitude formation; agenda-setting; expansion of people's belief systems; value clarification. Under the affective heading, the media may be perceived as creating fear or anxiety; increasing or decreasing morale; and establishing a sense of alienation.

In terms of the third category, behaviour, the effects may be to activate or de-activate; formulate issues and influence their resolution. They may stimulate a range of behaviours from political demonstrations to altruistic acts such as donating money to good causes. The authors cite the model as avoiding 'a seemingly untenable all-or-nothing position of saying either that the media have no significant impact on people or society, or that the media have an unbounded capacity to manipulate people and society'.

Where the model is open to most serious criticism is in its assumption that the societal structure and the media structure are independent of one another and that these are in some sort of equilibrium with audience. In many cases the media are so interlinked with power structures that a free interaction is more likely in theory than in practice. See COGNITIVE (AND AFFECTIVE); CULTURAL APPARATUS; HEGEMONY; MEDIATION; POWER ELITE.

Band-wagon effect See NOELLE-NEUMANN'S SPIRAL OF SILENCE MODEL OF PUBLIC OPINION, 1974.

Bandwidth Range of frequencies available for carrying data and expressed in hertz (cycles per second). The amount of traffic a communication channel can carry is roughly proportional to its bandwidth. See BROADBAND.

BARB Broadcasters' Audience Research Board, limited company jointly owned by the BBC and ITCA (Independent TV , Channel 5, BskyB and the Institute of Practitioners in Advertising.) See AUDIENCE MEASUREMENT.

Barnlund's transactional models of communication, 1970 In 'A transactional model of communication' in K.K. Sereno and C.D. Mortensen, eds, *Foundations of Communication Theory* (US: Harper & Row, 1970), Dean C. Barnlund attempts to address the 'complexities of human communication' which present 'an unbelievably

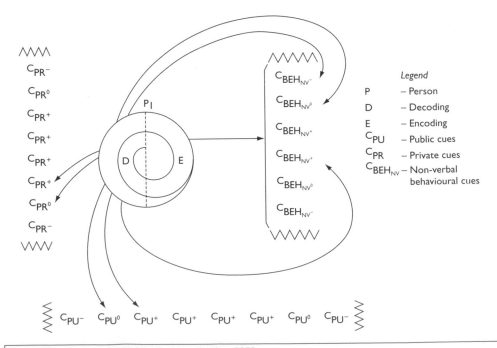

Barnlund's transactional models of communication, 1970

difficult challenge to the student of human affairs'. His model pays due respect to this complexity. For Barnlund, communication both describes the evolution of meaning and aims at the reduction of uncertainty. He stresses that meaning is something 'invented', 'assigned', 'given' rather than something 'received': 'Meanings may be generated while a man stands alone on a mountain trail or sits in the privacy of his study speculating about internal doubt.'

Within and around the communicant are *cues* of unlimited number, though some carry more weight – or valence – than others at any given time. Barnlund's model indicates three sets of cues, each interacting upon one another. These are *public* cues, *private* cues and *behavioural* cues. DECODING and ENCODING are visualized as part of the same spiralling process – continuous, unrepeatable and irreversible.

Public cues Barnlund divides into *natural* – those supplied by the physical world without the intervention of people, such as atmospheric conditions, natural occurrences – and *artificial* – those resulting from people's modification and manipulation of their environment. For example, Barnlund places his communicant, Mr A, in a doctor's waiting room which contains many public artificial cues – a pile of magazines, a smell of antiseptic, a picture by Joan Miró on the wall. Private cues emanate from sources not automatically available to any other person who enters a communicative field: 'Public and private cues may be verbal or non-verbal in form, but the critical quality is that they were brought into existence and remain beyond the control of the communicants.' The third set of cues – behavioural – are those initiated or controlled by the communicant him/herself and in response to public and private cues, coloured by the communicant's 'sensory-motor successes and failures in the past, combined with his current appetites and needs' which will establish 'his set towards the environment'.

In the second diagram, INTRAPERSONAL COMMUNICATION becomes INTERPERSONAL COMMUNICATION, with the multiplication of cues and the introduction of the message (M). Barnlund

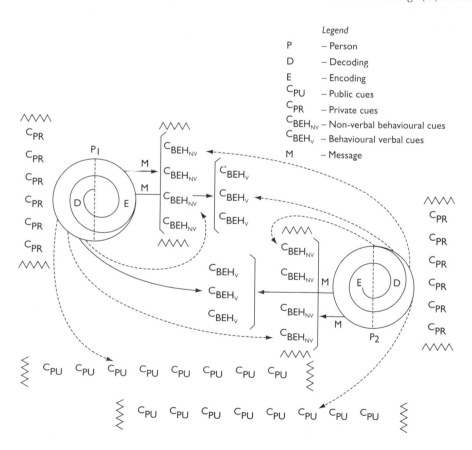

emphasizes the *transferability* of cues. Public cues can be transformed into private ones, private cues may be converted into public ones, while environmental and behavioural cues may merge. In short, the whole process is one of *transaction*, and few models have explored so impressively the inner dynamics of this process as Barnlund's, which also has useful application to the dynamics of MASS COMMUNICATION. See *TOPIC GUIDE* under COMMUNICATION MODELS.

Barrier signals Used as personal defence mechanisms in communication situations, gestures such as the placing of hands and arms across the body, or folding the arms. In the business world, the classic defensive barrier is the desk. On its role in the relationship between the executive and this modern version of the old moated castle and drawbridge, much has been written – about the size and dominance of the desk, its angle to the office door, the distance between the desk and the chair placed for those who approach the boss's territory. In *Manwatching: A Field Guide to Human Behaviour* (UK: Jonathan Cape, 1977), Desmond Morris would have us believe of the executive desk that 'many a businessman would feel naked without one and hides behind it gratefully every day, wearing it like a vast wooden chastity belt'.

Basic needs See MASLOW'S HIERARCHY OF NEEDS.

Bass's 'double action' model of internal news flow, 1969 A development of two earlier classic models addressing the processes of media news production – WHITE'S GATEKEEPER MODEL, 1950 and McNELLY'S MODEL OF NEWS FLOW, 1959. In his article, 'Refining the gatekeeper concept' in *Journalism Quarterly*, 46 (1969), A.Z. Bass argues that the most important 'gates' in the exercise of GATE-KEEPING are located within the news organization. Bass divides the operation into a newsgathering stage and a news processing stage.

Writers, reporters and local editors are closer to the 'raw' news, the event, than those involved in Stage II of the gatekeeping process, while those involved at Stage II are closer to the power centre of the organization and therefore more subject to the organization's norms and VALUES and to pressures from competing stories. See MALETZKE'S MODEL OF THE MASS COMMUNICATION PROCESS, 1963.

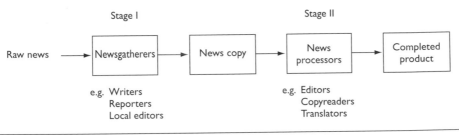

Bass's 'double action' model of internal news flow, 1969

Baton signal Chiefly manual gestures with which we beat time to the rhythm of spoken expression and which give emphasis and urgency. They are the stock-in-trade of declamatory communication, especially that of politicians. Not only the hands are employed in baton signals, but the head, shoulders and feet. See NON-VERBAL BEHAVIOUR: REPERTOIRE.

'Battle of the Somme, The' See 'SOMME, THE BATTLE OF THE'.

BBC See BBC DIGITAL; BBC, ORIGINS; BBC WORLDWIDE; BROADCASTING; BROADCAST-ING LEGISLATION; PUBLIC SERVICE BROADCASTING (PSB); RADIO BROADCASTING; REI-THIAN; SELSDON COMMITTEE REPORT ON TELEVISION, 1935; TELEVISION BROADCAST-ING; ULLSWATER COMMITTEE REPORT ON BROADCASTING, 1936. See also *TOPIC GUIDE* under BROADCASTING.

BBC America Launched in March 1998, BBC America comprises a broadcasting partnership between the BBC and the Discovery Channel of the US, issuing via cable and pay-TV channels worldwide, the 'best of the Beeb'.

BBC Digital The UK BBC anticipated, in 2001, the eventual shift from analogue to digital transmission of TV and RADIO, with a digital supplement to BBC1, giving viewers equipped with digital sets, or set-top conversion boxes, access to a broader range of programmes, including an interactive facility, than those available to viewers with analogue sets. The same extra provision became available to viewers of BBC2. On air shortly afterwards were the following new services: CBBC, a channel for children aged between six and thirteen; CBeebies, for children under six; BBC4, an in-depth culture channel; BBC News 24 and BBC Choice aimed at a young adult audience, eventually to be retitled BBC3, and given the go-ahead by government in September 2002.

Interactive services across all digital channels come under the umbrella term BBCi. In addition, BBC Parliament covers all aspects of government, at home and in the European community. With the collapse in 2002 of ITV Digital, a pay service, the BBC was permitted by government to take up the shortfall in digital services, making these an impressive – and *free* – alternative to existing commercial digital channels.

Access to digital radio via the BBC has been available since 1995 on BBC Radio 1, 2, 3, 4 and 5 Live. From 2002 five new services came on stream – BBC 5 Live Sports Extra; 6Music, aimed at rock and pop fans; 1Xtra, targeting young audiences interested in contemporary black music; BBC7, broadcasting comedy, book readings and drama for all ages; and BBC Asian Network. The longstanding BBC World Service became available in the UK digitally in 2002. The BBC's digital transmitters were planned to reach some 85 per cent of the UK population by 2004, though by 2005 there were still many areas unable to access Freeview channels via a digibox.

BBC: Government White Paper, 1994 The future of the BBC was guaranteed for another ten years by the White Paper, *The Future of the BBC: Serving the Nation, Competing Worldwide*. In renewing the corporation's charter, the White Paper confirmed that the BBC would continue as the main provider of PUBLIC SERVICE BROADCASTING (PSB). It should contribute to the growth of cable and satellite services; further develop commercial TV services worldwide; continue to provide a broad spectrum of TV and radio programmes; guarantee special support for news, current affairs and educational programmes; and cover cultural and sporting activities which 'bring the nation together'. As well as recommending giving more attention to the views of audience on matters of taste and decency, the White Paper proposed the merger of the Broadcasting Standards Council with the Broadcasting Complaints Commission, the function of the new council to monitor standards and provide guidance. See COMMUNICATIONS ACT (UK), 2003.

BBC, origins The BBC began life as the British Broadcasting Company, incorporated on 15 December 1922 and receiving its licence to broadcast on 18 January 1923. It was a private company made up chiefly of manufacturers of broadcasting equipment. The company was incorporated with 100,000 shares of stock worth £1 each. Any British wireless manufacturer could join by purchasing one or more shares, making a £50 deposit and agreeing to the terms that had been drawn up by the negotiating manufacturers and the Postmaster-General.

The six largest manufacturers, in return for guaranteeing the continuing operation and financial solvency of the company, were given control. Although other manufacturers could buy stock and be admitted to membership, the principals could choose six of the company's nine directors and these in turn had the power to select its chairman. Each wireless set owner had to pay a 10 shilling (50p) licence fee to the Post Office annually and the government agreed to issue licences only to people using receivers made by members of the company. Thus the manufacturers were guaranteed protection against competition.

The company was to establish eight broadcasting stations in different parts of the British Isles. Only news originating from four established NEWS AGENCIES (such as the Press Association and Reuters) could be used in broadcasting and there was to be no advertising. By April 1923 the Postmaster-General had appointed a seven-man investigating committee to review the status of the British Broadcasting Company, headed by Sir Frederick Sykes, with a mandate to consider 'broadcasting in all its aspects'.

The Sykes Committee faced questions on widespread evasions of the equipment monopoly and condemnation by Beaverbrook newspapers of the control of the six. After 34 meetings, the Committee recommended – and the government accepted – a single receiver licence of 10 shillings to cover all types of radios, and the ban was raised on foreign receivers. Most importantly, Sykes forecast the eventual replacement of private by public operation: '... we consider that the control of such a potential power [of broadcasting] over public opinion and the life of the nation ought to remain with the State, and that the operation of so important a national service ought not to be allowed to become an unrestricted commercial monopoly'.

However, Mazzoleni is of the opinion that to attribute Berlusconi's electoral success solely to his media power is a short-sighted reading of the complexity of the Berlusconi phenomenon. Rather his message, greatly aided by the power to communicate it across the nation, 'was successful because it found several ears ready to listen to it'. Further, Berlusconi understood perhaps more clearly than any other media mogul that today's elections are not only fought out on the television screen, they are about grabbing popular attention by combining the emotive with the entertaining.

Though Berlusconi's first premiership was short-lived – he resigned office within months – it set agendas for the future of political communication; and to prove that his electoral success was not a flash in the pan, Berlusconi was returned to office in the Italian elections of 2001. His position as prime minister has allowed him indirect control over state broadcasting, and a study by researchers at the University of Pavia in 2002 found that the time allocated on state broadcasting to the political opposition had been reduced by 10 per cent. Between May and July 2000 government airtime on RAI 2 news bulletins received 61 per cent of airtime compared with the opposition's 19 per cent.

As one opposition spokesman, Paoli Gentiloni, was quoted as saying, 'RAI news programmes are increasingly the voice of the government, while the space reserved for the opposition has been drastically reduced.' On Berlusconi's own channels the opposition received less than 5 per cent of political airtime on two channels and 23 per cent on the Channel 5 news programme. See *TOPIC GUIDE* under MEDIA: OWNERSHIP & CONTROL.

Bernstein's wheel, 1984   Refers to a model designed by David Bernstein to aid the planning of an organization's communication activities, for example public relations and associated activities. At the hub of the wheel is the organization. This in turn is located in the context of its industrial or commercial sector and its country of origin. Each of these contextual factors will, of course, have an impact on the nature of the communication activities.

The inner circle of the wheel represents the options available as regards channels of communication that may be used to reach the designated PUBLICS: advertising, correspondence, point of sale, public relations, personal presentation, impersonal presentation, product, literature and placement media. At the outer circle of the wheel are the various publics to be reached: the trade, the media, government, financial, customers, general public, internal, local and influential groups. A message may of course be designed to reach several publics and it may be appropriate to divide them into primary and secondary publics or audiences.

The wheel can be spun such that the inner circle can turn within the outer circle so that channels can be matched to publics. Thus the wheel can be used when planning which types of publics need to be reached and by what means. Several channels may be used to reach any one public. In *Company Image and Reality* (UK: Holt, Rinehart & Winston, 1984) David Bernstein argues that the wheel is designed to 'stimulate some fresh thoughts and encourage the thinker to regard corporate communications as a totality rather than a series of discrete messages to discrete audiences'. He continues, 'A company needs to take a holistic view of communication because it is communicating all the time (even if it doesn't want to or doesn't realize it), to all of those nine publics.'

Beveridge Committee Report on Broadcasting, 1950   Both from a theoretical and a practical point of view the Committee chaired by Lord Beveridge conducted the most thorough examination of broadcasting in Britain since its inception. Beveridge went to considerable lengths to identify and discuss the dangers of monopoly, as then held by the BBC. Nevertheless proposals for competitive broadcasting were rejected on the grounds that programmes would deteriorate in quality if there were rival corporations. Beveridge was equally firm in believing that broadcasting should be independent of government control, and declared against suggestions that the power of the BBC should be curbed through closer parliamentary supervision.

To prevent broadcasting becoming an uncontrolled bureaucracy, Beveridge recommended more active surveillance of output by the BBC's Board of Governors and a 'Public Representation Service' to bridge the gap between the BBC and the general public. Additionally, the Committee proposed regional and functional devolution of some of the corporation's activities, more comprehensive reports by the BBC on its work, and five-year reviews by small independent committees. A major recommendation which made no headway was that the monopoly of broadcasting be extended to local authorities and universities, allowing them to operate FM radio stations.

Commercial broadcasting in the US style was not approved of: 'Sponsoring ... puts the control of broadcasting ultimately in the hands of people whose interest is not broadcasting but the selling of some other goods or services or the propagation of particular ideas.' Interestingly, four of the eleven committee members (including Lord Beveridge) dissented from the majority verdict against any form of commercial advertising. See *TOPIC GUIDE* under COMMISSIONS, COMMITTEES, LEGISLATION.

Bias, biased From the French, *biais*, slant; a one-sided inclination of the mind. The student of communication approaches this term with extreme caution, for bias generally belongs to the realm of PERCEPTION, and other people's perceptions at that: like beauty, bias lies in the eye of the beholder, whose vision is coloured by VALUES and previous experience. The accusation of bias tends to be predicated on the assumption that there is an opposite – OBJECTIVITY; that there is an attainable ideal called IMPARTIALITY; that freedom from bias is not only possible but desirable. To speak, publish or broadcast without bias would imply the use of LANGUAGE which is value-free. Yet however careful we might be in what we say, we disclose something of ourselves, what shaped and formed us; what counts with us, what we value. When other people appear to call that value into question, we may be tempted to classify them as biased.

* Barrie Gunter, *Measuring Bias on Television* (UK: University of Luton Press, 1997).

Bibliotherapy Or 'book therapy'; help with human problems by means of books. Used chiefly with young people, bibliotherapy has also successfully been introduced to the elderly in long-stay hospital wards or other institutions.

Bifurcation of belief See IMPARTIALITY.

Bigotry An inability and/or unwillingness to consider views, beliefs, values and opinions other than the ones you already hold. The term refers to the rigid way in which an individual may hold his/her views, beliefs and so on. Bigotry is often allied with PREJUDICE. Clearly bigotry is a cause of NOISE within INTERPERSONAL COMMUNICATION. As regards the process of MASS COMMUNICATION one area of debate is whether or not television programmes designed to ridicule bigotry, particularly racial bigotry, succeed in doing this among all sections of the viewing audience.

Two notable examples here are *Till Death Us Do Part*, a very popular comedy in the UK in the late 1960s and early 1970s on BBC1 and its American counterpart, *All in the Family*. *Till Death Us Do Part* focused on the bigotry of its central character, Alf Garnett. Johnny Speight who devised the programme intended to ridicule Alf Garnett's bigotry but as Angela Barry argues in 'Black mythologies: representations of black people on British television' in John Twitchin, ed., *The Black and White Media Book* (UK: Trentham Books, 1990), the overall effect of the programme was the opposite.

The public airing of Alf Garnett's views gave them a real 'legitimacy'. Similar research was done on *All in the Family* (whose leading character Archie Bunker matched Alf Garnett for bigotry) by Neil Vidmar and Milton Rokeach. Their article 'Archie Bunker's bigotry: a study in selective perception and exposure' in the *Journal of Communication*, Winter 1974, concluded that the programme, whatever its intentions, often reinforced the bigotry of those viewers whose prejudice it most sought to challenge. See RACISM.

Binary opposition See POLARIZATION; SEMANTIC DIFFERENTIAL; WEDOM, THEYDOM.

Bit See COMPUTERS IN COMMUNICATION.

Black English See COMMUNICATION: INTERCULTURAL COMMUNICATION.

Blacklisting See HUAC: HOUSE UN-AMERICAN ACTIVITIES COMMITTEE.

Blogging Derives from weblogging, the practice by thousands worldwide of 'diary writing' for consumption on the Internet. Fascination with other people's lives, their intimate thoughts and reflections, is only one factor explaining what draws visitors to blogging. For example, Salam Pax, recording his experiences from the heart of Baghdad during the Iraq War (2003), provided a unique insight into the situation of an ordinary Iraqi subject to the awesome firepower of the coalition forces of the US and the UK. A woman's take on the military occupation of Iraq, *Baghdad Burning: Girl Blog from Iraq*, written under the pseudonym Riverhead, was published in 2005 in the US by the University of New York Press and in the UK by Marion Boyars. The book was a prize winner in the LETTRE ULYSSES AWARDS for the art of reportage, 2005.

In 'Disruptive technology: Iraq and the Internet', published in *Tell Me Lies: Propaganda and Media Distortion in the Attack on Iraq* (UK/US: Sage, 2004), edited by David Miller, Alistair Alexander cites blogging as a support and pressurize those in power to take some desired action. Access to the mass media is often crucial for a pressure group's successful campaign. Media personnel may also initiate campaigns to raise their audience's awareness of certain issues – child abuse, for example. Indeed such campaigns can be seen as part of the mass media's AGENDA-SETTING role. One focus for media research has been the measurement of how effective campaigns are.

Campaign for Press and Broadcasting Freedom UK organization founded by John Jennings in 1979 as a broad-based non-political party pressure group dedicated to making Britain's media more open, diverse and accountable. Specifically the Campaign has worked for the RIGHT OF REPLY, freedom of information legislation and more community-based and 'alternative' newspapers. It is a stalwart supporter of PUBLIC SERVICE BROADCASTING (PSB). The Campaign publishes a bi-monthly bulletin, *Free Press*.

---

* www.cpbf.org.uk

Campaign for Quality Television Report (UK), 1999 Written by Steven Barnett and Emily Seymour on behalf of the charity dedicated to promote PUBLIC SERVICE BROADCASTING (PSB), *A Shrinking Iceberg Travelling South* highlighted the decline in serious drama and current affairs reporting in UK television. The authors' research found that the single or one-off play had been largely replaced by drama series dominated by police/detective stories; that homegrown TV drama had suffered relegation in face of American imports.

A *domestic* agenda was the key feature of NEWS and information services. As for investigative JOURNALISM, the report found that there is scant room for 'speculative' investigations and very little programme innovation. 'Within the BBC,' comment Barnett and Seymour, referring to 30 confidential interviews with senior producers, 'there is concern that current affairs has lost its sense of direction and that internal structural changes have weakened its creative potential.' Formed in 1988, the Campaign for Quality Television was relaunched in 1995. See CASUALIZATION; TELEVISION DRAMA.

Captive audience advertising See ADVERTISING: AMBIENT ADVERTISING.

Cards See CIGARETTE CARDS; PICTURE POSTCARDS.

Caricature A distorted REPRESENTATION of a person, type or action. Though we generally associate caricature with humorous cartoons, the process of distortion has played an important role in art. Known to the Egyptians and Greeks, caricature was revived by Italian artists of the Renaissance and developed throughout Europe in the eighteenth century. In England, artists such as Rowlandson (1756–1827) combined high-quality draughtsmanship with trenchant social and political satire. Though the most famous, *Punch* was only one among many magazines carrying cartoons in the nineteenth century. In England, *Vanity Fair* (founded 1868) proved a rival. In the US, *Puck* (1876), in France, *Le Rire* (1894), in Germany, *Simplicissimus* (1896), made the cartoon the most impactful form of printed illustration prior to the regular use of photography. The best known of all US magazines carrying cartoons, the *New Yorker*, was founded in 1925.

Carnivore Original title of computer software enabling the FBI in the US to 'spy' on global e-mailing by responding to the use of certain words; renamed DCS 1000 in order to conceal its teeth and its tracks. See HACKER, HACKTIVIST; REGULATION OF INVESTIGATORY POWERS ACT (RIPA) (UK), 2000; SURVEILLANCE SOCIETY.

Cartoons In fine art, a cartoon is the final preparatory drawing for a large-scale painting, tapestry or mosaic. The Leonardo cartoon in the National Gallery, London, is a notable example – ready for final working, but never completed by the artist. In modern terms, the cartoon is a humorous illustration or strip of illustrations. In 1841 a series of fine art cartoons was designed for paintings in the new Houses of Parliament in London. The satirical magazine *Punch*, founded in that year, poked fun at the drawings, with sketches entitled 'Punch's Cartoons'.

According to Alan Coren in his Foreword to W. Hewison's *The Cartoon Connection* (UK: Elm Tree Books, 1977), cartoons were born 'in the far Aurignacian days of 20,000 BC', when 'a squat, hirsute, browless man one morning dipped his stick in a dark rooty liquid, bent straight again, and, on the cave-wall of Lascaux, drew a joke about men running after buffalo'.

Hewison calls the cartoon 'drawn humour' and lists the following cartoon categories: (1) recognition humour (where the viewer recognizes the workings of human nature); (2) social comment (very often recognition humour with a message); (3) visual puns; (4) zany (or screw-ball); (5) black humour (or sick, or bad taste); (6) geometric (where, for example, lines are made to fall in love with dots); (7) faux naif (pretended naivety) – 'when an ideas man can draw but cannot develop a satisfactory comic style of cartoon drawing, he quite often throws in the towel and adopts a deliberately childlike style'; and (8) the strip cartoon, the originator of which was Wilhelm Busch (1832–1904).

On the screen, Walt Disney has dominated the field of the animated cartoon but there have been many others: Paul Terry's *Terrytoons*, Pat Sulliven's *Felix the Cat*, Bob Cannon's *Gerald McBoing-Boing*, Ernest Pintoff's Human Rectangle *Flebus*, Tex Avery's *Chilly Willy*, the endlessly warring *Tom and Jerry* created by William Hanna, Joe Barbera and Fred Quimby, along with countless others such as *Top Cat*, *Scooby Doo* and the *Flintstones*, Walter Lantz's *Woody Woodpecker* and Terry Gilliam's contributions to *Monty Python's Flying Circus*.

Among those artists who have attempted to push the cartoon on film in an innovative direction are the Hungarian John Halas and his wife Joy Batchelor, Richard Williams and Bob Godfrey. In recent years Matt Groening's *The Simpsons* became arguably the world's most watched TV cartoon. Today's TV and movie cartoons benefit from computer-generated imaging.

Casualization In the UK in the late 1980s and 1990s, the casualization of jobs by shifting full-time to part-time appointments, and the offering of short-term work contracts, was particularly prevalent in the media and has continued into the new millennium. A good many of those who left the various BROADCASTING organizations have entered the freelance market or set up small independent production companies. More and more work traditionally done 'in-house' has been offered on a freelance basis or to independent production companies, many of which also employ a significant number of workers on short-term contracts or as freelances.

Catalyst effect Where a book, newspaper, film, TV or RADIO programme has the effect of modifying a situation, or taking a mediating role. The actual presence of TV cameras may, it is believed, influence the course of events. The debate continues as to whether such effects are substantial or marginal, for reliable proof is hard to come by. See MEDIATION.

Catharsis From the Greek, 'purging', catharsis is the effect upon an audience of tragedy in drama or the novel. The Greek philosopher Aristotle perceived the function of great tragedy to be the release of pent-up emotions in the audience. As a consequence, the mind is cleansed and purified. The so-termed *catharsis hypothesis* suggests that violence and aggression in films and on TV have a therapeutic effect. Exponents of this idea argue that the involvement in fantasy aggression may serve as a form of displacement, providing a harmless 'release' from hostile impulses which might otherwise be acted out. See EFFECTS OF THE MASS MEDIA.

CCTV: closed-circuit television One of the key means of public and private SURVEILLANCE contributing to what Bryan Appleyard in a UK *Sunday Times* article, 'No hiding place' (15 April 2001) describes as 'the final turn of the screw' in the transformation of Britain into a 'surveillance state' (see SURVEILLANCE SOCIETY). Appleyard's estimate at the time of writing was that over 1.5 million CCTV cameras were in operation in the UK and some, 'as in the London borough of Newham, use facial recognition software that automatically identifies target individuals'.

The author worries that 'a police state with powers of control and surveillance beyond the wildest dreams of Hitler and Stalin could be established in Britain within 24 hours ... But the weirdest thing of all is that we really don't care'. It would seem that the public 'have such fear of crime, and such a mute acceptance of the seizure of power by the authorities, that we are actually comforted by the thought that we are being watched all the time'. See ECHELON; REGULATION OF INVESTIGATORY POWERS ACT (RIPA) (UK), 2000.

CD: compact disc See MP3.

Ceefax Trade name of the teletext service offered by the BBC since September 1974, giving viewers access to information on a wide range of services. The commercial television equivalent is Teletext.

Celebrity See JOURNALISM: CELEBRITY JOURNALISM.

Cellular radio Comprises RADIO frequencies divided up into 'cells' of air waves facilitating, in particular, personal communications systems. For example, anyone operating a car telephone will be switched communication network, the sooner he/she will be in possession of all the information at the disposal of the group. Influence is closely related to possession of information because the possessor has the power to choose what information to pass on, and to whom. Communication networks differ in the degree of centrality and the number of levels of centrality possible within them.

Centres for research into the media See RESEARCH CENTRES (INTO THE MEDIA).

Certification of films (UK) For several years until December 1982, the BRITISH BOARD OF FILM CEN-SORS had the following system of certification: X, denoting films with high sex and violence content or other disturbing subject matter which those under 18 were not permitted to see in cinemas; AA films from which children under 14 were barred; A films to which children were admitted if accompanied by an adult; and U-certificate films admitting all.

These were replaced in 1982 with 18 (permitting admission for those 18 and over); 15 (replacing AA, and raising the admission age from 14 to 15); PG (Parental Guidance, a symbol used in the US, and intended to show that a film contains some scenes which individual parents may feel unsuitable for children); and U as before. A 12 certificate was introduced in 1989, mainly to target the first film in the *Batman* series.

In August 2002 the British Board of Film Classification, under pressure from a number of sources, including parents and children, made an adjustment to the 12 certification by adding a 12A rating, meaning that children could see formerly restricted films – such as *Spider-Man* – so long as they were accompanied by an adult over 18.

The 12A certificate marked the arrival of former civil servant Sir Quentin Thomas as chief censor. It brought Britain into line with other countries, including the US, Canada, Japan, Ireland, New Zealand and Spain. The first film to carry a UK 12A certificate was *The Bourne Identity* starring Matt Damon. 12A certification requires that posters advertising such films should carry warnings about scenes involving violence, sex and bad language. The 12 rating remains for film videos. See H-CERTIFICATE.

Chamberlain, Lord See LORD CHAMBERLAIN.

Channel Each MESSAGE-carrying signal requires its route along which it is transmitted from the sender to the receiver and along which FEEDBACK may be obtained. Channels may be physical (our voices or bodies), technical (the telephone) or social (our schools, media, etc.). In business organizations or institutions they may be vertical, hierarchical, formal and predominantly one-way – from the boss downwards; or horizontal, democratic, informal and two-way as between workmates and groups with common tasks, interests and sympathies. Like country paths, channels need to be kept open and frequented – and sometimes repaired – if they are to continue to be recognized as viable. See COSMOPOLITE AND LOCALITE CHANNELS; JAKOBSON'S MODEL OF COMMUNICATION, 1958; PHATIC (LANGUAGE); SHANNON AND WEAVER'S MODEL OF COMMUNICATION, 1949.

Channel capacity C.E. Shannon and W.E. Weaver use this term to describe the upper limit of information that any communication system can handle at a given time. To discover this limit, it is first essential to know how much uncertainty – or *entropy* – a given signal will eliminate. See REDUNDANCY.

Channel 4 (UK) Under the direction of Jeremy Isaacs, in 1982 C4 became the UK's fourth TV channel, the 'quality' arm of commercial television. The new organization quickly became a major sponsor of independently made movies, drama series and documentaries. From the start the channel set out to challenge set ways and attitudes. Much of its programming was international in theme, whether the subject was poverty in the developing world or American football. The new channel proved the argument for *broad*casting, mixing popular viewing with minority-interest programmes and showing that the entertaining could be combined with the serious without sacrificing standards.

C4 became the first channel to provide a full hour of news daily. It was to create a high reputation for the funding of feature films, some of which, like *Four Weddings and a Funeral* (1994), proved worldwide cinema successes. The BROADCASTING ACT, 1990, cleared the way for C4 to negotiate directly its own advertising revenue. The Welsh fourth channel is called Saniel Pedwar Cymru (S4C). See COMMUNICATIONS ACT (UK), 2003; OFCOM: OFFICE OF COMMUNICATIONS (UK).

Channel 5 (UK) The Independent Television Commission of the UK awarded Britain's fifth national terrestrial TV channel to Channel 5 Broadcasting in October 1995. It began broadcasting in January 1997 and is now known as five.

Chapultepec, Declaration of, 1994 Adopted 11 March in Mexico City by the Hemisphere Conference on Free Speech, organized by the Inter American Press Association (IAPA), the Declaration states, 'A free press enables societies to resolve their conflicts, promote their well-being and protect their liberty.' The defence of the freedom of the press is absolute and unqualified: 'No law or act of government may limit freedom of expression or of the press, whatever the medium.' Chapultepec rejects prior CENSORSHIP (Clause 5), licences for the importation of paper, newsgathering equipment and the assigning of RADIO frequencies (Clause 7), and asserts that no news medium or journalist may be punished for publishing the truth or for criticizing or denouncing government (Clause 10). See NEW WORLD INFORMATION ORDER; TALLOIRES DECLARATION.

Characteristics of mass communications See MASS COMMUNICATION: SEVEN CHARACTERISTICS.

Chequebook journalism A euphemism for bribery – newspapers paying someone for exclusive rights on his or her story. The police pay their 'snouts' or 'grasses' for the common good; the press pay their informants for tomorrow's headline, to serve the public's 'right to know' and to boost sales in the war of circulation.

Children, Young People and the Changing Media Environment Title of a major research project carried out in 12 countries during 1997–98, involving a survey of almost 15,000 children and young people. Directed by Sonia Livingstone of the Media Research Group of the London School of Economics and Political Science, in collaboration with George Gaskell and Moira Bovill, the survey's ongoing findings about how young people use the media were published in a special issue of the *European Journal of Communication*, December 1998 – 'Young People and the Changing Media Environment'.

Themes addressed in the research project and summarized in the *EJC* are Young People's Ownership and Uses of New and Old Forms of Media in Britain and The Netherlands; Patterns of Old and New Media Use among Young People in Flanders, Germany and Sweden; Family Lifestyles and Media Use Patterns; Media Use and the Relationships of Children and Teenagers with their Peer Groups; and Global Culture in Practice – a look at children and adolescents in Denmark, France and Israel.

The survey revealed valuable data for further investigation. For example, only 64 per cent of British children possessed a shelf of books compared with 95 per cent of the Dutch children questioned, and personal ownership of a computer in the UK was 48 per cent compared with 85 per cent in Holland. British children, however, watch more TV, the researchers explaining this as being in part due to the 'enviable reputation for producing quality programmes … in Britain'.

A research team led by Dafna Lemish reported on interesting initial perspectives concerning young people – French, Danish and Israeli – and their mediated relations with global CULTURE. They write that 'media seem to connect young audiences to the social "centre" of humankind', while the Internet is seen as 'another type of transnational social space'. Young people seem at ease with the *hybridity* of modern culture: '… What we understand from our informants is that the meeting between the global and the local can be [that] of coexistence and conflation, rather than assimilation vs isolationism.'

* David Buckingham, *Small Screens: Television for Children* (UK/US: Leicester University Press, 2002).

Chronology News narratives on TV are often compared to those of fictional stories (see STORYNESS) but there are obvious differences, an important one being divergence over chronology. 'In news,' writes Allan Bell in *The Language of News Media* (UK: Blackwell, 1991), 'order is everything but chronology is nothing.' Indeed, in the news narrative the climax is reported first whereas in a story this usually comes at the end. Chronology has a low priority in the construction of news stories to the point where AUDIENCE has to be highly news-literate to follow what is going on. Bell says, 'The time structure of news stories can make the shape of a difficult film or novel look straightforward in comparison.' See AGENDA-SETTING.

Cigarette cards: cultural indicators A US company, Allen Ginter, produced the forerunner of the first British cigarette card when it packed with its Richmond Gem brand a pair of oval cards held together by a stud, one section of which was a calendar for 1884, with UK parcel postage rates on the back. By the 1890s the larger British tobacco companies were issuing cards, beginning with advertisements then progressing to series on particular themes such as soldiers, ships, royalty, sport and famous beauties.

The first company to issue photographic cigarette cards on a large scale was Ogdens which, in 1894, began its Guinea Gold and Tabs cards covering, in the next 13 years, practically every facet of life of that period. In the early 1900s there were around 50 companies issuing cards in the UK and Ireland. Reflecting the dominance of the British Empire, the cards represented many military issues, along with major inventions of the time – the motor car and the aeroplane. Exploration and discovery, and the Edwardian craze for collecting things – birds' eggs, butterflies, porcelain – were prominently reflected in the choice of subject matter, as were the music hall and the scouting movement.

Early in the First World War (1914–18) the Wills company actually issued cards as miniature recruiting posters while in 1915 and 1916, Gallahers put out several series of Victoria Cross Heroes. Carreras issued Women on War Work and Raemaker's War Cartoons portraying the Germans as barbarians.

Later examples of these cultural ephemera were Gallahers' Boy Scouts, Fables and Their Morals; Wills' Cinema Stars and Radio Celebrities. Ogdens produced a series on Broadcasting. With the approach of the Second World War (1939–45) Carreras produced Britain's Defences (1938), Players issued Aircraft of the RAF in the same year and in 1939 Modern Naval Craft. The most ambitious cigarette card enterprise of the period was the Imperial Tobacco Company's Air Raid Precautions, made available in a variety of cigarette brands.

Cigarette card production remained popular in the post-war era, though the 1960s saw a marked decline. In the 1970s came the much sought-after series from Player, The Golden Age of Motoring, packed in Doncella cigars. The Golden Age continued with Steam (1976), Flying (1977) and Sail (1978). See PICTURE POSTCARDS.

Cine-clubs Played an important role in the development of cinema in many countries. Where in the commercial film theatres, popular entertainment monopolized programmes, the cine-clubs showed new experimental and often non-fictional work. John Grierson (1898–1972) organized the first British showing of Sergei Eisenstein's *Battleship Potemkin* at the London Film Society (formed in 1925) in 1929, along with his own seminal documentary *Drifters*. Minister of Propaganda in Nazi Germany, Goebbels, outlawed all cine-clubs because of their 'subversive' nature and a similar fate befell the cine-club movement in pre-Second World War Japan.

The Depression and the failure of the media to meet head on the causes of depression helped give belated birth to the US cine-club movement. The Workers' Film and Photo League, soon renamed the National Film and Photo League, was formed in New York in 1930. Members of the League made films as well as watched them, concentrating on filming the hunger marches and other mass protests of the time. Among their creations was a Workers' Newsreel which the League persuaded some commercial cinemas to screen.

Cinema See CINEMATOGRAPHY, ORIGINS; FILM.

Cinema legislation The first legislation in the UK relating to cinema use was the Cinematograph Act of 1909. It concerned the licensing of exhibition premises and the safety of audiences. In 1922, the Celluloid and Cinematograph Film Act drew up safety rules for premises where raw celluloid or cinematograph film was stored and used. The Cinematograph Film Production (Special Loans) Act, 1949, established the National Film Finance Corporation and in the same year came the British Film Institute Act.

The Cinematograph Films Act, 1957, provided a statutory levy on exhibitors and exhibitions to be collected by Customs & Excise and paid to the British Film Fund Agency which would use the monies to support film production in the UK and the work of the Children's Film Foundation. This made the formerly voluntary levy compulsory. The Cinematograph (Amendment) Acts of 1982 extended provision of the 1909 Act to include 'all exhibitions of moving pictures for private gain', bringing under regulation pornographic cinema and video 'clubs'. The Acts exclude from regulation bona fide film societies.

The Films Act, 1985, abolished the Cinematograph Films Council and the Eady Levy, and dissolved the National Film Finance Corporation, replacing it with the British Screen Finance Consortium. The government provided a 'starter' of £1.5m for five years to the loan fund of the BSFC whose function would be to raise funds independently of state support. See BROADCASTING LEGISLATION.

CinemaScope Wide-screen process copyrighted by 20th Century Fox in 1953 but invented much earlier by Henri Chretien.

Cinématographie Word first used by G. Bouly in 1892 in a French patent specification for a movie camera.

Cinematography, origins Among the earliest moving-picture inventions was the *Thaumatropical Amusement* of Englishman Henry Fitton (1826). Exploiting the phenomenon of PERSISTENCE OF VISION the

Thaumatrope consisted of a round box inside which were a number of discs, each with a design on it. When the discs were twirled round, the images merged and gave the impression of a single movement.

Joseph Plateau's *Phenakistoscope* (1833), a circular design opposite a mirror, worked the same little miracle. The ZOETROPE, or 'wheel of life', invented by Englishman W.G. Horner (1834), offered a revolving drum with strip sequences inside, enabling figures to jump, gallop or even do cartwheels. Emile Renauld's *Praxinoscope* of 1877 improved on the Zoetrope by removing the slots of the drum and using mirrors to reflect the images, thus avoiding the dizziness to viewers caused by the Zoetrope. The wonder of this device was extended with the *Projecting Praxinoscope* using a revolving disc-blade shutter to project animated images on to a screen.

The main impetus in the development of cinematography came, however, from another direction. Working in the US, English photographer Edward Muybridge (1830–1904) in the 1870s took multiple photographs of animals, birds and humans in movement. His most famous experiment was the one in which a line of cameras, using exposures of less than one-thousandth of a second, 'filmed' a galloping horse. The horse triggered each camera as it passed – and proved, incidentally, that there are moments in a horse's movement when all its hooves are clear of the ground.

The next step was the projection of these in-sequence pictures. William Friese-Green (1855–1921) in 1890 revealed the potential of moving film when he set up a small slide projector in which the usual slide carrier had been replaced by a glass disc bearing a ring of pictures. Friese-Green's revolving disc was later demonstrated, to eager crowds, in the window of his studio in Piccadilly.

In France, meanwhile, Etienne Jules Marey (1830–1904) had invented a photographic 'gun' (1882) to take pictures of birds in flight and soon followed this with a camera capable of snapping 60 pictures a second on a paper-based film. In the US, Thomas Alva Edison (1847–1931) produced his *Kinetograph* to take moving pictures and his KINETOSCOPE to show them. The viewer looked through a peephole in the foot-high box. The 50 feet of film ran for about 13 seconds. 'Kinetoscope parlours' were set up in which people could view films by putting a coin in a slot.

The most important year in the development of cinematography was 1895, with the invention of projectors in the US by Thomas Armat and Woodville Latham, in France by the Lumière brothers – Auguste (1862–1954) and Louis (1864–1948) – and in the UK by Robert Paul. With the arrival of the Lumières on the scene, the cinema was truly born. Their vision and entrepreneurialism turned experiment into performance, private screenings into public, commercial profit. 'What did I do?' Louis Lumière is reported to have said. 'It was in the air.' Auguste Lumière was less modest than Louis: 'My brother,' he said, 'invented the cinema in one night.' On 28 December 1895, the Lumières, already highly successful in the photographic business, opened in the Salon Indien, in the Grand Cafe on the Boulevard des Capuchines. Seats were priced at one franc. Within weeks they were a worldwide success. Immediately the Lumières trained a brigade of cameramen-cum-projectionists and sent them abroad to several foreign countries; in quick time, some 1200 single-shot films were produced, including the Diamond Jubilee procession in London.

Cinéma vérité Or *Catalyst* cinema. In a 1961 DOCUMENTARY, *Chronique d'un Été* (Chronicle of a Summer), Jean Rouch, instead of simply recording the daily routines of Parisians, challenged them to face the camera and answer the question, 'Tell us, are you happy?' Rouch and co-producer Edgar Morin were suddenly on-camera participants. Their subjects, having been filmed, were invited to see the film rushes. Their discussion of these was filmed and recorded, and used as part of the end-product.

The style was named *cinéma vérité* in homage to the Russian movie pioneer Dziga Vertov and translated from the term used by Vertov and his associates, *kino pravda*, film truth. Erik Barnouw in *Documentary* (UK: Oxford University Press, 1974) writes, 'The direct cinema documentarist took his camera to a situation of tension and waited hopefully for a crisis; the Rouch version of cinéma vérité tried to precipitate one. The direct cinema artist aspired to invisibility; the Rouch cinéma vérité was often an avowed participant.'

Cinerama Extra-wide screen system invented by Fred Waller and first demonstrated in *This is Cinerama* (1952). Three projectors, electronically synchronized, created a three-section picture on the screen, giving a disturbing visual wobble at the joins. The first film story using the process was *How the West Was Won* (1962). Shortly afterwards the three-camera system was abandoned in favour of 'single-lens Cinerama', practically identical to CINEMASCOPE, though with higher definition.

Citizen journalism See JOURNALISM: CITIZEN JOURNALISM.

Citizen Kane of the global village Description of media mogul Rupert Murdoch by Alex Brummer and Victor Keegan in a *Guardian* article (13 May 1995) entitled 'Planet Rupert takes on the galaxy'. The authors examine the growth and growth of the Murdoch global empire. Kane was the fictional newspaper mogul in Orson Welles' film masterpiece *Citizen Kane* (1941), rather more than loosely based upon the life of the American newspaper baron, William Randolph Hearst (1863–1951) – the Rupert Murdoch of his age. See MURDOCH EFFECT.

Civil inattention Phenomenon of INTERPERSONAL COMMUNICATION observed by Erving Goffman in *Behavior in Public Places* (US: Free Press, 1963) where, after initial EYE CONTACT, a person quickly withdraws visual attention from another to avoid any further recognition or need for further contact. As Goffman says, 'In performing this courtesy the eyes of the looker may pass over the eyes of the other, but no "recognition" is typically allowed.' The ritual of civil inattention Goffman explains is one that 'constantly regulates the social intercourse of persons in our society'. See INDICATORS.

Clapper board See SHOT.

Claptrap See VERBAL DEVICES OF SPEECH-MAKING.

Class A vital factor in the analysis of interpersonal and mass communication is the concept of class; and the most significant impact on the development of that concept was made by the German philosopher Karl Marx (1818–83). For him, class denoted a relationship to the *means of production* in any given society. Marx identified two main classes: the owners of the means of production (land, factories) whom he called the *bourgeoisie*, and those who were obliged to sell their labour to the owners to make a living – the *proletariat*. Although aware of other classes, he considered them of minor importance.

Marx argued that as a result of their position in the economic order, members of each class shared common experiences, lifestyles and certain political and economic interests. He believed that there was and would remain, in a capitalist society, an inevitable conflict between the interests of the bourgeoisie and the proletariat. He further argued that GROUP identity, class consciousness and collective political and economic action would develop in the course of economic and political conflict. Proletarian class consciousness was particularly likely to emerge as its members were thrown into serious difficulties and close daily associations at work.

The dominant class – the bourgeoisie – would, according to Marx, seek to impose its culture upon the rest of society. Its culture would become the *dominant* culture, its IDEOLOGY the dominant ideology. Consequently the communication systems of society would reflect the dominant culture of the bourgeoisie and also the conflict between the two classes. From a Marxist viewpoint, control of many facets of the mass media by the ownership of capital gives that class the opportunity to disseminate its own culture and ideology. Such control, in Marxist terms, plays a vital role in the maintenance of HEGEMONY.

The term is also commonly used when what is meant is *social* class. Social class membership is based, primarily, upon occupation rather than ownership or non-ownership of the means of production. For the ADVERTISING industry and media management, social class is a significant factor in the profile of an audience. Market researchers are primarily interested in income and spending power. For those media organizations that are dependent on advertising revenue, the social class composition of their AUDIENCE is of obvious importance. The inter-relationships between the social class structure and the communication processes of society are complex and research in this area is wide-ranged. Of particular concern is whether the narrowness of social class backgrounds of those who control and work in the media is reflected in its output. See *TOPIC GUIDE* under MEDIA: VALUES & IDEOLOGIES.

Classic FM Commercial radio station broadcasting nationwide in the UK from the autumn of 1992. Its menu of popular classics presented in a lively and unpatronizing way and a policy of winning audience loyalty through competitions and sponsored musical events has proved a notable success.

'Clean up TV' movement Brought together in Birmingham in 1963 by Mary Whitehouse and others; later called itself the National Viewers' and Listeners' Association (NVLA). Over the years the movement has succeeded in gaining access to practically every forum in which the issues of broadcasting are discussed; additionally, the NVLA has been active as a 'morality watchdog' in other arts, especially the theatre and publishing. The basis of NVLA thinking is that of traditional Christian ethics; the belief that the VALUES of chastity and the family underpin all that's best in western society, and that such values are constantly under threat and have to be protected. Of equal concern to the NVLA is the increase in the display, in film, on TV and in the theatre, of scenes of violence. See BROADCASTING STANDARDS COUNCIL; CENSORSHIP; MORAL ENTREPRENEURS.

Climate of compliance See KUUKI.

Climax order In the process of persuading others, the order in which arguments and evidence are placed is of considerable importance. Research has been conducted into the climax order and anti-climax order, that is when the best point of an argument is reserved until last (climax) or used at the outset (anti-climax). The two orders have varying advantages depending on the particular conditions under which the communication is presented, including the audience's predisposition and the type of matter being transmitted. Similar concepts are the Law of PRIMACY and the Law of RECENCY.

Clipper chip A microchip, called the spy in the computer, the 'sleeping policeman on the superhighway of information'. It was feared in the mid-1990s that it would become a compulsory element in US-made computers allowing government agencies, by means of an electronic back door, to snoop on data into and out of computers. Such was the determination of users of the INTERNET and their campaign against the clipper chip that the Clinton government temporarily retreated from its plans.

However, in February 1996 Clinton signed a Telecommunications Bill requiring that from 1998 all TV sets with a screen size of 13 inches or more should be fitted with a V (for violence)-chip. In the same month the European parliament voted in favour of a similar measure – the insertion of V-chips into every new TV set sold in Europe under the Television Without Frontiers directive. See ENCRYPT; PRIVACY.

Clique A close-knit group of people within a social system whose communication is largely with each other. *Clique analysis* is used to determine communication groupings within a social system and its main tool is SOCIOMETRICS.

Closed text See OPEN, CLOSED TEXTS.

Closure Occurs in a communication situation when one participant, usually the receiver of information, closes down attention, and thus deflects the message or the messenger, or terminates an encounter. The reasons for closure may relate to the unacceptability of the MESSAGE: it may conflict with the attitudes, beliefs or VALUES of the receiver; it may be an 'uncomfortable truth' which causes the receiver a feeling of DISSONANCE. Also, it may have something to do with the messenger rather than the message – personal dislike of the sender on the part of the receiver or a simple unwillingness to receive this kind of message from this messenger – or it may simply reflect a wish to terminate the encounter and move on.

The means of closure will involve NVC (non-verbal communication) as well as verbal strategies. The term is also used in relation to NARRATIVE, in the sense of *narrative closure*. This does not mean bringing the narrative to a close, but employing narrative devices to close down alternative readings or interpretations. See OPEN, CLOSED TEXTS; PREFERRED READING.

Cocktail party problem In *On Human Communication* (US: MIT Press, 1966), Colin Cherry writes, 'One of our most important faculties is the ability to listen to, and follow, one speaker in the presence of others. This is such a common experience that we may take it for granted; we may call it "the cocktail party problem". That is, how do we filter out a barrage of communication messages, selecting one to concentrate upon?' Cherry experimented with two different taped readings being played at once, with the instruction to the subject to concentrate on one and ignore the other.

Though the tapes produced a 'complete babel', and though very wide-ranging texts were used, considerable success in deciphering the message was demonstrated, illustrating the importance of 'our ingrained speech habits at the acoustic, syllabic, or syntactic levels'. Cherry and his colleagues also experimented to see what happened when a subject was asked to read a text out loud while simultaneously listening to another one. This process, of testing the subject's ability to select from competing message channels, they called 'shadowing'.

Code of broadcasting (UK) See OFCOM: OFFICE OF COMMUNICATIONS.

Code of semes See CODES OF NARRATIVE.

Codes A code is generally defined as a system into which signs are organized, governed by consent. The study of codes – other than those *arbitrary* or fixed codes such as mathematics, chemical symbols, MORSE

CODE etc. – emphasizes the social dimension of communication. We have codes of conduct, ethical, aesthetic and LANGUAGE codes (see ELABORATED AND RESTRICTED CODES).

Non-verbal communication is carried on through what have been classified as *presentational codes*: gesture, movement of the eyes, expressions of the face, tone of voice. A *representation code* can be speech, writing, music, art, architecture, etc. Speech itself has non-verbal characteristics: *prosodic codes* affect the MEANING of the words used, through expression or pitch of voice.

The media are often referred to as employing *broadcast* and *narrowcast* codes in gearing content, level and style to expected audiences. In *Introducing Communication Studies* (UK: Methuen, 1982), John Fiske writes, 'Narrowcast codes have acquired the function in our mass society of stressing the difference between "us" (the users of the code) and "them" (the laymen, the lowbrows). Broadcast codes stress the similarities among "us" (the majority).' In the case of TV, *Coronation Street* would represent the broadcast code and a production of Shakespeare's *King Lear* a piece of narrowcasting, though economically speaking, in terms of advertising, narrowcast may simply indicate the target audience of the advertiser.

Aesthetic codes are crucially affected by their cultural context, some of it highly conventional, some AVANT-GARDE, subject to textual rather than commonly recognized cues to meaning. Much modern art, for example, has been encoded in visual languages accessible to only a small number of people. However, over time, innovative aesthetic encoding becomes conventionalized. The obscure code has become familiar. A case in point is Surrealism, whose intention was to shock cultural convention, yet whose dream symbols and often disturbing juxtapositions of objects have become a commonplace of mass advertising. What began as a code specific to itself has been transformed into one given its meaning by cultural convention. See CODES OF NARRATIVE; DECODE; DOMINANT, SUBORDINATE, RADICAL; ELITE; HIGHBROW; SEMIOLOGY/SEMIOTICS.

Codes of advertising practice See ADVERTISING STANDARDS AUTHORITY (ASA); OFCOM: OFFICE OF COMMUNICATIONS.

Codes of narrative Roland Barthes in *S/Z* (UK: Basil Blackwell, 1990; translated from the French by Richard Miller) applies a number of narrative codes in a book-length analysis, or deconstruction, of a 23-page short story, 'Sarrasine', written by Honoré de Balzac in 1830. Barthes describes 'five major codes under which all the textual signifiers can be grouped' in a narrative. The *Proiaretic* or *Action* code (the Voice of Empirics) tells us of events – of what happens – and thus is instrumental in the sequence of the story.

The code of the *seme* or sign ('semantically the unit of the signifier') refers to character and is categorized by Richard Howard in the Preface to *S/Z* as the *Semantic* code (though Barthes does not actually use this term in the text). Barthes speaks of this as the Voice of the Person. Under the *Hermeneutic* or *Enigma* code (the Voice of Truth) 'we list the various (formal) terms by which an enigma can be distinguished, suggested, formulated, held in suspense and finally disclosed'. *Cultural* or *Referential* codes 'are references to a science or a body of knowledge' – 'physical, physiological, medical, psychological, literary, historical, etc.'. These are the Voice of Science. Finally there is the *Symbolic* code, the Voice of Symbol.

Barthes writes of the codes that they 'create a kind of network, a *topos* [Greek: a place, location] through which the entire text passes (or rather, in passing, becomes text)'. This taxonomy of codes is widely used in the analysis of texts of all kinds. Nowhere, however, does Barthes suggest that such coding is prescriptive, discrete or exact. He writes, 'The code is a perspective of quotations, a mirage of structures; we know only its departures and returns.' Barthes talks of a 'galaxy of signifiers, not a structure of signifieds'. For him the text 'is not unitary, architectonic, finite' and the approach to it is characterized by 'blanks and looseness of analysis'. The meaning of the 'readerly' as contrasted with the 'writerly' text is ultimately elusive. The 'blanks' and 'looseness of analysis' will be like 'footprints making the escape of the text'.

Cognitive (and affective) That area or domain of human behaviour which can be described as intellectual – knowing, understanding and reasoning – is often referred to as the *cognitive*. A substantial amount of media communication is aimed at producing cognitive responses in the receiver. That area which is involved with attitudes, emotions, VALUES and feelings is termed the *affective*. Obviously the two overlap and intertwine.

Whether the content of a MESSAGE is cognitive or affective in its orientations will greatly influence the mode chosen for its communication. If the content of a message is judged to be of cognitive intent, then LANGUAGE will generally be couched in neutral terms; presentation will strive after objectivity and balance. An affective message will be more likely to be framed in emotive language, its imagery directed towards emotional responses.

However, much recent media research has been directed towards a more critical analysis of the allegedly objective modes of cognitive messages. There is concern as to whether the dissemination of apparently neutral information – especially if that dissemination is of some FREQUENCY and CONSISTENCY of treatment – influences an audience's perception of national and world events. From the mass of available information, the media select and reject. They give emphasis – and legitimacy – to some issues rather than others, and they set the order of priorities (see AGENDA-SETTING) as well as seeking to establish links between occurrences and their causes in the minds of the audience. See EFFECTS OF THE MASS MEDIA; GLASGOW UNIVERSITY MEDIA GROUP.

Cognitive capture See IMPARTIALITY.

Cognitive dissonance See CONGRUENCE THEORY; DISSONANCE.

Cold media, hot media See HOT MEDIA, COLD MEDIA.

Collective representations Describe the role played by community in telling stories about itself, in particular those musical or dramatic forms, images and artefacts that speak for and about popular tastes, beliefs, VALUES and preoccupations. At the same time the term describes the way the community may adopt images and artefacts produced for it, works of art, for example, and assign to them significance rooted in popular needs and uses. The collective production of MEANING, says Wendy Griswold in *Cultures and Societies in a Changing World* (US: Pine Forge Press, 1994), 'tries to take away the mystery about the creation of art, ideas, beliefs, religion, and culture in general by revealing the many social activities, such as interaction, cooperation, organization, and contestation, involved in the formulation of what we designate as cultural objects'. See CULTURE; POPULAR CULTURE; EXPECTATION, HORIZONS OF.

Collocation The tendency of words to occur in regular association; words set together through customary usage such as 'fair' and 'play', 'auspicious' and 'occasion'.

Collodion or wet-plate process See PHOTOGRAPHY, ORIGINS.

Colloquialism An expression used in common, informal speech, but not as far removed from acceptable modes as SLANG. If your comments 'cut no ice' with somebody, that is a colloquialism; if you are told to 'keep yer 'air on', that is slang. It is a modest distinction, for as Ronald Ridout and Clifford Witting say in *The Facts of English* (UK: Pan Reference Books, 1973), 'the slang of yesterday becomes the colloquialism of today'. See DIALECT; JARGON; REGISTER.

Colonization Term used to describe the process by which various cultural material is acquired from a variety of contexts and then reassembled to construct particular messages. In this process the MEANING of the original signs is often changed, if not subverted; their use may appear to celebrate differences between people but the goal to which they are put may have as its purpose the REINFORCEMENT of the DOMINANT CULTURE, and the denial of differences and the conflict which they bring.

Advertising messages contain many examples of colonization. For example, the signs and symbols widely associated with certain YOUTH CULTURES are often employed to sell goods and services to various audiences – whether young people themselves or older consumers who are presumed to identify with a particular youth culture. Ironically whilst youth cultures are often a site of resistance and challenge to the dominant culture, their signs and symbols are in this way used to draw them further into the dominant culture, for instance through encouraging certain patterns of consumption and the use of financial services such as banking services.

Colour TV The first regular TV service in colour began in the US in 1954; 1960 saw the first colour service in Japan, seven years ahead of Britain. In 1969 there were 100,000 colour sets in use in the UK; by the same month in 1972 there were 1.6m and twice that 12 months later. Ferguson produced the first full-size colour receiver using transistors throughout, in 1967. Transistors consumed a quarter of the power of traditional valve receivers. They ran cooler and were more reliable.

Later came integrated circuits, doing away with many discrete components. The surface acoustic wave (SAW) filter further refined the accuracy of colour reception, as did improved shadow-mask tubes. Here stripes of colour rather than dots achieved registration of the picture's red, green and blue components without the need for any of the many correction circuits previously required.

Comics The first newspaper comic-strip is generally considered to be that which appeared on 16 February 1896 in the *New York Sunday World*. It was a three-quarter page feature in colour called 'The Great Dog Show in M'Googan's Avenue'. Kids in the city's slum backyards were organizing their own dog show; the hero, dressed in a bright yellow nightgown, soon became the 'Yellow Kid' and 'Hogan's Alley' achieved immediate popularity as a long-running comic-strip (see YELLOW KID).

The idea was not new. English cartoonist Thomas Rowlandson (1757–1827) created a comic character, Dr Syntax, who was popular with the public, and considerably earlier William Hogarth (1697–1764) included speech 'balloons' in his engravings satirizing London life. George Orwell took comics seriously enough to write about them. In 'Boys' Weeklies' (1939), published in *Selected Essays* (UK: Penguin, 1957), Orwell analysed the social and political connotations of early publications in the genre. What seemed to characterize comics in Orwell's day was their social changelessness, deep down if not in the surface detail. Orwell did find differences between the older and the new generation of weeklies, however: in the new, 'better technique, more scientific interest, more bloodshed, more leaderworship'; in 'social outlook there is hardly any advance'.

As life appears to have become more complex, and society more complicated, the STEREOTYPE of the hero has had a sustaining appeal. Picture-strip heroes such as Clark Kent, alias Superman, who first made his appearance in *Action Comics* (1938) in the US, have not only led popular (and charmed) lives on the printed page but have translated into immensely popular film heroes. The debate concerning comics, and comic books, centres around the extent to which they seem to legitimize dominant social values.

At the same time concern is expressed about the subversive potential of so-called *comix*, which offer a more pluralist, and sometimes radical, reading, as well as a more aesthetically conscious approach. This kind of comic also addresses adult audiences and is often anti-authority in essence. See CARTOONS.

Commanders of the social order Term used by Herbert I. Schiller in *Culture, Inc. The Corporate Takeover of Public Expression* (UK: Oxford University Press, 1989), referring to the vast transnational corporations which, he argues, have come to dominate and shape CULTURE, establish prevailing discourses, set political, economic and cultural agendas, and call the tune of mass media. Schiller talks of the PRIVATIZATION of public space: in a literal sense (public areas being transformed into privately owned and controlled shopping malls and pleasure domes) and in an intellectual sense, through the 'corporatization' of arts, literature and media. He cites the extent to which the entire worlds of information (libraries, museums, universities, mass communication) and of expression (architecture, music, art) and of public spectacle (sport) have been colonized by corporations, particularly in the US, but increasingly in the rest of the world. See AUDIENCE: ACTIVE AUDIENCE; BERLUSCONI PHENOMENON; CONSENSUS; ELITE; HEGEMONY; MANUFACTURE OF CONSENT; POWER ELITE; PRESS BARONS; PUBLIC SPHERE. See also *TOPIC GUIDE* under MEDIA: OWNERSHIP & CONTROL.

Commercial confidentiality A CENSORSHIP device employed to prevent the media transmitting, or the general public receiving, information, on the grounds that such information might be commercially damaging (regardless of whether that information might be in the public interest). One particularly sensitive area of commerce which is shrouded in mystery is the arms trade.

Britain is, for example, among the world's top arms-trading nations. Its government maintains an arms marketing and advisory service, the Defence Exports Services Organization, yet this organization is notoriously secretive whenever journalists seek to find out about its work, invariably answering that information cannot be supplied for reasons of 'commercial confidentiality'. Louis Blom-Cooper, chairman of the Press Council in 1990, expressed the view that 'traditional English law places a higher value on commercial interests than on the public's right to know'. See FREEDOM OF INFORMATION ACT (UK), 2005.

Commercial laissez-faire model of (media) communication In their Introduction to *The Manufacture of News* (UK: Constable, 1973) joint editors Stanley Cohen and Jock Young cite two general, and polarized, models which attempt to explain the intentions and impact of media on their audiences – the mass manipulative model and the commercial *laissez-faire* model. In the first, 'the public is seen as an atomized mass, passive receptacles of messages originating from a monolithic and powerful source'. From the perspective of the political Left it is big business – the hierarchy of capitalism – which is the seemingly all-powerful manipulator.

From the perspective of the political Right, the media in this model are seen as manipulating 'standards' by lowering them.

Drawn from the *laissez-faire* (leave well alone) model of the economy, the commercial *laissez-faire* model mirrors the freedom of the marketplace where producers compete with one another to sell their products to consumers. Thus media corporations are seen as having to compete for the attention and loyalty of their consumers, the audience. Researchers using this model tend to argue that the consumer is sovereign and that media corporations have to tailor their products to suit consumer wishes, tastes and needs. The focus of their research is, therefore, often upon the mechanisms by which such tailoring is achieved.

The commercial *laissez-faire* model emerged as a critique of the mass manipulative model. It is generally the PREFERRED READING of journalists and media people themselves. Because there is competition, the argument goes, there is consequently 'variety and diversity in information and opinions presented in the mass media and ... such variation minimizes the chances of manipulation'. This summary having been made in Cohen and Young's Introduction, the rest of the book's fascinating collection of reports and analyses is a remorseless exposé of fallacies perceived in the commercial *laissez-faire* model. See EFFECTS OF THE MASS MEDIA. See also *TOPIC GUIDE* under COMMUNICATION MODELS.

Commercial radio Although PIRATE RADIO attempted to buck the BROADCASTING monopoly of the BBC during the 1960s, legitimate commercial broadcasting in the UK was not in operation until the 1970s, following the Conservative government's Sound Broadcasting Act of 1972. The IBA had, by 1983, 37 commercial RADIO stations operating under licence throughout the UK and plans for over 60 commercial stations.

In the US the first commercial radio was KDKA of Pittsburgh, which went on the air on 2 November 1920 with a broadcast of the returns of the Harding–Cox presidential elections. In 1921 there were eight commercial radio stations; by 1922, 564. Development of radio in the US was spectacular and chaotic. In 1927 (the year that the BBC, by Royal Charter, was given a monopoly of radio broadcasting in the UK) Congress passed a Radio Act setting up the Federal Communications Commission to allocate wavelengths to broadcasters. Four radio networks were created as a hedge against monopoly – National Broadcasting Commission (NBC), Columbia Broadcasting Service (CBS), Mutual Broadcasting System (MBS) and the American Broadcasting Company (ABC) – while the FCC worked towards the growth of projects of educational interest.

Despite the BBC's monopoly in the UK, commercial broadcasts in English were transmitted from abroad as early as 1925. Radio Paris, broadcasting from the Eiffel Tower, presented a fashion talk in English, sponsored by Selfridges. Only three listeners wrote to the station to say they had heard the broadcast but the commercial lobby was undaunted. In the 1930s Captain L.F. Flugge, who had arranged the fashion talk, formed and ran the International Broadcasting Company. The IBC's Radio Normandy transmitted 15-minute shows for several hours a day from 1931 and by the following year 21 British firms were paying sponsorship money for commercial broadcasting, and the UK was being beamed at commercially from the Netherlands, Spain and Luxembourg.

The IBC actually set up offices in Portland Place, London, and had its own outside broadcasting vehicles, each painted black with 'Radio Normandy 274 metres' on the side. An important part of the company's operation was the International Broadcasting Club, formed in 1932, with free membership. By 1939, the IBC had 320,000 members.

Radio Luxembourg began broadcasting on 1191 metres long wave in 1933, its first two sponsors being Zam Buk and Bile Beans. Though the Post Office conducted a sustained campaign to close down these commercial stations, it was Adolf Hitler and the Second World War that did the trick: many transmitters were either destroyed by the Nazis or taken over. Radio Luxembourg became Hitler's major PROPAGANDA weapon against the British. The notorious Lord Haw-Haw (William Joyce), an Irishman committed to the German cause, broadcast daily recommendations to the British to lay down their arms, from the most powerful transmitter in Europe.

Of the commercial stations, Luxembourg was the only one to start up again after the war (finally closing down in 1992). The first accredited commercial radio station on British soil was Manx Radio which began broadcasting in 1964. With the election of the Conservatives in 1970, the Minister of Posts and Telecommunications produced a White Paper, *An Alternative Service of Broadcasting,* proposing a network of about 60 commercial stations under the Independent Television Authority (to be renamed the Independent

Broadcasting Authority). Opposition spokesman Ivor Richards called it 'nothing more than the establishment of 60 pop stations'.

From the beginning, in 1972, local independent radio was to broadcast on stereo VHF as well as medium wave. The first FRANCHISES were awarded in 1973, to bring into existence the all-news London Broadcasting Company (LBC) and Capital Radio for London, with regional stations following soon afterwards. Additional franchises were granted by the IBA in 1981. By 1988 there were 40 independent local radio stations (compared with 27 BBC local stations).

The BROADCASTING ACT, 1990, separated out the statutory overseeing of radio and television, creating for TV (in place of the IBA) the Independent Television Commission (ITC) and for radio the Radio Authority. These bodies were empowered to assign frequencies, appoint licensees and regulate programming and advertising. They were also required to draw up and periodically review codes of practice concerning programmes, advertising standards and other matters. Both the Radio Authority and the ITC ceased to exist with the inauguration of the Office of Communications (OFCOM), born out of the COMMUNICATIONS ACT (UK), 2003. See TELEVISION BROADCASTING.

Commissions/committees on the media See *TOPIC GUIDE* under COMMISSIONS, COMMITTEES, LEGISLATION.

Commoditization of information The notion that information is something upon which the possessor can put a price; thus information is bought and sold because it is a commodity rather than a public service. The process constitutes an important issue, and might also be termed the *privatization* of information. Herbert I. Schiller in 'Critical research in the information age', in *Journal of Communication,* Summer 1983, writes, 'The privatization of information is observable in all sectors of society … A new international division of labour, no less inequitable than its predecessor, is being created practically before our eyes.'

Schiller refers to a 'gale of technological and industrial change whipping across the United States and other industrialized countries'. This has had far-reaching effects on the way we regard, and use, information: 'In sum, long-term, deep structural forces are making communication the central process in global, national and local social organization. At the same time, the most powerful national and transnational decision-making groups are initiating and deploying new information technologies to consolidate and extend their positions.' See CORPORATIONS AND MEDIA; HEGEMONY; INFORMATION GAPS; MEDIA IMPERIALISM; MOBILIZATION; POWER; POWER ELITE; TECHNOLOGICAL DETERMINISM.

Commonality In terms of language, beliefs, culture, general outlook, that which is *shared* within a community; that which those who make up the community have in common.

Common sense In the study of media communication and its links with culture and politics, the term 'common sense' connotes an over-readiness to believe in the apparently obvious. The Italian philosopher Antonio Gramsci (1891–1937) defined common sense as being a composite of the attitudes, beliefs and assumptions of the mass of the people, and operating within a hierarchical social order.

Common sense tends towards conformism to the IDEOLOGY of the dominant social order, and in part is the product of that ideology. It accepts 'the way things are' – the status quo – as 'the way things should be'. Indeed such structures and circumstances are so obvious (so commonsensical) that they do not warrant being questioned. Gramsci believed that what he termed the 'chaotic aggregate of disparate conceptions' comprising common sense should be challenged by intellectuals and the complacency of common sense explained and exposed. Many commentators have focused on the role the media play in nurturing and reinforcing rather than unpacking commonsensical visions of society. See EXNOMINATION; HEGEMONY.

Communication While the definitions of communication vary according to the theoretical frames of reference employed and the stress placed upon certain aspects of the total process, they all include five fundamental factors: an initiator, a recipient, a mode or vehicle, a message and an effect. Simply expressed, the communication process begins when a MESSAGE is conceived by a *sender*. It is then ENCODED – translated into a signal or sequence of signals – and *transmitted* via a particular MEDIUM or CHANNEL to a *receiver* who then decodes it and interprets the message, returning a signal in some way that the message has or has not been understood.

What has been termed NOISE, or interference, may impede the message. This may be internal (resistance to the message or to the sender, for example, on the part of the receiver) or external (actual noise, distraction, language level, etc.). During the communication process, sender, message and receiver are subject to a multitude of cues which influence the message, such as a person's appearance, his/her known status or the expression on his/her own face as the message is communicated or responded to (see BARNLUND'S TRANSACTIONAL MODELS).

While INTERPERSONAL COMMUNICATION is that which occurs between two or more people, INTRAPERSONAL COMMUNICATION is what you say within and to yourself. Inner thoughts, impressions, memories interact with external stimuli – the decor of a room, a painting on the wall, a beautiful landscape, a row of slum houses, a jostling crowd, a teacher at the front of the class, your friend's good or bad mood – to create a silent discourse, continuously changing and renewing itself and influencing your perceptions of self and the world.

It is important to hold in mind, as Raymond Williams points out in *Keywords* (UK: Fontana, 1976), the 'unresolved range of the original noun of action, represented at its extremes by "transmit", a one-way process, and "share" ... a common or mutual process'. This polarity of meaning – of the one-way process as against aspects of communion, of cultural *exchange* – is fundamental to the analysis of communication, hence the attempt to generalize the distinction in such phrases *as manipulative* communication and *participative* communication.

Frank Dance in 'Toward a theory of human communication' in the book he edited, *Human Communication Theory: Original Essays* (US: Holt, Rinehart & Winston, 1967), observes that communication is something that changes even while one is in the act of examining it; it is therefore an interaction and a *transaction.* Dance and C. Larson in *The Functions of Human Communication: A Theoretical Approach* (US: Holt, Rinehart & Winston, 1976) detail their examination of 126 definitions of communication. They specify notable differences but common agreement that communication is a *process.* The authors conclude with a definition of their own: 'The production of symbolic content by an individual, according to a code, with anticipated consumption by other(s) according to the same code.' Or as Colin Cherry succinctly puts it in *On Human Communication* (US: MIT Press, 1957), communication is 'essentially a social affair'.

Of course a painter or a poet may quarrel with this definition. He/she might claim that the process of communication is one that essentially exists between artist, medium, subject matter and style and that the eventual viewer, reader or listener is of little account at the moment of encoding. It is open to debate whether, if a painting is stored in an attic or the poem burnt, any meaningful communication has taken place. Also, the painter or poet's work, once presented for consumption by others may be decoded – interpreted – in as many ways as there are people, each one reprocessing the work of art according to his/her own needs, norms, VALUES, CULTURE, EXPECTATIONS and SOCIALIZATION.

T.R. Nilson in 'On defining communication' in *Speech Trainer*, 1957, and reprinted in K.K. Sereno and C.D. Mortensen, eds, *Foundations of Communication Theory* (US: Harper & Row, 1970), distinguishes between communication which is *instrumental,* that is intended to stimulate a response, and *situational* in which there need not be any intention of evoking a response in the transmission of stimuli. As early as 1933, Edward Sapir differentiated between *explicit* and *implicit* modes of communication, a perspective supported by Baker Brownell in *The Community: Its Philosophy and Practice for a Time of Crisis* (US: Harper & Bros., 1950), who speaks of *direct* and *indirect* communication. The latter Brownell defines as being a 'process wherein something converted into symbols is carried over from one person to another', while the former is a function of the 'identification of people with one another'.

A precept that few commentators would challenge is that it is *impossible not to communicate.* By saying nothing, by remaining blank-faced, by keeping our hands stiffly to our sides, we are still communicating, however negatively. We are still part of the interaction whether we like it or not. For Jurgen Ruesch, communication is 'all those processes by which people influence one another' ('Values, communication and culture', in J. Ruesch and G. Bateson, eds, *The Social Matrix of Psychiatry,* US: W.W. Norton, 1951). At first we may resist the claim that whatever we do we are exerting an influence. Yet by trying not to influence we are arguably still affecting the patterns of communicative action, interaction and transaction. In our absence from the scene – from our family or work group, for example – as well as in our presence, we may still exert influence, however little, however unintended. See COMMUNICATION: INTERCULTURAL COMMUNICATION; COMMUNICATION, NON-VERBAL (NVC); SEMIOLOGY/SEMIOTICS.

Communication, functions Many and varied listings have been made by communications analysts. The following eight functions are usually quoted as being central: *instrumental* (to achieve or obtain something); *control* (to get someone to behave in a particular way); *information* (to find out or explain something); *expression* (to express one's feelings or put oneself over in a particular way); *social contact* (participating in company); *alleviation of anxiety* (to sort out a problem, ease a worry about something); *stimulation* (response to something of interest); and *role-related* (because the situation requires it). See JAKOBSON'S MODEL OF COMMUNICATION.

Communication integration See INTEGRATION.

Communication: intercultural communication Occurs between individuals from differing cultural backgrounds. Cultural differences are a potential source of much miscommunication and misunderstanding. According to Larry Samovar and Richard Porter in *Communication Between Cultures* (US: Wadsworth/Thomson Learning, 2001), 'intercultural communication will have two major points of contact: international and domestic. International contacts are those between people from different countries and cultures'. The authors point out that what also needs to be considered is that 'within each culture there are numerous co-cultures and specialized cultures. These provide the opportunity for domestic points of intercultural contact'. This is especially likely to be the case in multicultural societies such as those of Britain and the United States.

William B. Gudykunst and Young Yun Kim in *Communicating With Strangers: An Approach to Intercultural Communication* (US: McGraw-Hill, 1997) argue that intercultural communication is that 'between people from different societal cultures', but that rather than being a special case, 'the underlying process of communication between people from different cultures or subcultures is the same as the underlying process of communication between people from the same culture or subculture'. They suggest that the essential feature of such encounters is that people are communicating with strangers; that is, 'communicating with people who are unknown and unfamiliar, including people from another culture and people from our own culture or subculture who are in an environment new to them'.

To explore the dynamics of this process they propose a model which focuses on the influence of four categories of conceptual filter: *cultural, sociocultural, psychocultural* and *environmental*. They argue that 'each of these types of filters influences how we will interpret messages encoded by strangers and what predictions we make about strangers' behaviour. Without understanding strangers' filters, we cannot accurately interpret or predict their behaviour'.

LANGUAGE and NON-VERBAL COMMUNICATION clearly vary across cultures but the impact of this variable arguably goes further than causing the obvious problems of translation in intercultural encounters. There are those who support the SAPIR-WHORF LINGUISTIC RELATIVITY HYPOTHESIS. This proposes that as language determines thought, people with different languages actually perceive the world differently rather, that is, than perceiving it in the same way but expressing their perceptions in different languages. This hypothesis remains controversial but a number of researchers would argue that whilst language may not determine thought, it does influence it. Richard Hudson, for example, in *Sociolinguistics* (UK: Cambridge University Press, 1996) comments, 'In short, language does affect thought in ways that go beyond the rather obvious effects of the specific lexical items. On the other hand, language is not the only kind of experience which does affect thought'.

There is also a range of other cultural variables to be considered. Geert Hofstede, for example, in *Culture's Consequences: International Differences in Work-Related Values* (US: Sage, 1980) identified four variables that he considered important: those of *individualism-collectivism* (see below), *uncertainty avoidance, power distance*, and *masculinity* and *femininity*. Earlier, F. Kluckhohn and F. Strodtbeck in *Variations in Value Orientations* (US: Row Peterson, 1961) argued that five value orientations underpin cultural differences: *human nature* orientation, *person–nature* orientation, *time* orientation, *activity* orientation and *relational* orientation.

One key cultural variable identified by a number of researchers is whether a culture is predominantly, though not exclusively, collectivistic or individualistic. Cultures in which collectivistic tendencies predominate stress the importance of the ties and obligations attached to group membership. These will exercise considerable and general influence over members (for example, the family, faith groups). The interests of the in-group are seen as more important than those of individuals whose duty is to abide by the norms and values of the in-group. There are often marked differences between the manner in which in-group members communicate with each other and their communication with members of out-groups.

In contrast, cultures in which individualistic tendencies predominate stress the importance of the individual and the individual's aims, interests, achievements and self-development. Individuals are expected to be self-reliant and to take responsibility for themselves and their close family. Individuals may be members of a number of in-groups – most of which will have relatively limited and specific influence over their members. Individuals are encouraged to be competitive, to speak out and to stand out. There are likely to be fewer marked differences between the ways in which people communicate with in-group and out-group members.

It should be borne in mind, however, that people in any culture may have both collectivistic and individualistic orientations even though one will tend to be stronger. Further, not all people will necessarily identify strongly with the predominant tendency of the culture in which they live.

An important influence of the individualism–collectivism variable on communication lies in its relationship to the use of what Edward Hall in *Beyond Culture* (US: Doubleday, 1976) termed *high-* and *low-context* communication. High-context communication relies heavily on the aspects of the context – for example, the status differences between the communicators – to provide MEANING and considerable use is made of non-verbal signs. Hall writes, 'When talking about something that they have on their minds, a high context individual will expect his interlocutor to know what's bothering him, so he doesn't have to be specific. The result is that he will talk around and around the point, in effect putting all the pieces in place except the crucial one. Placing it properly – this keystone – is the role of the interlocutor. To do this for him is an insult and a violation of his individuality.'

As Gudykunst and Kim argue, 'High-context communication can be characterized as being indirect, ambiguous and understated with speakers being reserved and sensitive to listeners.' High-context communication is favoured by collectivistic cultures, such as that of Japan, in which the centrality of in-group membership ensures the degree of shared knowledge and understanding of contextual factors, essential for its effective use.

Individualistic cultures, such as that of European Americans, meanwhile, favour low-context communication. Here, such a degree of shared knowledge and understanding of contextual factors cannot be taken for granted so meaning is made obvious and less use is made of non-verbal signs – especially silence. As Gudykunst and Kim comment, 'Low-context communication … can be characterized as being direct, explicit, open, precise and consistent with one's feelings.'

Whilst the cultural variable of individualism/collectivism may predispose individuals to favour one pattern over another, they may in certain circumstances employ the contrasting pattern. So whilst those in individualistic cultures may generally employ low-context communication, in certain situations, for example when talking to a longstanding friend, they may use high-context communication.

In cross-cultural encounters confusion and possible conflict can occur when high context meets low context. Those from collectivistic, high-context communication cultures, for example, may find the direct, open approach of those from individualistic, low-context cultures socially inept and tactless; whilst those from individualistic, low-context cultures may get frustrated with the failure of those from collectivistic, high-context communication cultures to 'get to the point'.

Individualism and collectivism also affect the coding and decoding of mass media artefacts such as advertisements. For example, Sang-Pil Han and Sharon Shavitt conducted a study entitled Persuasion and Culture: Advertising Appeals in Individualistic and Collectivistic Societies, reported in *Journal of Experimental Social Psychology* 30(4), 1994, investigating the possible influence of individualism and collectivism on the encoding and decoding of a selection of magazine advertisements used in the US (individualistic culture) and South Korea (collectivistic culture). They concluded that in the United States advertisements were more likely to employ appeals to the individual whereas those in Korea focused on the benefits that a product or service could offer a group. Their study of the decoding of advertisements concluded that, 'in the U.S. advertisements emphasizing individualistic benefits were more persuasive, and ads emphasizing family or ingroup benefits were less persuasive than they were in Korea.'

'In both studies, however,' Han and Shavitt found, 'product characteristics played a role in moderating these overall differences. Cultural differences emerged strongly … for advertised products that tend to be purchased and used with others, but were much less evident for products that are typically purchased and used individually.'

The influence of cultural variables interplays with other key factors – for example, social identities, those of age, GENDER, social CLASS and ethnicity. Thus, for example, the GENDERLECTS noted by Deborah Tannen in *You Just Don't Understand: Men and Women in Conversation* (UK: Virago, 1992) could be expected to modify the degree to which, say, the cultural variable of individualism influences a person's communicative performance. Also part of the equation are psychocultural influences such as stereotyping, ETHNOCEN-TRISM and PREJUDICE, and environmental influences such as population density and terrain.

Encounters between people of different cultures can also be reflected in language; a pidgin, for example, may be generated. In trading and doing business with the English in the Far East, the Chinese and other peoples, such as the Malays, communicated in a very basic, utilitarian mode of half-English. Pidgin is a Chinese corruption of the word 'business' but the term is more widely used to to denote such basic means of communication. According to Elizabeth Closs Traugott and Mary Louise Pratt in *Linguistics* (US: Harcourt Brace Jovanovich, 1980), a pidgin may be 'roughly defined as a language that is nobody's native language'.

Pidgins are developed in situations where people with differing native languages are brought together, some often in a relatively powerless position, and have to communicate. Pidgins, though, tend to meet only the basic needs of communication and are very reliant on the accompanying use of NON-VERBAL COM-MUNICATION for their effectiveness. Creoles are normally developed by the children of pidgin speakers and these are more complex and more flexible languages. Over time, through the process of *decreolization*, a Creole often changes to resemble more closely the predominant or prestige language which was its base, if this language is still used in the area. This was the case with Jamaican Creole. In Britain, British Black English, derived largely from Jamaican Creole, is widely used by people of African-Caribbean origin as a linguistic marker of ETHNIC identity, and typically is part of a linguistic repertoire that also includes other varieties of English. See APACHE SILENCE; ASSERTIVENESS; M-TIME, P-TIME.

* Martin Montgomery, *An Introduction to Language and Society* (UK: Methuen, 1986; Routledge, 1993); Fred E. Jandt, *An Introduction to Intercultural Communication* (US/UK/India: Sage, 4th edition, 2004); H.C. Triandis, *Individualism-collectivism* (US: Boulder: Westview, 1995).

Communication, interpersonal See INTERPERSONAL COMMUNICATION.

Communication, intrapersonal See INTRAPERSONAL COMMUNICATION.

Communication: mobile concept of See MOBILIZATION.

Communication models See *TOPIC GUIDE* under COMMUNICATION MODELS.

Communication, non-verbal (NVC) Michael Argyle in *Bodily Communication* (UK: Methuen, 1988) identifies the main codes of NVC: TOUCH and bodily contact; spatial behaviour (PROXEMICS and ORIENTA-TION); appearance; FACIAL EXPRESSION; GESTURE and HEAD NODS; POSTURE; gaze (eye movement and EYE CONTACT); and NON-VERBAL VOCALIZATIONS. Varyingly NVC conveys much of what we wish to say, and much of what we would wish to withhold. Common functions of non-verbal communication include: the conveying of interpersonal attitudes; the display of emotional states; self-presentation; the regulation of interaction; the giving of meaning to verbal communication; the maintenance of interest in a communicative encounter; the provision of advance warning of the kind of verbal communication to follow; and, very importantly, the provision of FEEDBACK in communication.

Affiliation, sexual attraction, rejection, aggression, dominance, submission, appeasement, fear, grief, joy are often best expressed – and in some cases can only be expressed – through NVC. The amount of NVC in the repertoire of different peoples and nations varies considerably in range, emphasis, frequency and rules for use.

Some non-verbal signs appear to be universal, for example the eyebrow flash used in greeting. There are also many cultural differences in non-verbal communication, for example the rules regarding proximity, that is the amount of space or distance people should keep between them when communicating. These are different for Middle Eastern countries when compared with our own. The use of non-verbal communication may also be influenced by aspects of an individual's personality. Extroverts, for example, are thought to be more expansive in their use of gestures. Some GENDER differences have been noted in the use of NVC. Several studies have shown that women are more likely to touch each other in conversation than men are.

Ambiguity often surrounds the interpretation of non-verbal signs, not least because quite a lot of body movement is not communicative in intent and it may be difficult for the receiver to know whether a particular sign was intended to communicate a message or not. Judy Gahagan in *Social Interaction and its Management* (UK: Methuen, 1984) argues that the ambiguity surrounding the interpretation of non-verbal signs is essential to one of their major functions in communication – dropping hints. People may wish such messages to be open to varied interpretation so that the hint can be retracted later, if necessary. Non-verbal signs thus provide what Gahagan calls 'diplomatic flexibility'. As she remarks, 'Non-verbal communication is a language adapted for hints and innuendo.' See ACCENT; FAST; NON-VERBAL BEHAVIOUR: REPERTOIRE; OBJECT LANGUAGE; SILENCE.

* Desmond Morris, *People Watching* (UK: Vintage, 2002).

Communication postulates See POSTULATES OF COMMUNICATION.

Communication theory See *TOPIC GUIDE* under COMMUNICATION THEORY.

Communications Act (UK), 2003 Legislation bringing far-reaching changes to the landscape of telecommunications and broadcasting in Britain; and creating a 'super regulator' in the Office of Communications (see OFCOM). Telecommunications and BROADCASTING are seen in the Act to be twin parts of the same pattern of technological CONVERGENCE. Because of the interface between all technological means of communication, the philosophy is that attempts to regulate those means is self-defeating and bad for business in an increasingly competitive, and increasingly global, communications world.

Deregulation is therefore the key aim of the Act; and it makes sense as far as technology is concerned. However, critics have shown considerable unease about the removal of regulations concerning broadcasting, where divergence or fragmentation rather than convergence has been the dominant trend. There is the suggestion that what has been in the minds of the legislators is enabling the media industry to profit from deregulation rather than the interests of the audience in terms of quality programming.

What will continue to be regulated will be controlled with a 'light touch'. Rules concerning CROSS-MEDIA OWNERSHIP are largely abandoned; there is now no bar to foreign ownership of British media and thus no impediment to corporate media interests worldwide competing for swathes of British commercial broadcasting. This part of the Act prompted a clamour of protests in the UK from broadcasters, journalists and politicians, particularly members of the House of Lords. Across the Atlantic, *Time* magazine expressed its astonishment, writing on 20 May 2002 that the legislation 'threw open the airways to non-EU countries in a way not yet seen in Europe. The rules are a free-for-all: national newspapers and media giants like AOL Time Warner, Viacom and Disney can now buy commercial TV channels, while US concerns like Clear Channel are free to snap up radio stations.' Gillian Doyle agrees: in 'Changes in media ownership' in *Sociology Review* (February 2004), she writes, 'In effect these changes allow unprecedented opportunities for major commercial radio and television broadcasters to expand their share of the UK media market.'

The Act scraps the following regulatory rules: (1) those preventing single ownership of ITV; (2) those preventing ownership of more than one national commercial radio licence; (3) those preventing joint ownership of TV and radio stations; (4) those obstructing large newspaper groups from acquiring Channel 5 TV or radio licences; and (5) those preventing non-European ownership. All this, the Act's policy statement says, 'brings benefits for consumers and for businesses'. In other words, broadcasting is business, and audiences exist first and foremost as consumers. Yet, as Professor Steven Barnett of the University of Westminster points out in a posting on the MediaEd.org.uk website (2003), 'less regulation and more unfettered competition leads inexorably to a poorer service for consumers and an impoverished creative and cultural environment'.

Ofcom has taken over regulatory responsibilities from five bodies: the Broadcasting Standards Commission, the Independent Television Commission (ITC), the Office of Telecommunications (Oftel), the Radio Authority and the Radiocommunications Agency. It has a 'statutory duty to further the interests of citizens and consumers by promoting competition and protecting consumers from harmful or offensive material'. It is empowered to conduct research, develop policies, create codes of practice, consult widely, make recommendations concerning not only independent broadcasting but the BBC (which in terms of control does not, at least at the time of writing, come under Ofcom's remit), and deal with complaints.

Pressure from various bodies, including many MPs and a media committee chaired by Lord Puttnam, brought about government modifications to the original Bill. A 'public interest plurality' clause was inserted into the Act, allowing the Secretary of State to block any deals which might be judged to compromise plurality. 'How this is defined,' writes Barnett, 'and more importantly whether government ministers will have the political courage to thwart the corporate ambitions of powerful newspaper proprietors, remains to be seen.' See BRITISH MEDIA INDUSTRY GROUP; COMMANDERS OF THE SOCIAL ORDER; REGULATORY FAVOURS.

Communications conglomerates See CONGLOMERATES: MEDIA CONGLOMERATES.

Communications Decency Act (US) Law passed overwhelmingly by the US Congress and signed by President Bill Clinton in February 1996, designed to ban porn on the Internet (see INTERNET: MONITORING OF CONTENT). The measure has faced a number of formidable and ongoing obstacles; first, the means of exercising censorship on the net; second, arriving at any definition of 'decency' (as compared, for example, with 'obscenity') which can win CONSENSUS in America; third, controlling indecency across frontiers (it is easy for American citizens to 'emigrate' across the net by transmitting under the guise of 'anonymous remailers'); and fourth, persuading other nations to introduce similar legislation. Perhaps the strongest impediment to the Communications Decency Act has been the United States' Constitution, the First Amendment of which prohibits Congress from 'abridging the freedom of speech'. See REGULATION OF INVESTIGATORY POWERS ACT (RIPA) (UK), 2000.

Communications gap Failure of understanding usually as a result of a lack of information, especially between different age groups, economic classes, political factions or cultural groups. See INFORMATION GAPS.

Communicative rationality Jürgen Habermas in his vast and seminal work on communication and the public sphere, *The Theory of Communicative Action, Vol. 1: Reason and Rationalization* (US: Beacon, 1981) and *Vol. 2: The Critique of Functionalist Reason* (UK: Polity, 1983) poses the notion of communicative rationality as being characterized by truth, appropriateness and sincerity. The operation of these criteria in public life rests upon the existence of free, open and egalitarian DISCOURSE – an 'ideal speech situation' – which in turn makes understanding between elements of society more likely. Communicative rationality rests essentially on an equality of opportunity to participate in communication; still a dream aspiration as far as most societies are concerned.

Communicology The study of the nature, process and meanings systems of all forms of communication in what Dean C. Barnlund has described as 'the totality of time, space, personality and circumstance' (in 'A transactional model of communication', K.K. Sereno and C.D. Mortensen, eds, *Foundations of Communication Theory*, US: Harper & Row, 1970).

Community radio Because RADIO BROADCASTING is the cheapest form of MASS COMMUNICATION it lends itself to 'grass roots' use by communities of interest – whether geographical, cultural or political. Its potential is to be run by and for local communities, special interests and followings. The development of local radio in the UK has made some progress towards the community ideal, but full independence, in terms of appointments, policy, financing, programming etc., remains at levels other than the local one.

Though the term 'community radio' was probably first used in the UK by Rachel Powell in a pamphlet *Possibilities for Local Radio* (UK: Centre for Contemporary Cultural Studies, University of Birmingham, December 1965), the idea goes as far back as the BEVERIDGE REPORT, 1950, which proposed the use of VHF frequencies to 'establish local radio stations with independent programmes of their own. How large a scope there would be in Britain for local stations broadcasting programmes controlled by Universities or Local Authorities or public service organizations is not known, but the experiment of setting up some local stations should be tried without delay.'

In 1962 the PILKINGTON REPORT recommended that the BBC provide 'local sound broadcasting' on the basis of 'one service in some 250 localities', stations having a typical range of five miles. The 1971 government White Paper launched COMMERCIAL RADIO, but radio broadcasting through the next decades was to remain under the duopoly of the BBC and the IBA.

Pressure to produce a 'third' force in broadcasting in the UK, to consist of highly individual and genuinely local stations, grew in the 1980s. Throughout the country groups dedicated to the furtherance of community radio multiplied, providing information, and exerting pressure at national and local levels. The question that needs to be asked in identifying and characterizing community radio is whether, as well as aiming to serve the perceived interests of the community, radio is also run *by* the community.

Though the most familiar model is generally associated with PUBLIC SERVICE BROADCASTING (PSB) initiatives, variations on community radio are to be found throughout the world, particularly in the United States. Here, in January 2000, the Federal Communications Commission (FCC) approved the use of Low Power FM (LPFM) or micro-radio services that would be used for community-orientated programming, to serve schools, civic clubs, state and local governments, churches and other non-profit-making organizations.

However, the full-scale development of this *microcasting* met with the obstacle of vested interest as represented by corporate radio. The National Association of Broadcasters (NAB), working on behalf of the commercial sector, pressurized Congress for legislation that had the effect of eliminating the majority of the new voices, on the grounds of possible interference with high-power transmission.

As INTERNET services have expanded, so has interest in, and development of, web radio, often referred to as 'webcasting'. Both public and private radio broadcasters already make available programmes on the web, but the opportunities for individuals, groups and communities to offer alternative broadcasting services through the net are strictly limited. Web radio draws benefit from low start-up costs and relatively cheap equipment, but as Hans Ullrich Muhlenfeld points out in an article for the *European Journal of Communication*, March 2002, one of the main hazards in the way of the profileration of web radio is *licensing*.

In 'Research note: mass communication as participation. Web-radio in Germany: legal hazards and its contribution to an alternative way of mass communication', the author says that legal complexities, not helped by varying approaches to licensing in the different states within Germany, limit the contribution web radio can make to 'an alternative way of communication as much as the technological possibilities would allow'. Indeed, 'quite the opposite is true. The legislature forces radio enthusiasts into an outlaw position or a difficult economic situation.' He regrets that currently 'the development of web-radios in Germany can be considered as just another way to transmit well-established ideas and ideologies'. See CONGLOMERATES: MEDIA CONGLOMERATES; PRIVATIZATION.

Compassion fatigue The effect of world suffering upon mass media audiences may turn into what has been termed *compassion fatigue* in which the exposure to suffering becomes too much to take in. In an article 'Living in limbo' in the *Guardian* (21 April 1989), William Shawcross writes, 'Like Aids, Compassion Fatigue is a contemporary sickness. The symptoms are first a rush of concern for a distant and obviously suffering group, followed by tedium and a feeling of withdrawal that sometimes descends into disdain.'

Compassion fatigue is 'nurtured by the speed and plethora of communications that bewilder and disorient people everywhere'. Shawcross finds this phenomenon a 'truly terrifying sickness. Those it afflicts do not waste away physically – it is their humanity that is harmed'. The compassion factor is further strained by the nature of NEWS itself, restlessly and hungrily switching its focus of attention from one disaster to another.

The most thorough record of the causes and processes of compassion fatigue is to be found in Susan D. Moeller's book *Compassion Fatigue: How the Media Sell Disease, Famine, War and Death* (US/UK: Routledge, 1999). Defining it as a 'defence mechanism against the knowledge of horror', Moeller is highly critical of what she terms 'formulaic coverage' of world disasters which, in American reporting, suffers what she sees as *Americanization of events* (see EVENT: AMERICANIZING OF).

Ultimately, Moeller argues, the fault lies in piecemeal, often haphazard, selective and potentially hysterical media coverage of foreign news: 'Compassion fatigue, and even more clearly, compassion avoidance are signals that the coverage of international affairs must change', and that, she asserts, means a need for 'great reporters, producers and editors' and a will 'to invest in such an un-sexy news beat as international affairs'. She urges that events beyond our shores should be reported 'day in day out, year in year out'; in short, 'to get back to the business of reporting all the news, all the time'. See COUPS AND EARTHQUAKES SYNDROME.

Competence In LINGUISTICS, a term used to describe a person's knowledge of his/her own language, its system of rules; his/her competence in understanding an unlimited number of sentences, in spotting grammatical errors, etc.

Compliance, climate of See KUUKI.

Compliance, identification and internalization See INTERNALIZATION.

Complicity of users Term employed by Cees J. Hamelink to describe the reluctance of audiences to be told the truth about crises, particularly war situations but also in cases concerning government and corporate matters. In 'Ethics for media users' published in the *European Journal of Communication*, December 1995, Hamelink cites findings that indicated nearly eight out of ten Americans supported restrictions on information imposed by the Pentagon while six out of ten said they believed the military should have exercised greater censorship.

At the nub of market research into consumption behaviour is motivation. Why do people watch a TV commercial, what makes them pay attention and heed the message?

Regularly cited are three major reasons for a positive audience response: (1) social utility – watching commercials in order to gain information about the 'social significance' of products or brands, and the association of advertising objects with social roles and lifestyles; (2) communication utility – watching in order to provide a basis for later interpersonal communication; (3) vicarious consumption – participating at second hand in desired lifestyles as a means of indirect association with those people possessing glamour or prestige. See VALS TYPOLOGY.

Contagion effect Power of the media to create a craze or even an epidemic. Examples of this are the so-called Swastika Epidemic of 1959–60 where an outbreak of swastika daubing in the US was accelerated by media coverage, and the UK Mods vs Rockers seaside battles in the 1960s. Debate continues on whether media coverage 'worsens' or prompts street riots, often named Copycat Riots.

Stanley Cohen in 'Sensitization: the case of the Mods and Rockers' in *The Manufacture of News* (UK: Constable, 1st edition, 1973), edited by Cohen and Jock Young, writes, 'Constant repetition of the warring gangs' image … had the effect of giving these loose collections a structure they never possessed and a mythology with which to justify the structure' and the court scenes at which those arrested by the police were tried were 'arenas for acting out society's morality plays'.

In relation to 'loose connections' being given a 'structure', claims have been made by commentators in the aftermath of the 9/11 terrorist assault on New York's Twin Towers that the directing of attention to al-Qaeda had a similar contagion effect: even though there was very little evidence that al-Qaeda was a worldwide organization, treating it as such has been in danger of becoming a SELF-FULFILLING PROPHECY. See EMPOWERMENT; MORAL PANIC.

Content analysis Research into mass media content identifies, categorizes, describes and quantifies short-term and long-term trends. An early and most valuable descriptive trend study was that of Ernst Kris and Nathan Leites in 1947. In 'Trends in 20th century propaganda' in B. Berelson and M. Janowitz, eds, *Reader in Public Opinion and Communication* (US: Free Press, 1947), the authors traced the trend in propaganda from the First World War (1914–18) to the Second (1939–45), identifying a changing style towards a less emotional, less moralistic and more truthful orientation.

Content analysis serves an important function by comparing the same material as presented in different media within a nation, or between different nations; or by comparing media content with some explicit set of standards or abstract categories. On the basis of the existing body of quantitative and qualitative research, several broad generalizations may be hazarded about the content of MASS COMMUNICATION: what is communicated by the mass media is a highly selected sample of all that is available for communication; what is received and consumed by the potential AUDIENCE is a highly selected sample of all that is communicated; more of what is communicated is classifiable as entertaining rather than informative or educative; and, because the mass media are aimed at the largest possible audience, most material is simple in form and uncomplicated in content. See AUDIENCE MEASUREMENT; ETHNOGRAPHIC (APPROACH TO AUDIENCE MEASUREMENT); GLASGOW UNIVERSITY MEDIA GROUP. See also *TOPIC GUIDE* under RESEARCH METHODS.

Control group In comparative research methods, the neutral body against which a test group is measured. Thus, in the case of AUDIENCE MEASUREMENT, the test group is exposed to a TV programme, for example, and their responses analysed against identical monitoring of the control group who have not seen the programme.

Control of the media See MEDIA CONTROL.

Conventions Established practices within a particular CULTURE or SUB-CULTURE. Conventions are identifiable in every form of communication and behaviour, some strict, like rules of grammar, others open to wider application, such as dress. Conventions are largely culture-specific and context-specific. It is an accepted convention that a candidate dresses smartly for a job interview, yet it would be deemed unconventional if he or she appeared on the beach clad in the same manner.

Media practices have established many conventions that have become so familiar they appear 'the natural way to do things'. TELEVISION news holds to the convention of having on-screen newsreaders;

documentaries generally hold to the convention of having a voiceover narration. Innovators – for example in the arts – break with convention. The shock of the new often stirs among the conventional a sense of affronted VALUES. The chances of the new becoming conventionalized will depend on various factors, such as opinion leaders, prevalent tastes and fashions, even newsworthiness. See LEADERSHIP; REDUNDANCY.

Convergence The coming together of communication devices and processes; a major feature of the development of media technology in the 1990s onwards. In *Of Media and People* (US: Sage, 1992), Everette E. Dennis writes of forms converging 'into a single electronically based, computer-driven mode that has been described as the nearly universal integration of systems that retrieve, process, and store text, data, sound, and image', in short, multimedia. Dennis points out that convergence is far more than 'the stuff of hardware and software: it is the driving force that has spurred major change in the media industries and almost everywhere else'.

Convergence has operated at the technical and operational level and at the level of ownership and control. Just as individual items of hard and software have been centralized into one multimedia outfit, so media production has been centralized into fewer corporate hands, most of these transnational. With convergence has come a blurring of media functions: with the aid of a modem, the telephone permits us to surf the INTERNET or, regulation permitting, to summon up channels of screen entertainment. We can work from home, shop from home, summon up the world from home (if we are lucky enough to be able to pay for the technology).

A further question is whether technical and operational convergence will lead to transcultural convergence and extend the reach of what some would see as the already well-established strategy of cultural and MEDIA IMPERIALISM. For those that support this thesis, GLOBALIZATION fosters homogeneity and works in the interests of the powerful producers of cultural artefacts often located in western countries – especially the US – whilst undermining the indigenous cultures of the less powerful receivers of such artefacts.

However, such a view is seen by others as underestimating the degree to which those who receive such artefacts adapt them in the process of absorbing them into the host culture. The resultant blend may limit the degree of convergence. It should also be noted that artefacts destined for a wide market are often tailored to take account of differentiation within the market and in this process characteristics of the differing host cultures may be considered in the construction of the artefact. Moreover, the flow of cultural artefacts is arguably more complex than the cultural or media imperialism thesis suggests. A number of theorists point to the essential heterogeneity of culture(s) and argue consequently that it is unlikely that cultural convergence would occur. See CYBERSPACE; DIGITIZATION; MOBILIZATION. See also *TOPIC GUIDE* under MEDIA: PROCESSES & PRODUCTION.

Conversational styles In a study of conversation among friends at dinner, entitled *Conversational Style: Analyzing Talk Among Friends* (US: Ablex, 1984), Deborah Tannen identifies different conversational styles which she terms 'High Considerateness' and 'High Involvement'. Each style has different priorities. The 'High Considerateness' style places a premium on being considerate of others in conversation, of not interrupting, of listening to what someone is saying. The 'High Involvement' style, meanwhile, is characterized by enthusiastic involvement in a conversation and this may be at the expense of giving sufficient space to others.

One style is not necessarily better than the other but often reflects cultural differences; for example, in her study, the Briton was the most considerate of all. However, this categorization can help explain problems in INTERPERSONAL COMMUNICATION. To the highly considerate speaker the highly involved speaker may seem an exhibitionist whilst the highly involved speaker may perceive the highly considerate speaker as aloof or distant.

Co-orientation approach See McCOMBS AND SHAW'S AGENDA-SETTING MODEL OF MEDIA EFFECTS, 1976.

Copycat effect See CONTAGION EFFECT.

Copyrighting culture See CULTURE: COPYRIGHTING CULTURE.

Core nations, peripheral nations Cees Hamelink makes this differentiation with regard to the distribution of information in and between nations in 'Information imbalance: core and periphery' in *Questioning The* these groups a tendency to denigrate popular cultural capital. Popular cultural capital, meanwhile, can be seen as a rich source of responses to, including resistance to, social subordination. See CULTURE; HIGHBROW; TASTE CULTURES; YOUTH CULTURE.

* Pierre Bourdieu, *Distinction* (UK: Routledge, 1984) and *The Field of Cultural Production* (UK: Polity Press, 1993).

Cultural diamond See GRISWOLD'S CULTURAL DIAMOND MODEL.

Cultural Indicators research project See MAINSTREAMING.

Cultural industry See FRANKFURT SCHOOL OF THEORISTS.

Cultural memory That which the community recalls, re-encodes in a process of making sense of the present. Cultural memory contrasts with what has been termed *instrumental* or *electronic* memory, that which can be numerically encoded and recorded, as on a computer. In *Communication, Culture and Hegemony: From the Media to Mediation* (UK: Sage, 1993), Jésus Martín-Barbero writes, 'In contrast to instrumental memory "cultural memory" does not work with pure information or as a process of linear accumulation'; rather, it is 'articulated through experience and events. Instead of simply accumulating, it filters and weighs.'

It is not, says Martín-Barbero, 'a memory we can use, but the memory of which we are made'. What threatens cultural memory inflicts damage on culture itself, particularly in cultures where tensions exist, dramatically, between tradition and progress. Says Martín-Barbero, a part of whose book focuses on media development in South American countries, 'In the dilemma of choice between under development and modernization, cultural memory does not count and has no place': a situation he and other scholars of cultural change view with dismay.

Cultural metaphor Generally an image, or a series of images, seen to represent a culture. The expression 'an Englishman's home is his castle' attempts to classify the English – perhaps even stereotype them – by means of a dominant image or practice. In this case a number of characteristics are drawn together in the image of home as something to be defended as though it were a castle – private, self-contained, constructed to be resistant to outside intrusions and influences.

According to Martin J. Gannon and associates in *Understanding Global Cultures: Metaphorical Journeys Through 17 Countries* (US: Sage, 1994), the use of identifying metaphors can assist us in grasping the nature of our own and other cultures. Gannon confirms the saying quoted above, arguing that the dominant cultural metaphor of Britain is the house, with its solid, firm foundations, rooted in the past; a place of privacy, walls and hedges. He and his associates take the view that 'the dynamics of the culture of a particular nation can be best understood through the use of one dominant metaphor that reflects the basic values that all or most of its members accept without question or conscious thought'.

The authors cite in detailed chapters of explanation the following metaphors that represent some of the cultures on their 'metaphorical journey': American football (US), the dance of Shiva (India), the family altar (China), the opera (Italy), wine (France), lace (Belgium), ballet (Russia), the symphony orchestra (Germany), the bullfight (Spain), the kibbutz (Israel), the garden (Japan), the stuga or summer home (Sweden), the marketplace (Nigeria) and the coffee house (Turkey). For Ireland, home of the Blarney Stone, the authors perhaps appropriately select as the country's presiding metaphor, conversation.

Cultural modes The *literate* mode is rooted in the written word; the *oral* mode is spoken or visual. Traditionally they have been aligned to CLASS differences; that is, the upper, better-educated classes have lived by a literate mode of cultural interaction, the *dominant* CULTURE, while the more 'untutored' classes have relied upon oral modes. With the advent of electronic media the oral mode has become increasingly assertive. It is essentially the mode of film and television, though both media still tend to be run by a class educated in the literate mode and whose perceptions are conditioned by such a mode.

Cultural or citizen rights and the media In 'Rights and representations: public discourse and cultural citizenship', in *Television and Common Knowledge* (UK: Routledge, 1999), edited by J. Gripsrud, Graham Murdock poses the following citizen rights – what citizens have the right to expect from the mass media: (1) the right to information; (2) to have access to 'the greatest possible diversity of representations of personal and social experience'; (3) to knowledge, that is, access to 'frameworks of interpretation' that facilitate understating of the links between issues, the causes that lead to effects, and the processes by which knowledge is assembled and represented to the public; and (4) to participation in a contemporary context where there is a demand from individuals and groups 'to speak about their own lives and aspirations in their own voice'.

The exercise of 'full citizenship', Murdock argues, depends upon the media's fulfilling these rights of information, experience, interpretation and participation. See *TOPIC GUIDE* under MEDIA ETHICS; MEDIA ISSUES & DEBATES; MEDIA: VALUES & IDEOLOGY; REPRESENTATION.

Cultural racism See RACISM.

Culture The sum of those characteristics that *identify* and *differentiate* human societies – a complex inter-weaving of many factors. The culture of a nation is made up of its LANGUAGE, history, traditions, climate, geography, arts, social, economic and political norms, and its system of VALUES; and such a nation's size, its neighbours and its current prosperity condition the nature of its culture.

There are cultures within cultures. Thus reference is made to working-class culture or middle-class culture. Organizations and institutions can have their own cultures (see ORGANIZATION CULTURES). We refer to cultural *epochs* resulting from developments – social, political, industrial, technological – that create cultural change. Mass production and the mass media have contributed immensely to cultural change, giving rise to what critics have termed mass culture and disapprovingly portrayed as manufactured, manipulated, force-fed, marketed like soap powder and, because of its unique access to vast audiences, open to abuse of the mass by the powerful.

Alan Swingewood, in *The Myth of Mass Culture* (UK: Macmillan, 1977), argues, however, that there 'is no mass culture, or mass society; but there is an ideology of mass culture and mass society'. The ideology is real enough, but the thing itself he describes as myth: 'If culture is the means whereby man affirms his humanity and his purposes and his aspirations to freedom and dignity then the concept and theory of mass culture are their denial and negation.'

Culture is transmitted through SOCIALIZATION to new members of a social group or society. The media play an important role in this process. A central concern of culturalist studies of the media is the degree to which the media's output may both reflect and communicate the culture of the more powerful social groups in that society at the expense of the less powerful. By asserting one culture against others, the media help to nurture a *dominant culture* and relegate rival cultures to the realms of deviance.

* Raymond Williams, *The Long Revolution* (UK: Chatto & Windus, 1961, and Penguin, 1965) and *Culture* (UK: Fontana, 1981); Richard Hoggart, *The Uses of Literacy* (UK: Penguin, 1958); James Curran and Michael Gurevitch, *Mass Media and Society* (UK: Edward Arnold, 1991, and subsequent editions); Nick Stevenson, *Understanding Media Cultures* (UK: Sage, 1995); Colleen Roach, ed., *Communication and Culture in War and Peace* (UK: Sage, 1995); Peter Brooker, *Cultural Theory: A Glossary* (UK: Arnold, 1999); Andrew Tudor, *Decoding Culture: Theory and Method in Cultural Studies* (UK: Sage, 1999); Ben Highmore, *Everyday Life and Cultural Theory: An Introduction* (UK: Routledge, 2001); Brian McNair, *Striptease Culture* (UK: Routledge, 2002); David Hesmondhalgh, *The Cultural Industries: An Introduction* (UK: Sage, 2002); Arthur Asa Berger, ed., *Making Sense of Media: Key Texts in Media and Cultural Studies* (UK: Blackwell, 2005); James Curran and David Morley, *Media and Cultural Theory* (UK: Routledge, 2005).

Culture: consumer culture Arguably consumer culture is the prevailing culture of late modernity in western societies. Don Slater in *Consumer Culture & Modernity* (UK: Polity Press, 1997) argues that 'it is more generally bound up with central values, practices and institutions which define western modernity, such as choice, individualism and market relations'. For Slater its 'defining feature' is that it 'denotes a social arrangement in which the relation between lived culture and social resources, between meaningful ways of life and the symbolic and material resources on which they depend, is mediated through markets'. The media and cultural industries obviously play a pivotal role in the operation of consumer culture and the nature of this relationship is the focus of much research. See CONSUMERIZATION.

Culture: copyrighting culture In the global context of communication, and in view of the open-access properties of the INTERNET, a question of growing importance is, to whom does a TEXT or work belong? (See TEXT: INTEGRITY OF THE TEXT.) R.V. Bettig, in *Copyrighting Culture: The Political Economy of Intellectual Property* (US/UK: Westview Press, 1996), addresses this concern, arguing that with information/knowledge becoming one of the chief commercial industries in the current age, the control of CULTURE has fallen to a number of transnational corporations (TNCs) through their ownership of copyright.

TNCs fear copyright piracy on a world scale and their ambition is to extend, globally, measures to protect intellectual property from piracy. The Berne Convention laid initial guidelines on protection that eventually materialized in the Agreement on Trade-related Aspects of Intellectual Property Rights (TRIPS) of the World Trade Organization. This included the extension of protection to databases; computer programs being classified as literary works and therefore subject to copyright.

Texts are not only protected, their universal access – working within a global free market – is also protected; thus, for example, the attempts by one country to protect its own cultural products from cultural 'invasion' become an area of contention. The result, fears Bettig, threatens to be an economic domination of the information-rich nations over the information-poor.

Economic dominance brings with it ideological influence. Copyright becomes a device for the COM-MODITIZATION and PRIVATIZATION of knowledge where 'the views and accounts of the world held by the capitalist class and aligned class factions and groups are broadly disseminated and persistently publi-cized'. Global agreements, however, in practice have the mother of all battles in the war against piracy. See DOWNLOADING; INFORMATION COMMONS.

Culture: globalization of Considered by many commentators as a paramount trend in the late twentieth century, in which cultures and cultural practices of chiefly western nations, America in particular, spread through the world, dominating native, home-grown cultures. The media are seen to be the channels through which the globalizing torrent has poured; and those channels have been largely under the direction and con-trol of transnational corporations. Under the umbrella of globalization we encounter a couple of key, linked and interactive phenomena: CONSUMERIZATION and MEDIA IMPERIALISM.

With cultural dominance, fear some commentators, comes ideological dominance, and that IDEOLOGY centres around the processes of production and consumption and the targeting of audiences in their role as consumers. Todd Gitlin in his chapter 'Prime time ideology: the hegemonic process in television entertain-ment' in *Television: The Critical View* (US/UK: Oxford University Press, 1994), edited by Horace Newcomb, believes, 'In the 20th century, the dominant ideology has shifted toward sanctifying consumer satisfaction as the premium definition of "the pursuit of happiness".'

Corporate domination of the economy extends to corporate dominance worldwide of CULTURE, at least those cultures through which profits may be obtained. It is not happiness alone that global corporatization promises, says Gitlin, but liberty, equality and fraternity: all can 'be affirmed through the existing private commodity forms, under the benign, protective eye of the national security state'.

The vision of a world dominated by American cultural products (not to mention products of other kinds, such as Coca-Cola and McDonald's burgers – see McDONALDIZATION) is challenged by observers who see in localism a force of resistance, or if not resistance, assimilation. Roland Robinson offers us a useful term in this respect – *glocalization* (in 'Globalization or glocalization?' in the *Journal of International Communication* 1, 1994), that is, the ability of people in their own cultures to deal in their own way with the cultural imports from the West, to absorb them, to adapt them, to glocalize them.

John B. Thompson in *The Media and Modernity: A Social Theory of Media* (UK: Polity, 1995) urges us to see trends of dominance within historical perspectives: 'Rather than assuming that prior to the importation of Western TV programmes etc. many Third World countries had indigenous traditions and cultural heritages which were largely unaffected by external pressures, we should see instead that the globalization of communi-cation through electronic media is only the most recent of a series of cultural encounters, in some cases stretch-ing back many centuries, through which values, beliefs and symbolic forms of different groups have been super-imposed on one another, often in conjunction with the use of coercive, political and economic power.'

Thompson maintains that the media-imperialist position underestimates the power of audiences to make their own meanings from what they read, listen to or watch. 'Through the localized process of appropriation,' Thompson believes, 'media products are embedded in sets of practices which shape and alter their significance.'

Evidence for the process of glocalization is offered by Tamar Liebes and Elihu Katz in *The Export of Meaning: Cross Cultural Readings of Dallas* (US: Oxford University Press, 1990; UK: Polity, 1993). Their researches indicated that the American soap *Dallas* was read in quite different ways by people of different origins, cultures and outlooks. It was *Dallas* which was dominated, not the audience for *Dallas*.

Majid Tehranian in his chapter 'Ethnic discourse and the new world dysorder' in *Communication and Culture in War and Peace* (UK: Sage, 1993), edited by Colleen Roach, argues that the levelling out which is said to be a benefit of globalization is more apparent than real. In fact the 'levelling' has camouflaged 'a hegemonic project by a new modern, technocratic, internationalist elite' speaking 'the language of a new international, a new world order'. However, Tehranian perceives the 'periphery' reacting against the 'core' in a number of potentially conflictual, even explosive, ways.

He speaks of *countermodernization* as a significant contemporary trend, in which pressure GROUPS such as some traditional religions react against modern ideas and dominant ideologies – the resurgence, for example, of fundamentalist religion in the face of scientific and technological advances; while a contrary trend, *demodernization*, is expressed by the voices of environmentalists or feminists; and by those 'localites' (as contrasted with 'cosmopolites') whose advocacy is inspired by the notion that 'small is beautiful'.

The nature and degree of globalization of culture will continue to be fiercely debated and such debate will inevitably have to take into account inequalities of wealth, provision and media technology across nations. See NEWS: GLOBALIZATION OF; INFORMATION GAPS; SLAPPS. See also *TOPIC GUIDE* under GLOBAL PERSPECTIVES.

* Malcolm Waters, *Globalization* (UK: Routledge, 1995); Peter Golding and Phil Harris, eds, *Beyond Cultural Imperialism* (UK: Sage, 1996); Daya Kishan Thussu, ed., *Electronic Empires: Global Media and Local Resistance* (UK: Arnold, 1998); Barry Smart, ed., *Resisting McDonaldization* (UK: Sage, 1999); George Monbiot, *Captive State: The Corporate Takeover of Britain* (UK: Macmillan, 2001); Mike Savage, Gaynor Bagnall and Brian J. Longhurst, eds, *Globalization and Belonging* (UK: Sage, 2004).

Culture: intercultural communication See COMMUNICATION: INTERCULTURAL COMMUNICATION.

Culture of deference Journalist Richard Norton-Taylor in an article 'Pressure behind the scenes', subtitled 'A history of deference, and cosy relationships in Westminster, have made self-censorship acceptable' (UK: *Index on Censorship* 4 & 5, 1991), writes of a 'deep-seated culture of deference' existing between many British editors and journalists in their relationship with those in authority (see POWER ELITE). This, Norton-Taylor claims, arises out of an anxiety to be accepted by and be a part of the Establishment. The deference has its 'origins in the centralization of the British state and in Britain's imperial past – where there was virtually unchallenged consensus about the Empire's "civilizing mission".'

Deference, says Norton-Taylor, continues to be applied to institutions of the state such as Whitehall, the monarchy, the courts and Parliament. This deference also helps create and supports CONSENSUS against 'enemies', against foreign rivals, in war or in business. See JOURNALISM.

Culture: popular culture Something of a redundant term in that all culture is to a degree 'popular'; otherwise if it is 'unpopular' – that is, if it does not attract or involve an AUDIENCE – it vanishes. The term has come to mean the culture of 'ordinary people', of the working class, the non-elite majority as contrasted with so-termed *high* or *highbrow* culture. Popular culture generally signifies cohesion, high culture difference – difference, that is, from popular culture and those with whom it is associated.

Popular culture has traditionally been looked down on as something banal, trashy, unchallenging or even potentially harmful: an ELITE standpoint. In their time, theatricals, dancing, wassailing, 'pulp fiction', the PRESS, POSTERS, postcards, COMICS, SOAP OPERA, the hit parade and the cinema have varyingly been defined as the kind of culture which contains the potential for subversion – usually of 'standards'.

According to the French philosopher Pierre Bourdieu, popular culture is basically associated with that section of the population who lack both economical and CULTURAL CAPITAL. Since at least the 1960s popular culture has become the focus of critical attention and re-evaluation: it is studied – analysed, measured, in short, taken seriously.

In *Cultures and Societies in a Changing World* (US: Pine Forge Press, 1994), Wendy Griswold writes, 'Scholars examining previously despised works, genres and systems of meaning found them to contain complexities and beauties; at the same time, deconstructing previously esteemed works, genres and systems of meaning, they found widespread representations of class, hegemony, patriarchy, and illegitimate canonization.'

Culture, whether popular or 'elitist', *cultivates*, hence its fascination for researchers, commentators and students of media. Television, it has been claimed, has appropriated popular culture and by doing so redefined the term to mean 'that which is popular on TV'. The nature of participation by the populace in generating and taking part in popular culture has not been lost on TV programme-makers: audience participation is the key to popular quiz and competition programmes and to so-termed REALITY TV series such as *Big Brother*, in many cases turning that which traditionally has been private and intimate into public display. See AUDIENCE: ACTIVE AUDIENCE; ETHNOGRAPHIC (APPROACH TO AUDIENCE MEASUREMENT); RESPONSE CODES.

* Dominic Strinati, *An Introduction to Studying Popular Culture* (UK: Routledge, 2000); Annette Hill, *Reality TV: Audiences and Popular Factual Television* (UK: Routledge, 2005).

Cultures of organizations See ORGANIZATION CULTURES.

Custom audience research That which is commissioned or undertaken by a company or client into AUDI-ENCE response to the media marketing of its product or services, generally targeting specific media outlets. Such studies produce rich, focused data while at the same time incurring doubts concerning the objectivity of that data. In contrast, *syndicated* studies are grander in scope as, like the Nielsen ratings, they measure the audiences of multiple media outlets of audience response.

As Peter V. Miller says in 'Made-to-order and standardized audiences: forms of reality in audience measurement' published in *Audiencemaking: How the Media Create the Audience* (US: Sage, 1994), edited by James S. Ettema and D. Charles Whitney, 'The unique, made-to-order nature of the custom study is both its chief benefit and its major cost.' He goes on, 'The syndicated study offers comparative, longitudinal information about audiences that can be used to sell advertising space and time. Unlike the custom study, the syndicated effort provides the advertisers with a standard way to judge alternative vehicles for their messages.' See AUDI-ENCE MEASUREMENT.

Cut-off In INTERPERSONAL COMMUNICATION, actions which block – cut off – incoming visual signals when people are under stress: hands over eyes, deflected glance, glazed look, eyes shut, etc. See GESTURE.

Cybernetics The study of communication FEEDBACK systems in human, animal and machine. Taken from the Greek for 'Steersman', the term was the invention of American Norbert Wiener, author of *Cybernetics: or Control and Communication in the Animal and the Machine* (US: Wiley, 1949). Essentially an interdisciplinary study, Cybernetics ranges in its interest from control systems of the body to the monitoring and control of space missions. Cybernetics concerns itself with the analysis of 'whole' systems, their complexity of goals and hierarchies within contexts of perpetual change. The Greek steersman used the feedback of visual, aural and tactile indicators to chart his passage through rough seas. Today we have computers: the potential for accuracy and rapidity of feedback and control is vastly greater, and so is the potential for disaster should the feedback systems go wrong.

Cyberspace (See also INTERNET and NEW MEDIA.) Term probably first used by William Gibson in his novel *Neuromancers* published in America by Ace Books in 1984. Gibson describes cyberspace as 'a consen-...al hallucination ... [People are] creating a world. It's not really a place, it's not really space. It's notional space.' By pressing computer keys, and by grace of a modem and telephone line, the operator has access to potentially infinite information and endless exchanges with other users.

Network systems offer to the computer-explorer vast research possibilities, all for a monthly rental equal to that of a TV set. We can write direct, through e-mail, to the President of the United States or to Bill Gates, president of Microsoft. We can call up information from the Library of Congress, check the strength of the market in Hong Kong or book a holiday in the Caribbean.

We can join pressure groups and 'globalize' the issues that concern us. The net alters for us both time and space. New York, Alaska or Alice Springs could be in the next room for all that distance counts in cyberspace; and national boundaries need no longer be barriers. Indeed, in cyberterms, national and geographical divisions are an out-of-date way of viewing the world.

According to Mark C. Taylor and Esa Saarinen in *Imagology: Media Philosophy* (UK: Routledge, 1994), itself a mercurial sortie into cybergraphics, chief among cyberspace's characteristics is speed. 'Power,' the authors declare, 'is speed' and the 'swift will inherit the earth.' Some commentators claim that control, traditionally exercised by governments and powerful groups such as the transnational corporations, is shifting away from centres to peripheries, from organizations to individuals forming their own, hierarchy-free associations. In a number of countries the electronic highways of information, knowledge and ideas are seen as a threat to hierarchy and authority.

Some commentators see cyberspace as a force for dismantling patriarchal structures in society and altering existing gender relations. Is cyberequality on its way? American academic Cheris Kramarae is not so sanguine. In 'A backstage critique of virtual reality' in *CyberSociety: Computer Mediated Communication and Community* (US: Sage, 1995), edited by Steven G. Jones, Kramarae argues, 'Cyberspace, like earthspace, is not developed as a viable place for women.' She talks about 'malestream publications and other forums' and views 'cybersex' as something where game, play and match will continue to reflect sexist attitudes and behaviour.

Fears about the posting of paedophile information on the net, of information exchange between extremist factions, of freely available information on how to make weapons of mass destruction have surfaced on to public agendas to the point where, in many countries, those in authority have sought to 'fence in' the open prairies of cyberspace by legislation. Such moves have prompted many expressions of concern about the CENSORSHIP of the net.

As Darin Barney says in *Prometheus Wired: The Hope for Democracy in the Age of Network Technology* (US: University of Chicago Press, 2000), 'The key to network systems is surveillance.' He quotes David Lyon in his book *The Electronic Eye: The Rise of the Surveillance Society* (US: Minnesota University Press, 1994) who believes that to 'participate in modern society is to be under electronic surveillance'.

There are fears that the major CONGLOMERATES are successfully intent on colonizing cyberspace, converting the open prairie into virtual shopping malls. Many analysts take the view that the net is unlikely to be a bridger of the gap between information-rich and information-poor, that it is failing to redress the balance between core and periphery; and some are of the opinion that cyberspace is largely off limits to the poor, the ill-educated and the unemployed. See CORE NATIONS, PERIPHERAL NATIONS; INFORMATION GAPS; REGULATION OF INVESTIGATORY POWERS ACT (RIPA) (UK), 2000; SURVEILLANCE SOCIETY; WIKI, WIKIPEDIA. See also *TOPIC GUIDE* under CYBERCULTURE: THE NET, THE WEB.

* David Gauntlett and Ross Horsley, eds, *Web Studies* (UK: Arnold, 2nd edition, 2004).

Cylinder or rotary press The most important technical development in PRINTING history following the invention of movable type was the steam-driven cylinder press invented by Friederich Koenig. Born in Saxony, Koenig moved to London in order to set up a works to manufacture the new machines (1812). He demonstrated that a cylinder press machine could take off impressions at the rate of over 1000 an hour. On 28 November 1814 one of the presses was used to print *The Times*. Its editor, John Walter, described the press as 'the greatest improvement connected with printing since the discovery of the art itself'. As a result of its advantage in using Koenig's press, *The Times* became the dominant and most influential newspaper of the nineteenth century in the UK. See *TOPIC GUIDE* under MEDIA: TECHNOLOGIES.

→ D

Daguerreotype Early photograph produced in the manner of Louis Daguerre (1789–1851), a French theatrical designer who teamed up with Joseph Nicèphore Nièpce (1765–1833), a founding father of photography, in 1830. Nièpce died three years later but Daguerre continued their work, fixing images on metal plates coated with silver iodide, which he treated with mercury vapour in a darkroom. Daguerre was eventually able to reduce the exposure time of a photograph from eight hours to between 20 and 30 minutes. His daguerreotype was taken up by the French government in July 1839 and revealed to the world at a meeting of the Académies des Sciences in August. No prints could be made from a daguerreotype; thus Daguerre's method was a cul-de-sac in photography, though a vastly successful one at the time. See PHOTOGRAPHY, ORIGINS.

Dance's helical model of communication, 1967 The earliest communication models were linear; their successors were circular, emphasizing the crucial factor of FEEDBACK in the communication process. Frank E.X. Dance in 'A helical model of communication', in the book he edited, *Human Communication Theory* (US: Holt, Rinehart & Winston, 1967), commends the circular model as an advance upon the linear one but faults it on the grounds that it suggests that communication comes back full-circle, to exactly the same point from which it started, an assumption which is 'manifestly erroneous'.

The helix or spiral, for Dance, 'combines the desirable features of the straight line and of the circle while avoiding the weaknesses of either'. He goes on, 'At any and all times, the helix gives geometric testimony to the concept that Communication while moving forward is at the same moment coming back upon itself and being affected by its past behaviour, for the coming curve of the helix is fundamentally affected by the curve from which it emerges.' Dance's helical model parallels theories of education put forward by Jerome Bruner, and generally referred to as the spiral curriculum. See *TOPIC GUIDE* under COMMUNICATION MODELS.

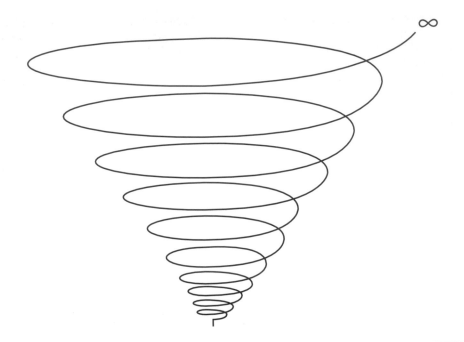

Dance's helical model of communication, 1967

Data mining In a 1998 publication, *Data Mining: Staking a Claim on Your Privacy* (Canada: IPC), Ann Cavoukian, Ontario (Canada) Information and Privacy Commissioner, defines data mining as 'a set of automated techniques used to extract buried or previously unknown pieces of information from large data bases'. The Commissioner states that 'successful data mining makes it possible to unearth patterns and relationship, and then use this "new" information to make proactive knowledge-driven business decisions'.

The process illustrates the penetrative power of surveillance (see SURVEILLANCE SOCIETY) made possible by computer networking. Extensively used by governments and business, data mining identifies patterns and trends in the seemingly disparate activities of citizens, such patterns and trends being used as indicators of future policy and promotion. See PRIVACY.

Data protection The increasing use of computers and sophisticated information technology has greatly magnified the harm to individual PRIVACY that can occur from any collection, storage or dissemination of personal information, and many countries have legislated against data abuse. Sweden, Denmark, Norway, Luxembourg, West Germany and France have all legislated to protect both the public and private sectors of society. In the US and Canada data protection legislation applies only to the public sector and compliance with it is voluntary.

In the UK, the report of the Lindop Committee (*Report of the Committee on Data Protection*, 1978) urged the need for individuals to have a right of veto on what information was passed on about them, and how this would operate in the context of 'the interests of the rest of society, which include the efficient conduct of industry, commerce and administration'. In 1984, the DATA PROTECTION ACT entered the Statute Book, and began operation in 1987 (see next entry).

CRYPTOGRAPHY, or what in modern parlance is termed *privacy transformation*, can be employed to 'scramble' data prior to storage in order to guard against accidental or deliberate disclosures of information. The problem here is how the key or code to the scrambling process is to be protected. In the US, the Hellman-Diffie method allowed for different keys for the scrambling and unscrambling processes. An alternative to this is the so-called *electronic signature* which works by reversing the roles of scrambling and unscrambling keys. Another mode is PIN – personal identity number – where everybody is issued with a personal key. PIN is already in use for the authorization of electronic funds transfers. See ECHELON; PRETTY GOOD PRIVACY (PGP). See also *TOPIC GUIDE* under MEDIA: FREEDOM, CENSORSHIP.

Data Protection Act (UK), 1984 The purpose of the Act is 'to regulate the use of automatically processed information relating to individuals and the provision of services in respect of such information'. From November 1987 the public has been able to check whether any organization holds information on them; to see a copy of that information, known as personal data; to complain to the Data Protection Registrar about the way data have been collected or used; to have inaccurate computer records corrected, or deleted in certain circumstances; and to claim compensation through the courts if the 'data subject' has suffered damage by the loss or destruction of personal data, or through an unauthorized disclosure or because of inaccuracy.

Designed to bring Britain into line with the Council of Europe Convention for the Protection of Individuals with regard to Automatic Processing of Personal Data, the Act provides for the establishment of a data watchdog, the Data Protection Registrar, and outlines eight DATA PROTECTION PRINCIPLES.

The test of any act protecting the citizen is the size and scope of the exceptions. There are three unconditional exemptions from registration: personal data required to be exempt for the purpose of safeguarding national security; data which its user is required by law to make public; and personal data held by an individual and 'concerned with the management of his personal, family or household affairs or held by him only for recreational purposes'. Subject access is barred on matters of prevention or detection of crime, the apprehension or prosecution of offenders or the assessment or collection of any tax or duty.

Data protection principles Listed in the DATA PROTECTION ACT (UK), 1984, are the following eight principles governing data protection for computer users handling personal data: computer users must (1) obtain and process the information fairly and lawfully; (2) register the purposes for which they hold the data; (3) not use or disclose the information in a way contrary to those purposes; (4) hold only information which is adequate, relevant and not excessive for the purposes; (5) hold only accurate information and, where necessary, keep it up to date; (6) not keep any information longer than is necessary; (7) give individual access to information about themselves and, where appropriate, correct or erase the information; (8) take appropriate security measures. Persons feeling that any computer user has broken one or more of the above principles may complain to the Data Protection Registrar. See PRIVACY; SECRECY.

Decency: Communications Decency Act, 1996 See COMMUNICATIONS DECENCY ACT (US).

Decisive moment French photographer Henri Cartier-Bresson (1908–2004) used this term to describe the instant when pressing the shutter release button produced the desired image. Indeed some critics believe that Cartier-Bresson's timing, his ability to be at the ready when destiny appeared to be bringing highly photogenic elements together, his instinct for the decisive moment, qualifies him to be considered the finest of all twentieth-century photographers.

Declaration on the Mass Media (UNESCO General Council, 1978) See MEDIA IMPERIALISM.

Decode The process of interpreting, analysing and understanding the nature of messages – written, spoken, broadcast, etc. This requires not just an understanding of the words, signs or images used but also a sharing of the VALUES and assumptions that underpin their encoding into a message by the transmitter. A focus for research in communication studies is the extent to which the receiver decodes the message in the way the encoder or sender would prefer. This is an important element in the debate on the power and influence of the media.

If the message is received by an AUDIENCE which does not share the same codes or values as the sender, it will be interpreted in an 'aberrant' way, that is, a different meaning will be assumed to that which was intended, hence the term *aberrant decoding*. In short, it is a difference of 'reading' the message derived from a difference of experience, perception or evaluation. See PREFERRED READING. See also *TOPIC GUIDE* under COMMUNICATION THEORY; LANGUAGE/DISCOURSE/NARRATIVE.

Deconstruction The process of deconstruction, as a mode of textual and intertextual analysis, is chiefly associated with the ideas of the French philosopher Jacques Derrida and his method of 'close-reading' of minute particulars in a text. The search is not for an ultimate MEANING; on the contrary, Derrida sees meaning as *undecidable*: signifiers within linguistic contexts refer to further signifiers, texts to further texts in an infinite web of INTERTEXTUALITY. Deconstructors such as Derrida seek to pry behind the dominant expressions of a TEXT, regarding these as serving to exclude subordinate terms. The technique is to *reverse* and *displace*, thus bring about an upending – an overthrow – of the hierarchies which rule all forms of expression.

In the words of Madan Sarup in *An Introductory Guide to Post-Structuralism and Postmodernism* (UK: Harvester Wheatsheaf, 1993), 'Deconstruction disarticulates traditional conceptions of the author and undermines conventional notions of reading and history ... It kills the author, turns history and tradition into textuality and' – we must gratefully note – 'celebrates the reader.' If *self* can be constructed as a text then self is subject to deconstruction, which displaces the notion of a *stable* self (see EISENBERG'S MODEL OF COMMUNICATION AND IDENTITY, 2001). The only coherence it would seem is fragmentation, leading to the conclusion that there can be no meaning, only interpretation.

Sarup's phrase 'textual undecidability' usefully sums up the position of the deconstructors, as does the term 'labyrinth of deconstruction' used by Christopher Norris in *Deconstruction: Theory and Practice* (UK: Methuen, 1982).

* Jacques Derrida, *Writing and Difference* (UK: Routledge & Kegan Paul, 1976); Christopher Norris, *Derrida* (UK: Collins, 1987).

Decreolization See COMMUNICATION: INTERCULTURAL COMMUNICATION.

Deep Dish TV See PAPER TIGER TV; TELEVISION: ACCESS TELEVISION.

Deep focus Film-making technique in which objects close to the camera and those far away are both in focus at the same time.

Deep structure Though the term was first used by Charles Hockett, the concept was given widest currency by fellow US linguist Noam Chomsky in 'Current issues in linguistic theory' in J. Foder and J. Katz, eds, *The Structure of Language: Readings in the Philosophy of Language* (US: Prentice Hall, 1964). In its original form, deep structure is an underlying abstract level of sentence organization, which specifies the way a sentence should be interpreted.

For Chomsky the deep and surface structures, and the relationship between them, provide the essential base of language which, far from being merely a sequence of words strung together, is rather a series of organized structures (see STRUCTURALISM). This deep structure, or level, supplies information that enables the reader or listener to distinguish between alternative interpretations of sentences which have the same surface form, or sentences which have different surface forms but have the same underlying meaning.

When, for example, a publisher replies to a budding author, 'I will waste no time in reading your manuscript', he presents a surface structure with alternative possible meanings. Yet by altering the surface structure of the sentence 'The dog chased the cat' to 'The cat was chased by the dog', the underlying idea is not altered. The transformations that might occur between deep and surface structure can be passive ('My father was warned by the doctor to give up smoking'), negative ('My father was not warned to give up smoking'), in question form ('Was my father warned to give up smoking?') or as an imperative ('Father was told – "Stop smoking!"'). See *TOPIC GUIDE* under LANGUAGE/DISCOURSE/NARRATIVE.

* Noam Chomsky, *Language and Mind* (UK: Harcourt Brace Jovanovich, 1968).

Deep throat Journalists' parlance for 'anonymous sources'. Perhaps the most famous was the unknown telephone informant calling himself 'Deep Throat' who set *Washington Post* reporters Carl Bernstein and Bob Woodward on the trail in the WATERGATE scandal that eventually led to the resignation of President Richard Nixon. In 2005 Deep Throat revealed his identity, winning worldwide media attention. He was Mark Felt, at the time of the revelations number two at the American FBI, responsible for the investigation into the burglary at the Democratic National Committee HQ in the Watergate apartment in 1972. Felt kept his secret for 33 years.

Defamation Any statement made by one person that is untrue and may be considered injurious to another's reputation, causing shame, resentment, ridicule or financial loss, is regarded as defamation under the Defamation Act (UK) of 1952. In permanent form, such as expressed in print, records, films, tapes, photographs, images or effigies, defamation is classified as *libel*. In temporary form, such as in spoken words or gestures, defamation is classified as *slander*.

No legal aid is granted to plaintiffs or defendants in defamation cases, thus persons even with the most genuine case for grievance at reports about them in the PRESS etc. must think twice before deciding to incur vast legal expenses in defending their reputation.

The 1996 Defamation Act is, in the words of a *Guardian* Leader of 26 June 1996, 'a generally sensitive attempt to impose practical rules upon the difficult relationship between the media and those who allege they have been defamed by them'. However, the late addition of the 'Hoffman clause' (brought by Lord Hoffman in the House of Lords and later approved by the House of Commons) concerning defamation and Members of Parliament, meets with disapproval, raising 'issues of privilege which go much further than the draftsmen can ever have intended'.

The clause devolves control over parliamentary privilege from the House as a whole to individual MPs, allowing them to waive parliamentary privilege in order to have the same rights as an ordinary citizen to take the media to court for alleged libel.

At first sight the amendment seems just: an MP has a right to make the media prove the truth of allegations. However, barrister Andrew Nicol, writing in the *Guardian* of 27 June 1996, states that the 'problem with such arguments is that they ignore the difference between journalistic evaluation of a story and the process of establishing the truth of a proposition in court'; in future mere doubt about whether truth can be proved in court may persuade nervous publishers to hold back on a story.

Nicol cites the 1963 decision by the US Supreme Court that if such conditions applied to public officials they would be an unconstitutional restriction on freedom of speech. Under the Hoffman clause, if an MP waived parliamentary privilege it would mean that no source material could be accepted as evidence unless the originator appeared in court to verify that information. This could destroy at a stroke the generally honourable tradition of the media protecting its sources. 'The information,' says Nicol, 'may, for instance, come from a reliable source but one who for good reason would not wish to testify in court.' See *TOPIC GUIDE* under MEDIA: FREEDOM, CENSORSHIP.

Defensive communication Occurs when people hear what they do not wish to hear. DISSONANCE arises when messages cut across, or contradict, VALUES and assumptions, and the reaction varies from not concentrating on the MESSAGE to deliberately misrepresenting or misunderstanding the sender's motive as well as his/her message.

Climates of threat create defensive tactics just as supportive climates help reduce them. If we know that we are being tested or evaluated, for example, our communication response will be guarded. Equally we might resort to defensive tactics if we feel the communicator of the message is intent on winning control, exerting superiority. We are less defensive in situations in which spontaneity, empathy, equality and a sense of open-mindedness about the nature of the message are predominant.

Deference, culture of See CULTURE OF DEFERENCE.

Deliberative listening See LISTENING.

Democracy and the media Both the word democracy and the idea are of Greek origin. *Demos* means citizen body; thus democracy is rule by the citizens, suggesting the right of all to decide on what are matters of concern, and possessing the power to decide on those matters. Democracy implies a vote for every citizen of a certain age, regular elections, a genuine choice of parties to *represent* citizens, and a range of rights – free speech, security from arbitrary arrest, the freedoms of belief, movement and association.

The media can be seen – and they often see themselves – as WATCHDOGS of democracy; journalists as articulators and defenders of democracy, the eyes and ears of the public. In his analysis of whether new technologies, in particular computer networks, enhance or diminish democracy, Darin Barney in *Prometheus Wired: The Hope for Democracy in the Age of Network Technology* (University of Chicago Press, 2000) identifies three elements he considers essential in *any* serious definition of democracy – equality, participation and 'a public sphere from which sovereignty emanates'.

Barney speaks of equality of *ability* as well as opportunity; and participation that is meaningful rather than 'frivolous or merely symbolic'. By this he suggests that 'democratic participation must be clearly and decisively connected to the political decisions that direct the activity of the participants' community'. Participation is not, he argues, confined to freedoms of 'consumer choice', the preferred interpretation of democracy by business. In Barney's view many self-proclaiming democracies would not pass the test of equality, participation and power through 'collective decisions'.

It has often been suggested that the media, through argument and advocacy, made democracy possible (see JOURNALISM). From Tom Paine's *The Rights of Man* (1891) through the age of the radical press during the nineteenth century, the cause of democracy was championed by journalists and editors, often risking life and liberty to make their case. Within a modern democracy, the media has an ongoing responsibility to exercise vigilance – to nurture, protect and celebrate a range of features that keeps democracy healthy, and prevents it from corruption, manipulation, misuse and apathy. These might be described as *satellites* of democracy, facilitators, the absence of which threaten the democratic process; they include full and fair transmission of information, PLURALITY of opinions and diversity of media provision.

Their enemies are monopolization of media-outlets by the few (see CONVERGENCE), the profits-generated insistence on treating people as consumers rather than citizens (see CONSUMERIZATION) and the consequent displacement or marginalization in media channels of information, critical analysis, debate and investigation. In this sense, considering the nature of media ownership (see *TOPIC GUIDE* under MEDIA: OWNERSHIP & CONTROL), the media are as likely to subvert democracy, or at least relegate it in importance, as to be its defender and advocate. See AGORA; DISCURSIVE CONTESTATION; DISENFRANCHISEMENT (OF READERSHIP); FRAMING; PUBLIC OPINION; PUBLIC SERVICE BROADCASTING (PSB); PUBLIC SPHERE. See also *TOPIC GUIDE* under MEDIA: POLITICS & ECONOMICS; MEDIA: VALUES & IDEOLOGIES.

Demographic analysis The collection and interpretation of data about the characteristics of people other than their beliefs, VALUES and attitudes. Specifically, *demography* is the study of population, while *demology* is the theory of the origin and nature of communities.

Demonization What the media do, particularly the popular PRESS, to those whose views they perceive to be dangerous, destabilizing, bad for business or subversive. The process of demonization begins with *personalization*, that is, focusing on the personal characteristics or attributes (invariably negative) of the leader or spokesperson advocating a cause or raising an issue, which the demonizers do not support. Having rendered the cause or issue a 'personal' matter associated with an individual, the aim of the media concerned is to destroy the credibility of the spokesperson and by so doing undermine, in the public mind, the cause for which he/she speaks. See FOLK DEVILS; LOONY LEFTISM.

Denotation See CONNOTATION.

Dependency theory The degree to which audiences are dependent upon the mass media constitutes one of the chief debates about the functions and effects of modern communication systems. In 'A dependency model of mass media effects', in G. Gumpert and R. Cathcart, eds, *Inter/Media: Interpersonal Communication in the Media* (US/UK: Oxford University Press, 1979), Sandra J. Ball-Rokeach and Melvyn DeFleur believe, 'The potential for mass media messages to achieve a broad range of cognitive, affective, and behavioural effects will be increased when media systems serve many unique and central information systems.' The fewer the sources of information in a media world, the more likely the media will affect our minds and thoughts, our attitudes and how we behave. Further, that influence will have increased potential 'when there is a high degree of structural instability in the society due to conflict and change'.

However, just as the audience may be changed by the information/messages it receives, in turn the media systems themselves are changed according to AUDIENCE response. It is not one-way traffic. In the cognitive or intellectual sphere, the authors cite the following possible media roles: (1) resolution of ambiguity, and relatedly limiting the range of interpretations of situations which audiences are able to make; (2) attitude formation; (3) AGENDA-SETTING; (4) expansion of people's systems of beliefs (for example, the tremendous growth in awareness of ecological matters); (5) clarification of values, through the expression of value conflicts (see DEVIANCE).

The media play a significant role in the establishment and maintenance of 'we feeling', that is, communal solidarity and oneness; equally they may work towards the alienation of sections of the population who are traditionally discriminated against – women, blacks, asylum-seekers, etc.

At critical decision-making times, such as elections, people have become increasingly dependent on the media, especially TV, for election information and guidance. Ball-Rokeach and DeFleur argue that the greater the uncertainty in society, the less clear are people's frames of reference; consequently there is greater audience dependence on media communication. See BALL-ROKEACH AND DEFLEUR'S DEPENDENCY MODEL OF MASS COMMUNICATION EFFECTS, 1976; EFFECTS OF THE MASS MEDIA. See also *TOPIC GUIDE* under COMMUNICATION THEORY.

Deregulation Describes the process whereby channels of communication, specifically radio and TV, are opened up beyond the existing franchise holders. Another term in current use, 'privatization', emphasizes the practical nature of the shift from public to commercial control, driven by the development of VIDEO, CABLE TELEVISION and SATELLITE and accelerated by DIGITIZATION. Regulation is associated with public service communications, for example PUBLIC SERVICE BROADCASTING (PSB), deregulation with the ambitions and practices of the private sector of the communications industry. See COMMUNICATIONS ACT (UK), 2003; CONGLOMERATES: MEDIA CONGLOMERATES; CONSUMERIZATION.

Deregulation, five myths of In 'The mythology of telecommunications deregulation' (*Journal of Communication*, Winter 1990), Vincent Mosco of Carleton University identifies five influential assumptions about the deregulation of telecommunications, which he describes as myths (see here Roland Barthes' definition of MYTH): deregulation lessens the economic role of government; benefits consumers; diminishes economic concentration; is widely supported; and is inevitable. Because deregulation is clearly in the interest of the non-public sector, particularly corporations profiting from the free market, it is in the sector's interest to establish the benefits of deregulation as a natural truth – unquestionably a good thing.

'Whatever their basis in fact,' writes Mosco, 'these myths continue to reflect significant political and economic interests. Moreover, they help to constitute those interests with a shared belief system ... promoting the dismantling of a public infrastructure and massive income redistribution up the social class ladder.' Mosco goes on, 'In the long run they want to advance the transformation of information from a public resource into a marketable commodity and a form of social management control. Deregulation is more than a policy instrument; it serves as a cohesive mythology around which those who would benefit from these short- and long-run interests might rally.'

Desensitization Process by which audiences are considered to be made immune, or less sensitive to, human suffering as a result of relentless exposure to such suffering in the media. A constant media diet of violence, real or fictional, is widely believed to 'harden up' people's tolerance of violence. See COMPASSION FATIGUE.

Detachment, ideology of See IMPARTIALITY.

Determiner deletion A common stylistic practice of journalists where the characteristics of a person and the name are linked without use of 'the' or 'a', in the interests of verbal economy while at the same time having the effect of *labelling* the named person. An example might be: 'Ex-jailbird six-times married Joe Bloggs yesterday told the press ...' or '"Kiss-and-tell" Minister's former live-in lover claims ...'. Allan Bell in *The Language of News Media* (UK: Blackwell, 1991) describes this practice as a form of *titleness* that gives instant NEWS VALUE to the person being reported. See HYPHENIZED ABRIDGEMENT; LABELLING PROCESS (AND THE MEDIA).

Determinism See TECHNOLOGICAL DETERMINISM.

Developmental news That which developing nations consider will help rather than harm their prospects. 'Western news' is seen by developing nations as essentially the pursuit of 'bad' news, and bad news hurts. The term implies government monopoly of information flow in the interests of giving a developing country a 'good name' and runs counter to western notions of free comment. The aspirations to a reporting tradition of social responsibility rather than sensation-seeking are honourable; and the dangers, of press subservience to government, obvious. See INFORMATION SOCIETY; MEDIA IMPERIALISM; NEW WORLD INFORMATION ORDER. See also *TOPIC GUIDE* under NEWS MEDIA.

Deviance Social behaviour that is considered unacceptable within a social community is deviant; and the defining of what constitutes deviance depends upon what norms of conduct prevail at any given time in a society. Of primary interest in the analysis of deviance is the question – who defines deviance and why? There are two main views on this: the first maintains that the definition of what is deviant behaviour stems from a general CONSENSUS within society; the second argues that it is the most powerful groups within a society which define as deviant behaviour that which may constitute a threat to themselves or their dominant position in society.

Particular interest has been focused on the role of the media in shaping definitions of deviance and then responding to those. While from a moral standpoint the media may disapprove of deviant behaviour, there

Digitization is seen to be both empowering (to the already powerful) and potentially disempowering (to those with less of it in the first place). In relation to the trend towards deregulation, Hamelink argues that 'tension between public good and private commodity is increasingly resolved to the latter's advantage'. Consequently the 'erosion of the public sphere by implication undermines diversity of information provision ... everything that does not pass the market threshold because there is not a sufficiently large percentage of consumers, disappears. That may be good for markets, it may be suicidal for democratic politics and creative culture.' See COMMUNICATIONS ACT (UK), 2003; DISEMPOWERMENT; DOWNLOADING. See also *TOPIC GUIDE* under MEDIA: TECHNOLOGIES.

* Jan van Dijk, *The Deepening Divide: Inequality in the Information Age* (US/UK: Sage, 2005).

Direct cinema Term used to describe the work of post-Second World War DOCUMENTARY film-makers in the US, such as Albert Maysles (*Salesman*, 1969, and *Gimme Shelter*, 1970), who coined the phrase, Stephen Leacock (*Don't Look Back*, 1968) and Frederick Wiseman (*High School*, 1968). New, lightweight equipment and improved synchronous sound recording facilities made the work of these observer-documentarists an inspiration for film-makers in many other countries. Direct cinema went out into the world and recorded life as it happened, in the 'raw'. An earlier, and British, link with this mode of film-making was Free Cinema, a short-lived 'collective' of directors in London, organized by Karel Reisz (*Momma Don't Allow*, 1956) and Lindsay Anderson (*O Dreamland*, 1953). Direct cinema film-makers had the technical edge on free cinema because of the availability of superior sound recording. See CINÉMA VÉRITÉ.

Disconfirmation See CONFIRMATION/DISCOMFIRMATION.

Discourse A form, mode or GENRE of LANGUAGE use. Each person has in his/her repertoire a whole range of possible discourses – the language of love, of authority, of sport, of the domestic scene. In a media sense, an example of a discourse would be the NEWS, reflecting in its choice of language and style of presentation the social, economic, political and cultural context from which the discourse emanates.

Gunther Kress in *Linguistic Processes in Sociocultural Practice* (Australia: Deakin University Press, 1985) provides the following useful explanation of discourse: 'Institutions and social groupings have specific meanings and values which are articulated in language in systematic ways. Following the work particularly of Michel Foucault, I refer to these systematically-organized modes of talking as discourse. Discourses ... give expression to the meanings and values of an institution.

'Beyond that, they define, describe and delimit what is possible to say and not possible to say (and by extension what is possible to do or not to do) with respect to the area of concern of that institution, whether marginally or centrally. A discourse provides a set of possible statements about a given area, and organizes and gives structure to the manner in which a particular topic, object, process is to be talked about. In that it provides descriptions, rules, permissions and prohibitions of social and individual action.'

The analysis of discourses is central to the study of media which is essentially about how TEXTS are encoded and how the MEANING of those texts, operating within and influenced by contexts, is decoded. Discourses are, in the words of John Fiske, 'socially produced' and a 'socially located way of making sense of an important area of experience'. Reality is a constant part of experience – how is it reconstructed into discourse? And how is it influenced by other discourses? (See INTERTEXTUALITY.)

All discourses are framed within *narratives* of one form or another. In news, or indeed in fiction, the story is what happens, the discourse how the story is told and the CONNOTATIONS or meanings embedded within it – the PREFERRED READINGS. Discourses struggle for attention; some are dominant and thus hold the public key to the definition of reality. They rigorously conform to *conventions* that work through mechanisms of information control (see AGENDA-SETTING; CONSENSUS; DISCOURSE OF POWER; GATEKEEPING) and are IDEOLOGY-driven (see DEMONIZATION; PHOTOGRAPHIC NEGATIVIZATION; NEWS VALUES; WEDOM, THEYDOM).

Ultimately discourse is about ruling explanations and thus contributes to the nature of MYTH. Christopher P. Campbell in *Race, Myth and the News* (US: Sage, 1995) sees myth not as the 'grand storytelling tradition associated with ancient cultures' but in the 'sense of the stories that modern societies unwittingly create to reduce life's contradictions and complexities'. This is what the discourse of news does, it 'comprises continuing stories which uphold and consolidate myth which ultimately focuses on order and disorder'. Campbell argues that 'News is a way of creating order out of disorder, offering cultural meanings, resolutions and reassurances'.

Discourse serves (and services) myth and the desired end-product is COMMON SENSE; in other words a state of affairs in which that which is defined by discourses is so patently commonsensical that it cannot be seriously contradicted. Campbell identifies the *divisive* rather than *cohesive* potential of commonsensical discourse: 'The danger of the commonsense claim to truth is in its exclusion of those who live outside the familiar world it represents.' See DOMINANT DISCOURSE. See also *TOPIC GUIDE* under LANGUAGE/DISCOURSE/NARRATIVE.

Discourse analysis Form of MASS COMMUNICATION analysis that concentrates upon the ways in which the media convey information, focusing on the language of presentation – linguistic patterns, word and phrase selection (lexical choices), grammatical constructions and story coherence. In particular, discourse analysis sets out to account for the textual form in which the mass media present IDEOLOGY to readership or audience. See CONTENT ANALYSIS; MODES OF MEDIA ANALYSIS.

Discourse of power The French philosopher Michel Foucault (1926–84) wrote that *all* arguments as to the truth are driven by the will to power, that is to exert control. Clearly, in terms of the media, discourses are perceived as means of exerting influence and control over audiences. Foucault saw the field of a discourse in the same way that a physicist sees the electromagnetic field: it is defined not by its will to truth but by its will to power. A discourse seeks power and that is what marks out its range. See HEGEMONY; IDEOLOGY.

Discursive communication Susanne Langer in *Philosophy in a New Key* (US: Harvard University Press, 1942) differentiated between what she named *discursive* communication – prose and logic – and *non-discursive* communication, such as poetry, music and ritual.

Discursive contestation Situation, usually occurring in the transmission of NEWS, where the AUDIENCE is permitted room to challenge or disagree; where news TEXTS passing through *frames* of production, are more open (to interpretation) than closed. News formats either facilitate discursive contestation or close down its potential.

Simon Cottle in 'Television news and citizenship: packaging the public sphere', published in *No News is Bad News: Radio, Television and the Public* (UK: Longman, 2001), edited by Michael Bromley, talks of how 'incredibly "restricted" some news formats are when reporting news stories'. Conventionalized TV news formats frame and discursively 'seal' the text from alternative interpretations. However, where 'words are spoken by accessed voices', that is by members of the public rather than media professionals, news texts are more open to discursive contestation.

Cottle argues that formats should work towards what he terms 'participatory control' or alternative frames where 'social actors are granted resources and news space to present in their own ways, and in their own words, their own frameworks of understanding'.

The author presents an analysis in tabular form of his studies of TV news formats (the result of a research project, UK News Access, funded by Bath Spa University College). He lists ten British TV news and presentational formats, varying from the 'tight' frame of newscaster only to the more discursive frame of live group interviews. He summarizes his findings by saying that 'nearly half of all TV news items ... provide few if any opportunities for direct access and discursive engagement by non-news voices, and such voices that are referenced remain the discursive prisoners of the news presenters and their informing news frame'. See DISEMPOWERMENT; FRAMING: MEDIA.

Discursive gap Term used by Roger Fowler in *Language in the News: Discourse and Ideology in the Press* (UK: Routledge, 1991). The 'gap' is that which exists between the mode of address of the newspaper – formal, bureaucratic – and that of the perceived reception mode of the reader, informal and personal, especially readers of the popular press. Fowler argues that 'the fundamental device in narrowing the discursive gap is the promotion of oral models within the printed newspaper text, giving an illusion of conversation in which common sense is spoken about matters on which there is consensus'.

He believes 'the basic task for the writer is to word institutional statements (those of the newspaper, and those of its sources) in a style appropriate to interpersonal communication, because the reader is an individual and must be addressed as such. The task is not only stylistic, but also ideological: institutional concepts have to be translated into personal thought.' In brief, the press employs a range of devices to simulate a sense of 'orality' which has the writer sitting next to the reader around the kitchen table or in the pub and joining in a process of 'co-production'; the product being CONSENSUS, an apparently shared vision of the world.

British film director, producer and theorist John Grierson (1898–1972) is thought to have been first to use the word documentary, in a New York *Sun* review (1926) of Robert Flaherty's film *Moana*, a study of the way of life of the South Seas islanders. In fact, 'documentary' is as old as the cinema itself. Louis Lumière's early short films of 1895, one showing the demolition of a wall, another of a train coming into a station, can be described as documentaries.

The founding father of documentary film-making in the UK and later in Canada, Grierson never claimed scientific objectivity for such films. For him the documentary was far more than a straightforward reconstruction on film of reality. He spoke of the 'creative use of actuality' in which the director re-formed fact in order to reach towards an inner truth. Indeed when documentarists have felt it necessary to get at the truth of a subject as they perceive it, they have not held back from fictionalization, often using actors, often turning the real-life person into an actor recreating a scene.

In the 1930s FILM documentary ran parallel with RADIO documentary – the BBC showed considerable innovative enterprise in this field, especially its Manchester studio – and, in the US, many impressive publications combined documentary evidence with outstanding photography. The themes were very often those of the Depression: concern at the plight of the poor, the unemployed, the alienated; and the mode was largely to have the people speak for themselves rather than distance the impact of their experience by using the mediation of a commentator.

The documentary approach has been a recurring feature in modern theatre, especially from the 1960s. Historical or contemporary events on stage are far from new: Aeschylus dramatized the victory of Marathon (490 BC) and Shakespeare reconstructed history, often to fit the perceptions of the Tudor monarchy, in a third of his output.

German dramatist Rolf Hochhuth won worldwide attention with his documentary drama *The Representative* in 1963, on the subject of the Papacy and the Jews during the Second World War (1939–45). He followed this up with *Soldiers* (1967) based upon the alleged involvement of British Prime Minister Winston Churchill in the wartime death of the Polish General Sikorski. In the UK, Peter Brook's highly successful *US* (1966) was an indictment of American involvement in the Vietnam War.

On-stage documentaries, in the US often termed the Theater of Fact, have frequently been presented with the aid of official and press reports, original diaries, projected photographs, tape recordings and newsreel films. In the case of the Royal Court production, *Falkland Sound* (1983), a moving and damning recollection of the Falklands War (1982) was presented through the letters home of a young naval officer killed in action.

Faction and dramadoc are terms mainly associated with TV documentaries in which actors recreate historical lives, such as the BBC's *The Voyage of Charles Darwin* (1978) or play the part of famous people of the immediate past, such as Thames Television's *Edward and Mrs Simpson* (1978), Southern TV's *Winston Churchill – The Wilderness Years* (1981), and ITV's *Kennedy* (1983). To TV producers faction has come to represent an ideal synthesis of education, information and entertainment, albeit highly selective and deeply coloured by contemporary perspectives.

Just as documentary has borrowed from fictional narratives, fiction has taken on the 'guise' of documentary. Such works are described as 'mock' documentaries and they aim to examine the borderline between the real and the invented. A memorable example is Woody Allen's *Zelig* (1983) in which he achieved remarkable results by combining newsreels, stills and live footage (see Craig Hight and Jane Roscoe's *Faking It: Mock-Documentary and the Subversion of Factuality*, UK: Manchester University Press, 2001).

The popularity of REALITY TV has in the new millennium been matched by increased interest on the part of audiences in documentary film for both the cinema and TV screens, with outstanding documentaries such as Kevin Macdonald's *Touching the Void* (2003), Errol Morris's *The Fog of War* and Andrew Jarecki's *Capturing the Friedmans* (both 2004), each with powerful stories to tell and conveying a dramatic sense of immediacy – indeed making the claims of authenticity put forward for reality TV pale in comparison.

Immensely popular on both sides of the Atlantic have been Michael Moore's documentaries, *Bowling for Columbine* (2002), a savage indictment of the US gun culture, and *Fahrenheit 9/11* (2004), a critical exploration of the Iraq War of 2003 and alleging links between President George Bush and top Saudi families including the bin Ladens. *Fahrenheit 9/11* won the prestigious Palme d'or best film award at the Cannes Film Festival. It was the first time that a documentary had won the top prize since Jacques Cousteau's award for *Silent World* in 1956. See CINEMATOGRAPHY, ORIGINS; CINÉMA VÉRITÉ; DIRECT CINEMA; FLY ON THE WALL; RADIO BALLADS; SOAPS: DOCU-SOAPS.

Dolly A trolley on which a camera unit can be soundlessly moved about during shooting; can usually be mounted on rails. A 'crab dolly' will move in any direction.

Domestication of the foreign See NEWS: GLOBALIZATION OF.

Dominant culture See CULTURE.

Dominant discourse In a general sense, DISCOURSE is talk; converse; holding forth in speech and writing on a subject. We are referring both to the content of communicative exchanges and to the level at which those exchanges take place, and in what mode or style as well as to whom the discourse is addressed. A dominant discourse is that which takes precedence over others, reducing alternative content, subordinating alternative approaches to 'holding forth'. All public discourse is socially and culturally based, thus it follows that the dominant discourse is usually that which emanates from those dominant in the social and cultural order. See ELITE; IDEOLOGY; HEGEMONY; POWER ELITE.

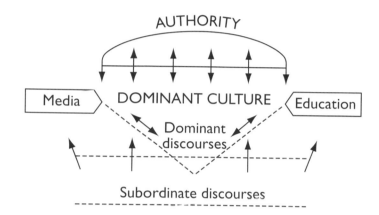

Dominant, subordinate, radical Three categories of response in terms of the reading of media messages on the part of AUDIENCE are posed by Frank Parkin in *Class, Inequality and Political Order* (UK: Paladin, 1972). Do we accept what we are told, only half accept or substantially reject it? Parkin argues that it is our place in the social structure that conditions our response. Stuart Hall in 'The determination of news photographs' in Stanley Cohen and Jock Young, eds, *The Manufacture of News* (UK: Constable, 1st edition, 1973) supports Parkin's view, with the same categories but different terminology.

The dominant system of response (Hall calls it a *dominant code*) signifies that the dominant values and existing society are wholly accepted by the respondent; the subordinate response (Hall's *negotiated code*) indicates general acceptance of dominant VALUES and existing social structures, but the respondent is prepared to argue that a particular group – blacks, unemployed, women – within that structure may be unfairly dealt with and that something should be done about it. The radical response (Hall's *oppositional code*) rejects the PREFERRED READING of the dominant code and the social values that produced it.

David Morley's researches into audience response, published in *The 'Nationwide Audience'* (UK: British Film Institute, 1980), gave substance to Parkin and Hall's division of response, but also emphasized other response-conditioning factors such as education, occupation, political affiliation, geographical region, religion and family. More recent commentators have expanded on the response codes mentioned here; for example, a *popular* response may be characterized by *inattention* on the part of audience or the rejection of media messages because 'they have nothing to do with us'. See EFFECTS OF THE MASS MEDIA; ETHNOGRAPHIC (APPROACH TO AUDIENCE MEASUREMENT); POLYSEMY. See also *TOPIC GUIDE* under AUDIENCES/CONSUMPTION & RECEPTION OF MEDIA.

Double exposure Two pictures superimposed upon one another on the same piece of film. Like reverse motion, double exposure in filming began by being a simple visual curiosity before it became a fully fledged means of artistic expression. It was first used in still photography, where double or multiple exposure images produced what was described as 'spirit photography'. Georges Meliès (1861–1938) used it in his films from

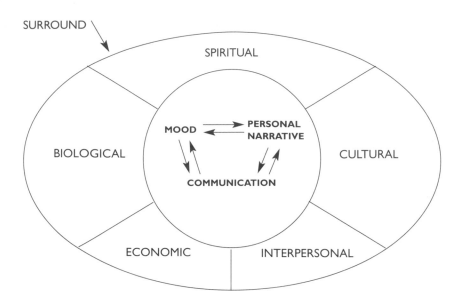

SURROUND

SPIRITUAL

MOOD → PERSONAL NARRATIVE
←

BIOLOGICAL

CULTURAL

COMMUNICATION

ECONOMIC

INTERPERSONAL

Eisenberg's model of communication and identity, 2001 (the identity process, with three subprocesses operating within a surround)

psychological orientation to the world around us; to others within the context of that world. It concerns our sense of power – power to take hold of our lives, shape them, and this connects to the stories we construct about ourselves, our identity; facilitating (or otherwise) what Eisenberg terms our 'narrative possibility'.

The three core elements are interdependent and interactive, and the sense of empowerment will depend on the nature of communication, to put it briefly, less target orientated, less occupied with the 'ideology of clarity', of objectivization, less individualised, less defensive of self, value and ideology and more communal – in essence, more connective, indeed orientated towards the cultivation of a 'planetary identity'.

While Eisenberg does not wish to minimize the importance of 'understanding' in communicative exchange, he sees in uncertainty its value as mystery, a vital counterbalance to strategies that endanger sympathetic communion with others, for as the author acknowledges, 'Despite unprecedented advances in science and culture, brutal dictatorships, medieval forms of torture and genocide persist' – all in the name of truth-assertion and the notion of identity as something fixed and permanent. The stories we tell ourselves, our construction of identity through self-narrative, are predicated on the nature of communication itself, its ability to accommodate the 'fundamental indeterminacy of the future', which Eisenberg argues, 'is an essential quality of human experience'. See *TOPIC GUIDE* under COMMUNICATION MODELS.

Elaborated and Restricted Codes In *Class, Codes and Control Vol. 1* (UK: Paladin, 1971), Basil Bernstein posed a now-famous classification of language codes, the Elaborated and Restricted Codes based upon researches into the language use of children. Bernstein maintains that there are substantial differences in speech between middle-class and working-class children, the former using the Elaborated Code, the latter the Restricted Code.

The determinant of the code in each case is the nature of the social relationships and influences to which the child is exposed. A close-knit, traditional working-class community, Bernstein argues, tends to use the Restricted Code because a high degree of shared MEANING is assumed. In the more typically loose-knit middle-class communities there are fewer grounds for making assumptions about shared meaning and therefore a more explicit, Elaborated, code is used. This is not to say that the middle classes do not possess their own Restricted Codes in particular social or professional situations. The important point is that they can move with ease from a Restricted to an Elaborated Code.

The Restricted Code tends to be less complex than the Elaborated, with a small vocabulary and simpler sentence structure. It tends to be spoken rather than written. It is easy to predict (high in REDUNDANCY) whereas the Elaborated Code is less easy to predict (high in *entropy*). The Restricted Code is orientated towards social relations, towards COMMONALITY, while the Elaborated Code represents an emphasis on individuality and individual differences.

The one is the language of the street, the home, the playground, the pub; the other, very largely, the language of school; the language of formal education. Thus, Bernstein indicates, within the educational context, the user of the Restricted Code is placed at a disadvantage. He does not argue that the Elaborated Code is superior to the Restricted Code, only that it is different and more useful for upward social mobility.

Bernstein's claims prompted considerable debate, some of it critical, and a number of researchers would argue that his classification was inflexible. Martin Montgomery, for instance, in *An Introduction to Language and Society* (UK/US: Routledge, 1995), argues that 'there is, for example, in the final analysis hardly any linguistic evidence to support the division of speech into two mutually exclusive codes or speech variants. And by the same token, Bernstein's treatment of the social structure looks with hindsight somewhat rigid and schematic'. See *TOPIC GUIDE* under LANGUAGE/DISCOURSE/NARRATIVE; REPRESENTATION.

---

* Basil Bernstein, 'Social class, language and socialization', an extract from his major work, in J. Corner and J. Hawthorn, eds, *Communication Studies* (UK: Arnold, 1993).

Electronic democracy See TELEVISION: INTERACTIVE TELEVISION.

Electronic mail: e-mail The sending and receiving of e-mails – texts of all kinds through the 'postal' system of the computer – has become the fastest-growing means of communication in business, within institutions, and between friends, families and total strangers across the world. It has proved a useful tool in the exchange of knowledge, the provision of advice, the two-way transmission of research data and the sharing across social and national boundaries of myriad problems. It serves as a link between GROUPS and communities of like interest, all at the price of a local phone call.

In 1992 only 2 per cent of the American population used the e-mail service. This had risen in 1998 to 15 per cent. The rise in what has been referred to as 'computer babble', both for business and leisure use, is such that e-mails now constitute a problem as much as an opportunity. The *Wall Street Journal* has gauged that a typical worker in a European company deals with an average 150 e-mails a day. Allowing time to read these and reply, they would take some four to five hours to process – a dramatic example of information overload. The *Journal* reported that an executive returning to the States from a business trip in Europe found 2000 e-mails waiting to be dealt with.

E-mails are also very public statements, open to the scrutiny of those not intended to read them. Then there has been the growth of junk e-mails – *spam*; and, more seriously, *phishing*, using spam e-mails to redirect online banking users to fake sites, with often devastating financial consequences for the victims. Even more serious still is *spoofing* where spammers use header information to convince you that their message is genuinely from your bank or any other source which is confidential.

The future effectiveness of net industries will depend on systems of *authentication*, that is, making sure that communications sent are valid and legitimate, while at the same time blocking off unwanted sources. One system pitching for industry standard ENCRYPTION is Domain Keys Identified E-mail (DKIM) originating from Yahoo! and Cisco Systems. This puts a unique electronic 'signature' on each e-mail. A public key is held on record and a user's private key on any DKIM server. A point at issue is whether such systems should be part of commercial packages or open-source applications. See *TOPIC GUIDE* under CYBERCULTURE: THE NET, THE WEB; MEDIA: TECHNOLOGIES.

Electronic newsgathering Referred to as ENG, the gathering of sound and vision NEWS reports electronically, usually transmitted via telephone links or from transmitter vans. Much lighter and more compact than traditional film or TV cameras, electronic equipment records on to cassette, bypassing the film processing stage: pictures from the scene of action can be transmitted directly or stored electronically. EFP – electronic field production – is an advance on ENG, making location programmes of all kinds possible without having the cameras tied to an outside broadcasting (OB) vehicle.

Elite A small group within a society who may be socially acknowledged as superior in some sense and who influence or control some or all sectors of the society. Several definitions of the term *elite* exist and these influence the precise focus of research into the relationship between the media, elites and society.

Early writers generally see the elite as a ruling elite or oligarchy whose power is general and affects most

Euphemism In polite circles, 'belly' is not referred to, but 'stomach' is acceptable. That is a euphemism, the rendering of blunt, harsh or unpleasant terms in mild, inoffensive or quaint LANGUAGE. Thus 'to die' may be rendered euphemistically as 'to pass away'; a 'bookie' may prefer to seek more status by calling him/herself a 'turf accountant'. In advertising, 'budget items' are preferred to 'cheap goods'. In business, people are not 'sacked' but 'the labour force is slimmed' or 'downsized'.

Some euphemism is justifiable in INTERPERSONAL COMMUNICATION, for example at times of grief and tragedy; some are insulting to language and to human intelligence and dignity, such as the terminology of armed conflict where 'demographic targeting' means the destruction of cities in situations of war, 'support structure' is civilians, 'collateral damage' is dead civilians and an 'intelligence producing facility' is a torture chamber.

In their chapter 'Doublespeak' in *Weapons of Mass Deception: The Uses of Propaganda in Bush's War on Iraq* (US: Tarcher/Penguin; UK: Constable and Robinson, 2003), Sheldon Rampton and John Stauber cite 'shaping the security environment' as polite language for controlling people at gunpoint, while 'critical regions' is doublespeak for 'countries we want to control'.

A recent euphemism in the UK has been the term 'entitlement card' broached by the Home Office to disguise its true intention of being an ID card serving the government's 'entitlement' to know all about you.

Euronet A consortium of national computer interests in a number of European countries, working towards the creation of a mutually compatible interconnection of European databases. Euronet is designed for reasons as much political as economic, as a method of ensuring that in the long term the economic control of Europe remains in European hands, and thus, inextricably, the control of information.

European Community and media: 'Television Without Frontiers' Title of a Council of Europe directive, October 1989, the first attempt by the European Community to regulate and institutionalize BROADCASTING between member states; revised in 1997. The directive requires EC members to guarantee unrestricted reception for audiences across Europe and to avoid any strategies likely to limit retransmission in their territory of any EC broadcasts that meet Community conditions. The directive lays down a policy of minimum regulation, granting equal rights to commercial operators and public service broadcasters while at the same time requiring no legal obligations to enhance public discourse.

Facing the TWF initiative in 2005 was the monumental task of legislating for the vast increase in INTERNET and mobile phone traffic. Pressure for further DEREGULATION came from major corporations such as Time Warner, News International, Bertelsmann and Microsoft, lobbying under the umbrella of the International Communications Round Table (ICRT). See FAIRNESS DOCTRINE (USA); PRIVATIZATION.

Europe: cross-border TV channels Since the 1980s the number of cross-border TV channels has risen to over 100, some 80 of these holding a licence from the UK Independent Television Commission (ITC, replaced by OFCOM in 2003), whose licences are cheap and easy to obtain, the prime criterion being that such stations are based in the UK.

Among the major cross-border players are Arte, BBC Prime, BBC World, Bloomberg, Cartoon Network, CNN International, Discovery, Eurosport, Fox Kids, MTV, National Geographic and Sky News, most of which are UK registered.

The expansion of cross-border transmission was made possible, and encouraged by, three key factors: (1) DEREGULATION which occurred through Europe (and elsewhere) during the 1980s and 1990s; (2) the European Community's 'Television Without Frontiers' directive (see above), Article 2 of which prevents member states barring broadcasting emanating from other member states; and (3) the possibilities brought about by SATELLITE TRANSMISSION. See LOCALIZATION.

Event The occurrence which gives rise to media coverage will have fulfilled one or more, or an amalgam, of NEWS VALUES. In the analysis of media, different forms of event can be identified. Primarily there is the *key event* triggering media and subsequently public attention. Such an event may, as in terrorist attacks in one country or city, trigger a worldwide sense of crisis.

In 'The impact of key events on the presentation of reality' in the *European Journal of Communication*, September 1995, Hans Mathias Kepplinger and Johanna Habermeier suggest a useful typology of the causes and communicative functions of events (see diagram). The coverage of events, especially if they give grounds for concern about causes and consequences, stimulates the 'activities of pressure groups who see an

Communicative functions	Causes		
	Genuine (independent of the media)	Mediated (influenced by the media)	Staged (for the media)
Key events			
Similar events			
Thematically related events			

— Topic

Kepplinger and Habermeier's model of media events, 1995

---

opportunity of gaining media attention, since their concerns fit in with the established topic. The consequence is an increased number of mediated and staged events.'

Equally, such coverage tends to exert 'pressure upon decision-makers in politics, business, administration, etc.'. The authors give the example of how safety rules for petrol tankers may be changed as a result of media conjecture about possible, rather than actual, accidents. Coverage of key events will, say Kepplinger and Habermeier, enhance the coverage of similar or related events, and add interest and urgency to events thematically linked.

Of course the nature of coverage will vary between media, for example between daily and weekly newspapers or between broadsheets and tabloids. The authors note a tendency in the reporting of key events to give the impression of an *accumulation* of such events (hence the sense of crisis) whereas what is actually happening is an accumulation of another kind: similar stories, being gathered together from the past as well as the present, are being reinvigorated and intensified as they compound information about the new key event.

Key events thus trigger apparent waves of such events when in reality only one has occurred: 'Here one has to take into account that the news coverage creates a false impression that events accumulate and problems become more urgent.' (See next entry.)

Event: Americanizing of Practice, in the US, of reporting world events in relation to American interest or interests. As Susan D. Moeller points out in *Compassion Fatigue: How the Media Sell Disease, Famine, War and Death* (US/UK: Routledge, 1999), 'The American filter, the notion of relevance to the United States, is very important.' Speaking of the American public, Moeller says, 'Since our knowledge about the lands outside our borders is minimal, even the abbreviated version of events which makes it into news has to be translated for us' (see ETHNOCENTRISM).

In her conclusion to her analysis of COMPASSION FATIGUE and how the media can strive to avoid creating or reinforcing it, Moeller believes that the Americanizing of events '(once called the "Coca-Colonization" of events) can be a positive force to attract the public's attention to a far-off event, but it should not be the defining characterization of that event' for 'once in play, the Americanization can become a crutch, simplifying a crisis beyond recognition, and certainly beyond understanding'.

The author concedes that 'Americans are already too self-involved' and she blames the media's 'entrenched news net and news priorities' as the cause 'of their neglect of certain events or countries'. See HISTORICAL ALLUSION.

PHOTOGRAPHY; HOLLYWOOD; IMAX; KINETOSCOPE; KULESHOV EFFECT; MARCH OF TIME; McGUFFIN; MONTAGE; MULTIPLE IMAGE; MUSICAL: FILM MUSICAL; NATIONAL FILM ARCHIVE; NEWSREEL; NEW WAVE; OMNIMAX; PERSISTENCE OF VISION; RUSHES; SHOT; SLOW MOTION; 'SOMME, THE BATTLE OF THE'; SPECIAL EFFECTS; SYNCHRONOUS SOUND; VAMP; VIDEO; WESTERN; WILLIAMS COMMITTEE REPORT ON OBSCENITY AND FILM CENSORSHIP (UK), 1979; ZOOM LENS; ZOOPRAXOGRAPHY.

Film censorship See CENSORSHIP; CERTIFICATION OF FILMS.

Filmless camera Launched by the Japanese in 1987, the all-electronic camera is instant, avoids the need for chemical processing, can project its pictures from a standard television monitor and permits its images to be transmitted down a TELEPHONE line or fed into a computer for further processing.

Film noir Term used by French film critics, notably Nino Frank, to describe a particular kind of dark, suspenseful thriller. A classic of the GENRE is French director Marcel Carné's *Le Jour se Lève* (1939) – 'Day Arises' – starring Jean Gabin. We see the last doomed hours of a man wanted by the police for murder. He has barred himself in his attic bedroom in an apartment block. He is totally surrounded. He has no chance; but then, Carné makes clear, the man never did have a chance. At dawn he shoots himself and, as he lies dying, his alarm clock goes off, reminding him of his otherwise intolerable life as a worker.

Described as 'symbolism with a three o'clock in the morning mood', film noir gained substantial currency in the US, generally thriving between the early years of the Second World War and the late 1950s, and ranging from John Huston's *Maltese Falcon* (1941) to Orson Welles' *Touch of Evil* (1958). Hollywood film noir, says Michael Walker in the Introduction to *The Movie Book of Film Noir* (UK: Studio Vista, 1992), edited by Ian Cameron, features 'heroes who are frequently victims of a hostile world'. Such movies are characterized by a 'distinctive and exciting visual style, an unusual narrative complexity' and 'a generally more critical and subversive view of American ideology than the norm'.

Women in film noir, writes E. Ann Kaplan in *Women in Film Noir* (UK: British Film Institute, 1980), edited by Kaplan, are 'presented as desirable but dangerous to men'. They 'function as the obstacle to the male quest. The hero's success or not depends on the degree to which he can extricate himself from the woman's manipulations'. Billy Wilder's *Double Indemnity* (1941), with Fred MacMurray as the (willingly) manipulated male victim and Barbara Stanwick as the alluring manipulator, is a classic example of the genre.

* Foster Hirsch, *Film Noir: The Dark Side of the Screen* (US: Da Capo Press paperback, 1983).

First impressions There is evidence that we tend to give too much attention to the initial information we may receive about an individual, and relatively less to later information that may be contradictory; that is, we are biased towards primacy effects (see PRIMACY, THE LAW OF). There is some evidence that negative first impressions in particular can be resistant to change.

First impressions can clearly count in situations where most of the information is received about a person in a fairly short, discrete period of time, as in an interview. In this instance there might be little opportunity for first impressions to be modified.

In some circumstances – as when a considerable time gap intervenes between sets of information received about an individual or when there is regular, close contact with that individual – first impressions can be modified. Here the later information received may have greater impact. This is known as the *recency* effect, because it is the more recent information that is the more influential. See *TOPIC GUIDE* under COMMUNICATION THEORY.

Five filters of the news process See CONSENT: MANUFACTURE OF.

Five myths of deregulation See DEREGULATION, FIVE MYTHS OF.

Flak Term used by Edward Herman and Noam Chomsky in *Manufacturing Consent: The Political Economy of the Media* (US: Pantheon, 1988; US: Vantage paperback, 1994) to describe a 'negative response to a media statement or programme, and this may resemble flak in its wartime sense: a blitz taking the form of letters, telegrams, phone calls, petitions, lawsuits, speeches and bills before Congress, and other modes of complain, threat, and punitive action'.

The authors argue that 'if flak is produced on a large scale, or by individuals or groups with substantial resources, it can be both uncomfortable and costly to the media'. Used by the powerful such as the great corporations, flak is intended to inhibit media activity, or bring about the cessation of that activity. Flak can be aimed at media activity indirectly as well as directly 'by [in the case of corporations] complaining to their own constituencies (stockholders, employees) about the media, by generating institutional advertising that does the same, and by funding right-wing monitoring or think-tank operations designed to attack the media'. See CONSENT· MANUFACTURE OF.

Flashback A break in the chronology of a NARRATIVE in which events from the past are disclosed to the reader, listener or viewer, and which have a bearing on the present situation. Flashback was a device used very early in the history of the cinema. D.W. Griffith's epic *Intolerance* (1916) is made up of four flashbacks. Used with a narrator, the form achieved its greatest popularity in the cinema in the 1930s and 1940s. Orson Welles' *Citizen Kane* (1941) is made up entirely of a dazzling series of flashbacks. Equally inventive is the flashback narrative of the Ealing comedy, Robert Hamer's *Kind Hearts and Coronets* (1949).

Flat-screen technology Called 'roll-up TV'; the late 1990s saw a race to develop flexible liquid crystal display (LCD) technology that would replace bulky TV sets reliant on the cathode-ray tube, with light, high-definition screens which could be hung like paintings on a wall. Flat screens made their first appearance in early laptop computers, but these lacked colour fidelity and image resolution. The so-termed Malvern screen, developed at the Worcestershire headquarters of the imaging department of the UK's Defence Evaluation and Research Agency (DERA) employs, as later laptop computers have done, ferroelectric crystals, but operating at different voltages and alignments. When not in use the screen can be used to display works of art or photographs. DERA's prime motive in developing the Malvern screen has been to produce roll-up, animated electronic maps, or miniature screen displays built into a pilot's helmet.

Fleet Street Until the 1980s, the home of most of Britain's major national newspapers; indeed the name had become the generic term for the nation's PRESS; a figure of speech (see METONYMY). The advent of new technology linked with the cost-cutting ambitions of newspaper owners, both of which led to bitter conflict with the print unions, caused an exodus from 'The Street' of all the major titles.

* Laura Melvern, *The End of the Street* (UK: Methuen, 1986).

Flops Floating point operation per second, the means by which the speed of computers is measured.

Flow See PROGRAMME FLOW.

Fly on the wall Popular title given to a GENRE of DOCUMENTARY film-making, for the cinema or TV, in which the camera remains concealed, or is handled so discreetly that the subjects forget they are being filmed. Richard Denton, producer of the BBC documentary series *Kingswood: A Comprehensive School* (1982), describes the approach in 'Fly on the wall – designed to invade privacy', *Listener* (13 January 1983) as attempting 'to remove the process of filming so far from the consciousness of the contributors that they will, in theory, forget its existence and so behave in a markedly more natural, truthful and realistic manner'.

Denton speaks of two distinct problems: 'The first concerns the question of accuracy and context ... The second, and probably more important, problem concerns privacy.' Outstanding examples of the fly-on-the-wall approach were the BBC's *Police* series (1982), the work of Roger Graef and Charles Stewart, and Channel 4's *Murder Squad* (1992). Of particular interest for fly-on-the-wall documentarists has been *family interaction.* First in the UK to win fame by exposing their lives to the eye of the camera was the Wilkins family of Reading, featured in the BBC series *The Family* (1974). In 1999 Granada Television screened the lives of a mixed-race family from Leeds, in *Family Life.* See CINÉMA VÉRITÉ; DIRECT CINEMA.

Focus groups Frequently employed in market research; members of a group are brought together by a researcher to discuss aspects of a product, be it soap powder, a political party or a television programme. The group is often chosen to be a representative SAMPLE of all those who are thought to be the actual or potential consumers of the product. As a qualitative research method, use of focus groups allows for in-depth discussion and exploration of consumers' orientations towards and evaluations of a product. Focus groups are also widely used by governments and political parties as a gauge of public opinion on proposed or actual policies. See *TOPIC GUIDE* under RESEARCH METHODS.

Foe creation See WEDOM, THEYDOM.

Folk culture Term generally applied to the CULTURE of pre-industrial societies. Such societies have certain distinguishing features that are thought to affect the elements of their culture: work and leisure are undifferentiated; there is relatively little division of labour; the communities are small and social action is normally collectivist as opposed to individualist. Thus folk songs, for example, are usually firmly rooted in the everyday experience and beliefs of both the AUDIENCE and the performer.

Folk devils Stanley Cohen in *Folk Devils and Moral Panics* (UK: MacGibbon & Kee, 1972, 3rd edition 2002) argues that societies are subject to periods of moral panic in which certain groups are picked out as being a special threat to the VALUES and interests of society. The media and in particular the press play an important role in transmitting this sense of outrage to the general public.

These groups or individuals are usually those transgressing the values of the dominant hierarchy. It is further argued by Cohen and others that the castigation of such groups, such folk devils, by the media is a mechanism by which adherence to dominant social norms is strengthened along with support for the forces of law and order and an extension of their powers. See LOONY LEFTISM.

Footage Length of film expressed in feet.

'Footprint' Term used to describe the area in which a signal from a communications satellite can be received. See SATELLITE TRANSMISSION.

Four stages in audience fragmentation See AUDIENCE: FRAGMENTATION OF.

Fourteen-Day Rule (UK) In the period after the Second World War (1939–45) the BBC entered into an agreement with government whereby it would not try to usurp the functions of the House of Commons as the supreme forum of the nation by BROADCASTING on issues due to be debated in Parliament. An embargo was placed upon all such issues until 14 days after Parliament had debated them. It was a crippling intrusion upon the editorial rights of the Corporation, and the BEVERIDGE COMMITTEE REPORT ON BROADCASTING (UK), 1950, called for the abandonment of the Rule. Nevertheless, successive governments held tenaciously to it.

In 1956 the House of Commons set up a Select Committee to investigate the workings and effects of the Rule: it recommended a reduction to seven days. Pressure from broadcasters and the press continued unabated and within a year the Rule was abandoned altogether (1957). See *TOPIC GUIDE* under MEDIA: FREEDOM, CENSORSHIP; MEDIA HISTORY.

Four Theories of the Press See PRESS, FOUR THEORIES OF.

Fourth estate The eighteenth-century parliamentarian Edmund Burke (1729–97) is thought to have been the originator of this phrase describing the press and its role in society. According to Burke's definition, the other three 'estates' were the Lords Spiritual (the Church), the Lords Temporal (the judiciary) and the Commons. 'And yonder,' he is believed to have said in Parliament, 'sits the Fourth Estate, more important than them all.'

The implication is that the press, like the other estates, serves the state, as differentiable from government, and thus functions as a force for social, cultural and national cohesion. Underlying this argument is the assumption that while governments might be in error, the state is benign if not sacrosanct. A glance at states ancient and modern would suggest otherwise. The classifying of the press as the Fourth Estate points up the ambivalent role of media in society: does it tell the truth, the whole truth and nothing but the truth? Or because the priorities of state seem to require it, manipulate, conceal or deny that truth? See ELITE; GUARD DOG METAPHOR; MEDIA CONTROL; POWER ELITE; WATCHDOGS. See *TOPIC GUIDE* under MEDIA HISTORY.

Fragmentation of audience See AUDIENCE: FRAGMENTATION OF.

Framing: interpersonal Conversations are often framed by METASIGNALS that let observers and participants know what kind of activity is going on so that they are better able to interpret the conversation. For example, is the conversation a serious argument or horseplay?

Such signals also allow people to recognize what Erving Goffman in *Frame Analysis* (US: Harper & Row, 1974) terms the *alignment*, that is the relative positions with regard to STATUS, intimacy and so on, being taken by the participants, themselves included. If A, for instance, explains something to B in a condescending manner, A is taking a superior alignment with regard to B.

In *You Just Don't Understand: Men and Women in Conversation* (UK: Virago, 1992), Deborah Tannen argues that protective comments and gestures from men towards women 'reinforce the traditional alignment by which men protect women'. She goes on to argue that 'the act of protecting frames the protector as dominant and the protected as subordinate'. However, arguably because men and women are fundamentally tuned to interpret some aspects of conversation differently, the difference in relative status signalled by such comments may be more apparent to men than women. Women may simply interpret them as indicating a desire to protect or be supportive rather than as indicative of women's traditionally subordinate status in society. See GENDER; GENDERLECTS.

Framing: media The process by which the media place reality into frame; and the study of the process of framing is at the core of media analysis, hence the length of this entry. Framing constitutes a NARRATIVE device. What is *not* on the page of a newspaper is 'out of frame'; what does not appear within the frame of the TV is off the public agenda. For the NEWS, there is the world – and 20 minutes to put it in the frame. *Time*, then – the shortness of it – is an important deciding factor. For a soap opera, time also poses problems of framing. There are 30-minute slots to be filled, each to conclude with unfinished business, preferably dramatic and suspenseful, while not being so dramatically 'final' that the series cannot continue day by day, week by week. Presented with such a time-frame, soaps require many characters and many plots. To facilitate this requirement (and to capture and retain AUDIENCE attention) scriptwriters divide up the frame into quick-bite scenes – framing within frames.

What happens outside the creative frame – audience measurement, for example – influences the nature of the frame and what goes on inside it. Robert Entman in 'Framing: toward clarification of a fractured

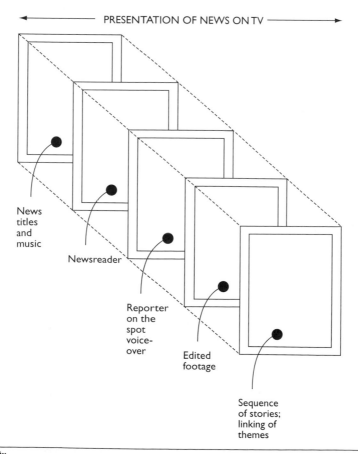

PRESENTATION OF NEWS ON TV

News titles and music

Newsreader

Reporter on the spot voice-over

Edited footage

Sequence of stories; linking of themes

Framing reality

paradigm' in the *Journal of Communication* 4 (1992) says that a crucial task of analysis is to show 'exactly how framing influences thinking' for 'the concept of framing consistently offers a way to describe the power of a communicating text'.

He argues, 'Analysis of frames illuminates the precise way in which influence over a human consciousness is exerted by the transfer (or communication) of information from one location such as speech, utterance, news report, or novel – to the consciousness.' Essentially, framing constitutes *selection* and *salience*; what is perceived to be most meaningful, the one serving the other. Entman suggests that framing serves four main purposes: (1) to define problems; (2) to diagnose causes; (3) to make moral judgements; and (4) to suggest remedies.

These will function varyingly according to the text, but they operate in four locations in the communication process: the *communicator*, the *text*, the *receiver* and the *culture*. Communicators 'make conscious or unconscious framing judgments in deciding what to say, guided by frames (often called schemata) that organize their belief systems'. Before we frame, we are in a frame. The text will not only be framed by the framer within a frame, it will be shaped by a number of factors – requirements concerning format and presentation, aesthetic considerations, notions of professionalism and pressures to meet the expectations of convention.

When the text comes to be 'read', the frames as presented may be at variance with the frames that guide the receiver's thinking. For Entman the culture is 'the stock of commonly invoked frames ... exhibited in the discourse and thinking of most people in a social grouping'. 'Framing in all four locations includes similar functions: selection and highlighting, and use of the highlighting elements to construct an argument about problems and their causation, evaluation and/or solution. This approach is useful in analysing the encoding of messages and gauging their effectiveness. It emphasizes the subjective nature of encoding by recognizing the 'invisible' schemata – psychological templates – which, however hard we try to be objective and impartial, deeply influence our actions.

For successful communication – that is, winning the interest and attention of the audience, and perhaps even going beyond that in terms of gaining the audience's assent or approval – there seems to be a need for a meeting of schemata: a common ground. The communicator selects, then attempts to give salience to those parts of the story which may fit with the existing schemata in a receiver's belief system.

Much of what we know about the past, about history, is itself in frames – in ancient palaces and tombs, on triumphal arches, the walls and ceilings of great monasteries and cathedrals. These artefacts do not necessarily tell us what life was like in those days; rather, they tell us what was considered salient by those with power to make decisions. In *The Nature and Origins of Public Opinion* (US: Cambridge University Press, 1992), J.R. Zaller says that framing is a central power in the democratic process: it is political elites who control the framing of issues. Such framing, Zaller believes, not only influences public opinion but is capable of defining it.

At a practical level, framing is governed by professional conventions, indeed by ritual: newspapers are framed by deadlines and publication times. TV news is framed with music, graphics, headlines and newsreaders, each ritual presence reinforcing and increasing the salience of the frame, its dominance over alternative frames. The study of media is an example of what Entman calls *counterframing* in that it attempts to call the ritual frames into question by analysing them in the light of possible alternative frames.

In 'Framing European politics: a content analysis of press and television news', in the *Journal of Communication*, Spring 2000, Holli A. Semetko and Patti M. Valkenburg identify five key frames in which the media present the news – *attribution of responsibility, conflict, economic consequences, human interest* and *morality*. In their researches, the authors found less divergence between press and TV and more between serious and sensationalist press; the first operating within the attribution of responsibility frame, the second in the human interest frame. See *TOPIC GUIDE* under MEDIA: PROCESSES & PRODUCTION.

* Dietram A. Scheufele, 'Framing as a theory of media effects', *Journal of Communication*, Winter 1999.

Franchise Contractual agreement; most commonly associated with the licensing to broadcast, for fixed periods, of commercial television and radio companies.

Franchises for Independent Television (UK) Royal Assent to the TELEVISION ACT, 1954, was received on 30 July and on 4 August the Independent Television Authority (later to become the Independent Broadcasting Authority) was set up by the Postmaster-General under the chairmanship of Sir Kenneth Clark. The first commercial television franchises were issued in 1955, with the Associated Broadcasting Company

(ATV) beginning its first London transmission on 24 September 1955, and its first Midlands transmission on 17 February 1956.

Franchises from 1993 (UK) What the *Guardian* called 'the biggest shake-up in television's 36-year history', with an estimated loss of some 2500 jobs, occurred in October 1991. The Independent Television Commission (ITC) chaired by George Russell announced the winners of the 'auction' for 16 regional commercial TV franchises, including a breakfast TV licence, to extend over ten years and commencing on 1 January 1993.

Four existing stations lost their renewal bids: Thames Television (replaced by Carlton Communications), Television South (Meridian Broadcasting), Television South West (Westcountry Television) and the breakfast station TV-am (Sunrise Television). The stations empowered to continue broadcasting through the 1990s were: Granada Television (for the north-west), London Weekend, Yorkshire, Anglia Television, Tyne-Tees (north-east), Harlech Television (Wales), Ulster Television, Channel Television (Channel Islands), Central Television (Midlands) and the Scottish channels Grampian, Border and Scottish Television. Russell declared that though the process had caused 'undoubted turmoil' within ITV, 'the quality and the viewers will win out'. This point of view was not shared by George Walden in an article 'Is this merely a lottery, or is it a serious business?' (*Daily Telegraph*, 17 October 1991). 'Sadly,' he wrote, 'what has been at stake in this lottery is the quality of British television.'

The Times leader of 17 October called the whole affair an 'ITV auction fiasco' and said, 'The government should never ask such a task again ... auctioning terrestrial commercial television was always intended to benefit the Treasury not the television viewer. The result must be fewer resources available for programme-making and thus for competing with the cheap products on offer from the American television industry.'

The original plan of the Conservative government was to auction off the franchises to the highest bidder in a blind sale. This was later modified by the introduction of a so-called 'quality threshold'. Eight of the 16 licences did not go to the highest bidder and 13 applications were judged not to have passed the quality threshold. One notable characteristic of the new franchise winners was the declared policy of running lightly staffed publisher–broadcaster stations, on the lines of Channel 4, buying in programmes from independent producers rather than the companies originating most of their own material.

Frankfurt school of theorists Founded in 1923, the Institute for Social Research in Frankfurt became the meeting point of several young Marxist intellectuals among whom were Theodor Adorno, Herbert Marcuse and Max Horkheimer. The members of the 'school' placed at the forefront of their thinking and analysis the centrality of the role of IDEOLOGY in mass communication. When Hitler came to power in 1933, the Institute moved to New York and until 1942 it was affiliated to the Sociology Department of the University of Columbia. In 1949, Horkheimer led the Institute back to Frankfurt, though Marcuse remained in America.

The Frankfurt school posed the questions: Why had the prospect of radical change in society so little popular or natural support? Why was there so little consciousness of the need for politically radical change – indeed how had that sense of need been apparently eliminated from popular consciousness? Marcuse, in *One Dimensional Man* (UK: Sphere Books, 1968), contended that in advanced societies capitalism appears to have proved its worth; by 'producing the goods' it is deemed a successful system and therefore one which has rendered itself immune to criticism.

The Frankfurt school believed that culture – traditionally transcendent of capitalist ethic and thus in many ways potentially subversive of it – had been harnessed by the mass media (see HEGEMONY). Classical art had been popularized, yes; but in the process of media adoption it had been deprived of its *oppositional* values (see DOMINANT, SUBORDINATE, RADICAL). The Frankfurt school has had considerable influence upon thinking about the media and its power to shape cultures, but has been criticized for condemning existing reality without proposing how it might be changed for the better. See AUDIENCE: ACTIVE AUDIENCE; CULTIVATION; CULTURAL APPARATUS; DOMINANT DISCOURSE. See also *TOPIC GUIDE* under COMMUNICATION THEORY.

* Rolf Wiggershaus, *The Frankfurt School: Its History, Theories and Political Significance* (UK: Polity Press paperback edition, 1995).

Freedom of Information Act (UK), 2005 The right of access by citizens to information of public interest is enshrined in legislation in many countries, in particular the United States. In the UK in 1994 the Conservative government under John Major took a tentative step towards creating a degree of open government with its Code of Practice on Access to Government Information. In opposition, the Labour Party made no secret of its intention to end secret government, the future Labour Prime Minister Tony Blair promising that a Freedom of Information Act, should Labour be elected, would 'signal a new relationship between government and people; a relationship which sees the public as legitimate stakeholders in the running of the country'. The basis of this relationship was to be freedom of information.

Once elected, the New Labour government delayed implementing FOI (freedom of information) legislation, eventually producing an Act which a *Guardian* leader of 31 December 2004 described as 'a pale shadow of the 1997 white paper', *Your Right to Know*. The Act, which became law at midnight on 31 December 2004, gives the public rights of access to Parliament, government departments, local authorities, the National Health Service and education, but not the security services or the courts. Coming into force at the same time as the Act were Environmental Information Regulations (EIRs), implementing an EU directive freeing up previously closely guarded information about the environment and increased rights of access under the DATA PROTECTION ACT (UK), 1984.

A welcome step towards more open government, the Act nevertheless is cluttered with exemptions. The provision of information can be denied if it is likely to prejudice interests such as international relations, defence, the enforcement of the law, economic and commercial interests. As the *Guardian* leader pointed out, 'About 75 per cent of the disclosures in the Hutton and Butler enquiries … would not be permitted under the new law.' (See HUTTON REPORT (UK), 2004.)

Freedom of information does not come cheaply. If the cost of finding and extracting information exceeds set limits the authority is empowered to say 'No', though in many straightforward cases, the service is free.

The Act also created the role of Freedom of Information Commissioner but drew back from granting him or her independent powers, subjecting the Commissioner's actions to the will of government ministers. A notable case of ongoing CENSORSHIP and resistance to open government was New Labour's refusal through 2004 and 2005 to make public the advice offered to Cabinet by Lord Goldsmith, the attorney general, on the legality or otherwise of the invasion and occupation of Iraq in 2003. See HUMAN RIGHTS ACT (UK), 2000; REGULATION OF INVESTIGATORY POWERS ACT (RIPA) (UK), 2000; SURVEILLANCE; TERRORISM: ANTI-TERRORISM, CRIME AND SECURITY ACT (UK), 2001. See also *TOPIC GUIDE* under MEDIA: FREEDOM, CENSORSHIP.

Frequency In a non-technical sense, and as used in relation to the media, frequency is the degree of repetition of topics of NEWS or information in the press and on RADIO or TV. The more frequently a topic inhabits news headlines and news stories, the more likely it is to continue to do so; to be defined and accepted as 'important', and to have media impact.

Negative frequency operates when stories are overlooked, or edged to the margins of attention. Consequently they rarely have the chance either to improve their status as news or impart the full weight of their argument. The term may also be used to refer to the way in which news items fit the frequency – the *timescale* – of the mode of communication. See CONSISTENCY; EFFECTS OF THE MASS MEDIA; IMMEDIACY; INTENSITY; NEWS VALUES.

Front See SELF-PRESENTATION.

Front region, back region See IMPRESSION MANAGEMENT.

Functionalist (mode of media analysis) Interprets social behaviour in terms of its contribution to the assumed overall goals of society, recognizing a CONSENSUS within society of common norms and VALUES. The main focus of functionalist analysis is upon the ways in which social systems maintain *equilibrium*. A functionalist would consider any social or cultural element in relation to its contribution to the survival, integration or stability of society. The communication process features as a major component in the 'servicing' of equilibrium.

Structural functionalism, a mode of analysis developed by US sociologist Talcott Parsons, identifies common features of a complex industrial society that are central to its survival. These include the delineation and maintenance of boundaries (social, cultural, etc.); the definition of major structural units of society and the connections between them; and an overriding concern with system maintenance. This school of analysis has been particularly strong in the US.

Within the functionalist perspective, activities that contribute to the survival of a system are known as *eufunctions*; those which contribute to disturbance are known as *dysfunctions*. A distinction is also made between manifest and latent functions, the one intended and recognized by the participants, the other neither intended nor recognized.

The functionalist approach makes challengeable assumptions about consensus over the goals of society, leaving untouched important questions about the source of these goals and the degree to which an identified source may influence the nature of the social structure and social action. Its tendency is to legitimize the status quo and to emphasize the predominance of the whole over the parts, overlooking alternative means of achieving the same or similar functions. See MARXIST (MODE OF MEDIA ANALYSIS).

Functions of communication See COMMUNICATION, FUNCTIONS.

Functions of mass media See NORMATIVE THEORIES OF MASS MEDIA.

→ **G**

Gagging order Issued by judges to restrain the publication or broadcast of information where it is considered that such information breaches the law. Companies in the UK may seek gagging orders to prevent communication to the public that seems a threat to *commercial confidentiality*; individuals may seek the imposition of such orders to protect their personal PRIVACY.

The HUMAN RIGHTS ACT (UK), 2000, emanating from the European Convention of Human Rights, forbids, for example, publication of details of a person's health. Deemed a 'private matter' this nevertheless raises difficult questions when a person's individual 'health' – say if he or she is a health worker suffering from HIV – may have implications for the public. See *TOPIC GUIDE* under MEDIA: FREEDOM, CENSORSHIP.

Galtung and Ruge's model of selective gatekeeping, 1965 Whenever 'newsworthiness' is discussed and analysed, the names of Johan Galtung and Mari Ruge are likely to be mentioned before all others. Their article 'The structure of foreign news: the presentation of the Congo, Cuba and Cyprus crises in four foreign newspapers' in the *Journal of International Peace Research* 1 (1965), and reprinted in *The Manufacture of News* (UK: Constable, 1973), edited by Stanley Cohen and Jock Young, has proved a focal point for those who ask the questions: What qualifies as news? And what makes one item of news predominate over another?

The model represents the way in which events pass through the GATEKEEPING processes of the media – initially the perceptions of media people as to whether the event qualifies as news, then the selection according to a set of news criteria (I to IX) alone or in combination. For details of the criteria identified by Galtung and Ruge, see NEWS VALUES. See also *TOPIC GUIDE* under COMMUNICATION MODELS.

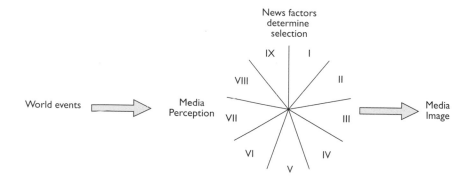

Galtung and Ruge's model of selective gatekeeping, 1965

Games See TRANSACTIONAL ANALYSIS.

Gantt chart Named after Henry Lawrence Gantt and originally developed in the early twentieth century. The chart is still widely used in the communications field to plan and track the schedule of activities required for events, programmes or campaigns. Basically activities are plotted from top to bottom (with the initial activity at the top and the last at the bottom) along the vertical axis against a time-frame plotted along the horizontal axis.

Gatekeeping To reach its intended target, every MESSAGE has to pass through many 'gates'; some will be wide open, some ajar, some tightly closed. At work, the boss's secretary is the archetypal gatekeeper. She may be under instruction to welcome callers or delay them, by letter, by telephone or physically by 'guarding' the boss's door. Writing about gatekeepers in the media, Stuart Hood in 'The politics of television' in Denis McQuail, ed., *Sociology of Mass Communications* (UK: Penguin, 1972) says, 'A news bulletin is the result of a number of choices by a variety of "gatekeepers". They include the editor who decides on the day's coverage, or the organizer who briefs the camera crews and reporters and allocates assignments, the film editor who selects the film to be included in the bulletin, the copy-taster who chooses the stories from the tape to accompany the film, the sub-editor who writes the story and the duty editor who supervises the compilation of the bulletin, fixes the running order of the stories and gives it its final shape.'

The selection or rejection of material is made according to a set of criteria determined by a number of factors – the gatekeeper's class background, upbringing and education and his/her attitudes to the world (VALUES); plus the values, norms and traditional wisdom of the organization for which the gatekeeper works.

The process and effect of gatekeeping in the media have undergone substantial modification in the age of electronic transmission. The age of scarcity of channels has been transformed to an age of BANDWIDTH abundance. Consumers of communication now have at their fingertips the power to evade traditional modes of gatekeeping. Text, pictures, the latest movies, pop tunes have become available online; and if gatekeeping has always been a process of manipulation by the communicators as well as selection, the consumer can do this too with the images and texts that he or she can summon up.

As populations access the net in increasing numbers, there is the potential for a shift of control from producer to consumer. This, at the same time, threatens to lessen the ability of governments to exercise intervention in the form of regulation and censorship. The very freedom of expression that electronic data exchange offers people worldwide will prompt governments to seek to curb this freedom – a possibility which will be made more viable once all transmission forms share the same digital network. See AGENDA-SETTING; CONSENSUS; DIGITIZATION; GALTUNG AND RUGE'S MODEL OF SELECTIVE GATEKEEPING, 1965; MR GATE; NEWS VALUES; WHITE'S GATEKEEPING MODEL, 1950. See also *TOPIC GUIDE* under MEDIA: PROCESSES & PRODUCTION; NEWS MEDIA.

Gender Our gender or gender identity refers to our categorization, and that of others, of ourselves as either male or female. According to Richard D. Gross in *Psychology: The Science of Mind and Behaviour* (UK: Hodder & Stoughton, 1987), gender is a cultural term and one's gender role 'refers to the behaviours, attitudes, values, beliefs and so on which a particular society expects from, or considers appropriate to, males and females on the basis of their biological sex'. Definitions of appropriate behaviour for males and females can vary from one CULTURE to another and, over time, within a particular culture or society. Conflict also exists within our own society regarding the precise definition of what should constitute appropriate behaviour for the different gender roles.

It is arguable that maintenance of a gender identity requires the individual to carry off a performance in line with expectations others hold of suitable behaviour for the identity claimed. Judith Butler, for example, in *Gender Trouble: Feminism and the Subversion of Identity* (US/UK: Routledge, 1990) stresses the crucial importance of performance, and thus of verbal and non-verbal communication, in the construction of gender identity. Such expectations reflect assumptions about gendered behaviour within the society, communities and social groups to which an individual belongs – expectations which may, of course, conflict.

Expectations and assumptions about appropriate gender behaviour can be challenged and such challenges extend to the assumption that gender can be neatly divided into either male or female categories. A transvestite, for example, in playing out this role adopts the appearance and other aspects of performance usually associated with those of the opposite sex. There has been much research not only into the degree to which verbal and non-verbal communication shape and reflect gender identity but also into the effect the media may have on the formation and reinforcement of gender identities and roles.

Ideas about appropriate gender behaviour also lie at the heart of notions of femininity and masculinity and include assumptions about sexual preferences. A current area of research focuses upon media portrayal of sexual preferences and, in particular, its portrayal of those preferences assumed to be minority preferences, for example those of lesbians and gay men. Larry Gross in 'Minorities, majorities and the media' in Tamar Liebes and James Curran, eds, *Media, Ritual and Identity* (US/UK: Routledge, 1998) argues that traditionally in much of the US media, portrayals of lesbians and gay men have been limited and stereotypical, with the underlying message being that such identities are deviant. See FEMINISM; GENDERED GENRE; GENDERLECTS; HE/MAN LANGUAGE; MALE-AS-NORM; NEWS: THE 'MALENESS OF NEWS'; PATRIARCHY; PLEASURE: ACTIVE AND REACTIVE: REPORT-TALK, RAPPORT-TALK; REPRESENTATION; SELF-IDENTITY; SELF-PRESENTATION; SEMIOTIC POWER; STEREOTYPE; QUEER THEORY.

Gender and media monitoring Especially since 1995 when the United Nations Fourth Conference on Women took place in Beijing, China, women's groups have focused intensively on the degree to which media globally have asserted male over female interests, at the same time representing women in stereotypical ways. The conference affirmed the need for systematic and ongoing monitoring of the media, judging that evidence was the key to influencing hearts, minds and practices. The weight of research evidence would be the driving force behind lobbying for fairer representation.

* Margaret Gallagher, *Gender Setting: New Agendas for Media Monitoring and Advocacy* (UK: Zed Books with the World Association for Christian Communication, 2001).

Gendered genre Term used in cultural analysis to denote GENRES of film or television which are seen to appeal to one GENDER rather than another. For example, SOAP OPERAS have traditionally been seen to be primarily directed at female audiences whilst crime series are perceived to appeal more to male audiences. The TEXT and its NARRATIVE patterns typically reflect such differences in AUDIENCE and in part, though not uncritically, assumptions about gender roles and typical masculine and feminine behaviour.

Soap operas, for instance, concentrate on the family and local neighbourhood and the interplay of interpersonal relationships within these contexts, whereas the crime series focuses on action, heroic deeds and male bonding. Some researchers have argued that the concept of gendered genre over-simplifies the potentially complex relationship between the text, its narrative form, its authors and its audience.

The term *gendered viewing* describes the different perspectives, ways of seeing, *between* genders in relation to cultural, social and historical contexts. This is not simply a matter of the ways men look, or perceive, compared with the way women perceive, for as Mary Ellen Brown asserts in *Soap Opera and Women's Talk: The Pleasure of Resistance* (US: Sage, 1994), 'gender role characteristics of the one sex can be displayed by people of either sex'. Indeed, the 'simple delineations of masculine and feminine are also somewhat inappropriate because they imply masculinity as central and femininity as marginal'.

Brown's book explores the ways in which women view – and use – soaps to assemble DISCOURSES of resistance through what she terms GOSSIP NETWORKS. Brown writes, 'Both soap operas and gossip claim for women a space and time in which there is freedom to play with dialogue – dialogue that does not necessarily advance the plot but is simply there for pleasure. All of these aspects fly in the face of dominant conventions.' See FEMINISM; GENRE; SEXISM. See also *TOPIC GUIDE* under GENDER MATTERS.

Genderlects In *You Just Don't Understand: Men and Women in Conversation* (UK: Virago, 1992), Deborah Tannen argues that in conversation while men 'speak and hear a language of status and independence', women 'speak' and hear a language of 'connection and intimacy'. These fundamentally different orientations and their influence on perception are, she argues, important factors in creating confusion and misunderstanding in conversations between men and women.

These differences have led Tannen to conclude that men and women speak different *genderlects* and her book examines examples of how male and female differences in orientation and consequently in interpretation can be observed in many different contexts. See REPORT-TALK, RAPPORT-TALK.

* Mary Crawford, *Talking Difference: On Gender and Language* (UK: Sage, 1995).

Gender signals Male and female signals in interpersonal conduct and appearance that label or place emphasis upon the sex of the signaller. See GESTURE; PROXEMICS.

Generalized other As contrasted with SIGNIFICANT OTHERS; representing society at large – the organized community or social group which, in the words of George Herbert Mead in *Mind, Self and Society From the Standpoint of a Social Behaviourist* (US: University of Chicago Press, 1934), 'gives the individual his unity of self'. Mead argues that 'it is in the form of the generalized other that the social process influences the behaviour of individuals involved in it and carrying it on'. Thus the generalized other exercises a degree of control over the conduct of its members; and its norms and VALUES are important determining factors in the individual's thinking. The *significant other* – a parent, friend, group leader or public figure – may varyingly reinforce, modify, challenge or counteract the influence of the generalized other. See SYMBOLIC INTERACTIONISM.

Genre Term deriving from the French, meaning type or classification. In literature the major classic genres were epic, tragedy, lyric, comedy and satire, eventually to be followed by the novel and short story. Genres, working at least approximately to basic ground rules of form and style, are categories to be found in all modes of artistic expression. In films there are genres of the WESTERN, gangster movies, FILM NOIR, science fiction, romantic comedy, horror, disaster, costume drama, etc. In TELEVISION there are SITCOMS, SOAPS, detective and police series. Genres are rarely discrete or singular entities. They are subject to influence by other genres, and are often a mixture of genre elements.

Indeed part of the pleasure audiences derive from genre TEXTS is their inventiveness, the way the CODES of different genres have been knowingly manipulated, sometimes to satirical effect. In short, what attracts and fascinates is their INTERTEXTUALITY. Writing in *Acts of Literature* (UK: Routledge, 1992), French philosopher Jacques Derrida is of the opinion that there is 'no genreless text'; thus the way is open to classify TV news, party political broadcasts, weather reports, quiz shows, chat shows and consumer programmes as genres. See NARRATIVE. See also *TOPIC GUIDE* under LANGUAGE/DISCOURSE/NARRATIVE.

Gerbner's model of communication, 1956 This is described by Denis McQuail in *Communication* (UK: Longman, 2nd edition, 1993) as perhaps 'the most comprehensive attempt yet to specify all the component stages and activities of communication'. Below is a modified version of George Gerbner's model as presented in 'Towards a general model of communication', in *Audio Visual Communication Review* 4. M is responder to E (event) and may be human or machine (such as a microphone or camera). Gerbner's emphasis is upon the considerable variability in the perception of an EVENT by a communicating agent and also in the way the MESSAGE is perceived by a receiver. He speaks of the essential 'creative, interactional nature of the perceptual process'. Equally important is the stress placed upon the importance of context to the 'reading' of messages, and of the open nature of human communication.

For Gerbner the relationship between form and context in the communication process (S = Signal) is dynamic and interactive. It is also concerned with access and control, dimensions which inevitably affect the

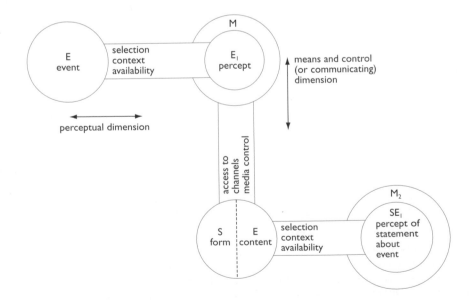

Gerbner's model of communication, 1956

nature and content of communication messages – their selection, shaping and distortion. At the level of the mass media this is obvious, but access and control also operate at the level of interpersonal communication – teachers in classrooms, for example, speakers at public meetings, parents in the home situation.

Back on the horizontal axis, Gerbner stresses the importance of *availability*. A literate electorate may have the capacity to read all the facts about a political situation, all the pros and cons of an industrial dispute but that capacity can only operate, and the pros and cons be properly weighed, if the necessary facts are made available. What Gerbner's model does not do is address itself fully to the problems of how MEANING is generated. The form or code of the message (S) is taken for granted, whereas the advocate of SEMIOLOGY/SEMIOTICS would argue that meaning is of the essence. See *TOPIC GUIDE* under COMMUNICATION MODELS.

Gestural dance A term that has been used to describe the way in which gestures are employed to achieve interactional synchrony between participants in an encounter. For example, the smooth handing over of the conversational floor from speaker to listener is achieved by a combination of prolonged gaze, falling intonation, returning of the hands to a rest position and possibly the use of a gesture towards the listener to invite a contribution. The listener may have indicated a wish to speak by the use of rapid HEAD NODS.

Gestural echo See POSTURAL ECHO.

Gesture Michael Argyle in *Bodily Communication* (UK: Methuen, 1988) divides gestures and bodily movements into three main categories: *Emblems, Illustrators* and *Self-touching*. Emblems are movements, often hand movements, that can easily be translated into speech in terms of their MEANING (they may often stand in for speech) within a particular GROUP or CULTURE. The use, in Britain, of the thumbs-up gesture to mean OK would be an example. Illustrators are those gestures used to illustrate or accompany speech, often to aid explanation; for example, gestures used when giving directions. Self-touching normally indicates information about an individual's emotional state, such as the scratching of the face when anxious.

In *Manwatching: A Field Guide to Human Behaviour* (UK: Jonathan Cape, 1977), Desmond Morris defines a gesture as 'any action that sends a visual signal to an onlooker'. Incidental gestures may be unintentional, accidental, but they still communicate messages, such as mood information. Primary gestures are those that are intended – a wave, a nod, a wink.

Morris offers six categories of gestures. (1) *Expressive*, shared by other animals as well as humans, and including facial expression and manual gesticulations. (2) *Mimic gestures*, exclusively human, 'the essential quality of a Mimic Gesture is that it attempts to copy the thing it is trying to portray'. This category Morris subdivides into *social* mimicry (or 'putting on a good face'); *theatrical* mimicry; *partial* mimicry (pretending your hand is a gun, for example); and what he terms *vacuum* mimicry – gestures to indicate hunger or thirst. (3) *Schematic* gestures are those in which imitations become abbreviated or abridged, a gestural shorthand. (4) *Symbolic* gestures represent moods and ideas, such as the SIGN to indicate that you consider someone is 'round the twist'. (5) *Technical* gestures constitute specialized signal systems recognized only by those in the trade or profession, such as those employed by a TV studio manager or a fireman to his colleagues. (6) *Coded* gestures are based upon formal systems, such as deaf-and-dumb sign language, semaphore and the tic-tac signalling of the race-course.

Many gestures carry universal meaning but in general the gesture is critically dependent upon the cultural context in which it is made and specific contexts of timing and situation as well as the combination of gestures, for rarely do they exist alone, or without vocal accompaniment. See BARRIER SIGNALS; BATON SIGNAL; COMMUNICATION, NON-VERBAL; CUT-OFF; METASIGNALS; NON-VERBAL BEHAVIOUR: REPERTOIRE; PROXEMICS; SALUTATION DISPLAY; SHORTFALL SIGNALS; TIE-SIGNS. See also *TOPIC GUIDE* under INTERPERSONAL COMMUNICATION.

Ghost-writer One who does literary work for someone else, usually a celebrity, who takes the credit.

Glasgow University Media Group Set up with a grant from the UK Social Science Research Council, the Group has published research findings that have won considerable attention and not unexpectedly drawn fire from the media under investigation. By 1982 the Group had published three major works tabulating its exhaustive research into the way TV handles the NEWS. First came *Bad News* (UK: Routledge & Kegan Paul, 1976), which exploded the generally held image of broadcasters being substantially more objective and reliable in news reporting than the PRESS. 'Our study,' wrote the eight authors of the original study, 'does not support a received view that television news is "the news as it happens".' The Group had monitored all TV news broadcasts over a six-month period, from January to June 1975. Notable among the Group's findings was evidence of a bias in TV against the activities of organized labour and a relentless emphasis upon effects rather than causes.

Later publications by the Glasgow University Media Group have been *More Bad News* (UK: Routledge & Kegan Paul, 1980), *Really Bad News* (UK: Writers and Readers' Publishing Co-operative, 1982) and *War and Peace News* (UK: Open University Press, 1985) about media coverage of the Falklands War, the Miners' Strike of 1984 and Northern Ireland. The theoretical base from which the Group works may be summarized by a quotation from *More Bad News*: 'news is not a neutral and not a natural phenomenon: it is rather the manufactured production of ideology'.

The Group was back in the news again in 2002 with research findings suggesting that TV news has failed to inform young people about the Israeli–Palestinian conflict. Reporting the findings of the Group in a UK *Guardian* article (16 April), 'Missing in action', Greg Philo writes, 'If you don't understand the Middle East crisis it might be because you are watching it on TV news.' The research group interviewed 12 small audience groups involving 85 people with a cross-section of ages. These were asked a series of questions on the Middle East situation, and then the same questions were posed to 300 young people between the ages of 17 and 22. It was found that 'many of those questioned had little understanding of the reasons for the conflict and its origins'.

The conclusions drawn from this research were that the failure to place events into a historical *context* occurred as a result of TV news existing 'in a very competitive market' subject to anxiety about audience ratings: 'In this respect it is better to have great pictures of being in the middle of a riot with journalists ducking stones than to explain what the conflict is about.' The reluctance to contextualize, says Philo, also lies in the political roots of the conflict in which 'Israel is closely allied to the United States and there are very strong pro-Israeli lobbies in the US and to some extent in Britain.' See RESEARCH CENTRES IN THE MEDIA (UK). See also *TOPIC GUIDE* under RESEARCH METHODS.

---

* Greg Philo and Mike Berry, *Bad News from Israel* (UK: Pluto, 2004).

Glasnost Openness; Russian term for greater freedom of expression and less state secrecy. The word became universal currency with the election to leadership in the Soviet Union of Mikhail Gorbachev, who welcomed rather than shunned world publicity, and demonstrated an openness within the Russian nation and in communication with other countries not experienced since the early days of the Russian Revolution (and experienced only fitfully since). Linked with *glasnost* has been *perestroika*, meaning reconstruction, reform in relation to government practices and expectations.

Global culture and young people See CHILDREN, YOUNG PEOPLE AND THE CHANGING MEDIA ENVIRONMENT.

Globalization See COMMODITIZATION OF INFORMATION; CONGLOMERATES; CONSUMERIZATION; CONVERGENCE; CULTURE: GLOBALIZATION OF; GLOBALIZATION OF MEDIA; GLOBALIZATION, THREE ENGINES OF. See also *TOPIC GUIDE* under GLOBAL PERSPECTIVES; MEDIA ISSUES & DEBATES; MEDIA: OWNERSHIP & CONTROL.

Globalization of media As early as the 1960s Marshall McLuhan was describing the world as an electronic village and his phrase 'global village' is now part of the language of mass communication. Certainly electronic transmission of information has become global and the institutions, the transnational corporations (TNCs) responsible for that transmission, are global in scale and intention. The similarity with village life is more obscure. Thanks to global transmission we are theoretically capable of knowing what is happening in backyards or back gardens worldwide. It is feared that what we may be permitted to see there will come to look more and more like what is happening in our own backyards, as familiar as American apple pie.

Globalization is also a process of CONVERGENCE, of hardware and software, of systems of ownership and control. Globalization brings the world to our TV screens, and through the INTERNET to our computers. Information in and out converges; services (computer shopping, for example) converge with the capacity to summon up data for our individual needs. With the DIGITIZATION of information, turning every element of data – words, pictures, sound – into digits that can be transmitted terrestrially, through the telephone line and cable, via satellite, or all of them together, the possibility of the control of multi-media sources falling into fewer and fewer corporate hands deserves to stimulate global concern.

Just as the technology of media converges, so do operation systems. Traditional regulations preventing cross-media ownership were modified or dismantled throughout the 1990s. News International, the flagship of the Murdoch dynasty (see CITIZEN KANE OF THE GLOBAL VILLAGE; MURDOCH EFFECT) operates globally in every conceivable field of mass communication, and where it does not operate alone, it is a decisive part of other conglomerate activities in the media field. For example, in May 1995 News International formed a $2bn link with the American telecommunications giant, MCI, rival of the all-powerful US company AT&T. The deal put Murdoch's empire directly on to the carrier system of the superhighway, establishing Murdoch as a galactic superstar.

An observer from outer space might survey the current media scene, in which Murdoch feasts the globe with his vast library of films from the Fox archives, with US football, UK Premier League soccer, Rugby League and cricket; dominates European satellite transmission with Britain's BSkyB satellite and Asian satellite services with Star TV (not to mention his control of Australia's Channel 7 and the Delphi Online Internet Service) and conclude that a synonym for globalization is 'Murdochization' and that the true name of McLuhan's global village is Rupertsville. However, the Murdoch empire is not the world's biggest media-corp; that distinction falls to AOL Time Warner. See EUROPE: CROSS-BORDER TV CHANNELS; GLOBAL MEDIA SYSTEM: THE MAIN PLAYERS; LOCALIZATION; MOBILIZATION. See also *TOPIC GUIDE* under GLOBAL PERSPECTIVES; MEDIA TECHNOLOGIES.

* Terri Rantanen, *The Media and Globalization* (UK/US: Sage, 2005).

Globalization of news See NEWS: GLOBALIZATION OF.

Globalization: three engines of According to the Group of Lisbon publication *Limits to Competition* (US: MIT Press, 1995), the three engines driving globalization are *liberalization, deregulation* and *privatisation*, the first permitting companies to move capital and operations to locations offering competitive terms (such as low wages). DEREGULATION allows liberalization and, as a consequence, leads to PRIVATIZATION of public utilities.

Ultimately, many commentators fear, these three engines of global financial and industrial activity undermine, if not dismantle altogether, the welfare state of individual nations. The authors of *Limits to Competition* argue that at the core of the dismantling process is the conviction that the more labour costs are cut and related social benefits are reduced, the better will be the country's competitiveness. As the media are so substantially a part of the portfolios of TNCs (transnational corporations) the danger is that they will either advocate these trends or hold back from the public responsibility of subjecting them to critical scrutiny.

Global jukebox Name given to the *Live Aid* for Africa rock concert held jointly at Wembley Stadium, UK, and the John F. Kennedy Stadium, Philadelphia, US, on 13 July 1985. This, the first worldwide rock concert of its kind, was the brainchild of its principal organizer, rock musician Bob Geldof, and it was held to raise money for famine victims in the Sudan, Ethiopia and the Sub-Sahara.

Global media system: the main players Fewer than 15 transnational corporations (TNCs) dominate world media ownership. The ranking of these is subject to rapid shifts resulting from mergers, but the current players at the top of the media tree are: AOL Time Warner, Vivendi, Viacom, Disney, Sony, Bertelsmann, News Corporation, Segram (snapped up by Vivendi in 2000), PolyGram and General Electric.

The giant of giants is AOL Time Warner (owning *Time* magazine, Time Life Books, Warner Music Group, America On Line, Warner Bros films, HBO cable channel, CNN, etc.). A close challenger is Disney (ABC, film studios, theme parks, record production, book publication, global cable TV channels, etc). Close business links between the media giants are a key feature of operations, alliances between them being more common than direct competition. Rupert Murdoch's News Corp has equity joint ventures in long-term alliances with AOL Time Warner, Viacom, EMI, Granada TV and Globo of Brazil. Disney is involved in joint ventures with Bertelsmann, NBC and Hearst Newspapers (not to mention Coca-Cola and McDonald's). Bertelsmann of Germany is in joint enterprises with (in addition to Disney) AOL Time Warner, Sony, Pearson Publications (UK) and the BBC.

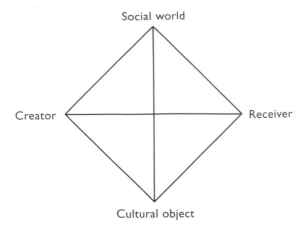

Social world

Creator

Receiver

Cultural object

Griswold's cultural diamond model, 1994

Groups A good deal of communication takes place within groups of one type or another. Charles H. Cooley, one of the initiators of research into group behaviour and communication, in his work, *Social Organization* (US: Scribner, 1909), classifies groups into two main types. *Primary* groups such as the family are defined as groups in which there is face-to-face communication; in which norms and *mores* are produced; in which roles are allocated and in which a feeling of solidarity is enjoyed.

Secondary groups, such as social class groups, are much larger aggregates. Several researchers have sought to determine the communication processes that take place within groups and in particular the inter-relationship between a group's CULTURE, ROLES, STATUS structure, cohesiveness, size and type, and its communication processes.

The performance of individuals is often affected by group membership. Being in a group can enhance or inhibit individual performance depending on such factors as the nature of the task, the degree of effective leadership, the cohesiveness of the group and the flexibility of its communication networks. These factors also determine the quality of group decision-making.

In certain circumstances individuals may feel they need to make less effort in a group situation and become social *loafers*, alternatively they may be motivated to work harder and become social *labourers*. At times individuals may be prepared to work harder to make up for their less energetic group members and contribute to social *compensation*.

Certain dynamics also appear to come into play when groups make decisions. Robert A. Baron and Donn Byrne provide some examples, in *Social Psychology* (US: Allyn & Bacon, 1994 edition), noting that, 'groups often demonstrate group polarization, a tendency to shift toward more extreme views. Two other potential difficulties faced by decision-making groups are *groupthink* … and an inability to pool unshared information.'

A small primary group particularly has the potential to influence the perceptions of its individual members and thus the way in which they interpret and respond to communication from sources both within and outside the group. Secondary groups are not without influence either, in the communication process. Basil Bernstein argues, in 'Social class, language and socialization', in *Communication Studies: An Introductory Reader* (UK: Arnold, 1993), edited by John Corner and Jeremy Hawthorn, that a relationship exists between membership of a social class group and the LANGUAGE code adopted. See CONCURRENCE-SEEKING TENDENCY.

Grub Street Description of any form of literary or journalistic drudgery. According to Dr Johnson (1709–84) Grub Street was 'originally the name of a street near Moorfields in London, much inhabited by writers of small histories, dictionaries and temporary poems, whence any mean production is called grub street'.

Grunig and Hunt: four models of public relations practice, 1984 Proposed by James Grunig and Todd Hunt in *Managing Public Relations* (US: Harcourt Brace Jovanovich, 1984), these models have been widely used for analysing public relations performance. Practices based on *The Press Agentry/Publicity* model focus activities on gaining publicity, on one-way communication with the audience through the mass media. There is little concern with gaining FEEDBACK and evaluating the effectiveness of messages. The *Public Information* model is seen to stem from the view of public relations propounded by Ivy Lee – an early public relations practitioner – which emphasizes informing the audience on issues by the presentation of facts, details and figures.

Additionally Grunig and Hunt argue most practitioners of this model inform the public, 'with the idea of making the organization more responsible to the public'. Clearly, however, any presentation of information can be selective. This model does allow for two-way communication with the audience and is an approach much used by government institutions and agencies.

The authors make the case that the need for propaganda, mainly as a consequence of the First and Second World Wars, led to the development of the *Two-Way Asymmetric* model. This focuses upon the role of public relations in the process of persuading audiences to change their attitudes and behaviour, and is associated strongly with another early public relations practitioner, Edward Bernays. The model acknowledges that research on human behaviour is useful for constructing persuasive programmes and campaigns. In particular, research on the audience's existing interests, values and attitudes is considered important, as the audience is seen as best persuaded by messages in line with these.

Finally there is the later *Two-way Symmetric* model associated with Scott Cutlip and Allen Center as well as Bernays. This model stresses the need to engage with the audience in order to establish a harmonious relationship – for example, between an organization and its PUBLICS. This requires that, rather than just seeking to persuade its publics, the organization takes into consideration the needs and goals of its publics and adapts its own policies and practices to the feedback received from them. Whilst expressing a preference for the Two-way Symmetric model, Grunig and Hunt note the choice of approach for any particular programme or campaign will be contingent upon situational factors.

GSR Galvanic skin response: a measure of stress and emotion caused to individuals by others, especially when spatial territories have been invaded – that is, someone coming too close for psychological comfort. See PROXEMICS; SPATIAL ZONES.

Guard dog metaphor A variation of (and in contrast to) the WATCHDOG metaphor; representing one of the traditional functions of mass media. The term suggests that the media perform as a *sentry*, not for the community but for special interest GROUPS that have the power and influence to establish and maintain their own security systems (see POWER ELITE). In 'A guard dog perspective on the role of media' in the *Journal of Communication*, Spring 1995, George A. Donohue, Phillip J. Tichenor and Clarise N. Olien of the University of Minnesota argue that the guard dog media 'are conditioned to be suspicious of all potential intruders, and they occasionally sound the alarm for reasons that individuals in the master households, that is, the authority structure, can neither understand nor prevent. These occasions occur primarily when authority within the structure is divided.' In communities where there is no apparent conflict within power structures 'the media are sleeping guard dogs'.

The guiding principle appears to be: support the powerful unless the powerful are intruders. 'Where different local groups have conflicting interests,' say Donohue *et al.*, 'the media are more likely to reflect the views of the more powerful groups.' Consequently the guard dog role works towards internal cohesion. The metaphor contrasts with that of the media's perceived role as *watchdog*. The role in this case is one of surveillance of the powerful on behalf of and in the interests of the public. The media serve as freedom-seekers-and-defenders, hence the titles of so many early newspapers – *Sentinel, Voice of the People, Champion, Justice, Poor Man's Guardian, Observer, Enquirer* and *Advocate*.

A third 'dog' in the repertoire of the media is that of the lapdog. As Donohue *et al.* point out, 'A lapdog perspective is a total rejection of the Fourth Estate view on all counts.' The lapdog is submissive to authority and oblivious 'to all interests except those of powerful groups' and serves to frame all 'issues according to the perspectives of the highest powers in the system'.

While the guard dog is characterized by deference as contrasted with submissiveness, at least it recognizes the existence of, and gives attention to, conflict. The greater the social differentiation within a community or nation, the more extensive is the reporting of conflict. Where there is 'power uncertainty' the media are likely to 'display a tendency to concentrate on individuals while accepting the structure. In doing so, the media of uniformity. If, as Jacques Ellul and a number of other commentators believe, efficiency has fast become the key determinant of human affairs in modern society (see TECHNIQUE: ELLUL'S THEORY OF TECHNIQUE), then hegemonic power, in the hands of the state and the corporate system, is likely to increase rather than diminish. See ELITE; IDEOLOGICAL STATE APPARATUSES; McDONALDIZATION. See also *TOPIC GUIDE* under MEDIA: VALUES & IDEOLOGY.

* Jacques Ellul, *The Technological Society* (US: Knopf, 1964); Antonio Gramsci, *Selections from the Prison Notebooks* (UK: Lawrence & Wishart, 1971).

Helical model of communication See DANCE'S HELICAL MODEL OF COMMUNICATION.

Helical scan See TELERECORDING.

Heliological metaphor See VISIONS OF ORDER.

He/man language Dale Spender in her book *Man Made Language* (UK: HarperCollins, 1990 edition) refers to the principle by which for several centuries the terms *he* and *man* have been used to include women, for example, *man*kind. This principle has, according to Spender, not only the effect of contributing to the perspective of MALE-AS-NORM, of males as more worthy, but also helps to construct the invisibility of women in language, thought and reality. Not everyone, of course, either agrees with or employs this principle, and it has become the focus of some critical scrutiny in recent decades.

Herman and Chomsky's propaganda model See CONSENT, MANUFACTURE OF.

Hermeneutic code See CODES OF NARRATIVE.

Hermeneutics The science of interpretations or understanding. The word is taken from the Greek, *hermeneuein*, and derives from Hermes, messenger of the gods; it means to make things clear, to announce or unveil a MESSAGE. In film study, a hermeneutic code, or 'code of enigma', explains by one device or another the mysteries of the plot – the situation or predicament characters find themselves in – and indicates the process of resolution.

Heterophily See HOMOPHILY.

HICT Project Household Uses of Information and Communication Technology: a major research project funded by the UK's Economic and Social Research Council. Its task has been to investigate the domestic use of TV, VCR, home computer and telephone technology. It was initially carried out by a team including Andrea Dahlberg, Eric Hirsch, Sonia Livingstone, David Morley and Roger Silverstone, with the Centre for Research into Innovation, Culture and Technology at Brunel University. The researchers studied 20 families living in the south-east of England, using ethnographic/participant observation methods followed up by a diversity of other approaches – time-use diaries, mental maps or brain patterns illustrating the perceived spatial location and significance of various technologies; and even scrutinizing family photo albums.

The notion of the household as a 'moral economy' is posed by the Brunel team. Are the location and use of such communication technology a reflection of the 'ordering' of the household, of relative degrees of power and status, of priorities; does it enhance or pose barriers to family interactivity; and how are differences over the uses of such technology resolved within the community of the household?

In *Consuming Technologies: Media and Information in Domestic Spaces* (UK: Routledge, 1992), edited by Silverstone, Hirsch and Morley, the authors write, 'To understand the household as a moral economy ... is to understand the household as part of a transactional system, dynamically involved in ... the production and exchange of commodities and meanings.' See *TOPIC GUIDE* under RESEARCH METHODS.

Hidden agenda When the underlying objective of an act of communication is different from that which is stated. See IMPRESSION MANAGEMENT.

Hidden needs Vance Packhard in *The Hidden Persuaders* (UK: Penguin, 1960, with updated editions) cites eight 'hidden needs' which the adman can cater for. These are: emotional security; reassurance of worth; ego-gratification; creative outlets; love objects; a sense of power; a sense of roots; and immortality. See ADVERTISING; MASLOW'S HIERARCHY OF NEEDS; VALS TYPOLOGY.

Hierarchy Classification in graded subdivisions. The hierarchy of a company starts at the top with the chairperson or managing director; a social hierarchy is dominated by the ELITE classes who varyingly influence those CLASS divisions below them. In the media, the dominant hierarchy are the owners, top executives, major shareholders, boards of directors, etc. See ORGANIZATION CULTURES.

High- and low-context communication See COMMUNICATION: INTERCULTURAL COMMUNICATION.

Highbrow Someone considered to be a member of the intellectual and cultural ELITE, whose tastes are, by definition, considered to be aesthetically superior to those of the majority, is deemed highbrow. Highbrow tastes are limited to the few. The terms middlebrow and lowbrow are used to indicate a level of intellectual capacity of cultural appreciation judged against the standards of the highbrow elite. See CULTURAL CAPITAL.

High fidelity See GRAMOPHONE.

High-speed photography One of the wonders of modern technology, but a preoccupation of photographers from the earliest pioneering days, the high-speed flash process slows down, or magnifies, time: the splash of a drop of water, the trajectory of a bullet, can be reduced to slow motion that permits astonishing revelations. Foremost among developers of ultra-high-speed electronic flash photography as a tool of scientific analysis was the American Harold Edgerton, inventor of the stroboscope.

The term *stroboscopic photography*, or strobe photography, refers to pictures of single or multiple exposure taken by flashes of light from electrical discharges, permitting objects moving at their natural speeds to be observed in slow motion, the rate of the slow motion depending on the frequency of the strobe and object. When the flash frequency exactly equals that of the rotation or vibration, the object is illuminated in the same position during each cycle, and appears stationary.

Mechanical cameras such as the register-pin intermittent action camera are capable of 500 frames a second; for faster objects, there is the rotating prism camera at 1500 frames a second, slowing time down between 200 and 400 times. Even faster is the rotating mirror camera, capable of 10,000 pictures a second – a capacity which, however, is dwarfed by the image tube electronic camera which can take a million-million pictures a second.

In contrast to high-speed photography, *time-lapse photography*, by taking pictures at timed intervals of seconds, minutes, hours or days, speeds up, or telescopes, time. In a few moments of film we can see the germination of a seed, the hatching of an egg or blow-fly maggots consuming a dead mouse. Audiences in the 1930s delighted in the time-lapse spectacle, in *Four Minutes to Brighton*, of travelling, via film, at 760mph on the Brighton Belle. Apollo astronauts on the moon used time-lapse photography. Both high-speed and time-lapse photography are employed most widely to answer two questions: how is it done, and what went wrong? See PHOTOGRAPHY, ORIGINS.

Historical allusion The practice in NEWS reporting of making reference – alluding to – events in the past perceived as being similar to current events, recognized by AUDIENCE as such, and potentially capable of adding to the NEWS VALUE of a story. For example, a convenient (and often all too easy) way to DEMONIZE an 'enemy' leader is to compare him to Hitler, the activities of 'enemy' peoples to Nazis, and to use past terminology such as 'holocaust' and 'death camps'.

Such language was used prominently by the western media to describe events in Serbia, Bosnia and Croatia during the 'ethnic cleansing' of the 1990s. For example, a *New York Times* editorial of 4 August 1992 declared that 'the chilling reports from Bosnia evoke this century's greatest nightmare, Hitler's genocide against Jews, Gypsies and Slavs'. Two days later, the *Chicago Tribune* asked, 'Are the Nazi era death camps being reprised in the Balkans? Unthinkable, you say? Think again ... The ghost of World War II genocide is abroad in Bosnia ...'.

Following the terrorist assault on the US Pentagon and the World Trade Center in New York on 11 September 2001 (9/11), and the subsequent build-up to war by the US and UK, the British Prime Minister Tony Blair was compared in the media – varyingly and queryingly – with the pugnacious war-leader Winston Churchill, the nineteenth-century PM William Gladstone (whose mission was to 'pacify Ireland') and the gunboat-happy British Foreign Secretary Lord Palmerston. Blair's public performance following the London bombings of July 2005 was similarly described as Churchillian and recalled the London Blitz during the Second World War.

Such use of analogies and metaphors is seen generally to serve to place events into contexts familiar to

Hypodermic needle model of communication More a METAPHOR representing a view of the effects of the mass media, the hypodermic needle 'model' has formed a point of general reference in crediting the media with power over audiences. The basic assumption is that the mass media have a direct, immediate and influential effect upon audiences by 'injecting' information into the consciousness of the masses.

The AUDIENCE is seen as impressionable and open to manipulation. Like other early models of communication flow from the media, it overlooks the possible effects of INTERVENING VARIABLES (IVs) in the communication process and presents the masses as being unquestioning receptacles of media messages. This sense of the all-powerfulness of the media is a central feature of early mass society research. It is now regarded as crude and simplistic. See AUDIENCE: ACTIVE AUDIENCE; COMMERCIAL LAISSEZ-FAIRE MODEL OF (MEDIA) COMMUNICATION.

Hypothesis The first step of the research cycle is the formulation of a hypothesis. This will usually be based on an idea or hunch gained by the researchers from their own reading of earlier studies and/or their own observations of society. Starting with this basic idea a researcher usually proposes a working hypothesis that will guide the research. The hypothesis proposes a relationship between certain social phenomena: for example, that people from a higher-education background are more likely to read what is regarded as the quality press.

Not all hypotheses are expressed as formal statements. Some can be a general collection of ideas about particular social phenomena. All hypotheses, though, must be capable of EMPIRICAL testing; that is, they must be capable of being proved or disproved by facts and argument. The hypothesis will determine the nature of the research design – the method of collecting the information that will prove or disprove the hypothesis.

Once this information has been collected and analysed the hypothesis is reviewed. It may be proved, disproved or amended. Indeed in many cases the original hypothesis may have been modified during the data collection stage of the research. Alternatively it may be decided that further evidence is required before any conclusion is reached.

Hypothesis of consonance See NEWS VALUES.

 I

Iconic Describes a SIGN which, in some way, resembles its object; looks like it, or sounds like it. Picture-writing is iconic, as is a map. ONOMATOPOEIA (word sounds that resemble real sounds) is iconic. In SEMIOLOGY/SEMIOTICS the iconic is one of three categories of sign defined by American philosopher C.S. Peirce (1834–1914). Where the *iconic* describes or resembles, an *index* is connected with its object, like smoke to fire, while the *symbol* has no resemblance or connection, and communicates MEANING only because people agree that it shall stand for what it does. A word is a symbol. The categories are not separate and distinct. One sign may be made up of all three categories. See *TOPIC GUIDE* under LANGUAGE/DISCOURSE/NARRATIVE.

Ideational functions of language The use of language to explore, interpret, construct and express views about ourselves and the world. Another major function of language, the interpersonal function, is that of establishing and maintaining relationships with others. Clearly both functions are often present in communicative encounters and the two are often related.

Identification The degree to which people identify with and are influenced by characters, fictional or otherwise, in books, radio, films and on TV, has fascinated media analysts, especially in areas of behaviour where that identification might lead to anti-social activity such as violence. 'To identify with' has two common meanings: to participate in the situation of someone whose plight has caught one's sympathy; and to incorporate characteristics of an admired person into one's own identity by adopting that person's system of values.

Identification is used in a more specific sense when we discuss the degree of influence persons, institutions and the media may have on others. In 'Processes of opinion change', *Public Opinion Quarterly* 25 (1965), Herbert Kelman explores three basic processes of social influence with reference to opinion change and to communication. These are *compliance*, *identification* and *internalization*. The first position in this 'social influence theory' refers to the acceptance of influence in the hope of either receiving a reward or avoiding punishment. Identification in this sense occurs 'when an individual adopts behaviour derived from another person or a group because this behaviour is associated with a satisfying self-defining relationship to this person or group'.

As with compliance, change or influence is reliant upon the external source and 'dependent on social support'. Internalization occurs when the proposed change, the influence, is fully believed in, accepted, taken fully on board, because the influenced person 'finds it useful for the solution of a problem or because it is congenial to his own orientation, or because it is demanded of his own values'.

Linked to the analysis of the extent to which identification takes place is the interest in how we identify along lines of age, CLASS or GENDER.

Identity See SELF-IDENTITY.

Idents Channel identities; snapshot films, reminding TV viewers in graphic, computer-generated form which channel they are tuned to. Idents are designed to establish an image of the channel, a channel branding. The generic ident is basically suitable for any programme introduction while specific idents create images closely reflecting the nature of particular programmes or series.

Ideological presumption Describes the view that journalists and the NEWS media are necessarily and unavoidably ideologically implicated in the MESSAGE systems and DISCOURSES to which they contribute. In *The Foucault Reader* (US: Random House, 1984) the French philosopher Michel Foucault states that the social relations of power produce and constitute knowledge, and that socio-economic power lies at the root of what we are, what we believe and what we are shown – through the media. The position locates journalists as *cultural workers*, in the service of those with power and authority.

The view is challenged by Matthew Kieron in 'News reporting and the ideological presumption' published in the *Journal of Communication*, Spring 1997. He declares that the 'presumption' is 'either false, incoherent or trivial'; it is 'overextended, misplaced and distortive'. Kieron argues that we should, in our scrutiny of journalism, acknowledge that in broadly free societies there are sufficient variables in interpretation and approach to escape the grip of the voice of authority.

Ideological state apparatuses This term derives from the work of the French philosopher Louis Althusser (1918–90). Ideological state apparatuses (ISAs) are those social institutions which, according to Althusser, help shape people's consciousness in a way that secures support for the IDEOLOGY of those who control the state, that is, the dominant ideology. Such institutions include education, the family, religion, the legal system, the party-political system and the mass media. The dominant ideology is thus represented as both natural and neutral. As a result it becomes almost unseen, taken-for-granted.

In contrast there is what Althusser calls the RSA (*repressive state apparatus*), the law, police, military; brought into operation – using coercion or the threat of it – when the ISA is failing, through persuasion, to secure its objectives of social control. Authority relies on the media to serve as an ISA and to support situations when the RSA is brought into action. See COMMON SENSE; DISCOURSE; ELITE; HEGEMONY; MYTH; POWER ELITE. See also *TOPIC GUIDE* under MEDIA: POLITICS & PRODUCTION; MEDIA: VALUES & IDEOLOGY.

Ideology An ideology is a system of ideas and beliefs about human conduct which has normally been simplified and manipulated in order to obtain popular support for certain actions, and which is usually emotive in its reference to social action. Karl Marx (1818–83) used the term to apply to any form of thought that underpins the social structure of a society and which consequently upholds the position of the ruling class. The twentieth-century French philosopher Louis Althusser (see above), drawing on the work of Marx, saw ideology as being an unconscious set of VALUES and beliefs that provide frames for our thinking and these help us make sense of the world.

Ideology can often be found to be hiding (or hidden) under terms such as 'common sense', the 'common sense view', which Marx would claim was merely the view of the ruling CLASS translated by repeated usage through channels of communication into wisdom as apparently natural as fresh air – a process sometimes referred to as *mystification*. Within society there may be a variety of contending ideologies at play, representing different sets of social interests, each seeking to extend recognition and acceptance of its way of making sense of the world, its own capacity to give order and explain social existence.

Language itself may be seen not as a neutral medium but as ideological, thus in its use ensuring that ideology is present in all discourses. Each may seek to become the dominant ideology and it can be argued that the capacity to make use of the channels of mass communication is crucial to either achieving or maintaining this position.

The use of the media in this respect is the focus of much media research and analysis. German sociologist Karl Mannheim (1893–1947), in *Ideology and Utopia* (1936), distinguishes between ideas that defend existing interests, the status quo, which he terms *ideologies* and ideas that seek to change the social order, which he terms *utopias*. See CONSENSUS; CULTURAL APPARATUS; DISCOURSE; DOMINANT DISCOURSE; HEGEMONY; IDEOLOGICAL STATE APPARATUSES; MALE-AS-NORM. See also *TOPIC GUIDE* under MEDIA: VALUES & IDEOLOGY.

* Mike Cormack, *Ideology* (UK: Batsford, 1992); Tuen A. van Dijk, *Ideology: A Multidisciplinary Approach* (UK: Sage, 1998).

Ideology of detachment See IMPARTIALITY.

Ideology of romance An aspect of HEGEMONY in which the perceptions and attitudes of women, in particular teenage girls, are 'shaped' by DOMINANT DISCOURSES into accepting the roles of wife and mother within an essentially patriarchal social structure. Wendy Halloway in 'Gender difference and the production of subjectivity' in *Changing the Subject: Psychology, Social Regulation and Subjectivity* (UK: Methuen, 1984), edited by J. Henriques *et al.*, calls this mode of communicative conditioning a *'to have and to hold'* discourse which links acceptable behaviour with monogamous relationships.

The ideology of romance can be found expressed and reinforced in magazines, films, pop songs, ADVERTISING and SOAP OPERAS. It is, in the view of Mary Ellen Brown, author of *Soap Operas and Women's Talk: The Pleasures of Resistance* (UK: Sage, 1994), an ideology that 'can leave young women few options'. At the same time the ideology of romance can be seen as a rational response to, and a means of coping with, material and economic subordination, encapsulated in the song *Diamonds are a Girl's Best Friend*. Says Brown, 'Such romantic ideology positions young women in such a way that they can easily decide to buy into the system.' Most feminist writers would argue that the ideology of romance is coterminous with the notion of the *ideology of dependence*.

Ideology of silence The belief, held chiefly by governments, that the best way of 'getting things done' in, for example, attempts to win the release of political prisoners or hostages, is by secret, behind-the scenes diplomacy. The same rule would apply in cases where one government may feel obliged, perhaps through public pressure, to protest to another country. The problem in such cases is that there is no real proof that a protest has been made and consequently no evidence as to the nature of that proof.

In an article, 'Against silence', in *Index on Censorship* (February 1987), Jacob Timerman, formerly a political prisoner in Argentina, expands on the notion of the ideology of silence and concludes that 'the only way to solve problems of decency and civilization is to speak out'.

Idiolect An individual's personal dialect which incorporates the individual variations that exist between people in their use of punctuation, grammar, vocabulary and style. No two people are likely to express themselves in exactly the same way.

Idiot salutations See PHATIC (LANGUAGE).

Image A likeness; a representation; a visualization. The term can have several meanings depending on the context in which it is used. It may refer to a visual representation of reality such as is seen in a photograph; it can also refer to a mental, imaginative conception of an individual, event, location or object as, for example, one conjures up an image of a character in a novel. The image does not merely reproduce, it interprets; it has added to it certain meanings. The writer, artist, architect, photographer and advertising image-maker all use assemblies of signs in order to represent or suggest states of mind, or abstractions. Van Dyck's equestrian portrait of Charles I portrays the monarch on a noble steed against a background suffused with dramatic light. All the details of this painting converge to create an image of kingship, thus a process of *symbolization* has taken place.

The purpose of image-creation obviously varies, but all images are devised in order to evoke responses of one kind or another, usually emotional. Images often serve as psychological triggers effecting responses that are not always easy to articulate. Advertisements regale us with images of the good life; they play upon our perceived needs (see HIDDEN NEEDS; MASLOW'S HIERARCHY OF NEEDS). Image is also something we present of ourselves – our best face, the way we want the world to perceive us. Politicians work at their images more than most, and these are portrayed to fit in with the image appropriate to a public figure whose aim is to impress voters by his or her qualities of leadership and trustworthiness.

Sometimes we talk of a person whose image 'has slipped', which seems to indicate the connection between image and *performance* (see IMPRESSION MANAGEMENT) and that it relates to an ideal. For the artist, whatever his or her medium, imagery is central to expression. It is a part of STYLE and a key to the construction of MEANING. See METAPHOR. See also *TOPIC GUIDE* under REPRESENTATION.

Image, rhetoric of In its contemporary use, the word *rhetoric* is interchangeable for persuasion or PROPAGANDA; thus the rhetoric of the image indicates the use of images as a means of persuasion; of inculcation or reinforcement of ideological positions. The power of the image is employed, particularly in the NEWS, to *empower* the overt or covert MESSAGE. Such images have the effect of closing off, by their dramatic and emotional nature, alternative ways of reporting and interpreting realities.

IMAX Canadian film projection system developed in the 1970s, notable for the vastness of its screen for 70mm film; installed in the UK in 1983 at the National Museum of Photography, Film and Television in Bradford, and later in London. See OMNIMAX.

Immediacy A prime NEWS VALUE in western newspaper, radio and television newsgathering and presentation. At the centre of decision-making and of news control is the time factor, usually related to the daily cycle. In his article 'Newsmen and their time machine', in *British Journal of Sociology* (September 1977), Philip Schlesinger points out that in industrialized societies an exceptional degree of precision of timing is necessary in our working lives. 'Especially noteworthy are those who operate communication and transport systems ... Newsmen ... are members of a stopwatch culture.'

Immediacy shapes and structures the approach to newsgathering. The report of an event must be as close to the event as possible, and ideally the event should be reported as it happens. The pure type of immediacy would be the live broadcast. News, says Schlesinger, is 'hot' when it is most immediate. 'It is "cold", and old, when it can no longer be used during the newsday in question.' Immediacy is not only a vital factor in the selection of a story for treatment; it also helps fashion that treatment. Pace is what counts in presentation, especially in TV news, where the priority is to keep the audience 'hooked'.

The danger with such emphasis on immediacy is that news tends to be all foreground and little background, all events and too little context, all current happening and too little concentration on historical and cultural frameworks. Schlesinger rounds off his article by saying that it is plausible to argue 'that the more we take note of news, the less we can be aware of what lies behind it'. See EFFECTS OF THE MASS MEDIA. See also *TOPIC GUIDE* under NEWS MEDIA.

Immersion The degree to which the virtual, the invented – as in VIRTUAL REALITY – submerges the real perception system of the user. The more that VR works to the exclusion of contact with the real, physical world, the more it is classified as being immersive. The prospect of near-total immersion, on the part of some users, is a matter of interest and concern. As Frank Biocca says in 'Communication within virtual reality: creating a space for research' in *Journal of Communication*, Autumn 1992, 'If people eventually use VR technology for the same amount of time that they spend watching television and using computers, some users could spend 20 or more years "inside" virtual reality'.

Impact of the mass media See EFFECTS OF THE MASS MEDIA.

Impartiality Just as Professor Stuart Hall doubts the existence, in media terms, of OBJECTIVITY, so Philip Schlesinger, in a remarkable study of the workings of BBC News, has cast doubt on the possibility of impartiality. Between 1972 and 1976, Schlesinger had a unique research opportunity to conduct in the newsrooms of Broadcasting House and the Television Centre, London, fieldwork which attempted 'to grasp how the world looks from the point of view of those studied' – the reporters, correspondents, editors and managing editors in the most prestigious media organization in the world. He interviewed over 120 BBC news staff and spent 90 days in observation. His findings were published in *Putting 'Reality' Together. BBC News* (UK: Constable, 1978; Methuen/University Paperback, with new Preface, 1987).

Several key words framed the basic principles of news production: *balance, objectivity, responsibility, fairness, freedom* from bias; and these were, in the 'ordinary discourse of newsmen', for the most part 'interchangeable'.

media rarely shatters unaccountable power. Publicity better resembles the throwing of snowballs into a blizzard – or the blowing of bubbles into warm summer's air.'

The term 'blizzard' has also been used to describe the multiple and interacting images we encounter daily, brought to us with ever-new associations by the media (see TEXT). For the French cultural critic Jean Baudrillard the sheer volume of signifiers in the contemporary world of mass communication, so readily and regularly detached from their original SIGNIFICATION, means that meaning is too lost in the blizzard to be worth the trouble of attempting to define it. Consequently in this cultural blizzard anything can be made to mean anything. See Chapter 5, 'Baudrillard's blizzards' in Nick Stephenson's *Culture, Social Theory and Mass Communication* (UK: Sage, 1995) in which Baudrillard's 'irrationalism' is challenged.

Information commons Equivalent to 'common land', that is space or territory accessible, by right, to the public, without charge; thus information commons relate to public space, or the public *domain*, with regard to information and expression. Some commentators fear that the public domain as typified by our shared culture, has long been subject to a process of *enclosure*, or PRIVATIZATION, in which cultural artefacts and practices, once part of the information commons have been turned into private property accessible only as commodity.

A particular area of concern is copyrighting which has extended far beyond the protection of the works of writers, artists, musicians etc. into images, sounds, acronyms and names. In a tom.paine.com online article (1 August 2002), entitled 'Stopping the privatization of public knowledge: the endangered public domain', David Bollier of the Annenberg School of Communications, Philadelphia, talks of 'content autocrats' dedicated to copyright enforcement operating in an atmosphere of 'fully fledged cultural pathology'. The enforcement of copyright in the courts has proved a serious intrusion upon the freedoms of cultural expression, believes Bollier. He cites McDonald's threatening 'every food business that uses "Mc" in their names' or Mattel threatening 'legal action against art photographers who use images of Barbie dolls to comment on American beauty ideals'. See CULTURE: COPYRIGHTING CULTURE; NEW MEDIA.

Information gaps Many scholars have focused their studies on the inequality in the distribution of information among different groups in societies. Such inequalities are mostly the result of educational or social CLASS differences with the advantage being enjoyed by the better-educated and those in the higher-status groups. The role of the mass media in creating, widening or narrowing information gaps has prompted widespread concern.

There are differing kinds of gaps depending on the nature of the information.

Gaps – between *information-rich* and *information-poor* – may close or widen with time. It had been thought that the increasing flow of information from the mass media might help to narrow such gaps, but the evidence here is mixed. Whilst the media may have the potential to close gaps it seems that an advantage remains with those with most communication potential and new gaps open as old ones are closed. Gaps exist between groups within the same societies, but the greatest inequalities are between developed and less developed nations, most of the channels of global communication being controlled by the former.

This means that not only have the developed nations the potential to acquire and disseminate more information, they also have the potential for considerable control of the flow and content of the information going to less developed nations. Thus the majority of information flowing from info-disadvantaged countries is *raw*, compared with the *mediated* information that flows in the other direction. Information gaps can also be generated, reinforced or modified through patterns of interpersonal communication. See DIFFUSION; DISCURSIVE GAP; J-CURVE; MEDIA IMPERIALISM; MISINFORMED SOCIETY.

* Jan van Dijk, *The Deepening Divide: Inequality in the Information Society* (US/UK: Sage, 2005).

Information society The Japanese were the first to apply the tag to this stage in the growth of the industrial era in which information has become the central and most significant 'commodity'. Through the development of computers and associated electronic systems, such aspects of national and international life as class relationships, government, economics and diplomacy are being visualized as functions of information transfer. Indeed we are at the point when information and wealth are practically one and the same thing.

With the development of satellite surveillance it is now possible for a country highly advanced in informatics to know more about the topography of, say, a developing nation than that country's own government does. And information is power that crosses national boundaries with greater ease than invading armies.

Information is not only a commodity but a social and cultural resource, raising questions of social allocation and control, with such associated problems as PRIVACY, access, commercial privilege and public interest. See COMMODITIZATION OF INFORMATION; MEDIA IMPERIALISM; MISINFORMED SOCIETY; MOBILIZATION; NEW MEDIA.

Information suburbs See TECHNOLOGICAL DETERMINISM.

Information technology (IT) Microelectronics plus computing plus telecommunications equals IT. Its formal definition is framed as follows in a UK Department of Industry publication (1981) for Information Technology Year (1982): 'The acquisition, processing, storage and dissemination of vocal, pictorial, textual and numerical information by a micro-electronics-based combination of computing and telecommunications.'

Information Technology Advisory Panel (ITAP) Report on Cable Systems See CABLE TELEVISION.

Infotainment Term used to describe the trend towards enhancing the entertainment value of factual programmes in order to increase their popularity with audiences. There are concerns, expressed by a number of analysts, that NEWS and current affairs coverage may become trivialized by such an approach. See DOCUMENTARY.

Inheritance factor The TV programme which captures a viewer's attention paves the way for those that follow. See BUTTON APATHY.

Inner-outer directed See VALS TYPOLOGY.

Inoculation effect In the processes of persuasion, a relative immunity in an AUDIENCE may be induced by 'inoculation' prior to a concerted exercise in persuasion: if an audience is forewarned about an attempt to persuade it, when that attempt occurs, they are more capable of defence against influence. Studies have shown that the inoculation effect can also be achieved by generating counter-arguments in people through exposure to a mild version of arguments against their opinions as well as to arguments supporting their existing views. This seemed to 'inoculate' them against being persuaded later by more robust arguments against their beliefs, opinions and attitudes.

Insert shot In film, close-up inserted into a dramatic scene, usually for the purpose of giving the AUDIENCE a view of what the character on the screen is seeing, such as a newspaper headline, the title of a book, a cigarette, a letter, etc. See SHOT.

Institution The term institution is generally applied to patterns of behaviour which are established, approved and usually of some permanence. Such patterns of behaviour are normally rational and conscious. The term can be applied to both the *abstract* – for example, religion – and the *concrete* concept of an institution, such as a media organization. The patterns of behaviour to which this term is applied can vary, from simple routine acts to large complexes of standardized procedures governing social relationships in a large section of the population.

All institutions embody a particular complex of norms, VALUES, ROLES and role structures. They also, often, evolve relationships with other institutions. FUNCTIONALIST analysis tends to represent institutions as performing the functions essential to the maintenance of society and views them as being mutually sustaining. Some research has, however, indicated the relative *autonomy* of most institutions and the often conflicting goals to be found within them. Much research into the mass media has concentrated upon their *corporate* role as major social institutions, upon their norms, VALUES and relationships with other major social institutions.

Insult signals Generally defined as those signals which are always insulting, no matter what the context in which the signal has been made; though these do vary substantially between nationality and nationality. Such signals may communicate lack of interest, boredom, superiority, contempt, impatience, rejection and mockery. *Dirt signals* appear to be universal and refer to human and animal waste products on the basis, presumably, of: cleanliness = good; filth = bad. Picking the nose with forefinger and thumb in Syria means 'Go to blazes' while in the UK a gesture of derision is to pull an imaginary lavatory chain at the same time as holding the nose. In Greece, pushing the flat of the palm towards another's face is the ultimate insult signal. Called the *moutza*, the signal represents a thrusting of filth into the opponent's face, and has ancient roots (see RELIC GESTURES).

Beyond the insult signal is the *threat signal*, an attempt to intimidate without, necessarily, recourse to blows. Threat signals are mostly violence substitutes rather than prologues to violence, because such signals are checked, held back and distance maintained between threatener and threatened. Also, such signals are often redirected – to the insulter's own body, such as mock strangulation.

Of *obscene signals*, the phallic-displaying gesture is as old as civilized man. The Romans for example referred to the middle finger as the impudent and obscene finger. The more expressive forearm jerk is common throughout the western world and is employed particularly in France, Italy and Spain as a threatening insult by one male towards another; however, in the UK, the signal tends to be more a crude sexual comment than a direct insult. The V-sign, with palm facing the communicator, is the most potent gestural insult in Britain along with its single-finger variant. See COMMUNICATION, NON-VERBAL (NVC); NON-VERBAL BEHAVIOUR: REPERTOIRE.

Integrateds See VALS TYPOLOGY.

Integration New ideas and behaviour vary in the degree to which they are incorporated into the continuing operations and way of life of members of a SOCIAL SYSTEM or sub-system. The term *communication integration* is used to describe the degree to which the members/units of a social system are interconnected by INTERPERSONAL COMMUNICATION CHANNELS.

Integration: vertical and horizontal Vertical integration occurs when an enterprise owns and controls all the processes and stages involved in production. An example is where a film company initiates ideas and facilitates all aspects of production, marketing and ADVERTISING, and has direct or associate interest in product dissemination and consumption, including related promotional merchandise. In contrast, horizontal integration indicates concentration of ownership across rather than within products and producers – in media terms, CROSS-MEDIA OWNERSHIP and control.

Integrity of the text See TEXT: INTEGRITY OF THE TEXT.

Intellectual property See CULTURE: COPYRIGHTING CULTURE; TEXT: INTEGRITY OF THE TEXT.

Intelsat Acronym for International Telecommunications Satellite (Consortium), an organization of over 70 member nations formed to control and promote work in global communications by means of satellites. See SATELLITE TRANSMISSION.

Intensity Some NEWS stories receive much more concentrated, more intense, coverage by the media than others, and tend to dominate or stifle competing stories. Intensity, if appropriate in terms of timing, and if given the promise of frequency, abetted by consistency of coverage, equals *influence*, at least in the sense of making audiences aware.

General elections provide useful illustrations of the intensity of media coverage. National attention is focused on the event (usually more on personalities than issues) and the legitimacy of the event is given substance and flavour. In contrast, local elections derive neither substance nor flavour from the media, who largely ignore them. See DISPLACEMENT EFFECT; EFFECTS OF THE MASS MEDIA; NEWS VALUES.

Interaction The reciprocal action and communication, verbal or non-verbal, between two or more individuals, or two or more social groups. Successful negotiation of social interaction requires considerable mastery of the verbal and non-verbal communication deemed appropriate to the social situation and the social ROLES being performed. As Judy Gahagan comments in *Social Interaction and its Management* (UK: Methuen, 1984), 'The mere presence of others introduces a degree of control over our demeanour that we do not display when we are alone ... This control over demeanour suggests we follow quite strict sets of rules of conduct.' Most of these rules however are unwritten and learned, often unconsciously, through the process of SOCIALIZATION. There are arguably more rituals and rules involved in our everyday social interaction than we realize.

Gahagan notes, 'We are in fact quite unaware of their existence until someone does something "odd".' See IMPRESSION MANAGEMENT; INTERPERSONAL COMMUNICATION; SELF-MONITORING; SELF-PRESENTATION.

Interactive television Allows viewers to respond to programmes in ways ranging from seeking further programme information to making contact with programme-makers or providing instant FEEDBACK to questions put to them. The now familiar 'red button' invites the viewer into more specialised scenarios, the best offering viewers the chance to question writers, film-makers, actors, sports people, etc., and to comment on their work.

Early predictions for interactive TV suggested a new age of instant public response, of quick-fire referendums, of elections and other polls 'going electronic'. We await the full momentum of that age, for the greater potential for interactivity of the Internet may have checked, if not stalled, the use of TV as an interactive medium – unless, of course, the TV and the computer are one and the same device, as typified by the multifunctional mobile phone (see MOBILIZATION). However, for the majority of users the sophisticated mobile serves largely as an entertainment centre, interactivity focusing on the personal and the popular rather than issues of social or political concern. See REALITY TV.

Interactivity In the simulation of VIRTUAL REALITY, interactivity describes the process by which the user exerts control over the form and content of the mediated environment.

Intercultural communication See COMMUNICATION: INTERCULTURAL COMMUNICATION.

Internalization See IDENTIFICATION.

International Commission for the Study of Communication Problems Report, 1980 See MACBRIDE COMMISSION.

International Federation of Journalists (IFJ) Organization whose testament is that 'the promotion of a new world order of information is first and foremost the business of journalists and the trade unions and not of states, governments or any pressure group of whatever kind'. The IFJ is made up chiefly of western journalists and was formed to monitor and counteract moves through the United Nations Educational, Scientific and Cultural Organization (UNESCO) to 'impose', through government legislation, a NEW WORLD INFORMATION ORDER. See MACBRIDE COMMISSION; MEDIA IMPERIALISM; WORLD PRESS FREEDOM COMMITTEE.

International Law Enforcement Telecommunications Seminar (ILETS) See INTERNET: MONITORING OF CONTENT.

International Programme for the Development of Communication (IPDC) See MACBRIDE COMMISSION; MEDIA IMPERIALISM; NEW WORLD INFORMATION ORDER.

Internet (See also CYBERSPACE.) Worldwide network of interlinked computer systems exchange of digital information – texts, sounds, pictures or video. One of the few global communication systems *not* owned or controlled by the transnationals; in fact the Internet is not 'owned' by anyone (yet). The net was first established in the 1960s as an American military project, ARPANet, to link computers at research establishments and to form a network of information distribution which could survive a nuclear attack.

The use of the net, and the information available via websites, has grown exponentially, but take-up has, in global terms, been uneven. In 1998 four trillion e-mails were sent in the US, and that was still only representative of 15 per cent of the population. The *Wall Street Journal* has calculated that a typical worker in a European company deals with some 150 e-mails a day.

Few businesses can have grown as fast as the industry in websites. In western nations every self-respecting company, local authority, educational establishment, human rights agency or pressure group now has its own growing website. This applies also to the media organizations such as the BBC which, according to Fletcher Research, became in 1999 the second largest among the UK's top ten websites, beaten to pole position only by Yahoo! which is essentially an Internet 'gateway' to other services, while the BBC is a content provider. Thus RADIO and TELEVISION, the BBC's market specialisms, are joined to a PRESS function: the BBC puts into print, pictures and sound its vast archives of material (see CONVERGENCE). Additionally the BBC's commitment to Internet use is nurturing interest that in turn will encourage growth in the numbers of people coming online.

It has been claimed for the net – with some justification – that it is today's version of the AGORA, the open space in which public DISCOURSE can be conducted without the MEDIATION of those in authority and without the GATEKEEPING and AGENDA-SETTING of the mass media. Citizens speak to citizens, groups to groups, across geographical and political boundaries; and certainly governments are worried about the freedom of access to and use of information which computer-mediated communication allows.

Another key question concerning Internet use is how far it is a *leveller,* that is, through the ease of exchange, helping to level up opportunities for peoples of different economic, cultural and political status. Does the net help the poor – individuals, communities and nations – or does it somehow threaten to increase the INFORMATION GAP between them and better off individuals, communities and nations? In 'The internet and knowledge gaps: a theoretical and empirical investigation' (*European Journal of Communication,* March 2002), Heinz Bonfadelli focuses on the *digital divide,* identifying four barriers preventing people benefiting fully from the information society (see INTERNET: MONITORING OF CONTENT).

These are (1) a continuing lack of basic computer skills 'and connected fears and negative attitudes especially among older and less educated people'; (2) restrictions on *access* to the necessary hardware and software – in short, expense; (3) the lack of user friendliness and (4) the actual use of the net. Bonfadelli quotes research that suggests the 'higher the educational background [of the user], the more people use the Internet in an instrumental way, and the lower the educational background, the more people seem to use the Internet only for entertainment purposes'. See BLOGGING; DOWNLOADING; MOBILIZATION; NEW MEDIA; PODCASTING; WIKI, WIKIPEDIA.

Internet: monitoring of content The 'freedom' of the net has long been a matter of public concern, on the one hand by those in authority anxious about websites preaching political and racial hatred or providing PORNOGRAPHY, and on the other hand by those fearful of ambitions held chiefly by governments, to censor network exchange. Some commentators have argued that the key to network systems is not freedom but SURVEILLANCE. As Darin Barney points out in *Prometheus Wired: The Hope for Democracy in the Age of Network Technology* (US: University of Chicago Press), 'networked computers have emerged as surveillance technology par excellence'.

In May 1999 it was reported that European Commission ministers were planning to require manufacturers and operators to build in 'interception interfaces' to the Internet and all future digital communication systems. Details are set out in *Enfopol 19,* a restricted document leaked to the Foundation for Information Policy Research, based in London. In an article 'Intercepting the Internet' in the UK *Guardian* (29 April 1999), freelance writer Duncan Campbell reports on plans requiring 'the installation of a network of tapping centres throughout Europe, operating almost instantly across all national boundaries, providing access to every kind of communications including the net and satellites'.

According to Campbell, the plans were formulated by an organization founded in 1993 by the American FBI: the International Law Enforcement Telecommunications Seminar (ILETS), made up of police and security agents from some 20 countries. ILETS has had success in persuading the European Community to adopt its recommendations contained in a document drawn up in Bonn in 1994, the International Requirements for Interception. These have become law in the US.

At meetings in subsequent years, ILETS has tightened further its monitoring requirements. So far, the major obstacle to the fulfilment of the demands listed in *Enfopol 19* has been the cost of enforcement. However, the ease with which governments introduce laws of restriction, and the determination of those governments to spy on the net, promises a serious reining in of Internet freedoms. See REGULATION OF INVESTIGATORY POWERS ACT (RIPA) (UK), 2000. See also *TOPIC GUIDE* under MEDIA: FREEDOM, CENSORSHIP.

* Robert Burnett and P. David Marshall, *Web Theory* (UK/US: Routledge, 2003); David Gauntlett and Ross Horsley, eds, *Web Studies* (UK: Arnold, 2nd edition, 2004); Jan van Dijk, *The Network Society* (US/UK: Sage, 2nd edition, 2005).

Internet: wireless internet The use of the net without cables or wires; transmission of Internet messages by wireless technology. Developed in the late 1990s wi-fi, as it is termed, employs a technical standard known as 802.11b, using the radio spectrum 2.4GHz, and operating through 'data clouds' between multi-directional antennae.

Originally used in rural areas where cabling up proved too costly, wi-fi has moved into cities. Essentially, it is a local operation, its reach though restricted offering opportunities for community interactivity. It remains, in the UK, illegal to use wi-fi for public access networks, but the likelihood is that regulation will be changed and satellite BROADBAND – expensive for individuals but a real possibility when access is shared by groups of users – might obviate the cost of cabling: no more trench digging, perhaps, for the Internet future might just 'lie in the clouds'. See MOBILIZATION.

Interpersonal communication Describes any mode of communication, verbal or non-verbal, between two or more people. While the term MEDIO COMMUNICATION has often been used to specify interpersonal communication at a greater than face-to-face distance, such as when the communication is by letter, e-mail or telephone, it is most useful to keep the definition as wide and unprescriptive as possible.

Gail and Michele Myers in *The Dynamics of Human Communication* (US: McGraw-Hill, 1985) write, 'Interpersonal communication can be defined … in relation to what you do with it. First, you can use communication to have an effect on your "environment", a term which means not only your immediate physical surroundings but also the psychological climate you live in, the people around you, the social interchanges you have, the information you want to get or give in order to control the questions and answers of your living. Second, you use communication to improve the predictability of your relations with all environmental forces, which act on you and on which you act to make things happen.'

A great many factors affect the sending and receiving of MESSAGES within the process of interpersonal communication, only some of which can be mentioned here. In constructing a message the sender may be influenced by his/her SELF-CONCEPT and perception of the receiver(s) and the knowledge, beliefs, attitudes, VALUES, assumptions and experiences on which they rest; his/her personality; the role he/she is playing at the time; the state of his/her MOTIVATION; his/her communicative competence and the context in which the communicative encounter takes place. All these factors and others affect decisions about SELF-PRESENTATION. They also influence the receiver(s) and how he/she will interpret messages sent.

Barriers often arise in interpersonal communication and these are categorized by Richard Dimbleby and Graeme Burton in *More Than Words: An Introduction to Communication* (UK: Routledge, 3rd impression, 1997) into three main types: *technical* (physical barriers such as a noisy environment); *semantic* (barriers arising from an inability to understand the signs, verbal or non-verbal, being used by one or more of the persons involved in the transaction); and *psychological* (barriers caused by a range of psychological factors – for example, the message may be perceived as a threat to one's values). Common errors made in the process of social perception, such as stereotyping, also constitute psychological barriers to effective communication.

Speech and non-verbal communication are the main means by which messages are sent in interpersonal communication; non-verbal communication being particularly important in providing FEEDBACK and in regulating interaction. Interpersonal communication is also affected by the context in which it takes place, in GROUPS or organizations, for example, and factors found there such as norms, MORES, power relationships and so on. Good interpersonal communication skills are valued and many techniques have been developed to try to improve them, ASSERTIVENESS TRAINING and TRANSACTIONAL ANALYSIS being but two examples. There is of course a rich interplay between the messages received in interpersonal and MASS COMMUNICATION and our reflection on them in the process of INTRAPERSONAL COMMUNICATION. To complicate matters further most of the factors influencing the process of interpersonal communication are formed and shaped through that process. See *TOPIC GUIDE* under INTERPERSONAL COMMUNICATION.

* Michael Argyle, *The Psychology of Interpersonal Behaviour* (UK: Penguin, 1994) and *Bodily Communication* (UK: Methuen, 1988) by the same author; Richard Ellis and Ann McClintock, *If You Take My Meaning: Theory Into Practice in Human Communication* (UK: Edward Arnold, 1990); John Corner and Jeremy Hawthorn, eds, *Communication Studies: An Introductory Reader* (UK: Arnold, 1993); Michael Burgoon, Frank G. Hansaker and Edward Edwin J. Dawson, eds, *Human Communication* (UK: Sage, 1994); J. Devito, *Human Communication: The Basic Course* (UK: Addison-Wesley/Longman, 2000).

Interpretant C.S. Peirce (1839–1914), generally regarded as the founder of the American strand of SEMIOLOGY/SEMIOTICS, used the word interpretant in his model defining the nature of a SIGN, which 'addresses somebody, that is, it creates in the mind of that person an equivalent sign, or perhaps a more developed sign. The sign which it creates I call the interpretant of the first sign. The sign stands for something, its object' (from J. Zeman, 'Peirce's theory of signs' in T. Sebeok, ed., *A Perfusion of Signs*, US: Indiana University Press, 1977). The interpretant, then, is a mental concept produced both by the sign itself and by the user's experience of the object. Peirce's sign and interpretant find a parallel in the *signifier* and *signified* of the father of the European strand of semiology, Swiss linguist Ferdinand de Saussure (1857–1913).

Intertextuality See TEXT.

Intervening variables (IVs) Those influences which come between the encoder, the message and the decoder are referred to as *intervening variables*, mediating factors which influence the way a MESSAGE is perceived and the nature and degree of its impact. Time of day, mood, state of health can all constitute intervening variables. More importantly family, friends, peer groups, respected persons, opinion leaders, etc., are capable of significant mediation between what we are told and what we accept, believe or reject.

Whilst people may act as intervening variables between media messages and audience, the media may also be intervening variables between people: the TV socializes the child as do parents. It also 'comes between them' in the sense that it can stop interaction, modify it, improve it, re-channelize it (not to mention the DISSONANCE it might cause in a family when, for example, it provokes controversy). See S-IV-R MODEL OF COMMUNICATION. See also *TOPIC GUIDE* under COMMUNICATION MODELS.

Intervention Chiefly describes the policy and practice of governments to 'intervene' in, and attempt to control, the nature and flow of information. Intervention operates through laws, regulations and SURVEILLANCE. From earliest times governments have, with justification, believed that communication is power – that it is an agent of change – and that such power is a threat to existing power structures. Intervention remains high on the agenda of contemporary governments apprehensive about the freedoms of access and expression brought about by online services. See ENCRYPT; CENSORSHIP; CLIPPER CHIP; INTERNET: INTERNET: MONITORING OF CONTENT; NEWS MANAGEMENT.

Interviews Though there are many forms of interview and many different reasons for conducting them, the common goal is that of gaining more information from and understanding of other people, through a planned process of questions and answers. PRESS and television journalists use interviews as a means of collecting information and opinions. Interviews can be used to provide entertainment, as in chat shows; they are the most common means of selecting people for jobs or students for courses; they are a major method of data collection in the social sciences.

The kinds of questions widely used in interviews are: (1) open questions; these are broad, usually unstructured and often simply introduce the topic under discussion in a way that allows the interviewee a good deal of freedom in answering; (2) closed questions; these are restrictive, offering a fairly narrow range of answers from which the interviewee must choose; (3) primary questions; these introduce the subject or each new aspect of the subject under discussion; (4) subsidiary or secondary questions; these follow up the answers to primary questions; (5) neutral questions; these do not suggest any preferred response; (6) leading questions, which suggest a preferred response and are not normally used in research interviews. See *TOPIC GUIDE* under RESEARCH METHODS.

Intimacy at a distance See PARASOCIAL INTERACTION.

Intimization Mode of dealing with information, especially NEWS, and focusing on human interest; presented in a manner which is intimate and personal, termed 'matters of personality' by Liesbet van Zoonen in 'A tyranny of intimacy? Women, femininity and television news' in *Communication and Citizenship: Journalism and the Public Sphere* (UK: Routledge, 1991) edited by Peter Dahlgren and Colin Sparks. Van Zoonen is referring specifically to Dutch TV and argues that the increasing use of women presenters in the media is 'part and parcel of the intimization that seems to permeate most news' and risks being 'yet another articulation of traditional femininity' and what she calls 'the gendered nature of private sphere values'.

Intrapersonal communication That which takes place within ourselves: our inner monologues; our reflection upon ourselves, upon our relationships with others and with our environment. What goes on inside our heads (or hearts) is conditioned and controlled by our *self-view* and that self-view has emerged from a vast complex of past and present influences – on the view we perceive others holding about us, on our past achievements and failures, on memory-banks of good, bad and neutral actions and impressions.

Our concept of self interacts with our view of the world. Having been formed by experience, it is shaped and modified by subsequent experience, though rarely straightforwardly. The psychologist, for example, speaks of the *extrovert* personality and the *introvert* personality. On the face of it, the extrovert is characterized by a confidence in public performance that may indicate inner assurance, while the introvert may demonstrate a public shyness or guardedness reflective of inner uncertainty.

However, the outer confidence may well be a role, as in a play or performance, which may conceal an altogether different inner image or performance. The so-called introvert, on the other hand, may, through the richness or assurance of inner resources, have opted out of public role playing, or selected the role of introvert as a public defence mechanism.

Arising from both inner and outer stimuli, intrapersonal communication is a convergence, a coming-together, of both. A piece of music stirs in us, perhaps, previous memories; these memories of people or places may join with immediate impressions of events to create an ongoing DISCOURSE, between ourselves in the past, our former selves and our selves, perceiving and perceived, in the present.

Through intrapersonal communication we come to terms (or fail to come to terms) with ourselves and with others. Through it we create bridges or battlements; we make connections or we sever them; we open ourselves up or we establish self-defences. Most of us, it is important to note, are, as it were, on our own side. We use intrapersonal communication as a means of self-assurance, of confidence-building or confidence-maintenance as well as self-discovery (or indeed self-delusion). It is what makes us unique.

Investigatory Powers Act (RIPA) (UK), 2000 See REGULATION OF INVESTIGATORY POWERS ACT (RIPA) (UK), 2000.

Invisibility That is, invisible to the public as represented by media. The case is put by many commentators that certain sections of the population are overlooked, neglected, denied rightful attention by media, as though they did not exist. Ethnic minorities are seen to be 'invisible' or 'absent' in mainstream representations, except when they are viewed as a 'problem' in which case the spotlight of attention is trained upon them. Nations as well as individuals and groups are cloaked in invisibility, fulfilling NEWS VALUE only when there is trouble, conflict, a perceived threat to order.

Visibility then comes at the price of STEREOTYPING and the nurturing of 'us and them' (or WEDOM, THEYDOM attitudes). Tuen van Dijk in *Racism and the Press* (UK: Routledge, 1991) writes that 'minorities continue to be associated with a restricted number of stereotypical topics, such as immigration problems, crime, violence (especially "riots"), and ethnic relations (especially discrimination), whereas other topics, such as those in the realm of politics, social affairs and culture are under-reported'. See *TOPIC GUIDE* under MEDIA ISSUES & DEBATES.

Issue proponents GROUPS or individuals, often SIGNIFICANT OTHERS, who promote, or help determine, the ranking of an issue on the media agenda. See AGENDA-SETTING.

Issues Those social, cultural, economic or political concerns or ideas which are, at any given time, considered important, and which are the source of debate, controversy or conflict. What is an issue for one social group may not be considered such by another. Environmental issues have arguably grown out of middle-class concern, in particular among the younger, often college-educated members of that class.

Of vital interest to the student of communications are such questions as: How are issues disseminated? Why do some issues 'make it' to the national forum of debate while others fall by the wayside? What are the characteristics of a 'successful' issue? What prolongs an issue? What factors, other than the resolution of the issue, are involved in the decline in attention paid to an issue? And, running through all these questions, what role do the processes of communication play in the definition, shaping and promoting of issues?

The media are, of course, themselves an issue, like all institutions wielding power and influence, and the issues involving the role of the media in society are meat and drink for the student of communication. This has been given due acknowledgment in communication and media study syllabuses. Among the many issues of current interest involving the media are: censorship; media ownership and control, including the role of conglomerates in worldwide media activity; the part played by the media in the REINFORCEMENT of the STATUS QUO in society; in SOCIALIZATION; in their claim to act as the so-called FOURTH ESTATE; in policing the boundaries of social and political dissent and in being largely unquestioning advocates of the capitalist consumer-orientated society. See DEVIANCE; EFFECTS OF THE MASS MEDIA; LABELLING PROCESS (AND THE MEDIA); McCOMBS AND SHAW'S AGENDA-SETTING MODEL OF MEDIA EFFECTS, 1976; MEDIA CONTROL; MAINSTREAMING; MEDIA IMPERIALISM; NEWS VALUES. See also *TOPIC GUIDE* under MEDIA ISSUES & DEBATES.

➔ **J**

J-Curve One focus of communications research has been the part played by personal contact in the diffusion of information about NEWS events featured in the mass media. The assassination of President Kennedy in 1963 and the speedy diffusion of the news of the EVENT gave an impetus to this research.

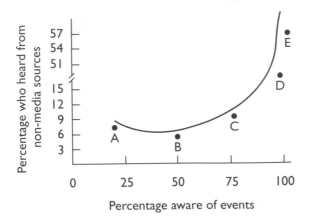

J-Curve of news diffusion

The J-Curve arose from the conclusions of B.S. Greenberg and stems mainly from his work on the Kennedy assassination when he investigated the first sources of knowledge about 18 different news events. It represents the relationship between the overall extent of awareness people have of such an event and the proportion of those learning of it through interpersonal sources.

Greenberg argues that news events can be divided into three groups as regards the manner of their diffusion and the involvement of personal contact in it. Type 1 events are important to the few people who may be affected by them but are of little concern to the general public. Such events, though reported in the media, will most generally be diffused by personal contact – the announcement of an engagement, for example. Type 2 events such as those in typical main news stories are generally regarded as important and command the attention of a large number of people.

News of such events is not likely to be passed on as information through personal contact, although they may be discussed as it will be taken for granted that most people will either know of such news or that it is not of vital interest to them. An example here might be an earthquake in another country. Type 3 events are dramatic, important and of very wide interest. Such events, like the assassination of President Kennedy, the death of Diana, Princess of Wales, the destruction of New York's World Trade Center by passenger planes hijacked by terrorists or the London bombings of 2005, get speedy and all-enveloping coverage from the media. They also mobilize interpersonal sources and the proportion of those who learn of the events from personal sources will be considerably higher than for Type 2 news items.

Such events are, however, rare and are usually related to crisis situations. In the case of the Kennedy assassination, Greenberg and Parker found that the extent and speed of diffusion was amazing: 99.85 per cent of the US population knew of the event within five hours of its occurrence. About 50 per cent of people first heard about it through personal sources and of these a fairly high proportion were strangers – revealing the degree to which people departed from established communication patterns.

By plotting the proportion of people eventually aware of all types of events against the proportion who heard about them first from personal contacts, it was possible to group them into five categories and the line joining these five categories was J-shaped, as shown in the diagram. A is in Type 1, B, C, D are in Type 2 and E is in Type 3. It can be seen that the size of the total audience increases progressively but the proportion of those receiving information from interpersonal sources does not; the proportion is higher for some of Type 1 than for Type 2 but highest for Type 3. See *TOPIC GUIDE* under COMMUNICATION THEORY.

Jakobson's model of communication, 1958 A linguist, Roman Jakobson was concerned with notions of meaning and of the internal structure of messages. His model is a double one, involving the *constitutive factors* in an act of communication; each of these factors is then locked on to the *function* it performs.

Thus the constitutive factors are:

	Context	
Addresser	Message	Addressee
	Contact	
	Code	

The functions form an identically structured model:

Referential
(Reality orientation of message)

Emotive	*Poetic*	*Conative*
(Expressive)	*Phatic*	(Effect of a message on addressee)
	Metalingual	

Phatic here refers to the function of keeping the channels of communication open and Metalingual is the function of actually identifying the communication code that is being used. See REDUNDANCY. See also *TOPIC GUIDE* under COMMUNICATION MODELS.

Jargon The specialist speech of groups of people with common identity – of religion, science, medicine, art, trade, profession, political party, etc. We can have educational jargon, cricket jargon, sociological jargon – that is, the in-language of people with specialist knowledge or interest. For those creating and operating jargon, it is a useful and vital means of communicating quickly between expert and expert. For those outside, jargon appears to be an unnecessarily complicated alternative to plain speaking, and a barrier to good communication. Without the growth of jargon words and expressions in Communication and Media Studies, this dictionary would not have been deemed necessary.

JICNARS scale Administered by the Joint Industrial Committee for National Readership Surveys in the UK, JICNARS measures AUDIENCE according to social CLASS, occupation and perceived economic status: *Category A* (upper middle class; business and professional people, considerable private means); *Category B* (middle class, senior people of reasonable affluence; respectable rather than luxurious lifestyle); *Category C1* (white-collar workers, tradespeople, supervisory and clerical jobs), *C2* (blue-collar, skilled workers); *D* (semi-skilled or unskilled members of the 'blue-collar' class) and *E* (those at the lowest level of subsistence, casual workers, those unemployed and/or dependent on social security schemes).

This classification has come under increasing criticism over the years, especially the emphasis upon targeting the occupation of the head of a household, traditionally male. More 'with it' methods of gauging patterns of consumption have concentrated on the notion of lifestyle as reflected in people's aspirations. The best known of these is VALS (Values and Lifestyles). See HICT PROJECT.

Jingoism Extreme and uncritical form of national patriotism. The word derives from G.W. Hunt's song, written at the time of the Russo–Turkish War (1877–78) when anti-Russian feeling in the UK was running high and the prime minister, Benjamin Disraeli, ordered the Mediterranean fleet to Constantinople: *We don't want to fight, but by Jingo if we do/We've got the ships, we've got the men, and got the money too.* The Falklands War of 1982 stirred up similar sentiments in Britain's popular press which used language as declamatory and as sensational as anything employed during the Boer War, the two world wars or the British invasion of Suez (1956).

From the *Sun* ('The paper that supports our boys'): '74 Days That Shook the World!', 'Lions Who Did The Impossible – By land, sea and air, our boys never faltered in their fight against tyranny' and, on the front page, in three-inch-high type, 'We've Won!' (15 July 1982). With the NATO bombing of Serbia in 1999, the Sun showed that it had not lost its jingoist panache. Under the resounding headline 'Clobba Slobba' (referring to the Yugoslav leader Slobodan Milosevic), the paper trumpeted 'Our boys batter Serb butcher in Nato bomb blitz'. And at the foot of the page, 'We go in: See pages 2, 3, 4, 5, 6, 7 and 8'. Again from the *Sun* during the allied invasion of Iraq, 2003: 'How Major Dunc's Rats Raised Hell', and 'Harriers KO Nest of Vipers' (24 March, 2003). In contrast, the *Sun's* rival, the *Daily Mirror* took a critical rather than jingoistic stance: 'This War's NOT Working' (1 April 2003).

Jingoism is at its most familiar in the reporting of sport between nations as a trawl of the UK tabloids at

word in 1450 (in the West, that is, the Chinese had developed printing much earlier) there have been ample cases of conformity and rebellion (if not revolution) in journalism.

In the nineteenth century the courageous editors of the radical press, such as Richard Carlile and Henry Hetherington, spent many years of their lives in prison for writing about and publishing beliefs that ran counter to those of the ruling elite. In the twentieth century hundreds of journalists and news photographers have been killed while reporting events throughout the world and the twenty-first century has seen no diminution in the death-toll of the bringers-of-news.

In journalism there will always be the biased and the spurious; there will continue to be invasion of PRIVACY, nationalist hype, shameless and malicious STEREOTYPING, wallowing in scandal – all 'examples' of contemporary journalism in action. There will also continue to be high-quality investigative journalism which, in the words of John Keane in 'The crisis of the sovereign state' (in Raboy and Dagenais) 'seeks to counteract the secretive and noisy arrogance of the democratic Leviathan'; which 'involves the patient investigation and exposure of political corruption and misconduct'; which sets out to 'sting political power, to tame its arrogance by extending the limits of public controversy and widening citizens' involvement in the public spheres of civil society'. See DEMOCRACY AND THE MEDIA; EMBEDDED REPORTERS; MEDIASPHERE; NEWS MANAGEMENT IN TIMES OF WAR; PUBLIC SPHERE; WATCHDOGS. See also *TOPIC GUIDE* under MEDIA ETHICS; MEDIA: FREEDOM, CENSORSHIP; MEDIA: ISSUES & DEBATES; NEWS MEDIA.

Journalism: celebrity journalism The preoccupation in modern print journalism with recording the activities, sayings, scandals of celebrities; described by Peter Hamill in *News is a Verb* (US: Ballentine, 1998) as a virus, and 'the most widespread phenomena [*sic*] of the times'. Hamill is of the view that 'true accomplishment is marginal to the recognition factor. There is seldom any attention paid to scientists, poets, educators or archeologists.'

Big names are the constant focus of attention to the exclusion of other subjects. The obsession with celebrity worries many media watchers for coverage of celebrity *displaces* the reporting of events, the analysis of ISSUES which are *in* the public interest as contrasted with being *of* interest to the public; the issue here being the swamping of important information by populist entertainment. In a UK *Guardian* article, 'Get a grip on reality' (26 May 2003), Nick Clarke wrote of the hold celebrities have both on the nation's newspapers and on TV. On one July day, flicking through the tabloids, he found no fewer than 58 pages dedicated to celebrity. Clarke's concern was that 'for millions of readers this material represents the bulk of their news diet'.

He charges editors with allowing 'the boundaries between fact and fiction to become blurred and sometimes – to the inexpert eye – indistinguishable'. Clarke takes the view that 'so great is the dominance of the celebrity/television culture, that it has started to distort the way in which we view the world around us … No wonder the "real" world has struggled to compete with the pseudo-existence on the screen.' See REALITY TV.

Journalism: citizen journalism With the advent of the multi-purpose mobile phone, in particular its capacity to transmit instantly online images, still and moving, newsgathering has been opened up to the man and woman in the street. Citizen journalism is about being close to, or involved in, events as they happen and transmitting pictures to the mass media often ahead of professional news teams. The capacity and potential of citizen reporting of news as it breaks was most dramatically illustrated during the terrorist bombings in London, the first wave of which occurred on 7 July 2005.

Within minutes of the carnage of 7/7, newsrooms in and around the capital were swamped with images and video footage, some of the material actually transmitted by the victims. Mobile footage was on national news within 30 minutes while still pictures were soon to dominate the front pages of the press worldwide.

Commentators have seen in citizen journalism a shift in power from mass communication, dominated as it is by corporate ownership, towards more democracy, more popular involvement in the news process. At the same time, concern has been registered at the possible unreliability of images published from unsolicited, unchecked sources, as well as issues of privacy. See BLOGGING.

Journalism: 'postmodern journalism' Shares characteristics with celebrity journalism; a broad and overarching term to describe a trend in journalism away from serious reporting; in particular emphasizing the personal over the political. It can be summed up as more tabloid, more consumerist. It focuses on discontinuities, celebrating difference over commonality, stressing the confessional over the reportorial, serving more as 'therapy' than cognitive enlightenment.

Such journalism, print or broadcast, strives for the intimate but turns this into a public spectacle. Referred to as 'therapy news', it focuses on feelings, 'emotionalizing' events rather than striving after objectivity. Compassion is prominent yet tends to be selective in its targeting. 'This confessional and therapy style of news,' write Deborah Chambers, Linda Steiner and Carole Fleming in *Women and Journalism* (UK/US: Routledge, 2004), 'is characterized by a profoundly selective tolerance of some people's failings and misfortunes. It usually taps into sympathy for victims drawn largely from white, middle-class, heterosexual social groups of the same nationality as the national or regional newspapers and broadcast programmes. It ignores the misery and distress of migrants and refugees, drug addicts or prostitutes and of millions of people in developing nations suffering from starvation and war.'

Postmodern journalism works towards the decontextualization of events and, by skirting issues of power, it takes politics out of everyday life. In the words of Chambers *et al.* it 'systematically devalues issues concerning economic, social and cultural power and techniques of critical engagement and investigation'. Ultimately, what happens in this postmodernist scenario is the conversion of news into entertainment. See POST-MODERNISM.

Journalism: Project for Excellence in Journalism (US, 1995) Examined American media over a period of 20 years, noting major shifts of emphasis, from the serious to the popular, from hard news towards INFO-TAINMENT; crime, scandal and celebrity being emphasized. The project noted the increase in reports of scandal from 0.5 per cent in 1977 to 15 per cent in 1997. Human interest stories went from 8 per cent in 1977 to 16 per cent 20 years later.

Jump cut Where two scenes in a TV news report are of the same subject, taken from the same angle and distance, the 'jump cut' is to be avoided; to get round this 'jump' from one shot to virtually the same, usually of someone being interviewed, a 'cutaway' shot is inserted – that is, a reaction shot from the interviewer.

Juxtaposition jump-cut See SOUND-BITE.

→ K

Katz and Lazarsfeld's two-step flow model of mass communication and personal influence See ONE-STEP, TWO-STEP, MULTI-STEP FLOW MODELS OF COMMUNICATION.

Kepplinger and Habermeier's Events Typology See EVENT.

Kernel and satellite See NARRATIVE: KERNEL AND SATELLITE.

Kineme A segment or fraction of a whole communicative GESTURE; a kinetic parallel to a phoneme (element of verbal language). The term was invented by Ray Birdwhistell. In *Kinesics and Context* (US: University of Philadelphia, 1970), Birdwhistell draws up a vocabulary of 60 kinemes which he found in the gestural/postural/expressive movements of American subjects. He maintains that these kinemes combine to form large units (*kinemorphs*) on the analogy of *morphemes* (or words). An example would be waving a fist or prodding the air with a finger while at the same time smiling or looking angry. See KINESICS.

Kinesics The study of communication through GESTURE, posture and body movement. In *Communication* (UK: Open University, Block 3, Units 7–10, 1975), the OU course team loosely classify kinesics under five headings: (1) information (indicating, for example, welcome or 'keep away'); (2) communication markers (head and body movements to give emphasis to a spoken message); (3) emotional state (as expression of feeling); (4) expression of self (in the way you sit or walk or hold yourself) and (5) expression of relationship (revealing attitude to others by how close you stand to someone, how you angle, tilt, shift your body in relationship to others or by the way hair or clothes are touched, a tie adjusted). See COMMUNICATION, NON-VERBAL; NON-VERBAL BEHAVIOUR: REPERTOIRE; PROXEMICS; TOUCH.

Kinetoscope Early form of film projection invented in 1887 by Thomas Alva Edison (1847–1931) and his assistant K.L. Dickson. On 14 April 1894, the first Kinetoscope Parlor was opened on Broadway, New York. The Kinetoscope was a wooden cabinet furnished with a peep-slit and an inspection lens through which a single person could view the endless loop of celluloid film that passed below it. It was driven by a small electric motor and illuminated by an electric lamp. Edison's lasting contribution to cinematography was his use of celluloid film 35mm wide, with four perforations for each picture. See CINEMATOGRAPHY, ORIGINS.

'Kite' co-orientation approach See McLEOD AND CHAFFEY'S 'KITE' MODEL, 1973.

Knowns, Unknowns In *Deciding What's News* (US: Pantheon, 1979) Herbert Gans says that those who are famous in society, *knowns*, appear at least four times more frequently in TV news bulletins than *unknowns*. The POWER ELITE and celebrities generally tend to be both the source and subject matter of news stories; and by being so they further qualify themselves to appear on the news as knowns. Gans states that fewer than 50 individuals regularly appear on US news. It is not only the actions of knowns that qualify as newsworthy, but their speech. As Allan Bell says in *The Language of News Media* (UK: Blackwell, 1991), 'Talk is news only if the right person is talking.' Meanwhile the dominance of the headlines by knowns, by the elite, leads to other actors, other talk, being ignored. See NEWS VALUES.

KPFA Radio In the US, the first listener-supported independent RADIO station, founded by Lewis Hill in 1949, broadcasting from Berkeley, California. Sister stations were later introduced – KFPK in Los Angeles (1959) and WBA1 in New York (1960). Working under the umbrella link of the Pacific Foundation the outspokenness of the stations proved a thorn in the side of government and the establishment in America. In 1970 KFPT went on air in Houston, Texas. It was firebombed twice by the Ku Klux Klan, but broadcasts continued.

Kuleshov effect Lev Kuleshov (1899–1970) was in at the sunrise of Russian cinema. He was film designer, film-maker and film theorist. In 1920 he was given a workshop to study film methods with a group of students. His Kuleshov effect, demonstrated in 1922, proved how, by altering the juxtaposition of film images, their significance, for the audience, could be changed.

In 1929 he wrote 'The content of the shot in itself is not so important as the joining of two shots of different content and the method of their connection and their alternation.' An experiment, aimed at proving his theory, showed a close-up of an actor playing a prisoner. This is linked to two different shots representing what the prisoner sees: first a bowl of soup, then the open door of freedom. Audiences were convinced that the expression on the man's face was different in each instance, though it was the same piece of film. See MONTAGE; SHOT.

Kuuki Japanese term, shared by the Chinese and Koreans, meaning a *climate of opinion requiring compliance*. In an article entitled 'The future of political communication research: a Japanese perspective' published in the *Journal of Communication*, Autumn 1993, Youichi Ito, Professor at Keio University, Shonan Fujisawa, Japan, emphasizes that kuuki refers not so much to generalities but specifics. In 'Climate of opinion, kuuki, and democracy' in William Gudykunst, ed., *Communications Yearbook* 26 (US: Lawrence Erlbaum, 2002), the author states that kuuki, the pressure towards compliance, refers 'to a certain specific opinion, policy, or group decision'; and this is usually accompanied by 'threats and social sanction'.

As the author points out, the phrase 'climate of opinion' has a long history and was probably first used in the seventeenth century by the English philosopher Joseph Glanville (1638–80). Ito suggests a parallel with the German term 'zeitgeist', spirit of the times. He cites the Russo-Japanese war of 1905 in which the climate of opinion became in Japan one of fervent popular support for the war. The circulation of the pro-war newspapers at the time grew dramatically. That of the anti-war press shrank.

Because kuuki, like zeitgeist, is more spirit than the corporeal, it is neither as predictable nor as controllable as more customary shaping devices. However, when the climate is right, kuuki's power can carry a nation. Ito sees a strong connection here with Elisabeth Noelle-Neumann's 'spiral of silence' (See NOELLE-NEUMANN'S SPIRAL OF SILENCE MODEL OF PUBLIC OPINION, 1974).

Once the climate requiring compliance spreads through a group, community or nation the spirit of the time becomes conformity. Isolated, the individual once accustomed to speaking his or her opinions freely, senses threat and danger; and retreats down a spiral of silence. It might also be concluded that the media, conforming to the spirit of the moment, will also confirm it, and for their part reverse the spiral until it becomes a clamour that legitimizes and reinforces.

Kuuki can work for good or ill. When it is fired by JINGOISM 'it can be undemocratic and destructive … The most dangerous case,' writes Professor Ito, 'is when kuuki is taken advantage of by undemocratic groups or selfish and intolerant political leaders. Even if the situation is not as bad as this, kuuki can make people's viewpoint narrower and limit their policy options.'

Ito explains how kuuki may be nurtured by the media, by government or by the strength of public opinion. Each is a source of influence upon the others, operating in a tripolar way. Where two of the major actors work in unison, or alliance, the dominant partnership can force the third actor into line. Ito lists five conditions in which kuuki operates to powerful effect: when (1) the majority opinion accounts for the majority in more than two of the three sectors; government, mass media and the public; (2) when the majority opinion accounts for the majority across the three sectors; (3) when the majority opinion increases over time; (4) when the majority opinion is escalating; and (5) when the subject matter 'tends to stir up the "spirits" inherent in individuals such as basic values, norms, prejudices, antagonism and loyalty to the collective or patriotism'.

Ito states, 'When these conditions are met and kuuki is created, it functions as a strong political or social force, resulting in the minority side becoming ever-more silent and acquiescent and changing or modifying its opinion on policy, or its members resigning from their positions.'

→ **L**

Label libel A McLUHANISM. Marshall McLuhan (1911–80), media guru of the 1960s, wrote of the way that the mass media stick labels on people, trap them in STEREOTYPES, typecast them, pigeon-hole them, to the point that such generalizations become invidious and thus a mode of DEFAMATION.

Labelling process (and the media) Howard Becker in a classic study, *The Outsiders; Studies in the Sociology of Deviancy* (US: Free Press, 1963), analyses the process by which certain social actions or ideas and those who perform or express them come to be defined as DEVIANT; and which he calls 'the labelling process': 'The deviant is one to whom the label has successfully been applied; deviant behaviour is behaviour that people so label.'

Becker's work highlights the role that powerful social groups and individuals play in defining the limits of acceptable and unacceptable behaviour, through the labelling process. He argues that certain groups within society, moral entrepreneurs, are particularly able to shape, via the mass media, new images of deviancy and new definitions of social problems. See CRISIS DEFINITION; ISSUES.

LAD (Language Acquisition Device) According to linguists such as Noam Chomsky, LAD is an innate device within the human mind which allows us to acquire language. The LAD is a hypothetical model of this process and is grounded in the theory that human beings are programmed to acquire and create language and thus can develop competence in any language that they are exposed to, over a period of time. See DEEP STRUCTURE.

Lame A term used by William Labov in *Language in the Inner City* (US: University of Pennsylvania Press, 1972) to describe individuals who are relatively isolated, on the margins of a group and its culture. This relatively isolated position often shows itself linguistically in that such individuals will use less the significant linguistic features of the group or culture in question.

Language See *TOPIC GUIDE* under LANGUAGE/DISCOURSE/NARRATIVE.

Language pollution According to Gail and Michele Myers in *The Dynamics of Human Communication* (US: McGraw-Hill, 1985), this occurs 'when language is used by people to say what in fact they do not believe, when words are used, sometimes unwittingly, sometimes deliberately, to cover up rather than to explain reality, our symbolic world becomes polluted. This means that language becomes an unreliable instrument for adapting to the environment and for communicating'.

The authors identify three main types of language pollution and their common characteristics: *confusion* (unknown meanings), characterized by the use of foreign languages, unfamiliar words, technical JARGON and misused terminology; *ambiguity* (too many meanings), characterized by vagueness, the use of words with multiple definitions and the use of very general imprecise statements, or terms; and *deception* (obscured meanings), characterized by outright lies, distortion, and giving incomplete information or non-answers to questions.

Langue and parole In his *Cours de Linguistique Générale* (1916), published after his death, Ferdinand de Saussure (1857–1914) defined *La langue*, or language, as a system, while *La parole* represented the actual manifestations of language in speech and writing. The former he conceived as an 'institution', a set of interpersonal rules and norms; the latter, events or instances, taking their MEANING from, or giving meaning to, the system.

* F. De Saussure, *Course in General Linguistics* (English translation; UK: Fontana/Collins, 1974).

Lasswell's model of communication, 1948 A questioning device rather than an actual model of the communication process, Harold Lasswell's five-point approach to the analysis of the mass media has nevertheless given enduring service. It remains a useful first step in interpreting the transmission and reception of messages.

In 'The structure and function of communication in society' in Lymon Bryson, ed., *The Communication of Ideas* (US: Harper & Row, 1948) Lasswell suggests that in order to arrive at a due understanding of the MEANING systems of MASS COMMUNICATION the following sequence of questions might be put:

Who

Says *What*

In which *channel*

To *whom*

With what *effect?*

Assuming that the last question would include the notion of FEEDBACK, Lasswell's model could still do with an additional question: 'In what *context* (social, economic, cultural, political, aesthetic) is the communication process taking place?' Also Lasswell makes no provision for INTERVENING VARIABLES (IVs), those mediating factors that impact on the ways in which messages are received and responded to. It is useful to compare Lasswell's list to the verbal version of GERBNER'S MODEL OF COMMUNICATION, 1956. In 'Towards a general model of communication' in *Audio-Visual Communication Review* 4 (1956), George Gerbner offers the following formula:

1   Someone

2   perceives an event

3   and reacts

4   in a situation

5   through some means

6   to make available materials

7   in some form

8   and context

9   conveying content

10   with some consequence.

See *TOPIC GUIDE* under COMMUNICATION MODELS.

Latitudes of acceptance and rejection The greater the gap between an attitude a person already holds and that which another wants to persuade him/her to adopt, the less likely it is that any shift in attitude will occur. C.W. Sherif in *Attitudes and Attitude Change* (US: Greenwood Press, 1982) argues that our responses to attempts to challenge or change our attitudes are divided into three main types. (1) An individual's *latitude of acceptance* contains the opinions, ideas and so on about an issue that a person is ready to agree with or accept. (2) The *latitude of non-commitment* contains the range of opinions and ideas on the same issue that the individual is neutral about. (3) The *latitude of rejection* contains those ideas and opinions about an ISSUE that the individual finds unacceptable. Further, unacceptable statements tend to be interpreted as even more hostile and unfavourable than they really are – the *contrast effect*; while those that are not far removed from the latitude of acceptance may gradually be incorporated into it – the *assimilation effect*. See BOOMERANG EFFECT.

Law of minimal effects Point of view that the media have little or no effect in forming or modifying the attitude of audiences. See EFFECTS OF THE MASS MEDIA.

LBC: London Broadcasting Corporation The first COMMERCIAL RADIO station to come on air in the UK, in October 1973; followed a few days later by Capital Radio.

Leadership Leaders can generally be defined as individuals within GROUPS or organizations who have influence, who provide focus, coordination and direction for the activities of the group. It may be argued that the purpose of leadership is to enable the group to function effectively and achieve its goals, although in practice leadership may not always have this effect. Leadership may be and often is invested in one person but it can also be shared.

Leaders may be emergent or appointed. An emergent leader is one who comes to acquire the role of leader through the process of group INTERACTION. He or she may, for example, be the person with the best ideas or communication skills. An appointed leader is one who is formally selected; leaders in work situations are often appointed to their position.

A considerable amount of research has been conducted with the aim of trying to ascertain the qualities and interpersonal skills required for effective leadership and the type of leadership needed for the optimum performance of groups or organizations. An early perspective was the *trait* approach to leadership which argues that individuals who become leaders have certain personality traits or characteristics enabling them to cope well with leadership. The suggestion is that leaders are born, not made. However, this approach has been widely criticized for being simplistic and lacking in any hard evidence to substantiate its claims.

Another approach examines the varying *styles* of leadership that may be adopted and the characteristics of each style. An example here would be represented by the work of Robert Likert. In *The Human Organization* (US: McGraw-Hill, 1967), Likert identifies four main styles of leadership: *Autocratic, Persuasive, Consultative* and *Democratic*. Research into leadership styles tends to point towards the democratic leadership style as being superior to the others. However the *Contingency* approach to leadership argues that effective leadership depends on a leader being able to adjust his/her style to suit the context: factors in the context that are thought to influence the appropriate choice of style, include the nature of the tasks, the position of power held by the leader and the nature of the relationships between the leader and subordinates.

Another theory within the Contigency approach is the *Situational Leadership Theory* proposed by Paul Hersey and Ken Blanchard (1988). This maintains that key factors affecting the choice of effective style are the level of guidance and support a leader is willing to provide and the degree of readiness among subordinates as regards performance of the tasks.

Examples of key situational factors identified by a number of theorists as determining suitable leadership styles include the nature of the task, the characteristics of the group and the organizational CULTURE. More recently Daniel Goleman (2000) has identified six leadership styles: Coercive, Authoritative, Affiliative, Democratic, Pacesetting and Coaching. Goleman argues that effective leaders are able to use all these styles depending on the situation. He stresses the importance of *emotional intelligence* in the deployment of these styles.

The *functional* approach to leadership focuses on identifying the behaviour needed from leaders so that particular groups and organizations may achieve their goals. The implication here is that individuals can improve their leadership abilities. In *Organizational Behaviour* (US/UK: Prentice Hall, 2001) Andrzej Huczynski and David Buchanan identify two trends in contemporary thinking about leadership. One gives 'recognition of the role of heroic, powerful, charismatic, visionary leaders', whilst the other gives 'recognition of the role of *informal leadership* at all levels'.

One point all approaches are agreed on is that a good leader has to be a good communicator.

Leakage See FACIAL EXPRESSION.

Leaks A time-honoured way in which governments disseminate information, often through 'sources close to' the president or the prime minister; a way of authority manipulating the media. Leaks can always be denied. Sometimes, of course, leaks are genuine, that is they are true divulgences of information which those in authority would wish to be withheld. Here, those close to the centres of power, perhaps disagreeing with decisions about to be made or affronted at the potential mismanagement of power, disclose information with the intention of causing embarrassment and, through publicity, a change of policy. See DEEP THROAT; SECRECY.

Learned journals on communication See PERIODICALS FOR THE STUDY OF MEDIA.

Legislation See *TOPIC GUIDE* under COMMISSIONS, COMMITTEES, LEGISLATION.

Legitimation/delegitimation In *Ideology: A Multicultural Approach* (UK: Sage, 1998) Teun A. Van Dijk states that 'Legitimation is one of the main social functions of ideologies.' It is the process whereby a group, society or nation give a status of acceptance – legitimize – ways of doing or saying things. By the same token, a process of delegitimation occurs in which the 'We' or 'Us' of a situation seek overtly, or covertly, to deny acceptance to *other*, or what Van Dijk refers to as 'outgroups'. Reference, for example, to 'illegal' immigrants has the effect of delegitimating a host of different 'others' and, in the public mind, creates antipathy, fear (of the 'foreigner') and rejection.

Legitimation is very much about being a member of a group and relies in some part upon a recognition of what differentiates Us from Them (those who are not part of the group). Van Dijk speaks of an 'ideological square' in which four main positions are taken in relation to legitimation/delegitimation. The square serves as (a) a positive SELF-PRESENTATION and (b) a negative 'other' presentation.The positions are as follows: (1) express/emphasize information that is positive about Us; (2) express/emphasize negative points about Them; (3) suppress/de-emphasize information that is positive about Them and (4) suppress/de-emphasize information that is positive about Us.

Communicative strategies employed in legitimation/delegitimation DISCOURSES are numerous, depending on the nature of the communication and the contexts in which it takes place. They work through the *implicit*, by assumption; by implication, presupposition, assertion and manipulation; and their aim is the maintenance of power through the creation of compliance and consent. See HEGEMONY; IDEOLOGY.

Lettre Ulysses Award   Initiated in 2003, an international award for the art of reportage; made annually by the French cultural magazine *Lettre International* in partnership with the Aventis Foundation and with the support of the Goethe Institute. The Award, made in Berlin, carries prizes of 50,000, 30,000 and 20,000 euros. UK journalist Alexandra Fuller received the top award in 2005 for her book *Scribbling the Cat: Travels with an African Soldier* (US/UK: Penguin, 2004).

Lexis   Linguists' term to describe the vocabulary of a language: a unit of vocabulary is generally referred to as a *lexical* item or *lexeme*. A complete inventory of the lexical items of a language constitutes a dictionary, a lexicon. Lexicography is the overall study of the vocabulary of language, including its history.

Libel   A written accusation; any malicious, defamatory publication or statement. The spoken equivalent of libel is *slander*. Both constitute DEFAMATION and the law in the UK may impose heavy fines on those proved to have injured someone's good name. However, it is not possible to obtain legal aid in order to take, for example, a newspaper to court for libel in order to protect that good name.

Life positions   In his book, *I'm O.K. You're O.K.* (US: Harper & Row, 1969), Thomas Harris identifies four life positions that can be used in TRANSACTIONAL ANALYSIS for exploring and examining people's feelings, attitudes or positions towards themselves and others and the way in which these influence their social interaction. The I'm OK–You're OK position is one in which an individual believes in his/her own worth and that of others. It is a position in which we accept ourselves and others and base our transactions on this orientation. Harris argues that to reach this position requires conscious decision and effort.

Harris believes many people hold an I'm not OK–You're OK position as a result of early socialization which, in attempting to shape an individual's behaviour into a pattern that is socially acceptable, contains a lot of messages critical of the individual – that is, not OK messages. This position may lead to a feeling of inferiority that shows itself in defensive communication such as game playing.

Experiences in early childhood, especially abuse and neglect, may result in the individual forming the perspective that whilst he/she is OK, other people are not, hence the I'm OK–You're not OK position, which may show itself in a characteristically hostile, or aggressive communicative style. I'm not OK–You're not OK is the position of those who feel neither themselves nor others are OK. This negative perspective may show itself through a despairing and resigned attitude when communicating with others. Life positions influence the kinds of life SCRIPTS individuals write for themselves. See *TOPIC GUIDE* under INTERPERSONAL COMMUNICATION.

* Ian Stewart and Vann Joines, *TA Today* (UK: Lifespace, 1987); Amy and Thomas Harris, *Staying OK* (UK: Arrow Books, 1995).

Lifestyle   See STYLE; VALS TYPOLOGY.

Lighting cameraman   In a film crew, the lighting cameraman or woman is responsible for the pictorial composition of the film image as well as the arrangements for lighting.

Light Programme   One of three BBC radio channels until the introduction of Radio 1 in 1967, and a change of names for the rest: Light became Radio 2, Home Service became Radio 4 and the Third Programme

Radio 3. The Light Programme, for general entertainment RADIO, was created in the year the Second World War ended, 1945.

Lindup Committee Report on Data Protection, 1978 See DATA PROTECTION.

Linguistic determinism The proposition that the language of a culture determines the way in which the world is perceived and thought about. Thus in acquiring a language an individual is also acquiring a particular way of thinking about the world, a particular worldview. The two linguists closely associated with this position are Benjamin Lee Whorf and Edward Sapir whose Linguistic Relativity Hypothesis helped to establish this particular view on the relationship between language and thought. Though their proposition that language actually determines thought has been much questioned, many would accept that the language at an individual's disposal influences the way he/she thinks about the world. See SAPIR-WHORF LINGUISTIC RELATIVITY HYPOTHESIS.

Linguistics The scientific study of language. *Diachronic* or *historical* linguistics investigates how language use has changed over time; *synchronic* linguistics is concerned with the state of language at any given point in time; *general* linguistics seeks to establish principles for the study of all languages; *descriptive* linguistics is concerned with the analysis of the characteristics of specific language; *contrastive* linguistics explores the contrasts between different languages or families of languages while *comparative* linguistics concentrates on common characteristics. Among a profusion of other linguistics-related studies are *anthropological linguistics*, *biolinguistics*, *psycholinguistics* and *sociolinguistics*. See PARADIGM; SEMIOLOGY/SEMIOTICS; STRUCTURALISM.

Linotype printing Patented in 1894 by German immigrant to Baltimore, US, Ottmar Mergenthaler. The operator uses a keyboard similar to that of a typewriter. As each key is depressed a brass matrix for that particular letter drops into place. When the line is complete, the row of matrices is placed over a mould and the line of type is cast, the molten lead alloy setting almost at once. See MONOTYPE PRINTING; PRINTING.

Lip-sync Synchronization between mouth movement and the words on the film soundtrack.

Listening Though often taken for granted, listening is a crucial element in human communication. Gail and Michele Myers in *The Dynamics of Human Communication* (US: McGraw-Hill, 1985) point out that 'Listening is often not the natural process that it is often believed to be.' Poor listening can be the cause of many breakdowns in communication. Myers and Myers go on to identify ways in which listening can be improved and communication thereby made more effective.

Active listening reflects a certain attitude towards others, recognizing that what others say is worth listening to and that one should attempt to imagine how what is being said makes sense to the person saying it and the feelings involved. The receiver needs to listen to the sender without initially passing judgement on what is being said and then mirror back to the sender what was said in order to show and to check that he/she understood the message and the feelings that lie within it. This helps to build a supportive situation in which communication can take place. Active listening is also known as *empathetic listening*, whereas *deliberative listening* involves trying to determine, accurately, the content of the message.

Lithography Printing from stone, slate or a substitute such as zinc or aluminium, with greasy ink; invented in 1798 by Alois Senefelder.

Lloyd's List The oldest international daily newspaper, founded in 1734; perhaps most noted for its role as an almanac of world shipping movements and casualty reports.

Lobbying A process in which individuals or GROUPS seek to influence those in power. In the UK Parliament, the lobby is the passage through which MPs pass to record their votes. Lobbying includes any device – postal and electronic mailing through to financial contributions – to persuade other people, usually those in authority, to give an issue their support. Most major vested interests – such as the so-termed Gun Lobby in the US – see lobbying as an essential part of their strategies of persuasion or dissuasion.

Those wishing to influence a government are likely to engage public relations practitioners for whom lobbying is a specialized area of public relations practice. In *Effective Public Relations* (US: Prentice-Hall, 1994), S. Cutlip, A. Center and G. Broom describe lobbying as that 'part of public relations that builds and maintains relations with government primarily for the purpose of influencing legislation and regulation'. See ALTER-EU.

Lobby Practice A book of rules of conduct written by, and abided by, UK parliamentary lobby correspondents who operate from offices in the House of Commons and whose access to the centres of power is highly prized. The lobby system in the British House of Commons goes as far back as 1886. Correspondents meet daily at Downing Street, the home of the prime minister, and weekly on Thursdays in the Commons for a briefing by the PM's press secretary.

The system has been subjected to considerable criticism on the grounds of its secrecy, alleged cosiness and danger of collusion between government and privileged lobby correspondents. It has been varyingly called 'an instrument of closed government' and the 'real cancer of British journalism'. At the heart of the criticism is the fact that the lobby correspondents receive no more information than government wishes them to know; if they break the rules of Lobby Practice they know their privileges will be withdrawn. See PHILLIS REVIEW OF GOVERNMENT COMMUNICATIONS (UK), 2004.

Localization The process by which global media tailor their products for local markets and local audiences. The 1980s and 1990s saw a dramatic expansion of TV channels crossing national borders, and this trend was nowhere more manifest than in Europe. Companies such as MTV, CNN, Sky News, BBC Prime, BBC World and National Geographic have been reaching out for pan-European audiences.

Initially, channels such as MTV (launched in the US in 1981 and in Europe in 1987) operated in a global capacity, that is in the sense of an increasingly homogenous culture, offering a single brand regardless of national and regional differences. They were swiftly to recognize the importance of catering to local tastes.

Jean K. Chalaby in 'Transnational television in Europe: the role of pan-European channels' in the *European Journal of Communication* (June, 2002) writes that 'these cross-border players awoke to the reality of national boundaries and cultural and linguistic markers and realized that there were limits to the exportability of their programmes'.

Localization became an imperative, at first by opening local ADVERTISING windows, then by adapting programming itself, especially of entertainment, to local needs. Chalaby is of the view that localization is a practical and convenient step on the way towards further GLOBALIZATION rather than a force working against it. While the 'necessity for localization can be interpreted as evidence of the limits of cultural globalization', it nevertheless 'accelerates the process of globalization, notably because it allows global players to operate in a multinational environment'. True, the 'music may become local' but the 'expansion plan remains global'.

Localization is less evident in NEWS services such as CNN and BBC World. For them the reporting of international events is their key function. In contrast, channels dedicated to children's entertainment, such as Fox Kids or the Cartoon Network, demand localization, the originating language being converted to the 'home' language directly or through dubbing or subtitling.

Chalaby believes 'Localized channels are not so much a "hybrid" cultural form incorporating the local – as is sometimes suggested – than a bridge that helps the global reach the local.' See EUROPE: CROSS-BORDER TV CHANNELS.

Looking behaviour See CIVIL INATTENTION; EYE CONTACT.

Lookism Theory that the better looking you are the more successful you will be in life. The term was first used as early as 1978, in the *Washington Post Magazine* but more recently has been written about at length by American psychologist Nancy Etcoff in *Survival of the Prettiest: The Science of Beauty* (US: Little, Brown, 1999). In an age of images, the image dominates our perceptions, our thoughts and our judgements.

According to Etcoff even mothers love their offspring just a little bit less if they are less than handsome. In the world of work, says Dr Etcoff, 'Good looking men are more likely to get hired, at a higher salary than unattractive men.' She compares 'Looking' with sexism and racism. However these are conscious, easily recognized attitudes, while Lookism works at a subconscious level. We are largely unaware of favouring the beautiful.

Loony Leftism In the 1980s in the UK a mythology was created by local and national newspapers about the policies of Labour-led councils, particularly those in Greater London. 'Loony' became the catchword whenever councils such as Hackney, Haringey or Islington were mentioned; and the accusation arose from rumours that were simply untrue. For example, the *Daily Star* printed a headline story declaring that Hackney Council, in its attempt to stamp out racism and racist language in the borough, had banned the singing of 'Baa, Baa, Black Sheep' in playschools.

Hackney had never considered banning the nursery rhyme; however, newspapers throughout the country and in the rest of the world picked on this example of 'Loony Leftism'. Once in print, the story gained momentum and credence. Even Labour MPs took on board the Loony Left slogan. Similar press treatment was handed out to the authors of the Congestion Charge Scheme which came into force in London in February 2003. Prior to this, the press subjected the scheme, and its architect, Mayor Ken Livingstone, to vilification and scare stories.

The tabloid paper the *Sun* called Livingstone 'the madcap mayor', 'crazy', 'loopy', 'potty', 'barmy' and a 'crackpot'. Reference to 'Red Ken' appeared in the *Sun* 29 times and the 'Loony Left' ten times between January 2002 and May 2003. The broadsheet the *Daily Telegraph* referred to 'Red Ken' 31 times and the 'Loony Left' seven times, while the London *Evening Standard* referred to the 'Loony Left' 14 times. For detailed research findings on this topic, see *Culture Wars: The Media & the British Left* (UK: Edinburgh University Press, 2005) by James Curran, Ivor Gaber and Julian Petley.

Lord Chamberlain (UK) Until they were abolished in 1968 the powers of the Lord Chamberlain to censor plays in the British theatre went back as far as the reign of James I, though such powers were not defined by statute until 1737. All plays, except those performed by theatre clubs, were obliged to obtain a licence from the Lord Chamberlain's office. Each script was vetted for bad language, subversive ideas and any criticism of monarchy, Parliament, the Church, etc.

In 1967 a Joint Committee on Censorship of the Theatre was set up by government. This recommended freedom for the stage 'subject to the overriding requirements of the criminal law' and that managements and dramatists should be protected from 'frivolous or arbitrary' prosecutions. These recommendations formed the basis of Labour MP George Strauss's private member's bill, which became law, liberating the theatre from the Lord Chamberlain in the Theatres Act of September 1968.

Lowbrow See HIGHBROW.

LP See GRAMOPHONE.

→ **M**

MacBride Commission International Commission for the Study of Communication Problems under the chairmanship of Sean MacBride, former secretary general of the International Commission of Jurists, to hear, distil and report on evidence submitted with regard to media information interaction between the western and 'Third World' countries. In particular, the Commission was to report on the impact of western media technology, and the subsequent flow of western-orientated information, upon developing nations.

Set up by the United Nations Educational, Scientific and Cultural Organization (UNESCO) in 1978 with a committee of 'fifteen wise men and one woman', including Colombian novelist Gabriel García Márquez and Canadian media guru Marshall McLuhan, the Commission produced a 484-page report in 1980.

This urged a strengthening of Third World independence in the field of information gathering and transmission, and measures to defend national cultures against the formidable one-way flow of information and entertainment from western capitalist nations, chiefly the US. Faced with the antipathy and resistance of such nations, the Commission's recommendations, and its vision of a NEW WORLD INFORMATION ORDER were left dead in the water. See CHAPULTEPEC DECLARATION, 1994; INFORMATION GAPS; MEDIA IMPERIALISM; TALLOIRES DECLARATION, 1981; YAMOUSOUKROU DECLARATION. See also *TOPIC GUIDE* under GLOBAL PERSPECTIVES.

Machinery of representation In modern societies, the various forms of mass media have been named the 'machinery of representation' by Professor Stuart Hall in his chapter on media power and class power in *Bending Reality: The State of the Media* (UK: Pluto Press, 1986), edited by James Curran, Jake Ecclestone, Giles Oakley and Alan Richardson. Hall writes of the 'whole process of reporting and construction' through which reality is translated into media forms – forms that the AUDIENCE is expected to recognize as reality.

Yet reality, argues Hall, is not simply transcribed in 'great unassimilated lumps through our daily dose of newspapers or our nightly diet of television': 'They all work using language, words, text, pictures, still or moving; combining in different ways through the practices and techniques of selection, editing, montage, design, layout, format, linkage, narrative, openings, closures – to represent the world to us.'

The media exercise 'the power to represent the world in certain ways. And because there are many different and conflicting ways in which meaning about the world can be constructed, it matters profoundly what and who gets represented, what and who regularly and routinely gets left out; and how things, people, events, relationships are represented.' See DISCURSIVE GAP; HEGEMONY; LEGITIMATION/DELEGITIMATION; POWER ELITE; PREFERRED READING.

Magnum International cooperative agency of photo-journalists, formed in 1947. Among its early members were Henri Cartier-Bresson, Robert Capa, Marc Bresson and Inge Morath. Magnum's objectives have been: top-quality photography, independence, objectivity and control – by the members – over the use of their pictures.

* William Manchester, *In Our Time: The World as Seen by Magnum Photographers* (UK: Andre Deutsch, 1989).

Mainstreaming Professor George Gerbner and a team of researchers at the Annenberg School of Communications, University of Pennsylvania, conducted a massive and ongoing research project throughout the 1980s on the impact of television on cultural attitudes and attitude formation. A process is identified that Gerbner calls *mainstreaming*, whereby television creates a coming-together, a CONVERGENCE of attitude among viewers. In their article, 'The "mainstreaming" of America: violence profile No. 11' in *Journal of Communication* (Summer, 1980), Gerbner, Larry Gross, Michael Morgan and Nancy Signorielli write, 'In particular, heavy viewing may serve to cultivate beliefs of otherwise disparate and divergent groups towards a more homogeneous "mainstream" view.'

The authors' opinion is that TV's images 'cultivate the dominant tendencies of our culture's beliefs, ideologies, and world views' and that the 'size' of an 'effect' is far less critical 'than the direction of its steady contribution'. The light viewer is more likely to hold divergent views and the heavy viewer more convergent views: 'For heavy viewers, television virtually monopolizes and subsumes other sources of information, ideas and consciousness.' Convergence in this sense is to the world as shown on television.

Returning to this theme in an article for the American magazine *Et cetera* (Spring 1987), Gerbner writes, in 'Television's populist brew: the three Bs', 'The most striking political difference between light and heavy viewers in most groups is the collapse of the liberal position as the one most likely to diverge from and challenge traditional assumptions.' The three *Bs* referred to in Gerbner's article are the processes by which television brings about mainstreaming. First, television *blurs* traditional social distinctions; second, it *blends* otherwise divergent groups into the mainstream and, third, it *bends* 'the mainstream in the direction of the medium's interests in profit, populist politics, and power'.

In a study conducted in the UK in 1987, researchers from the Portsmouth Media Research Group, Anthony Piepe, Peter Charlton and Judy Morey (see their article 'Politics and television viewing in England: hegemony or pluralism?' in the Winter 1990 edition of the *Journal of Communication*) found that British television 'does not cultivate a single mainstream around which a heterogenous audience converges', as in the US, but that it contains two message systems and constructs two audiences: that for essentially news-related programmes, which keep pluralist options open, and that for soaps which do, the researchers confirm, hasten a mainstreaming tendency, particularly when heavy viewing is involved.

In 1994 a study of TV influence on political attitudes in Italy was published by Luca Ricolfi of the University of Turin. According to his findings, summarized in 'Elections and mass media. How many votes has television moved?' (*Il Mulino* 356), TV, public and commercial, had influenced 10 per cent of the Italian electorate and the commercial channels had significantly assisted the shift of voters from the Left and Centre to the Right. See CULTIVATION; CULTIVATION DIFFERENTIAL; EFFECTS OF THE MASS MEDIA; GLASGOW UNIVERSITY MEDIA GROUP; MACHINERY OF REPRESENTATION; MEAN WORLD SYNDROME; RESONANCE; SHOWBUSINESS, AGE OF; VIOLENCE ON TV: THE DEFENCE.

Male-as-norm In her introduction to *Man Made Language* (UK: Routledge & Kegan Paul, 1980) Dale Spender says, 'One semantic rule which we can see in operation in the language is that of the male-as-norm. At the onset it may appear to be a relatively innocuous rule for classifying the objects and events of the world, but closer examination exposes it as one of the most pervasive and pernicious rules that has been encoded.'

The rules of society are man-made and so, Spender argues, is the language we use – the 'edification of male supremacy'. Thus women are allotted a *negative semantic space*, illustrated by the way women are often referred to when they occupy a role traditionally the preserve of men. Suzanne Romaine in *Language and Society: An Introduction to Sociolinguistics* (UK: Oxford University Press, 2000) comments that in the British National Corpus of 1995 'I found the following usages: *lady* doctor (125 times), *woman* doctor (20 times), *female* doctor (10 times), compared to *male* doctor (14 times)'. Other terms used for male-as-norm in relation to language are *androcentralism* (male centred) and *masculist*, as well as *patriarchal*. See *TOPIC GUIDE* under GENDER MATTERS.

Maletzke's model of the mass communication process, 1963 What is so useful about the model constructed by German Maletzke and presented in *The Psychology of Mass Communications* (West Germany: Verlag Hans Bredow-Institut, 1963) is the comprehensiveness of the factors operating upon the participants in the mass communication process and at the same time of the complex interaction of such factors.

The SELF-IMAGE of the communicator corresponds with that of the receiver: both act upon and are influenced by the message which is itself constrained by the dictates of the medium chosen. To add to the complexity, the message is influenced by the communicator's image of the receiver and the receiver's image of the communicator. Maltetzke's is a model suggesting that in the communication process many shoulders are being looked over: the more shoulders, the more compromises, the more adjustments.

Thus not only is the communicator taking into due regard the medium and the nature of AUDIENCE, and perceiving these things through the filter of self-image and personality structure, he or she is also keenly responsive to other factors – the communication team, with its own special set of values (see NEWS VALUES) and professional practices. Beyond the team, there is the organization which in turn has to look over its shoulder towards government or the general public (see IMPARTIALITY).

Just as the communicator is a member of a team within an organizational environment, so the receiver is part of a larger context of reception: he or she is subject to influences other than the media message. Those influences may start in the living room of a family home, and the influencers might be the viewer's or reader's family, but there are contextual influences beyond that in the pub, at work, in the community.

Maletzke's model provides students of the media with a structure for analysis. By its complexity, by suggesting an almost limitless interaction of variables, it also indicates the enormous difficulty faced by research into the EFFECTS OF THE MASS MEDIA. As Denis McQuail and Sven Windahl say in *Communication Models for the Study of Mass Communication* (UK: Longman, 5th impression, 1998), 'This complexity is, no doubt, an important reason why mass communication research has been fairly unsuccessful in explaining

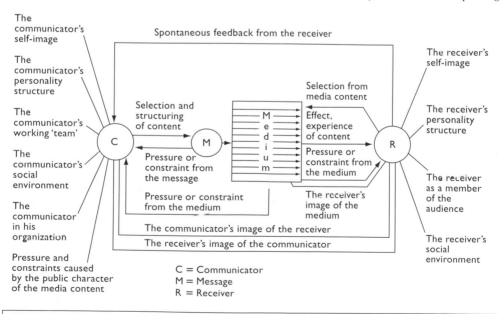

Maletzke's model of the mass communication process, 1963

and predicting outcomes of the mass communication process.' See *TOPIC GUIDE* under COMMUNICATION MODELS.

Manufacture of consent See CONSENT, MANUFACTURE OF.

March of Time Famous US newsreel series of the 1930s, and a classic example of media interaction. Roy Larsen, one of Henry Luce's aides on *Time* magazine, had arranged to have items from the magazine broadcast on RADIO, and these newscasts became so popular among listeners that they were developed into a network programme, *The March of Time*. One attraction was that the programme dramatized the news; actors played 'memorable scenes from the news of the week'.

In 1934, Louis de Rochement, under Larsen's supervision, adapted the radio format to film which, after early uncertainties, made a notable impact. The monthly film panoramas of American and international events alerted the public to the growing menace of Fascism. They carried an Academy award-winning report on life inside Nazi Germany (1938) and an even more powerful one on refugees. In 1935, 432 US cinemas were showing the *March of Time*, with its famous end-of-programme words 'Time ... marches on!' and by 1939 the number had trebled. The series continued until 1953. See DOCUMENTARY. See also *TOPIC GUIDE* under MEDIA HISTORY.

Marginality See DISPLACEMENT EFFECT.

Marketing Defined on the Chartered Institute of Marketing (UK) website (2005) as 'the management process responsible for identifying, anticipating and satisfying customer requirements profitably'. It goes on to state that, 'The central premise of marketing is that in order to be successful, and effectively satisfy customers, there are certain marketing fundamentals that you need to address.' These have been called the *Ps* of marketing: (1) the *product* or service must satisfy customer needs; (2) the *price* should be competitive and appropriate to the quality of the product and customers' pockets; (3) there will need to be effective *promotion* of the product or service to customers. It is here that the appropriate employment of a range of communication strategies and activities is vital. A promotional strategy may involve ADVERTISING, PUBLIC RELATIONS, sales promotion, personal selling and direct marketing activities.

(4) The product or service must be available in the right *place*, at the right time. Similarly, any promotional communication with the customer must be accurately located. (5) *People* are also a key element of the marketing process. All those who deal with the customer have the potential to influence the customer's perception of the product or service. Thus, the CIM argues, 'This means that they must be appropriately trained, well motivated and the right type of person.' Good INTERPERSONAL COMMUNICATION skills are crucial here.

(6) The *process* of marketing involves a myriad of activities, many of them communication activities, focused on delivery of the product or service to the satisfaction of the customer. (7) It is also important to provide customers with *physical evidence* that reflects the benefits and quality of the product given that they are not able to experience the product in advance.

The Ps need to be appropriately considered, with reference to the product, service and consumers, but 'together they form the basis for any marketing plan'. According to the CIM the first five of these Ps are important for the marketing of a product and all are important to the marketing of a service. Four of these Ps – Price, Product, Place, Promotion – are often described as being at the core of the marketing mix.

Frances Brassington and Stephen Pettitt in *Essentials of Marketing* (US/UK: Prentice Hall, 2005) discuss the rise of a contemporary approach to marketing known as *relationship marketing* – one that focuses on building the relationship between buyer and seller. This is typical of marketing activity in the business-to-business sector where 'the importance of enduring buyer–seller relationships as a major influence on decision-making' has been acknowledged. It is also increasingly used in other sectors. New technology has facilitated direct communication with individual consumers, the building of closer relationships with the ordinary customer and the nurturing of consumer loyalty.

Brassington and Pettitt further point out, 'Although relationship marketing over time focuses on customers' needs and attitudes as important points of concern, it can also embrace social and ethical concerns ...'. This may be the case especially where an organization has developed a Corporate Social Responsibility programme. A number of organizations have such programmes as a means of enhancing their reputation with both consumers and the wider national and international community. In part such programmes reflect a growing awareness that a significant number of consumers are concerned about the ethical behaviour, or otherwise, of companies. See CULTURE: CONSUMER CULTURE; MARKET RESEARCH; PEST; SWOT.

Marketing mix See MARKETING.

Market liberalism IDEOLOGY dominant in western countries, adopted worldwide after the fall of Soviet communism as a normative way of state, industrial and commercial governance; its key principle – *leave to market forces*. It is essentially the same as *capitalism* where all attempts to restrict free enterprise by state control or regulation are generally perceived to be ill-judged, an interference with the 'natural order of things'. Ownership of the means of production is essentially private: the 'public' denomination of private corporations has nothing to do with the public, rather, it denotes shareholding by other 'public' bodies and private individuals. Out of market liberalism has sprung the concept of the free press; policies urging PRIVATIZATION of all mass communication; and DEREGULATION.

John Keane in *The Media and Democracy* (UK: Polity Press, 1991) says that many market liberals 'love to talk of the need for a free communications market without censorship'. However, 'they are ... unsympathetic or hostile to citizens' attempts to extend the role of law, to reduce the arbitrariness and secrecy of political power'. Thus two competing principles are at work. The 'free market' process coexists within 'a powerful, authoritative state which acts as an overlord of the market'. This amounts to a position where there is liberty for some but not necessarily for all.

Keane believes market liberalism 'succours the old doctrine of sovereignty of the state – permission for the state to defend itself by any means should it feel threatened, including controlling and regulating the liberties of the public'. Should there at the same time appear to be a threat to the free market, then the free market will collude with the state in seeking out and identifying 'enemies of the state'. Private-sector media, in particular the PRESS, will have taken on the role of GUARD DOG. See COMMERCIAL LAISSEZ-FAIRE MODEL OF (MEDIA) COMMUNICATION; KUUKI; HEGEMONY.

Market research A term that covers the wide range of research activities that may be undertaken to investigate aspects of an existing or potential market. It may have a number of aims: for example, to discover whether there is a need for a proposed new service, to ascertain consumers' views on the need to modify an existing product, to test out ideas for promotional activities or to evaluate responses to a CAMPAIGN. With regard to its use in marketing activities, Brassington and Pettitt in *Essentials of Marketing* (US/UK: Prentice Hall, 2005) comment, 'Decisions on product range, packaging, pricing and promotion will all arise from a well-understood profile of the different types of need in the market' – it is the role of market research to help construct such profiles. Typical research methods include observational techniques, QUESTIONNAIRES, INTERVIEWS and FOCUS GROUPS. See CONSUMPTION BEHAVIOUR; SAMPLING; SEGMENTATION.

Market threshold Decisions on media production – whether to initiate, go ahead or continue with media enterprises – depend more and more on whether there is a sufficiently large percentage of consumers to warrant investment. The market threshold is the critical point at which a media artefact justifies, financially, its existence; and the greater the competition within the market, the more critical that threshold becomes. See PRODUCER CHOICE.

Marxist (mode of media analysis) Focuses on social conflict which is seen as being essentially derived from the mode of production in capitalist societies. Karl Marx argued that the CULTURE – and communication process – of a capitalist society reflects the NORMS and VALUES of that section of the community which owns the means of production: out of the dominant CLASS springs the dominant IDEOLOGY which the media serve to disseminate and reinforce in the 'disguise' of CONSENSUS.

Marxist analysts have employed three main strategies of research (also used by other, non-Marxist commentators): *structuralist, political/economic* and *culturalist*. The structuralist approach examines the ideology embodied in media content, concentrating on 'text' and the source of the ideology. The political/economic approach investigates the location of media power within economic processes, and the structure of media production. The culturalist approach commences from the standpoint that all societies are made up of a rich variety of group cultures, but seeks to indicate that some groups, therefore some cultures, receive a disproportionate representation in the media in the process of shaping and defining consensus and obscuring the roots of genuine conflict. See FUNCTIONALIST/SOCIAL ACTION (MODES OF MEDIA ANALYSIS); MACHINERY OF REPRESENTATION. See also *TOPIC GUIDE* under RESEARCH METHODS.

operate at individual or group level, like graffiti, through DRESS, song or even bumper stickers; they have expressed themselves through pamphlets, newspapers, novels, comics, street theatre, performance art and – not least in impact – PORNOGRAPHY.

Protesting at the disappearances of their loved ones in Argentina, the Mothers of the Plaza De Mayo communicated their message through *assembly*, wearing diapers as headscarves and carrying placards bearing the dates on which their loved ones were last seen alive: eventually images of their courage and resolution were transmitted around the world.

The INTERNET has been seen as potentially the most effective mode of alternative media, by its reach and accessibility and its interactive power. However, the risk of being colonized by the 'usual suspects', big business and government, through commercialization and legal restraint, has diminished optimism that struggles for justice and equality can be fought online. See NEW MEDIA; UNDERGROUND PRESS; WIKI, WIKIPEDIA.

* John D.H. Downing, *Radical Media: Rebellious Communication and Social Movements* (US/UK: Sage, 2001).

Media control Four categories of media control are generally recognized: *Authoritarian*; *Paternal*; *Commercial* and *Democratic*. They can apply to an individual communications system, such as ownership of a newspaper, or to a state pattern of control. The first indicates a total monopoly of the means of communication and control over what is expressed. The second is what Raymond Williams in *Communication* (UK: Pelican, 1966) terms 'authoritarianism with a conscience', that is, authority with VALUES and purposes beyond those concerning the maintenance of its own power. The third relates to control by market forces: anything can be said provided that you can afford to say it and that you can say it profitably.

Democratic control is the rarest category, implying active involvement in decisions by the workforce and, indeed, the readership or audience. Control works at different levels – at the *operational* level (editors, producers, etc.), at the *allocative* level (of funds, personnel, etc.) and at the *external* level (government, advertisers, consumers).

Trends in media control have been towards greater concentration of ownership; towards ownership by CONGLOMERATE organizations and subsequently a series of ever-diversifying control NETWORKS in which international finance has fingers in practically every communications pie, from newspapers to cinema, from records to satellites. Running parallel with these trends has been the development of multi-marketing of media products – books, films, TV series, video cassettes – with such products being packaged for worldwide consumption; audience maximization, and therefore profit maximization being the most important driving force. See GLOBAL MEDIA SYSTEM: THE MAIN PLAYERS; NEW MEDIA; NORMATIVE THEORIES OF MASS MEDIA; WORLD TRADE ORGANIZATION (WTO) TELECOMMUNICATIONS AGREEMENT, 1997. See also *TOPIC GUIDE* under MEDIA: OWNERSHIP & CONTROL.

Mediacy Term first given public prominence at the 1983 British Association conference by Michael Weiss and Carol Lorac of the Communication and Social Skills Project at Brighton Polytechnic. Deemed as important, in the education curriculum of the future, as literacy and numeracy are today, mediacy is defined by Weiss and Lorac as 'the ability to understand and manipulate recorded sound and vision. Information technology and video are the machinery of mediacy: its pen and paper.'

Media effects See EFFECTS OF THE MASS MEDIA.

Media: hot and cold See HOT MEDIA, COLD MEDIA.

Media imperialism Term used to describe the role western capitalist media play in dominating 'Third World' developing countries through communication systems.

Crucial to the notion of media or *cultural* imperialism is the understanding of the relationship between economic, territorial, cultural and informational factors. In the age of western economic colonialism in the nineteenth century the flow of information was a vital process of growth and reinforcement. Where the trade went, so followed developing media practice and technology, reflecting the VALUES and assumptions of those who owned and manned the service.

As developing countries reached independence much concern was felt at the degree of penetration by western media. In 1972, the General Conference of the United Nations Educational, Scientific and Cultural Organization (UNESCO) drew attention to the way the media of the richer sections of the world were a means towards 'the domination of world public opinion or a source of moral and cultural pollution'. Since then the movement towards a NEW WORLD INFORMATION ORDER has grown in vigour and strength.

In 1973, in Algiers, a meeting of heads of state of non-aligned countries agreed to take concerted action to promote a fairer, more balanced exchange of information among themselves and release themselves from dependence upon the exports of the richer nations, demanding the 'reorganization of existing communication channels which are the legacy of the colonial past ...'. By 1978, the UNESCO General Council agreed its new *Declaration on Mass Media* emphasizing the 'balanced' aspect of a concept of information based on the principle of 'free and balanced flow'.

Developing countries have long held a heart-felt belief that western agencies report only the bad news of what happens in their countries and that this bad news – based upon what Anthony Smith in his book *The Geopolitics of Information* (UK: Faber, 1980) terms 'aberrational' criteria for news selection – causes serious harm, especially when such countries are in need of western financial support and investment.

One proponent of the imperialist thesis, Herbert Schiller, writing in the late 1960s, saw American television exports as part of an attempt by the American military industrial complex 'to subjugate the world'. He argued that the declining European empires had been replaced by an emergent US empire; one arm of this empire being the US-based, transnational communications industries which Schiller saw as working in collaboration with western (predominantly US) political and military interests.

These communications industries were for the most part funded privately by advertising revenue and were thus extensively tied to commercial interests. The cultural artefacts exported, mainly from the US, to other countries were seen as promoting the values of consumer capitalism. As such they could be seen as either reinforcing these values where they already existed, as for example in western European countries, or as undermining traditional values and supplanting them with those of consumer capitalism in countries, such as Third World countries, where capitalist modes of production were non-existent or less developed. It was, for Schiller, a means by which the US could encourage, among other things, demand for its own products.

Schiller's thesis has met with some criticism. John B. Thompson in *The Media and Modernity* (UK: Polity Press, 1995), for example, argues that it overlooks the *multipolar* nature of the global economy in which Europe, Japan and South-East Asia have played an increasingly important role; the growing foreign investment in US communications such as that of Sony in Columbia, Tristar and CBS records; and the importance of other exporters of cultural artefacts such as Britain, Australia, Mexico, Brazil and India as regional producers.

Thompson believes that 'it would be quite implausible to suggest that this complex and shifting field of global power relations could be analyzed in terms of the thesis of cultural imperialism. The thesis is simply too rigid and one-dimensional to do justice to a global situation which is in considerable flux'.

Further, argues Thompson, the thesis tends to overlook the fact that whilst messages may be diffused on a global scale, many factors within the locale of their reception can affect the way in which they are *appropriated* by the audience. Both senders and receivers contribute to the construction of their meaning. Tamar Liebes and Elihu Katz, for example, in their classic study of audience reception of episodes of *Dallas*, the American SOAP OPERA, *The Export of Meaning: Cross-cultural Readings of 'Dallas'* (UK: Polity Press, 1993), demonstrate the impact cultural variables can have on the reading of television texts.

Schiller, in later writings, acknowledged these criticisms yet maintained that global domination by US culture has not significantly declined. Whatever the criticisms of the media imperialism thesis, the concentration of symbolic power mainly in the US as a result of the ongoing process of GLOBALIZATION of ownership within the media and cultural industries cannot be denied.

What is not in dispute are inequalities of wealth and therefore of cultural and media provision between so-called core nations and peripheral nations (see CORE NATIONS, PERIPHERAL NATIONS) and the serious and ongoing INFORMATION GAPS between them; gaps which are unlikely to be bridged until the *structures* of deprivation are removed.

It is not only the inequalities in the distribution of information which cause concern but the *flow* of that communication. Cees Hamelink in *World Communication: Disempowerment and Self Empowerment* (UK: Zed Books, 1995) says: 'Information flows across the globe are imbalanced, since most of the world's information moves among the countries in the North, less between the North and the South, and very little flows among the countries of the South' and this 'differential access to the management of information has put the developing countries at a serious disadvantage in the world political-economy.' This situation 'compromises their national sovereignty' and in so far as developing nations have increased 'their import capacity for communication technology, they have become more dependent upon the economic forces of the North'. See CONVERGENCE; GLOBAL MEDIA SYSTEM: THE MAIN PLAYERS; INTERNATIONAL FEDERATION OF JOURNALISTS (IFJ); MACBRIDE COMMISSION; NEWS AGENCIES; NEWS AID?; NEWS VALUES; NON-ALIGNED NEWS POOL; TALLOIRES DECLARATION; WORLD PRESS FREEDOM COMMITTEE. See also *TOPIC GUIDE* under GLOBAL PERSPECTIVES; MEDIA ISSUES & DEBATES; MEDIA: OWNERSHIP & CONTROL.

* Jonathan Benthall, *Disasters, Relief and the Media* (US: I.B. Tauris, 1995); James Lull, *Media, Communication, Culture: A Global Approach* (UK: Polity Press, 1995); Edward S. Herman and R.W. Chesney, *The Global Media: The New Missionaries of Corporate Capitalization* (UK/US: Cassell, 1997); George Monbiot, *The Capitalist State: the Corporate Takeover of Britain* (UK: Macmillan, 2001); Tehri Rantanen, *The Media and Globalization* (UK/US: Sage, 2004).

Media moguls: four sources of concern   The issue of global media ambitions on the part of transnational corporations (TNCs) prompts debate between those alarmed by the CONVERGENCE of ownership across the world, and others who accept its inevitability while at the same time arguing that 'media moguls' are not as all-powerful, or their progress as inevitable, as some commentators believe.

Such a debate was conducted on the openDemocracy website (www.opendemocracy.net) by analysts on both sides of the Atlantic. One contributor to this debate is James Curran who, in an online article, 'Global media concentration: shifting the argument' (23 May 2002) discussed what he perceives as four sources of concern in relation to what he sees as a 'pattern of domination'. First, Curran believes that 'the private concentration of symbolic power potentially distorts the democratic process'. He cites the example of Italian media mogul Silvio Berlusconi whose media empire helped catapult him 'into the premiership of Italy without having any experience of democratic office ... Berlusconi would not be ruling Italy now if he did not dominate a massive media empire that enabled him to manufacture a political party.'

The second concern 'is that the power potentially at the disposal of media moguls tends to be exerted in a one-sided way', usually rightist and consumerist-orientated. Curran refers to Rupert Murdoch, who 'may have presided over the subversive *Simpsons* but he is also the man who bullied his British journalists to follow a right-wing agenda ... part of a more general pattern in which shareholder interventions sometimes advance conservative or market-friendly positions, but more rarely their antithesis'.

Curran's third concern is that 'the concentration of market power can stifle competition'. He believes that a 'fundamental reason for the long-standing deficiencies of the British national press ... is that it has been controlled so long by an oligopoly'. Leading on from this is the fourth concern, a 'one-sided protection of our freedoms'; on the one hand 'a state of constant alert against the abuse of state power over media, reflected in the development of numerous safeguards', yet on the other hand 'not matched by an equivalent vigilance and set of safeguards directed against the abuse of shareholder power over the media'.

In other words, in the conflict between media power and public interest the latter is likely to lose out. One consequence of what Curran describes as 'the current quiescence' (in the face of the media's assertion of its own freedoms) 'is that media conglomerates have been able to persuade governments around the world to ease monopoly controls'. See BERLUSCONI PHENOMENON; CROSS-MEDIA OWNERSHIP; GLOBALIZATION OF MEDIA; GLOBAL MEDIA SYSTEM: THE MAIN PLAYERS; MURDOCH EFFECT; REGULATORY FAVOURS. See also *TOPIC GUIDE* under MEDIA: OWNERSHIP & CONTROL.

Media-Most   Media empire in Russia after the fall of Communism and the shift in that country towards a capitalist and democratic system. The 'Rupert Murdoch' of Media-Most was Vladimir Gosinsky whose independence, and indeed criticism, of the state government under Vladimir Putin led to the group's destruction and dismemberment. 'Through the selective application of tax and criminal law,' writes Jonathan Becker in 'Lessons from Russia: a neo-authoritarian media system' in the *European Journal of Communication* (June 2004), 'including the invasion of Media-Most premises by hooded and heavily armed tax police, the direct pressure of the Ministry of Press, Radio and Television and boardroom intrigue, Media-Most collapsed.' In Becker's view, 'The timing, form and tenacity of government actions sent a chill through non-state media, contributing to uncertainty and, no doubt, self-censorship.' See CENSORSHIP.

Media: new media See NEW MEDIA.

Media research centres See RESEARCH CENTRES.

Media species Classification of the public in terms of their attitudes to ADVERTISING. A 1997 report drawn from research by CIA Medialab in the UK defines the following public 'species': *cynics, acquiescents, enthusiasts* and *ambivalents*. The research arm of CIA Medianetwork, Medialab, conducted an 18-month survey using nationally representative focus groups; 25 per cent of these, named cynics, resent the intrusion of national ads and feel strongly about the capacity of advertisements to subvert. Acquiescents are better news for adworld. Comprising 21 per cent of the survey findings, they are easy-going, and they approve of ads that are funny, colourful and vivid. They do not care for national newspaper ads, or direct mail, which makes acquiescents feel vulnerable. Enthusiasts make up 35 per cent of respondents. They too seem unimpressed by national newspaper ads, but they enjoy TV commercials, often more than the programmes they accompany. The ambivalents are seen to be a rather inert band, resistant through being uninterested, and they take a fatalistic attitude to the effects/dangers of advertising. See VALS TYPOLOGY. See also *TOPIC GUIDE* under ADVERTISING/MARKETING.

Mediasphere Term posed and defined by John Hartley in *Popular Reality: Journalism, Modernity, Popular Culture* (UK: Arnold, 1996) to describe the positioning of media, its range and breadth of influence, in relationship to the PUBLIC SPHERE, and the notion of the *Semiosphere* put forward by Yuri Lotman in *The Universe of the Mind: A Semiotic Theory of Culture* (US: University of Indiana Press, 1990). Hartley sees the semiosphere – the sphere of cultural expression and cultural MEANING – as being in a constant process of interaction with the mediasphere and public sphere. He images the relationship as resembling Russian dolls: the public sphere fits within the mediasphere which in turn fits within the semiosphere.

The most salient feature of these interlocking spheres, argues Hartley, is JOURNALISM. It was journalism that originated and nurtured concepts of freedom, of human rights, within societies. It served a key function in, and in turn was served by, the success of the American and French revolutions. The public sphere of the nineteenth century was created by journalism. Hartley believes 'there would be no public' and consequently no progress towards the sovereignty of the people without the aid of journalistic writing. This served, and continues to serve, as a counterforce to subordination. Indeed it is 'the mechanism for making these [democratic] discourses generally available, and also for articulating the different forms of resistance'.

Ultimately, though, journalism's power to define and further the public sphere depends on readership. The changing nature of readership also alters the nature of the public and private spheres. Hartley believes that we have moved from the traditional *adversarial* mode of journalism, with its public, political and masculine bias, to a POSTMODERNIST phase, driven in particular by popular journalism (described by Hartley as 'the textual system of modernity').

This gives emphasis not to public life 'but to private meaning'. He identifies the following shifts in the nature of readership: from male to female, from old to young, from militant to meditative, from public to private, from governmental to consumerist and from law-making to identity-forming. Hartley describes the mediasphere as 'suffused with images and issues which connect popular readerships and popular meanings together ... the mainstream of contemporary journalism is fashion, gossip, lifestyle, consumerism and celebrity, and "news" is private, visual, narrativized and personalized'. It follows that the icon of the contemporary mediasphere is 'not the superpower but the supermodel'.

The shifts mentioned here are not, however, to be seen as having become disengaged from the past of journalism/readership: modern journalism is populist, yes. Yet it remains in the tradition of the radical journalism that helped give birth to the American and French revolutions. See DEMOCRACY AND THE MEDIA.

Media technology See *TOPIC GUIDE* under MEDIA: TECHNOLOGIES.

Media theory: purpose and uses In his Introduction to *Understanding Media Theory* (UK: Arnold, 2003), Kevin Williams says that the purposes of media theory are fourfold: to answer the question 'What is going on?'; to explain how and why; to suggest what might happen next and, taking prediction into account, to serve as a guide to future behaviour and performance. He identifies three *levels* of theory, each of which interacts with, influences and is influenced by the others in the contexts where communication takes place.

There is *commonsense theory* in which 'people have implicit understandings or ideas with which they make sense of the media'. Such a theoretical level is important because of the role it plays in public debate on the media, though often leading 'to simplistic portrayals of the role and influence of the media'. *Practitioner theory* relates to the ideas media practitioners have about their world. It is also referred to as *operational theory*, covering 'the accumulated practical wisdom found in most organizational and professional settings'.

Academic theory – the primary focus of Williams' book, and indeed of the study of media from GCSE and A-level to degree work and beyond – is what occupies scholarship, and as far as media study is concerned, involves a broad range of academic fields, including, as Williams lists them, sociology, psychology, social psychology, literary studies, anthropology, sociolinguistics, economics, political science, philosophy, history, law, rhetoric and speech communication, group and systems theory, 'and even mathematics'.

In the light of this diversity, says Williams, 'it is not surprising that there are conflicts over the assumptions, foci and methods of analysis in the field and that contradictory hypotheses and theories are put forward'. This, of course, is part of the fascination – indeed the open-endedness – of the study of media. Theories must be examined and re-examined, subjected to close and insistent scrutiny; in other words tested in terms of relevance and reliability, and it must not be seen as something 'detached from the day-to-day issues of ordinary men and women'.

Theory 'guides research by helping scholars organize how they gather facts and observe the world. But good theory should also help us to understand and make sense of our personal experience and the wider structures and processes of daily life, and how they shape our interaction with other people'. For Williams, the ultimate test of any theory 'is the extent to which it furthers our understanding of the world we live in'. As well as assisting us to develop our knowledge of mass media, theory helps us 'challenge the misleading ideas that have come to dominate public debate about their influence and involvement'.

In terms of subject interest, theory focuses in the main on the *production* side of texts, the *texts* themselves (see SEMIOLOGY) and the *reception* of those texts, all within the cultural, political, economic and environmental contexts in which communication takes place. During the early days of media study and research, the 1940s and 1950s, attention centred almost exclusively on the communicators and there was the assumption that what was transmitted was simply received. With the advent of USES AND GRATIFICATIONS THEORY the audience became important and it became plain that audiences put media to many uses, not always the ones intended by the communicators.

At around the same time, in the 1960s and 1970s, textual analysis came into its own (see DENOTATION; CODES; CONNOTATION; SIGNS). *Deconstruction* of texts became a key activity. Eventually interest turned to deconstructing the audience itself, using research methods such as those pioneered in ethnography (see ETHNOGRAPHIC APPROACH TO AUDIENCE MEASUREMENT). Today there is general agreement that to focus on one area of study to the neglect of others is to produce skewed results, and the validity and reliability of theory suffers. Ultimately, however, the purpose of theory can be summed up in one phrase – the search for MEANING. See *TOPIC GUIDE* under COMMUNICATION THEORY.

Mediation Between an EVENT and the reporting or broadcasting of it to an AUDIENCE, mediation occurs, that is, a process of interpretation – shaping, selecting, editing, emphasizing, de-emphasizing – according to the perceptions, expectations and previous experience of those involved in the reporting of the event; and in accordance with the requirements and characteristics of the means of reporting. Between the event of a car accident or a murder and the report of such an event a whole series of inter-mediating actions takes place. The event is translated into words or pictures; it is processed according to the demands of the MEDIUM – for headlines, for good pictures – and pressures such as time, space and contending messages.

Even when, in INTERPERSONAL COMMUNICATION, person A communicates a message to person B, which B conveys to person C, a process of mediation inevitably takes place: B may rephrase the message, give parts of it prominence and understate other parts, supplement or distort the information. Mediation is inescapable: much of our knowledge of life and the world comes to us at second hand, through the mediation of PRESS and TV; our perceptions of events are coloured by the perceptions, preoccupations, VALUES, of the mediators.

However, the *construct* of events is far from a monopoly of the mass media; it is further mediated, and the process modified or altered altogether, by those around us who exert influence – friends, relatives, work colleagues etc. – and other so-called intervening variables such as personal mood, time of day or state of health. See S-IV-R MODEL OF COMMUNICATION.

Mediatization Process whereby political or indeed any public activity, having become reliant for its audience/electorate upon the media for its messages to be communicated, adopts the principles and methods of media communication. In particular TV has become the medium and channel of political communication. Consequently political communication pays greater attention to entertainment value as practised by TV, for example PERSONALIZATION, simplification and an emphasis on using 'media-*genic*' players (see LOOKISM).

In 'Towards a "videocracy"?: Italian political communication at a turning point' in the *European Journal of Communication*, September 1995, Gianpietro Mazzoleni said of the situation in Italy at the time of the 1994 elections, 'The parties are increasingly unable to bring their message to the voters and have to do it by relying on the channels of mass communication. The toll that the parties must pay is the mediatization of their communication activities.' In consequence, media ceases to be the servant to and observer of political parties; and political parties become in thrall to the media, in their grip. Mazzoleni considers this a significant and far-reaching 'metamorphosis', in which the media take on the role of *kingmaker* – a case exemplified when media mogul Silvio Berlusconi, using the power of his own media empire, was, in 2001, elected prime minister of Italy for the second time. See BERLUSCONI PHENOMENON.

Media user ethics See TEN COMMANDMENTS FOR MEDIA CONSUMERS.

Media: uses of media by the young See CHILDREN, YOUNG PEOPLE AND THE CHANGING MEDIA ENVIRONMENT.

Medio communication That mode of communication between direct, face-to-face address and MASS COMMUNICATION; into this classification comes communication by letter, e-mail, fax or telephone.

Medium The physical or technical means of converting a communication message into a signal capable of being transmitted along a given channel. TV for example is a medium that employs the channels of vision and sound. John Fiske in *Introduction to Communication Studies* (UK: Methuen, 1982 and subsequent editions) divides media into three categories as follows. (1) *Presentational* media: the voice, face, body; the spoken word, GESTURE; where the medium is actually the communicator. (2) *Representational* media: books, paintings, photographs, etc., using cultural and aesthetic conventions 'to create a "text" of some sort'; they become independent of the communicator, being *works* of communication (whereas presentational media are *acts* of communication). (3) *Mechanical* media: telephone, radio, TV, film, etc., and they are *transmitters* of 1 and 2. The properties of the medium determine the range of CODES which it can transmit, and considerably affect the nature of the message and its reception.

Medium is the message One of the classic quotes of media literature and perhaps the best-known of Marshall McLuhan (1911–80). The 'medium is the message' is the first chapter heading in *Understanding Media: The Extensions of Man* (UK: Routledge & Kegan Paul, 1964; Routledge, 2002). What is said, McLuhan believes, is deeply conditioned by the MEDIUM through which it is said. The particular attributes of any medium help to determine the MEANING of the communication, and no medium is neutral. See McLUHANISM.

Message That which an act, or work, of communication is *about*. For purposes of definition and analysis it is sometimes necessary to treat the message as something separable from the *process* of communication; but ultimately a message can only meaningfully be examined in the context of other elements all of which are interlinked and interacting.

It is important to distinguish between the actual signal that carries the message and the message itself: a wink is a signal but what is its message? The answer depends on many factors – for example, who is winking, to whom and in what context? (See SIGN.) While message signals, in the form of visual or aural CODES, may be sent, the message may well not be understood. Thus an ambiguous smile may represent the signal that a message is being conveyed, but the receiver may fail to understand the message while recognizing the signal.

The message may draw its initial shape or purpose from the Sender or Communicator: it will be similarly influenced by the nature of the medium in which it is sent. The Receiver of a message may be close at hand, in sight of the Communicator, or some distance away. If the message involves INTRAPERSONAL COMMUNICATION, the Communicator and the Receiver may be one and the same. Both the signal and the intended message may encounter NOISE, that is, physical or psychological interference that will affect its meaningfulness. The message may elicit FEEDBACK which will further modify the message and indeed create a new communication situation and new signals and messages.

Denis McQuail in *Communication* (UK: Longman, 1975) writes that the simplest way of regarding human communication is 'to consider it as the sending from one person to another of meaningful messages'. We can rarely if ever be certain of how other people will interpret our signals, or whether we will 'get our message across'. Thus the message sent may be quite different from the message received, and while we think we are communicating a single message we may, unconsciously, be putting across all sorts of other messages too.

We are selecting in and selecting out a barrage of message-carrying signals all the time. We give attention to them if we are motivated to do so. The effectiveness of a message depends, at a basic, instrumental level, on the weight it carries in competition with other signals and messages but equally it depends upon the significance attached to it by the receivers.

This in turn depends upon the 'set' or preparedness, of the receivers for the Sender/Message/Medium. The message of a satirical cartoon, for example, might be completely lost if the reader knows nothing about the particular circumstances to which the cartoon refers. Even a knowledge of the facts may not be enough to facilitate the intended interpretation, because this may only occur if the reader shares the social, political or cultural values of the cartoonist. In short, whether we 'get our message across' depends partly upon the context in which it is received; and the VALUES, attitudes, perceptions and knowledge of the receiver as a crucial part of that context. See DOMINANT, SUBORDINATE, RADICAL; INTERVENING VARIABLES (IVs); METAMESSAGE; POLYSEMY; PREFERRED READING.

Metamessage The underlying message in a communicative act. This may differ from what on the surface appears to be the message. The metamessage is conveyed both verbally and, often more crucially, non-verbally. The metamessage carries information about the relationships of those involved in an encounter and the attitudes they have towards each other and the topic in question.

The interpretation of the metamessage is usually influenced by the way in which the message is communicated; non-verbal communication thus plays a vital role in the sending and receiving of metamessages. A simple question such as 'May I help you?' asked by someone in a higher-status ROLE, for example, can be interpreted as a friendly gesture or as an accusation of incompetence depending, in part, on the tone of voice adopted.

Metamessages can also help frame a conversation as they assist in defining the nature of the encounter by, for example, establishing the seriousness of the conversation and the relationships of those taking part.

Metaphor A figure of speech or a visual device that works by transporting qualities from one plane of reality to another: 'the camel is the ship of the desert'; 'life for Mary was a bed of roses'. Without metaphor there would be no scope for the development of either visual or verbal language; it would remain clinical and colourless.

Metaphor is not merely an expressive device but an integral part of the function of language as a *definer* as well as a reflector of reality. As a rhetorical device metaphor is central to the way media define reality, structure, maintain and monitor DISCOURSE, uphold (and sometimes challenge) hierarchies, service (and sometimes undermine) HEGEMONY. Metaphor provides us with the pictures by which we envision the world: we define time by metaphor ('time is money'); we view the public as inhabiting a 'space' (see AGORA); we define public argument and debate using metaphors of conflict and the notion of argument as 'war' is built into the CULTURE we inhabit.

Even where peace is being referred to, the media are more than likely to express it in military terms: 'War breaks out over classroom peace plans.' Press language is riddled with the bombast of conflict. Things are axed, chopped, smashed, slashed; knives are constantly out; prime ministers stick to their guns, oppositions are routed.

We use metaphor to define the nature of communication as *transmission* or as *ritual*. We talk of *homo narrens* (see NARRATIVE PARADIGM), casting the human being as the storytelling animal; or, with Erving Goffman, we may use the *dramaturgical* model, the metaphor of life as a stage.

In *An Introductory Guide to Post-Structuralism and Postmodernism* (UK: Harvester Wheatsheaf, 1993), Madan Sarap states that 'metaphors determine to a large extent what we think in any field. Metaphors are not idle flourishes – they shape what we do. They can help make, and defend a world view'. As well as being 'productive of insights and fresh illuminations', metaphors, according to Sarap, 'can encapsulate and put forward proposals for another way of looking at things'. They can serve as agents of change as well as weapons of reinforcement (see STEREOTYPE).

'Through metaphor,' says Sarap, 'we can have increased awareness of alternative possible worlds.' Few contemporary media phenomena have prompted so many and varied metaphors as the INTERNET. Early in its history it was described as an open prairie or a superhighway; in more recent terms, its SURVEILLANCE capacity has earned it the metaphor of electronic eye.

The so-called *mixed metaphor*, beloved of politicians seeking by their RHETORIC to attract media attention, contains in a statement two or more ineptly linked images: 'Lame ducks will be barking up the wrong tree if they think government is going to bail them out every time profits take a hammering.' Though the metaphorical allusions may be all over the place, the statement's underlying IDEOLOGY is, however, crystal clear. See EUPHEMISM; METONYMY; VISIONS OF ORDER.

See also *TOPIC GUIDE* under LANGUAGE/DISCOURSE/NARRATIVE.

Metasignal A signal that makes a comment about a signal, or a set of signals: it directs us to the accurate meaning of the signals. For example, two people appear to exchange blows: is the fight real or make-believe? Their smiling faces form the metasignal which indicates that, at least on the surface, what we are seeing is a play-fight.

Body posture is among the chief metasignals. Equally, *uniform* serves effectively in this capacity. We react differently to the policeman in uniform than we might to the same person in off-duty jeans and T-shirt. Desmond Morris in *Manwatching: A Field Guide to Human Behaviour* (UK: Jonathan Cape, 1977) says that 'in a sense the whole world of entertainment presents a non-stop Metasignal, in the form of the proscenium arch around the stage of a theatre, or the edge of the cinema or TV screen'. Audiences, he believes, can tolerate, and gain entertainment from, films and plays featuring dollops of death and mayhem because of the metasignals that indicate 'this isn't real'. Morris argues that though the actors may aim at maximum reality in their dark deeds, 'no matter how convincing they are, we still carry at the back of our minds (even as we gasp when the knife plunges home) the Metasignal of the "edge" of their stage'.

* Desmond Morris, *People Watching* (UK: Vantage, 2002).

Metonymy A figure of speech in which the thing meant is represented by something that is an attribute of the original. When we talk of the newspaper business, we refer to the press, something that stands for the whole.

As far as images are concerned, the metonym is a selection of one of those available to represent the whole; and from that selection flows our interpretation or understanding of the whole. Thus the selection of a piece of film of young people lounging at a street corner, or strike pickets in combat with the police, acts as the 'trigger of meaning' for the way the teenager or the striker is defined. For this reason, metonyms are powerful conveyors of reality, indeed so powerful that they can come to be accepted as actually being reality, the way things really are.

Micro-myth, macro-myth Philip Schlesinger in *Putting 'Reality' Together. BBC News* (UK: Constable, 1978; Methuen/University Paperback, 1987) examines the BBC news machine at work, and identifies what in his view are two myths entertained by those who work in BBC news: the *micro-myth* that production staff are permitted autonomy within the organization; the *macro-myth*, that the BBC is an independent organization, largely socially unattached. See IMPARTIALITY.

Milieu The social environment of the individual, group, CULTURE or nation.

Milton's paradox On the one hand the English poet John Milton (1608–74) is famous for his stalwart defence of the freedom of expression (see AREOPAGITICA); on the other Milton did not entirely practise what he preached. Dominant in Milton's own life was anti-Catholicism. The paradox arises from the difference between principle and practice: during the period of the Interregnum, 1649–60 (the Commonwealth of Oliver Cromwell) Milton was an official censor, though apologists argue that the poet was less involved in CENSORSHIP than in editing and supervision.

In 'Milton's paradox: the marketplace of ideas in post-Communist Bulgaria', in the *European Journal of Communication*, September 1997, Ekaterina Ognianova and Byron Scott believe that 'in a simplistic way at least, Milton represents a perennial conflict between general beliefs and specific behaviour, between concepts and practice when it comes to the question of how much freedom to permit'.

countries around the world; these agencies do not merely play a major part in establishing the international political agenda, but they have done so now for a hundred years. And for a hundred years they have been the main definers of world "news values", of what sort of things have become news.'

Of special interest to researchers has been the nature of the *flow* of information for which the agencies are responsible, and the degree to which that flow is *mediated*. What has been termed *raw* news flows from the periphery to the centre, but on the way it becomes *cooked* news – constructed according to western production criteria; while the flow of information from the centre is almost invariably cooked – shaped, that is, according to western news values. See EVENT; MEDIA IMPERIALISM; NEW WORLD INFORMATION ORDER; NON-ALIGNED NEWS POOL.

News Aid? Paul Harrison and Robin Palmer use this term in their book *News Out of Africa: Biafra to Band Aid* (UK: Hilary Shipman, 1986) to illustrate the ambivalent relationship between the media's coverage of the dramatic and distressing effects of famine in the 'Third World', particularly Africa. The authors note the media's long-term reticence, in news or current affairs programmes, to participate in a DISCOURSE about the underlying causes of such famine and ways in which famines might be prevented. Such reticence begs the question of whether or not coverage of the effects of famine, however galvanizing of public opinion and action in the short term, really aids finding a solution to the problem.

Indeed some commentators argue that the media's tendency to concentrate reporting of Third World countries around issues of natural disasters or conflict leads to the perpetuation of negative and stereotypical images of Third World citizens. Liam Kane in 'Media Studies and images of the "Third World"', in the Spring 1994 edition of *Media Education*, comments that '"Third World" people tend to be portrayed very negatively, as passive victims of an unexplained poverty'. The consequence, he goes on to argue, is that we can 'easily blame poverty on a combination of "natural disasters" and the supposed ignorance, laziness or backwardness of Asians, Africans, and Latin Americans'.

What are often overlooked are the structural causes of these problems; in both national and international inequalities in the distribution of resources and power. Also undervalued or not reported at all are the resilience and achievement of Third World citizens despite their often formidably adverse circumstances. Another fear is of course that concentration on the symptoms rather than the causes of disasters, like war and famine, may lead ultimately to a dulling of the audience's sensibility to them. See COMPASSION FATIGUE.

News: audience evaluation, six dimensions of In 'Research note: the effects of live television reporting on recall and appreciation of political news' in *European Journal of Communication*, March 2000, Roland Snoeijer, Claes H. de Vreese and Holli A. Semetoko examine 'the evaluative judgment that viewers make of television news'. They pose six *evaluative dimensions*: Credibility, Importance, Involvement, Attractiveness, Immediacy and Comprehensibility.

TV news scores highly in terms of audience belief in its credibility, in part because viewers not only see what is happening, but, as a result of SATELLITE TRANSMISSION, they can see events as they are actually happening. 'The concept of importance,' write the authors, 'refers to the implications or impact that a story is believed to have for society as a whole', viewers taking their cue from 'the importance of a story defined by newsmakers' (see AGENDA-SETTING). Involvement relates to NEWS VALUES and centres around personal likes and dislikes, interests and geographical proximity.

'Information,' consider the authors, 'is found to be attractive if it is vivid, lively and attention grabbing', though perceptions and responses vary in impact, some GROUPS of people 'finding it very attractive, others disturbing', and this dimension, as with credibility, applies to both the content and presentation of the news.

The speed at which TV news can report events – its immediacy – is highly appreciated by the audience for news. Finally, viewers need to believe that 'that they have received the information in a comprehensible way' and the success in this relates to the way news stories are structured and the way they tackle the complexity of events. See NEWS FRAMEWORKS.

News: audience for news The Pew Research Center of the US in a phone survey conducted between April and May 1998 identified six groups of news consumers in America. The results, stated the Center's research report, indicated 'how differently the generations are responding to the information explosion'. The news-consuming groups identified were: (1) the *Mainstream news* audience, deemed to have 'middle-of-the-road' preferences; newspaper readers who also regularly tune in to local and networked TV news shows; (2) the *Basically broadcast* audience, relying primarily for its news on TV; (3) the *Very occasional* audience which 'only follows the news when something major is happening'; (4) the *Constant* audience 'that watches, reads and listens to just about everything – seemingly indiscriminately'; (5) the *Serious news* audience, equally committed but more selective and (6) the *Tabloid* audience which 'rejects broadcast news and favours the *National Enquirer*, tabloid TV and the tell-all talk show'.

'Ironically,' the Pew report states, 'the daily newspaper, the oldest format, is the only news source used regularly by a majority of all groups.' See *TOPIC GUIDE* under AUDIENCES/CONSUMPTION & RECEPTION OF MEDIA.

News consensus See CONSISTENCY.

News elements: breaking, explanatory, deep background In an article 'Public broadcasting: imperfect but essential' posted on the openDemocracy website (www.openDemocracy.net), 26 June 2001, Jean Seaton identifies three central elements of news provision: (1) *Breaking news*, what she describes as 'attention-grabbing top stories that are often visually dramatic ... that attract audiences by virtue of their drama'; (2) *Explanatory* or 'understanding' news – longer-format news programmes such as the UK's Channel 4 early evening news, 'which provides some context to understand headlines and breaking news' and (3) *Deep background* news formats 'that track issues to the root'.

In Seaton's view, examples of the third element 'are rare – that's part of the problem', for she sees, in the light of new technologies, of digital CONVERGENCE and remorseless pressures of competition, the threat of cost-cutting and the undermining of deep background, investigatory JOURNALISM. She considers that 'mainstream broadcast news is wilting under the pressure of the market and is losing intelligence, style, authority and audience'. She argues that 'In a world of globalized corporate power, full scale detailed investigation is essential to provide the public with the truth about what is going on.' See DEREGULATION; NEWS, GLOBALIZATION OF.

News frameworks Consist of a shared set of assumptions by reporters and editors about what is newsworthy. These assumptions influence the selection of items for investigation and reporting and, to some extent, how they will be presented. This set of assumptions also enables journalists and editors to relate news items to an image of society in order to give them MEANING. Thus the framework can provide a 'ready reckoner' for constructing as well as selecting news that allows deadlines to be met. See FRAMING: MEDIA; NEWS VALUES.

News, globalization of Satellite technology coupled with trends in transnational media ownership and control have created global patterns of information transmission characterized by both CONVERGENCE and diversity. TV news services worldwide show marked similarities of content and narrative approach when stories of international dimensions are being reported. In contrast, diversity is maintained when national and local stories are dealt with.

In 'The global newsroom: convergences and diversities in the globalization of television news' in *Communication and Citizenship: Journalism and the Public Sphere* (UK: Routledge, 1991), edited by Peter Dahlgren and Colin Sparks, Michael Gurevitch, Mark R. Levy and Itzhak Roeh write that convergence is in part predicated by the availability, worldwide, of pictures and reinforces what the authors term a measure of 'shared professional culture', a certain 'commonality in news values and news judgments, across all services'.

However, diversity asserts itself in 'lesser items' suggesting 'that this sharing of news values is not complete and that national social and political differences, as well as journalistic norms between nations, also play a part in shaping patterns of news coverage'. Examples are cited of how globally available film footage is actually harnessed to national meanings – same pictures, different reading. This in the opinion of the authors is a practice offering 'an important antidote to "naive universalism" – that is, to the assumption that events reported in the news carry their own meanings, and that the meanings embedded in news stories produced in one country can therefore be generalized to news stories told in other societies'.

Gurevitch *et al.* identify what they call the 'domestication of the foreign': stories from abroad are 'told in ways which render them more familiar, more comprehensive and more compatible for consumption by different national audiences'. TV news then, anchored as it generally tends to be 'in narrative frameworks that are already familiar to and recognizable by news men as well as by audiences situated in particular cultures

Normative theories of mass media Building on an early work by American media analysts G.F. Siebert, T. Peterson and Wilbur Schramm, *Four Theories of the Press* (US: University of Illinois Press, 1956), Denis McQuail posits six normative theories of the mass media. In *Mass Communication Theory: An Introduction* (UK: Sage, 1983), McQuail lists (1) Authoritarian Theory; (2) Free Press Theory; (3) Social Responsibility Theory; (4) Soviet Media Theory; (5) Development Media Theory and (6) Democratic-Participant Theory.

By normative, we mean how the media should be, what is to be expected of them rather than what necessarily happens in practice; and it is out of the political, cultural and economic context that the normative principles arise. Central to the normative theory is the way the media 'behave' in relation to the state, and the dominant expectations that the state has of the role of the media.

The *Authoritarian Theory* thus appertains in a state in which press or BROADCASTING freedoms not only do not exist but are not considered by those in power, or those who support them in power, undesirable even as ideals. What Siebert *et al.* call 'Libertarian theory' McQuail terms the *Free Press Theory*, which is considered the chief legitimating principle for the print media in liberal democracies. Free and public expression is, implies this theory, the best way to arrive at the truth and expose error. It is a principle enshrined in the First Amendment of the American Constitution. This states that 'Congress shall make no law ... abridging the freedom of speech of the press.'

McQuail's analysis of this principle in practice is well worth noting, for he asks searching questions about whose freedom; about monopoly tendencies; about the close identification of notions of freedom with profit and private ownership.

The *Social Responsibility Theory* believes in freedom so long as it is harnessed to responsibility. Independence is desirable only so long as it is reconcilable with an obligation to society. In this sense, the media are perceived as fulfilling a role of public stewardship. They are the WATCHDOGS of the common good against government or private abuse of power or corruption. There is an emphasis on neutrality and balance; most of all, a belief in media accountability to society.

Soviet Media Theory (worth noting even though the Soviet system has passed away) derives from the postulates of Marx, Engels and Lenin. Here, the media serve the interests of the socialist state, the state being an embodiment of all the members of a classless society. Because the media are of the people, they belong to the people. In practice, of course, they belonged to the people's leadership. The tasks of media are to socialize the people into desirable NORMS as defined in Marxist doctrine; to educate, inform, motivate and *mobilize* in the aims and aspirations of a socialist society.

Development Media Theory has a.isen out of special needs in the developing nations of the 'Third World' (see MACBRIDE COMMISSION; MEDIA IMPERIALISM; NEW WORLD INFORMATION ORDER). This theory eschews bad news theory and favours positive reporting on the grounds that for developing nations, often struggling for economic survival in competition with western industrialized countries, reporting of disasters and setbacks can substantially injure the process of nation building.

The *Democratic-Participant Media Theory* emphasizes the individual rights of access, of citizen and minority GROUPS, to the media, in fact the right to *communicate*; to be served by the media according to a more democratic determination of need (see DEMOCRACY AND THE MEDIA). Thus the theory opposes the concentration of ownership and rejects the role of AUDIENCE as tame receiver. Media should be answerable, free of government or big-business intervention, small-scale, interactive and participative (see CAMPAIGN FOR PRESS AND BROADCASTING FREEDOM; COMMUNITY RADIO; RIGHT OF REPLY).

In a later publication, 'Mass media in the public interest: towards a framework of norms for media performance' in *Mass Media and Society*, edited by James Curran and Michael Gurevitch (UK: Edward Arnold, 1991), McQuail re-examines the validity of normative models because 'attempts to formulate consistent "theories" of the press' become increasingly difficult to sustain 'when media technologies and distribution systems are multiplying and when there is less consensus about basic values than in the past'. The dissolution of the Soviet Union is a case in point, though it is arguable that 'Marxist' media theory continues to apply in China and Cuba.

McQuail proffers a set of defining principles by which media performance can be judged, and these relate to community values. He cites the following as Public Communication Values: (1) *freedom*, acquiring its public definition through the independent status of the media, public access to channels and diversity of supply; (2) *equality*, which concerns openness, access and OBJECTIVITY (characterized by neutrality, fairness and truth); and (3) *order*, a classification relating both to order in the sense of solidarity and in the sense of control (the one operating bottom upwards, as it were, the other top downwards).

The principles interrelate, interact and are obviously in constant conflict with one another. McQuail acknowledges 'deep fissures and inconsistencies, depending on how they [the principles] are interpreted'. However, the application of these principles to the changing patterns of media operation provide 'the essential building blocks for a quite comprehensive, flexible and changing "social theory of media", relevant to our times and of practical value in the ever widening circle of public discussion of the role of mass media in society'. See McQUAIL'S ACCOUNTABILITY OF MEDIA MODEL, 1997.

Norms Shared expectations or standards of behaviour within a particular social group or society. Any type of established group will have norms, both peculiar to itself and shared with the wider community. Of those norms widely accepted in a society, some will operate on a high, some on a low CONSENSUS. Any individual's PERCEPTION and interpretation of experience will be influenced by the norms of the social groups and society to which he/she belongs. Individuals generally take such norms for granted. Communication between individuals likewise reflects certain norms, such as those of grammar and style of writing or norms of conduct that guide social INTERACTION.

Norms arise from such interaction between various individuals and social groups. Once developed, they are passed on through SOCIALIZATION to new members. Norms are not static: they are subject to renegotiation. They play a significant part in maintaining the social position of particular groups and individuals and constitute an influential agent of informal social control.

The media, as agents of communication and socialization, are in a position to both reinforce general societal norms and express the norms of certain social groups. In addition, the media have the potential to *shape* expectations of behaviour, particularly with regard to individuals or groups with whom the viewer, listener or reader is unfamiliar. It is this potential that has aroused considerable research interest. See CULTURE; MALE-AS-NORM; VALUES.

Northcliffe revolution New schooling in the late nineteenth century in the UK following the Foster Education Act of 1870 created a rapidly expanding readership of literature and NEWS. Alfred Charles William Harmsworth (1865–1922), later Lord Northcliffe, perhaps the most dynamic and extraordinary of the PRESS BARONS, built a press empire on the new flood-tide of literacy. Creator of the *Daily Mail* (1896) and the *Daily Mirror* (1903), Northcliffe combined a 'popular-educator' emphasis with a marketing sense that was energetic, imaginative, daring and ruthless. Northcliffe represents the fundamental shift towards the exploitation of, and increasing dependence upon, ADVERTISING as a means of newspaper finance.

Publicity was everything. Rivalry between papers, in terms of sensation-seeking and attention-grabbing stunts resembled, as it continues to do today, the Battle of the Titans. Raymond Williams in *The Long Revolution* (UK: Chatto & Windus, 1961) says, 'The true "Northcliffe Revolution" is less an innovation in actual journalism than a radical change in the economic basis of newspapers, tied to the new kind of advertising.' By 1908 Northcliffe's press empire included the *Mail*, the *Mirror*, *The Times*, two Sunday papers (*Observer* and *Dispatch*) and an evening paper (*News*) plus a host of periodicals such as *Tit-Bits* and *Answers* (whose circulation had leapt from 12,000 at its inception to 352,000 two years later).

Though the so-called Northcliffe revolution was chiefly characterized by the employment of new technology, the drive for mass circulations and the wholesale reliance on advertising as the prime source of press revenue, the 'flavour' of that revolution must not be overlooked, that is the style and content emanating from the Press Barons themselves. James Curran and Jean Seaton in *Power Without Responsibility: The Press and Broadcasting in Britain* (UK: Routledge, 6th edition, 2003), write 'Northcliffe and Beaverbrook shaped the entire content of their favourite papers, including their lay-out.'

When *The Times* changed the place in the paper of the weather report, Northcliffe raged, 'if it's moved again, whoever does it is fired'. Curran and Seaton speak of how the personal tastes of the press barons influenced the popular journalism of the time: 'Northcliffe had a lifelong obsession with torture and death: he even kept an aquarium containing a goldfish and a pike, with a dividing partition, which he would lift up when he was in need of diversion.' He told staff of the *Daily Mail* to find 'one murder a day'.

Meddling with content by newspaper proprietors was not, of course, new. It had gone on throughout the nineteenth century, but then interference had focused mainly upon political matters. What was different with

Northcliffe and his ilk was that the new proprietors meddled in everything. See NEWSPAPERS, ORIGINS. See also *TOPIC GUIDE* under MEDIA HISTORY.

* Kevin Williams, *Get Me A Murder A Day! A History of Mass Communication in Britain* (UK: Arnold, 1997).

N-step theory See OPINION LEADER.

NVC See COMMUNICATION, NON-VERBAL (NVC).

→ **O**

Object See SIGN.

Objectivity Professor Stuart Hall has expressed the view that objectivity, 'like impartiality, is an operational fiction' (in 'Media power: the double bind', *Journal of Communication*, Autumn 1984). In examining the media, analysts encounter the Famous Four – balance, CONSENSUS, IMPARTIALITY and objectivity – upon which all good reporting is said to be based. The questions arising from this precept are: Balance between what and what? Consensus among whom? Impartiality in what sense? Objectivity in whose eyes? Considering the complex processes of MEDIATION between an event and its report in media form, is it possible to have value-free information?

'All edited or manipulated symbolic reality,' says Hall, 'is impregnated with values, viewpoints, implicit theorizings, common-sense assumptions.' When there are differences between what is objective and what is not, whose opinion wins the day?

Hall says of consensus that it is 'structured dominance'. The prevailing definition usually rests with the POWER ELITE, the 'power-ideology complex' in any society whose control of and influence upon the media gives them a dominant say in the definitions of objectivity. See CULTURAL APPARATUS; ELITE; HEGEMONY; MACHINERY OF REPRESENTATION.

Object language According to Gail and Michele Myers in *The Dynamics of Human Communication* (US: McGraw-Hill, 1985) this term refers to 'the meanings you attribute to objects with which you surround yourself'. Such objects might be items of dress, for example clothes, hairstyle, fashion accessories; your house; your furniture; your car, and so on.

These and many other objects may say something about you to others: they can all be part of your SELF-PRESENTATION. These objects may not of course always convey to others the MESSAGE you wish them to. Others may not be aware of the symbolic value of the objects or simply read into them different meanings than the ones intended. You may of course be unaware yourself of messages that you may be sending to others through the objects you have. Object language may be particularly important when people are forming first impressions of one another. A great deal of ADVERTISING certainly works on the assumption that consumer objects have as their main appeal a *symbolic* rather than a purely functional value.

As Jib Fowles comments in *Advertising and Popular Culture* (US/UK: Sage, 1996), 'The individual looks at advertising imagery and the associated commodity in the attempt to find those pleasing signs that will define oneself in distinction to others. Still, those signs *must* be readable by others, so what the solitary consumer is buying is not so much self-definition in isolation as participatory symbols.'

In their book *Understanding and Sharing: An Introduction to Speech Communication* (US: Brown, 1979, reprinted 1985), authors Judy Cornelia Pearson, Paul Edward Nelson and Donald Yoder use the term *objectics*, the study of 'clothing, adornments, hairstyles, cosmetics and other artefacts that we carry with us or possess'. Object language conveys information about our age, sex, status, role, personality, relationships with groups and with other people, psychological and emotional state, self-concept, and the 'physical climate in which we live'. See COMMUNICATION, NON-VERBAL (NVC); SELF-CONCEPT.

Obscene signals See INSULT SIGNALS.

Obscenity and film censorship See WILLIAMS COMMITTEE REPORT ON OBSCENITY AND FILM CENSORSHIP (UK), 1979.

Obsolescence Generally, anything passing out of date or out of use. In a communications sense, it refers to the link between social habits and media-using habits. Obsolescence can be defined as the abandoning of formerly institutionalized modes of conduct related to some established cultural activity.

Oeuvre French for 'work', generally the complete works of an artist, writer, composer, etc. The word refers to the work of the mind as well as of hand and eye. Thus we may refer to the *oeuvre* of Pablo Picasso (1891–1973) and mean not only the items of his work – paintings, sculpture, pottery – but, by implication, the nature or character of that work. See OPUS.

Ofcom: Office of Communications (UK) A 'super-regulator' born of the COMMUNICATIONS ACT (UK), 2003, and assuming its responsibilities on 29 December 2003; inherited the duties of the Broadcasting Standards Commission (BSC), the Independent Television Commission (ITC), the Office of Telecommunications (Oftel), the Radio Authority and the Radio Communications Agency. Lord Currie of the Cass Business School at City University was appointed its first chairman and Stephen Carter, formerly senior UK executive of the advertising firm J. Walter Thompson, became Ofcom's first chief executive.

Ofcom has responsibilities across the spectrum of broadcasting and telecommunications in Britain, required by statute to 'further the interests of citizens and consumers by promoting competition and protecting consumers from harm or offensive material'. Ofcom consults, researches, produces codes and policies, and deals with complaints.

In May 2005 Ofcom published its Broadcasting Code for television and radio. This acknowledges European Community directives relating to TV and incorporates aspects of the Human Rights Act of 1998, in particular articles of the Convention relating to the rights to freedom of expression, thought, conscience and religion; personal privacy and freedom from discrimination. Section 1 of the Code lays down broadcasting benchmarks to protect the under-18s and deals with programme scheduling, the coverage of sexual and other offences in the UK involving under-18s; drugs, smoking, solvents and alcohol; violence and dangerous behaviour; offensive language; sex, nudity, excorcism, the occult and the paranormal.

Other sections of the Code deal with Harm and Offence; Crime ('To ensure that material likely to encourage and incite the commission of crime or lead to disorder is not included in television or radio services'), Religion; Impartiality and Due Accuracy; Elections and Referendums; Fairness ('To ensure that broadcasters avoid unjust or unfair treatment of individuals or organizations in programmes'); Privacy; Sponsorship and Commercial References and Other Matters. The Ofcom Contact Centre can be reached via e-mail at contact@ofcom.org.uk. See PRODUCT PLACEMENT; SPONSORSHIP OF BROADCAST PROGRAMMES (UK).

Official Secrets Act (UK) Born in a spy scare during the Agadir crisis of 1911, reinforced in 1920 during the 'Troubles' in Ireland, given further power as war broke out in 1939, the Act censors information, access to it and expression of it, which might be of use to the nation's enemies. It is easier to define what the Act does not cover rather than what it does. Without question, it is the single most comprehensive weapon of CENSORSHIP with regard to the activities of government in the UK, and has few parallels in the 'free' world.

For a time, the saving grace of the Act was the possibility of defending individual, group or media breaches of secrecy on the grounds that such a breach was in the *public interest*. This was excised from the Act by the Conservative government in 1990 and to date New Labour administrations have made no move to put it back.

Brian Raymond, solicitor to the civil servant Clive Ponting who was unsuccessfully prosecuted under the Act for revealing information about the sinking by a British submarine of the Argentinian battleship *Belgrano* with the loss of hundreds of lives during the Falklands War (1982) said: 'The obliteration of the public interest defence … amounts to a licence to cover up Government wrong-doing.' See D-NOTICES; REGULATION OF INVESTIGATORY POWERS ACT (RIPA) (UK), 2000; FREEDOM OF INFORMATION ACT (UK), 2005; SPYCATCHER CASE. See also *TOPIC GUIDE* under MEDIA: FREEDOM, CENSORSHIP.

Oligopolization Oligarchy is government by a small exclusive CLASS or group; in media terms, oligopolization is the process of communication systems falling into the hands of a small exclusive group of owners or corporations.

Omnimax Spectator-surrounding film projection technique developed, like IMAX, in Canada from a system invented by an Australian, Ron James. Though there are several Omnimax screens in North America, the first in Europe, with the largest screen in the world, operates at the 55-hectare Paris exhibition complex, Cité des Sciences et de L'Industrie at Porte La Villette, which opened in 1986.

La Gèode offers a projection screen covering 10,000 square feet and surrounds spectators with a complete hemisphere, exceeding the normal field of vision. Like Imax, Omnimax uses 70mm film which passes through the camera horizontally producing a 5×7cm film image, approximately nine times the image area of ordinary cinema film. Camera and projector use a 25mm fish-eye lens with a scope of 172 degrees. A massive light source is required to project such a gigantic picture and Omnimax has a 15kW water-cooled xenon lamp.

One-step, two-step, multi-step flow models of communication Basically these are refinements of the HYPODERMIC NEEDLE MODEL OF COMMUNICATION. The one-step model ignores the role of the OPINION LEADER in the flow of communication and presents the view that the mass media communicate directly to a mass AUDIENCE. There is no suggestion, however, that the messages reach all receivers equally or that they have the same effect on each individual in the audience. The model takes into account the influence of an individual's PERCEPTION, memory and SELECTIVE EXPOSURE on his/her particular interpretation of a MESSAGE.

A study conducted by Paul Lazarsfeld and others of the 1940 presidential election in the US threw doubt on the validity of the one-step theory. Reporting in *The People's Choice* (US: Duell, Sloan & Pearce, 1944), the authors found little evidence of the direct influence of the media; indeed people seemed more influenced by face-to-face contact with others. Lazarsfeld and his fellow researchers suggested that the flow of communication to the individual is often directed through an opinion leader who plays a vital role in both spreading and interpreting the information.

They thus proposed a *two-step model* of communication flow which later research has found to be generally useful. In highlighting the importance of the social context of the receiver in the process of the interpretation of mass communication messages this model differs significantly from earlier ones. It presents the mass audience as being composed of interacting and responsive individuals rather than of the socially isolated, passive atoms of earlier theories.

The *multi-step model* is a development of the other two, allowing for the sequential relaying of a message. It is not specific about the number of steps there will be in the relaying process nor does it specify that messages must originate from a source and then pass straight through the agencies of the mass media. The model suggests a variable number of relays in the communication process and that the receivers may receive the message at various stages along the relay network. The exact number of steps in the process depends upon the following: (1) the intentions of the source; (2) the availability of the mass media; (3) the extent of audience exposure to agencies of communication; (4) the nature of the message; (5) the importance of the message to the audience.

The model has often been used in recent research. Its advantage is that it allows the researcher to account for different variables in different communication situations. See *TOPIC GUIDE* under COMMUNICATION MODELS.

Onomatopoeia Words that imitate actual sounds are onomatopoeic, such as bang, thud, crackle, hiss, quack and twitter. They are mostly invented words. The first ever attempts at spoken language were very probably onomatopoeic and such words continue to be invented, not a few of them (zap, for example) starting life in comics and cartoons.

Open, closed texts Italian semiologist Umberto Eco has made this useful separation between TEXTS that are varyingly articulated, to either permit little or no interpretation on the part of AUDIENCE (*closed texts*) or to allow plenty of room for interpretation (*open texts*). A work of art – a poem, a painting, a piece of sculpture, for example – would represent an open text in that the intention of the writer, painter or sculptor is to express ideas or feelings which may be interpreted in different ways and at different levels.

The open text invites a sense of participation in the reader or viewer and the interaction that occurs between creator, creation and audience is one in which 'right answers' are less important than the possibility of a proactive response; and this may be subject to flux in differing instances and at varying times. PROPAGANDA would constitute closed text in that there is a rigorously PREFERRED READING: the decoder is expected to receive the message, and register its MEANING as intended by the communicator. Any divergence from acceptance would, to quote another term of Eco's, represent *aberrant decoding*. See ANCHORAGE; DECODE.

'Open source' creed Belief in the free availability of data online; put into practice by public-spirited computer programmers encouraging people to freely adapt software rather than allowing it to be patented by big companies. An example is Freenet developed by Ian Clarke at the University of Edinburgh. This is a decentralized information system designed to bypass government-approved and/or commercially based ISPs (Internet Service Providers). In the UK the potential for this free and anonymous exchange and interactivity stands at risk in face of invasive legislation, in particular the REGULATION OF INVESTIGATORY POWERS ACT (RIPA) (UK), 2000 (its reach substantially increased in 2002, its principles and practices also extended to other countries in the European Community).

Opera omnia Latin for 'All his works', the term denotes a total ban on an author's writings imposed by the Roman Catholic *Index Librorum Prohibitorum*, first issued in 1559. A few such prohibited writers have been David Hume, Emile Zola, Jean-Paul Sartre and Alberto Moravia. See CENSORSHIP; INDEX.

Opinion leader Someone able to influence informally other individuals' attitudes and/or behaviour in a desired way with relative frequency. He/she is a type of informal leader. Opinion leadership is earned and maintained by the individual's technical competence, sociability and conformity to the NORMS of the social system. When such leaders are compared to their followers several characteristics are of note: opinion leaders are more exposed to all forms of external communication; more *cosmopolite*; of a higher social status; and more innovative.

Opinion leaders are widely thought to play a vital role in the spreading of new ideas, VALUES and beliefs. As Paul Lazarsfeld has noted in several studies, opinion leaders can be important intermediaries in the process of communication, including mass communication, in that they have the potential to influence reaction, among those around them, to messages received.

An opinion leader whose range of influence is limited to one specific topic exercises *monomorphic* opinion leadership. This type of leadership is thought to be typical of modern, industrial societies as the complex technological base of such societies results in a sophisticated division of labour and considerable specialization of roles. Monomorphic opinion leadership can be related to what Randy Bobbitt and Ruth Sullivan in *Developing the Public Relations Campaign* (US: Pearson, 2005), term *N-step theory*. This proposes that 'individuals seldom receive information from only one opinion leader. Instead, they are likely to turn to different opinion leaders for each issue on which they form an opinion'.

An opinion leader whose influence covers a wide range of topics exercises *polymorphic* opinion leadership. This is generally thought to be more common in traditional societies. A respected, elderly member of a village, for example, might be consulted on a variety of matters ranging from marriage problems to methods of harvesting. See ONE-STEP, TWO-STEP, MULTI-STEP MODELS OF COMMUNICATION.

Opinion poll The process or processes by which public opinion is researched, the findings of which are widely and regularly published and broadcast, and are seen not only as evidence upon which governments, oppositions, public bodes etc. might act, but as an influence in their own right. For example, in election campaigns poll results are seen as vital indicators of the way the public intends to vote, but the headlines such opinion polls produce are also seen to influence the electorate, particularly if the findings suggest a CONSENSUS of opinion. For this reason, some countries ban the publishing of poll results in the immediate run-up to elections.

Oppositional code See DOMINANT, SUBORDINATE, RADICAL; POLYSEMY.

Optical-fibre cable See FIBRE-OPTIC TECHNOLOGY.

Opus Latin for 'work', a term most often applied to musical compositions in order of their creation; for example, Beethoven's Ninth Symphony is Opus 125.

Oral culture An oral CULTURE or SUB-CULTURE is one in which essentially most communication is by word of mouth. Pictures may also be used as a supplement but reading and writing play a minor role in the communication process.

Orality: primary and secondary In *Orality and the Technology of the Word* (US: Cornell University Press, 1982) Walter Ong in investigating the nature of the shift between oral and literate cultures differentiates between 'primary' and 'secondary' orality. The first refers to and describes *preliterate* societies, the second results from the introduction of electronic media into *literate* societies.

Order, visions of See VISIONS OF ORDER.

Organization cultures In examining the NORMS, VALUES and practices of business organizations in his *Understanding Organizations* (UK: Penguin, 1993 edition) Charles B. Handy identifies four forms of organizational CULTURE that affect the nature or 'profile' of the organization and its patterns of communication. Each culture has, according to Handy, its own presiding deity. (1) The *power culture* depends upon a central power source, with 'rays of power and influence' (and communication) spreading out from a central figure. Zeus, the chief of the gods of Ancient Greece, who ruled by 'whim and impulse, by thunderbolt and shower of gold', is seen as the patron god of this culture. An example of such a culture is the self-made business person running his/her own company (see BERLUSCONI PHENOMENON; MURDOCH EFFECT). Without such a 'spider', the web structure of the culture would collapse.

(2) The *role culture* is the classic bureaucracy, its model like a Greek temple, with the leadership – directors, governors, etc. – represented by the pediment, the various organizational departments, the pillars of the temple and the workers at the base. Here, plainly, the communication process, following lines of authority, is vertical and chiefly one-way. Apollo, the god of reason, is seen as the patron god of this organization, whose culture values logic and rationality. In media terms, the BBC would be a good example of a role culture.

(3) The *task culture* is a skills- or ability-orientated culture in which what an employee is capable of doing is more important than who he/she is in terms of position or role. The model is net-shaped, made up of interdependent strands; LEADERSHIP is exchangeable according to the task in hand. This culture, centred on task completion, is not seen by Handy as having any one overall presiding deity but Athena, the warrior goddess, and Odysseus, the champion of commando leaders, would best reflect its ethos. This so-called *matrix structure* is characterized by very flexible channels of communication, horizontal rather than vertical in direction, and is responsive to change. Examples from the media of a task culture would be a creative ADVERTISING agency or small companies producing film or VIDEO or designing and operating websites.

(4) The *person culture* is, in terms of business organizations, the rarest of the four. Here the organization exists only to serve the individuals within it. The model is of a cluster, a galaxy of individual stars, without hierarchical structures, constantly interchanging in form. Dionysus, the god of the 'self-oriented individual', is its ruling deity. As Handy says, 'Clearly not many organizations can exist with this sort of culture, since organizations tend to have objectives over and above the collective objectives of those who comprise them.' In its purest form, the kibbutz (small egalitarian Israeli community) is an example of the person culture. Cooperatives in the arts are examples of the people culture (see MAGNUM). The factors Handy cites as influencing organization cultures are history and ownership; size; technology; goals and objectives; the environment and the people.

In *The Empty Raincoat* (UK: Arrow Books, 1995) Handy discusses a new model for organizations, based on what he terms the *doughnut principle*. This, he argues, reflects the way in which the traditional models and cultures have changed and will continue to change in order to survive shifts in the technological and economic environment.

The doughnut consists of a *core* surrounded by *bounded space*. It is 'an inside-out doughnut, one with the hole on the outside and the dough in the middle'. It is a 'conceptual doughnut, one for thinking with, not eating'. The core contains 'necessary jobs and necessary people'. These full-time employees often organize the activities of the bounded space that contains many other people working for the organization as flexible workers tied to the organization by flexible and often short-term contracts.

Thus organizations will become much smaller in terms of the number of people they directly employ; consequently it is likely that more people will be self-employed or freelance workers. Within the television industry, for example, this method of working is now well established. See CASUALIZATION; PRODUCER CHOICE.

Orientalism Concept posed by Edward Said describing the STEREOTYPICAL image of Asia held by those in European cultures. Representation of the Orient arises from ETHNOCENTRIC attitudes with an imperialist ancestry, and results in a projected image of Asia and Asians as being exotic ('the lure of the Orient'), indolent, untrustworthy and devious; in short a misrepresentation by western commentators and analysts, of OTHER. In *Orientalism* (UK: Routledge, 1978), Said raises the question of whether anything can be truly or objectively represented. See also Said's *Culture and Imperialism* (UK: Chatto & Windus, 1993).

The potency of the term has been reinforced by new millennium events such as the war on ('Arab') terrorism conducted by the US in Afghanistan and, following 9/11 2001, the invasion of Iraq in 2003 by US and British forces. This was seen by many critics as underscored by Orientalist attitudes manifested by an ignorance of the complexities of Arab culture and a seeming indifference to the remonstrations of the Arab world. A chilling example of this came when, having totted up their own war dead, the Allies saw it as no business of theirs to count those of the 'enemy', whether they were combatants or innocent civilians. Ulimately Orientalism is about valuing some 'bodies' over others.

In August 2005 when the Israeli army expelled illegally-settled Israelis from the Gaza Strip, massive publicity in the western media focused on the heart-rending sight of residents forced from their homes. It was pointed out by some observers that no comparable attention had been paid to the expulsion of Palestinians and their families driven from their homes, often without warning, and with no compensation, over a number of years. It could equally be pointed out, taking NEWS VALUES into account, that the extra news-worthiness of the story arose from the surprising or the unexpected – clearance of Israelis by Israelis.

Orientation An element of non-verbal communication referring to the angle at which people sit or stand in relation to one another. Orientation can be used to convey a range of messages about relationships, mood, personality and social context. For example, if people are in a potentially hostile or competitive situation they usually face each other head on. See COMMUNICATION, NON-VERBAL (NVC).

Other A person, persons, group, social CLASS, community, race or nation who are not 'us' and who are defined by their difference from us; yet who by that difference contribute to our concept of self, as individuals, members of groups etc. There is the ranking of *generalized* other, as illustrated by the statement, 'Other people might like to shop on a Sunday, but for me it is still a day of rest'. Also, there are SIGNIFICANT OTHERS. These may be people, or types of people, whom we respect and whose opinions carry weight with us. They count in our lives, and they may be real or fictitious. They are often, or have the potential to be, ROLE models.

'Other' in general media use represents, by and large, those we disapprove of, dislike, fear; and the popular media use of Other works in *binary* fashion (see WEDOM, THEYDOM). In everyday communication, Other plays a key role in jokes – Irish jokes, Scottish jokes, etc. – each one relying for its effect upon a CONSENSUS about the negative qualities of the butt of that joke.

In TABLOID press headlines name-calling is a favourite device to put down Other and consequently boost the sense of superiority of Us over Them. When Other is perceived as a threat, the demarcation lines become more forcible; and of course in sport, Other is always the opposition – at which point Germans become 'Krauts' and the French become 'Frogs'. Other, then, is almost invariably those in opposition, those who are different in appearance or CULTURE and are seen in some way as a challenge to 'our' ways.

Outer-inner directed See VALS TYPOLOGY.

Out-take Piece of film that is not actually used in the completed version.

Overhearing Kurt H. Wolff in *The Sociology of Georg Simmel* (US: Free Press, 1950) uses this expression to describe how recipients of messages may proceed, usually below the level of awareness, to select certain parts for special attention, often distorting them, while at the same time overlooking ('overhearing') other parts entirely. In short, the human organism perceives to a considerable degree what it wants to perceive. See COCKTAIL PARTY PROBLEM; PERCEPTION; SELECTIVE EXPOSURE.

Overkill signals See SHORTFALL SIGNALS.

Ownership and control of mass media See BERLUSCONI PHENOMENON; GLOBALIZATION: THREE ENGINES OF; GLOBAL MEDIA SYSTEM: THE MAIN PLAYERS; MEDIA CONTROL; MURDOCH EFFECT; PRESS BARONS. See also *TOPIC GUIDE* under MEDIA: OWNERSHIP & CONTROL.

Oz Trial The longest-ever obscenity trial in the UK, lasting 26 days in the summer of 1971, centred on the *Oz School Kids Issue* (*Oz* 28). The three editors, Richard Neville, Felix Dennis and Jim Anderson, were eventually acquitted on the most serious charge of conspiring to corrupt the morals of children, but a majority of ten to one of the trial jury found *Oz* guilty of publishing an obscene article, sending such articles through the post and having such articles for profit and gain.

Oz Publications Ink Ltd received a total fine of £1000 with £1250 costs. Neville got a 15-month jail sentence and a recommendation that he be deported (he was Australian). Anderson received 12 months and Dennis nine. See CENSORSHIP; SPYCATCHER CASE. See also *TOPIC GUIDE* under MEDIA: FREEDOM, CENSORSHIP.

Packaging The style and the framework within which TV programmes are presented on our screens: good-looking announcers or interviewers, titling, music, the tailoring of programmes to suitable lengths, indeed any form of image-making for a media product. The word gives emphasis to the connection between the manufacture and sale of goods and the making and presentation of media products. Stuart Hood in *Hood on Television* (UK: Pluto Press, 1980) refers to TV announcers as the 'sales people of the air'. See LOOKISM.

Panopticon gaze A metaphor used by Michel Foucault (1926–84) in *Discipline and Punish* (UK: Penguin, 1979) to describe the exercise of power through the numerous and often subtle diciplinary practices and technology embedded within modern western organizations and societies. The panoptican (see also SURVEILLANCE SOCIETY) was originally a design, conceived by nineteenth-century social philosopher Jeremy Bentham (1748–1832), for establishments in which people could be be kept under supervision. The basic principle is that inmates, confined to separate compartments or cells, can be observed at any time but have no way of knowing when and if they are being observed. Consequently the feeling of being under constant surveillance is produced even though the observer will not in fact observe any one inmate continuously.

As Foucault writes, the result is 'to induce in the inmate a sense of conscious and permanent visibility that assures the automatic functioning of power. So to arrange things that the surveillance is permanent in its effects, even if it is discontinuous in its actions; that the perfection of power should tend to render its actual exercise unnecessary.' Foucault argues that the use of surveillance in the exercise of power and control has become widespread and has helped to create 'the disciplinary society' and that, further, the uses of disciplinary practices to control the indivdiual within prisons, organizations and societies share common features.

Contemporary examples of such practices within organizations might include performance-related pay, targets, monitoring of phone calls, e-mails, deadlines, schedules, career paths, 360-degree appraisal. These practices arguably operate to produce a sense of a *panopticon gaze* which in turn leads people to become self-disciplining through anticipation of the considerable degree of monitoring and surveillance of their activities.

These practices are potentially powerful instruments of socialization, ensuring conformity and order, particularly as they may often be taken for granted. Within the wider society arguably much modern communications technology, especially computer technology, facilitates the operation of the panopticon gaze, for example speed cameras and CCTV cameras.

Surveillance is also a recurrent theme running through the mass media: the tabloid press surveys the activities of celebrities; on REALITY TV shows like *Big Brother* surveillance is presented as a form of entertainment; whilst other programmes, for example *Crimewatch*, focus on enrolling the public's help in detecting criminals. Such coverage can be seen to contribute to a general sense, among the public, of being under surveillance. Indeed they may help us to see such surveillance as normal.

John E. McGrath poses an interesting question in *Loving Big Brother* (US/UK: Routledge, 2004), 'Could the obsessive repetition of CCTV imagery on television be, in some way, a means of narrativizing, of making sense, of the daily experience of being watched and recorded?' In making sense of such experience we may also, of course, consider how to protect our freedoms and how to resist pressures to conform. As McGrath points out, a substantial amount of the CCTV footage we see portrays deviant or excessive behaviour. It is arguable that it could just as well encourage deviance as conformity.

Paparazzo Aggressive, prying and often unscrupulous freelance photographer who specializes in taking pictures of celebrities; pursuing them wherever they go, armed with a thick skin and zoom lenses. The word is an Italian – Calabrian – surname. It was suggested by writer Ennio Flaiano as a name for a character in Federico Fellini's film *La Dolce Vita* (The Sweet Life), made in 1960. Paparazzi were accused of hounding Diana, Princess of Wales, to her death in 1997 and the press at that time made a number of resolutions to curb the use of 'intrusive' pictures.

Paper Tiger TV Media collective based in New York from 1981; an example of 'action' or 'alternative' media. A networking system of access and production, generally run on a volunteer basis, it aims to encourage grassroots resistance to the dominance of the media industry. In 1995 Paper Tiger received a grant to distribute programming by satellite to public access centres around the US. Its Deep Dish TV has become a nationwide organization with a steering committee and small full-time staff.

Paperwork Reduction Act (US), 1980 On the face of it, a welcome onslaught on the overproduction of bureaucratic paperwork; yet critics of this piece of American legislation view it with a degree of cynicism. In 'The tug-of-war over the First Amendment' published in *Questioning The Media: A Critical Introduction* (UK: Sage, 1990), edited by John Downing, Ali Mohammadi and Annabelle Sreberny-Mohammadi, Donna A. Demac and John Downing write that the Act was 'promptly used to curtail public access to government information' – in short, backdoor CENSORSHIP. Supervised and guided by the Office of Management and Budget, government agencies have used the Act to transfer the management of key information programmes to the private sector, thus furthering the retreat from public to private of information services.

Demac and Downing say that by 1985 'one-fourth of all government information was made available only in computer tapes, which put its utilization out of the financial and technical reach of the vast majority of citizens'.

Paradigm (paradigmic) Commonly used in the social sciences, the term refers to a framework of explanation within which theories from various schools of thought in a discipline are located and from which research operates. In *linguistics*, paradigm describes the set of relationships a linguistic unit, such as a letter or a word, has with other units in a specific context. The word is applicable in all SIGN systems, verbal, numerical, musical, etc. The alphabet is a paradigm, or set of signs, from which a choice is made to formulate the message. A *syntagm* is a combination of the chosen signs, a chain that amounts to MEANING. In language we can describe the vocabulary we use as *paradigmic*, and the sentence that vocabulary is formed into as *syntagmic.*

All messages, therefore, involve selection from a paradigm and combination into a syntagm. All the units in a paradigm must share characteristics that determine the membership of that paradigm, thus letters in the alphabetic paradigm, numbers in the numerical paradigm, notes in the musical paradigm.

Each unit within the paradigm must be clearly differentiable from other units; it must be characterized by distinctive features. Just as the paradigm is governed by shared characteristics and distinctive features, the syntagm is determined by rules or conventions by which the combination of paradigms is made – rules of grammar and syntax or, in music, rules of harmony. See PARADIGMS OF THE MEDIA, SEMIOLOGY/SEMIOTICS.

Paradigms of the media James Curran in 'Rethinking the media as a public sphere' in *Communication and Citizenship* (UK: Routledge, 1991), edited by Peter Dahlgren and Colin Sparks, has identified three paradigms that seek to explain the relationship between the mass media and the POWER structure of societies in which they operate: the *Marxist* or *Neo-Marxist*, the *Liberal-Pluralist* and the *Radical Democratic* paradigms.

The Marxist or Neo-Marxist school argue that it is those who own and control economic capital who are at the heart of a society's power structure and that such a position allows them to exercise power over cultural institutions, such as the mass media, in order to better pursue their economic goals. Media professionals may view themselves as autonomous but, it is argued, they have been socialized into and have *internalized* the NORMS and VALUES of the dominant CLASS.

Thus from this perspective, a key ideological contribution made by the mass media is that it provides the audience with frameworks for interpreting messages which encourage it to construct readings that are consistent with the interests of the dominant class. Critics of this tradition have argued, though, that it overlooks the degree of leeway which does exist for journalists to ask awkward questions and the need to consider the AUDIENCE and the audience's role in constructing the MEANING of mass media messages.

A competing paradigm is that offered by the Liberal-Pluralist tradition of media research, which argues that the mass media is and should be composed of a number of competing groups operating within a free market, though subject to state intervention when this is deemed in the public interest. Groups within the mass media tend to be seen as in competition for power and influence within society.

Media professionals, such as journalists, are seen to enjoy a considerable degree of *autonomy* over the production of media artefacts. Within this tradition some perceive the media to have a responsibility within society to behave as a WATCHDOG whose role it is to provide an arena for wide public debate about civil issues, facilitating the articulation of a *plurality* of views and values and in so doing to allow private individuals to exercise a form of informal control over the state.

This tradition has, however, been subject to much criticism for its failure to address the narrow social base from which media professionals are often drawn, resulting in those from working-class and/or ethnic backgrounds being under-represented; and the degree to which the political economy of media ownership, the CULTURE of media organizations and the place of these organizations in the political economy of a society, influence the content and reading of media artefacts.

The Radical Democratic paradigm, according to James Curran, offers a synthesis between the other two paradigms. Whilst this paradigm acknowledges the links between the ownership and control of media institutions and that of other key institutions and that the free market tends to be skewed in favour of the dominant class, it does not perceive the links to be so close that the media could be conceived as an arm of the ruling class. Rather the media is seen as 'caught in the crossfire', providing 'a battleground between contending forces. The way in which the media responds to and mediates this conflict affects the balance of social forces and, ultimately, the distribution of rewards within society'.

Journalists and media professionals are viewed as having day-to-day autonomy that allows them to make a difference and opens up the possibility for the committed radical journalism which would allow the media to act as a countervailing force and to further the cause of the less powerful. It also recognizes that not all journalists and media professionals work in media organizations which have one dominant owner, and argues that those working in BROADCASTING and in commercial media where ownership is dispersed among a number of shareholders, may enjoy considerable freedom to criticize the powerful. The structure of the media, however, is seen as being in need of reform if it is to achieve its potential for providing diverse debate within a democratic society. See DEMOCRACY AND THE MEDIA. See also *TOPIC GUIDE* under MEDIA INSTITUTIONS.

Paralanguage See NON-VERBAL VOCALIZATIONS.

Parallel processing Our visual capacity allows us to process many images simultaneously – in parallel; to record both foreground and background actions. In contrast, speech capacity depends upon *serial* processing: we hear one word or phrase at a time and process it before proceeding to subsequent data.

Paraproxemics Term used to classify the way TV handles the space between people in its programmes, echoing and simulating the real-life use of space (see PROXEMICS) by individuals; for example, the close-up, medium-range and distance camera shots paralleling the spatial zones of intimate, personal and social space. Joshua Meyrowitz in 'Television and interpersonal behaviour: codes of perception and response' in G. Gumpert and R. Cathcart, eds, *Inter/Media: Interpersonal Communication in a Media World* (US/UK: Oxford University Press, 1979) writes, 'the way in which a person is framed' [by the TV camera] may suggest an interpersonal distance between that person and the viewer'. Distance, in fact, shapes viewer response, with the TV screen becoming 'a kind of "extended retina" for the viewer'.

Parasocial interaction The illusion, contributed to both by the performer and the AUDIENCE in mass media communication, especially RADIO, TV and film, of an interpersonal relationship existing between them, free of MEDIATION. Characters (or *personae*) on air or film, actual or fictional, are often cited as being more 'real' to audiences than the real people they know.

In 'Mass communication and parasocial interaction: observation on intimacy at a distance', *Journal of Psychiatry* 19 (1956), D. Horton and R.R. Wohl write, 'The persona offers, above all, a continuing relationship. His appearance is a regular and dependable event, to be counted on, planned for, and integrated into the routines of daily life' and may be considered by his audience as 'a friend, counsellor, comforter, and model', but unlike all those real people around him, the persona is changeless. 'Typically, there are no challenges to a spectator's self ... that cannot be met comfortably.' Arguably the strongest relationship or interaction is that between audiences and fictitious characters, especially those in long-running series such as SOAP OPERAS.

Parental Guidance (PG) See CERTIFICATION OF FILMS.

Participant observation Some research evidence is collected by the researcher becoming a member of the group or social situation under observation. The researcher participates fully in the situation and those being observed may be unaware that he/she is a researcher. The advantage of this method of data collection is that the greater involvement of the researcher may facilitate an increased insight into and greater understanding of the behaviour being investigated. See ETHNOGRAPHIC (APPROACH TO AUDIENCE MEASUREMENT). See also *TOPIC GUIDE* under RESEARCH METHODS.

Partisan An adherent of a particular party or cause. The term is also used to describe actions as well as allegiances. Within media studies, much research has focused upon the political partisanship of the press and TV companies, that is upon the degree to which they may support one or other political party or faction, and colour their political coverage accordingly. If such coverage gives space to the views of two factions or parties it is generally described as being *bi-partisan*; if its tone is one of general disinterest, of being above party politics, it is described as being *anti-partisan*. Partisan perspectives may not, though, permeate political coverage only; they may pervade media presentations generally. See EFFECTS OF THE MASS MEDIA.

Passivity One influential and widely held PERCEPTION of the mass AUDIENCE is that it is largely passive and unreflective. There is little evidence for this, though assumptions carry weight, and are noticeable in content selection and approach, regardless of evidence. Modern media commentators insist on the diversity of response of audiences. James Curran and Jean Seaton in *Power Without Responsibility* (UK: Routledge, 6th edition, 2003) believe, 'The public is not a passive empty box merely waiting to be filled with the injunctions of advertisers. How people react to what they see is determined by their class, age and the beliefs they already hold.' See AUDIENCE: ACTIVE AUDIENCE; AUDIENCE MEASUREMENT; EFFECTS OF THE MASS MEDIA; EMPOWERMENT; INTERACTIVITY; PLEASURE: ACTIVE AND REACTIVE; RESISTIVE READING.

Paternity of the text See TEXT: INTEGRITY OF THE TEXT.

Patriarchy Society ruled by or dominated by men; patriarch means father, thus patriarchal relates to a CULTURE shaped and governed in the interests of men, with women in a subordinate, and in some cases, subject, role. Patriarchy is reflected in customs, NORMS and VALUES, the law, education, commerce, industry, the arts, sport and, not least, language. Many commentators have also identified patriarchy as being assertively alive in the media, though at least at the *operative* (rather than *managerial*) level substantial advances have been made by women in JOURNALISM and BROADCASTING. See NEWS: THE 'MALENESS' OF NEWS.

Patriot Act (US), 2001 See USA – PATRIOT ACT, 2001.

Pauper press See UNDERGROUND PRESS.

PeaceNet See TELEDEMOCRACY.

'Pencil of Nature, The' Title of the first book ever illustrated with photographs, published in England in 1844, the work of William Henry Fox Talbot (1800–77), inventor of the CALOTYPE process of photo-printing. The range of photographs pasted into *The Pencil of Nature* was extraordinary and included intimate, informal studies of Talbot's household at his home, Lacock Abbey. See PHOTOGRAPHY, ORIGINS.

People meter Electronic recording device used to measure individual TV viewing habits. Each member of a family has a portable keypad very like the TV's remote control device. Linked to the home by telephone lines, the system's central computer correlates each viewer's number with demographical data already on record.

People's Communication Charter Proposed by Cees Hamelink in *World Communication: Disempowerment and Self-Empowerment* (UK: Zed Books, 1995) in the light of his vision that the GLOBALIZATION of communication threatens to further divide the information-rich from the information-poor, at the personal, community and national levels. The Charter provides a valuable text in which issues are highlighted, rights and responsibilities spelt out.

The Preamble to the Charter opens with the affirmation that 'communication is basic to the life of individuals and peoples' and that 'communication is crucial in the issues and crises which affect all members of the world community'. It is mindful that 'communication can be used to support the powerful and to victimize the powerless' and that 'communication is fundamental to the shaping of the cultural environment of every society'.

Disempowerment is seen as a major trend; it occurs through the 'withholding of information, by distorting information, by overwhelming people with overloads of information, or by obstructing people's access to communication channels'. In consequence the Charter urges support to enable people to develop their own communication channels through which they can speak for themselves. Under General Standards, Article 1 declares the 'conviction that all people are entitled to the respect of their dignity, integrity, equality,

Phillis Review of Government Communications (UK), 2004 Examines the relationship between British government information services, the media and the public, identifying a lack of trust on the part of the public in the communications performance of government. The report by an independent committee chaired by Bob Phillis, chief executive of the Guardian Media Group, declares that favouritism, partisanship, collusion and distortion have become the key features of the relationship between government and media. The Government Information and Communication Service (GICS) was considered 'no longer fit for [its] purpose' and it was recommended that it be disbanded.

The report criticizes the lobby system (see LOBBYING; LOBBY PRACTICE) in which some media are favoured over others, chiefly because it can be relied on to provide the government with a 'good press'. It urges more *transparency*, more openness, as against briefings in 'a closed, secretive and opaque insider process' behind closed doors.

The report also voices serious concern about the role of the civil service in the communications process. It perceives an erosion of impartiality brought about by government pressure. As for the response of government information services to the public, the Phillis Review urges a speeding up of the official response rate to enquiries by members of the public, citing a case in which the Ministry of Defence took six years to respond to a query.

The public should be guaranteed a reply to enquiries within 20 days of receipt, a move the report believes could, along with other measures – such as reducing the power of ministers to veto the provision of information – address the problem of lack of trust on the part of the public, and its current disenchantment with government information services.

In its *Media Manifesto*, 2005, the CAMPAIGN FOR PRESS AND BROADCASTING FREEDOM describes the government's response to Phillis as 'lamentable', failing to act on the recommendation to cap the number of political advisers or limit their powers and 'in the face of opposition from political correspondents at Westminster, the Downing Street press office has backed away from changing the rules in order to allow lobby briefings to be televised'. See FREEDOM OF INFORMATION ACT (UK), 2005.

Phoneme The smallest unit in the sound system of a language. Each language can be shown to operate with a relatively small number of phonemes, some having as few as 15, others as many as 50. Phonemics is the study of the basic sounds of language.

Phone-tapping See PRIVACY.

Phonetics The science of human sound-making, especially sounds used in speech. Phonetics includes the study of articulation, acoustics or perception of speech, and the properties of specific languages.

Phonodisc First-ever VIDEO recording, developed by John Logie Baird (1888–1946) in 1928. This was a 10 inch 78rpm record, in every way similar to the acoustic discs already being produced for conventional sound recording. Despite its novelty, the Phonodisc, coming so early in the age of the development of TV, failed to succeed commercially.

Phonograph See GRAMOPHONE.

Phonology A branch of LINGUISTICS which studies the sound systems of languages. Its aim is to demonstrate the patterns of distinctive sound in spoken language and to make as general statements as possible about the nature of sound systems in languages throughout the world.

Photographic negativization See VISIONS OF ORDER.

Photography, origins Joseph Nicèphore Nièpce (1765–1833) and his brother Claude were the first to fix images of the CAMERA OBSCURA by chemical means in 1793, though the light sensitivity of silver nitrate had been known and written about as early as 1727 when Johann Heinrich Schulze, professor of anatomy at the University of Altdorf, published a paper indicating that the darkening of silver salts was due not to heat but to light.

1826 is generally recognized as the year in which the first photographic image was captured. Joseph Nièpce's reproduction of a roof-top scene on a pewter plate he called Heliographie – sun drawing. In 1830 he teamed up with Louis Daguerre (1789–1851), theatrical designer and co-inventor of the diorama. The death of Nièpce three years later left Daguerre to lead the field in France. He discovered that an almost invisible latent image could be developed using mercury vapour, thus reducing exposure time from around eight hours to between 20 and 30 minutes.

His DAGUERREOTYPE was taken up by the French government in 1839, and elicited from Paul Delaroche the immortal line, 'from today, painting is dead!' In the UK astronomer Sir John Herschel (1792–1871) read a paper 'On the art of photography' to the Royal Society, accompanied by 23 photographs. He was the first to use the verb *to photograph* and the adjective *photographic*, in 1840 to identify *negative* and *positive,* and 20 years later to use the term *snapshot.*

William Henry Fox Talbot (1800–77) won fame and fortune with his CALOTYPE (1841), the true technical base of photography because, unlike the daguerreotype, its negative/positive principle made possible the making of prints from the original photographs. The inventions and discoveries that followed helped to improve the effectiveness of the photographic process. Frederick Scott Archer's *collodion* or wet-plate process, details of which were published in 1851, greatly increased sensitivity; the use of gelatine silver bromide emulsion, invented in 1871 by Dr Richard Leach Maddox, and later improved upon by John Burgess, Richard Kennett and Charles Bennett, proved a considerable advance on the collodion method, and ushered in the modern era of factory-produced photographic material, freeing the photographer from the necessity of preparing his/her own plates.

CELLULOID was invented by Alexander Parkes in 1861 and roll film made from celluloid was produced by the Eastman Company in the US from 1889. By 1902, Eastman, manufacturer of Kodak, was producing 80–90 per cent of the world's output. Very swiftly photography became the hobby of the man in the street. Every tenth person in the UK – 4m people – was estimated to own a camera by 1900.

Colour film photography hit many technical snags in its development. A colour screen process was patented as early as 1904 by the Lumière brothers. They commercially introduced their Autochrome plates in 1907 when good panchromatic emulsion was available. However, exposure was about 40 times longer than that for black and white film.

Modern methods based on multiple-layer film and coupling components were simultaneously introduced by Kodak and Agfa. In 1935, Kodachrome, created by two American amateurs, Leopold Godowsky and Leopold Mannes, was marketed, a year ahead of Agfacolor. In both, transparencies were obtained suitable for projection as well as reproduction. Electronic flash was invented in 1931 by Harold E. Egerton. See CAMERA; FILMLESS CAMERA; HIGH-SPEED PHOTOGRAPHY; PHOTO-JOURNALISM; PHOTO-MONTAGE; TIME-LAPSE PHOTOGRAPHY. See also *TOPIC GUIDE* under MEDIA HISTORY.

Photogravure Engraving by photography, for purposes of printing, was invented by Englishman William Henry Fox Talbot (1800–77) in 1852. It was not until 1947 that the first machine to do a complete typesetting job by means of photography was invented.

Photo-journalism Despite the popularity of photography among the general public, the press were curiously slow to realize the possibilities of photographs. The *Daily Mirror* was first in the field in the UK at the turn of the twentieth century, but the use of photographs did not become commonplace until the end of the First World War (1914–18). In June 1919, the New York *Illustrated Daily News* at last fully acknowledged a vital means of communication 39 years after the feasibility of printing a half-tone block (reproducing light and shade by dots of different sizes and densities) alongside type had been demonstrated by Stephen H. Horgan in the New York *Daily Graphic.* It was not until the 1920s that photo-journalism in the modern sense began, with the introduction of the Ermanox camera and ultra-rapid plates.

Among the fathers of photo-journalism were Erich Saloman, Felix H. Man and Wolfgang Weber. With a camera hidden in his top hat, Arthur Barrett secretly took court photographs of the suffragettes, and, in February 1928, Saloman took sensational pictures of a Coburg murder trial. Man pioneered the picture story in, for example, *A Day in the Life of Mussolini,* 1934, and it was Man who founded *Weekly Illustrated* in the same year. He became chief photographer for *Picture Post,* founded in 1938, a position he held until 1945.

Photo-journalism was given increasing status over the years by many outstanding photographers. Henri Cartier-Bresson photo-reported visits to Spain (1933) and Mexico (1934); Robert Capa won undying fame with his war photography, especially his pictures taken during the Spanish Civil War (1936–39); Bill Brandt photographed the *English at Home* (1936) while Margaret Bowke-White, in *You Have Seen Their Faces* (1937), portrayed the conditions in the Deep South of the US, in particular the negro chain-gangs. Suppression of the photo-reportage of Bert Hardy from the Korean War (1950–53) by the proprietors of *Picture Post* led to the resignation of the magazine's outstanding editor, Tom Hopkinson.

Talented, fearless and concerned photo-journalists continue to the present, even in the age of TV and with

That was not the end of pirate radio, however. A widespread enthusiasm for radio broadcasting independent of the duopoly was sustained through the 1970s, and in the 1980s pirates began popping up all over, making illegal broadcasts from unlicensed transmitters in woodlands, on hilltops, in back bedrooms, in garages or even on the move. Today's pirates continue, with no less ingenuity, to evade the efforts of authority to curtail their activities, though the majority of today's 'piracy' is only an INTERNET website away. See BLOGGING; COMMERCIAL RADIO; COMMUNITY RADIO; PODCASTING. See also *TOPIC GUIDE* under BROADCASTING.

Pistolgraph See CAMERA.

Plagiarism From the Latin, 'plagiarius', kidnapper; the act of stealing from others their thoughts or their writings and claiming them for one's own.

Play theory of mass communication In *The Play Theory of Mass Communication* (US: University of Chicago Press, 1967), William Stephenson counters those who speak of the harmful effects of the mass media by arguing that first and foremost the media serve audiences as play-experiences. Even newspapers, says Stephenson, are read for pleasure rather than information and enlightenment. He sees the media as 'a buffer against conditions which would otherwise be anxiety producing'. The media provide communication pleasure.

Stephenson argues that what is most required by people within a national culture is something for everyone to talk about. For him mass communication 'should serve two purposes. It should suggest how best to maximize the communication-pleasure in the world. It should also show how far autonomy for the individual can be achieved in spite of the weight of social controls against him.' See *TOPIC GUIDE* under COMMUNICATION THEORY.

Pleasure: active and reactive Mary Ellen Brown in *Soap Opera and Women's Talk* (UK: Sage, 1994) speaks of the active and reactive pleasure of women viewers of soap operas. She argues that 'active pleasure for women in soap opera groups affirms their connection to a woman's culture that operates in subtle opposition to dominant culture'. It is this 'cult of the home and of women's concerns,' says Brown, 'recognized but devalued in patriarchal terms, that provides a notion of identity that values women's traditional expertise'.

On the other hand, reactive pleasure, 'while not rejecting the connection women often feel towards women's cultural networks and concerns, also recognizes that these concerns often arise out of women's inability to completely control their own lives'. Consequently they are able to 'recognize and to feel at an emotional level the price of oppression'.

Key to resistive soap opera groups is talking, the very act of which 'indicates the importance of connectedness to others'. Brown acknowledges that soaps are a genre 'designed and developed to appeal to women's place in society' and largely to keep her in that place, yet 'Although soap operas work at isolating women in their homes and keeping them busy buying household products, in fact many observations indicate that they actually bring women together'; thus, it would seem, paradoxically undermining HEGEMONY while aiming to underpin it.

Pluralism The view that modern industrial societies have populations that are increasingly *heterogeneous*, that is different in kind, divided by such factors as ethnic, religious, regional and CLASS differences. Such heterogeneity, it is argued, produces a diversity of NORMS, VALUES interests and personal perspectives within such societies. Technological developments, such as those fostered by the digital revolution, make it increasingly possible for the media and cultural industries to address and access the heterogeneous nature of audiences, niche advertising being but one example of this.

It can also be argued that a plurality of groups competes for power and influence within society. Power is seen, therefore, as being increasingly diffuse in terms of its distribution within these societies. This perspective is not without its critics. Some GROUPS are likely to have more power than others and will be in a better position to impose their values upon other groups. As far as the field of media studies is concerned, recent concentrations in media ownership throw some doubt on the degree to which power is becoming more diffuse in its distribution.

The proliferation of media outlets has not, in the view of some commentators, guaranteed for audiences a broader choice of programmes; indeed in the age of digitization there is the fear that more may prove to be less, and that consumerist criteria may reduce pluralism rather than extend it. See DIGITIZATION; ELITE; SOCIAL ACTION (MODE OF ANALYSIS).

Pluralist Many modes, many alternatives; in media terms, *diversity* – of ownership, style, content and standpoint. A pluralist society is one in which there are many choices and many interpretations of MEANING.

Podcasting Derives from the Apple Macintosh iPod music DOWNLOADING system.

A podcast is the RADIO equivalent of BLOGGING. It allows individuals and groups to run their own radio broadcasting service, downloadable via the INTERNET. As Ken Young, in a UK *Guardian* article (21 July 2005) 'One-man band', points out, 'With podcasting, the one man radio station was born.' Podcasts can be delivered by an automatic news feed system known as Really Simple Syndication (RSS), enabling broadcasts to be downloaded automatically whenever a station is being broadcast. Problems concern copyright on music and the risk that the authorities will seek to impose licensing regulations.

Polarization Refers to the tendency to think and speak in terms of opposites (see WEDOM, THEYDOM) or what have been termed *binary oppositions*. The English language abounds with terms denoting opposition. Reality, however, is more complex, and arguably few things can be seen meaningfully in terms of polar opposites. Our language then may tempt us into misleadingly simple perspectives.

As Gail and Michele Myers argue in *The Dynamics of Human Communication* (US: McGraw-Hill, 1985), 'Our language supports dividing the world into false opposites. Polarization consists of evaluating what you perceive by placing it at one end of a two-pole continuum and making the two poles appear to be mutually exclusive … If you are honest, you cannot be dishonest.'

Whilst there are situations in which genuine opposites are found, what we should be wary of is applying this perspective when it is not appropriate and in so doing denying the complexities of a situation, or debate, and the range of alternatives that can or may exist. See VISIONS OF ORDER.

Politics of accommodation (in the media) Potential conflict between various individuals and GROUPS within media corporations and between these corporations and a central social authority is seen by some commentators to be mediated by what Tom Burns in *The BBC: Public Institution and Private World* (UK: Macmillan, 1977) calls a 'politics of accommodation'. This is a negotiated compromise in which notions such as professional standards and the public interest are used as trading pieces. Negotiations of this type can be conducted at several levels: between the professionals and the management, between one corporation and another, and between a corporation and the government.

Even between rival media empires there can exist, temporarily at least, what might be termed *reciprocal silence*, an agreement to censor information that may, if publicized, be damaging to one or other side. A case in point is the silence exercised by the UK *Daily Mail* and its sister paper the *Mail on Sunday* over the controversial takeover of the *Mail's* rival, *Express* Newspapers, by porn king Richard Desmond, chief of the Northern and Shell company. The Labour government's approval in 2002 of this takeover was explained by some commentators – though not in the *Mail*, among Labour's harshest critics – as being linked with Desmond's £100,000 contribution to Labour Party funds.

Associated Newspapers (AN), owners of the *Mail* and *Sunday Mail*, turned out to have a legal agreement with Northern and Shell – a pact of reciprocal silence – not to report the controversy in return for the *Express* group's silence concerning allegations about the Rothermere family, owners of AN. Margaret McDonagh, the then Labour Party General Secretary, who banked the £100,000 for Labour, shortly afterwards joined Northern and Shell. See CONSENSUS; ELITE; ESTABLISHMENT; HEGEMONY; MEDIA CONTROL; MEDIATION; REGULATORY FAVOURS; STRATEGIC BARGAINING. See also *TOPIC GUIDE* under MEDIA INSTITUTIONS; MEDIA: POLITICS & ECONOMICS.

Polysemy Many meanings; broadly used, the term describes the potential for many interpretations in media TEXTS, or the capacity of AUDIENCE to read into such texts their own meanings rather than merely the PREFERRED READING of the communicators. For some commentators, audience is the 'victim' of media messages; for others, it is perceived as being capable of making its own diverse responses (see AUDIENCE: ACTIVE AUDIENCE; DOMINANT, SUBORDINATE, RADICAL). There is CONSENSUS among researchers that the extent of polysemy is to be viewed with caution.

As Celeste Michelle Condit writes in 'The rhetorical limits of polysemy' in *Television: The Critical View* (US: Oxford University Press, 1994), edited by Horace Newcomb, 'It is clear that there are substantial limits to the polysemic potential of texts and of decodings.' She recommends that we differentiate between the polysemy of texts and their interpretation by audience, and suggests the term 'polyvalence' to describe the meanings ascribed to texts by audience.

'Polyvalence occurs,' says Condit, 'when audience members share understandings of the denotation of a text but disagree about the evaluation of those denotations to such a degree that they produce notably different interpretations.' It is different from polysemy in that it reflects 'not a multiplicity or instability of textual meanings but rather a difference in audience evaluations of shared denotations'.

Condit describes her research findings based upon the response of two students to an episode of the American TV cop series *Cagney & Lacey* (11 November 1985) in which the issue of abortion is dealt with. 'Jack', a pro-lifer, and 'Jill', pro-choice, had no difficulty understanding the *denotational* aspects of the episode. Where they took diametrically opposite viewpoints was in their response to the programme which had a pro-choice message; their *connotational* reading. See OPEN, CLOSED TEXTS; OPINION LEADER; SIGNIFICANT OTHERS.

Polyvalence See POLYSEMY.

Pool system Practice, particularly in wartime, of governments chanelling media access to NEWS events through a regulated 'pool' of reporters; and consequently the 'pooling' of information for publication or broadcasting. This strategy of NEWS MANAGEMENT effectively censors journalists by corralling them, while at the same time claiming to offer prompt and reliable information on events. The first Gulf War (1991) offered a classic example of control through pooling. For a similar exercise in the control of war reporting, this time during the second Gulf War (2003), see EMBEDDED REPORTERS.

Poor Man's Guardian Title of perhaps the most influential radical newspaper in Britain during the nineteenth century, edited by Bronterre O'Brien, published by Henry Hetherington. It appeared between 1831 and 1835, and was described by George Jacob Holyoake, a campaigner against the Taxes on Knowledge levied by government on the press, as 'the first messenger of popular and political intelligence which reached the working classes'. Other radical papers of this turbulent period were Richard Carlile's *Gauntlet* (1833–34), Robert Owen's *Crisis* (1832–34), James Watson's *Working Man's Friend* (1832–33) and Fergus O'Connor's *Northern Star* (1837–52), principal organ of the Chartist movement. See STAMP DUTY; UNDERGROUND PRESS. See also *TOPIC GUIDE* under MEDIA HISTORY.

Popular culture See CULTURE: POPULAR CULTURE.

Populism According to some theorists one of the distinguishing features of a mass society is its populist nature. Legitimacy is given to those persons, ideas or actions that are thought to best express the popular will or meet the most widely shared expectations. One result, such theorists claim, is that a premium is placed upon the capacity of those in leadership positions to both create and placate popular opinion. The mass media tend to be seen as the agents through which such leaders control and exploit the masses.

Pornography Term originating from the Greek, 'writing of harlots'. Two sorts of pornography are usually differentiated: *erotica*, concentrating on physical aspects of heterosexual activity; and *exotica*, focusing on abnormal or deviationist sexual activity. Attitudes to pornography reflect a society's permissiveness and its current 'tolerance threshold', and also cast a light on prevailing social values.

Tolerance of pornography makes sense only if there is no felt risk; if pornography is thought to be linked with the abuse of women and children and the degradation of human relationships and family life, it will be fought against whether the link is proved or not. In any case, pornography itself often makes the link between sexuality and violence: hard porn is, by general definition, a DISCOURSE in dominance expressed through violence which, at the very least, poses examples of possible behaviour.

Of interest and concern is the indisputable fact that in many countries pornography is big business. Civic concern about the possible link between porn and violence was registered by the Minneapolis City Council in 1983. Exhaustive public hearings took place to provide a basis of information for a decision as to whether or not to add pornography as a 'discrimination against women' to existing civil rights legislation. The transcript of the Minneapolis hearings was published in 1988.

Quoting evidence from academic and clinical research on the effect of pornography on ordinary men, the report stated that, exposed to pornography, men become desensitized; they see themselves more likely to commit rape, less likely to respond sympathetically to women who are victims of rape or more likely to be lenient in their response to men who commit rape. According to the Minneapolis transcript, pornography which portrays women enjoying rape or violence or humiliation is most damaging.

As a result of the hearings the City Council passed a civil rights law enabling women victims of pornography to bring civil rights actions against the pornographers. However, the law was vetoed by the mayor and never implemented. A similar situation arose in Indianapolis where pornographers claimed they were being denied their constitutional right to free speech (under the First Amendment). Thus, in the courts, free speech took precedence over women's equality and safety from physical abuse.

In a UK *New Scientist* article, 'Flesh and blood' (5 May 1990), on the effects on men of pornography, Mike Baxter writes, 'The weight of evidence is accumulating that intensive exposure to soft-core pornography desensitizes men's attitudes to rape, increases sexual callousness and shifts their preferences towards hard-core pornography. Similarly, the evidence is now strong that exposure to violent pornography increases men's acceptance of rape myths and of violence against women. ... Many sex offenders claim they used pornography to stimulate themselves before committing their crimes.'

The arrival and expansion of the INTERNET, with its relative freedom from control and overview, has offered global opportunities for pornography, along with the pornography of race hatred (see CYBER-SPACE). Any system that combines the privacy of output and input with potentially universal access will be abused. It has been argued that for women exercising their right to explore the net there is as much danger from predators as there is on the streets at night. See CENSORSHIP; DESENSITIZATION; REGULATION OF INVESTIGATORY POWERS ACT (RIPA) (UK), 2000; STEREOTYPE; WILLIAMS COMMITTEE REPORT ON OBSCENITY AND FILM CENSORSHIP, 1979.

Postcards See PICTURE POSTCARDS.

Posters Printed posters have had a short but vivid history, dating from the 1870s when the perfection of techniques in colour LITHOGRAPHY first made mass production possible. Posters have been described as the art gallery of the street and indeed the form has appealed to many artists, such as Henri Toulouse-Lautrec (1864–1901), members of the Art Nouveau movement and the graphic designers of the Bauhaus and the De Stijl group. Posters have served every mode of PROPAGANDA, social, political, religious, commercial. The arresting clarity of their images, combined with words used dramatically, emotively, humorously have often continued to impress long after the ideas, events or products they relate to have faded from attention.

So immediate and memorable are posters, and so widely recognized, that they have formed a regular inspiration for image-makers: imitated, reproduced, turned into cult objects, transmuted into other meanings. For example, many different uses have been made of Alfred Leete's famous poster (1914) 'Your Country Needs You', in which Lord Kitchener points out towards the audience, offering a formidable challenge to all those who have not yet volunteered for service in the First World War.

In peacetime, between elections, ADVERTISING dominates the poster contents of the billboards, sometimes with bold, witty and memorable images such as the Guinness adverts or Benetton's striking socio-political images. Posters come into their own in time of protest or revolution. Some of the finest posters were designed and printed during and after the Russian Revolution of 1917, while the Spanish Civil War (1936–39) stimulated the production of hundreds of hard-hitting, passionate and often tragic images. See *TOPIC GUIDE* under MEDIA HISTORY.

Postmodernism Term referring to cultural, social and political attitudes and expression characteristic of the 1980s and 1990s, following the modernist period of psychoanalysis, functional, clean-line, machine-inspired architecture, abstract art and stream-of-consciousness fiction. Wendy Griswold in *Cultures and Societies in a Changing World* (US: Pine Forge Press, 1994) writes 'Many people believe that society has entered this new stage beyond modernity, a postindustrial stage of social development dominated by media images, in which people are connected with other places and times through proliferating channels of information.'

If hope and anxiety were features of modernism, says Griswold, 'the postmodern person is characterized by a cool absence of illusion. Modern minds were sceptical, Postmodern minds are cynical.' The prevailing cynicism is wary of traditional attempts at explaining the evolution of society. It discards the affirming or 'grand narratives' (*metanarratives*) of the past that subscribed to the view of the inevitability of human progress, what might be described as the Enlightenment position. Reality itself is an uncertainty: being a creation of language and existing in socially produced DISCOURSE, it represents an infinitely movable feast.

Marxism has been rejected by postmodernist thinkers such as Michel Foucault, Jacques Derrida, Jean-François Lyotard and Jean Baudrillard as having 'totalizing ambitions', that is offering grandiose explanations of reality which cannot be sustained. They therefore reject the central tenet of Marxism, its belief in the emancipation of humanity.

The postmodernist position derives much of its vision from the German philosopher Friedrich Nietzsche (1844–1900), in particular his profound antipathy to any system and his rejection of the view expressed by an earlier German thinker, Georg Wilhelm Friedrich Hegel (1770–1831), of history as progress. Instead of such totalizing, postmodernism embraces *fragmentation* (and this includes views on the fragmentation of time itself and therefore of concepts of the past and present). It homes in on micro-situations. The stress is on the local. Taking a deeply sceptical position, postmodernists declare that progress is a MYTH. If there are no unities, then nothing figures; if nothing figures, nothing matters and if nothing matters then anything goes.

Thus in architecture postmodernism scorns traditional forms while unapologetically plagiarizing them. It has varyingly been described as a culture of surfaces, of self-aware superficiality characterized by the ephemeral and discontinuity. In the postmodernist approach, writes Norman K. Denzen in a review, 'Messy methods of communication research' in the *Journal of Communication* (Spring 1995), all 'criteria are doubted, no position is privileged'.

Taken to a logical conclusion such a standpoint facilitates cultural freedom and unshackled PLURALISM; it could also unhinge freedom from responsibility on the ground that a definition of responsibility could be arrived at only on a personal, micro-level, hence the accusation made in some quarters that postmodernism is the cultural arm of the COMMODITIZATION of information and knowledge.

Madan Sarup in *An Introductory Guide to Post-Structuralism and Postmodernism* (UK: Harvester Wheatsheaf, 1993) says of Baudrillard, 'Personally I find many of his insights stimulating and provocative but, generally, his position is deplorable. In Baudrillard's world truth and falsity are wholly indistinguishable, a position which I find leads to moral and political nihilism.' The danger for a postmodernist world resides in a view expressed by Lyotard that power has increasingly become the criterion of – the *synonym* for – truth. See DECONSTRUCTION; MEDIASPHERE. See also *TOPIC GUIDE* under COMMUNICATION THEORY.

* David Harvey, *The Condition of Postmodernity: An Inquiry into the Origins of Cultural Change* (UK: Blackwell, 1990); J.-F. Lyotard, *The Postmodern Condition* (UK: Manchester University Press, 1984); Frederic Jameson, *Postmodernism, or, The Cultural Logic of Late Capitalism* (UK: Verso, 1991); Christopher Norris, *Uncritical Theory: Postmodernism, Intellectuals and the Gulf War* (UK: Lawrence & Wishart, 1992); Angela McRobbie, *Postmodernism and Popular Culture* (UK; Routledge, 1994); John Hartley, *Popular Reality: Journalism, Modernity, Popular Culture* (UK: Arnold, 1996); George Myerson, *Heidegger, Habermas and the Mobile Phone* (UK: Icon Books, 2001).

Post-synchronization Or *dubbing*. In film-making, the process of adding new or altered dialogue in the original language to the soundtrack of a film after it has been shot. See SYNCHRONOUS SOUND.

Postulates of communication To define the fundamental attributes of the communication process is possibly a more fruitful area of analysis than struggling for an all-embracing and acceptable definition of communication. C.D. Mortensen in *Communication: the Study of Human Interaction* (US: McGraw-Hill, 1972) poses a single, basic postulate, that 'Communication occurs whenever persons attribute significance to message-related behaviour'; and then follows this up with five secondary postulates.

These are: (1) Communication is dynamic. (2) Communication is irreversible. (3) Communication is proactive (as opposed to *reactive*). Mortensen says here, 'The notion of man as a detached bystander, an objective and dispassionate reader of the environment, is nothing more than a convenient artefact. Among living creatures man is the most spectacular example of an agent who amplifies his environment.' We are shapers, not mere recipients. (4) Communication is interactive. (5) Communication is contextual. See *TOPIC GUIDE* under COMMUNICATION MODELS.

Postural echo Occurs when people – friends, lovers, etc. – unconsciously imitate or 'echo' each other's GESTURES and postures. Desmond Morris in *Manwatching: A Field Guide to Human Behaviour* (UK: Jonathan Cape, 1977) describes postural echo as 'part of a natural body display of companionship'. He writes, 'Because acting in unison spells equal-status friendship, it can be used by dominant individuals to put subordinates at their ease.' See TIE-SIGNS.

Posture An element of non-verbal communication, a person's posture can be used or taken to indicate a range of aspects of behaviour. For instance, people often make judgements about others' states of mind from their body posture and certain postures do seem to communicate something of the way a person feels. Optimism, confidence and dominance, for example, are often associated with an upright posture whereas depression tends to be associated with a slouching, shrinking posture. Posture can be used to provide a variety of messages in feedback and can also be used to communicate our attitude to others.

Positive feelings towards others are often shown, in part, by a leaning-forward posture in conversation, and by POSTURAL ECHO. Conversely, negative feelings can be indicated by leaning back from others. High status can be signalled by an upright posture. Aggressive attitudes towards others can be demonstrated by a progressively more exaggerated exhibition of high status or dominant behaviour. Shifts in posture can be used to mark stages in a conversation. See COMMUNICATION, NON-VERBAL (NVC).

Power This has been defined, and written about at length, by many theorists in many different disciplines, but a useful working definition is that provided by John B. Thompson in *The Media and Modernity: A Social Theory of the Media* (UK: Polity Press, 1995): power is 'the ability to act in pursuit of one's aims and interests, the ability to intervene in the course of events and to affect their outcome. In exercising power, individuals employ the resources available to them; resources are the means which enable them to pursue their aims and interests effectively.' Whilst the individual may be the basic building block of the power structure of any society, some blocks are arguably a lot bigger than others as some individuals have personally considerably more resources than others.

Further, as Thompson argues, 'While resources can be built up personally, they are also commonly accumulated within the framework of institutions, which are important bases for the exercise of power. Individuals who occupy dominant positions within large institutions may have vast resources at their disposal, enabling them to make decisions and pursue objectives which have far-reaching consequences.'

A concept closely related to that of power is *influence*. Charles B. Handy in *Understanding Organizations* (UK: Penguin, 1993) describes the relationship between power and influence thus: 'Influence is the process whereby A modifies the attitudes and behaviour of B. Power is that which enables him to do it.' The exercise of power and influence, in addition to resources requires what French and Raven term a 'power base' (quoted in B. Raven and J. Rubin, *Social Psychology*, US: John Wiley, 1983) and at the same time the selection of appropriate methods of influence. In turn this is predicated to a considerable extent on the acceptance of, or acquiescence in, the exercise of power by those subjected to it.

John B. Thompson offers a distinction between the differing *sources* of power and categorizes these into four main types: *economic, political, coercive* and *symbolic.* Of course these often overlap and the way in which they do so is in itself an indication of the often complex and at times mutually supportive relationships that exist within the overall power structures. Varying forms of power are often concentrated in institutions. *Economic power* is based in ownership or control of those resources required for the productive activity involved in transforming human, material and financial resources into goods and services, for sale or exchange in a market in order to generate a means of subsistence. This might also be described as *corporate power.*

Political power stems from the authority, usually of governments and those bodies invested with *authority,* to organize the activities of individuals, GROUPS or organizations and nations. *Coercive power* expresses itself through the use of force and can be found in a diverse range of power relationships. Most states, for example, whatever their form of government, have resources that underscore their political power with the ability to employ physical force when the exercise of power by persuasion seems likely to fail.

Very different but not necessarily less effective is *symbolic power*, which Thompson defines as stemming from 'the activity of producing, transmitting and receiving meaningful symbolic forms'. He sees such activity as being 'a fundamental feature of social life. ... Individuals are constantly engaged in the activity of expressing themselves in symbolic forms and in interpreting the expressions of others; they are constantly involved in communicating with one another and exchanging information and symbolic content.' To do so, individuals draw upon the various 'means of information and communication' such as access to the channels of communications, communicative competence, knowledge and acknowledged expertise in areas of symbolic exchange. The mass media serve as key operators of symbolic power.

The pivotal role that the media play in transmitting information about politics and politicians to a wide audience, in *power-broking*, has resulted in their being referred to as the FOURTH ESTATE; that is, they rank alongside the judiciary, the Church and government as exercisers of power and influence. Indeed it is the media who play an essential role in communicating to the public the nature, location and distribution of power in the community and the power-relationships operating within it; hence the central interest among media analysts and researchers in the media's capacity to influence, shape, reinforce or undermine the

screen. His apparatus was crude but effective, containing all the essentials – a source of light with a reflector behind it and a lens in front, a painted glass slide and a screen. Kircher's astonished audience spoke of black magic. Undaunted, the inventor published a description of his findings.

The projection of moving pictures was first demonstrated by Baron Von Uchatius (1811–81) in 1853. He used a rotating glass slide, a rotating shutter and a fixed lens. An improved version contained a rotating light source, fixed slides and a series of slightly inclined lenses whose optical axes met on the centre of the screen. See CINEMATOGRAPHY, ORIGINS.

Project of self See SELF-IDENTITY.

Prolefeed The rubbishy entertainment and spurious news piped to the proletariat by the Party in George Orwell's novel *Nineteen Eighty-Four* (1949).

Propaganda Usually deliberate manipulation by means of symbols (words, gestures, images, flags, monuments, music, etc.) of other people's thoughts, behaviour, attitudes and beliefs. The word originates with the Roman Catholic Congregation for the Propagation of the Faith, a committee of cardinals in charge of the missionary activities of the Church since 1622. Propaganda works through emphasizing some factors and excluding others, often emotively appealing to anxieties, fears, prejudices and ignorance of the true facts. Propaganda can be blatant (see RADIO DEATH) or work by stealth, often using entertainment as a means of 'sugar-coating' messages.

In the world of contemporary politics, propaganda takes the form of NEWS MANAGEMENT or *spin*; and a profession of *spin doctors* now 'doctor' facts in ways intended to favourably propagate to the public the ideas, policies and performance of government. Propaganda, whether it is that of governments, companies, institutions, charitable organizations or the world of sport, aims to create in the public mind a favourable impression. This might be termed *white* propaganda. In contrast, propaganda that sets out to create in the public mind a bad impression – of other countries, for example, other ethnic groups, foreigners, asylum-seekers, minorities, that is defining them as 'enemy' – might be termed *black* propaganda.

Garth J. Jowett and Victoria O'Donnell in *Propaganda and Persuasion* (US: Sage, 1999) identify three forms of propaganda: *white, black* and *grey*: 'White propaganda comes from a source that is identified correctly, and the information in the message tends to be accurate … Although what listeners hear is reasonably close to the truth, it is presented in a manner that attempts to convince the audience that the sender is the "good guy".

'Black propaganda on the other hand,' explain the authors, '… is credited to a false source and spreads lies, fabrications and deceptions. Black propaganda is the "big lie", including all types of creative deceit.' DISINFORMATION would be an example of black propaganda. Grey propaganda lies 'somewhere between white and black. The source may not be correctly identified, and the accuracy of the information is uncertain.'

Sheldon Rampton and John Stauber in *Weapons of Mass Deception: The Uses of Propaganda in Bush's War on Iraq* (US: Tarcher/Penguin; UK: Constable & Robinson, 2003) write, 'Whereas democracy is built upon the assumption that "the people" are capable of rational self-governance, propagandists regard rationality as an obstacle to efficient indoctrination. Since propaganda is often aimed at persuading people to do things that are not in their own best interests, it frequently seeks to bypass the rational brain altogether and manipulate us on a more primitive level, appealing to emotional symbolism.'

The authors talk of 'corporate spin doctors, think tanks and conservative politicians' who have 'taken up the rhetoric of fear for their own purposes'. See ADVERTISING; BRAINWASHING; CONSENT, MANUFACTURE OF; DEMONIZATION; EFFECTS OF THE MASS MEDIA; LOBBYING; PSYOPS; PUBLIC RELATIONS (PR); RHETORIC. See also *TOPIC GUIDE* under LANGUAGE/ DISCOURSE/NARRATIVE.

Propaganda model of mass communication See CONSENT, MANUFACTURE OF.

Property: intellectual property See CULTURE: COPYRIGHTING CULTURE.

Propinquity A significant determinant of group membership, propinquity is liking through *proximity*; when people are close together physically there is a strain towards amicability which aids group formation, more reliably than with physically distant persons. See GROUPS.

Propp's people In a study of Russian folk tales, Vladimir Propp classified a range of stock characters identifiable in most NARRATIVES (see his *Morphology of the Folk Tale* published in 1968 by the University of

Texas Press). These may be individualized by being given distinguishing character traits but they are essentially functionaries enabling the story to unfold. Propp describes a number of archetypal story features: the *hero/subject* whose function is to seek; the *object* that is sought; the *donor* of the object; the *receiver*, where it is sent; the *helper* who aids the action and the *villain* who blocks the action.

Thus in one of the world's best-known folk tales, Red Riding Hood (heroine) is sent by her mother (donor) with a basket of provisions (object) to her sick granny (receiver) who lives in the forest. She encounters the wolf (villain) and is rescued from his clutches – and his teeth – by the woodman (helper).

This formula can be added to and manipulated in line with the requirements of the GENRE, but it does allow us to differentiate between *story level* and *meaning level*, between the denotive and the connotive, between the so-termed *mimetic plane* (the plane of representation) and the *semiosic plane* (the plane of MEANING production). See CODES OF NARRATIVE.

Prosodic signals Timing, pitch and stress of utterances to convey MEANING.

Proxemics The study of the way people approach others or keep their distance from others: the analysis of what we do with space as a dimension of non-verbal communication (see COMMUNICATION, NON-VERBAL (NVC)). There appear to be definite features that mark the distance people observe between each other in communication situations. Within three feet is intimate; up to about eight feet is personal; over that distance is semi-public or social. The proximity between communicators differs, obviously, according to the nature of the MESSAGE, and varies between cultures, classes and nations.

The personal but not intimate distance of Arabs, for example, can be as little as 18 inches – intimidating for an English listener. Middle-class distances tend, it has been found, to be slightly greater than those maintained between working-class communicators. Proxemics extends to the way we allocate space to those extensions of ourselves – rooms, houses, towns, cities – and the manner in which we occupy those extensions. See PARAPROXEMICS.

* Edward T. Hall, *The Hidden Dimension: Man's Use of Space in Public and Private* (UK: Bodley Head, 1966).

PR: public relations See PUBLIC RELATIONS (PR).

PSB (Public Service Broadcasting) See PUBLIC SERVICE BROADCASTING (PSB).

Pseudo-context In his sharply critical assessment of the impact of TV on society, in *Amusing Ourselves to Death* (UK: Methuen, 1986), American author and communications professor Neil Postman says of a pseudo-context that it is 'a structure invented to give fragmented and irrelevant information a seeming use'. However, the pseudo-context offers us no useful function for the information in terms of action, problem-solving or change. TV is the culprit in this fragmenting process. All that is left for what Postman calls the 'decontextualization of fact' by the non print media, particularly TV, is to amuse. All knowledge, having been fragmented, is reduced to a trivial pursuit. See EFFECTS OF THE MASS MEDIA.

PSI Parasocial identification; that is, members of an AUDIENCE associate with fictitious characters as portrayed in the media, or with well-known personalities whom they regularly 'meet' through the mediation of radio, TV, etc. See PARASOCIAL INTERACTION.

Psycholinguistics The study of the interplay between language acquisition, development and use and other aspects of the human mind.

Psychology This discipline seeks to explore the way in which individual behaviours are linked together to form a 'personality'. Its focus is upon the experience and behaviour of the individual, upon the individual's reaction to certain physiological and/or social conditions. Some areas of social psychology are concerned with the behaviour of individuals in small groups or crowds; here there is some overlap between this discipline and that of SOCIOLOGY.

* Valerie Walkerdine and Lisa Blackman, *Psychology and the Media* (UK: Macmillan, 1999).

Psyops US shorthand for psychological operations; the equivalent UK term is 'information support'; an arm of PROPAGANDA. Psyops work in a number of ways to promote 'fact' and 'truth' in support of state action, especially in times of conflict and war. David Miller in 'The propaganda machine', a chapter in the book he edited, *Tell Me Lies: Propaganda and Media Distortion in the Attack on Iraq* (UK: Pluto, 2004), writes that such operations are 'entirely outside of democratic control'. They appear 'not to be constrained by adhering to any standard of truthfulness', operating 'on the basis that anything goes so long as it is calculated that it can be got away with'.

The author is of the view that the use of psyops shows contempt for the process of democracy 'since the lies are constructed to misinform and persuade – in part – the electorate of the US and UK as well as world opinion'. He is referring in particular to the techniques and processes of persuasion which supported the invasion and occupation of Iraq in 2003 by US and British forces; alluding in particular to the 'evidence' put forward to the public of weapons of mass destruction (WMDs) that posed a threat to the invading nations; weapons that were never found.

Public communication Alternative term to *mass media* or *mass communication* and one preferred by some writers, among them Raymond Williams.

Public communication values See NORMATIVE THEORIES OF MASS MEDIA.

Public cues See BARNLUND'S TRANSACTIONAL MODELS OF COMMUNICATION, 1970.

Public data access See TELEDEMOCRACY.

Public Interest Disclosure Act (UK), 1999 See WHISTLE-BLOWING.

Public Occurrences Both Foreign and Domestic Title of the first American newspaper, founded in Boston on 25 September 1690 by Benjamin Harris. The paper survived for one issue only, being immediately suppressed by the Governor and Council of the then British colony.

Public opinion The Greek AGORA is traditionally seen as the birthplace and location of public opinion. It was an open space where free citizens gathered to discuss and ideally shape the affairs of state. By its nature public opinion lacks the structure of, for example, ELITE opinion and there are difficulties both of definition and identification. The modern-day OPINION POLL tests samples of the whole public; market and audience research have pursued increasingly sophisticated, technology-aided modes of opinion measurement. For such research, measurement is of TASTES, expectations, needs, VALUES and behaviour as well as opinions. For the student of media, the public is examined from the point of view of how the media *represent* public opinion, purport to speak for it, indeed, to define it; and to shape it especially in the light of perhaps the most important and specific expression of public opinion – voting.

Susan Herbst and James R. Beniger in 'The changing infrastructure of public opinion' published in *Audiencemaking: How the Media Create the Audience* (US: Sage, 1994), edited by James S. Ettema and D. Charles Whitney, explore the connections between the concept of public opinion and the means by which public opinion is measured, the one being influenced by the other; thus what public opinion is in any situation is to a degree defined by how it is defined and measured. The authors say that 'both polling and voting embrace a conception of public opinion as the aggregation of individual opinions and both provide means for elite management of those opinions'.

They identify three historical phases in the evolution of public opinion infrastructures. The first was located in the salons of mid-eighteenth-century France (see SALON DISCOURSE). Here the political and intellectual elite gathered socially to discuss all matters from art to philosophy, not the least affairs of state and the nature of government. This elite model of public opinion found a modestly downmarket parallel in the coffee houses of London presided over by such 'agorans' as Dr Samuel Johnson (1709–84). These 'spaces' for DISCOURSE were only one aspect of the infrastructure; what formed an extension of them were the writings of those novelists, poets, scientists and philosophers who attended the salons or met in the coffee houses.

Towards the middle of the nineteenth century the press became the dominant residence of public opinion, but the newspapers were increasingly reflecting, both in the UK and US, the development of political parties. Herbst and Beniger believe that 'in concert with the newspapers that shared their ideologies, political parties were a critical component of the late-19th century American infrastructure of public opinion expression and assessment'. In fact PRESSURE GROUPS of all kinds, including trades unions, contributed to the group-based model of public opinion.

New media technology such as RADIO and more efficient measurement practices contributed to what Herbst and Beniger term 'a shift from publics to audiences'. What had, until the emergence of audience-measurement techniques (such as the Audimeter-based NIELSEN RATINGS in the States), been an aggregate of opinions, was now a profile of *differences* leading to what in ADVERTISING terms was to become SEGMENTATION. The ability to discriminate between shades of opinion as far as this audience model is concerned indicates advancing degrees of rationalization, and this, state Herbst and Beniger, 'works best for those at the top of a given system'. See INFORMATION COMMONS; MEDIASPHERE.

Public radio Term used in Australia to refer to COMMUNITY RADIO.

Public relations (PR) According to the Chartered Institute of Public Relations website (2005), 'Public Relations is about reputation – the result of what you do, what you say and what others say about you … Public Relations is the discipline which looks after reputation, with the aim of earning understanding and support and influencing opinion and behaviour. It is the planned and sustained effort to establish and maintain goodwill and mutual understanding between an organization and its publics.'

Many companies and institutions in both the public and private sector have PR departments dedicated to creating and sustaining their good image and reputation with a variety of publics: for example, shareholders, taxpayers, clients, customers and employees. Public relations personnel may work alongside those in ADVERTISING and MARKETING but their role is essentially focused on building relationships and fostering the two-way communication channels required to achieve this aim.

Shirley Harrison in *Public Relations: An Introduction* (US/UK: Routledge, 1995) writes, 'The most common public relations activities undertaken by practitioners are media relations, publicity and publications, corporate public relations and provision of information.' See BERNSTEIN'S WHEEL; GRUNIG AND HUNT MODEL, 1984; LOBBYING; OPINION LEADER; PEST; PIE CHART; PUBLICS; STAKEHOLDERS; SWOT.

Public relations news (PRN) See NEWS: PUBLIC RELATIONS NEWS (PRN).

Publics A term used within public relations practice to refer to specific groups that are or might become an intended audience for communication activities: pressure groups, customers, competitors, local communities and opinion leaders. As Paul Baines, John Egan and Frank Jefkins note in *Public Relations: Contemporary Issues and Techniques* (UK: Elsevier Butterworth-Heinemann, 2004), 'The identification of the "publics" of public relations is fundamental to the planning of a PR programme, for unless the publics are defined it is impossible to select the media that will best convey our messages to them'.

Relevant publics will vary from one organization or individual client to another and from one programme or campaign to another; they will also vary over time. As with any communication activity, knowledge of the public (audience) is crucial when making decisions about the construction as well as the delivery of messages. A PR activity may, of course, have a number of publics, each of which might need to be approached, to some extent, in a different manner. The concept can also be used in identification of potential future publics.

A number of researchers have proposed means of classifying publics. James Grunig and Todd Hunt in *Managing Public Relations* (US: Harcourt Brace Jovanovich, 1984) note, for example, the four categories derived from James Grunig's studies. Grunig divided up publics in terms of their levels of likely activity as regards a PR programme and identified four main types of public: (1) publics that are active on all issues; (2) publics that are apathetic on all issues; (3) publics interested in single issues; and (4) publics that are active only on issues that involve nearly everyone in the population, that is controversial topical issues. Any one individual's position may of course change over time and one aim of a campaign, for example, might be to convert apathy into some form of active engagement. See BERNSTEIN'S WHEEL (1984); GRUNIG AND HUNT MODEL (1984); OPINION LEADER.

* Scott M. Cutlip, Allen H. Center and Glen M. Broom, *Effective Public Relations* (US: Prentice Hall, 1994); Allen H. Center and Patrick Jackson, *Public Relations Practices* (US: Prentice-Hall, 2003).

Public service broadcasting (PSB) Refers to any BROADCASTING system whose first duty is to a public within a DEMOCRACY, serving to inform, educate and entertain, and to regard AUDIENCE as constituting citizens, members of communities and individuals rather than merely consumers. PSB is essentially the creation of government in the first instance though for this reason safeguards are built in to the system so that its operation is (relatively) free of government control and influence. Financing of PSB is usually through some form of taxation or licence, subject to periodic revision by government; or in the case of commercial television, by means of ADVERTISING.

The BBC, in the UK, represents for many the classic example of public service broadcasting (see BBC, ORIGINS). It was created by Act of Parliament and is subject to *regulation* laid down by Parliament. The

Quotas Limits placed upon the import of foreign printing, film and broadcast material to protect indigenous, home-grown media products. Quotas are immensely difficult to establish and sustain and, with the modern shift of emphasis from producers to consumers (through the availability of video, DVD, cable transmission and satellite transmission) import controls will be even less effective. For quotas to work, it would be necessary to rival the attraction-value of the materials available – cheap, packaged, of proven success with audiences. See MEDIA IMPERIALISM.

Quota sample See SAMPLING.

QWERTY Arrangement of letters on the traditional TYPEWRITER keyboard, devised in 1873 to overcome jamming problems on the world's first production machine, a Remington.

 R

Racism Discrimination against individuals or GROUPS of people on the basis of assumed racial differences. The term is problematic in that there is some argument as to whether the concept of race is useful anyway in describing biological differences between people. Racism, though, rests on the belief that different races with specific characteristics can be meaningfully identified. At an individual level such discrimination takes the form of PREJUDICE, whereas the term racism is often used to describe the way in which such discrimination is embedded into the structure of a society.

Cultural racism refers to the perpetuation, consciously or unconsciously, of such discrimination and the beliefs and VALUES on which it rests through the cultural institutions of a society, for example, education and the mass media. As Stuart Hall notes in 'The whites of their eyes: racist ideologies and the media' in *The Media Reader* (UK: BFI Publishing, 1990), edited by Manuel Alvarado and John O. Thompson, 'The media are … part of the dominant means of ideological production. What they "produce" is precisely representations of the social world, images, descriptions, explanations and frames for understanding how the world is and why it works as it is said and shown to work. And, amongst other kinds of ideological labour, the media construct for us a definition of what race is, what meaning the imagery of race carries, and what the "problem of race" is understood to be. They help to classify our world in terms of the categories of race.'

One important focus of current media research is the role that the media play in shaping and perpetuating racism and racist STEREOTYPES. Research suggests that negative and stereotypical images of ethnic minorities abound and present an image of them as inferior, marginal and a potential source of social problems. Simon Cottle in *Ethnic Minorities and the Media* (UK: Open University Press, 2000), edited by Cottle, argues that 'over recent decades a considerable body of research conducted in both the UK and the US has examined the media's representations of ethnic minorities.

'The collective findings of this research effort generally make depressing reading. Under-representation and stereotypical characterization within entertainment genres and negative problem-orientated portrayal within factuality and news forms, and a tendency to ignore structural inequalities and lived racism experienced by ethnic minorities in both, are recurring research findings.'

Manuel Alvarado, Robin Gutch and Tana Wollen argue in *Learning the Media* (UK: Macmillan, 1987) that the portrayal of black people on television largely falls into four main categories: the *exotic*, for example coverage of tribal dancing used to welcome members of the royal family when visiting various Commonwealth countries; the *dangerous*, for example coverage of immigration as an issue that presents coloured immigrants and asylum-seekers as a threat; the *humorous*, where humour may well serve to reinforce notions of racial differences to the detriment of coloured people; and the *pitied*, for example media coverage of famines in Africa and of western attempts to provide aid, which tend to represent famine as resulting from the inadequacies of the people and their governments rather than as a legacy of western colonialism.

Tuen A. van Dijk in 'New(s) racism: a discourse analysis approach', published in Cottle's *Ethnic Minorities and the Media*, analyses the contribution news coverage in the press makes to *new racism*, which opts for a more subtle negative portrayal of ethnic groups rather than the more obvious and open racism of the past. Van Dijk writes that 'most mentions of "terrorists" especially also in the US press) will stereotypically refer to Arabs. Violent men who are our friends or allies will seldom get that label.

'For the same reason, "drug barons" are always Latin men in South America, never the white men who are in the drugs business within the US itself.' New racism extends to selection of stories for news coverage and van Dijk argues that as regards news about immigrants and ethnic minorities, there is 'a preference for those topics that emphasize Their bad actions and Our good ones'. The consequence, he concludes, is that 'Systematic negative portrayal of the Others, thus vitally contributed to negative mental models, stereotypes, prejudices and ideologies about the Others, and hence indirectly the enactment and reproduction of racism.' See BIGOTRY; COMPASSION FATIGUE; ETHNOCENTRISM; MEDIA IMPERIALISM; NEWS AID?; OTHER. See also *TOPIC GUIDE* under MEDIA ISSUES & DEBATES.

* John Twitham, ed., *The Black and White Media Book* (UK: Trentham Books, 1990); Tuen van Dijk, *Racism and the Press* (UK: Routledge, 1992); Karen Ross, *Black and White Media: Black Imagery in Popular Films and Television* (UK: Polity, 1996); Oscar H. Gandy Jr, *Communication and Race: A Structural Perspective* (UK: Arnold, 1998); Steve Fenton, *Racism, Class and Culture* (UK: Macmillan, 1999); Sarita Malik, *Representing Black Britain: Black and Asian Images on Television* (UK: Sage, 2001); Norman K. Denzin, *Reading Race* (UK/US: Sage, 2002).

Radical press See MEDIA: ALTERNATIVE (OR RADICAL MEDIA); UNDERGROUND PRESS.

Radical suppression of potential (technology) See SUPERVENING SOCIAL NECESSITY.

Radio See RADIO BROADCASTING.

Radio ballads Form or GENRE of musical DOCUMENTARY inspired in the UK by radio producer Charles Parker, and compiled by folk singers Ewan McColl and Peggy Seeger, beginning in 1958 with *The Ballad of John Axon*. The introduction of high-quality portable tape-recorders to the BBC enabled Parker and his team to create new patterns of vocal sound, interlaced with sound effects (real, not studio-simulated) which served as an 'impressionistic' means of describing the lives and work of ordinary people. John Axon was a train driver, killed in a crash, and the nature of his life was recreated in ballad and recollection. *Singing the Fishing* (1960), taking for its theme the hard life of the North Sea fisherman, won the Italia Press award. The BBC withdrew financial support from this pioneering team in 1964. See RADIO DRAMA.

Radio broadcasting The First World War (1914–18) had given impetus to the development of radio for military purposes, and the training of wireless operators. Visionaries of the age saw the possibility of wireless programmes as an exciting extension of wireless messages – a 'household utility' that would create a world of sound, of voices and music; that would annihilate distance and offer undreamed-of opportunities for CULTURE, entertainment and information. With the ending of the war, crystal sets tuned in by their 'cat's whisker' became immensely popular. The valve, called the 'magic lantern of radio', developed between 1904 and 1914, soon usurped the place of the crystal.

The first 'broadcast' of music and speech was made by an American, R.A. Fissenden, in 1906. The American Radio and Research Company was broadcasting concerts twice and three times a week as early as 1916, though KDKA of Pittsburgh won the earliest renown as a pioneer in the field (on air, 1920).

A ban imposed on 'amateur' radio in Britain at the outbreak of the First World War was not lifted until 1919, but in February 1920 the Marconi Company in the UK began broadcasting from Writtle/Chelmsford, though later in the year the Post Office withdrew permission for these broadcasts. However, on 14 February 1922, the first regular broadcasting service in Britain was again beamed from Writtle, organized by the Experimental Section of the Designs Department of Marconi. Their London station, 2LO, began broadcasting on 11 May of the same year.

The Post Office, faced with nearly 100 applications from manufacturers who wanted to set up broadcasting stations, and realizing the need to have some sort of control of the air waves, proposed a consortium of companies to centralize broadcasting activity: the British Broadcasting Company was born, and John Reith appointed its managing director (see BBC, ORIGINS). The BBC, set up by Royal Charter, came into existence on 1 January 1927. It was to hold a monopoly on broadcasting in the UK until commercial radio was legalized in the SOUND BROADCASTING ACT (UK), 1972.

From its beginning, radio broadcasting in the US was financed by ADVERTISING; from its beginning, radio broadcasting in the UK was free of advertising; the one was predominantly local, the other a national public service and eventually a national institution. No study of the evolution of broadcasting in the UK can avoid also being an analysis of the philosophy, vision and practices of the BBC's Managing Director and later Director General John (later Sir John) Reith. Varyingly called the Napoleon of Broadcasting, and Prospero, the all-powerful magician, Reith disliked politics and politicians, viewed commerce with disdain (and commercialism with contempt). He forged a definition of PUBLIC SERVICE BROADCASTING (PSB) that dominated broadcasting, both radio and TV, for generations and, even in the age of the dispersal of control, affects us still.

Radio newsreaders wore dinner jackets and bow ties to read the NEWS, a symbol of the aloofness and distancing characteristic of Reith and much of the output of the BBC. There was even a Pronunciation Committee. Yet the Corporation resisted criticisms from the popular press that its tastes were too elitist. It was to give drama and classical music, as well as many other forms of music, a new structure and a new popularity. Equally, there was room for developing the special potentials of radio in outside broadcasts, drama documentary, discussion programmes and fireside talks.

The greatest fear of the broadcasters was, and continues to be, government interference. Reith's caution was as monumental as the extent of his control. His desire to render the BBC beyond political reproach led to the Corporation often censoring itself so as to be one step ahead of being censored. The risks to the BBC were not imagined. During the General Strike of 1926 Winston Churchill wanted the government to commandeer the Corporation, a move Reith managed to resist – but at a price: during the strike no representative of organized labour was permitted to broadcast, and the leader of the opposition, Ramsay MacDonald, was also banned.

With the introduction and swift public take-up of television, radio lost dominance and for a time looked as if it would be displaced as a major player on the stage of mass communication. In the 1990s and into the new millennium, both the BBC and commercial radio responded to the challenge, diversified, took audience tastes into account as never before, introduced new channels, new programme modes, adopting digital broadcasting with alacrity. Radio acquired a dynamic new profile not only for music but for talk programmes, sport, the arts, drama and comedy. See WIRELESS TELEGRAPHY. See also *TOPIC GUIDE* under BROADCASTING.

* Asa Briggs, *The History of Broadcasting in the United Kingdom* (UK: Oxford University Press, four vols, 1961, 1965, and vols 3 and 4, 1979); P.M. Lewis and J. Booth, *The Invisible Medium: Public Commercial and Community Radio* (UK: Macmillan, 1989); Paddy Scannell and David Cardiff, *A Social History of British Broadcasting: Vol. 1 1922–1939: Serving the Nation* (UK: Blackwell, 1991); Andrew Crissell, *Understanding Radio* (UK: Routledge, 1994) and *An Introductory History of British Broadcasting* (UK: Routledge, 1997); Stephen Barnard, *Studying Radio* (UK: Arnold, 2000); Caroline Mitchell, ed., *Women and Radio* (UK: Routledge, 2000); Michele Hilmes, ed., *Radio Reader: Essays in the Cultural History of Radio* (US/UK: Routledge, 2001); Asa Briggs and Peter Burke, *A Social History of the Media: From Gutenberg to the Internet* (UK: Polity, 2002).

Radio Cracker See COMMERCIAL RADIO.

Radio Death Or Hate Radio; nickname given to Rwanda's Radio Television Libre des Milles Collines (Thousand Hills Television Radio) which, following the assassination of President Juvenal Habyarimana, conducted an intensive campaign of hatred against the minority tribe, the Tutsis (9 per cent of the population as against 90 per cent Hutu). RTLM proved the power of radio in a land almost without TV and with an illiteracy rate of over 50 per cent of the population. A broadcast in April 1994 claimed that 'by the 5th May the elimination of the Tutsis should be finished'. In the first week of the killing spree upwards of 200,000 people were murdered as Hutu militia combed the countryside.

In 1995 REPORTERS SANS FRONTIÈRES (REPORTERS WITHOUT BORDERS), a Montpellier-based group of journalists set up in 1987 to defend press freedom worldwide, initiated a civil lawsuit in Paris against the founders and organizers of Radio Death alleging their responsibility for genocide, violation of humanitarian law and crimes against humanity.

In response to the torrents of hatred emerging from RTLM, Radio Gatashya was formed and took to the air for the first time in August 1994 in Goma – its own nickname, Humanitarian Radio – providing an information service of help and support to the thousands of refugees. In a BBC Radio 4 documentary, *War Radio*, broadcast in December 1998, journalist Misha Glenny compares the propagandist radio of Rwanda with that of local stations in Bosnia during the late 1990s, emphasizing that as language is the *essence* of radio's power, so it is the essence of ethnic and other differences.

Listeners learn how ethnic groups previously sharing a common language began, through radio, to introduce words and terms that served as markers of difference. The antidote to a MEDIUM that lies as it dominates is not, Glenny concludes, to shut it down but to match it with rival radio which is professional and a respecter of the truth. It is argued that all United Nations peacekeeping enterprises should be supported by a radio service which from the beginning of UN activity is 'on air' in the battle for hearts and minds.

In June 2000 a Belgian-born announcer on Radio Death, Georges Ruggiu, was sentenced by an international criminal tribunal to 12 years' imprisonment on two counts of inciting the Hutu massacres of Tutsis in Rwanda.

Radio drama The first ever radio play was Richard Hughes' *Danger* (1923), about a couple trapped in a mine, but the play that appears to have had the most substantial impact as a work in a new MEDIUM was Reginald Berkeley's *The White Chateau*, broadcast by the BBC to an audience of over 12m on Armistice Day 1925, and telling an extremely harrowing story of the trench war.

Since that time hundreds of writers have been given a start in their professional lives by radio, one of whose many virtues is cheapness: today, a 30-minute radio play requires one day's studio time; an hour-long play, two days. The radio playwright need not concern him/herself with the massive costs of scene changes; there is little need to keep costs down by writing plays for two people and an armchair. The whole world of time and space is at the writer's command.

Most importantly, there is the awaiting imagination of the listener. The best radio plays take listeners on a journey into their imagination, where the play is given its own unique setting, the characters a unique appearance – all with the help of voices, sound-effects and silence; an art form, as the poet W.H. Auden once said, that is 'not spoiled by any collision with visual reality'.

Radio drama possesses the characteristic of intimacy: it has made the interior monologue, the soliloquy, a dramatic device perhaps more convincingly acceptable than on the stage; at the same time, because its stage is contained by no proscenium arch or screen-frame, because its 'stage-set' is actually the mind of the listener, radio also lends itself successfully to epic drama: Shakespeare can be marvellous on radio.

Among writers who took an early interest in radio as a serious art form was the Irish poet Louis MacNeice (1907–65). His verse plays broadcast during and after the Second World War, such as *The Story of My Death* (1943) and *The Dark Tower* (1946) impressively explored the potential of radio, while in 1953 another poet, Welshman Dylan Thomas (1914–53), gave to the world one of the best-known and most loved plays for radio, *Under Milk Wood*. The play was first broadcast on 25 January 1954, with a distinguished all-Welsh cast and produced by Douglas Cleverdon.

For 30 years Val Gielgud as Head of Radio Drama at the BBC guided the evolution of the radio play, himself producing and writing. Throughout its history, radio drama has witnessed a strong tradition of able producers such as Cleverdon, Lancelot Sieveking, Donald McWinnie and Alfred Bradley, nurturing writers who later became famous: Harold Pinter, Stan Barstow, Giles Cooper, Allan Prior, Alun Owen, William Trevor, Henry Livings, Peter Terson, Alan Plater, David Rudkin and Tom Stoppard.

Despite its creative potential, radio as a dramatic medium has acquired less status, and been paid less attention than other, more glamorous media, and less than it deserves. However, the BBC continues to broadcast between 200 and 300 radio plays a year, classical drama as well as new works. See TELEVISION DRAMA; 'WAR OF THE WORLDS'.

Radio: independent radio; Radio Luxembourg; Radio Normandy See COMMERCIAL RADIO.

Radio Northsea PIRATE RADIO station, UK, which began broadcasting off the coast of Essex immediately prior to the general election of 1970. Mindful of the Labour government's antipathy to COMMERCIAL RADIO and the Conservatives' support for it, Radio Northsea broadcast pro-Tory propaganda at an election in which the 18–21 age group were voting for the first time.

Many constituencies in London and the south-east were marginal seats. Labour lost the election; in the constituencies nearest Radio Northsea, the swing against Labour was greatest. At the Royal Opening of Parliament on 2 July 1970, the Queen's Speech confirmed that legislation would be introduced for local radio stations 'under the general supervision of an independent broadcasting authority'.

Radio 1, Radio 2, Radio 3, Radio 4, Radio 5 Live (BBC) Radios 1 to 4 have broadcast in their present form from 1967; Radio 5 took to the air in August 1990, to be revamped into Radio 5 Live in March 1994. Prior to 1967 there was the Home Service, catering for news, plays, talks, comedy shows and magazine programmes – the Talk channel; the Light Programme, largely for popular music and entertainment; and the Third Programme, serving the world of classical music and drama. During the 1960s PIRATE RADIO invaded the air waves with pop music which attracted large audiences. The Marine Broadcasting (Offenders) Act, 1967, made such stations illegal. BBC's Radio 1 was created to meet the new demand and successfully competes with COMMERCIAL RADIO stations for the attention of popular music fans.

Radio 2 took on a similar if not identical role to that of the Light Programme, Radio 3 that of the Third Programme and Radio 4 became Britain's premier talk radio channel. For its richness, diversity and sheer quality of output, Radio 4 must rank among the world's finest radio services. Faced with competition from

CLASSIC FM, Radio 3 has proved itself responsive to audience needs without sacrificing (too much) quality.

Radio 5 was to be a speech-led service catering for the needs of children and young people, sharing air-time with news and sport. Just when this pioneering new channel was beginning to win listeners and to pro-duce programmes of originality, the BBC abandoned the adventure of, in the words of Controller of Radio 5 Pat Ewing, introducing 'a new generation to speech radio', and opted for Radio 5 Live, more general in orientation, often crossing lines with Radio 4 but, in terms of its sports coverage, unexcelled. See BBC DIG-ITAL. See also *TOPIC GUIDE* under BROADCASTING.

RAJAR Radio Joint Audience Research; research body of both the commercial radio and PUBLIC SER-VICE BROADCASTING sectors in the UK. RAJAR contracts out its radio research work to an independ-ent company, Ipsos-RSL. Areas of audience research reported by RAJAR are 'weekly reach', 'average hours' listening on the part of audience, and 'share of listening' between public and private stations. The weekly reach and share listening figures comprise RATINGS.

Random sample See SAMPLING.

Ratings See AUDIENCE MEASUREMENT.

Reaction shot When a person is being interviewed on television there are regular *in-cuts* where the viewer is offered a glimpse of the reactions of the reporter or interviewer – nodding, smiling, acknowledging. When interviews take place on location rather than in the studio, such reaction shots are usually filmed separately and 'edited in' later. See SHOT.

Readership See MEDIASPHERE.

Reading Just as, in modern usage, we refer to TEXT as any human-made artefact, rather than merely a print-ed text, so we refer to reading as a process which is a response to all texts. Use of this term suggests a more positive, attentive and interpretative reaction to a text rather than merely looking. We read critically; we analyse, while at the same time modern usage accepts the more open nature of 'readings' – their POLY-SEMY (or many-meaningness). A *work*, as Roland Barthes has defined it, emanates from a creator, an encoder – writer, artist, composer, for example – but the *text* belongs in the sphere of reading and thus becomes, as it were, the property of the decoder.

It does not necessarily follow that all readings are of equal value for, inevitably, there are informed as con-trasted with uninformed readings. Recognition of *competence* has to be considered, and this would involve what Noam Chomsky has termed 'linguistic competence', as well as knowledge, experience, training and a degree of EMPATHY. The study of media communication is largely about learning to read competently, with PERCEPTION and understanding. See *TOPIC GUIDE* under TEXTUAL ANALYSIS.

Realism That which is portrayed as 'reality' in art, literature, theatre, film fiction or documentary and photo-graphy. It constitutes an imitation of *perceived* reality, a simulation. Because it is the result of a range of choices concerning subject matter and aesthetics, realism is a *construct* of reality rather than a reproduction of it, influ-enced by VALUE and IDEOLOGY and convention. Socialist realism in Russian cinema, for instance, focused on the realities of the lives of workers, on the land or in factories, but such portraits of reality were highly charged with the ideology of the Soviet system in the ways that labour was idealized rather than por-trayed by means of a critical READING of the system.

Susan Strehle in *Fiction in the Quantum Universe* (US/UK: University of Carolina Press, 1992) suggests the use of the term 'actualism' rather than 'the old mechanistic reality' because it has 'its roots not in things [or facts] but in acts, relations and motions'. The term corresponds to ACTUALITY, an approach pioneered by early radio DOCUMENTARY makers to allow real situations to be communicated with a minimum of inter-vention from the programme-maker. Yet however absent seems to be the hand of MEDIATION it is (in actu-ality) ever-present.

Peter Dahlgren in *Television and the Public Sphere: Citizenship, Democracy and the Media* (UK: Sage, 1995) says of TV texts that 'realism' (his inverted commas) is a 'very central feature' but one which is highly problem-atical. We should constantly remind ourselves, Dahlgren believes, that 'all representation involves construc-tion'. In discussing TV the author talks of the 'pleasure of verisimilitude'. Essentially TV is 'mimetic', it imitates reality rather more than it interprets it. In Dahlgren's view this limits the potential TV has for POLYSEMY and thus, in this context, the representation of alternative realities.

In 'Reading realism: audiences' evaluations of the reality of media texts', *Journal of Communication* (December 2003), Alice Hall poses tests of the authenticity of realism – whether the text is plausible; whether it is typical and factual; the following convinces in terms of emotional involvement; achieves narrative consistency and whether it is sufficiently persuasive of audience perceptions of what is real. See *TOPIC GUIDE* under REPRESENTATION.

Reality TV Perhaps best described as 'live documentary'; a prime example being, in the UK, Channel 4's *Big Brother*, versions of which have been produced in many other countries worldwide. While participants in reality TV are real people (rather than actors), and while the story of their interactions is unscripted and not known in advance, such programmes are essentially *contrivances* of reality, highly mediated by the TV production team, and highly manipulated from start to finish.

The participants are painstakingly vetted prior to selection. Once chosen, though they are 'real' people they are placed into a situation that requires *performance*. They become actors in front of cameras and millions of viewers, knowing full well that the performance of the realities of self-presentation will be judged by a 'participatory' audience.

Such programmes as *Big Brother*, the BBC's *Castaway* or ITV's *Popstars: The Rivals* have been described as docu-soaps with gameshow appeal, and they chiefly target younger-generation audiences. Their popularity, the unscripted sensation-seeking of many participants, and the encouragement of such sensationalism on the part of the popular press, have provoked criticism and a degree of righteous indignation.

France's near-equivalent to *Big Brother*, entitled *Loft Story* (in which men and women are housed together in a loft under 24-hour TV surveillance) prompted street riots, protest marches and an Anti-*Loft Story* day of action. Screened on M6, the pay-to-view-channel, *Loft Story* threatened to knock TFI, the main state broadcaster from its number one slot in the viewer ratings. TFI reported *Loft Story* to the Audiovisual High Council. In a UK *Guardian* article, 'In search of loft principles' (21 May 2001), Emily Bell wrote, 'What *Loft Story* has highlighted for the French, and maybe for the rest of us, is the issue of ratings versus responsibility and trash versus culture.'

In 2002 there were even stirrings of protest from tabloid commentators. Garry Bushell ('King of Telly!') in a piece 'Why British telly is going down the pan' in the *News of the World* (2 June) reported that the most thrilling thing that happened in the *Big Brother* house was that 'one of the assembled mutants soiled the toilet seat. For pity's sake enough!' Across the red-tops, Charlie Catchpole of the *Daily Star* (3 June) under a headline, 'Bruv's enough to drive you mental' declared, 'Yup. Watching paint dry is now a recognized pastime for almost six million people.'

Perhaps the *Daily Mirror's* Kevin O'Sullivan ('Anti-Big Brother Correspondent') summed up what is the kernel of 'reality' TV, its fascination for audiences and for the popular press, when he wrote, 'Put any group of dumb animals in an enclosed environment and before long their thoughts will turn to breeding.' Despite such comments, Channel 4, desperate to boost its audience share, programmed *Big Brother* seven nights a week in 2002, incurring accusations that its special text-messaging service could lead to soaring phone bills, especially among children.

Three years later, the popularity of 'reality TV' seemed undiminished. Feminist writer and academic Germaine Greer even volunteered to join the *Celebrity Big Brother* household in 2005, only to walk out, claiming that the programme was 'an object lesson in bullying'. At the *Media Guardian* Edinburgh TV Festival in the summer of 2005, former Director General of the BBC, Greg Dyke, voiced profound concern at the direction of reality shows, aiming for more provocative situations and scenarios, to the point when 'we are turning it [reality TV] into a freak show ... I worry that at some stage something terrible will happen, something really unpleasant and that will be the end of the genre'.

* Richard Kilborn, *Staging the Real: Factual TV Programming in the Age of Big Brother* (UK: University of Manchester Press, 2003); Mark Andrejevic, *Reality TV: The Work of Being Watched* (US/UK: Rowman & Littlefield, 2004); Annette Hill, *Reality TV: Audiences and Popular Factual Television* (UK: Routledge, 2005).

Reassurance, structure of See NEWS.

Received pronunciation (RP) That mode of pronunciation in English which is free of regional ACCENT and aspires to a generally accepted standard; derives from the speech of the court and of public schools; traditionally the 'vocal sign' of the educated person, adopted as the norm for BBC broadcasters, and eventually being termed 'BBC English'. RP no longer has the prestigious status or the dominance it once had. Regional accents have been 'in' since the 1960s, though RP has retained a substantial foothold in national broadcasting.

Receiver See SENDER/RECEIVER.

Recency effect See FIRST IMPRESSIONS; PRIMACY, LAW OF.

Reception studies In recent years particular research emphasis has been placed upon the ways that AUDIENCES receive media messages; how they react to their reading, listening and viewing; and what audiences do with that experience, what MEANINGS they make of it. Such reception studies have, as far as television is concerned, shifted from a prime focus on audience response to news and current affairs to the investigation of audience reception of popular GENRES, such as SOAP OPERAS. See AUDIENCE MEASUREMENT. See also *TOPIC GUIDE* under AUDIENCES/CONSUMPTION & RECEPTION OF MEDIA.

* Tony Wilson, *Watching Television: Hermeneutics, Reception and Popular Culture* (UK: Polity Press, 1995); Sonia Livingstone, *Making Sense of Television: The Psychology of Audience Interpretation* (UK: Routledge paperback, 1998); Pertii Alasuutari, ed., *Rethinking the Media Audience* (UK: Sage, 1999).

Record player See GRAMOPHONE.

Redundancy In communication terms, redundancy refers to that which is conventional or predictable in any message. Its opposite is *entropy*, that which is unexpected and surprising, of low predictability. John Fiske in *Introduction to Communication Studies* (UK: Methuen, 1982) says, 'The English language is about 50 per cent redundant. This means we can delete about 50 per cent of any utterance and still have a usable language capable of transmitting understandable messages.'

Redundancy is established through frequent use until it becomes a convention, both technical, in terms of correctness, and social, in terms of general acceptability. It is essential if the MEANING of messages is to have wide currency and be 'on wave-length' with the codes and reference tables of the receiver.

The entropic challenges these codes and reference tables with novelty – new expression, new thought, overturning predictability and probability. The art of the avant-garde is entropic, at least in its initial phase, it speaks in a language the general public find difficult to understand, and is often provocative. Of course the shock of the new passes: yesterday's outrage is today's fashion, yesterday's entropy is today's redundancy.

A scan of the popular arts reveals their reliance on the conventional forms and practice that make up redundancy – the predictable rhymes and metres of pop songs, for example, the repetitive refrains of folk songs. Fiske writes, 'Redundancy is generally a force for the status quo and against change. Entropy is less comfortable, more stimulating, more shocking perhaps, but harder to communicate effectively.' See PHATIC LANGUAGE; SHANNON AND WEAVER'S MODEL OF COMMUNICATION, 1949.

Referent The actual object, entity in the external world to which a SIGN or linguistic expression refers. The referent of the word table is the object 'table'.

Referential code See CODES OF NARRATIVE.

Reflective-projective theory of broadcasting and mass communication Posed by Lee Loevinger in 'The ambiguous mirror: the reflective-projective theory of broadcasting and mass communication' in Gary Gumpert and Robert Cathcart, eds, *Inter/Media: Interpersonal Communication in a Media World* (US/UK: Oxford University Press, 1979). Loevinger states that 'mass communications are best understood as mirrors of society that reflect an ambiguous image in which each observer projects or sees his own vision of himself and society'. The media reflect images of society but not of the individual.

'While the mirror can pick out points and aspects of society, it cannot create a culture or project an image that does not reflect something already existing in some form in society.' BROADCASTING can clarify or distort images of society; it can focus broadly or narrowly. According to the theory, the media 'are most unlikely to become instruments of social reform or great public enlightenment'. Thus violence on TV reflects the existence of and tolerance of violence in society. See *TOPIC GUIDE* under COMMUNICATION THEORY.

Reflexivity Self-monitoring in terms of COGNITIVE practice; but more significantly for the analysis of the individual's self-positioning within a fast-changing society in which NORMS, VALUES and practices are rendered less certain, less distinct. Reflexivity is central to the construction of identity. It operates intuitively and aesthetically as well as cognitively, and mass communication is seen to be an agency in the control of or liberation of self-interpretation in relation to the READING of and reaction to media TEXTS. Reflexivity makes critical use of NARRATIVES, personal and collective, through which sense is forged out of experience. See SELF-IDENTITY.

Refutation The employment of counter-arguments, evidence and proof to dispute the arguments of another person. Strictly speaking, to disprove allegations.

Register Term describing the compass of a voice or instrument, the range of sound tones produced in a particular manner. The soprano and the bass sing in different registers. The word also describes the structures of language used in varying social contexts: its levels of vocabulary, sentence construction, tones and inflexions. Thus the register adopted by an infant school teacher in his/her class will differ from the register selected for the staff room, just as a scientist will adjust his/her register between conversations held with scientific colleagues and with casual acquaintances in the local pub. In printing, register refers to the exact adjustment of position, as of colours in a picture, or letterpress on opposite sides of the page.

Regulation of Investigatory Powers Act (RIPA) (UK), 2000 One of the most far-reaching pieces of government SURVEILLANCE legislation, RIPA extends blanket powers of interception on TELEPHONE and INTERNET traffic to not only the police and security agencies such as MI5 but to a broad spectrum of government departments as well as local government. In 2002 what had initially been claimed to be a means of tracking online crime was suddenly opened out to be what a UK *Guardian* leader, 'British liberty RIP' (11 June 2002), called 'a mockery of the right to privacy that the Human Rights Act is supposed to protect'. RIPA was seen to 'have profound civil liberty implications'.

The Act opens up all telephone messages and e-mails to official scrutiny. In addition it empowers employers to monitor the e-mail exchanges of their employees. It obliges Internet Service Providers (ISPs) to install 'black boxes' which record all server traffic. It makes illegal any ENCRYPTION that might deny access by the authorities. Refusal on the part of individuals or GROUPS to declare keys to encryption is punishable by up to two years' imprisonment. Unwittingly, ISPs become the snouts of government and its agencies.

In future, the 'spy-in-the-wire' will know who you talk to, when, what you talk about and where you have been talking from. It can accumulate vast amounts of information about you which will be made available to people you have never met, never heard of, about whom you know nothing. The fact that information about you has been gathered and stored is kept secret from you, and you will not know how that information is to be used and for what purpose.

Roy Greenslade in an article 'I arrest you for e-mailing' (*Guardian*, 31 July 2000) believed that 'The passing of the RIP act denies everyone the freedom, and the privacy, we thought the internet had provided. It robs journalists and their sources – including that most potent and essential of tipsters, the whistleblower – of their rights, and quite possibly, threatens their liberty.' The issue of interception warrants by those in authority has to be kept secret; and it is a criminal offence to publicize that a demand for an encryption key has been made.

Sections 21 to 25 of the Act grant the state powers to gather data from Internet traffic where the following might be considered to be at risk: national security, the detecting or preventing of crime, matters of disorder, traffic which may be deemed to be in the interests of the UK's economic well-being, public safety, public health, the levying/collecting of taxes, and for any purposes the Secretary of State specifies, subject to Parliamentary approval.

Caspar Bowen, Director of the Foundation for Policy Research, declared in a UK *Tribune* article (26 June 2001), 'that Britain now has the most draconian snooping laws in the world and the law infringed basic human rights'.

The opportunity, grasped by the Labour government in 2002, of tightening the screw of surveillance, was offered by the events of 11 September 2001 and the terrorist attack on the US Pentagon and New York's World Trade Center. It also resulted in the UK government influencing the rest of the European Union to fall into line. Welcoming the EU's ready embrace of this new tranche of data-spying, the UK Home Office issued the following statement: 'The UK is very pleased that the [European] council and parliament have reached agreement on a text that will ensure that the fight against terrorism and other crime will be given the appropriate weight', conceding that 'It is, of course, important to protect people's fundamental rights and freedoms, but, as the tragic events of September 11 show, this must be balanced with the need to ensure that the law enforcement community can do its job.'

John Wadham, director of Liberty, condemned the Act and its European extension: 'This violates,' he believed, 'a fundamental principle of privacy, which is that data collected for one purpose should not be used for another.' The editor of *StateWatch*, Tony Bunyan, summed up the Act, and official attempts at CENSORSHIP generally, with the comment, 'The problem with wanting to monitor a few people is that you end up having to keep data on everyone.'

The question, widely asked, has been – human rights issues apart – will RIPA succeed in its stated aim of catching criminals? The *Guardian* leader of 11 June 2002 doubted it: 'Ironically, such Orwellian surveillance will be of little help in tracking terrorists or organized crime cells. They can avoid identification by using pre-paid mobile phones or web-based e-mail from public terminals.' The prediction was all too tragically proved when the authorities eased security surveillance in July 2005 at the very moment that London was targeted by terrorist bombers, none of whom was known to the police or the security services. *TOPIC GUIDE* under MEDIA: FREEDOM, CENSORSHIP.

Regulatory favours In an age when multinational corporations have acquired local, national and global voice by investing in media, it comes as no surprise to observe them using that voice to promote corporate interests, to employ those media to pressurize government to grant them favours. Jeremy Tunstall and Michael Parker in *Media Moguls* (UK: Routledge, 1991) use the term *regulatory favours*, which governments cede to big media-owning companies in return for a 'good press'. These favours principally constitute the abolition or waiving of media regulations that might hinder expansionist interests.

When, in May 2002, the UK government announced plans for the further DEREGULATION of BROADCASTING, a *Guardian* leader carried the headline, 'Murdoch gets his way: New Labour rolls over for Rupert', referring to the decision that the way was to be made clear for Rupert Murdoch to expand into terrestrial TV in Britain. In an article in the same issue, media correspondent Emily Bell, under the headline 'Murdoch must have done a deal' talks of an 'unexpected act of munificence' and suggests that 'someone in the cabinet office checked the calendar and realized they had missed Rupert's birthday by six weeks, and they just happened to have a spare channel [Channel 5] kicking around in the cupboard'. See CONGLOMERATES; GLOBAL MEDIA SYSTEM: THE MAIN PLAYERS; POLITICS OF ACCOMMODATION (IN THE MEDIA); PRIVATIZATION; STRATEGIC BARGAINING. See also *TOPIC GUIDE* under MEDIA: POLITICS & ECONOMICS.

Reinforcement There has been much argument over the role of the mass media in reinforcing, in under-pinning, certain social and political VALUES and structures. Considerable attention has been given to two areas: the media's portrayal of violence and the role of the mass media in political communications.

There are those who claim that the frequent incidence of violence in the media has contributed to an increase in acts of violence in society. Research evidence, however, gives few clear pointers as to the nature or extent of any media influence. One school of thought rejects the notion that the media directly encourage violent behaviour in all viewers but argues that the media violence may reinforce already existing tendencies to violence in some viewers.

This position is open to question. As Sonia Livingstone in an article, 'On the continuing problem of media effects', published in *Mass Media and Society* (UK/US: Arnold, 1996), edited by James Curran and Michael Gurevitch, comments, 'It is difficult to know what beliefs people might have espoused but for the media's construction of a normative reality, and difficult to know what role the media plays in the construction of those needs and desires which in turn motivate viewers to engage with the media as they are rather than as they might be.'

Paul H. Lazarsfeld, Bernard Berelson and Hazel Gaudet in a classic study of the effects of political communication by the mass media on voting behaviour, *The People's Choice* (US: Columbia University Press, 1948), were of the opinion that the media's main effect is to reinforce *existing* political preferences. The notions of *selective perception*, SELECTIVE EXPOSURE and *selective recall* are used to explain how the same output can reinforce the diverse views, values and beliefs of a mass audience. It is suggested that the audiences, rather than being passive receptacles for media output, select from the output those messages which are in accordance with their own prior dispositions and give attention to these, a point confirmed by Garth J. Jowett and Victoria O'Donnell reviewing research into the effects of persuasion and propaganda in their work *Propaganda and Persuasion* (US: Sage, 1999). They state: 'Selectivity in the perception of messages is generally guided by preexisting interests and behaviour patterns of the receivers ... mass communication effects tend to take the form of reinforcement rather than change.'

Whilst in recent years there has been a tendency to adopt a more multiculturalist perspective in many areas of broadcasting this may result in the inadvertent reinforcement of more subtle negative attitudes. For example, Simon Cottle in *Ethnic Minorities and the Media* (US/UK: Oxford University Press, 2000), edited by Cottle, concludes from his study of regional TV news programmes in the UK that despite attempts to present a multiculturalist perspective, 'such "multiculturalist" representations ... may actually serve to reinforce culturally sedimented views of ethnic miniorities as "Other" and simultaneously appear to give the lie to ideas of structural disadvantage and continuing inequality'. See AUDIENCE: ACTIVE AUDIENCE; EFFECTS OF THE MASS MEDIA; POLITICS OF ACCOMMODATION (IN THE MEDIA); RESONANCE.

Reithian Attitudes to BROADCASTING as typified by the first Director General of the BBC, Sir John Reith (1889–1971), who dominated the rise of broadcasting in the UK like a colossus. Dour, high-principled, autocratic, paternalist and a Scottish Presbyterian to boot, Reith was appointed General Manager of the newly formed British Broadcasting Company in December 1922. His philosophy was that broadcasting was a heaven-sent opportunity to educate and enlighten the people in the ways of quality, and that 'giving the people what they wanted' was the way to perdition.

This 'Tsar of Savoy Hill' as the press called him, believed, in the words of the *New Statesman* on Armistice Day 1933, 'in the medicinal effects of education – a cultural dictatorship'. Though George Lansbury MP said of Reith, 'I have always felt that Sir John Reith would have made a very excellent Hitler for this country', Clement Attlee saw advantages: 'He puts up a splendid resistance to vested interests of all kinds.'

Elitist, imperious and sabbatarian, Reith nevertheless created in the BBC an organization resistant to commercialism, favouring the arts, serious debate and notions of public responsibility. Reith strove for IMPARTIALITY but never achieved *balance*: coverage of royal activities in the 1920s and 1930s was not in any way matched by coverage of the activities of the Labour movement and the unions and, during the General Strike of 1926, the BBC remained strictly 'neutral': it stayed silent. Reith, the 'Napoleon of Broadcasting', as Colonel Moore Brabazon called him, resigned as 'DG' (Director General), as his own staff spoke of him, in 1937. See BBC, ORIGINS. See also *TOPIC GUIDE* under MEDIA HISTORY; MEDIA INSTITUTIONS.

Relationship marketing See MARKETING.

Relic gestures Those physical gestures that have outlived their original situation, yet continue to be used to effect even though their derivation is no longer obvious or explicable. Such gestures survive not only from historical past but from a human's infantile past. For example, the rocking to and fro of disaster victims in the face of intolerable grief.

Repertoire of non-verbal behaviour See NON-VERBAL BEHAVIOUR: REPERTOIRE.

Repetitive strain injury (RSI) Brought on by regular and intensive use of, for example, computer keyboards and thus the 'disease of journalists' as well as secretaries; resulting in severe pain in the hands, arm, neck and back. Once RSI has taken hold it is difficult and sometimes impossible for the sufferer to carry on working.

Reporters: embedded reporters See EMBEDDED REPORTERS.

Reporters Sans Frontières (Reporters Without Borders) Montpellier-based group of journalists set up in 1987 to defend press freedom worldwide, and campaign on behalf of journalists in trouble. Produces valuable data on the plight of reporters, photographers and film-makers – those injured, imprisoned or killed in bringing home the news.

Report-talk, rapport-talk This is one way in which men and women's conversational style differs according to Deborah Tannen in her *You Just Don't Understand Me: Women and Men in Conversation* (UK: Virago Press, 1992). Men, she argues, are confident with public speech or what she calls *report-talk*, whether this be in a formal or an informal situation where several people are in conversation.

In these situations, when the company is mixed, men typically participate more in conversation than women and in part their performance may be a way of establishing status and control. In a more private setting, though, this difference in the participation rate between men and women may change or even reverse.

Here *rapport-talk*, with which women, Tannen argues, are more comfortable, is more appropriate. Rapport-talk is used for establishing and reinforcing intimacy. These differences reflect the different GENDER-LECTS that Tannen argues men and women use, which in turn reflect one main difference in their use of conversation: men using conversation to establish *status* and control, women to establish *intimacy*. See *TOPIC GUIDE* under GENDER MATTERS.

Representation A core function of media is to re-present to AUDIENCES the realities of 'the world out there'. Most of our knowledge of that world is brought to us via the media; and our perception of reality is MEDI-ATED by newspapers, TV, advertisements, films, etc. The media *image* the world for us. They do this by means of selection and interpretation which operate through GATEKEEPING and according to AGENDAS which are suffused by IDEOLOGY. The media represent to us the past as well as the present, and representations – or interpretations – of the past affect our perceptions of the present. Out of such representations arise issues concerning, for example, the representation of women, of race, asylum-seeking, poverty, minorities.

What we as audience know of Africa and Africans, of Serbs and Albanians, of Israelis and Arabs, of Muslims and Sikhs, is what we have experienced through the reports and pictures brought to us by the media. The study of media representation, therefore, is central to cultural, media and communication stud-ies. Because it is impossible to represent the world in all its massive complexity, media representation has to be viewed as a 'version' of reality, in which FRAMING has taken place according to criteria such as NEWS VALUES or pressures to propagandize, sensationalize, binarize (that is, divide 'us' from 'them' – see WEDOM, THEYDOM) or seek to impose MEANING upon webs of complexity. Representation is essen-tially about *definition*, and media representation tends to be about promoting certain definitions, and there-fore meanings, over others; thus endeavouring to affect the preferences of the public. See DISCOURSE. See also *TOPIC GUIDE* under REPRESENTATION.

Representation, machinery of See MACHINERY OF REPRESENTATION.

Representation of crime on screen See CRIME: TYPES OF CRIME ON SCREEN.

Representative sample See SAMPLING.

Repressive state apparatus See IDEOLOGICAL STATE APPARATUSES.

Repressive use of the media See EMANCIPATORY USE OF THE MEDIA.

Re-regulation The notion that DEREGULATION of media – essentially BROADCASTING – has actual-ly meant fewer regulations and more freedom is challenged by Karen Siune and Wolfgang Truetzschler in *Dynamics of Media Politics* (UK: Sage, 1992). The authors write 'What has frequently been referred to as dereg-ulation has turned out to be regulation in another form, and the concept of "re-regulation" is much more appropriate.' The more systems are fragmented, the authors argue, the more detailed rules are created con-cerning minor but still significant aspects of media structure; in contrast to the former overall framework 'that provides only vague outlines'.

Research centres (into the media) In the UK there are centres of research into culture and the media at the universities of Birmingham, Cardiff, Glasgow, Leeds, Leicester, London, Loughborough, Portsmouth, Sheffield and Stirling. At Birmingham there is the Centre for Contemporary Cultural Studies; in Cardiff the Tom Hopkinson Centre; in Glasgow the GLASGOW UNIVERSITY MEDIA GROUP; in Leeds the Centre for Television Research; in Leicester the Centre for Mass Communication; in Loughborough the Communication Research Centre; in Portsmouth, the Media Research Group; in Sheffield the Centre for English Cultural Tradition; and in London the Media Research Groups at Goldsmith's College and the London School of Economics and Political Science.

Resistance (of audience to media) See DOMINANT, SUBORDINATE, RADICAL; POLYSEMY.

Resistive reading Occurs when the AUDIENCE chooses not to accept without question the PREFERRED READING of media messages. Considerable research has been conducted into the capacity of audiences, and of segments of audiences such as women, to react independently to DOMINANT DISCOURSES: hence the *active-audience* thesis. See AUDIENCE: ACTIVE AUDIENCE; DOMINANT, SUBORDI-NATE, RADICAL; EMPOWERMENT.

Resonance Term used by George Gerbner and fellow researchers at the Annenberg School of Communications, University of Pennsylvania, Philadelphia, to describe a condition experienced by television viewers when what they see matches their expectations. If what they see confirms their vision of the world, of reality, that vision *resonates*. It is reinforced. In 'The "mainstreaming" of America: violence profile no. 11' (*Journal of Communication*, Summer 1980) Gerbner, Larry Gross, Michael Morgan and Nancy Signorielli state that where TV reality and a person's experience or PERCEPTION of reality are in alignment, 'the combination may result in a coherent and powerful "double dose" of the television message'.

For example, city dwellers living in centres of high crime will find TV's violent imagery congruent with their experience. 'These people receive a "double dose" of messages that the world is violent, and consequently show the strongest associations between viewing and fear.' See EFFECTS OF THE MASS MEDIA; MAINSTREAMING; MEAN WORLD SYNDROME.

Response codes See DOMINANT, SUBORDINATE, RADICAL; POLYSEMY.

Restricted code See ELABORATED AND RESTRICTED CODES.

Reterritorialization According to James Lull in *Media, Communication and Culture* (UK: Polity Press, 1995), reterritorialization means 'first that the foundations of cultural territory – ways of life, artefacts, symbols and contexts – are all open to new interpretations and understandings', and second, 'implies that culture is constantly reconstituted through social interaction, sometimes by creative uses of personal communications technology and the mass media'. Thus *cultural territory* is potentially dynamic and changing, so reshaping is constantly possible.

Rhetoric Traditionally, the theory and practice of eloquence, whether spoken or written; the use of language so as to persuade others. The word is almost always used today as a term of criticism: rhetoric is the style in which bare-faced persuasion – politicking – is used. It is emotive; it belongs to speeches and while it is very often resounding it is rarely eloquent because it trades in empty phrases and endless repetitions. It is essentially redundant in that it tells supporters what they already know and antagonists what they know and don't want to hear.

Rhetoric is the stock-in-trade of the press, and of the popular press in particular. Practically every front-page headline is rhetorical in that it is soaked through with the ideological attitudes of the newspaper, not least the belief in what sells newspapers, what commands attention, what readers want to be told. Indeed it might be said that one of the prime functions the popular press sets itself is to translate actuality into rhetoric: complex issues are translated into the simplifying mode of MYTH, of WEDOM, THEYDOM, Militant and Moderate, Order and Disorder, Black and White, Management and Unions, Dries and Wets. See NEWS VALUES; OTHER. See also *TOPIC GUIDE* under LANGUAGE/DISCOURSE/NARRATIVE.

Rhetoric of numbers Phrase used by Itzhak Roeh and Saul F. Feldman to describe how the press, the popular press in particular, use numbers and amounts for *rhetorical* rather than *factual* purposes. The authors' analysis of the headlines of two Hebrew dailies, one ELITE, one popular, is reported on in 'The rhetoric of numbers in front-page journalism: how numbers contribute to the melodramatic in the popular press', published in *Text* 4/4 (1984).

Rhetoric of the image See IMAGE, RHETORIC OF.

Right of reply A long-established practice in continental countries, the right of reply in the UK press has been argued for long, hard and generally unsuccessfully. Such a right would require newspaper editors to publish within a given time the replies of individuals or organizations who allege serious press misrepresentation, or face a special court and a fine if found to be in error. It is argued that such a right would act as a deterrent to editorial bias and unethical practices. Newspapers do publish apologies but these are usually for printing factual errors that might land them with libel actions. See CAMPAIGN FOR PRESS AND BROADCASTING FREEDOM; PEOPLE'S COMMUNICATION CHARTER.

Rights and the media See CULTURAL OR CITIZEN RIGHTS AND THE MEDIA.

Riley and Riley's model of mass communication, 1959 John W. Riley Jr and Matilda White Riley in 'Mass communication and the social system', in *Sociology Today: Problems and Prospects* (US: Basic Books, 1959; Harper Torch Books, Vol. 2, 1965), edited by R.K. Merton, L. Broom and L.S. Cottrell Jr, pose a model in which the process of communication is an integral part of the social system. For Riley and Riley, both the Communicator (C) and the Recipient (R) are affected in the message process of sending, receiving, reciprocating, by the three social orders: the *primary group* or groups of which C and R are members; the larger *social*

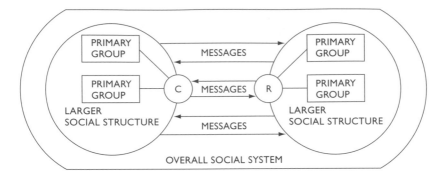

Riley and Riley's model of mass communication, 1959

structure, that is the immediate community – social, cultural, industrial – to which they belong, and the *over-all social system*. All of these are in dynamic interaction, with messages flowing multi-directionally.

The mass media audience Riley and Riley perceive as being neither impassive nor isolated but 'a composite of recipients who are related to one another, and whose responses are patterned in terms of these relationships'. See *TOPIC GUIDE* under COMMUNICATION MODELS.

RIPA See REGULATION OF INVESTIGATORY POWERS ACT (RIPA) (UK), 2000.

Ritual, rites of passage A ritual can be seen as a carefully constructed act of communication, a focused organization of symbols, loaded with a range of meanings significant for the individuals or social GROUPS concerned. Some rituals involve a great deal of ceremonial activity whilst those of everyday life may be fairly simple. Rituals can be religious or secular. They operate to give individuals or groups a sense of collective identity and security.

Rites of passage is a term used to refer to those rituals that mark the transition from one status, stage or state to another either by the whole community or, more commonly, by individuals. The ceremonies which mark such changes provide a symbolic confirmation of the change of social identity involved: a wedding ceremony would be an example of one such ceremony, redolent with symbols reflecting socio-cultural VALUES and expectations.

Rogers and Dearing's agenda-setting model, 1987 Published in *Communication Yearbook 11* (US: Sage, 1987) and examined in *Communication Models for the Study of Mass Communication*, McQuail and Windahl, eds, (UK: Longman, 2nd edition, 1997), this development by E.M. Rogers and J.W. Dearing of previous AGENDA-SETTING models is a welcome acknowledgement of the competing agendas in the public sphere. In their *Yearbook* article 'Agenda-setting, where has it been, where is it going?' the authors see the public agenda as existing separately from, though locked between, the policy agenda, of the state, of government and the media, each subject to influence by the others.

The triad of agendas is itself influenced by a number of contextual factors 'out there' – for example, spectacular news stories. There are substantial factors that shape one, two or all agendas but which may also temper, or restrict, the effectiveness of those agendas, such as personal experience or what Rogers and Dearing call 'real world indicators' of the importance of an agenda issue. In this sense, reality remains something other than what is constructed in the media, or 'fed to' the public as reality by those who promote the policy agenda.

One problem with the model is its linearity in that it does not sufficiently indicate the interactive nature of competing agendas. It also presents the public agenda as being in the same league, in terms of power, as the other agendas. Lastly, the model could arguably have a fourth agenda added to it, the *corporate* agenda, in order to reflect the increasingly dominant role in all aspects of policy, public debate and media operation, played by transnational companies on the global stage.

This Dictionary's authors would pose here a modest alternative to Rogers and Dearing, which emphasizes the *interactive* nature of the dominant agendas while shifting the public agenda into no less central a position,

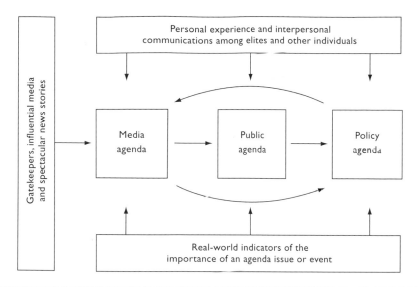

Rogers and Dearing's agenda-setting model, 1987

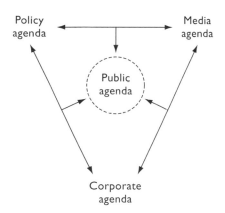

Tripolar model of competing agendas

but one which is by its nature less defined, inevitably more diffuse and thus more open to influence. See REGULATORY FAVOURS. See also *TOPIC GUIDE* under COMMUNICATION MODELS.

Roles A social role consists of the expected behaviour associated with a particular social position. Thus the social position of a 'journalist' identifies a body of behaviours expected of a journalist, that is the role of the journalist in society. Role is a relational term. People play roles within a context in which other people are also playing roles. Roles within society or a social group carry with them responsibilities, obligations and rights.

There is some evidence that the role a person or group occupies within a given social context can influence the pattern of communication adopted. Basil Bernstein, for example, argues in 'Social class, language and socialization' in *Language and Social Context* (UK: Penguin, 1972), edited by P.P. Giglioli, that selective access to the elaborated language code may well result from the fact that there is selective access to the social roles which require its use (see ELABORATED AND RESTRICTED CODES).

Behaviour identified with a role is not necessarily rigidly prescribed. Through interaction with others, 'dishes' or antennae. Most communication satellites receive and transmit simultaneously from a number of earth stations.

TV pictures were first transmitted via satellite on 10 July 1962 when Telstar was launched at Cape Canaveral, US, and circled the earth every 157.8 minutes, enabling live TV pictures transmitted from Andover, Maine, to be received at Goonhilly Down, Cornwall and in Brittany (11 July). In 1964 the unmanned Syncom relayed pictures of the Olympic Games from Tokyo. The first commercial communications satellite was Early Bird, which marked the beginning of regular TV transmission via satellite (2 May 1965).

The UK franchise for a three-transponder direct-broadcast satellite (DBS) was granted in 1986, with a start date of 1990. After financial and investment doubts which led to early backers such as the BBC withdrawing from DBS plans, the contract for Britain's first two DBS channels was awarded to British Satellite Broadcasting (BSB). Rupert Murdoch's Sky Satellite arrived ahead of BSB, beginning programme transmission in the UK in March 1989.

Between them, the rival companies estimated to have spent £1.25bn, yet by October 1990, such were the colossal start-up expenses, that BSB was forced into a merger with Sky. The 'squarial' dish, created to bring BSB programmes into the home, suddenly became scrap. The founding principle of the free market – that competition is the basic dynamic of success – was itself 'squarialized'. Sky took on the initials of BSB, becoming British Sky Broadcasting (BSkyB). Corporate monopoly of satellite transmission joined that of those other 'free enterprise' industries in the UK, rail transport, gas, water and electricity.

Murdoch's ambition to make News Corp a global provider of TV programming was marked in the 1990s with the acquisition of Star Television in Asia. In November 1995 News Corp joined with the Globo Organization of Brazil, Grupo Televisa of Mexico and Telecommunications Inc. of the US to set up a satellite TV service for the Latin American and Caribbean markets with estimated total launch costs of $500m. See COMMUNICATIONS ACT (UK), 2003; CROSS-MEDIA OWNERSHIP. See also *TOPIC GUIDE* under MEDIA: TECHNOLOGIES.

Scanner Mobile control room used in outside TV broadcasts.

Scheduling Process by which programmes or types of programme are 'timetabled' in order to attract maximum audiences, and keep them attracted in the face of competition from rival programmes. The aim of the programme scheduler is to minimize the danger of audiences switching off or, even worse, over. Low-appeal programmes are usually placed against weak opposition, or they are 'hammocked', that is placed in between 'bankers', trusting to the INHERITANCE FACTOR. Conversely there is the so-called 'pre-echo' effect where anticipation of a really popular programme can induce viewers to switch on earlier and thus watch a preceding programme with less popular appeal.

Scheduling techniques assume a high degree of passivity on the part of an audience, and might be said seriously to underestimate audience potential for variety and challenge. Competitive scheduling above all reduces the range of choice open to the viewer simply by making risk-taking more difficult.

Schema (plural: schemata) A schema is basically a framework or pattern, stored in the memory, which preserves and organizes information about some event or concept. The framework may be expanded as new information about the event or concept is acquired. It is argued by several researchers concerned with learning and memory, that existing schemata affect our PERCEPTION of new information and that there is a tendency for us to try to fit new information into our existing frameworks, at least initially.

Schemata themselves can form cross-linkages to provide a wider mental or conceptual map of an area of knowledge or experience. This perspective on the way in which we receive and process information has important implications for the analysis of the way in which we send and receive messages in the communication process.

Schramm's models of communication, 1954 Wilbur Schramm built on SHANNON AND WEAVER'S MODEL OF COMMUNICATION, 1949 (the Mathematical Theory of Communication), but was more interested in mass communication than in the technology of communication transmission. In 'How communication works' in W. Schramm, ed., *The Process and Effects of Mass Communication* (US: University of Illinois Press, 1954) the author poses three models (see diagram).

Shannon and Weaver's 'Transmitter' and 'Receiver' become 'Encoder' and 'Decoder', and their essentially linear model is restructured in Schramm's second model to demonstrate the overlapping, interactive nature

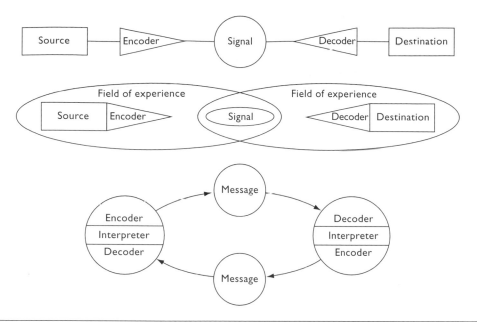

Schramm's models of communication, 1954

of the communication process and the importance of what the Encoder and Decoder bring with them to the communication situation, their 'Field of Experience'. Where that field of experience overlaps is the Signal. Schramm's third model emphasizes FEEDBACK, and in doing so points up the circularity of the communication process. See *TOPIC GUIDE* under COMMUNICATION MODELS.

Scripts These are described by Eric Berne in *What Do You Say After You Say Hello?* (UK: Corgi Books, 1975) as 'a preconscious life plan' by which an individual structures 'longer periods of time – months, years or his whole life'. Scripts are developed in our early years but then have the capacity to influence and shape our transactions with others. A script contains within it an individual's self-concept and his/her general perception of and orientation towards other people and the world. It thus forms a basis for action. Berne identifies a number of possible scripts individuals may have as a result of their early experiences.

One example is the 'You Can't Trust Anybody' script. An individual with this script would obviously be suspicious and distrustful of others and act accordingly. Such a script has obvious implications for communication with others. Berne argues that individuals tend to seek proof that their scripts are valid, by behaving in a way or interpreting behaviour in a manner that will reinforce them. So to a greater or lesser extent behaviour might be script-driven. Scripts can obviously be limiting but can, of course, be changed.

In *TA Today* (UK: Lifespace, 1987) Ian Stewart and Vann Joines discuss three main types of script: Winning, Losing (or *hamartic*, from the Greek, meaning basic flaw) and Non-winning (or *banal* scripts). A 'winner' is an individual who achieves the goals he/she has set for him/herself. It is also implied that these are met, 'comfortably, happily and smoothly'. A loser does not achieve set goals or does but is unhappy or damaged as a result. The Losing script may resemble Ancient Greek drama when the basic flaw seems to lead inexorably to tragic finale. A Non-winning or banal script is one focused on playing safe and not taking risks. It may result in small gains and losses but the individual will remain a 'non-winner'. It seems that many people have a mixture of scripts: winning in some aspects of life whilst losing in others. See TRANSACTIONAL ANALYSIS.

Secondary viewing Term describing the circumstances in which TV viewing forms an accompaniment to other activities such as homework and reading.

Segmentation Refers in a specific sense to the constituent nature of TV – chopped up into segments, of NEWS, comedy, drama, commercial, DOCUMENTARY, quiz shows etc. John Fiske in 'Moments of everyday performances is important both to the development and maintenance of the self-concept, and thus also to self-identity. Disturbances in such performances constitute, therefore, a threat, 'Life may not be much of a gamble, but interaction is'. Competent performances require considerable day-to-day control and the appropriate employment of personae.

As Kath Woodward comments in *Understanding Identity* (UK: Arnold, 2002), 'Identity involves the inter-relationship between the personal and the social; between what I feel inside and what is known about me from the outside.' Psychoanalytic theories, such as those of Freud and Jung, focus more on internal process-es and the conflict between inner desires and the demands of others, of society. These theories view much of our behaviour as influenced by forces within the unconscious. Self-knowledge is therefore limited and self-identity partial, provisional and vulnerable to fracture.

For Freud there is an inevitable conflict between what he argued are the three components of an individ-ual's personality: the id, the ego and the superego. The id reacts to basic biological instincts and operates on the 'Pleasure Principle' in that it encourages behaviour that seeks pleasure and avoids pain. The ego, accord-ing to Richard D. Gross, in *Psychology: The Science of Mind and Behaviour* (UK: Hodder Arnold, 2005), can be 'described as the "executive" of the personality, the planning, decision-making, rational and logical part of us'. The ego operates on the 'Reality Principle'. It is concerned with the social consequences of our behav-iour and the resulting judgements others would make. Thus it seeks to control influences from the id that would, if acted on, result in social criticism or rejection. The superego contains our ideas about what is moral-ly right or wrong. It also seeks to control influences from the id, through the ego, if they are likely to result in behaviour of which our own superego would disapprove. The ego may, though, on occasion counsel against behaviour in line with the superego's demands.

Gross comments, 'the ego, the person's conscious self, is caught in the middle of opposing sets of demands, it is the battleground on which three opposing factions (reality, the id and the superego) fight for supremacy'. The id lies in the unconscious part of the mind, whilst parts of the ego and superego are in the conscious and parts in the unconscious mind. The ego mediates between these factions to obtain a compro-mise and, according to Freud, is aided by three processes: Dreams, Neurotic Symptoms and Defence Mechanisms. We are not, however, usually aware of the operation of these processes. The Defence Mechanisms, for example – Repression, Denial, IDENTIFICATION, Sublimation, PROJECTION – in par-ticular can be seen to have consequences for the study of social interaction and for the analysis of responses to mass media messages. See TRANSACTIONAL ANALYSIS.

Another perspective on self-identity, that offered by Anthony Giddens in *Modernity and Self-Identity* (UK: Polity Press, 1991) considers the impact of societal influences upon the formation of self-identity. Giddens defines self-identity in the conditions of late modernity as 'the self as reflexively understood by the person in terms of his or her biography'. Whilst self-identity is seen as normally having a degree of continuity it is 'such continuity as interpreted reflexively by the agent'. Self-identity also involves cognitive awareness of the self: 'To be a "person" is not just to be a reflexive actor, but to have a concept of a person.' Self-identity is an inte-gral element of the SELF-CONCEPT.

Giddens further argues that although concepts of what a 'person' is may vary across cultures, 'The capac-ity to use "I" in shifting contexts, characteristic of every known culture, is the most elemental feature of reflexive conceptions of personhood.' Self-identity, Giddens argues, requires self-conscious thought and action; it is not 'something that is just given ... but something that has to be routinely created and sustained in the reflexive activities of the individual'. It is an ongoing project, for in the conditions of late modernity self-identity has to be explored, developed and modified against a background of changing circumstances.

Giddens identifies four influences evident in the structure of post-traditional societies which create the plurality of choices that make difficult the struggle of maintaining a coherent self-identity and which make necessary a *project of self.* Identities can be achieved only through choice – 'we have no choice but to choose' – given that much of the tradition which allowed them to be ascribed or indicated has lost its hold.

Individuals inhabit a 'pluralization of lifeworlds' in which they have to present a number of different identities as they move from one social sphere to another, often negotiating differing expectations of their behaviour as they do so. What Giddens terms 'methodological doubt' is yet another feature of late modernity; certainty is seen as fragile as truth is seen as contextual and authority and reason provisional. 'Mediated expe-rience' is seen to be at the heart of social life. Through the mass media and travel a vast range of 'lifeworlds' are presented to audiences, thus increasing the range of options available in the construction of identities.

Further, such identities have to be adjusted to cope with the range of changes that an individual is likely to encounter in such a society, the change to self-identity that usually accompanies a divorce being but one example. Giddens argues that little help is available to individuals in making such choices, although artefacts within consumer CULTURE may promise guidance, self-help manuals, for example. The ability to control SELF-PRESENTATION and in doing this to actively construct and reconstruct bodily appearance is seen by Giddens as essential to maintaining a coherent self-identity.

Don Slater notes in *Consumer Culture & Modernity* (UK: Polity Press, 1997) that another influence on late modernity – 'commercialization' – has resulted in 'a greater fluidity in the use of goods to construct identities and lifestyles'. It has also resulted, arguably, in individuals perceiving themselves, in part, as consumers; a perception which would reinforce the notion that individuals must make choices.

There are, of course, innumerable attempts to appeal to aspects of the self in ADVERTISING and marketing. The danger, warns Giddens, is that 'the project of self becomes translated into one of possession of desired goods and the pursuit of artificially framed styles of life ... The consumption of ever-novel goods becomes a substitute for the genuine development of self.'

For Slater, 'consumer culture "technicizes" the project of self by treating all problems as solvable through various commodities'. Also, 'identity can be seen as a saleable commodity'. Individuals may feel under pressure to 'sell' themselves in various social situations. Arguably many commodities are promoted on the grounds of their value to the individual in his/her task of constructing and maintaining self-identity. See IMPRESSION MANAGEMENT; MASLOW'S HIERARCHY OF NEEDS; SELF-CONCEPT; SELF-MONITORING.

Self-image See SELF-CONCEPT.

Self-monitoring This term refers to the degree to which people are sensitive to and able to respond to the demands of social situations with regard to their own behaviour. Richard D. Gross in *Psychology: The Science of Mind and Behaviour* (UK: Hodder & Stoughton, 1986) identifies high and low self-monitors. High self-monitors are motivated to and able to assess the demands of different situations and adjust their SELF-PRESENTATION and general behaviour accordingly.

Low self-monitors, on the other hand, tend to behave in a similar fashion regardless of the situation, and their behaviour is more likely to be influenced by their own internal states. High self-monitors appear much more able to conceal their own moods, feelings and so on. Evidence suggests that high self-monitors have better social skills; for example, they can interpret non-verbal communication more accurately than low self-monitors.

Self-presentation Term used to describe the way in which we behave and communicate in differing social situations. It carries with it the implication that to some degree we consciously present ourselves to others in any given situation. The feedback we gain from self-presentation plays a role in shaping and changing our self-concept. Erving Goffman in *The Presentation of Self in Everyday Life* (US: Anchor, 1959; UK: Penguin, 1971) employs the dramaturgical perspective to analyse social interaction. Goffman writes, 'life itself is a dramatically enacted thing. All the world is not, of course a stage, but the crucial ways in which it is not are not easy to specify ... In short, we all act better than we know how.'

Goffman puts forward several useful concepts that have become influential in analysing self-presentation. A key concept is that of *persona*. The persona is the character we take on to play a part in a particular social situation. Different situations will usually require us to play different parts and therefore adopt different personas. So, for example, the persona an individual would adopt when visiting a folk festival with friends might be very different from the persona he/she would adopt in carrying out his/her work role as a High Court judge or an attorney.

The persona is part of our way of dealing with different people and the demands of different social situations. Once chosen for a particular situation it influences how we communicate in that situation. The ability to choose an appropriate persona for a situation and communicate accordingly can be seen as an important communication skill, as can the ability to shift from one persona to another as situations demand it. Also, it is likely that the role a person is playing may dictate the kinds of persona it would be appropriate to adopt in any given situation.

Goffman uses the term *performance* to describe the act of self-presentation and in many cases these performances can be seen as staged. In staging a performance in everyday life we would use props just as actors would on a theatre stage; obvious examples here are dress, cars and furnishings. A well-established pattern of action that may be used as part of a performance is known as a *routine*. An example here would be a characteristic display of temper.

According to Goffman we also perform from behind a *front* which he defines as 'that part of the individual's performance which regularly functions in a general and fixed fashion to define the situation for those who observe the performance'. Standard parts of the front are the setting, for example one's home and the personal front – age, dress, sex. See CONFIRMATION/DISCOMFORMATION; IMPRESSION MANAGEMENT; SELF-MONITORING. See also *TOPIC GUIDE* under INTERPERSONAL COMMUNICATION.

Self-regulation Although BROADCASTING in the UK has traditionally been regulated by acts of Parliament and governing charters, the press has been self-regulating. The Press Council was an advisory body, set up by the newspaper industry; its successor, the PRESS COMPLAINTS COMMISSION, which started work 1 January 1991, has similarly no statutory powers. The question often asked is whether the press, dominated by a handful of media barons, can be left to regulate itself – that is, be judge of its own malpractices. A negative view of self-regulation has been taken by the CAMPAIGN FOR PRESS AND BROADCASTING FREEDOM in its publication, *Free Press*. The June 1991 issue declared 'The CPBF is sceptical that the PCC will take any meaningful steps to redress press abuses.'

In the wake of the death of Diana, Princess of Wales in 1997, issues of self-regulation were widely discussed and the UK newspaper industry responded to public concern by agreeing to criteria for respecting PRIVACY and curtailing media intrusion. In any event, the UK Labour government's incorporation into British law of the European Convention on Human Rights (see HUMAN RIGHTS ACT, 2000) made the privacy of the individual a legal right in Britain for the first time. See CALCUTT COMMITTEE ON PRIVACY AND RELATED MATTERS, 1990. See also *TOPIC GUIDE* under BROADCASTING.

Selsdon Committee Report on Television (UK), 1935 The task of Lord Selsdon's Committee was 'to consider the development of Television and advise the Postmaster-General on the relative merits of several systems and on the conditions under which any public television should be provided'. The Report recommended that the BBC be made the initiating body, and that the cost of TV broadcasting be borne from the revenue derived from the existing 10-shilling radio licence fee. See *TOPIC GUIDE* under COMMISSIONS, COMMITTEES, LEGISLATION.

Semantic code See CODES OF NARRATIVE.

Semantic differential The analysis of semantic differential is one of three traditional empirical methods of measuring AUDIENCE response to the media, the others being CONTENT ANALYSIS and the investigation of uses and gratifications (see USES AND GRATIFICATIONS THEORY). In exploring semantic – or MEANING – differentials, analysts concentrate on people's attitudes, feelings and emotions towards certain concepts and VALUES as actuated by media performance. The values under scrutiny are presented in preliminary form by words or statements.

These are then selected and expressed as binarily opposed concepts (Offensive – Not Offensive, for example) on a five- or seven-point scale. Binary opposition is the most extreme form of significant difference possible. A sample audience, or selected group, is tested on the scale or scales, and the results averaged. The method was given currency by Charles Osgood in *The Measurement of Meaning* (US: University of Illinois Press, 1967). See *TOPIC GUIDE* under RESEARCH METHODS.

Semantics A major branch of linguistics in which the MEANING of language is analysed. The study of the origins of the form and meaning of words is etymology, a branch of semantics. The crucial point about the study of semantics is that it is an exploration of change – how the context of usage, historical, social, cultural, etc. – alters the meanings of words and expressions used. When King James II observed that the new St Paul's Cathedral was amusing, awful and artificial he did not intend to be derogatory about Sir Christopher Wren's masterpiece; rather he meant that it was 'pleasing, awe-inspiring, and skilfully achieved'.

The differences are, of course, far from merely evolutionary. What, for example, is the meaning of the word equality? Its definition is modified by the perceptions and VALUES of all those who use it, and the situation in which it is used. As Simeon Potter points out in *Our Language* (UK: Penguin, 1950), 'Men frequently find themselves at cross-purposes with one another because they persist in using words in different senses.

Their long arguments emit more heat than light because their conceptions of the point at issue, whether Marxism, democracy, capitalism, the good life, western civilization, culture, art, internationalism, freedom of the individual, equality of opportunity, redistribution of wealth, social security, progress, or what not, are by no means identical. From heedless sloth, or sheer lack of intelligence men do not trouble to clarify their conceptions.' Semantics, therefore, must lie at the heart of any serious study of communication processes. See *TOPIC GUIDE* under LANGUAGE/DISCOURSE/NARRATIVE.

Semiology/semiotics Deriving from the Greek *semeion*, sign; semiology is the general science of sign systems and their role in the construction and reconstruction of MEANING. All social life, indeed every facet of social practice, is *mediated* by language conceived as a system of signs and representations, arranged by codes and articulated through various discourses. Sign systems, believes the semiologist, have no fixed meaning. The perception of the sign system rests upon the social context of the participants and the interaction between them.

Semiology examines the SIGN itself, the CODES or systems into which signs are organized and the CULTURE within which these codes and signs operate. The primary focus of semiology is upon the TEXT, preferring the term *reader* (even of a painting, photograph or film) to receiver because it implies a greater degree of activity, and that the process of reading is socially and culturally conditioned. The reader helps to create the meaning and significance of the text by bringing to it his/her experience, values and emotional responses.

There is special emphasis on the link between the reading and the IDEOLOGY of the reader. 'Wherever a sign is present,' writes V.N. Volosinov in *Marxism and the Philosophy of Language* (US: Seminar, 1973), 'ideology is present too. Everything ideological possesses a semiotic value'; or as Umberto Eco says, 'Semiology shows us the universe of ideologies arranged in codes and sub-codes within the universe of signs' (in 'Articulations of the cinematic code' in *Cinematics* 1, undated).

The theories of Swiss linguist Ferdinand de Saussure (1857–1913) provided the foundation stone of semiology. His lectures, *Cours de Linguistique Générale* (1916) were published after his death by two pupils, Charles Bally and Albert Sechehaye. De Saussure set out to demonstrate that speech is not merely a linear sequence like beads on a string but a system and structure where points on the string relate to other points on the string in various ways (the so-called *syntagmic* structure) and operate in a network of relationships with other possible points which could substitute for it (the *paradigmic* structure).

The American logician and philosopher C.S. Peirce (1834–1914) approached the structure of language with a wider-angle lens, conceiving semiotics (the term preferred in the US) as being an interdisciplinary science in which sign systems manifested in structures and levels could be analysed from philosophical, psychological and sociological as well as linguistic points of view. Peirce and other philosophers, such as Charles Morris and Rudolph Carnap, saw the field as divisible into three areas: *semantics*, the study of the links between linguistic expressions and the objects in the world to which they refer or which they describe; *syntactics*, the study of the relation of these expressions to each other; and *pragmatics*, the study of the dependence of the meaning of these expressions on their users (including the social context in which they are used).

The terminology of semiology/semiotics is complex and daunting, but the names Peirce gave to his categories are worth quoting here: the sign he called an *icon* resembles the object it wishes to describe, like a photograph; an *index* establishes a direct link between the sign and its object (smoke is an index of fire); finally, the *symbol* where there is neither connection nor resemblance between sign and object. A symbol communicates only because there is agreement among people that it shall stand for what it does (letters combined into words are symbols).

Semiology has come to apply, as a system of analysis, to every aspect of communication. There is practically nothing that is not a sign capable of meaning, or signification. The work of the French philosopher Roland Barthes (1915–80) has exercised particular influence on our understanding of areas such as music, eating, clothes and dance as well as language. See PARADIGM; MYTH. See also *TOPIC GUIDE* under COMMUNICATION THEORY; LANGUAGE/DISCOURSE/NARRATIVE.

Semiosic plane See MIMETIC/SEMIOSIC PLANES.

Semiotic power The power, by members of the public – AUDIENCE, consumers – to turn the consumerist signs and symbols which dominate contemporary life to their own uses. The case is put by John Fiske who, while acknowledging the power of ADVERTISING and consumerist PROPAGANDA generally, gives substantial credit to individuals to exercise a 'semiotic power' – resistance – of their own.

Our initial impression of the public flocking, for example, to an enticing new shopping mall might be to see it as a clear indicator of corporate influence at work. However, Fiske argues in his chapter 'Shopping for pleasure' in *Reading the Popular* (US: Unwin Hyman, 1989) that 'the department store was the first public space legitimately available to women' and the 'fashionable commodities it offers provide a legitimated public identity and a means of participating in the ideology of progress'.

For Fiske 'the meanings of commodities do not lie in themselves as objects, and are not determined by their conditions of production and distribution, but are produced finally by the way they are consumed'. While he readily agrees that resistance from the bottom up in society is difficult and rarely likely to be effective beyond the micro-level of everyday life, this is not a reason to deny its existence. He writes, 'Scholarship that neglects or devalues these practices seems to me to be guilty of a disrespect for the weak that is politically reprehensible.'

Big companies may make style, in clothes or more broadly in lifestyle, but such styles are not followed slavishly. Rather they are appropriated: 'Women, despite the wide variety of social formations to which they belong, all share the experience of subordination under patriarchy and have evolved a variety of tactical responses that enable them to deal with it on a day-to-day level. So, too, other subordinated groups, however defined – by class, race, age, religion, or whatever – have evolved everyday practices that enable them to live within and against the forces that subordinate them.'

Fiske refers to people as forging their own meanings out of the signifiers available to them, exerting semiotic power, and though working only at the micro-level of society 'may well act as a constant erosive force upon the macro, weakening the system from within so that it is more amenable to change at the structural level'. See AUDIENCE: ACTIVE AUDIENCE.

Sender/receiver In early transmission models of the communication process, a message was seen to be conveyed, simply, from a sender to a receiver. *Transmitter* was also used, while the linguist Roman Jakobson preferred *Addresser* and *Addressee* (see JAKOBSON'S MODEL OF COMMUNICATION, 1958). The terms *author/reader* and *encoder/decoder* recognized both the complexity, and interactive nature of communication and the role of CODES and encoding in that process. In these cases due weight was given to the TEXT which was encoded and decoded as well as the *context* in which the encoding/decoding takes places. Such terms acknowledge the critical nature of the reception of messages and the diverse ways in which such messages are interpreted.

At the same time they reflect the shift of emphasis away from a preoccupation with *sending* to a fuller recognition of the *power* that rests in reception; hence the importance of research into audience uses of media. See DECODE; ENCODE; SEMIOLOGY/SEMIOTICS.

Sensitization The process by which the media can alert the public, and specific social groups, to the fact that certain social actions are taking place, or to the possibility that certain social actions might take place. Stanley Cohen, for example, concludes in 'Sensitization: the case of the Mods and Rockers' in *The Manufacture of News: Deviance, Social Problems and the Mass Media* (UK: Constable, 1973 and subsequent editions), edited by Cohen and Jock Young, that media coverage of the bank holiday activities of the Mods and Rockers gangs, at certain southern holiday resorts in the mid-1960s, played a significant role in 'reinforcing and magnifying a predisposition to expect trouble: "Something's going to happen"'.

Cohen argues that once this perception had been established there was a tendency to interpret new, similar incidents in the same manner and fairly trivial events, normally overlooked, received media attention. Thus, 'Through the process of sensitization, incidents which would not have been defined as unusual or worthy of attention ... acquired a new meaning.' In this particular case sensitization was the first step in a process of media coverage which, Cohen argues, significantly affected the course of real events.

A more recent example is provided by Kenneth Thompson in *Moral Panics* (US/UK: Routledge, 1998) in discussion of the moral panic aroused in the mid-1990s about female violence and girl gangs. Thompson argues that the well-publicized attack on actress, model and celebrity Elizabeth Hurley by four teenage girls served as a catalyst for considerable subsequent media coverage about the so-called rise in violent behaviour among girls and in the increase in the number of violent girl gangs. See LOONY LEFTISM.

Sentence meaning, utterance meaning In his two-volume work, *Semantics* (UK: Cambridge University Press, 1977), John Lyons makes a useful distinction in the matter of 'meaning' versus 'use' in our employment of language. Sentence meaning is directly related to the grammatical and lexical (choice of words) meaning of a sentence, while utterance meaning includes all 'secondary' aspects of meaning, particularly those related to the context in which a linguistic exchange takes place. It is this distinction, between sentence and utterance meaning that allows a person to say one thing and actually mean something else.

Set A state of mental expectancy which is grounded in pre-formed ideas about some future event. The impact of a message is always influenced, to some extent, by the mental set of the receiver. See SCHEMA (PLURAL: SCHEMATA).

Seven characteristics of mass communications See MASS COMMUNICATIONS: SEVEN CHARACTERISTICS.

Sexism Discrimination against people on the grounds of assumed differences in their qualities, behaviours and characteristics resulting from their sex. Such discrimination may be targeted against men as well as women, but generally women are seen as its main victims. Sexism may manifest itself in an individual as a form of prejudice or bigotry, but more fundamentally concern focuses on the degree to which such discrimination is embedded within the structure and language of a society. In this respect the role that the media may play in generating or perpetuating this discrimination has been a theme of considerable recent research. See FEMINISM; GENDER; MALE-AS-NORM; STEREOTYPE. See also *TOPIC GUIDE* under GENDER MATTERS; MEDIA ISSUES & DEBATES.

S4C The Welsh counterpart of CHANNEL 4 (UK) – Saniel Pedwar Cymru. Approximately half the channel's output is in Welsh to serve the 500,000 Welsh-speakers in Wales.

Shadowing See COCKTAIL PARTY PROBLEM.

Shannon and Weaver's model of communication, 1949 Developed by Claude Shannon and Warren Weaver to assist the construction of a mathematical theory of communication which could be applied in a wide variety of information transfer situations, whether by humans, machines or other systems. It is essentially a linear, process-centred model.

Shannon and Weaver were engineers working for the Bell Telephone Laboratories in the US and their objective was to ensure maximum efficiency of the channels of communication, in their case telephone cable and radio wave. However, in *Mathematical Theory of Communication* (US: University of Illinois Press, 1949), they claim for their theory a much wider application to human communication than solely the technical one. Within the framework of their model of transmission, the authors identify three levels of problems in the analysis of communication: Level A (technical), Level B (semantic – the meaning as emanating from the Transmitter's mode of address) and Level C (effectiveness in terms of reception or understanding on the part of the Receiver). Shannon and Weaver's model was constructed mainly to tackle Level A problems, and the assumption seems to be that to sort out the technical problems by improving encoding will, almost automatically, lead to improvements at Levels B and C.

Shannon and Weaver stressed the importance of REDUNDANCY in telephonic communication, that is the practice of inserting words, salutations, phrases, expressions not strictly relevant to the central message. Such a practice, conducted by all of us in everyday conversation, serves a vital purpose. As far as exchanges on the telephone are concerned Shannon and Weaver estimated that as much as 50 per cent of the conversation can be lost, say as a result of crackle on the line, yet the gist of the message would still be understood. See CHANNEL CAPACITY; CYBERNETICS; REDUNDANCY. See also *TOPIC GUIDE* under COMMUNICATION MODELS.

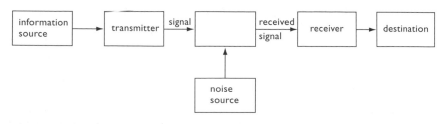

Shannon and Weaver's model of communication, 1949

Shawcross Commission Report on the Press (UK), 1962 The five-member Commission chaired by Lord Shawcross, lawyer and former Labour minister, declared that the real enemy of good-quality newspapers was competition; and competition threatened diversity. 'Within any class of competitive newspapers,' said the Report, 'the economies of large-scale operation provide a natural tendency for a newspaper which already has a large circulation to flourish, and to attract still more readers, whilst a newspaper which has a small circulation is likely to be in difficulties.'

Shawcross offered no radical solution to the problems his Committee had delineated, trusting in the free market, albeit reluctantly: 'there is no acceptable legislative or fiscal way of regulating the competitive and economic forces so as to ensure a sufficient diversity of newspapers'.

The Report put forward an idea for a press amalgamations court which should scrutinize proposed mergers of all daily or Sunday papers with sales over three million, and to give the go-ahead only if the court considered such mergers to be no threat to public interest. In 1965 the Monopolies Commission was created by the Labour government under Harold Wilson, by means of the Monopolies and Mergers Act, which ruled that issues were to be decided by government, not the courts. See *TOPIC GUIDE* under COMMISSIONS, COMMITTEES, LEGISLATION.

Shortfall signals In interpersonal contact, a shortfall signal is, for example, a smile of greeting that disappears too soon; in other words, it fails to carry conviction as a true smile of greeting. In the main, shortfall signals consist of simulated warmth in salutation. The evasive glance, the pulled-away glance, the frozen smile, the smile of mouth without eyes – all of these and many more are INDICATORS of personal unease about the encounter.

The explanation may be because the person you greet is someone you dislike or fear, though the shortfall signal may have as much to do with personal mood, and preoccupation, as anything else. Conversely, there is the so-called *overkill signal*, where the greeting is too friendly, too effusive, the handshake too forcible. The overkill signal may be a simulation of sincere greeting; on the other hand, when people of different cultures or nations meet, one person's shortfall may be another's overkill. See GESTURE; PROXEMICS.

Shot In film-making, the shot is the equivalent, in writerly terms, of a word, a phrase, a sentence or a paragraph. The director of a movie shoots film; each shot is the length at which a camera works continuously from a still or moving position. A 'take' may constitute a series of shots or a continuous shot. It is visually defined by the use of the clapperboard held in front of the camera.

The board has the title of the film written on it, and the number of the take; the clapper is extended and then closed at the moment of the take. A correspondent on the function of the clapperboard, Peter Heinze, writing from the European Institute for the Media, says its prime function is to give the editor 'a synchronous point both on the picture and the sound track, without which it is difficult – sometimes impossible – to match the picture to the sound, and thus have words mouthed "in sync"'. Heinze adds that it is true that on optical tracks (both variable area and variable density) it is possible to match the two by sight, the standard way is to listen for the 'clap'.

There are many types of shot: low and high angle, tilted; tracking, where the camera rests on a crab and track device and follows the action into or across the picture. The zoom lens allows the CU (Close Up), MCU (Medium Close Up) and the BCU (Big Close Up). There is the wide-angle shot and the pan where the camera swings across the scene; there is the still shot and the slow motion shot. Final decisions about how long a shot will be, which shots will be used and in what order come at the editing stage of film-making. See MONTAGE.

Showbusiness, age of The present age of advancing communications technology has been given many titles – the Age of Information, the Telecommunications Age, the Age of the Global Village. Neil Postman in *Amusing Ourselves to Death* (UK: Methuen, 1986) calls it the Age of Showbusiness, a period in which TV dominates the lives of the community, turning people, in his view, into a population 'amusing ourselves to death'. In the Age of Showbusiness, Postman argues, all DISCOURSES are rewritten in terms of entertainment; substance is translated into IMAGE and the present is emphasized to the detriment of historical perspectives.

Postman's criticism is targeted upon the commercial TV of his native America but his points are worth examining in wider contexts at a time when PUBLIC SERVICE BROADCASTING (PSB) looks nervously to its own future. According to Postman, TV 'does everything possible to encourage us to watch continuously. But what we watch is a medium which presents information in a form that renders it simplistic, nonsubstantive, non-historical and non-contextual; that is to say, information packaged as entertainment.' See CONSUMER SOVEREIGNTY; EFFECTS OF THE MASS MEDIA; MAINSTREAMING; PILKINGTON COMMITTEE REPORT ON BROADCASTING (UK), 1962; PSEUDO-CONTEXT.

Sign In communication studies, a little word that triggers complex explanations. Father of semiology/semiotics, Swiss linguist Ferdinand de Saussure (1857–1913) regarded language as a 'deposit of signs'; he viewed the sign as a phenomenon comprising an 'acoustic image' and a concept (the thing signified). A word or combination of words in a language refers to, is an indicator of, some externally existing object or idea. Charles Peirce (1834–1914), the American philosopher and logician, posed a triangular relationship involving the activation of the sign (as in the diagram below).

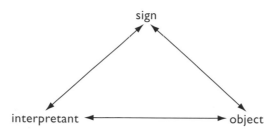

The object is that which is described by the sign, but the sign only signifies – has MEANING – in the process of it becoming a mental concept (*interpretant*), or what de Saussure named the *signified*. The point to emphasize here is that the sign depends for its meaning on the context in which it is communicated. Edmund Leach in *Culture and Communication* (UK: Cambridge University Press, 1976) says signs do not occur in isolation; 'a sign is always a member of a set of contrasting signs which function within a specific cultural context'. Also, a sign conveys information only when it is combined with other signs and symbols from the same context. 'Signs signal', writes Donis A. Dondis in *Contact: Human Communication and its History* (UK: Thames & Hudson, 1981), edited by Raymond Williams, 'they are specific to a task or circumstance'.

Of course there are not only different kinds or levels of meaning (or signification), there are many different kinds of sign. Peirce divided signs into three categories: the *icon, index* and *symbol*. These, like the triangular sign–object–interpretant are interactive, and they are overlapping. The icon is a resemblance or a representation of the object – a photograph or a map would constitute an iconic sign. An index is a sign connected or associated with its object – an indicator: smoke is an index of fire, for example.

The symbol may have no resemblance whatever to the object or idea. It is arbitrary. It comes about by choice, it exists by convention, rule or assent. It means something beyond itself. As Dondis neatly points out, 'Signs can be understood by animals as well as humans; symbols cannot.' They 'are broader in meaning, less concrete'. Raymond Firth, in *Symbols, Public and Private* (UK: Allen & Unwin, 1973), adds a fourth sign type to Peirce's three – *signal*, a sign with an emphasis on 'consequential action', a stimulus requiring some response.

Signs combine to form systems or codes, from the basic MORSE CODE or Highway Code to, for example, the complex codes of musical notation. See LANGUE AND PAROLE; JAKOBSON'S MODEL OF COMMUNICATION, 1958; TRIGGER EVENTS. See also *TOPIC GUIDE* under LANGUAGE/DISCOURSE/NARRATIVE.

Signal The physical manifestation of a message which allows it to be conveyed. See SHANNON AND WEAVER'S MODEL OF COMMUNICATION, 1949.

Signature files Commercial practice of adding information, advertising material, ongoing publicity at the bottom of e-mails; both in the outgoing stream of e-mail communication and in response to incoming e-mails. A flexible and effective marketing tool.

Significant others The analysis of the effects of a media message, of its impact, relies on the response not only of the direct respondent, but of those persons close to, influential upon the respondent – relatives, friends, work colleagues. These are 'significant others'. In the case of a child watching TV commercials, his/her response may be conditioned and modified by parents, brothers and sisters, friends. See INTERVENING VARIABLES (IVs); OPINION LEADER; OTHER.

Significant symbolizers G.H. Mead in *Mind, Self and Society* (US: University of Chicago Press, 1934), uses this term to indicate how the social organization of a society, human or animal, needs the support of reliable, regular and predictable patterns or signs if it is not to be destroyed by accumulating discrepancy and misinformation. The symbol or symbolizer, whether vocal sound, GESTURE or SIGN, achieves meaningful definition only when it has the 'same effect on the individual making it as on the individual to whom it is addressed'. Thus, according to Mead, a person defines him/herself by 'talking to himself in terms of the community to which he belongs'. Through contact with 'significant' (meaningful) objects of the social world a person develops a coherent view of him/herself and of his/her relations with others. See INTERPERSONAL COMMUNICATION; INTRAPERSONAL COMMUNICATION.

Signification One of the most valuable contributions made by Swiss linguist Ferdinand de Saussure (1857–1913) to the study of language was his idea of differentiating between the name, the naming and the MEANING of what has been named. This process enabled the linguist more effectively to examine the *structural* elements of communication. Saussure contrasted the *significant* (or signifier) with *signifié* (or that which is signified).

The relationship between these, the physical existence of the sign, and the mental concept it represents, becomes signification which, for Saussure, is the manifestation of external reality or meaning. Signification, it is important to realize, is culture-specific as is the linguistic form of the signifier in each language. Saussure terms the relationship of signs to others in the sign system, *valeur*, and it is valeur that primarily determines meaning. Thus meaning is an active force, subject to constant change, the result of dynamic interaction. See SEMIOLOGY/SEMIOTICS.

Signification spiral Stuart Hall and co-authors in *Policing the Crisis: Mugging, The State and Law & Order* (UK: Macmillan, 1978) use this term for the process by which discrete, local problems and occurrences are linked by the media into a framework of NEWS coverage in such a way as to suggest the existence of a more widespread and serious social problem.

They argue that, for example, during the 1970s there emerged a signification spiral in which problems previously presented as atypical or parochial – such as student protest, industrial unrest and mugging – were presented by the media as part of a wider concern: the breakdown in law and order. See FOLK DEVILS; DEMONIZATION; SENSITIZATION.

Significs Enquiry into questions of meaning, expression and interpretation, and the influence of language upon thought.

Silence In certain circumstances silence is as effective a means of communication as speech. In *The Dynamics of Human Communication* (US: McGraw-Hill, 1985), Gail and Michele Myers state: 'Silences ... are not to be equated with the absence of communication. Silences are a natural and fundamental aspect of communication, often ignored because misunderstood.' Silences are used to give meaning to verbal communication but can also communicate a range of information in their own right such as feelings of anger, a state of mourning or preoccupation with one's own thoughts. There are many kinds of silence and we often need other non-verbal or verbal cues to help us identify what is meant when someone is silent.

Being aware of the range of meanings that silence may convey, and the ability to accurately interpret them and react sensitively to them, is an important communicative skill as in the ability to fill an embarrassing gap in a conversation. There is a tendency in our culture to perceive silence caused by lapses during a conversation as awkward. Myers and Myers point out that masking behaviours, which include coughing, whistling and sighing, are often employed to cover up such lapses until someone thinks of something to say. The use and acceptability of silence does vary from one culture to another. See APACHE SILENCE; COMMUNICATION, NON-VERBAL (NVC); SILENCE: STRATEGIC SILENCE.

Silence, spiral of See NOELLE-NEUMAN'S SPIRAL OF SILENCE MODEL OF PUBLIC OPINION, 1974.

Silence: strategic silence In NEWS selection, that which is omitted. R. Lenz in 'The search for strategic silence: discovering what journalism leaves out' in *American Journalism* 8(1) (1991), perceives the working of ideology in reportorial omission and that such omission often says more about the selection process, and those who do the selecting, than what is included in news bulletins. That version of reality constructed by journalists, writes Lentz, 'relies upon the production of meanings based not only upon published content but upon ways in which some things are not "seen", or if seen, not recorded, as part of the social transaction between readers and creators of editorial matter'. The term *absence* is often used in this context.

Sincerity test (by the media) Some commentators claim that a by-product of political BROADCASTING is the way TV appearances by influential public figures are assessed by audiences for honesty and sincerity. Equally, the skilled public figure can use TV to project the desired image of honesty and sincerity in order to gain public support.

Sit-com Situation comedy on TV, the comedy growing out of context and recurringly generated or fuelled by amiable antagonism of one kind or another. Where the SOAP OPERA demands a substantial range of characters the sit-com generally focuses upon narrow circles of acquaintance and relationship such as families or groups of friends. Rarely does the narrative of one instalment of a sit-com continue from the previous one or continue to the next, again contrasting with the soap whose narrative key is balancing a number of ongoing stories and spinning these along over days and weeks.

Each instalment of a sit-com begins with a situation that is resolved within a single timescale. Characters may be rounded, even complex, but rarely do they, or the situations they are involved in, develop or change. This does not mean that they are sealed against the events of the real world; indeed they often reflect real-world conditions and make use of current issues and trends. For example, the UK sit-com *Men Behaving Badly* explored, amusingly and wittily, the 'gender war' of the 1990s in which men had to adjust to the threat to their traditional dominance by women confident that the future is theirs. Writers of sit-coms have succeeded in creating diverse themes, from comedy in prison – *Porridge* – to comedy in space – *Red Dwarf* – to aliens on earth – *Third Rock from the Sun*. The Korean War was the setting for one of the best and most incisive sit-coms, *MASH*, starring Alan Alda, while the zany antics of New York's thirtysomethings in *Friends* proved a worldwide success.

The best sit-coms prove to have a long and recurring screen life: *The Phil Silvers Show* and *Dad's Army* have been introduced and reintroduced to succeeding generations of audience. Notable sit-coms from the UK stable have been *Till Death Us Do Part, Steptoe and Son, The Likely Lads, Rising Damp, The Good Life, Fawlty Towers, Last of the Summer Wine, Birds of a Feather, Father Ted* and *Goodness Gracious Me*, from the US, a few of many notable sit-coms have been *Bewitched, Rhoda, Taxi, Cheers!, Cybill, Roseanne* and *Frasier*.

Site The theoretical or physical space where a struggle over MEANING and the power to reinforce a particular meaning occurs.

Situational proprieties Erving Goffman in *Behaviour in Public Places* (US: Free Press, 1963) employed this phrase to describe rules of behaviour common to interpersonal and group situations which oblige participants to 'fit in'; to accept the particular normative behaviour suitable for a successful, dissonance-free interaction. Such properties might be to avoid making a scene or causing a disturbance; refrain from talking too loudly or too assertively; hold back from attempting to dominate proceedings or, in contrast, to check oneself from withdrawing from what is going on.

S-IV-R model of communication Derives from general theories of learning/communication, where the relationship between stimulus (S) and response (R) is regarded as providing the key to both learning and communication. Actually it is a teaching-orientated model rather than learner-centred, and implies a predominantly one-way traffic of information from teacher to pupil. The IV stands for INTERVENING VARIABLES, those factors in the communication situation that help, hinder or modify the response to the intended message. These variables are innumerable: NOISE (technical or semantic), lack of motivation or concentration, personal problems and, very importantly, the influence of other people – peer groups, friends, parents, etc. See MEDIATION; OTHER; SIGNIFICANT OTHERS. See also *TOPIC GUIDE* under COMMUNICATION MODELS.

Slander A false or malicious report by spoken word or by SIGN or GESTURE. In law, slander may constitute DEFAMATION – of character or reputation – and may be subject to heavy fines. However, no legal aid is granted in the UK for defamation cases. LIBEL is the written or printed equivalent of slander.

Slang Colloquial language whose words and usages are not generally acceptable within formal modes of expression. The word was not used until about 1756. Prior to that it was called *cant*, and referred to the secret language of the underworld, of thieves and rogues; also termed *argot*. Slang usually begins as in-group language, then moves into popular use. For example, the criminal world's slang nouns for policeman (coppers,

An era which, to a modern generation, had seemed a closed book, curtained off by official reluctance to examine a past of terror following the Spanish Civil War, had the curtains of forgetfulness drawn back; and all at once, the nation focuses on its past as never before.

Elizabeth Nash, writing from Madrid, in a news report entitled 'Spain gripped by soap set in dark years of Franco's rule' (UK *Independent*, 9 August 2002), says, 'The series has caught the imagination of all generations of Spaniards: those who remember Franco relish the authenticity of every detail; youngsters who never knew him are fascinated by this window on their otherwise silent and invisible history.' See EMPOWERMENT; FEMINISM; GENDER; GENDERED GENRE; GOSSIP NETWORKS; NARRATIVE.

* Ien Ang, *Watching Dallas: Soap Operas and the Melodramatic Imagination* (UK: Methuen, 1985; Routledge paperback, 1996); David Morley, *Family Television: Cultural Power and Domestic Leisure* (UK: Comedia, 1986); David Buckingham, *Public Secrets: EastEnders and its Audience* (UK: British Film Institute, 1987); Yvonne Tasker, 'Having it all: feminism and the pleasures of the popular' in Sarah Franklin, Celia Lury and Jackie Stacey, eds, *Off-Centre: Feminism and Cultural Studies* (UK: HarperCollins Academic, 1991); Mary Ellen Brown, *Soap Opera and Women's Talk* (UK: Sage, 1994); Robert C. Allen, *To Be Continued: Soap Operas Around the World* (UK: Routledge, 1995); Charlotte Brunsdon, *Screen Tastes: Soap Opera to Satellite Dish* (UK: Routledge, 1997).

Soaps: docu-soaps Popular variant of the fictional soap, presenting documentary series in the fashion of soaps with the same emphasis on characters the audience can readily identify with, real-life situations intercut with parallel situations in the typical manner of soaps. Examples in the UK have been *Airport, Driving School* and *Hotel.*

Such programmes have tended to supplant serious, probing documentaries and are largely the result of the intense pressures of competition. Their fascination lies in the actuality of the mini-dramas and their sense of immediacy. Where docu-soaps are different from fictional soaps is in the freedom the 'characters' are given to comment on the mini-dramas that fill their working days.

Social action (mode of media analysis) Stresses the role of the individual as a potent force within a dynamic social system. It sees conflict as central to the process of change, in particular conflict between GROUPS seeking influence, power and status. Social action analysis concentrates on the media as a special group both reflecting and involved in the conflicts that concern social change, or resistance to it. A pluralist society, of competing ideologies and varying, changing definitions of truth and meaning, is acknowledged by social action analysis as are the complex influences at work upon media and media audiences and the interaction between them. See FUNCTIONALIST (MODE OF MEDIA ANALYSIS); MARXIST (MODE OF MEDIA ANALYSIS); PLURALISM. See also *TOPIC GUIDE* under RESEARCH METHODS.

Social action broadcasting A broad term describing RADIO and TV programming that sets out not only to analyse current social problems and issues and bring them to public attention, but to encourage people to take action in response to what they have heard or seen. In the UK such programmes range from the BBC's adult literacy series *On the Move* or *Crimewatch UK* to Capital Radio's *Helpline.* Information on social action broadcasting is disseminated by the National Volunteer Centre in its publication *Media Project News* which produces a twice-yearly Directory of Social Action Programmes.

Social anthropology The study of the evolution of human communities and cultures.

Social class See CLASS.

Social influence theory See IDENTIFICATION.

Socialization The shaping of human behaviour through experience in and knowledge of certain social situations: the process by which individuals are made aware of the EXPECTATIONS others have of their behaviour; by which they acquire the NORMS, MORES, VALUES and beliefs of a social group or society; and by which the CULTURE of a social group or society is transmitted. Socialization continues throughout life as individuals change their ROLES and membership of social GROUPS.

There exist what are commonly known as *agents of socialization.* In modern industrial societies, the family, school and friendship groups are thought to be the most significant agents in shaping the behaviour of the individual. The mass media are also agents of socialization and are considered to be particularly influential in transmitting awareness and expectations concerning a wide range of societal behaviour.

Individuals and societies may undergo radical change; if so, *re-socialization* may occur – the peeling away of learned patterns of behaviour and their replacement with quite different ones. There is interest as to the media's potential role in this process: its capacity as a disseminator of PROPAGANDA, for example, could be of significance. Additionally, media organizations are themselves social institutions and as such have their own patterns of behaviour, attitudes and beliefs into which their members are socialized. The degree to which the culture of media organizations affects their output is a considerable source of interest. See *TOPIC GUIDE* under MEDIA: VALUES & IDEOLOGY.

Social lubricators Richard Hoggart in *Speaking to Each Other* (UK: Chatto & Windus, 1970) uses this term to describe those people involved in the research, design and presentation of material aimed at aiding the smooth running of a technologically advanced society: communications experts, public relations officers and advertising executives, for example. See PUBLIC RELATIONS (PR).

Socially unattached intelligentsia See IMPARTIALITY.

Social perception See PERCEPTION.

Social system Consists of a collective of people who undertake different types of tasks in order to achieve common goals and solve common problems. The term can be applied to a group of two or more individuals, complex organizations or whole societies. For the members of a social system to cooperate there must be a shared language and some cultural similarities between them, although within the overall system there may be a variety of sub-cultures and language CODES, as well as other individual differences. All social systems are liable to undergo transition, a process by which the structures and functions are altered. One focus for research has been the role of the communication of innovation in the process of social change. See SOCIALIZATION.

Societally conscious See VALS TYPOLOGY.

Sociolinguistics The study of the way in which an individual's linguistic behaviour might be influenced by the social communities to which he/she belongs. It investigates also the linguistic variations found between groups, and their identification through language.

Richard A. Hudson in *Sociolinguistics* (UK: Cambridge University Press, 1996) comments that 'in sociolinguistics … the social questions are in full focus'. Areas within the field include the study of dialects, codes, registers, pidgins, Creoles, the relationship between language and thought, and gender differences in the use of language. A number of aspects of contemporary research as well as debates within sociolinguistics are of relevance to the study of interpersonal communication. See *TOPIC GUIDE* under INTERPERSONAL COMMUNICATION; LANGUAGE/DISCOURSE/NARRATIVE.

Sociology French philosopher Auguste Comte (1798–1857) was the first to use the word. The discipline attempts a scientific and systematic study of society, employing precise and controlled methods of inquiry. It is concerned with social structure; social systems; social action; the various GROUPS, institutions, categories and classes which go to make up a society or social system; the CULTURE and lifestyle of a society and the groups of which it is composed; the processes of socialization by which such cultures are communicated and maintained; and the types and allocation of social roles. Social groups, their inter-relationships and INTERACTION, and their conditioning of individual behaviour could be seen as the building blocks of the discipline.

Sociometrics (and media analysis) Sociometrics is the analysis of small GROUPS, their coherence and the interpersonal relationships and communication within them. This mode of analysis has been extended and applied within media studies to ascertain the nature of the relationships between owners of media organizations and owners of other industrial or commercial concerns and the degree to which they are interlocking. The purpose of such a sociometric map of capitalism is to discover whether or not shared positions in and patterns of social and economic life produce recognized shared interests and a common cluster of beliefs, VALUES and perspectives which feed back into and influence media organizations and their products.

Increasingly, owners of communications concerns are also owners of other businesses, and these contacts are reinforced by overlapping directorships. Board members of top media corporations have been found to hold membership of elite London clubs also favoured by directors of leading financial institutions and some business corporations. Of course evidence of points of contact does not necessarily constitute evidence of shared values, beliefs and perspectives, or deliberate influence of media products. See CONVERGENCE. See also *TOPIC GUIDE* under RESEARCH METHODS.

'Somme, The Battle of the' First-ever film DOCUMENTARY of war; records the first day of the battle of the Somme, 1 July 1916, during which the British Army suffered 57,000 casualties, almost a third of these killed. *The Battle of the Somme* was not filmed secretly but was produced with permission of the Secretary of State for War, David Lloyd George, whose words were read out at the first screening of the film on 10 August 1916, scarcely more than a month after the events the film so tellingly describes. Lloyd George's breathtaking openness (to us now) was based upon a belief that to tell the public the truth would reinforce support for the war: 'You are invited,' he wrote, 'to witness by far the most imposing picture of the war that our staff has yet procured.'

It was true that the film was popular. Shot by Geoffrey Malins and J.B. McDowell, *The Battle of the Somme* was seen by over 20 million people in the UK, practically half the population. Perceived as PROPAGANDA by the British Army, the film had the opposite effect to that intended. People were horrified by what they saw, and government immediately learnt that in times of war truth is better concealed than revealed.

Rarely again did countries at war permit such frank revelations of the harrowing experiences of conflict to be shown, uncensored, to the public. The exception was the Vietnam War in which film and reports of carnage eventually turned public opinion in the US against the war. In succeeding twentieth- and twenty-first-century wars censorship has been resolutely applied. Where censorship has proved less easy to impose, as in the wars in Bosnia and Kosovo, documentary footage has had a profound effect on public opinion worldwide. A video, *The Battle of the Somme: Official Pictures of the Army in France*, is available from the Imperial War Museum, London. See EMBEDDED REPORTERS; NEWS MANAGEMENT IN TIMES OF WAR. See also *TOPIC GUIDE* under MEDIA HISTORY.

Sound-bite Term originally derived from RADIO but which has come to apply equally to TV; describes a film or tape segment within a NEWS story, in which a reporter talks to a source such as a politician or an eyewitness. With the advent of more sophisticated technology for handling news reports, the use of jump-cutting has added to the complexity and the drama of the sound-bite. The *ellipsis* jump-cut splices two or more segments of the same person speaking in the same setting: these are classified as single sound-bites. The *juxtaposition* jump-cut places together contrasting segments, usually from different settings, in such a way as to make evident the discontinuity. These tend to be treated as separate sound-bites.

Research into the nature and degree of sound-bites in news broadcasting in the US indicates that contemporary news employs far more, and far shorter, sound-bites than in the past. In 'Sound-bite news: television coverage of elections, 1968–1988' in *Journal of Communication*, Spring 1992, Daniel C. Hallin reports that the average sound-bite has been shrinking, from more than 40 seconds in length in 1968 to under 10 seconds in the 1980s. The conclusion Hallin draws from this is that the news is now much more *mediated* than the TV news of the 1960s and 1970s.

He writes, 'Today's television journalist displays a sharply different attitude towards the words of candidates and other newsmakers. Today, those words, rather than simply being reproduced and transmitted to the audiences, are treated as raw material to be taken apart, combined with other sounds and images, and reintegrated into a new narrative.'

Hallin cites three reasons for the sound-bite revolution, as apposite in the twenty-first century as when he was writing: the technological one already mentioned, the weakening in political consensus and authority following Vietnam and WATERGATE, and the discovery by the TV industry in the US that news was big business if, that is, presentation was 'punchy' enough to attract and retain audience attention. Ironically, the approach derives from the very people journalists often accuse of manipulating the media – political campaign managers – so-called 'spin doctors' whose techniques of packaging candidates have centred around sound-biting images, one-liners, the use of triumphalist music, etc.

Dan Hallin acknowledges that modern news is far more 'professional', far more varied, slicker than in the past, but he identifies serious worries. 'First and simplest, it is disturbing that the public never has the chance to hear a candidate – or anyone else – speak for more than 20 seconds', especially as showing 'humans speaking is something television does very effectively'. Also the modern pace of exposition raises questions concerning audience comprehension, the ability of viewers to understand what is coming at them at such speed. Not the least concern is that sound-bite journalism emphasizes techniques over substance: the very sin the journalist accuses the spin doctor of committing. See JOURNALISM; NEWS MANAGEMENT. See also *TOPIC GUIDE* under NEWS MEDIA.

* David Stayden and Rita Kirk Whillock, eds, *Soundbite Culture: The Death of Discourse in a Wired World* (US/UK: Sage, 1999).

Sound broadcasting See RADIO BROADCASTING.

Sound Broadcasting Act (UK), 1972 Gave the go-ahead to COMMERCIAL RADIO in the UK. The name Independent Television Authority (ITA) was changed to Independent Broadcasting Authority (IBA), and the IBA was empowered to create a new group of contractors in up to 50 British cities to run local commercial radio stations and collect advertising revenue in a manner similar to that of the TV programme companies. The first commercial radio stations went on the air in October 1973.

Sound, synchronous See SYNCHRONOUS SOUND.

Source An individual, group or institution that originates a message. In media terms, the source is where information starts, and it is an axiom of good reporting that the material supplied by the source is reliable and true. Best practice suggests that single sources be checked against other sources. It is also a matter of journalistic principle that in some cases the source of information, especially if it is of a particularly sensitive or sensational nature, is kept secret; that the provider of information is assured of anonymity (see DEEP THROAT).

Where the information provided by the source is perceived to impugn those in authority, by suggesting corruption or other wrong-doing, reporters may be charged with criminal offences if they refuse to divulge their sources. If they give in to pressure, retreat from the guarantee of *confidentiality*, it is unlikely that they will be trusted with sensitive information ever again; on the other hand, they may end up in jail, as happened to *New York Times* journalist Judith Miller in 2005 after she refused to reveal the source of an inquiry into the leaking of the name of a CIA undercover agent.

The mass media are often criticized for over-reliance on official sources, or failing to question information which has been supplied to them by those in authority. Equally they are seen to pay selective attention to sources, valuing some, ignoring others. At worst, they serve the interests of the powerful by transmitting PROPAGANDA as if it were NEWS. See NEWS VALUES.

Source domination See PRIMARY, SECONDARY DEFINERS.

Spatial behaviour See ORIENTATION; PROXEMICS.

Spatial zones Those areas and distances which individuals maintain between each other, depending on the nature of the relationship between them. Edward T. Hall, 'inventor' of PROXEMICS (see his book, *The Silent Language*, US: Anchor Books, 1973), has specified four of these spatial zones: *intimate, personal, social* and *public* (each with a near and far phase). See INTERPERSONAL COMMUNICATION.

Special effects The 'real' gorilla in *King Kong* (1933) was just 18 inches high – that is special effects. Simulations of earthquakes, explosions, floods, fires, storms, of the interior of hell, of war in space or 40 fathoms deep is the job of the special effects wizards who today command fees as great as film stars. Special effects can, by dazzling defiance of the possible, make the success of a film. *Star Wars* (1977), directed by George Lucas, was raised from the humdrum and the banal to the spectacular by special effects; and computer graphics have provided an exciting new dimension to the art, with, first in the field, Walt Disney's $18m *Tron* (1982). The financial success of such movies as *Jurassic Park* (1993) and *Titanic* (1997) owed much to their special effects. The problem with effects is that they frequently became the main player in the NARRATIVE, a case of style dominating over content, as some critics pointed out in reviewing *Star Wars: Episode II: Attack of the Clones* (2002).

Speed photography See HIGH-SPEED PHOTOGRAPHY.

Spin doctor See NEWS MANAGEMENT; SOUND-BITE.

Spiral model of communication See DANCE'S HELICAL MODEL OF COMMUNICATION.

Spiral of silence See NOELLE-NEUMANN'S SPIRAL OF SILENCE MODEL OF PUBLIC OPINION, 1974.

Spoiler Device used by one or more newspapers to detract from a rival paper's scoop story; usually by running a different version of the story as told by lesser characters.

Sponsorship There is scarcely any field of the arts, sport, entertainment or media that is not to a greater or lesser extent dependent on sponsorship; and this sponsorship originates for the most part from industry, business and commerce. However, it could be said that sponsorship is as old as the pyramids; indeed the pyramids constitute one of the most impactful examples of state sponsorship. Tombs, yes, but also symbols of the pharaohs' will to dominate the lives of their subjects. The pyramids were a constant reminder to the Egyptians that 'We are here.' Similarly, sponsorship of the arts by monarchs and the Church was at base born of a desire to enthrone the sponsor in the minds and memories of the people.

Some powers of monarchy and the Church have been inherited by big business, as well as certain duties within the community. A company or corporation will sponsor a major art exhibition designed to give pleasure and illumination to thousands. And those thousands will in turn, so it is hoped, acknowledge the communal benefit made possible by the sponsoring company. Thus culture comes to us through the arch of sponsorship. At the same time the company will benefit by association.

To sponsor Mozart or Rembrandt is somehow to be touched by their greatness. Their quality rubs off on the sponsor. The danger is for Mozart to be hijacked from the public domain and transformed into yet another device for selling goods – processed, packaged and 'profitized'. Such is the awareness in public bodies of this danger that codes are written to regulate the degree of sponsorship and its nature.

Sponsorship of broadcast programmes (UK) Responsibility for establishing rules concerning sponsorship and broadcast programmes in the UK, and monitoring its practice, rests with the Office of Communications (see OFCOM). Sponsorship is dealt with in Section 9 of the Ofcom Broadcasting Code. The BBC does not come under Ofcom regulation in this matter.

The Code states that sponsorship may occur subject to certain conditions: there must be *transparency, separation* and *editorial independence.* It must be made clear that while a sponsor may have financed a programme, or materially supported that programme, it has not influenced the programme's content and that the acknowledgment of sponsorship makes clear the difference between itself and the programme. Excluded from any form of sponsorship are news bulletins and news desk presentations on radio, and news and current affairs programmes on TV.

Subsection 9.5 of the Code states, 'A sponsor must not influence the content and/or scheduling of a programme in such a way as to impair the responsibility and editorial independence of the broadcaster', while Subsection 9.6 rules that there 'must be no promotional reference to the sponsor, its name, trademark, image, activities, services or products and no promotional generic references' and the sponsor 'must also have no other direct or indirect interest in the editorial content of the sponsored programme. Non-promotional references are permitted only where they are editorially justified and incidental.'

Item 9.14 requires that 'Sponsorship must be clearly separated from advertising. Sponsor credits must not contain advertising messages or calls to action. In particular, credits must not encourage the purchase or rental of the products or services of the sponsor or a third party.' See ADVERTISING STANDARDS AUTHORITY (ASA).

Spot news Term used to describe unexpected or unplanned news events, such as natural disasters, air crashes, murders or assassinations, often referred to as *breaking* news, and to be distiguinshed from *diary stories* which are known well in advance and can be planned for by the newspaper, RADIO or TV news team – such as news conferences, state visits, elections or budgets. The *running story* is that which is ongoing and may stretch over several days or weeks, such as strikes, wars and famines; all stories that transcend the newsday cycle.

Sputnik First artificial satellite, launched into space by the Russians in 1957. See SATELLITE TRANSMISSION.

Spycatcher case A book by former British secret service employee Peter Wright, first published in the US in 1987, and banned from publication in the UK, became the centre of the most celebrated case of attempted government censorship in the 1980s. *Spycatcher: The Candid Autobiography of a Senior Intelligence Officer* (US: Viking/Penguin, 1987) was not dissimilar in its revelations about the activities of MI5 to other books that had been permitted to appear, but Wright, having signed the OFFICIAL SECRETS ACT (UK), was deemed to have breached confidence and arguably set a precedent for other secret agents to 'spill the beans' on security.

The Conservative government was determined not only to prevent publication of *Spycatcher* in the UK but to block the intentions of newspapers such as the *Guardian,* the *Observer,* the *Independent* and *The Sunday Times* to publish extracts from Wright's book. At the same time, government law officers pursued the book across the world to the courts in Australia and Hong Kong stirring publicity and interest that made it a world bestseller. Only the British people were to remain in the dark about Wright's revelations.

The government did not prosecute under the Official Secrets Act but pushed its case on the grounds of *confidentiality,* that members of the secret service, having sworn never to divulge information about their work, must in law be held for ever to that allegiance. Eventually the Law Lords deliberated on the saga of

Spycatcher and in October 1988 rejected government demands for a blanket injunction against the publishing in the UK of extracts from Wright's book.

'In a free society,' said Lord Goff, one of the five Law Lords, 'there is a continuing public interest that the workings of government should be open to scrutiny and criticism.' The Law Lords attacked the government's conduct of the litigation and its claims that it is for government alone to judge what information must remain confidential. An estimated £3m was spent by the government on court proceedings.

This triumph for free speech was followed by government measures to revise the Official Secrets Act in order to achieve the kind of CENSORSHIP which had been so conspicuously rejected in the Lords' judgment. See *TOPIC GUIDE* under MEDIA: FREEDOM, CENSORSHIP; MEDIA HISTORY; MEDIA: POLITICS & ECONOMICS.

Stages in audience fragmentation See AUDIENCE: FRAGMENTATION OF.

Stakeholders A term used in public relations practice to refer to those who have an interest or stake in, and thus are likely to be affected by, the activities and plans of an organization or individual client. Stakeholders may not always be aware of their potential involvement. Paul Baines, John Egan and Frank Jefkins in *Public Relations: Contemporary Issues and Techniques* (UK: Elsevier Butterworth-Heinemann, 2004) identify four categories of stakeholders based on their relative levels of power and interest as regards a particular situation.

First, there are the 'key players' who have considerable power to affect the activities of a company or industry sector. Second, there are stakeholders with low levels of power but a high degree of interest in the situation and who will look to be kept informed of activities. Then there are those stakeholders with a high level of power but a low degree of interest in activities but who should still receive a satisfactory amount of information. Finally, there are stakeholders who have both low levels of power and interest: consequently relatively less effort may be expended to keep them informed. See PUBLICS.

Stamp Duty A government tax in late eighteenth- and nineteenth-century Britain on newspapers, with the express intention of controlling the numbers of papers and access to them by the general public. With news of the French Revolution (1789) across the water, Stamp Duty was raised to two pence per newspaper copy, with an additional Advertising Tax at three shillings per advertisement. In 1797 Stamp Duty was raised to three and a half pence, and the hiring out of papers was forbidden. In the year of the Battle of Waterloo, 1815, the duty went up to four pence and the Advertising Tax was also raised.

These *Taxes on Knowledge* as they were described eventually provoked the 'War of the Unstamped', the struggle of papers unable or unwilling to pay the duties. William Cobbett (1763–1835) in his *Political Register* dropped news so as to evade tax and concentrated on opinion. Unstamped, and costing two pence, Cobbett's periodical achieved sales of 44,000. 'Here, in these critical years,' writes Raymond Williams in *The Long Revolution* (UK: Penguin, 1965), 'a popular press of a new kind was emerging, wholly independent in spirit, and reaching new classes of readers.'

Two of the six Acts of 1819 were directed against the press and the 1820s and early 1830s featured clashes, fines, imprisonments and heroic defiance. In 1836 Stamp Duty was reduced from four pence to one penny, three years after the Advertisement Tax had been reduced from three shillings and sixpence to one shilling and sixpence per insertion. In 1853 the Advertising Tax was finally abolished; in 1855 the last penny of the Stamp Duty was removed and in 1860 the duty imposed on paper was abandoned. 'The era of democratic journalism had formally arrived,' writes Joel H. Wiener in *The War of the Unstamped* (US: Cornell, 1969) 'and the daily newspaper became the cultural staple of the social classes.' See NEWSPAPERS, ORIGINS; PRESS BARONS; UNDERGROUND PRESS. See also *TOPIC GUIDE* under MEDIA HISTORY.

Standards and practice in advertising See ADVERTISING STANDARDS AUTHORITY (ASA).

Status The concept of status derives from the work of the sociologist Max Weber, who argued that status, though linked to CLASS, is a distinct dimension of social stratification. Status is the social evaluation of an individual or group, the degree of prestige or honour that society accords him, her or it. Wealth and high income may confer status but do not necessarily do so. The reasons why individuals or GROUPS may enjoy considerable status within a community or society are complex, subject to change and derive from many sources: such as the degree of power or authority a person or group may have, the perceived social usefulness of the abilities of an individual or group or the level of education an individual has (see CULTURAL CAPITAL).

Occupation or the ownership of property may bestow status or require attributes such as a high level of education, hence the link between status and class. Status may be *ascribed*, that is based on fixed criteria over which a person may have no control – such as ancestry, ethnic affiliation, sex – or *achieved*, that is gained by endeavour or luck. Status given may not coincide with an individual's perception of his or her status.

Status must normally be endorsed by behaviour: such as the possession of objects, status symbols, accent, manners and social skills consistent with the status position. Much communicative behaviour is involved in the display of status, the use of accent and dress for example. The mass media carry many images of status. Advertisers in particular appeal to status-consciousness as a way of selling a wide range of products and services.

Status quo As things are: the way in which things are done or were done in a period of time under discussion. Within the social science disciplines the term is often used to mean the prevailing or recent social, economic or political system – the way it works, usually by tradition, and who in the community work it (see HEGEMONY).

There is some controversy within Media Studies as to whether or not the mass media generally play an important role in reinforcing the status quo by presenting it as the 'natural' or 'real' state of things, and by rarely, in their presentation of aspects of human life, calling it into question. Richard Hoggart in *Speaking to Each Other* (UK: Chatto & Windus, 1970) argues that the tendency to accept the status quo results in the mass media concentrating on entertaining people at the expense of exploring the nature of human existence – an exploration that might disturb the status quo. See COMMON SENSE; CONSENSUS; ESTABLISHMENT; POWER ELITE.

Stereophonic sound See GRAMOPHONE.

Stereoscopy The creation of the visual illusion of relief or three dimensions. The stereoscope was invented by Sir Charles Wheatstone (1802–75) in 1838. The process has had many applications. In photography, two separate photographs, taken from minimally different angles corresponding to the position of two human eyes are mounted side by side on a card. Viewed through the angled prisms of the stereoscope, they interact to give the appearance of depth or solidity.

In the cinema, experimental processes of stereoscopy were demonstrated as early as the 1930s. It was developed as Natural Vision, or 3-D, in the early 1950s but never caught on, mainly perhaps because members of the audience had to wear special glasses. Only in Russia has a stereoscopic process that does not require the wearing of glasses been developed, yet even there it does not appear to have been widely adopted. However, 3-D (with glasses) was brought experimentally to UK TV screens by ITV in 1982–83. See HOLOGRAPHY.

Stereotype Oversimplified definition of a person or type of person, institution, style or event; to stereotype is to pigeon-hole, to thrust into tight slots of definition which allow little adjustment or change. Stereotyping is widespread because it is convenient – unions are like this, Arabs are like this, Jews are like this, teenagers, women, gays, asylum-seekers are like this. Stereotyping is often, though not always, the result of or accompaniment to PREJUDICE. It serves the media well because they are in the business of instant recognition and ready cues. It is very rare that we actually know any stereotypes: we only read of them, hear of them or have them 'framed' for us on TV. See HALO EFFECT; LABELLING PROCESS (AND THE MEDIA); SELF-FULFILLING PROPHECY. See also *TOPIC GUIDE* under MEDIA ISSUES & DEBATES.

* Michael Pickering, *Stereotyping: The Politics of Representation* (UK: Palgrave, 2001).

Stopwatch culture See IMMEDIACY.

Storyboard Sequence of sketches or photographs used by the director or the producer of a film to sketch out, scene by scene, and sometimes frame by frame, the film's progression, its sight and sound.

Storyness See NARRATIVE.

Strategic bargaining Between the subject of media interest, for example politicians, and the media, there is an interaction in which one gives to the other in return for a service: the media get a story, the politician gets publicity, preferably favourable. As Ralph Negrine says in *Politics and the Mass Media in Britain* (UK: Routledge, 1989), 'Each feeds off the other, each informs the other and the subsequent reactions are reciprocal and continuous ... The product of the interaction or bargaining is the media content to which the public at large attend.' See CULTURE OF DEFERENCE; REGULATORY FAVOURS. See also *TOPIC GUIDE* under MEDIA: POLITICS & ECONOMICS.

Strategic silence See SILENCE: STRATEGIC SILENCE.

Strategy A term sometimes used to describe a communicative act that has been planned to some extent beforehand, which is deliberate and which has a clear purpose. Strategies can become a matter of habit. An example here might be the strategy used by a door-to-door salesperson. There are many different kinds of strategies used in INTERPERSONAL COMMUNICATION and we learn to use them through experience. Some, like the greetings strategy, are commonly used by many people, some we invent for ourselves to deal with particular situations and some may be specific to certain groups or circumstances.

Stringer Name given in the NEWS reporting business to a non-staff reporter.

Structuralism A twentieth-century term of wide definition to describe certain traditions of analysing a range of studies – linguistics, literary criticism, psychoanalysis, social anthropology, Marxist theory and social history. Swiss scholar Ferdinand de Saussure's *Cours de Linguistique Générale* (1916), translated *Course in General Linguistics* (1954), is probably the initial key work in this movement, later developed and diversified by Claude Lévi-Strauss and Roland Barthes. Structuralism is something of an umbrella term linked with the study of SIGN systems or SEMIOLOGY/SEMIOTICS.

Structuralists would argue that language has both a natural and a cultural source. The natural source refers to language as a genetic endowment of the human race, and this is framed within a network of meanings derived from the CULTURE of society. Structuralism explores the deep and often unconscious assumptions about social reality that underlie language and its use. In particular, it examines the way language is employed to construct MEANING from social events. However, assumptions about social reality are themselves also a product of social conditioning. Thus different cultures and sub-cultures, and indeed individuals, may generate different patterns of meaning from the same objective event or situation. See POSTMODERNISM. See also *TOPIC GUIDE* under COMMUNICATION THEORY.

Style A means by which the individual or group expresses identity (see IDENTIFICATION; SELF-IDENTITY), attitudes and VALUES, about self, about others and about society. Style takes many forms – hair style, dress style, aesthetic style, or a complete pattern of living – lifestyle. A teenager may adopt the style of a teenage sub-culture, in dress, language, behaviour for several linked reasons: to secure a sense of personal identity, to acquire a sense of belonging, of being 'in' with a favoured group, as a gesture of rebellion (against the conventional style of parents, for example, or the older generation in all shapes and forms) and to achieve STATUS, that is a status awarded him/her by others in the favoured group, and peers generally.

Defiance of society at large is often cited as a reason why certain styles are adopted; this may or may not be true in all cases, but what is certain is that society often interprets such styles as acts of defiance or rejection, and the arbiters in this process of interpretation (or MEDIATION) are the mass media. Coverage by the media, researchers have found, tends to overdramatize the significance of style, to create STEREOTYPES and summon up exaggerated fears in the community.

In the world of the arts style is that particular set of characteristics of approach and treatment which gives a work its identity. As with styles in hair or dress, styles are first created, then imitated. In painting, the style of Paul Cézanne (1839–1906) is highly distinctive and instantly recognizable by anyone with a particular interest in art. However, it took Cézanne many years to develop that style which was a visible manifestation of everything he believed about visual art; thus style represents the outer part of a whole structure that is made up of personality, experience, learning, theory, belief – and fused, if the style is successful. Those coming after may slavishly imitate the style of the master or, like the Cubists in the case of Cézanne, assimilate the style and then recreate it, thrusting it in new directions. See CULTURE; FOLK DEVILS; LABEL LIBEL; LABELLING PROCESS (AND THE MEDIA); YOUTH CULTURE. See also *TOPIC GUIDE* under REPRESENTATION.

Sub-culture Alternatives to the dominant CULTURE in society, sub-cultures have their own systems of NORMS, VALUES and beliefs and in some cases their own language CODES. Such systems are often expressions of rejection of or resistance to the dominant culture. Members of sub-cultures are often those to whom the dominant culture awards low, subordinate and/or dependent status: youth, for example. Each sub-culture represents the reactions of a particular social group to its experience of society.

Some sub-cultures and their members may be labelled *deviant* by others in society. It has been argued that because of the fragmented social nature of modern society, the mass media play an increasingly important role in relaying images of such sub-cultures both to their own members and to members of the dominant culture. Dick Hebdige in *Subculture: The Meaning of Style* (UK: Methuen, 1979, reissued 2002) writes that in doing so the media tend to accommodate the sub-cultures within the framework of the dominant culture, thus preserving the CONSENSUS; a procedure which he calls the 'process of recuperation'.

Subliminal Signals that act below the threshold of conscious reception. Most familiarly we use the word in reference to subliminal ADVERTISING, the trick of flashing up on the screen, or recording on tape, messages so rapid that they are not consciously recorded but which may subsequently affect future attitudes or behaviour.

In the UK subliminal advertising is illegal and its use in other media is banned by the Institute of Practitioners in Advertising. In the US there is no such control. Many department stores use subliminal seduction to counteract shoplifting. Messages such as 'I am honest, I will not steal' are mixed with background music and continually repeated. One retail chain reported a drop of a third in thefts in nine months as a result of its subliminal conscience-coaxing.

Computer games escape rules concerning subliminal messages. The UK *Sunday Times* published a major story 'Children "drugged" by computer games' (8 October 1995), concerning the Time Warner game *Endorfun*. The messages are there, admit the manufacturers, but they are positive, one message being 'I forgive myself completely'. Randeep Ramesh, author of the article, quotes the opinion of Howard Shevrin, Professor of Psychology at the University of Michigan: 'It does not pay to fool around with subliminal messages. The results may not be good if you are the wrong person for the wrong message.' See SLEEPER EFFECT. See also *TOPIC GUIDE* under MEDIA: PROCESSES & PRODUCTION.

Subtitle Or striptitle, a text near the bottom of the projected image, usually providing a translation of foreign-language dialogue. These days it is possible with foreign-language films screened on TV to generate subtitles electronically so that the words are not actually on the film itself. In some multilingual areas, such as Cairo, where three or more titles in different languages and scripts are required, subtitles are projected on to separate screens at the sides and bottom of the main screen.

Super density (SD) discs Successors to the compact disc (CD), with more than 25 times the capacity of current CD-ROMs. As with the old rivalry between different video systems (VHS and Betamax) there is global rivalry between the SD format (SDI-DVD – digital video disc) favoured by Time Warner and MGM/UA and that of the co-inventors of the CD, Sony and Philips, called the MultiMedia Compact Disc. Both systems are in most respects identical without being compatible.

Supervening social necessity Notion that social or cultural pressures give the impetus to technological development, serving as *accelerators* in the process of change. Brian Winston suggests this feature in 'How are media born?' in *Questioning the Media: A Critical Introduction* (UK: Sage, 1990), edited by John Downing, Ali Mohammadi and Annabelle Sreberny-Mohammadi. He cites the arrival of TV in the US as being accelerated by the 'rise of the home, the dominance of the nuclear family, and the political and economic need to maintain full employment' after the Second World War. Winston argues that 'supervening social necessities are at the interface between society and technology'. They may operate as a result of the needs of corporations or because of new or rival technologies.

As well as accelerators, social necessities may serve as *brakes* upon technological developments, which 'work to slow the disruptive impact of new technology. I describe the operation of these brakes as the "law" of the suppression of radical potential, using "law" in the standard social science sense to denote a regular and powerful general tendency.' In this case, new technology, though available, is resisted, checked or even suppressed. Says Winston, 'The brakes ensure that a technology's introduction does not disrupt the social or corporate status quo.'

Winston is of the view that while TV had been 'accelerated' after 1945, it had been 'braked' prior to the war: 'Thus in the case of TV, the existence of facsimile systems, the rise of radio … and the need not to destroy the film industry all acted to suppress the speed at which the new medium was introduced, to minimize disruption.' Winston returns to, and expands on his analysis of the development of media technologies in his book *Media Technology and Society: A History from the Telegraph to the Internet* (UK: Routledge, 1998). See TECHNOLOGICAL DETERMINISM. See also *TOPIC GUIDE* under MEDIA: TECHNOLOGIES.

Surround See EISENBERG'S MODEL OF COMMUNICATION AND IDENTITY, 2001.

Surveillance Keeping watch; used in a media sense, the word indicates the way that listeners, viewers or readers employ the media with the aim of gleaning information from them: 'TV news provides food for thought' or 'I like to see how big issues are sorted out.' Equally surveillance implies the process of authority and its agencies keeping watch on the public. See USES AND GRATIFICATIONS THEORY.

Surveillance society New technology has vastly increased and speeded up access to personal data by those in authority or those individuals or organizations involved in financial, administrative or commercial transactions with members of the public. Each time we use a Switch card, each time we dial a telephone number, we offer notification of our activities, our whereabouts and our lifestyle. David Lyon in *The Electronic Eye: The Rise of Surveillance Society* (US: University of Minnesota Press, 1994), identifies four domains of surveillance in contemporary life – government administration, policing and security, the workplace and the consumer marketplace; and for Lyon a key characteristic of surveillance is that it operates *across* boundaries.

The concept of a surveillance society is not new. The English philosopher, social and legal reformer, Jeremy Bentham (1748–1832), in a proposal for the humanitarian treatment of prisoners, suggested the construction of what he called a *panopticon.* This was a circular building of cells with a central watchtower from which constant surveillance of the prisoners would take place, without their being certain at any given time that they were being directly observed. They would be well aware, of course, of the presence of surveillance and this knowledge would, without coercion, rule their behaviour until, so Bentham theorized, their good behaviour would become self-regulating.

For several commentators the panopticon has become a metaphor for our own times. In particular, the French philosopher Michel Foucault (1926–84) has focused on the 'all-seeing' panopticon (see PANOPTICON GAZE). In *Discipline and Punish* (UK: Penguin, 1977) he likens the panopticon to the Christian God's infinite knowledge and to computer monitoring of individuals in advanced capitalism. He argues that surveillance as represented by the contemporary panopticon creates subjects responsible for their own subjection (see PRIVACY).

We are subject to surveillance not only as citizens but as AUDIENCE for media. In an article entitled 'Tracking the audience', in *Questioning Media: A Critical Introduction* (US: Sage, 1990), edited by John Downing, Ali Mohammadi and Annabelle Sreberny-Mohammadi, Oscar Gandy Jr remarks how the fragmentation of audience for media, rendered possible by new technology, has resulted in a desperation among programme-makers that has led to two strategies aimed at survival. These Gandy identifies as *rationalization,* that is 'the pursuit of efficiency in the production, distribution, and sale of goods and services', and *surveillance* which 'provides the information necessary for greater control'. Increasingly, says Gandy, 'the surveillance of audiences resembles police surveillance of suspected criminals' and people are less and less aware that their behaviour as audience is being measured.

Gandy argues, 'Perhaps the greatest threat these computer-based systems for audience assessment represent is their potential to worsen the balance of power between individuals and bureaucratic organizations. Personal information streams out of the lives of individuals much like blood out of an open wound, and it collects in pools in the computers of corporations and government bureaucracies.' Resistance to such powers is, in Gandy's view, 'almost nonexistent, and what little there is may be seen as passive and defeatist'.

While recognizing that a 'nearly invisible minority simply refuses to enter the system of records, giving up the convenience of credit cards and acquiring goods and services under assumed names or aliases', Gandy fears that 'to escape the information net means to become a nonperson'. It is a high risk, for one 'maintains privacy through the loss of all else'. See CCTV: CLOSED-CIRCUIT TELEVISION; ECHELON; INTERNET: MONITORING OF CONTENT; REGULATION OF INVESTIGATORY POWERS ACT (RIPA) (UK), 2000; USA – PATRIOT ACT, 2001. See also *TOPIC GUIDE* under MEDIA: FREEDOM, CENSORSHIP; MEDIA ISSUES & DEBATES.

Survivors and the media A research report by Ann Shearer, 'Survivors of the media' (UK: John Libbey, 1991), commissioned by the Broadcasting Standards Council of the UK, found that insensitive media coverage adds to the distress of survivors of disasters and their bereaved relatives. Intrusions by media into PRIVACY, harassment, distortion and distasteful detail in what was reported, were identified by a sample of 54 people who had lost loved ones as damaging and hurtful. Many comments placed the worst blame at the doors of the press.

Sweetheart deals Term used to describe the informal practice by commissioning editors of BROADCASTING organizations of awarding ex-employees with a favoured STATUS when commissioning programmes from the independent production sector. A significant number of those formerly employed in broadcasting organizations entered the independent production sector when broadcasting organizations progressively downsized their labour force from the late 1980s to the mid-1990s. See CASUALIZATION.

SWOT Analytical approach widely used to scan and evaluate the internal and external environment of an organization. It can also be employed to evaluate specific organizational activities, for example the design of new products, as well as in planning MARKETING and PUBLIC RELATIONS campaigns. The approach taken is to analyse Strengths, Weaknesses, Opportunities and Threats. In *Planning and Managing Public Relations Campaigns*, (US/UK: Kogan Page, 2000) Anne Gregory provides some examples: *Strengths* may include good leadership and a loyal workforce; complacency and conservative approaches to investment may be identified as *Weaknesses*; potential *Opportunities* may include the acquisition of competitors and expansion into new markets, while being taken over by a conglomerate or the danger of becoming overstretched may be possible *Threats*.

Gregory comments further that those involved in corporate communications need to be aware of such contextual factors as they will shape their activities – 'For example, we will need to mount a marketing communications campaign if our product line is to be expanded ... An international corporate and government relations campaign will be required if we are to expand into China ...'.

Sykes Committee Report on Broadcasting, 1923 See BBC, ORIGINS.

Symbol Any object, person or EVENT to which a generally agreed, shared MEANING has been given and which individuals have learned to accept as representing something other than itself: a national flag represents feelings of patriotism and national unity, for example. Symbols are almost always culture-bound. See ICONIC; METAPHOR; MYTH; SEMIOLOGY/SEMIOTICS; SIGN; SIGNIFICATION.

'Symbolic annihilation of women' (by the media) See NORMS.

Symbolic code See CODES OF NARRATIVE.

Symbolic convergence theory Professor Ernest G. Bormann in his article 'Symbolic convergence theory: a communication formulation' in the *Journal of Communication*, Autumn 1985, writes of 'shared fantasies' which 'provide group members with comprehensible forms for explaining the past and thinking about the future – a basis for communal and group consciousness' (see NARRATIVE PARADIGM).

Bormann posits a three-part structure to the theory: (1) the part which deals with the discovery and arrangement of recurring communicative forms and patterns that indicate the evolution and presence of a shared group consciousness; (2) the part which consists of a description of the dynamic tendencies within communication systems 'that explain why group consensuses arise, continue, decline, and disappear' and the effects such group CONSENSUS has in terms of meanings, motives and communication within the group: the basic communication process is the dynamic of people sharing group fantasies; (3) that part of the theory which consists of the factors which explain why people share the fantasies they do and when they do.

By 'fantasy' Bormann means the creative and imaginative shared interpretation of events 'that fulfil a group psychological or rhetorical need'. What the author terms 'rhetorical fantasies' are the result of '*homo narrans* in collectives sharing narratives that account for their experiences and their hopes and fears'. Such rhetorical fantasies may include 'fanciful and fictitious scripts of imaginary characters, but they often deal with things that have actually happened to members of the group or that are reported in authenticated works of history, in the news media, or in the oral history and folklore of other groups and communities'.

The sharing of fantasies brings a 'convergence of appropriate feelings among participants ... when members of a mass audience share a fantasy they jointly experience the same emotions, develop common heroes and villains, celebrate certain actions as laudable, and interpret some aspect of their common experience in the same way'.

This Bormann names *symbolic convergence*. While the 'rational world paradigm' claims that there is an objective truth that speakers can mirror in their communication and against which its logic and argument can be tested and evaluated (and therefore regards MYTH and fantasy as untrue, as the recounting of falsehoods), for those giving credence to shared fantasies, 'the stories of myths or fantasy themes are central'.

An underlying assumption of the theory seems to be that fantasies are not only creative but benign. It would be interesting to apply symbolic convergence theory, the notion of *homo narrans*, to fantasies entertained about racial superiority, where fantasy becomes a nightmare. See *TOPIC GUIDE* under COMMUNICATION THEORY.

* E.G. Bormann, *Communicative Theory* (US: Holt, Rinehart & Winston, 1980); *The Force of Fantasy: Restoring the American Dream* (US: Illinois University Press, 1985).

Symbolic interactionism Term associated with the ideas of American scholar Herbert Blumer and crystallized in his book *Symbolic Interactionism: Perspective and Method* (US: University of California Press, 1969; first paperback edition, 1986). Blumer sees 'meaning as arising in a process of interaction between people'. The meaning of an object or a phenomenon for one person 'grows out of the ways in which other persons act towards the person with regard to the thing', that is the thing's *symbolic value*. Symbolic interactionism sees MEANING as a social product, as a creation 'formed in and through the defining activities of people as they interact'. All meanings, emphasizes Blumer, are subject to a constant and recurring 'interpretative process'; and this is a 'formative process in which meanings are used and revised as instruments for the guidance and formation of action'. Although G.H. Mead (1934) does not appear to have used this term, his approach to the study of human communication and its role in the formation of the SELF-CONCEPT stresses the importance of the symbolic nature of social interaction. See SELF-IDENTITY; SEMIOLOGY/SEMIOTICS; SEMIOTIC POWER.

Symmetry, strain towards Concept posed by Theodore Newcomb in 'An approach to the study of communicative acts', *Psychological Review* 63 (1953). The act of communication is characterized, believes Newcomb, by a 'strain towards symmetry', that is towards balance and consistency. See CONGRUENCE THEORY; INTERPERSONAL COMMUNICATION; NEWCOMB'S ABX MODEL OF COMMUNICATION, 1953.

Synchronic linguistics See LINGUISTICS.

Synchronous sound In film, sound effects synchronized with the visual image were first used commercially in 1926, in *Don Juan*, but it was *The Jazz Singer* in November 1927 that caused the sensation among audiences and marked the birth of the 'talkies'. Warner Brothers had been heading for oblivion in the cut-throat world of the HOLLYWOOD studios when the company adopted a system developed by the Bell Telephones Laboratories which reproduced sound from large discs, matching sound and picture by mechanical linkage. Nothing in the cinema was ever the same again.

The talkies marked the end of many careers made in the silent era but created new opportunities for actors from the theatre, writers, musicians, vaudeville and RADIO stars. As a technical possibility, synchronous sound had been inviting interest from movie-makers from as early as 1902. In that year Monsieur Gaumont gave an address to the Société Française de la Photographie, on film and employing synchronous sound. Indeed two years earlier Herr Ruhmer demonstrated what he called 'light telephony' to record sound directly on to the film itself – the first soundtrack.

Following the inventions of the thermionic valve by John Fleming in 1904 and the audion vacuum tube by Lee De Forest in 1907, amplification of sound by comparatively simple electric methods was feasible: the studios were simply not interested, fearing, perhaps, the impact language differences might have on the universal appeal of film as mime, whose only verbal language was easily translatable titling (see reference to *suppression of radical potential* in SUPERVENING SOCIAL NECESSITY).

Though Lee De Forest's Phonofilm of 1923 demonstrated how light waves could synchronize sound and image, and though the Germans had developed the finest early sound system of all, Tri-Ergon, the continuing profitability of the silent movie blinded the studios to two significant facts: the potential of silent film had practically been exhausted; and audiences were becoming bored.

Lights of New York (1928) was the first all-talking picture and within a year thousands of cinemas had been equipped for sound. Warner's VITAPHONE disc was soon replaced by optical sound systems where images and sound were put together on the same film, to make the married print where sound synchronization with the picture could not be lost. As sound recording techniques developed, dialogue, sound-effects and music were recorded separately, using a magnetic sound process, and then mixed at a later stage, thus allowing latitude for changes and creative editing.

The introduction of sound did not rescue the cinema from the general economic slump that followed the Wall Street Crash of 1929. During 1931, cinema attendances in the US dropped by 40 per cent and in 1932 the movie business lost between $4m and $5m. However, it was probably the new dimension of sound in the cinema that enabled the industry to rally so quickly.

The talkies interacted substantially with RADIO, the one drawing technical and creative ideas as well as talented personnel from the other. By 1937, 90 per cent of US-sponsored national radio programmes in the US were transmitted from Hollywood. See *TOPIC GUIDE* under MEDIA HISTORY; MEDIA: TECHNOLOGIES.

Synergy The establishment of relationships between differing areas and/or organizations within the cultural and media industries that allow for greater efficiency in the production and promotion of two or more cultural/media artefacts. An example of synergy is when the launching of a new film is accompanied by the promotion of a wide range of related merchandise. Conglomerates (see CONGLOMERATES: MEDIA CONGLOMERATES) are in an enviable position to take advantage of the benefits of synergies.

Examples of synergic partnerships have multiplied until they become a NORM and involve a range of sponsors and beneficiaries, thus McDonald's synergized with Disney to promote *Monsters, Inc.* (2002) while Harry Potter, books and movies, benefit from and benefit Coca-Cola. Perhaps the classic synergic relationship is between sport and big business.

Syntactics A branch of SEMIOLOGY/SEMIOTICS; the study of the SIGNS and rules relating to signs, without reference to MEANING.

Syntagm See PARADIGM.

Syntax The combination of words into significant patterns; the grammatical structure in sentences.

 T

Tabloid, tabloidese, tabloidization In '"Tabloidization" of news: a comparative analysis of Anglo-American and German press journalism' (*European Journal of Communication*, September 1999) Frank Esser writes that the term 'tabloid' orginally referred to a pharmaceutical trademark for the concentrated form of medicines as pill or tablet: 'This narcotic tabloid effect and the fact that it is easy to swallow have been readily transferred to the media.'

The term, in the UK, is used to refer to the size of a newspaper (in comparison with the *broadsheet* format), but in general 'tabloidese' describes the nature of news content and style. Esser quotes Marvin Kalb, director of the Shorenstein Center on the Press, Politics and Public Affairs at Harvard University: tabloidese is characterized by 'a downgrading of hard news and upgrading of sex, scandal and infotainment'. At the micro level, states Esser, tabloidization 'can be seen as a media phenomenon involving the revision of traditional newspaper and other media formats driven by reader preferences and commercial requirements' while at the macro level it 'can be seen as a social phenomenon both instigating and symbolizing major changes to the constitution of society'.

Esser's study focuses on the micro level of the tabloidization process, meaning 'a change in the range of topics being covered (more entertainment, less information), in the form of presentation (fewer longer stories, more shorter ones with pictures and illustrations) and a change in the mode of address (more street talk when addressing readers)'. He argues that the nature, evolution and relative predominance of tabloidization varies between America, the UK and Germany; thus it is an 'extremely problematic term' and can 'therefore only be analyzed with reference to the respective media cultures and journalistic traditions' of the countries in question.

For example, tabloidization has never taken hold in Germany to the extent that it has in the UK; in part because, as far as sex scandals are concerned, Germany has a strong PRIVACY law that 'also protects public figures'. He cites research evidence showing that extensive coverage of scandals can increase public disillusionment with public life, hence the fears which many commentators have 'that a shift towards sensation, emotion and scandal may have some negative effects on democracy'.

Currently the term tabloidization is used specifically to describe what many critics see happening both to the serious, broadsheet newspaper, and to TV NEWS, in the sense that they are 'getting more and more like the tabloids', matching them for populist content and design, and demonstrating the same fascination for covering the lives and antics of celebrities. In other words, the accusation is that while the tabloids – in the UK referred to as the red-tops – are already dumbed down, the dumbing-down process is actually what is happening to traditionally serious media. See *TOPIC GUIDE* under LANGUAGE/DISCOURSE/NARRATIVE.

* Rodrigo Uribe and Barrie Gunter, 'Research note: the tabloidization of British tabloids', *European Journal of Communication* (September 2004); Martin Conboy, *Tabloid Britain* (UK: Routledge, 2005).

Tactics and strategies Term used by Michel de Certeau in *The Practice of Everyday Life* (US: University of California Press, 1984) when analysing everyday cultural consumption, to draw the distinction between the strategies of the powerful controllers of the cultural industries and the tactics of the relatively powerless ordinary consumers in finding their own space for creating MEANING by adapting to their own use mass-produced cultural artefacts.

Some of these tactics subvert or resist the intentions and intended messages of the powerful. De Certeau's distinction, whilst acknowledging that audiences/consumers may be active in their consumption, does not imply that they have by any means the degree of power over cultural consumption exercised by those who own and control the cultural industries.

A rather different approach to differentiating between tactics and strategies is adopted by public relations practitioners. The term tactics refers to all the different operational tools that could be employed to communicate with an audience, such as a news conference or press release. Strategies refer to the overall plan within which such tactics might be used. They tend to look at the long-term, broad goals whilst any individual tactic tends to be focused on short-term, specific objectives. See AUDIENCE: ACTIVE AUDIENCE; SEMIOTIC POWER.

Tag questions The addition of phrases such as 'Isn't it?' or 'Don't you think?' at the end of a statement as tag questions, according to some linguists, suggests tentativeness on behalf of the speaker, and weakens the impact of what is said. However, there is some debate here. Tag questions can serve a range of functions, some relating to the content of speech, others relating to the facilitation of interaction and the relationships and attitudes of the participants to one another.

When used to facilitate interaction, tag questions do not seem to be associated with tentativeness, indeed, the tendency here is for tags to be associated with powerful speakers. Several studies suggest that women use more tag questions than men when acting as facilitators in an interaction.

Take See SHOT.

Talkies See SYNCHRONOUS SOUND.

Talloires Declaration, 1981 Concerned at the attempts by the United Nations Educational, Scientific and Cultural Organization (UNESCO) seemingly to impose upon world information systems a 'New Order' which would be characterized by far-reaching controls, representatives from news organizations of 20 countries met in the French village of Talloires in May 1981. They issued a declaration which insisted that journalists sought no special protected status, as was perceived to be UNESCO's intention, and that they were united in a 'joint declaration to the freest, most accurate and impartial information that is within our professional capacity to produce'. The declaration asserted that there could be no double standards of freedom for rich and poor countries. See MACBRIDE COMMISSION; MEDIA IMPERIALISM; NEW WORLD INFORMATION ORDER. See also *TOPIC GUIDE* under GLOBAL PERSPECTIVES.

Tamizdat See SAMIZDAT.

Taste In a media sense, the notion of good or bad taste generally relates to decisions about how much and how far; the answers to these questions depend upon AUDIENCE expectations and readiness, and the degree of access and immediacy. A photograph of an execution, reproduced in a newspaper or magazine, is sufficiently controlled by the frame of print and the fact that the event took place in the past, to escape the accusation of bad taste.

However, there were vigorous protests when, on TV news, a Vietcong prisoner had a pistol put to his head, and the trigger pulled. This was bringing, as it were, too much reality into the sitting room. It may have been the truth, ran the argument, but somehow the reproduction and presentation turned reality into theatre, indeed into macabre entertainment. As such it appeared an insult to human dignity, to that of the victim and to that of the audience cast in the role of voyeurs.

Taste can also be used to refer to the cultural or aesthetic tastes of an individual or group and such tastes can be used as signifiers of economic and CULTURAL CAPITAL and used as a means of social distinction. This perspective on taste owes much to the work of Pierre Bourdieu outlined in *Distinction: A Social Critique of the Judgment of Taste* (US: Harvard University Press, 1984). He argued that an individual's taste was significantly influenced, though not totally determined, by his/her class background and thus aspects of taste could be read as both a product and signifier of class affiliation.

Bourdieu uses the term *habitus* to refer to the collection of unconscious dispositions that individuals may have as a result of their location within the class structure; these may then influence tastes, body image and bodily communication: a person might buy an Armani suit but he/she will also need to look at ease wearing it, to carry off the statement it may make about his/her social position.

Bourdieu's view that class significantly influences an individual's tastes has been criticized, in part because some commentators argue that class distinction in modern-day society is less easy to define than in the past, and generally considered of diminishing importance. However this is not to say that people are unaware of the signs of distinction located in some tastes. See COMMUNICATION, NON-VERBAL (NVC); CONSUMPTION BEHAVIOUR; CULTURE: CONSUMER CULTURE; CULTURE: POPULAR CULTURE; OBJECT LANGUAGE; SELF-IDENTITY.

* Mike Featherstone, *Consumer Culture and Postmodernism* (US/UK: Sage, 1991); Fran Martin, ed., *Interpreting Everyday Culture* (UK: Edward Arnold, 2003).

Taxes on knowledge See STAMP DUTY.

Taxonomic conquistadors Term used by Bill Nicholls in *Blurred Boundaries: Questions of Meaning in Contemporary Culture* (US: University of Indiana Press, 1994) to describe the agencies, sociological and marketing, that subject humans to classification or SEGMENTATION. Nicholls admits the dangers inherent in placing people into (often stereotypical) slots but concedes that 'with no categories at all culture itself would disappear'. The use of the term conquistadors suggests that such taxonomies – lists of classification – have an enforcing and shaping capacity through powers of persuasion and of inclusion/exclusion. See AUDIENCE DIFFERENTIATION; AUDIENCE MEASUREMENT; VALS TYPOLOGY.

Technique: Ellul's theory of technique In a number of books written between the 1950s and 1990, Jacques Ellul saw contemporary society as being dominated by technological advances each aiding the MEDIATING power of mass communication; and together leading to a society in which efficiency and consequently conformity become the key determinants of human affairs. Ellul uses the term technique to suggest the generality of attitudes to, and uses of, machines in everyday life, applying equally to social production as to material production.

His view is a bleak one, seeing efficiency, brought about by the wholesale adoption by those who rule and those who are ruled, as being both authoritarian in tendency and beyond the control of governments: 'Technical advance,' says Ellul in *The Technological Society* (US: Knopf, 1964), 'gradually invades the state, which in turn is compelled to assume forms favourable to this advance.' Politicians Ellul sees as 'impotent satellites of the machine, which with all its parts and techniques, apparently functions as well without them'. However, the politicians do not step down. Instead they create an illusion of politics and political leadership.

Ellul anticipates the response that the information age has brought about a more involved public in the political process. For him the sheer volume of information works to reinforce the technological society by overwhelming the citizen. In a detailed analysis of Ellul's theory of technique in 'Hegemony, agency, and dialectical tension in Ellul's technological society' in the *Journal of Communication* (Summer 1998), Rick Clifton Moore writes: 'This is not to say that all of the blame for the political illusion must be laid at the feet of the state and the media. Ellul's orientation suggests the complicity of the citizens themselves ... The modern citizen is much too willing to accept the comfortable route of technique, rather than make difficult choices that would require humanness.'

The public, in Ellul's view, is subject to, and in thrall to, the 'spectacle-orientated society' in which everything is 'subordinated to visualization' and 'nothing has meaning out of it'. In today's society, Ellul says, there are many, and powerful, deterrents of human freedom. A key question is whether, in societies where 'covetousness and the desire for power' are human constants across all cultural boundaries, there is sufficient agency among citizens to achieve freedom. See HEGEMONY; IDEOLOGICAL STATE APPARATUSES; IDEOLOGY; McDONALDIZATION; SEMIOTIC POWER; SURVEILLANCE SOCIETY. See also *TOPIC GUIDE* under MEDIA: TECHNOLOGIES.

Technological determinism The view that if something is technically feasible then it is both desirable and bound to be realized in practice. Evidence points to the fact that such determinism is only partly convincing. Much technology usage is a by-product of technology devised for other purposes. RADIO became an 'inevitability', for example, largely because its determinant was radar, required to fulfil military needs, while satellites had a long record of military/political functions before they began to beam sporting events to the peoples of the world.

Set against notions of technological determinism is a second theory, *symptomatic technology*, which argues that technology is a by-product of a social process which itself has been otherwise determined. In *Television: Technology and Cultural Form* (UK: Fontana, 1974), Raymond Williams says that basically both theories are in error because in different ways they have 'abstracted technology from society' instead of examining the crucial interaction between them. Of course part of that interaction is the belief in technological determinism, and the risk of it becoming a SELF-FULFILLING PROPHECY.

Dwayne Winseck in 'Pursuing the holy grail: information highways and media reconvergence in Britain and Canada' in the *European Journal of Communication*, September 1998, argues that contrary to 'the belief that technological factors determine how media are organized', the primary drivers of media evolution 'are machinations between governments and industries, visions of how markets should evolve, and ideas about whether communication constitutes just another commodity or is something more imbued with cultural consideration and public service values'. See INTERNET; SUPERVENING SOCIAL NECESSITY. See also *TOPIC GUIDE* under MEDIA ISSUES & DEBATES.

Technology of the media See *TOPIC GUIDE* under MEDIA: TECHNOLOGIES.

Teenagers and media use See CHILDREN, YOUNG PEOPLE AND THE CHANGING MEDIA ENVIRONMENT.

Telecommunication *Tele* means far off, at a distance; a telecommunication is communication by TELEGRAPHY or TELEPHONE, with or without wires or cables. In telephony and telegraphy, signals are transmitted as electric impulses along wires. In RADIO and TV the signals are transmitted through space as modulations of carrier waves of electromagnetic radiation. See TELETEXT; WIRELESS TELEGRAPHY; WORLD TRADE ORGANIZATION (WTO) TELECOMMUNICATIONS AGREEMENT, 1997.

Teledemocracy Term used to describe theories that telecommunications serve to advance democracy by extending information and widening access to information; by counteracting through the use of computers and modems, the advantages of the information-rich over the information-poor. Local networks, using computers whose capacities have advanced as the prices have dropped, demonstrate the potential to link up nationally and internationally, favouring access to individuals and communities.

As evidence of teledemocracy the work of such alliances as PeaceNet, founded in San Francisco in 1986, EcoNet, London's GreenNet and the computer-communication project Public Data Access (PDA) is cited. PDA was responsible in the US for the dissemination of research into the exceptionally high correlation between toxic-waste sites and the location of minority communities. Sceptics, however, hold to the view that in an age when information has become increasingly *commoditized*, it is the all-powerful agencies of information – governments, multi-national corporations – who control the 'electronic highways' and that such highways are less public and free and increasingly private and subject to tolls.

A true gauge of teledemocracy is the health of NEWS coverage, and whether that news converage receives sufficient and increasing investment (in comparison with programme money going into entertainment). In a specific sense, the teledemocracy infers closer links between electorates and governments, encouraging greater interactivity through consultations (seeking out public opinion expressed electronically in various ways). Governments, however, have been slow to institute referendums via telecommunications, despite the success of TV in particular in seeking out and receiving public FEEDBACK, via correspondence, telephone, e-mail and audience-activating programmes. See DEMOCRACY AND THE MEDIA. See also *TOPIC GUIDE* under MEDIA: POLITICS & ECONOMICS

Telegenic Looking good on TV, a factor that has had particular significance in the domain of politics. There is no proof that it does not help to be handsome. See LOOKISM.

Telegraphy Only after the discovery of the magnetic effect of electric current was telegraphy possible. The first telegraph consisted of a compass needle that was deflected by the magnetic field produced by electric currents which flowed through the circuit whenever the transmitting key was depressed and contact established. The first patent for an electric telegraph was taken out by William Fothergill Cooke and Charles Wheatstone in June 1837 and later in the same year they demonstrated a five-needle telegraph to the directors of the London and Birmingham railway.

A year later the Great Western Railway connected Paddington and West Drayton by telegraph line which soon gave a considerable boost of publicity to telegraphy: in 1845 a suspected murderer was spotted boarding a London-bound train at Slough; the news was telegraphed to Paddington and the man was arrested on arrival and later found guilty and hanged.

In the US, Samuel Morse's first working telegraph of 1837 depended on the making and breaking of an electric current: an electromagnetically operated stylus recorded the long and short dashes of MORSE CODE on a moving strip of paper. After much persuasion, the US Congress, in 1843, voted to pay Morse (1791–1872) to build the first telegraph line in America, from Baltimore to Washington. It was in the following year, using the Morse Code on this line, that Morse transmitted his famous message 'What hath God wrought!'

Development of telegraphy was swift. By 1862 the world's telegraph system covered some 150,000 miles, including 15,000 in the UK. A method of printing the coded telegraph messages had been invented in 1845 and was developed in the US as 'House's Printing Telegraph'. In 1850 a telegraph cable had been laid across the English Channel. In 1858 the Atlantic was spanned by telegraph cable. The duplex telegraphy of Thomas Alva Edison (1847–1931) made it possible to transmit two messages simultaneously over the same line. Soon, four- and five-message systems followed, and ultimately the teleprinter. Picture transmission by telegraphy resulted from the development work of English physicist Shelford Bidwell, the first such transmissions taking place in 1881. See TELEX.

'The significance of telegraphy,' writes James W. Carey in *Communication as Culture* (UK: Routledge, 1992) 'is that it led to the selective control and transmission of information. The telegraph operator was able to monopolize knowledge, if only for a few moments, along a route; and this brought a selective advantage in trading and speculation.' It also ushered in a new language of JOURNALISM, what Ernest Hemingway called 'the lingo of the cable' – terse, precise; as Carey puts it, 'a form of language stripped of the local, the regional, and colloquial ... something closer to a "scientific" language, a language of strict denotation in which the connotative featurers of utterance were under rigid control'.

Telegraphy continues to be widely used by news services, the Stock Exchange telex service, public message services, certain police and fire alarm systems and private-line companies for data transmission. See TELEPHONE; WIRELESS TELEGRAPHY. See *TOPIC GUIDE* under MEDIA HISTORY.

* Brian Winston, *Media, Technology and Society: A History: From the Telegraph to the Internet* (UK: Routledge, 1998).

Telematics Term referring to the merging of telecommunications and computers, brought about by DIGITIZATION. The 1s and 0s of the computer are converted into tones relayed over telephone lines and then reconverted at the other end of the line by another computer. Thus information can be held centrally, dispatched rapidly, updated easily and networked internationally. This trans-border data flow (TBDF) is enhanced by SATELLITES, the advantage of whose use is that transmission costs do not rise in relation to the distance being covered (as is the case with microwaves and cables); so long, that is, as the communication falls within the 'footprint' of the same satellite.

Telephone In his early years, the Scotsman Alexander Graham Bell (1857–1922) knew Charles Wheatstone (1802–75), co-inventor of TELEGRAPHY, and also Alexander John Ellis, an expert in sound. Ellis showed Bell that the vibration of a tuning fork could be influenced by an electric current. He was able to produce sounds very like those of a human voice. Bell, teaching deaf-mutes in Boston, Massachusetts, experimented on a musical telegraph (1872). He produced artificial 'ear-drums' from sheets of metal and linked these with electric wire.

In 1876 Bell succeeded in passing a vocal message along a wire to an assistant in another room. The first telephone switching system was installed in New Haven, Connecticut, in 1878. However, while claiming credit for 'his' invention, and being acknowledged down the years as the inventor of the telephone, Bell must surrender the accolade to an unknown Italian, Antonio Meucci (1808–89), who demonstrated his 'teletrofono' in New York in 1860. Alas, Meucci's poverty (he could not afford the $250 needed to patent his 'talking telegraph') and his failure to secure financial backing left the way open for Bell – who had shared a laboratory with Meucci and thus had access to his findings – to file a patent and pursue a lucrative deal with Western Union.

A hundred years later, the US telephone system, largely the monopoly of the company Bell founded, was handling an average of over 240m phone conversations a day and, as Maurice Richards points out in *The World Communicates* (UK: Longman, 1972), the telephone system had 'developed into a communications network infinitely more versatile than could have been envisaged by the pioneers'.

Now telephone lines serve complex computer data systems; documents are transmitted via telephone – a scanning head records the light and shade of the document as it turns on a rotating drum, translating intensity of tone into electrical impulses for transmission over the wire to be re-translated at the receiving end. Telephone lines also carry telex services.

Microwave transmission techniques now allow telephone calls through air, free of wires, poles or underground conduits. Transmitting from point to point, tall towers now beam as many as 1500 calls on a single carrier wave. The London Post Office Tower has a potential load capacity of 150,000 telephone calls and capacity to transmit 100 TV channels.

Mobile phones (see MOBILIZATION) can be said to be the technological advance that more swiftly than any other became a means of communication on a mass scale, to the point where their use began to be seen as a public nuisance. Their increasing sophistication (and the fact that they had become a STYLE accessory) created a new crime – mobile mugging, setting the manufacturers the challenge of making the devices inoperable except by the legitimate owner. Today, in addition to phoning in the traditional way, and text-messaging, users of mobiles can tune into the INTERNET as well as RADIO and TV broadcasts, download music and play computer games.

Belatedly, in the summer of 2002, justice was done to the memory of the Florentine, Antonio Meucci. The US House of Representatives voted in favour of recognizing Meucci as the true father of telecommunications, 113 years after his death. See *TOPIC GUIDE* under MEDIA HISTORY; MEDIA: TECHNOLOGIES.

Telephone tapping See PRIVACY.

Telerecording Introduced in 1947, the first telerecording equipment consisted of a special 35mm film camera pointed at the screen. Picture quality was poor as a result of incompatibility between the camera shutter and TV's scanning process. The Ampex Corporation of America produced a definitive answer using a 'quadruplex' technique: a two-inch-wide tape travelled at normal speed while a rapidly spinning drum carrying four heads recorded tracks across the tape rather than along it, thus achieving the high and constant speed required.

The Ampex machine was in service in the US in 1956 and in May of the following year Associated Rediffusion in the UK installed the first pair of recording machines in Europe. The BBC followed suit shortly afterwards. Helical scan recorders were an advance upon the quadruplex machines. Instead of recording across the tapes, the spinning head-drum laid down tracks almost parallel to its length. Gradually, in the late 1970s, these machines took over from quadruplex though there were problems over product compatibility. Ampex and Sony agreed a common standard, known as C-format, and helical scan became the norm.

Teletext Data in textual or graphic form transmitted via the TV screen; the BROADCASTING version of viewdata, which is telephone-linked. In the UK, the BBC provides its CEEFAX information service; the commercial television equivalent was, until 1993, the Oracle service. In the auction for such services, empowered by the BROADCASTING ACT (UK), 1990, the licence winner was Teletext UK, a consortium headed by Associated Newspapers and Philips, the electronics company.

Telethon A live TV discussion or entertainment programme, often lasting for several hours, during which the public may ring in with questions and comments, and to make donations, and guest stars appear, all in aid of charity.

Television See *TOPIC GUIDE* under BROADCASTING.

Television: access television Term describing alternative, generally grassroots media; exemplified in the US by PAPER TIGER TELEVISION and its offshoot, Deep Dish TV (DDTV), funded through grants, bequests and donations; operating with minimal staffs backed by teams of helpers and targeting public access channels.

Access TV aims to cover ISSUES and events perceived to be neglected or marginalized by mainstream, commercial media. John D.H. Downing (with Tamara Villareal Ford, Geneve Gil and Laura Stein) in *Radical Media: Rebellious Communication and Social Movements* (US/UK: Sage, 2001), writes that 'access television may be understood as an institution that provides citizens with some of the necessary tools for self-governance' within the framework of democratic practices.

Downing *et al.* see this happening in three ways: (1) access TV 'enables its users to reinterpret, reframe, and refute the artefacts, messages, and ideologies of commercial culture from within a dominant forum for political communication'; (2) it creates for users 'a space in which to represent themselves and their interests to the larger community'; and (3) it 'permits the exercise of democratic functions of speech that are largely absent from commercial media'.

In these ways, access (or radical) TV proves to be a 'feasible and appropriate forum in which to respond to the hegemonic position of the larger medium'. However, standing in the way of the greater democratic potential of access television is 'its predominantly local orientation, and its marginalization as a sphere of public debate'. What advocates and participants should work for, believe the authors of *Radical Media*, is 'a policy environment more conducive to democratic communication'. See CULTURAL OR CITIZEN RIGHTS AND THE MEDIA; DEMOCRACY AND THE MEDIA.

Television Act (UK), 1954 Gave birth to commercial television in the UK; the Act set up the Independent Television Authority (later to be named the Independent Broadcasting Authority with the coming of COMMERCIAL RADIO). A rigorous set of controlling rules was imposed on the Authority which required 'that nothing is included in the programmes which offends against good taste or decency or is likely to encourage or incite to crime or to lead to disorder or to be offensive to public feelings or which contains any offensive representation of or reference to a living person'.

A proper balance was required in subject matter and a high general standard of quality. Due 'accuracy and impartiality' were required for the presentation of any news given in programmes, in whatever form. There were also to be 'proper proportions' in terms of British productions and performance in order to safeguard against the dumping of American material.

Of vital significance in the Act were the elaborate precautions that were made to prevent advertisers gaining control of programme content. The governing body of ITV set up by the Act was similar in size and function to that of the BBC, with seven to ten governors each serving for five years and dismissible at the behest of the Postmaster-General. Like the BBC, the ITA was to have a limited period of existence, followed by Parliamentary review and renewal. See SOUND BROADCASTING ACT (UK), 1972.

Television broadcasting Technical developments in the UK, the Soviet Union and the US combined to make TV a feasibility by 1931 when a research group was set up in Britain under Isaac Shoenberg (1880–1963), who had had considerable experience in radio transmission technology in the Soviet Union. He furthered the evolution of a practical system of TV broadcasting based on a camera tube known as the Emitrion and an improved cathode-ray tube for the receiver. Shoenberg elected to develop a system of electronic scanning which proved far superior to the mechanical scanning method pioneered by Scotsman John Logie Baird (1889–1946), who had first demonstrated his system publicly in 1926.

The BBC was authorized by government to adopt Shoenberg's standards (405 lines) for the world's first high-definition service, which was launched in 1936; a system that proved sufficiently successful to continue in the UK until 1962, when the European continental 625-line system was introduced. In the US, TV was slower to develop. It was not until 30 April 1939, at the opening of the New York World's Fair, that a public demonstration was made by the National Broadcasting Company (NBC).

The BBC's nascent TV service closed down during the Second World War (1939–45), which also hampered TV development in America, though by 1949, there were a million receivers in the US and, by 1951, 10 million. In the UK, TV transmission resumed in June 1946. Swiftly TV became, in terms of reach, diversity and popularity of content, the most influential and most powerful form of mass communication. The arrival of colour, transmission by cable and satellite, the possibilities of VIDEO recording and eventually DIGITIZATION confirmed and carried forward the Age of Information while at the same time turning it into the Age of the Image.

While TV has displaced, and sometimes marginalized other forms of communication, it has also proved their willing customer, borrowing and adapting forms from print, RADIO and cinema, in turn proving for them a constant source of material: how, for example, would popular newspapers survive without 'stories' from TV dramas such as SOAPS? TV fact and fiction have become so much a part of the culture of the modern age that they have become its benchmarks and its reality.

What's real is what is on TV; who appears on TV is deemed real. If an event does not appear on TV it is argued (at a metaphysical level) that the EVENT has really not taken place. Because of the nature of the medium, TV accentuates the image over the word, the dramatic over the analytical, and critics such as Neil Postman, in *Amusing Ourselves to Death* (UK: Methuen, 1986), claim that TV transforms all things into pure entertainment.

TV delivers audiences to advertisers; in turn advertisers use TV to reinforce the dominance of the image, in their case the image arising from imperatives of consumerism. TV news is seen to be a window on the world, a view attracting critical attention from media analyists who see in its underlying intentions frameworks essentially western in orientation, highly selective and thus offering a skewed vision of the world.

TV is where partnerships are forged, between sport and business. It is the venue of lifestyle, the route to celebrity, and for these and many other reasons it is a battleground between those who are ambitious to control it, the axis of the ongoing struggle between public and private ownership. The study of the effects, influence, impact and power of the media largely centres on TV and the questions prompting answers are legion: does TV and its blizzard of images confuse rather than clarify; does it distract rather than aid attention; does it fulfil the fears of those who (subscribing to the notion of a so-termed three-minute culture) claim that it robs viewers of the ability to concentrate for more than a few moments at a time; does its constant plethora of images of violence desensitize audiences to examples of violence in the real world? In brief, what *cultural differences* has TV brought about? See *TOPIC GUIDE* under BROADCASTING; MEDIA INSTITUTIONS; MEDIA: POLITICS & ECONOMICS; MEDIA: POWER, EFFECTS, INFLUENCE

* Anthony Smith, ed., and Richard Patterson, associate ed., *Television: An International History* (UK: Oxford University Press, 1998); Asa Briggs and Peter Burke, *A Social History of the Media: From Gutenberg to the Internet* (UK: Polity, 2002).

Television drama In an interview printed in *The New Priesthood: British Television Today* (UK: Allen Lane, 1970) edited by Joan Bakewell and Nicholas Garnham, TV playwright Dennis Potter (1935–95) said of TV, 'It's the biggest platform in the world's history and writers who don't want to kick and elbow their way on to it must be disowning something in themselves.' While the PILKINGTON COMMITTEE REPORT ON BROADCASTING (UK), 1962, found that the chief 'crime' of TV was triviality, much of TV drama (from the very first drama production on experimental TV, the BBC's *The Man with a Flower in his Mouth* by Luigi Pirandello on 14 July 1930) has been a striking exception to that judgement. In fact few might argue with the claim that TV's most substantial achievement has been to encourage generations of quality dramatists working specially for the medium, and a canon of plays, from both the BBC and commercial TV companies, to rival anything produced in the live theatre during the same post-Second World War period.

In the early days of TV drama, plays were stage-bound or, more accurately, studio-bound, both in concept and execution, taking for their model the theatre rather than the cinema, but the ideas of young directors making their mark during the 1960s, excited by the possibility of film drama, prevailed. Nell Dunn's *Up the Junction* (BBC, 1965) marked the first occasion when virtually the whole story was done on film. The camera was seen to be as important as the pen; indeed the camera in many ways became the pen. The social and sometimes political themes favoured by many writers and directors took the cameras more and more out of the studio and into 'real life', and many plays looked like, and had the impact of, documentary.

Produced by Tony Garnett, written by Jeremy Sandford and directed by Ken Loach, *Cathy Come Home* (BBC, 1966) detailed the decline into tragedy of a homeless family in affluent Britain. The sense of reality was almost unbearable: the camera was often hand-held, the scenes staged so realistically that the audience was tempted to forget it was watching something constructed, not something happening before their very eyes.

The intimacy, the close scrutiny of humans under stress at which film and TV can excel, has rarely been used to more disturbing effect than with John Hopkins' quartet of plays *Talking to a Stranger* (BBC, 1966), described as the first authentic masterpiece of television. The immediacy of the medium was stunningly demonstrated in Colin Welland's epic *Leeds United!* (BBC, 1974) about Leeds clothing workers who struck spontaneously in 1970 for an extra 10 pence an hour: the camera became part of the ongoing action to such an extent that it was impossible to detect what had been scripted and what was happening for real.

Much of this kind of drama obviously grew from the opportunities of the moment, and from improvisation, a method used most notably by Mike Leigh, who works with actors for long periods before filming, encouraging them to 'become' the characters and eventually invent or improvise their speech and actions.

Such experimental screen drama was soon to hit the buffers of economic necessity. In a 1982 publication for the IBA, *Television and Radio,* David Cunliffe, then Head of Drama at Yorkshire TV, wrote: 'The inescapable fact is that over the last few years the television single play has spiralled in production costs and plummeted in popularity.' Having moved from the studio to location, plays had become 'nearly Hollywood-size movies'. Cunliffe cited dramas such as Potter's LWT series, *Rain on the Roof, Blade on the Feather* and *Cream in My Coffee* as works that, despite their quality as drama, appealed to 'relatively small sections of viewers'. The death knell had more or less been sounded for the one-off play and increasingly in the following years dramatists turned to writing TV serials (which have more over-time impact and are more saleable commodities on the international programme market) and adapting classics such as novels by Jane Austen and Charles Dickens.

Today crime dominates TV drama, in mini or long-running series: cops, prosecutors, forensic scientists, psychologists specializing in crime are in, the recipes for the GENRE being tweaked here and there – by reaching for greater and greater actuality or by reversing traditional NARRATIVES (by putting women in charge of men for a change) or by abandoning the good-guys/bad-guys format in preference for closer examination of criminals as individuals. Much contemporary crime drama on TV seeks to explore the pressures on personal relationships, on marriages, on families, resulting from the dedication of those employed to protect the law and apprehend the lawbreakers.

In a rare case of cross-channel cooperation, the BBC and Channel 4 in 1996, combined in the production of Dennis Potter's last two plays for TV, *Karaoke* and *Cold Lazarus*. They proved Potter's epitaph, but also seemed to close the chapter in TV drama of which he was the most outstanding exemplar. See CAMPAIGN FOR QUALITY TELEVISION REPORT (UK), 1999.

* John Tulloch, *Television Drama: Agency, Audience and Myth* (UK: Routledge, 1990); David Paget, *No Other Way to Tell It: Dramadoc/Docudrama on Television* (UK: Manchester University Press, 1998).

Television news: inherent limitations In analysing the degree of 'informedness' between viewers of TV news and readers of newspapers, two American researchers found that TV makes for less effective *retention* than the printed page. John P. Robinson and Dennis K. Davis in 'Television news and the informed public: an information-processing approach', *Journal of Communication* (Summer 1990), found that in none of their studies 'do viewers of TV news programs emerge as more informed than newspaper readers'.

They identify seven inherent limitations of TV as an information medium: (1) a TV newscast has fewer words and ideas per news story than appear in a front-page story in a quality newspaper; (2) attention to a newscast is distracted and fragmented compared to attention when reading; (3) TV newscasts provide little of the repetition of information, or redundancy, necessary for comprehension; (4) TV viewers cannot 'turn back' to, or review, information they do not understand or that they need to know to understand subsequent information; (5) print news stories are more clearly delineated, with headlines, columns etc.; (6) TV news programmes fail to coordinate pictures and text; and (7) TV has more limited opportunity to review and develop an entire story. It is the authors' view that 'while TV has the power to evoke empathy and interest, time and other constraints prevent this power from being exercised'. See *TOPIC GUIDE* under NEWS MEDIA.

'Television without frontiers' See EUROPEAN COMMUNITY AND MEDIA: 'TELEVISION WITHOUT FRONTIERS'.

Telex Worldwide link-up system providing a rapid means of communicating written messages, via teleprinter among subscribers, combining the speed of the telephone with the accuracy and authority of the printed word. A printed copy of the message is available at both the sending and receiving teleprinters. Calls can be made to any telex subscriber in the UK and overseas 24 hours a day and messages may be transmitted to a subscriber even though his/her machine is unattached, provided it remains switched on. A telemessage (inland) and a telegram (overseas) can also be sent from a telex teleprinter to a Post Office telegraph office or to Cable & Wireless telegraph offices for onward transmission at normal telephone rates, and incoming telemessages can be accepted directly on the teleprinter.

Telstar Communications satellite launched on 10 July 1962; transmitted the first live TV pictures between the US and Europe. See SATELLITE TRANSMISSION.

Ten commandments for media consumers In 'Ethics for media users' published in the *European Journal of Communication* (December 1995), Cees J. Hamelink discusses the role the viewer, reader and listener should adopt in relation to the 'quest for freedom, quality and responsibility in media performance', arguing that the consumer must not only beware of the nature of media messages but be proactive in responding to them. The ten 'commandments' Hamelink suggests in order to assist the consumer with moral choices concerning the media are as follows. Thou shalt: (1) be an alert and discriminating media consumer; (2) actively fight all forms of censorship; (3) not unduly interfere with editorial independence; (4) guard against racism and sexist stereotyping in the media; (5) seek alternative sources of information; (6) demand a pluralist supply of information; (7) protect thine own privacy; (8) be a reliable source of information; (9) not participate in chequebook journalism and (10) demand accountability from media producers.

The author, however, cautions against over-reliance on such a code of user response, for moral issues and dilemmas ought to be addressed according to situation and context, a point well made when we take a global view of the 'commandments'. A pre-existing code must not be imposed on a situation; rather, the situation must be examined in the light of evolving and changing approaches to moral dilemmas. See *TOPIC GUIDES* under MEDIA ISSUES & DEBATES; MEDIA: VALUES & IDEOLOGY.

Tenth art See VIDEO GAMES.

Terrestrial broadcasting That which is transmitted from the ground and not via SATELLITE.

Territoriality The need in humans and animals to establish and maintain private territory. Several elements of SPATIAL BEHAVIOUR may be employed by both individuals and groups to mark and defend territory – for example, the use of furniture and belongings to signify claim to a particular space.

Terrorism: Anti-Terrorism, Crime and Security Act (UK), 2001 Following the destruction of New York's World Trade Center Twin Towers on 11 September 2001, the UK government hastened to tighten the law on a whole range of matters, some of them directly affecting media communication. The 125-clause Terrorism Act permits confidential information about an individual helped by any government agency to be disclosed to the intelligence services and the police – for any criminal investigation, not just for investigations of alleged terrorist offences.

Liberal-Democrat MP Simon Hughes said of the Act that it was 'a mixture of the welcome, the reasonable, the worrying and the completely unacceptable'. Clause 93 makes it a punishable offence for anyone to refuse a police request to remove a disguise, such as a mask or face paint. Following the terrorist bombings on the London Underground in July 2005 plans for further punitive legislation were announced by the UK government with the comment by the Prime Minister, Tony Blair, 'Let no one be in any doubt. The rules of the game are changing'. See REGULATION OF INVESTIGATORY POWERS ACT (RIPA) (UK), 2000.

Terrorism as communication The main aim of terrorist activity in liberal democracies is publicity. The existence of a free press, and TV and radio companies independent of government authority within societies which subscribe to the sanctity of the individual's right to life, provides fertile ground for headline seeking by acts of terror such as hijacks, abductions, assassinations and bombings. 'The modern terrorist makes maximum use of mass media,' wrote Dan van der Vat in *Index on Censorship* 2 (1982). 'Little more than a century ago, before the invention of the rotary press, he would have been inconceivable; he came into his own only in the last 15 years or even less, when television became an instantaneous medium, capable of sending live pictures round the globe by satellite.'

On 11 September 2001 the United States became victim of the most dramatic, daring and devastating act of terrorism with the destruction of the Twin Towers of New York's World Trade Center by means of hijacked passenger aircraft, and a similar onslaught on the country's military HQ, the Pentagon. In the case of New York, cameras recorded the tragedy as it happened. Millions of people across the world witnessed the vulnerability of even the most powerful nation in the world, and varyingly read messages into that sudden vulnerability.

Above all, acts of terror galvanise 'victim' governments into coercive responses. These range from the introduction of legislation inpinging on human rights and freedoms to all-out war against the perceived aggressor, as in Afghanistan and Iraq. Even the most well-set communities, confident of their values and ways of life, can be destabilised by terrorism. In a democracy, the ultimate danger is that the state will answer terrorism with terror: in such a situation, the role of the media (as watchdog or guard dog) becomes immensely important. In 2006 the Labour government pushed for the introduction of identity cards and for legislation against racial and religious hatred.

Text According to Tim O'Sullivan, John Hartley, Danny Saunders and John Fiske, in *Key Concepts in Communication* (UK: Methuen, 1983), text refers to 'a signifying structure composed of signs and codes which is essential to communication'. This structure can take a variety of forms: film, speech, writing, painting, records, for example. O'Sullivan *et al.* argue that the word text usually 'refers to a message that has a physical existence of its own, independent of its sender and receiver and thus composed of representational codes'.

Text is the focal point of study in SEMIOLOGY/SEMIOTICS. Texts are not normally seen as being unproblematic but as capable of being interpreted in a variety of ways, depending on the socio-cultural background and experience of the reader. The central concern of semiology is to discover the ways in which given texts can generate a range of meanings.

Occupying the special attention of analysts in recent years is the relationship between texts, the way they interconnect, interweave and interact upon one another. *Intertextuality* operates essentially in the perception and experience of AUDIENCE; a TV movie tells the story of a serial killer; TV news reports carnage caused by a madman loose with a machine gun; on the way to work the viewer sees a massive poster advertising the sequel to *The Silence of the Lambs*. What does he or she make of all this, and how does one text influence another in the mind's eye?

Of course intertextuality works at the level of simple publicity and promotion. A film may be writ large in our consciousness, but perhaps not only because of the power of the individual text: there will have been trailers, publicity material, interviews with the stars on TV; there will have been conversation about it.

The power of intertextuality is to blur the boundaries between individual texts. For example, which is the text in a promo-video – the chart-busting song of the rock group, the video of the performance, the presentation of that video on *Top of the Pops* or all of these as a package of texts which themselves link in with previous songs/videos by the group and by other groups, and features in fan magazines or celebrity appearances in support of AIDS research? Roland Barthes, the French media philosopher, was of the view that culture is a web of intertextuality and that texts tend to refer essentially to one another rather than anchor their referral in reality. See CODES; DECODER; ENCODER; MESSAGE; NARRATIVE. See also *TOPIC GUIDE* under LANGUAGE/DISCOURSE/NARRATIVE; TEXTUAL ANALYSIS.

Text: integrity of the text With the coming of the INTERNET, two major issues concern the producers of texts – books, articles, scripts, photographs, music, etc. – the questions of *integrity* of the text and of *paternity*. Copyright laws have until now protected the work of an author. While a book can be quoted from, it cannot be reprinted, reproduced in any way or altered without due permission. The Internet, as yet an open space for the communication of items of all kinds, uncontrolled by traditional regulation and so far evasive of what controls, legal and technical, might be applied, threatens to rob texts of integrity and to ignore their paternity (that is, the right of the author, composer, artist or performer to command 'ownership' of the text).

In short, networking is open to the abuse of SOURCE; indeed texts often soar through CYBERSPACE with little or no acknowledgement of source. Released from the tie of ownership, possibly doctored in whole or in part for whatever reason, are texts reliable any more? Does authorship continue to have any meaning?

The *moral rights* of paternity and integrity are enshrined in the Berne Convention. They are central to the UK's Copyright Designs and Patents Act (1988). The right of paternity is the right to be identified as the author of a copyright work, and that includes adaptations, film rights, etc. The major exception in the Berne Convention is authorship of the 'news of the day'. The UK Copyright Act also excludes from protection all work made for the reporting of current events, and this includes articles in newspapers and journals. See DOWNLOADING. See also *TOPIC GUIDE* under MEDIA ISSUES & DEBATES.

Texts See OPEN, CLOSED TEXTS.

Text: tertiary text The primary TEXT is that which is produced and transmitted – the painting, the poem, the poster, the film, what Roland Barthes terms the 'work'; the secondary text is that which members of an AUDIENCE receive, what is perceived as the text. The tertiary text results when the first two texts are translated into conversation between members of the audience, their families and friends. John Fiske uses the term in *Television Culture* (UK: Methuen, 1987) to denote the many uses media messages can be put to, interpretative, analytical, affirmative or rejective. The existence of the tertiary text indicates that audience has within its capacity the potential to be independent of the PREFERRED READING residing in the primary text or work (see AUDIENCE: ACTIVE AUDIENCE; EMPOWERMENT; RESPONSE CODES).

A more general use of the terms primary and secondary is current. The primary text is that which is produced, the secondary text, arising out of the first, may take many forms – publicity, trailers, critiques, interviews with the author or director, documentaries, translations into other creative forms (a novel into a movie or a TV series). Secondary texts at least begin as dependants upon the primary text; they are its satellites. However these may become more and more divorced from connection with the original until, arguably, they become primary texts in their own right. Where texts interact, interconnect and are interdependent we have what is termed *intertextuality*.

Thaumatrope Or 'wonder-turner'; a small cardboard disc, having different images on each surface, threaded on two pieces of silk or string which, when twisted, creates a joining of images, thus illustrating the phenomenon of PERSISTENCE OF VISION. The device was first produced by English doctor J.A. Paris in 1826. See ZOETROPE.

Theatre censorship See LORD CHAMBERLAIN.

Theories and concepts of communication See *TOPIC GUIDE* under AUDIENCES/CONSUMPTION & RECEPTION OF MEDIA; COMMUNICATION THEORY; COMMUNICATION MODELS; LANGUAGE/DISCOURSE/NARRATIVE; MEDIA: POWER, EFFECTS, INFLUENCE; MEDIA: VALUES & IDEOLOGY; REPRESENTATION.

Third-person effect Where we judge the impact/influence of the media to be stronger on others than ourselves; this effect is countenanced largely when the media message is negative or when persuasion by the MESSAGE is perceived to be less than desirable. In other words, *we* might not be affected, but others, usually differentiated from us by cultural or social difference, are more likely to be.

3-D The technique of filming and projecting movie pictures that gives the illusion of being three-dimensional. See STEREOSCOPY.

Tie-signs Any action – GESTURE or posture – that indicates the existence of a personal relationship is termed a tie-sign: linked arms, held hands, body closeness (or proximity), comfortable silence between two people, instinctive reciprocal movements. *Symbolic* tie-signs are wedding rings, lovers' tree engravings, etc. See COMMUNICATION, NON-VERBAL (NVC); PROXEMICS.

Time-lapse photography See HIGH-SPEED PHOTOGRAPHY.

Time-shift viewing Made possible by the introduction of the video or DVD recorder. By recording TV programmes, viewers are released from the schedules of the broadcasting companies to watch programmes of their choice whenever and as often as desired.

Touch Not the least important of the five senses, though often the most neglected. H.F. Harlow in *Learning to Love* (US: Albion, 1971) writes of his now famous experiments with baby monkeys. He had found that the deprivation of physical contact resulted in a failure to learn necessary responses to their own society. They became non-sociable, were unable to mate successfully or to rear their young.

Touch is an important ingredient in the transmitting of information, especially in the young when other channels of communication such as speech are undeveloped. In western society the incidence of touching between people begins to diminish when a child reaches the age of five or six, with males being touched less than females. It increases again in the teenage period, where touching and sex become equated to such an extent that touch becomes a sexual indicator unless applied by validated 'touchers' such as doctors, tailors or hairdressers.

CLASS, STATUS and ROLES are inextricably involved in touch-permission or touch-prohibition: a nurse may touch a patient, but it is not usual for a patient to touch the nurse, where it constitutes a trespass. Self-touching is acceptable, unless it becomes socially offensive (like nose-picking), as a form of substitution for the touch of others – face and head touching, hair stroking or hand wringing, for example.

Where we cannot touch other humans we substitute pets, stroking them and cuddling them, receiving (and perhaps giving) sensations of comfort. In illness and stress, in times of grief or great happiness, touching becomes more necessary and more acceptable. Touching can communicate reassurance, affection, friendship, courage-giving, support, sharing, understanding, invitation, desire, etc., as well as on occasions hostility and aggression. The practice varies considerably from class to class, CULTURE to culture and country to country and from hemisphere to hemisphere. See COMMUNICATION, NON-VERBAL (NVC); EYE CONTACT; GESTURE; INTERPERSONAL COMMUNICATION; NON-VERBAL BEHAVIOUR: REPERTOIRE; PROXEMICS.

Tracks In film-making, tracks are the portable 'railway lines' along which the camera, mounted on a dolly, moves. The term is also used to identify separate sound reels accompanying a film. These are harmonized into one at the dubbing stage of film production.

Traditional transmission US linguist Charles Hockett defined 16 design features characteristic of human language, of which traditional transmission is one, described in Hockett's 'The origin of speech', *Scientific American* 203 (1960). This design feature refers to the passing on of language from one generation to the next. 'Human genes,' Hockett writes, 'carry the capacity to acquire a language, and probably also a strong drive towards its acquisition, the detailed conventions of any one language are transmitted extra-genetically by learning and teaching.'

Traffic data Information about a message sent electronically – by whom, to whom and when (excluding the content of the message itself). Refers to e-mails, websites and TELEPHONE calls. Phone bills include all traffic data, time, destination and length of call. In the case of mobiles the data includes the base station used.

Transactional analysis Originally an approach to psychotherapy introduced by Eric Berne, transactional analysis is now more widely used as a technique for improving INTERPERSONAL COMMUNICATION and social skills. In essence it aims to increase the individual's awareness of the intent behind both his or her own and others' communication, and to expose and eliminate, or deal with, subterfuge and dishonesty.

The details of the framework are fairly complex and readers are referred to the works recommended below for an introduction to this area. Basically, however, transactional analysis investigates any act of interpersonal communication by considering what are called the 'ego states' of the communicators.

The hypothesis is that we are all able to function out of three 'ego states' that Berne identified as the Parent, the Adult and the Child. The states are produced by a playback of recorded data of events in the past involving real people; real times, places and decisions; and real feelings. Everyone is seen as carrying these voices inside them. We interact out of these 'ego states'.

The Parent is much influenced by the pronouncements of and examples set by our own parents and other authority figures, early in our life. It is concerned with our responsibility towards ourselves and others. It can be critical and set standards but it can also be protective and caring. The Adult within us is the part of us that rationally analyses reality. It collects information and thinks it through in order to solve problems, reach conclusions and judgements, and make decisions. The Adult develops throughout life and can arbitrate between the Parent and the Child. The Child is one of our most powerful states; it contains our feelings and carries our ability to play and act creatively. It can be spontaneous and risk-taking. It can also be rebellious or alternatively compliant or servile.

A *transaction* is a two-person interaction in which an ego state of one person stimulates an ego state of another. Transactions are analysed by assessing out of which 'ego state' people are speaking. We can distinguish these states in ourselves and others by such non-verbal cues as tone of voice or facial expression, as well as by the verbal content of the transactions. One of the chief values of transactional analysis is that it has the capacity to help clarify communication problems.

Other concepts commonly employed in TA are *Games*, LIFE POSITIONS and SCRIPTS. Eric Berne in *Games People Play* (UK: Penguin, 1964) describes a game as 'an ongoing series of complementary ulterior transactions progressing to a well-defined, predictable outcome'. Games are recurring sets of transactions, identifiable by their hidden motivations and the promise of psychological payoffs or gains for the game players.

The victim of the game is called a *mark*, and it is the known weakness of the mark, known as the *gimmick*, which allows the game player to hook his victim and achieve his/her desired *payoff*. Every game, Berne believes, whether played consciously or unconsciously, is essentially dishonest; generally taking the form of a defensive strategy in communication as far as the manipulator is concerned. Examples of such games played in everyday life, identified by Berne, are 'If it weren't for you' and 'See what you made me do'.

* Eric Berne, *What Do You Say After You Say Hello?* (UK: Corgi Books, 1975); Thomas A. Harris, *I'm O.K. You're O.K.* (US: Harper & Row, 1969); Ian Stewart and Vann Joines, *TA Today* (UK: Lifespace, 1987); Amy and Thomas Harris, *Staying O.K.* (UK: Arrow Books, 1995).

Transculturation The movement of cultural forms across geographical boundaries and periods of time resulting in cross-cultural interaction that may give rise to new cultural forms. See HYBRIDIZATION.

Transmission model of mass communication See ATTENTION MODEL OF MASS COMMUNICA-TION.

Trigger events See AGENDA-SETTING; TRIGGER EVENTS.

Truth, visualization of See VISIONS OF ORDER.

TV See TELEVISION.

Two-step flow model of communication See ONE-STEP, TWO-STEP, MULTI-STEP FLOW MODELS OF COMMUNICATION.

Typewriter A patent for an 'Artificial Machine or Method for Impressing or Transcribing of Letters Singly or Progressively one after another, as in Writing, whereby all Writing Whatever may be Engrossed in Paper or Parchment so Neat and Exact as not to be distinguished from Print' was taken out in the UK as early as 1714, but the first practical typewriter working faster than handwriting was probably that of American Christopher Latham Sholes (1868) who, after several improvements to his machine, signed up with E. Remington & Sons, gunsmiths, of New York. The first Remington machines were marketed in 1874.

1878 saw the introduction of the shift-key typewriter, followed by machines which for the first time allowed the typist to actually see what he/she was typing (1883). That jack-of-all-trades among inventors, Thomas Alva Edison (1847–1931), produced an electrically operated machine containing a printing wheel in 1872, though it was many years before a commercially viable electric machine was produced (by James Smathes in 1920).

IBM introduced the famous 'golf-ball' electric typewriter in 1961, allowing for different typefaces and type sizes to be used with the same machine. Today electronic typewriters (and even manual machines) continue to be manufactured and sold despite being to all intents and purposes displaced by the computer. See *TOPIC GUIDE* under MEDIA HISTORY; MEDIA: TECHNOLOGIES.

→ **U**

U-certificate See CERTIFICATION OF FILMS.

UK Gold Launched on 1 November 1992, UK Gold is a satellite and cable channel run jointly by BBC Enterprises and Thames Television based on their combined programme libraries.

Ullswater Committee Report on Broadcasting, 1936 This government-appointed committee under the chairmanship of Viscount Ullswater was given the task of making recommendations on the future of the BBC once its first charter expired on 31 December 1936. The report praised the BBC for its impartiality and catholicity but chided it for the heaviness of its Sunday entertainment. The Charter of the BBC was renewed for another ten years following the report; the number of governors was increased from five to seven and the ban on advertisements was to continue though sponsorship was to be permitted in the case of TV (a right the BBC only seldom exploited).

Like reports before and after it, Ullswater made clear the very serious public responsibility of BROAD-CASTING: 'The influence of broadcasting upon the mind and speech of the nation' made it an 'urgent necessity in the national interest that the broadcasting service should at all times be conducted in the best possible manner and to the best possible advantage of the people'. Two other matters elicited concern. The first related to criticisms of the monolithic nature of the BBC (under the rigorous direction of Lord Reith – see REITHIAN) and the Committee recommended more internal decentralization of control, especially towards the national regions.

The second concern, published in a Reservation written by Clement Attlee (1883–1967), future Labour Prime Minister, called into question the BBC's 'impartiality' at the time of the General Strike (1926): 'I think,' wrote Attlee, 'that even in war-time the BBC must be allowed to broadcast opinions other than those of the Government.' See PUBLIC SERVICE BROADCASTING (PSB). See also *TOPIC GUIDE* under COM-MISSIONS, COMMITTEES, LEGISLATION.

Ultra-violet/fluorescent photography Used in the examination of forged or altered documents, identifying certain chemical compounds, and in the examination of bacterial colonies. See HOLOGRAPHY.

Ulysses Award for the Art of Reportage See LETTRE ULYSSES AWARD.

Underground press Or radical, alternative or SAMIZDAT; those newspapers that are committedly anti-establishment, opposing in part or entirely the political and cultural conventions of the time; often publishing information or views seen as threatening by those in authority, and likely to incur CENSORSHIP.

In the UK the so-called 'pauper press' of the nineteenth century, finding its readership in the increasingly literate working class, was subject to harshly repressive measures by government. Editors such as William Cobbett, Henry Hetherington, William Sherwin, Richard Carlile and James Watson courted arrest and imprisonment and the shutting down of their presses as a routine professional hazard. Wooler's *Black Dwarf* stirred the government to wrath with its criticism of the authorities in their handling of the Peterloo Massacre (1819). Wooler escaped libel action on the plea that he could not be said to have written articles which he set up in type without the interventions of a pen.

Cobbett's *Weekly Political Register* had a substantial circulation despite the crippling STAMP DUTY that forced him to charge one shilling and a halfpenny per copy. Carlile's *Republican* was both republican and atheist; the Chartist *Oracle of Reason* incurred blasphemy prosecutions while Bradlaugh's *National Reformer* declared itself 'Published in Defiance of Her Majesty's Government'. So long as radical newspapers could fight off the need to win ADVERTISING, they could survive, despite prosecutions, relying on circulation alone. Edited by people close to the working class, they reflected the chief perspectives of the vanguard of the working-class movement and directed themselves to its increased politicization.

What beat the radicals of the nineteenth century was competition by papers more dedicated to entertainment and sensationalism, papers expanding through the power of advertisements and sensitive to the values and requirements of the advertisers. The radicals found themselves faced with the challenge – remain true to principles and thus risk being trapped in a ghetto of reduced readership, or to attempt to marry principles with popularization.

Radicalism retreated during the twentieth century but never surrendered. However, the costs of publishing and the reliance upon advertising proved increasingly formidable barriers to underground, radical or alternative newspapers and periodicals in the post-Second World War period (from 1945). In the 1960s there was a brief renaissance of protest: periodicals such as *Oz*, *IT*, *Frendz* and *Ink* in one way or another got up the nose of Authority, the *Oz Schoolkids Issue* earning for itself the longest-ever obscenity trial (see OZ TRIAL).

Distribution has proved yet another hazard for the small radical press. In the UK this is practically a duopoly of WHSmith and Menzies, whose hesitancy over providing the radical press with distribution outlets has been rather more to do with a view that radicals are just not good business rather than for ideological reasons.

In the March/April edition 1994 of *Free Press*, the news-sheet of the CAMPAIGN FOR PRESS AND BROADCASTING FREEDOM, Tony Harcup mourned the decline in the Thatcher/Major years of the radical regional press. In '*Northern Star* silenced', an obituary for the *Leeds Other Paper/Northern Star*, he points out that where in 1980 there had been more than 70 local alternative papers covering towns and cities in the UK, there were now only two, *Peninsula Voice* covering Cornwall west of Truro and Penzance, and the *West Highland Free Press*. The *LOP/Northern Star*, having survived 20 years, went into liquidation after 820 issues on 20 January 1994. It had been, in Harcup's words, 'a beacon of radical journalism … a thorn in the side of the local establishment'.

Ironically the paper had made as many enemies on the Left as the Right in local politics: 'The paper was too anarchistic for some Labour party members; too rank and filist for some union officials; too male dominated for some feminists; too pro-feminist for many men.' By 2005 the *Peninsula Voice* was no more, but the *West Highland Free Press* continues to serve its northerly outposts.

The future for radical JOURNALISM most probably lies not in print and paper but in the relatively cost-free 'pages' of the INTERNET, where the readership is both local and global. See BLOGGING; INDY MEDIA; JOURNALISM: CITIZEN JOURNALISM; PODCASTING. See also *TOPIC GUIDE* under MEDIA HISTORY.

* Stanley Harrison, *Poor Men's Guardians: A Survey of the Struggles for a Democratic Newspaper Press, 1763–1973* (UK: Lawrence & Wishart, 1974); Patricia Hollis, *The Pauper Press* (UK: Oxford University Press, 1970); Stephen Koss, *The Rise and Fall of the Political Press in Britain* (UK: Collins, 1990); Kevin Williams, *Get Me a Murder a Day!*

A *History of Mass Communication in Britain* (UK: Arnold, 1997); Elisabeth Eisenstein, *The Printing Press as an Agent of Change* (UK: Cambridge University Press, 1999); Chris Atton, *Alternative Media* (UK: Sage, 2001); Jeremy Black, *The English Press 1621–1861* (UK; Sutton, 2001); John D.H. Downing (with Tamara Vallareal Ford, Geneve Gil and Laura Stern), *Radical Media: Rebellious Communication and Social Movements* (US/UK: Sage, 2001).

Unitary, pluralist, core-periphery, breakup models of audience fragmentation See AUDIENCE: FRAGMENTATION OF.

Universality Principle that public services such as education, health and justice must be available to all within a society; applies equally to the notion of PUBLIC SERVICE BROADCASTING (PSB).

USA – Patriot Act, 2001 Surveillance measure that became law within a month of the terrorist attacks on New York and the Pentagon, 11 September 2001. Under its full title, Strengthening America by Providing Appropriate Tools Required to Intercept and Obstruct Terrorism, the Patriot Act, all 342 pages of it, provides the US government and its agencies with a formidable armoury of new powers to rein in civil liberties. Basically security agencies are granted extended powers to intercept wire, oral and electronic communications relating to terrorism; to share criminal investigation information; to seize voice-mail messages pursuant to warrants; to use DNA identification of terrorists and other violent offenders; to demand disclosure of educational records and to confiscate the assets of organizations suspected of planning or carrying out terrorism.

In its analysis of the Act, the Electronic Frontier Foundation talks of a 'rush job'; of 'sweeping new powers' that eliminate 'the checks and balances that previously gave courts the opportunity to ensure that these powers were not abused'. The EEF is of the view that 'The civil liberties of ordinary Americans have taken a tremendous blow with this law, especially the right to privacy in our online communications and activities', believing that 'there is no evidence that our previous civil liberties posed a barrier to the effective tracking or persecution of terrorists … the opportunities for abuse of these broad new powers are immense'.

Nancy Chang, Senior Litigation Attorney at the Center for Constitutional Rights, New York, called the Act 'a blatant power grab'. In *Silencing Political Dissent: How Post-September 11 Antiterrorism Measures Threaten Our Civil Liberties* (US: Seven Stories Press, 2002), she states that the Act 'grants the executive unprecedented, and largely unchecked, surveillance powers including the enhanced ability to track e-mail and Internet usage, conduct sneak-and-peek searches, obtain sensitive personal records, monitor financial transactions and conduct nationwide wiretaps'.

The author believes the Act 'sacrifices our political freedoms in the name of national security and upsets the democratic values that define the nation by consolidating vast new powers in the executive branch of government'. Chang sees terrorism status being conflated with immigration status in the Act. Its power, however, might be seen to embrace the potential activities of all forms of protesters – environmental or anti-globalization activists, for example – virtually outlawing direct action.

Use of media by the young See CHILDREN, YOUNG PEOPLE AND THE CHANGING MEDIA ENVIRONMENT.

Uses and gratifications theory View that mass media audiences make active use of what the media have to offer arising from a complex set of needs which the media in one form or another gratify. Broadly similar uses have been categorized by researchers based on questionnaires or interviews. An example is the *compensatory use* of the media – to make up for lack of education, perhaps, lack of STATUS or social success. Where the media have a *supplementing use*, the AUDIENCE may be applying what they see, hear and read in social situations as subject-matter for interpersonal exchange.

In 'The television audience: a revised perspective' in Dennis McQuail, ed., *Sociology of the Mass Media* (UK: Penguin, 1972) McQuail, Jay G. Blumler and J.R. Brown define four major categories of need which the media serve to gratify. (1) *Diversion* (escape from constraints of routine; escape from the burdens of problems; emotional release). (2) *Personal relationships* (companionship; social utility). (3) *Personal identity* (personal reference; reality exploration; value reinforcement). (4) *Surveillance* (need for information in our complex world – 'Television news helps me to make up my mind about things').

Blumler and Elihu Katz in the book of which they are editors, *The Uses of Mass Communication* (US: Sage, 1974), emphasize the social origin of the needs that the media purport to gratify. Thus where a social situation causes tension and conflict, the media may provide easement, or where the social situation gives rise to questions about VALUES, the media provide affirmation and REINFORCEMENT.

Uses and gratifications theory has been subjected to criticism by a number of commentators. In *The Export of Meaning: Cross-Cultural Readings of* Dallas (US: Oxford University Press; UK: Polity Press, 1993), Tamar Liebes and Elihu Katz state, 'The idea that readers, listeners, and viewers can bend the mass media to serve their own needs had gone so far [with gratificationists] that almost any text – or indeed no text at all – was found to serve functions such as social learning, reinforcing identity, lubricating interaction, providing escape etc. But it gradually became clear that these functions were too unspecified.' In other words, theorizing about use has to be linked to the TEXTS that are judged to fulfil audience needs. Then the complexity of audience use of texts can be more meaningfully examined. See COGNITIVE (AND AFFECTIVE); IDENTIFICATION; MASLOW'S HIERARCHY OF NEEDS. See also *TOPIC GUIDE* under COMMUNICATION THEORY.

Utterance meaning See SENTENCE MEANING, UTTERANCE MEANING.

 V

VALS typology Arnold Mitchell's *Nine American Lifestyles: Who We Are And Where We're Going* (US: Macmillan, 1983) describes a landmark in the documentation of human needs – a massive research project funded and carried out in America in 1980 by SRI International. The principle on which the research was based and which Mitchell's influential book articulates is that humans demonstrate their needs in their lifestyle and that both needs and lifestyle fluctuate according to circumstance and 'drive'. VALS stands for Values and Lifestyle.

The VALS approach, and its typology of categories of lifestyle, pigeon-holes people on an all-embracing scale. It has given a significant boost to marketing trends that have increasingly been preoccupied with *segmenting* people into consumer categories. VALS links the pursuit of lifestyle with personal growth: 'With this growth comes change, so that new goals emerge, and in support of these new goals come new beliefs, new dreams, and a new constellation of values,' writes Mitchell.

Though the main focus of research – ongoing rather than a one-off exercise – was upon the population of the United States, what Mitchell terms 'side spurs' of research explored VALS in five European countries – France, Sweden, Italy, West Germany and Britain. The VALS typology to a considerable degree reflects Abraham Maslow's notion of a hierarchy of needs (see MASLOW'S HIERARCHY OF NEEDS) and gives support to his categorization.

There are those for example at the bottom of the social pile, called *Survivors*, 'whose existence has shrivelled to the bleak reality of the moment and the fantasy world of television'. Higher up the pecking order of lifestyle are the *Achievers*. They 'are at the top … the driving and the driven people who have built "the system" and are now at the helm.' More than anything else 'Achievers have learned to live the comfortable, affluent, affable, outer-directed life, and in so doing they have set the standard for much of the nation.'

The typology identifies lifestyles as they are, or are becoming, and consequently has offered a model for change. Arnold Mitchell claims that VALS aids the 'eminently worthwhile' endeavour of choosing the kind of lifestyle 'a person, or a society of persons, would like in future'. At the same time he warns that the future holds a number of possible 'scenarios', some of brighter promise than others. The 'Hard Times' scenario, for example, would produce a very different VALS typology than the one Mitchell terms 'Bouncy Prosperity'.

Each scenario would favour lifestyle types in different ways, advantaging some, disadvantaging others. The Need-Driven in the scenario of Bouncy Prosperity would rise up the hierarchy of opportunity, adding to the ranks of the *Belongers* (usually the comfortably-off, middle-of-the-roaders with conservative tastes to match). On the other hand, VALS research seems to indicate 'the Societally Conscious segment would shrink' for many of their causes would have been addressed because there had been resources to deal with them.

With the Hard Times scenario 'There would be an increase in basic fear, insecurity, anxiety, dependence, rigidity, compulsiveness, and the desire for forceful leadership and for law and order.' See *TOPIC GUIDE* under ADVERTISING/MARKETING.

Values Each society, social group or individual has certain ideas, beliefs, ways of behaving, upon which is placed a value. A collection of these values, the criteria for judgement of one often acting as REINFORCEMENT for others, may amount to a *system* of values. Such a system, if it is not to cause DISSONANCE in a person, has either to be generally consistent or perceived as generally consistent.

Values are not merely systems of personal belief: they represent shared attitudes within social GROUPS and society at large, of approval and disapproval, of judgements favourable and unfavourable towards other individuals, ideas, objects (such as the value placed on property), social action and events. Like NORMS, values vary from one social group or society to another; and they change over time and in different circumstances.

An individual's perception and interpretation of reality will be influenced by the values of the social groups or society to which he/she belongs. The pervasiveness of such values ensures that they are enmeshed in all aspects of communication processes. The images and codes which are the stock-in-trade of the mass media are shaped by value systems; and their intention is to support and reinforce the value systems that shape them. Jeremy Tunstall in his Introduction to *Mass Sociology* (UK: Constable, 1970), edited by Tunstall, remarks that 'The media are saturated with social values of every kind.' These values come to the fore, achieve clearest definition, at times of crisis and conflict. See CULTURE; IDEOLOGY; MYTH; NEWS VALUES.

Vamp Early word for a sex-star in the movies. In 1914 producer William Fox (1879–1952) created a star by going to the farthest extreme away from screen idol Mary Pickford, symbol of purity and innocence, by imposing a parody of sensuality and eroticism on Theda Bara in the film adaptation of the Kipling poem *A Fool There Was*. The word 'vamp' was used in the publicity for the film, whose financial success helped Fox set up his own studio, among the most important of the 1920s.

V-chip See CLIPPER CHIP.

V-discs In 1943, during the Second World War (1939–45), record companies and musicians agreed to waive fees and contractual rights to a series of very high-quality musical offerings to the US forces. Such recordings, many of them by giants of the jazz world such as Benny Goodman, Louis Armstrong and Duke Ellington, are now prized by collectors.

Verbal devices in speech-making Max Atkinson in his illuminating study of the speech-making techniques of politicians and other well-known contemporary orators, *Our Masters' Voices: The Language and Body Language of Politics* (UK: Methuen, 1984), analyses various forms of what the *Shorter Oxford English Dictionary* terms *clap-traps* – linguistic or non-verbal devices to catch applause. Particularly successful, says the author, is the list of three, which stimulates audience response, reinforces that stimulus and then pushes it to the climax. Antithesis is also an effective claptrap ('I come to bury Caesar, not to praise him'). Atkinson cautions the would-be orator that these devices require skill, timing and judgement to be effective, and claptrap 'always involves the use of more than one technique at a time'. See *TOPIC GUIDE* under LANGUAGE/DISCOURSE/NARRATIVE.

Victim funds These were organized by the UNDERGROUND PRESS in the nineteenth century to help out fellow papers subjected to heavy government fines for evading the taxes on knowledge – STAMP DUTY, Advertising Tax, Paper Duty and State Security System Tax. In London alone between 1830 and 1836 there were at least 1130 fined for selling 'unstamped' papers. See NEWSPAPERS, ORIGINS.

Video The process of recording TV programmes on cassette tape proved to be one of the most popular technical developments in the late 1970s and the 1980s. Video permitted time-shift viewing, liberating the viewer from the restrictions imposed by television schedules. At the same time, films and TV programmes on video became commercially available, creating a situation in which it was possible to escape altogether TV as it was traditionally experienced.

With the arrival of video began a fast-accelerating process of audience *fragmentation* (see AUDIENCE: FRAGMENTATION OF); and this trend was given further impetus with the availability of the recordable digital video disc (DVD) in the 1990s.

Video, because it is reusable, and considerably cheaper than traditional film stock, has opened opportunities for film production, and indeed video soon became for aspiring film-makers the key medium of production. What was once a means of communication restricted to professionals and largely to the film industry, enabled individuals, cooperatives, pressure GROUPS, clubs, schools, Media Studies students in particular – anyone with a case to urge, beliefs or feelings to express, a story to tell – to counter, at least at the level of a local community, the dominant voices of the national broadcasters or mass media communicators generally. Where recordable DVD scores is in the quality of picture and sound, permitting the work of professionals and amateurs alike parity with standards expected 'in the trade'. See *TOPIC GUIDE* under MEDIA: TECHNOLOGIES.

* Sean Cubbitt, *Timeshift: On Video Culture* (UK: Comedia/Routledge, 1992).

Video games Like so many examples of popular CULTURE, the video game has incurred condemnation for being anti-social, a threat to the minds and mentality of the young, who are seen to be the main players, and loaded with harmful features. However, games have also achieved cultural status and have been claimed by some critics as amounting to an important art form, while 'cult status' is awarded to some of the protagonists of such games, the formidable Lara Croft, star of the *Tomb Raider* series, being the most notable. In *L'Univers Des Jeux Video/The Universe of Video Games* (France: Editions La Découverte, 1998), Alain and Frederic Le Diberder see video games as 'the 10th art' (cinema being the seventh, TV the eighth and comic-strips or 'graphic novels' the ninth).

The authors point to the following distinctive pleasures derived from video-game playing: competition, accomplishment, mastery of a system and spectacle. General concern is expressed about the long-term impact of playing games in which the central actions generally focus on violence and the destruction of enemies, and the subliminal *enculturalization* into what might be described as 'samurai mode', arising from the Japanese origin of most games.

A key trend in marketing has been the cross-pollination between films and games and the opportunity games-players have to read the 'the novel of the game'.

A highly readable commentator on the game scene, Steven Poole, in a UK *Guardian* article 'The new game plan' (27 November 1998), spotlighted the worrying ideologies that lurk behind so many video games. He refers to 'the increasingly subterranean political messages of video games', citing Sid Meier's city-building game, *Civilization*, 'in which capitalism is king and no matter how hard the player tries, it is impossible to run a hippy commune'.

With the convergence of digital technologies games feature on the menus of palmtop computers and mobile phones, though manufacturers have become sensitive to the use of the word 'games', preferring to market their products as multimedia entertainment centres. However they are described, video games are big business. The video game industry in the UK employs over 20,000 people with a net turnover of in excess of £200m a year.

* Steven Poole, *The Prometheus Engine* (UK: Fourth Estate, 1999).

Video nasties A market that developed in the 1980s of specially-made-for-video films of a singularly nasty, brutal and sexist nature. Court action in the UK in 1982 against several of these films led to their enforced withdrawal from circulation but, to the considerable disgust of Mary Whitehouse and the National Viewers' and Listeners' Association – among many others – there was no order made for their destruction. However, the Conservative government brought in rigorous controls of video nasties with the VIDEO RECORDING ACT, 1984 (see next entry).

In 1994 there was dramatically renewed interest in the possible effects of video nasties on behaviour following the Jamie Bulger trial in which two 11-year-old boys were convicted of murdering the small boy they had abducted. The judge in the trial, Mr Justice Morland, conjectured that the boys may have been influenced by seeing *Child's Play 3*, whose plot paralleled, to a degree, the real actions of the killers. Though this connection was dismissed by many in the TV and film industry, there was support from child psychologists, in particular from Elizabeth Newson, Professor of Development Psychology at the University of Nottingham, who spoke of the need for special concern when children – or indeed, adults – are repeatedly exposed to images of cruelty in the context of entertainment.

Video Recording Act (UK), 1984 Passed through Parliament in the UK with all-party support, MP Graham Bright's measure was designed to restrict the access of young persons to VIDEO NASTIES, many of which eluded the usual vetting process of the BRITISH BOARD OF FILM CENSORS.

The Act established by statute an authority (initially the BBFC) whose purpose was to classify video cassettes as suitable for home viewing and to censor those deemed unsuitable. Fines of up to £20,000 are liable for dealers and distributors breaking the law. All video works must be submitted for scrutiny, classification and certification unless they are educational or concerned with sport, religion or music.

However, if such videos 'to any extent' portray 'Human sexual activity' or 'Mutilation, torture or other acts of gross violence' or show 'human genital organs' they also have to be submitted to the censors. See CENSORSHIP; MORAL PANIC.

Viewers: light, medium and heavy Research into the amount and nature of TV viewing discriminates between the light viewer, generally classified as watching TV for two hours or fewer a day; the medium viewer, watching for between two and three hours a day and the heavy viewer watching for four hours or more a day. In the analysis of viewer response, special attention has been paid to the differences of attitude to issues and controversies that can be detected between light and heavy viewers, and thus the influence TV programmes may have on attitude formation and attitude change. See CULTIVATION; MAINSTREAMING; MEAN WORLD SYNDROME; RESONANCE.

Violence and the media See VIOLENCE ON TV: THE DEFENCE. See also *TOPIC GUIDE* under AUDIENCES/CONSUMPTION & RECEPTION OF MEDIA; MEDIA: FREEDOM, CENSORSHIP; MEDIA ISSUES & DEBATES; MEDIA: POWER, EFFECTS, INFLUENCE; REPRESENTATION.

* Barrie Gunter and Jackie Harrison, *Violence on Television. An Analysis of Amount, Nature, Location and Origin of Violence in British Programmes* (UK: Routledge, 1998); Karen Boyle, *Media and Violence* (US/UK/India: Sage, 2005).

Violence on TV: the defence The portrayal of violence on screen, whether in the cinema or on TV has long attracted controversy and is an ongoing ISSUE of our time. The dominent tendency among commentators is to deplore it, its nature, its extent and its amount. Simulated violence is seen to prompt some members of the AUDIENCE to re-enact that violence in real life; and violence is judged to desensitize viewers to the real thing.

Taking issue with these perspectives is Jib Fowles. In *The Case for Television Violence* (US: Sage, 1999), Fowles argues that contrary to the notion that screen violence breeds real violence, it is more likely to inhibit or reduce it: 'Television violence is good for people.' Recognizing in human beings an in-built violent impulse, Fowles says that society requires 'outlets' for this impulse. Violence is ever-present and has to be managed: 'In isolation, television violence may seem reproachable and occupy the foreground with a menacing intensity, but with a longer perspective it can seem comparatively like an improvement – a purer distillation of the age-old processes for containing and redirecting violence.'

We have to remember, says Fowles, 'that television violence is symbolic only ... Nobody actually suffers for our pleasure.' For the author, 'the assault on television violence is absolutely unwarranted'. It is 'simply the most recent and least damaging venue for the routinized working out of innate aggressiveness and fear'. The fuss over TV violence Fowles describes as a variant on the MORAL PANIC, which is usually accompanied by the fervour and 'extreme righteousness of the condemners as they lash out at conjured or magnified transgressions'; and the response 'is always out of proportion to whatever instigates it' (see THIRD-PERSON EFFECT). Fowles concludes: 'Perhaps, to give television violence its due, we need first to respect ourselves more fully, to have greater regard for the complex, semiviolent creatures that we are.'

As in addressing all theories, a cautionary note is perhaps required here, for cases occur from time to time in which the enactment of real violence echoes and sometimes directly simulates screen violence. The UK *Observer* (9 June 2002) reported under a headline 'Murder linked to horror trilogy' that French authorities were blaming the savage stabbing in Saint-Sebastien-sur-Loire by a teenager of a girl he had invited for a walk on the youth's seeming obsession with the *Scream* series of movies.

Two similar murders, by teenagers, had alerted the authorities to the possible influence the films exerted on impressionable young people. An *Observer* listing of what seemed to be copy-cat offences between 1999 and 2002 indicated that it was not only teenagers working out fantasies of violence on real-world victims, but older men too, or in the case of a murder in Massachusetts in 2000, a woman and two men wearing *Scream* masks.

In his *Observer* report, Paul Webster quoted psychiatrists worried 'about the inability of some young people to distinguish between reality and fiction'. Dave Grossman, American expert on the psychology and physiology of killing, would plainly challenge Jib Fowles' assertions. His belief, reported by Webster, was that 'repetition, desensitization and escalation reduced the normal human unwillingness to kill'.

Virtual reality Simulation of the real by technological means, using multi-media inputs – head-mounted display, data gloves, three-dimensional audio system and magnetic position tracker (to name the basics); what has been termed a 'technological cluster'. Generally, the simulation of the real exists in that 'window of realities', the TV monitor.

In a paper 'The ultimate display' for the Proceedings of the IFIPS Congress 2, published as early as 1965, Ivan Sutherland defined the VR dream: 'The screen is a window through which one sees a virtual world. The challenge is to make that world look real, act real, sound real and feel real.'

Virtual reality technology is three-dimensional and interactive. It is extensively used in engineering and architectural design, in medicine and telecommunications. It is potentially a vital component in reconstructing the past. At the first Virtual Reality Heritage conference in Bath, UK, November 1995, IBM's Brian Collins described the VR-aided reconstruction of a church that no longer exists, the Frauenkirche in Dresden, 50 years after its destruction by bombing. Using the few drawings and plans available, and colour photographs taken by the Nazis, VR technology provided a detailed reconstruction enabling the original to be rebuilt.

A more general application of the term virtual reality centres on the worlds 'out there' as brought to users of the computer, the INTERNET and the myriad experiences available online. It has become a matter of widespread concern that so many users seem to prefer life as it can be realized online. Mark Slouka in *War of the Worlds: Cyberspace and the High-Tech Assault on Reality* (US: Basic Books, 1995; UK: Abacus, 1996) talks of a 'culture of simulation' that blurs 'fiction and reality'; and this in his view risks creating in the public a fear 'of unmediated reality', especially considering our willingness to buy in to the virtual, that 'we're buying in to a fake'. It follows that reality itself 'is beginning to lose its authority'. See CYBERSPACE. See also *TOPIC GUIDE* under MEDIA ISSUES & DEBATES.

Virus: computer virus See COMPUTERS IN COMMUNICATION.

Visibility See GLOBAL SCRUTINY; PRIVACY.

Visions of order A notion long associated with the role and function of the journalist is that of 'bringer-of-light', of enlightenment. The French writer Jacques Derrida in *Writing and Difference* (UK: Routledge & Kegan Paul, 1978) posed the 'heliological metaphor', describing the journalist as a human version of the heliograph, recorder and transmitter of light, of revelation to AUDIENCE. The process is one of *envisioning* – offering a vision of the world: light for others to see by. In *The Politics of Pictures: The Creation of the Public in the Age of Popular Media* (UK: Routledge, 1992) John Hartley takes up this theme in a chapter entitled 'Heliography: journalism, and the visualization of truth'. What journalism brings to light, what it renders visible are, Hartley argues, 'distant visions of order'. It is not so much the actual truth that is brought to light as the *vision* of truth as visualized in terms of order.

The reader might raise the objection that journalism is really all about disorder rather than order; and this is exactly Hartley's point: what he calls 'a process of photographic negativization' takes place, 'where the image of order is actually recorded as its negative, in stories of disorder'. The 'distant vision of order' is not, however, of 'oneness'; rather, Hartley believes, ordering works on a basis of what the author terms WEDOM, THEYDOM – Us (good) and Them (bad). See JOURNALISM.

* Richard V. Ericson, Patricia M. Baraneh and Janet B.L. Chan, *Representing Order: Crime, Law and Justice in the News Media* (UK: Open University, 1991).

Vistavision Paramount's response to 20th Century Fox's CINEMASCOPE in the 1950s. The negative was made on 70mm stock and, to reduce graininess, converted to 35mm during printing.

Vitaphone Trade name of the first successful synchronous movie sound, introduced in 1926 by Warner Brothers. On 6 August at the Warner Theater in New York, John Barrymore starred in *Don Juan*, to the accompaniment of a Vitaphone 16-inch 33⅓rpm disc recording of voice and music. Curiously *Don Juan* caused less audience excitement than the Vitaphone shorts that accompanied it, such as the New York Philharmonic playing Wagner's *Tannhauser Overture*. The real sensation of the talkies was Warner's next picture, *The Jazz Singer* (1927) starring Al Jolson. There were, in fact, only 281 words spoken in the film, all of them ad-libbed by Jolson. See SYNCHRONOUS SOUND. See *TOPIC GUIDE* under MEDIA HISTORY.

Vocal cues All the oral aspects of speech except the words themselves; pitch – the highness or lowness of voice; rate – rapidity of expression; volume; quality – the pleasantness or unpleasantness of voice tone or delivery, and enunciation – pronunciation and articulation. See PARALANGUAGE.

Voiceover In film and TV film production, a framing device in which a commentator offers an explanation of what the AUDIENCE is seeing on screen. In feature films voiceover is often that of the chief character in a story though the DOCUMENTARY approach of an unidentified narrator is also common. Voiceover plays a significant role in shaping the MEANING of a film TEXT. It signals the way that audience is expected to read what is seen and heard. In this sense, voiceover closes down a text to a prescribed meaning, allowing the viewer little room for interpretation. See NARRATIVE; OPEN, CLOSED TEXTS.

Vox popping Collecting the opinions of large numbers of the general public (*vox populi* is Latin for 'voice of the people') in order to gauge public reaction to a current issue or topic.

→   **W**

War: four stages of war reporting According to Philip Knightley, author of the classic analysis of war reporting, *The First Casualty: A History of War Reporting* (UK: revised edition, Prion, 2000), first published in 1975, western coverage of military conflicts is highly predictable, and passes through four stages. These he discusses in a UK *Guardian* article, 'The disinformation campaign' (4 October 2001) following the terrorist attack on New York's World Trade Center (9/11).

Knightley calls stage 1, the crisis; in stage 2, the enemy leader is DEMONIZED; in stage 3, the enemy as a whole is demonized. Stage 4 focuses on atrocities. 'Comparing the leader with Hitler,' writes Knightley, 'is a good start because of the instant images that Hitler's name provokes' (see HISTORICAL ALLUSION): 'The crudest approach is to suggest that the leader is insane' and those who publicly question any of this 'can expect an even stronger burst of abuse'.

The simplest way of demonizing a whole people, says Knightley, is the atrocity story: 'Take the Kuwaiti babies story. Its origin goes back to the first world war when British propaganda accused the Germans of tossing Belgian babies into the air and catching them on their bayonets. Dusted off and updated for the Gulf War [1991] this version had Iraqi soldiers bursting into a modern Kuwaiti hospital, finding the premature babies ward and then tossing the babies out of incubators so that the incubators could be sent back to Iraq.'

This story, as well as others, was a fabrication, but it had served its propagandist function. See NEWS MANAGEMENT IN TIMES OF WAR. See also *TOPIC GUIDE* under NEWS MEDIA.

War of the Unstamped See STAMP DUTY; UNDERGROUND PRESS; VICTIM FUNDS.

'War of the Worlds' Title of the American CBS network radio adaptation by Howard Koch, produced and narrated by Orson Welles (1938), of H.G. Wells' famous story. Conveying the immediacy of a combat report from a war correspondent, the production actually convinced many listeners that an interplanetary war had broken out. However, reports to the effect that Orson Welles' radio 'hype' had caused panic in the streets have taken on the magic of legend, and become somewhat exaggerated in the telling. See IDENTIFICATION; PARASOCIAL INTERACTION.

Watchdogs The media pride themselves on their role as watchdogs of injustice, abuse and corruption; champions of public interest. The watchdog barks on behalf of the people, in their defence against the powerful, whether these are in government, business, industry or any walk of life where the interests of the public can be affected. The role of the watchdog may be seen as key to media functions and a guiding principle.

Research tends to point to the media being rather less than wholly effective in this capacity; generally to follow rather than initiate the investigation of abuse; indeed to be guilty of *omission* as much as commission (see GUARD DOG METAPHOR).

True 'watchdoggery' can come about only through genuine media independence – from ADVERTISING and sales revenue, from the influence of capital or institutional control. Fulfilling the role of watchdog becomes problematic when that role is seen to trespass upon the vested interests of those who own and control the watchdogs in question.

An arms manufacturing company with a portfolio that includes newspapers, radio and TV stations is unlikely to smile benignly on these media if, in the interests of the public, they wish to challenge arms manufacture and export. The result, usually, is not overt CENSORSHIP, but *self-censorship*. With the trend in recent years of CONVERGENCE of ownership, the risks of self-censorship, of failing to fulfil the role of public watchdog, have inevitably increased.

It is for this reason, among others, that media commentators express concern about convergences of

DEARING'S AGENDA-SETTING MODEL, 1987, this model is featured in an article 'Foreign news: news values and ideologies' by Jorgen Westerstähl and Folke Johansson, published in the *European Journal of Communication*, March 1994. Just as the environment or context is the centre and axis from which communicative action springs in ANDERSCH, STAATS AND BOSTROM'S MODEL OF COMMUNICATION, 1969, IDEOLOGY is the central 'generator' of news coverage according to Westerstähl and Johansson.

As reporting of news is coloured by a prevailing ideology of national interest, *proximity* and *importance* constitute two of four major criteria for news selection; proximity in the sense of geographic, cultural, political, linguistic or cultural closeness, affecting and being affected by another country's importance to 'us'. While the US is distant geographically from the UK it is nevertheless important – an ELITE nation. The Netherlands, in contrast, while being geographically close, is less 'important'. Events occurring in the US are therefore more likely to be reported than events in the Netherlands, unless those events have a direct relevance to the UK.

We recognize the NEWS VALUES as identified by Galtung and Ruge here – ethno-centrism and elitism in particular. The notion of *drama* is obvious enough but *access* is a welcome criterion: where reporting is possible, where reporters have access, there is greater likelihood that foreign events will be covered. The nature of that access is also critical. There was massive coverage of the Gulf Wars of 1991 and 2003, but access to the kind of information reporters wanted if a full picture of events was to be transmitted was severely curtailed by NEWS MANAGEMENT on the part of the military authorities and by ideological pressures requiring the activities of the 'home team' to be presented in the best light (See EMBEDDED REPORTERS; NEWS MANAGEMENT IN TIMES OF WAR).

Westerstähl and Johansson use their model to illustrate how coverage might run counter to traditional news values. They cite the case of the West's interest in Poland during the strikes and protests mounted by the Polish trades union Solidarity in the 1980s. The events were dramatic, yet Poland was neither near nor 'important'. The key to this special attention was, in the view of the authors, ideology. Solidarity's actions threatened the chief ideological rival to capitalism – Communism.

If performed in the West, Solidarity's actions would have incurred critical media attention: strikes are bad for business. However, such strike action taking place in an Iron Curtain country, and in the context of the Cold War, led to Solidarity's trade unionists being cast as heroes fighting for freedom against Soviet socialist totalitarianism.

'In our view,' write Westerstähl and Johansson, 'ideologies are the main source of deviation in news reporting from a standard based on more or less objectified news values.' See DISCOURSE OF POWER. See also *TOPIC GUIDE* under COMMUNICATION MODELS.

Westerstähl and Johansson's model of news factors in foreign news

Westminster view Opinion that the media in the UK take their cue from and align their perspectives to the standpoint of the activities of Parliament. This produces the simplistic equation – politics equals parliament, and can result in less than adequate coverage of political events which take place away from Westminster. See POLITICS OF ACCOMMODATION (IN THE MEDIA).

Whistle-blowing Whistle-blowers are individuals within an organization – industrial, commercial, govern mental, etc. – who can no longer keep silent about practices in that organization; perhaps because they perceive them as unsafe, corrupt, dishonest or misleading. Almost invariably whistle-blowers act out of con science. Their need for security is outweighed by a higher-order need, to square behaviour with a sense of VALUES (see MASLOW'S HIERARCHY OF NEEDS): they must speak out against the perceived abuse, even though their 'going public', by leaking information to the media, may result in dismissal.

In the UK a degree of protection is offered to whistle-blowers in the Public Interest Disclosure Act of 1999. Substantial compensation may be granted to whistle-blowers who have suffered victimization, or dis missal, as a result of their raising concerns about financial malpractices, breaches of contract, or cover-ups generally.

White's gatekeeper model, 1950 The existence of 'gate areas' along channels of communication was iden tified by Kurt Lewin in 'Channels of group life' in *Human Relations* 1 (1947). At such points, decisions are made to select out information passing through the gate areas. Lewin's particular study was concerned with decisions about household food purchases, but he drew a comparison with the flow of NEWS in mass com munication. David M. White in an article entitled 'The "gatekeepers": a case study in the selection of news', in *Journalism Quarterly* 27 (1950), applied Lewin's idea in a study of the telegraph wire editor of an American non-metropolitan newspaper, whom he called Mr Gate.

Today the model is acceptable only as a starting point for analysis of the GATEKEEPING process; indeed it is a useful exercise for the student to build on the model by adding important factors which White does not include, such as the organizational elements of the mass communication process that constrain and direct it. The model also indicates only a single gate and a single gatekeeper, where in practice news passes through many gatekeepers, official and unofficial, direct and indirect. White's model should be studied in relation to McNELLY'S MODEL OF NEWS FLOW, 1959, and GALTUNG AND RUGE'S MODEL OF SELECTIVE GATEKEEPING, 1965. See also *TOPIC GUIDE* under COMMUNICATION MODELS.

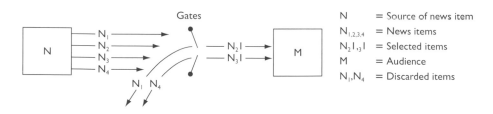

N	= Source of news item
$N_{1,2,3,4}$	= News items
$N_2 I_{,3} I$	= Selected items
M	= Audience
N_1, N_4	= Discarded items

White's gatekeeper model, 1950

Wi-fi See INTERNET: WIRELESS INTERNET.

Wiki, Wikipedia The brainchild of Jimmy Wales, and started up in January 2001, the Wiki is a website everyone can contribute to and edit; the *Wikipedia* is what thousands of contributors worldwide have assem bled. Wiki had become so popular by 2005 that 400 delegates attended the first Wikimania Foundation con ference in Frankfurt, Germany. 'What we are doing,' Wales told Sean Dodson of the UK *Guardian* ('Worldwide Wikimania', 11 August 2005) is building 'a world in which every person on the planet is given free access to the sum of human knowledge.' By the time of the conference the Wikipedia contained over a million and a half entries in 200 different languages, all contributed by 'wikipedians'.

'Never has such an anarchic idea produced such a democratic outcome as the Wiki,' writes Iranian blog ger journalist Hossain Derakhshan in a posting on the *OpenDemocracy* website (3 August 2005). Entries are made by members of the public for the use of the public: pose it, write it, alter it or any other entry: 'It's as if for every single change in an entry, a referendum is taking place.' Derakhshan sees great potential for the

Yellow journalism Phrase used in the US to describe newspapers involved in the internecine (dog-eat-dog) warfare of the popular metropolitan press empires of the late nineteenth century, a battle that has continued to the present day with mass-circulation tabloids competing for readership with all sorts of exploitative offers, lurid revelations and blockbuster bingo.

Yellow Kid Newspaper cartoon character, the possession of whose widely popular image – and the use of that image – was fought over by New York's press barons, Joseph Pulitzer (1847–1911) and William Randolph Hearst (1863–1951). The pictorial image was fast dominating the pages of newspapers at the beginning of the twentieth century, proving a circulation-booster and a marketing device. Pulitzer's *New York World* first featured Richard B. Outcault's cartoon *Shantytown* (renamed *Hogan's Alley*). Hearst 'raided' the *World's* Sunday edition, buying in the entire production team of the paper for his own newly purchased *Journal.* The gap-toothed Kid in his yellow smock, whose grin was recognized throughout the city on billboards and sandwich boards, joined the *Journal* as cartoon and promotional image. Soon Hearst was organizing the Yellow Fellow Transcontinental Bicycle Relay followed by a bike carnival in New York's Central Park.

In response, Pulitzer hired Richard Buks to continue the original cartoon strip and in 1895 two Yellow Kids were in competition. 'For contemporaries,' writes Andrew Wernick in *Promotional Culture: Advertising, Ideology and Symbolic Expression* (UK: Sage, 1991), 'the Kid's colour became emblematic of the effects of intensified consumerization on the whole character of the popular press.'

Visual appeal had become central to the process of promotion. When Hearst followed Pulitzer in issuing a full-colour Sunday supplement, the *Journal* announced its own 'eight pages of irridescent polychromous effulgence that makes the rainbow look like a lead pipe'. It is perhaps more than a coincidence that the most popular TV comic-strip, *The Simpsons*, continued with the effulgence of yellow. See *TOPIC GUIDE* under MEDIA HISTORY.

Youth and media See CHILDREN, YOUNG PEOPLE AND THE CHANGING MEDIA ENVIRONMENT.

Youth culture Since the Second World War (1939–45) considerable attention has been paid to the cultures and sub-cultures of young people – to their symbols, SIGNS, philosophies, MORES, NORMS, language and music. Music is an essential part of all youth cultures and sub-cultures, a mode of self-identification (see SELF-IDENTITY), and different GROUPS favour different musical styles and use music in different ways.

Youth cultures and sub-cultures differ not only over time but also between CLASS, sex and racial groups. Whilst they manifest significant differences there are some links between them and individuals may move from one to another. They adopt and adapt aspects of each other's cultural style and those of past youth cultures and sub-cultures. The more dramatic sub-cultures have attracted attention from the media and academics. Their often spectacular modes of expression offer contrast and challenge to society, usually communicated by STYLE – the hairstyle of the punks, for example.

The media have been a notable mediator of society's reaction to such challenges, and this role has been a focus of media research. Essentially youth culture is seen as deviant, or potentially deviant, and as a function of media is to patrol the boundaries between the norm and the deviant, particular interest is expressed in youth culture, often leading to DEMONIZATION and a tendency to work up concern that threatens to constitute a MORAL PANIC. See FOLK DEVILS; SENSITIZATION.

→ **Z**

Zapping, zipping The practice of TV channel-switching, especially when the commercials come on is referred to as zapping; made worryingly easy – as far as the advertisers are concerned – with the arrival of remote control and the PVR (personal video recorder). In France, an anti-zapping strategy designed to keep viewers glued to the commercials was introduced in the late 1980s: individual numbers placed in the corner of the screen offer viewers a bingo-style competition. A full line of numbers wins a cash prize. Zipping is fast-forwarding through recorded programmes, again most generally to escape the commercials.

Zinoviev letter, 1924 Probably forged by Russian émigrés and used as a 'Red scare' tactic by the *Daily Mail* to put the frighteners on the electorate immediately before the 1924 election. Labour lost the election and the Zinoviev letter probably made some difference if not a substantial one. It was a 1200-word document marked 'Very Secret', bearing the address of the 3rd Communist International, the organization in Moscow responsible for international communist tactics.

The letter was addressed to the Central Committee of the British Communist Party and its tenor was the need to stir the British proletariat to revolutionary action against their capitalist masters. Among other recommendations, the letter urged the formation of cells in the armed forces – the 'future directors of the British Red Army'.

The impact of the forged letter was due to its timing. It was 'intercepted' by the Conservative *Daily Mail* just a few days before the election of October 1924 and published four days before polling day. The *Mail* used a seven-deck (or lines) headline, topping the deck with 'Civil War Plot By Socialists' Masters'. With the exception of the *Daily Herald*, the entire British press swallowed and regurgitated the story. *The Times* discovered 'Another Red Plot in Germany' and on voting day the *Daily Express* warned, in red ink, 'Do Not Vote Red Today'. Labour lost 50 seats but gained more than a million votes.

Eventually (but always too late) the truth will out; and in February 1999 Gill Bennett, chief historian at the UK Foreign Office, produced a 126-page report, commissioned by then Foreign Secretary Robin Cook, pointing a sure finger of accusation at Desmond Morton, an MI6 officer and friend of Winston Churchill, as the official who supplied the *Mail* with its sensational disclosure. Also named is Major Joseph Ball, an MI5 officer who joined the Conservative Central Office in 1926. Bennett reported that the forged letter was 'probably leaked from SIS [the Secret Intelligence Service, alias MI6] by somebody to the Conservative Party Central Office'.

MI6 was at the centre of the scandal but Bennett could not be sure at this distance in time whether Admiral Hugh Sinclair, head of MI6, was party to the conspiracy. In a UK *Guardian* article 'The hidden hand' (4 February 1999) Robin Cook took the fullest opportunity to celebrate a 'remarkable exercise in openness' 75 years after the event, at the same time exonerating the Foreign Office from any blame, insisting that there was no institutional conspiracy and admitting that important questions remain unanswered, 'such as who forged the letter'. See DISINFORMATION; FREEDOM OF INFORMATION. See also *TOPIC GUIDE* under MEDIA: FREEDOM, CENSORSHIP; MEDIA: POWER, EFFECTS, INFLUENCE.

Zircon affair UK *New Statesman* journalist Duncan Campbell in 1986, made a series of six TV programmes for the BBC entitled *Secret Society*. The first of these was about a Ministry of Defence project – Zircon – to put a spy satellite into space, at an estimated cost of £5m. On 15 January 1987, Alisdair Milne, the BBC's soon-to-be-dismissed Director General, banned the Zircon programme on grounds of national security, a decision the *Observer* made public on 18 January.

The most notorious aspect of the Zircon affair was the police raids. Special Branch descended upon the *New Statesman* offices, upon Campbell's home as well as the homes of two other *Statesman* journalists, and finally there was a raid on the Glasgow offices of BBC Scotland, where all six of the *Secret Society* films were seized. Two days before, Milne had been sacked as the BBC's Director General.

The irony of the case is that Zircon was not really a closely guarded state secret; indeed the position of the proposed satellite was filed by the Ministry of Defence at the International Communications Union, an institution of which the former USSR was a member. Eventually the Zircon programme was transmitted by the BBC in September 1988, by which time the Zircon project had been cancelled. See *TOPIC GUIDE* under MEDIA: FREEDOM, CENSORSHIP; MEDIA: POLITICS & ECONOMICS; MEDIA: POWER, EFFECTS, INFLUENCE.

Zoetrope Or 'wheel of life'. Early nineteenth-century 'toy' in which pictures inside a spinning drum, viewed from the outside through slits, appear to be in motion. Invented in 1834 by Englishman W.G. Horner, the zoetrope simply but effectively demonstrated the phenomenon of PERSISTENCE OF VISION, the realization of which opened the way for the birth of cinema.

Zones In *The Hidden Dimension: Man's Use of Space in Public and Private* (UK: Bodley Head, 1966) Edward T. Hall identifies four distinct zones, or territorial spaces, in which most men and women operate. These are *intimate* distance, *personal* distance, *social* distance and *public* distance, each with its close and far phases. See PROXEMICS.

Zoom lens On a movie camera, a lens that can be adjusted automatically to give the effect of movement away from or towards the stationary camera.

Zoopraxography Pioneer photographer Eadward Muybridge (1830–1904) was not the inventor of cine-film but he made the first photographic moving pictures, a process he called Zoopraxography, 15 years before Lumière's first films. Muybridge described his Zoopraxiscope as being 'the first apparatus ever used, or constructed, for synthetically demonstrating movements analytically photographed from life'. In 1878 he set up an experiment at Palo Alto, California, to ascertain by photography, whether all four hooves of a galloping horse were ever simultaneously clear of the ground (they are); 24 cameras were aligned along the running track, each triggered off by the horse as it galloped past.

The Zoopraxiscope consisted basically of a spinning glass disc bearing the photographs in sequence of movement. The disc, when attached to a central shaft, revolved in front of the condensing lens of a projecting lantern parallel to and close to another disc fixed to a tubular shaft that encircled the other, and round which it rotated in the opposite direction.

By 1885 Muybridge had produced an encyclopaedia of motion: men and women, clothed and unclothed, performed simple actions such as running, drinking cups of tea or shoeing horses; and a massive and varied study of animals and birds in movement. His carefully catalogued work was published in 1887. See *TOPIC GUIDE* under MEDIA HISTORY.

APPENDIX: A CHRONOLOGY OF MEDIA EVENTS

This Chronology is drawn from many sources but our best thanks go to Patrick Robertson whose *The New Shell Book of Firsts* (UK: Headline, 1994), a remarkable piece of historical detective work, has been immensely helpful. *UK* is used in a generalized sense as a composite reference to England, Britain and the United Kingdom.

AD 105	Paper produced from pulp; invention attributed to Ts'ai Lun, China.
AD 704	First printed book, the *Dharani Sutra*, created in Korea from woodblocks on a scroll, and discovered in the foundations of the Pulguk Sa pagoda in Kyongju, South Korea, October 1966.
1174	First evidence of woodblock printing in Europe, by Benedictine monks at Engelberg, Switzerland, used to print capital letters in illuminated manuscripts.
1234	*Compendium of Rites and Rituals*, first book printed using movable type comprising 50 chapters, 28 copies of which were published in Korea. The type was made using a sand-moulding technique developed in 1102 for casting coins.
1451	*Donatis Latin Grammar*, two leaves of a 27-line publication, the first evidence of the use of movable type in Europe, possibly the same type as that used by John of Gutenberg in his 42-line Bible believed to have been printed at Mainz between 1451 and 1454, 48 copies of which survive, 36 printed on paper, 12 on vellum.
1454	Gutenberg prints the first calendar.
1461	Albrecht Pfister of Bamberg publishes the first books in the vernacular: Ulrich Boner's *Edelstein* and Johann von Tepl's *Ackermann aus Böhmen*.
1474	In Bruges, the Englishman William Caxton publishes *The Recuyell of the Histories of Troye*, a translation from original French text. Caxton moved to London where he printed in 1477 *The Dictes and Sayengis of the Philosophres*, a work of 74 leaves 'drawn out of frensche into our Englisshe tonge' by Anthony Earl Rivers.
1475	Jodocus Pflanzmann of Augsburg prints the first illustrated Bible.
1484	Caxton prints *Morte D'Arthur*.
1494	John Tate of Stevenage is the first to manufacture paper in England. Tate produced the first-known watermark in the UK – a star and circle.
1517	Martin Luther nails his 95 Theses, protesting against the sale of indulgences, on the church door at Wittenberg. The printing and distribution of his works ignites the Reformation and the division of Europe between Roman Catholic and Protestant faiths.
1526	William Tyndale's translation of the New Testament into English is published by Peter Schoeffer in Worms, Germany.

1527	Leipzig: printer Hanz Hergot executed for twice publishing *On the New Direction of Christian Life,* a pamphlet advocating common ownership of land and goods.
1536	Myles Coverdale's complete translation of the Bible into English published, probably in Cologne. This was printed in London by James Nicholson the following year.
1559	Roman Catholic church promulgates the Index Librorum Prohibitorum, a list of prohibited books; and in 1571 the Index Expurgatoris, of books permitted after censorship.
1588	Dr Timothy Bright introduces the first recorded system of shorthand. His system appeared under the title *Characterie; the art of short, swift, and secret writing.*
1608	The civil authorities of Norwich open the first municipal public library, chiefly for 'the use of preachers'. In 1656 Chetham's Library in Manchester became the first to employ a librarian. Chetham's was open to all. As late as 1849 it remained the only substantial collection of books fully accessible to the public. Manchester also took the lead with the lending of books. In 1852 the Manchester Free Library instituted a lending system, issuing over 70,000 books in its first year. This followed the Public Libraries Act of 1850.
1611	Issue in the UK of the Authorized Version of the Bible, the composite work of 46 translators and revisers.
1619	State of Weimar becomes the first to introduce compulsory education for all between the ages of 6 and 13. In the UK similar legislation had to wait until 1870.
1621	First *Corantos* published in London, followed in same year by first Proclamation against Corantos.
1637	Star Chamber Decree regulating printing, followed in 1643 with Ordinance for regulating printing, and in 1649 the first Printing Act.
1642	The *Mayflower* arrives in America from Plymouth, England, with a printing press on board.
1644	Publication of John Milton's *Areopagitica* presenting the case for the freedom of the press.
1649	UK: Charles I beheaded. During the period in power of the Lord Protector, Oliver Cromwell, and until the restoration of the monarchy in 1660, under Charles II, England becomes a hotbed of radical, chiefly religious, publications. John Lilburne issues *England's New Chaines Discovered.*
1650	At Leipzig, the first daily newspaper, the *Einkommenden Zeitungen,* is published by Timotheus Ritzsch. In the UK the *Perfect Diurnall* was published daily, except Sunday, between February and March 1660, though British readers had to wait until 1702 for the first successful daily, the *Daily Courant.*
1651	Publication of Thomas Hobbes' *Leviathan.*
1657	First classified advertisement in a UK paper printed in Thomas Newcombe's *Publick Advertiser,* the first English paper devoted entirely to advertising.
1660–1	Parliament prohibits publication of its proceedings.
1680	Royal Proclamation suppressing all newsbooks except those under licence from the authorities.

1693	In UK, the *City Mercury* is the first giveaway newspaper.
	London bookseller John Dunton issues the first women's magazine, the *Ladies' Mercury*.
1695	Parliament does not renew the Licensing Act.
1701	First provincial newspaper in the UK, the *Norwich Post*, a weekly, with an approximate circulation of 400–500 copies.
1702	First daily newspaper in Britain, the *Daily Courant*, is published in London.
1704	John Campbell publishes *Boston Newsletter*, the first newspaper in the US not to be a one-issue failure.
1709	English Copyright Act, the first enactment to secure the rights of authors and publishers by offering legal protection against 'pirating' of texts. A similar act was passed in France in 1793 and in the Grand Duchy of Saxe-Weimar in 1839 (the first to employ the 30-year term of protection after an author's death). The principle of international reciprocity of rights was established in the Berne Convention of 1886.
1712	In Britain, first 'Taxes on Knowledge' introduced – duties on newspapers and advertising and excise duty on paper.
1720s	Benjamin Franklin begins successful publishing career with *Pennsylvania Gazette*.
1725	Stamp Act in Britain applies 1712 regulations to all newspapers, whatever their size or format.
1739	Scotsman William Ged devises method of preserving pages of type for future reprints, using a mould made from plaster of Paris from which metal plates were made. In fear of their livelihoods, Scottish printers wrecked the invention; 60 years later it was revived by Firmin Didot, who reversed the process by creating the metal plate from sunken surfaces. Eventually stereotyping, as the process came to be known, was made a commercial proposition by amateur inventor Lord Stanhope, in 1805, at the Clarendon Press, Oxford.
	In 1829 the plaster and metal plates gave way to papier mâché, reducing time, weight and bulk – innovations happening at virtually the same time in Italy, France and England. Stanhope also improved the printing press by replacing the wooden press with an iron structure and by increasing the bed of the machine in order to produce one-pull larger-scale sheets.
1741	First magazines in US: Andrew Bradford's *American Magazine*, followed by Benjamin Franklin's *General Magazine*.
1757	UK: increases in taxes on newspapers; increased again in 1776, 1780, 1789 (the year of the French Revolution), 1797 and 1815.
1764	London: prosecution of firebrand editor/journalist John Wilkes for seditious libel published in the *North Briton*.
1770s	Thomas Paine in America. His *Common Sense* (1776), arguing powerfully for the separation of the States from English rule, will prove an immensely influential bestseller.
1771	Press permitted to report the proceedings of the House of Commons, followed by those of the House of Lords (in 1775).

The *Penny Magazine* of London becomes the first mass-circulation paper selling over 100,000 copies.

1833   Advertising Duty reduced, followed in 1836 with the reduction of Stamp Duty and Excise Duty on paper. It was not until 1853 that Advertising Duty was abolished. 1855 saw the abolition of Stamp Duty and 1861 Paper Duties.

US: *New York Sun*, concentrating on stories of sex and violence, published by Benjamin Day. This was followed in 1835 by the *New York Herald*, published by John Gordon Bennett, with specific pages dedicated to sport and finance.

1835   Henry Fox-Talbot, British pioneer in the development of photography, publishes a description in the February edition of the *Literary Gazette* of the positive–negative process, which would enable the reproduction of photographs in any number.

Fox-Talbot's work coincided with that of the Frenchman Louis Daguerre who was the first to commercially exploit photography. The daguerreotype used only the one-off positive, but it advanced exposure time from eight hours to only 15–30 minutes. The French government acquired the rights from Daguerre and Isidor Nièpce, heir of Nicèphore Nièpce (died 1833) who had gone into business with Daguerre. Thus the process became public property for all to use. Daguerre's own cameras were on sale before the end of the year.

1836   US: Samuel Morse builds his first telegraph.

1838   *The Times of India* founded.

Publication of the radical *Northern Star* (until 1852).

1839   In Paris, Alphonse Giroux manufactures for sale the first daguerreotype camera.

1842   *Illustrated London News* is founded.

Samuel Morse lays first submarine telegraph cable, New York Harbour.

1843   Giuseppe Mazzini obtains patent for a composing machine, though the idea had originated as early as 1682 with Johann Joachim Becher, a political economist.

Though some 1500 patents had by 1900 been registered in the US for composing machines those invented by Robert Hattersley and Charles Kastenbein dominated. With each, the chief problem was the need to justify the lines by hand, a problem resolved by Linotype and Monotype machines, and the punch-cutting machine of Linn Boyd Benton of Milwaukee in 1885.

A Saxon weaver, Friedrich Gottleb Keller, produces paper from wood pulp, another innovation suggested much earlier but not developed or taken up.

The first public telegraph service is introduced following the completion of the Great Western Railway telegraph line from Paddington to Slough. William Cooke, who had patented the system, transferred the licence, for an annual fee, to Thomas Home and the first paid telegrams were sent by Cooke's double-needle electro-magnetic telegraph along a 20-mile wire. Eventually the Electric Telegraph Company took up the licence and pioneered nationwide telegraphy. By 1847 two systems, north and south, were in operation, linking major towns and cities. Unification of the regions took place in November.

Foundation of the *News of the World*, *The Economist* and, in Newcastle, the *Miners' Journal.*

1844   Transmission of the first press telegram, from a Congress reporter in Washington, DC, to the editor of the *Baltimore Patriot*, by Morse telegraph. In the UK the first press telegraph was sent in the same year, from Windsor Castle to *The Times* via the Slough–Paddington telegraph, announcing the birth of Prince Alfred to Queen Victoria.

William Fox-Talbot's *The Pencil of Nature* is the first book in the UK to be published with photographs. This was issued by Longman in six parts.

Society of Women Journalists founded in London.

1846   London: *Daily News* founded, with Charles Dickens (briefly) as editor.

1847–8   Karl Marx and Friedrich Engels produce *The Communist Manifesto*. Having settled in the UK Marx produced his monumental work, *Das Kapital* (*Capital*) in 1859.

Paris: the photographic journal *Le Daguerreotype* published.

1848   In Havana, Cuba, Italian Antonio Meucci creates instrument with which he communicates between apartment floors with his invalid wife. However, it is 1860 before there is a public demonstration of the telephone, by Johann Philipp Reis of Germany, using a violin case for a resonator, a hollowed-out beer-barrel bung for a mouthpiece and a stretched sausage skin for a diaphragm. In 1861 Reis demonstrated an improved version to the Frankfurt Physical Society, transmitting verses and songs – albeit with very poor clarity – over a 300-foot line.

The editor of the UK *Morning Chronicle* employs Eliza Lyn Linton to write features and reviews. She later became the paper's Paris correspondent. On her return to the UK she became Fleet Street's first-ever full-time woman journalist. She became known for her antipathy to women's suffrage.

1850   UK: Public Libraries Act.

Philadelphia: Frederick Langenheim patents first photographic slides.

1852   J.W. Brett lays first submarine telegraph cable between Dover and Calais.

UK: House of Commons Press Gallery opens.

Surgeon John MacCosh is first British war photographer; 47 studies survive of his photo-coverage of the Second Burma War.

1853   Liverpool: the *Northern Daily Times* becomes England's first daily provincial paper.

1854   Paris: *Le Figaro* founded.

1855   Englishman Alexander Parkes invents celluloid.

Foundation of the *Daily Telegraph.*

In UK, newspaper tax abolished.

1858   First transatlantic telegram sent by John Cash, American name-tape manufacturer, from London to his New York representative. At £1 a word, it read: 'Go to Chicago.'

1860   Antonio Meucci demonstrates, in New York, his 'telefono' but has insufficient funds to patent his invention. Only in 2002 was he acknowledged, by the US House of Representatives, as the true originator of the telephone (rather than Alexander Graham Bell who had access to Meucci's materials and had shared a laboratory with him). However, it was Bell who patented a version of Meucci's device in 1876.

1865   Father Giovanni Caselli developed the first fax machine between 1857 and 1864. It was introduced for public service over the Paris–Lyons telegraph line in May 1865. However, the first office fax did not become commercially available until the Xerox LDX was demonstrated in the company's showroom in New York, May 1964. The Japanese firm Sharp introduced the first colour fax in 1984.

1866   Mahloon Loomis of Washington, DC, having described a system of radio signalling in a paper of July 1866, succeeds in October in broadcasting messages over a 14-mile distance. He was granted the world's first wireless patent in 1872. Lack of funds in a period of recession prevented Loomis developing radio commercially before his death in 1886. In the UK David Edward Hughes proved a significant pioneer into the phenomenon of radio waves, but he met with little encouragement. It was left to Heinrich Hertz, the German electrical scientist, to convince the scientific community of the existence and significance of radio waves, thus making possible the development of radio telegraphy and broadcasting.

1867   Invention of the typewriter by American Christopher Sholes.

1868   London: Press Association founded.

            New York: *Staats Zeitung* first newspaper to be printed on wood-pulp paper.

1870   UK: Education Act inaugurates systematic primary school education for all.

1870–1   Jessie White Mario becomes world's first woman war correspondent, covering the Franco–Prussian War for several US and British papers.

1872   Issue of first illustrated daily newspaper, the *New York Daily Graphic.*

1873   The *New York Daily Graphic* is first to publish a half-tone photograph (2 December) – an illustration of the city's Steinway Hall appeared on the back page.

1874   American writer Mark Twain becomes the first author to possess a typewriter – made by Remington. By 1890 in the US there were 30 manufacturers producing typewriters. In the UK none was on sale until 1889, from the Maskelyne British Typewriter & Manufacturing Company.

            In the same year George C. Blickensderfer's Connecticut company produced the first portable typewriter, the Blick. The introduction of the typewriter into business created new employment opportunities for women.

1876   Scotsman Alexander Graham Bell successfully initiates telephonic communication. Bell, of Edinburgh, patented the telephone on 9 March, and on 10 March, in Boston, US, the first truly coherent transmission took place – a message from Bell to his assistant, Thomas Watson: 'Come here, Watson, I want you.' The speaking telephone was demonstrated by Bell at the Centennial Exhibition, Philadelphia, 25 June. In July of the following year the first telephone line between two separate buildings was laid, in London, between the Queen's Theatre and Canterbury Hall. In the same year the first telephone exchange was created on behalf of the New England Telephone Company by Isaac D. Smith.

1877   Thomas Alva Edison of America patents the Phonograph, the first sound-recording system. The prototype being completed by Edison's mechanic, John Kruesi at West Orange, New Jersey, on 6 December, Edison proceeded to make history by reciting into the recording apparatus, 'Mary had a little lamb'. The Edison Speaking Phonograph Company began production in April 1879. The tin-foil cylinder provided so short a duration that public interest in the Phonograph declined.

            The wax-cylinder Graphaphone developed by Chichester Bell and Charles Sumner Tainter was patented in 1886, to be countered by Edison, his interest in recording renewed, with the Improved Phonograph. Edison Laboratories were the first to record music by an accredited musician, the boy pianist Josef Hofman, in 1888. There was no means of duplicating wax discs before 1892.

1878   The microphone demonstrated in London by Professor David Edward Hughes.

1880   The Radiophone, devised by Charles Sumner Tainter and Alexander Graham Bell, successfully transmits speech between the top of Franklin School, Washington, DC, and Bell's laboratory on 14th Street.

            Telephony without wires had been the invention of A.C. Brown of the Eastern Telegraph Company two years earlier. Reginald Fessenden produced the first conventional system of radio telephony capable of transmitting speech across distances regardless of obstacles between transmitter and receiver. He demonstrated his system for the first time, over a distance of a mile, 23 December 1900. His words were addressed to his assistant, 'Is it snowing where you are, Mr Thiessen?'

            UK: *Titbits* founded, followed in 1888 by *Answers* – two immensely popular weeklies.

1883   US: Joseph Pulitzer starts up the *New York World*.

1884   Lewis Waterman in the US creates the first fountain pen.

1885   Louis Aimé Augustin Le Prince, French-born but living in the US, projects the first moving pictures – on to a wall at the Institute for the Deaf, New York, applying in November 1886 for an American patent for an 'Apparatus for Producing Animated Pictures'. This was granted in January 1888 but reference to cameras and projectors was disallowed because of Dumont's British patent of 1861 (though this involved an arrangement of glass plates to form the facets of a prismatic drum and had nothing to do with the reproduction of moving images on a screen).

            On the point of going into commercial production in 1890, Le Prince boarded a train in Dijon, bound for Paris where it was his intention to demonstrate his invention to the secretary of the Paris Opera. He – and his apparatus – disappeared; a mystery that remains unsolved.

1886   *New York Herald Tribune* installs the first Linotype machine, the invention of Ottmar Margenthaler.

            Paris: *Le Petit Journal* becomes first paper to reach 1 million circulation.

1887   German Emile Berliner working in the US applies for a patent for the first gramophone or disc-recorder player. He demonstrated his invention at the Franklin Institute in Philadelphia in the following year. The hand-cranked gramophone was initially produced as a toy by Kammerer & Rheinhardt, Germany, using a five-inch vulcanized rubber disc at an approximate speed of

70rpm. Electrically operated machines were marketed by the United States Gramophone Company in Washington in 1894, using 7-inch records.

First overseas edition of a newspaper – *New York Herald* in Paris.

The Berliner Gramophone Company of Philadelphia produced the first shellac records in 1897. This company was also the first to create a recording studio and record shop. Double-sided discs were first manufactured in 1904 by the International Talking Machine Company, Germany, under the imprint Odeon Records.

San Francisco: William Randoph Hearst takes command of his father's paper, the *Examiner,* initiating a career as press baron to out-rival and out-live all his contemporaries. In 1895 he bought the *New York Journal,* which became the star and exemplar of Yellow Journalism.

Also in 1887, Monotype printing invented in the US by Tolbert Lanston. Commercially established by 1897, Monotype had the advantage over Linotype in that it cast each letter separately instead of in a compact line, thus making it easier to correct the text.

1888   George Eastman of Rochester, New York, produced first snapshot camera – the Kodak – for use by the general public. This used pre-loaded paper-roll film. It took 100 circular pictures 2.5 inches in diameter. Mass produced by the Eastman Company, Kodak No. 1 proved an immediate success in the US and worldwide.

In the same year John Carbutt of Philadelphia introduced celluoid film. This was made from celluloid sheets one-hundredth of an inch thick, and obtained from the Celluloid Manufacturing Company. However, the first celluloid roll film to be manufactured commercially was another Eastman coup. The Eastman Dry Plate Company produced roll film for its Kodak cameras, beginning in August 1889. The first colour roll film came much later, and was invented by Robert Krayn in Germany in 1910. Amateurs had a longer wait – until Kodrachrome produced three-colour roll film in 1936.

UK: *Financial Times* founded.

1889   UK's first Official Secrets Act.

Kansas City undertaker Almon B. Stowger patents the first automatic telephone exchange. The first exchange was opened at La Porte, Indiana, in November 1892. Dial telephones were introduced in 1896.

1890   Alfred Harmsworth, later Lord Northcliffe, publishes the first comic, the eight-page *Comic Cuts*, edited by Houghton Townley. Nearly 120,000 copies of the first edition were sold and this rose to 300,000 within a month. In October 1890 a rival to *Comic Cuts*, *Funny Cuts*, appeared with the first-ever front-page strip cartoon.

Telephoto lens invented by New Zealand geologist Alexander McKay.

London evening *Star* prints the first front-page newspaper headline, 16 July. This read 'Many Happy Returns of the Day – Wedding of Professor Stuart MP'.

1891   Peep-show projector, the Kinetoscope, developed by William Dickson at the instigation of his employer, Thomas Alva Edison, has first public showing in Edison's workshops in West Orange, New Jersey, to 147 representatives of the National Federation of Women's Clubs.

The first commercial showing took place at Holland Bros' Kinetoscope Parlor, Broadway, in April 1894. The films were produced by the Edison Co., which was thus the first-ever film production company. In the same year Greek showman George Trajedis installed six kinetoscopes in a converted Old Bond Street store in London, October, charging 2 pence per film.

1893   UK: first issue of the *Sketch*.

1894   The first commercially viable radio communication was the work of the Italian Guglielmo Marconi of Bologna. Experiments conducted in 1894 and 1895 led Marconi to offer his invention to the Italian Ministry of Posts and Telegraphs. Failing to elicit interest, the inventor moved to England where customs officials broke open his equipment, suspecting him of being an anarchist. Undaunted, Marconi settled in London and in 1896 applied for a patent for a method by which 'electrical actions or manifestations are transmitted through air, earth or water by means of electrical oscillations of high frequency'.

     The first public demonstration of Marconi's wireless took place on 12 December 1896. In the following year the Marconi Wireless Telegraph & Signal Company was formed.

1895   Brothers Auguste and Louis Lumière project the first-ever film on to a screen – *Workers Leaving the Lumière Factory*, 22 March, to members of the Société d'Encouragement a L'Industrie Nationale, at 44 rue de Rennes, Paris. On 28 December the Lumieres entertained a paying audience at the Grand Café on the Boulevard des Capuchines: cinema was born.

     William Randolph Hearst buys up the *New York Journal* having built up the *San Francisco Examiner*, given to him by his father, with sensational stories of gangsters and Hollywood sex scandals.

1896   First permanent cinema, the 400-seater Vitascope Hall, opens in New Orleans, 26 June, by William T. Rock. Admission was 10 cents, plus another 10 to view the Edison Vitascope projector. The 5000-seater Gaumont-Palace, formerly the Hippodrome Theatre, opened in Paris in 1910. The largest cinema ever built was the Roxy Theater in New York, with 6200 seats. In Berlin 300 cinemas were opened during 1908. In the UK by 1912 there were 4000 cinemas.

     J.H. Rigg of Leeds manufactures the first motorized cinema projector. An electrically powered model was demonstrated at the Royal Aquarium, London, 6 April.

     UK *Daily Mail* founded by Alfred Harmsworth, later Lord Northcliffe.

1897   First wide-screen film on 70mm stock introduced by Enoch J. Rector of the Veriscope Co., New York.

1898   The Telegraphone, the first magnetic recorder, is patented by Danish engineer Valdemar Poulsen employed by the Copenhagen Telephone Company. Demonstrated in public for the first time at the Paris Exposition of 1900, the Telegraphone used magnetized piano wire running between spools at 7 feet per second.

     Commercial production began in America in 1903. An improved model was used by Lee de Forest for experiments in talking film. The use of metal tape instead of wire came in 1929 with the Blattnerphone, again used in film production, at Elstree Studios.

     The use of plastic tape originated in Berlin with the Magnetophon produced by the firm AEG. This proved the archetype for all recorder developments from that time.

1900 Film: sound on disc demonstrated to a paying audience at the Paris Exposition. The first sound-on-film process was patented by French-born Eugene Lauste of Brixton in 1906. His first successful experiment in recording and reproducing speech on film came in 1910. He was ready to exploit his system commercially, only to be interrupted by the outbreak of war in 1914. He crossed the Atlantic with his idea but met with the same lack of interest as America itself entered the war.

1901 Marconi transmits messages by wireless telegraph from Cornwall to Newfoundland.

1902 Canadian-born Reginald Fessenden of the US introduces the first radio-telephone; makes the first transmission of speech by wireless.

    UK: Arthur Pearson founds the *Daily Express*.

    Alfred Harmsworth founds the *Daily Mirror*.

1906 Fessenden makes the first radio broadcast, using the 420-foot-high radio mast of the National Electric Signalling Company's radio station at Brant Rock, Massachusetts. On 24 December the programme began with Fessenden playing Gounod's 'O, Holy Night' on the violin, followed by him singing and reciting from St Luke's Gospel. The first gramophone record to be broadcast came next, a recording of Handel's 'Largo'. The transmission ended with Fessenden wishing his listeners a happy Christmas. The audience for the broadcast turned out to be ships' operators within a five-mile radius. Fessenden's second broadcast, on New Year's Eve, in better atmospheric conditions, was received as far away as the West Indies.

    In the UK the first radio broadcast came in the following year – from the radio room of HMS *Andromeda*. It was initiated by Lieutenant Quentin Crauford RN and transmitted to other ships at Chatham. News of the broadcast was not made known, for the Admiralty saw the possibilities of radio in military use, in particular as aiding communication between submarines and shore and other vessels.

1907 First regular experimental broadcasts conducted by Lee De Forest's Radio Telephone Company from the Parker Building, New York. Two years later De Forest introduced his mother-in-law Harriet Stanton Black to listeners. She gave the world's first broadcast talk; her theme was women's suffrage.

    Lord Northcliffe purchases *The Times*.

    UK: foundation of National Union of Journalists (NUJ).

    First patent, in London, Berlin and St Petersburg of all-electric television cathode-ray tube receiver, by Russian Boris Rozing. On 9 May 1911 Rozing succeeded in transmitting by wireless over distance 'a distinct image … consisting of four luminous bands'.

1909 US: National Board of Censorship of Motion Pictures established.

1911 UK Copyright Act requires copies of all British publications to be supplied to the British Museum and to five other copyright libraries.

    First Hollywood studio, the Nestor Studio, opened on Sunset Boulevard by David Horsley.

1912 Foundation, initially as the *Herald*, of the *Daily Herald*.

1913   The British Board of Film Censors, formed in 1912 by the Kinematograph Manufacturers' Association, begins operation.

1914   Price of *The Times* reduced to one penny.

First full-length feature film in colour, *The World, the Flesh and the Devil*, shown to the trade in February, and opened at the Holborn Empire in April. Kinemacolor was a two-colour system. Gaumont Chronochrome (1914) produced three colours, but three-colour processing was costly and slow in development.

Technicolor successfully produced, in 1932, the Disney cartoon *Flowers and Trees*; while the first feature-length film in Technicolor was Rouben Mamoulian's *Becky Sharp*, released in 1935.

1914–18   First World War.

1915   UK: *Daily Express* bought by Max Aitken, Lord Beaverbrook, for £17,500.

1916   Film, *The Battle of the Somme* – first-ever war documentary.

Clydeside workers are supported in their refusal to make munitions by the Labour paper *Forward*. It is suppressed.

1918   UK: first film society, the Stoll Picture Theatre Club, opens with a presentation by Baroness Orczy of *The Laughing Cavalier*.

1919   UK: Arthur Mee founds the *Children's Newspaper*.

1920   The Marconi Company begins radio transmission from its Chelmsford works on 19 January. On 15 June Dame Nellie Melba gives a 30-minute recital, from Chelmsford, sponsored by Lord Northcliffe. Her fee was £1000. In November transmissions from Chelmsford were suspended on the grounds that they interfered with radio communication to aircraft and ships. Broadcasts resumed from Marconi's Station 2MT at Writtle, February 1922. 2MT was the first regular broadcasting station in the UK.

1922   Marconi's new station 2LO broadcasts from Marconi House in the Strand, London. Along with three other radio stations, 2LO was merged into what was to become the British Broadcasting Company. Broadcasting from Writtle remained independent until it closed down on 17 January 1923. The first BBC programme was broadcast on 14 November 1922 from 2LO – a news bulletin put out at 6pm.

First play on radio, *The Wolf* by Eugene Walter, is broadcast by WGY Schenectady of New York, 3 August. In the UK *Cyrano de Bergerac* was presented by engineering staff at Marconi's experimental station 2MT Writtle, 17 October. The first play specially written for radio was Phyllis M. Twigg's *The Truth about Father Christmas*, a children's story, broadcast by the BBC, 24 December.

First programme of sound-on-film production at Berlin's Alhambra cinema using the Tri-Ergon process developed by Joseph Engl, Joseph Massolle and Hans Voght. In the US Lee De Forest's Phonofilm process is demonstrated to the first paying audience, at the Rialto Theater in New York in April 1923.

1924   UK: Sykes Committee Report on Broadcasting, followed in 1925 with the setting up of the Crawford Committee from which emerged the prime principles governing broadcasting in the

UK until the coming of commercial TV: monopoly, funding by licence, administration by an independent public corporation.

Publication in the *Daily Mail* of the notorious Zinoviev Letter, a fake, now considered to have emanated from the UK's own secret service, MI6.

Felix the Cat becomes the first film character to be merchandized. Licences issued on behalf of Felix's creator Pat Sullivan for Felix to 'feature' on packaging and later as a soft toy.

1925   Using a mechanical scanner for transmitting and receiving, Scotsman John Logie Baird (with others) creates the first television pictures on 30 October. Baird transmitted an image with gradations of light and shade using a primitive amalgam of parts, including an empty biscuit box for the lamphouse. For test purposes a dummy's head was used, to be replaced shortly afterwards by 15-year-old office boy William Taynton, who consented to be the first star of TV for the fee of half a crown.

Baird demonstrated his invention to the press on 7 January 1926, and gave a public demonstration on 27 January for members of the Royal Institution. Baird's mechanical system was soon to be overtaken by electronic TV transmission, first developed in Los Angeles by Philo T. Farnsworth in July 1929, though a more practical system developed by Russian-born Vladimir Zworykin of Westinghouse showed the way ahead. All modern TV systems derive from Zworykin's Kinescope and the Ionoscope, the camera tube he developed in 1933.

Lionel Guest and H.O. Merriman of London apply their electrical recording process to record the burial service of the Unknown Warrior at Westminster Abbey, proving that it was possible to substitute a microphone for the studio horn, thus location recording was born. The process was not pursued commercially, but location recording was set in progress in both the US and the UK in the same year. The all-electric record player, with loudspeaker amplification instead of the usual horn, was the Brunswick Panatrope, made by the Brunswick Company of Iowa. This year also saw the introduction of the automatic record-changer, built by 20-year-old Eric Waterworth of Hobart, Tasmania.

First issue of the *New Yorker*.

BBC broadcast first full-length play for radio, Reginald Berkeley's *The White Chateau*, 11 November.

1927   *The Jazz Singer*, using the Vitaphone synchronized disc system, opens at the Warner Theater on Broadway, 6 October. Directed by Alan Crosland and starring Al Jolson, the film is generally acknowledged to have inaugurated the age of sound cinema and marked the death knell for silent movies. There are only two talking sequences in the film and 281 words spoken, but the reception the film received on both sides of the Atlantic was phenomenal.

The Lights of New York, also from Warner Bros, was the first all-talking feature film. It was premiered at New York's Strand Theater, 6 July 1928. Fox Movietone's *In Old Arizona*, a western directed by Raoul Walsh, screened in December 1928 in Los Angeles, was the first all-talking sound-on-film feature. The first all-talking colour film was Warner Bros' *On With the Show*, screened at New York's Wintergardens, 1929.

1928   On 9 February John Logie Baird makes the first international TV transmission, sending 30-line images of his own face from London by land line to the transmitting station G2KZ at Coulsdon, Surrey, and then across the Atlantic to a receiving set manned by his assistant, Ben Clapp, at Hartsdale, New York State. On 3 July Baird became the first to transmit television in colour. Employing a Nikow scanning-disc with red, blue and green filters he screened red and blue scarves, a lighted cigarette and red roses. Baird was to be the first to demonstrate high-definition colour – at the Dominion Theatre, London, on 4 February 1938.

Walt Disney releases *Steam Boat Willie*, the first animated film using synchronous sound.

1929   Radar invented, by Scotsman Robert Watson-Watt.

              UK: first issue of the Communist *Daily Worker*.

1931   Experiments in electronic high-definition TV transmission are carried out by an EMI research team at Hayes, Middlesex, under the direction of Russian-born Isaac Shoenberg. The EMI system was demonstrated to the BBC in the following year – a film of the Changing of the Guard at Buckingham Palace, viewed on a 130-line cathode ray receiver with a five-inch square screen.

              RCA Victor launches the 33⅓rpm long-playing record. The first recording was of Beethoven's Fifth Symphony. However, the radiograms required to play the long-player were expensive in a time of acute recession and the venture was not a success. The LP did not come into its own until 1949 when Columbia issued microgroove records developed by Peter Goldmark – vinylite discs with a playing time of 23 minutes per side, and 224–300 grooves to the inch.

1932   Stereophonic cinema sound patented by French film-makers Abel Gance and André Debrie. Gance's eight-hour silent 1927 epic *Napoléon* was re-edited with added dialogue and sound-effects, and screened at the Paramount Cinema, Paris, in 1935. Warner Bros' *House of Wax* (1953) was the first feature film with complete stereo sound.

              The first stereophonic disc recordings are made by Arthur Keller of the Bell Telephone Laboratories. Made on wax masters at 78rpm, they were not produced commercially but were demonstrated at the Chicago World's Fair, 1933. The first stereo discs to be manufactured for sale were produced by Emory Cork of Stamford, US, in 1957.

1933   Chief of the German Navy's Signals Research Department, Dr Rudoph Kühnold produces the first working radar system. Radar in the UK was the brainchild of Robert Watson-Watt, superintendent of the radio research laboratory at Ditton Park. Experiments with radar in February 1935 led to the establishment of a number of air-defence radar stations which were to prove critical in the Second World War (1939–45).

1934   The Emitron electronic camera is an advance on the system developed by Shoenberg in 1931. In the following year Shoenberg inaugurated the 405-line system and on 1 November 1936 the EMI–Marconi system became standard as the BBC television service began operation from Alexandra Palace.

1935   Berlin: first television mobile unit comes into operation, employed at the opening of the Berlin TV station of the Reichs Rundfunk, 22 March. The first mobile units in the UK, designed by T.C. Macnamara, were used in the BBC's first major outside broadcast, of the Coronation, May 1937.

1936   First full-length animated film, *Snow White and the Seven Dwarfs* from the Disney Studios.

1938   Russian hypnotist, sculptor and journalist Lazlo Biró constructed a prototype ball-point pen with quick-drying ink. Having acquired British rights, Biró began manufacture in a disused

RAF hangar in 1944. In 1953 Baron Bic, in France, introduced the first 'throwaway' ball-point. In the UK, priced at 1 shilling, sales during 1959 totalled 53m.

1939–45   Second World War.

1939   US: William C. Huebner introduces photosetting of type.

Premiere of *Gone with the Wind.*

1940   UK: statutory newsprint rationing introduced; ended 1956.

1941   Release of Orson Welles' film masterpiece *Citizen Kane*, based on the life and lifestyle of American media baron William Randoph Hearst.

USSR: Tamara Lobova becomes first woman to shoot a feature film, *Suvarov*, released in January.

John Logie Baird demonstrates 3-D television in colour, a 500-line system, 18 December, at Sydenham.

The Communist *Daily Worker* is suppressed.

1944   Automatic digital computer, by American Howard Aiken, is followed in the next year by the electronic computer invented in the US by J. Presper Eckert and John W. Mauchly.

1945   BBC launches the Light Programme, now Radio 2, and, the following year, the Third Programme, now Radio 3.

1946   The Southwestern Bell Telephone Company of St Louis, US, offers the first commercial car phone service.

1947   Polaroid camera, by Edwin Land, US.

Soviet Union: first 3-D colour feature film, *Robinson Crusoe*, directed by A.N. Andreyevsky. Special spectacles were not required.

US: Private Commission on Freedom of the Press, founded by publisher Henry Luce and chaired by the chancellor of the University of Chicago, Robert Hutchens, to 'examine areas and circumstances under which the press of the United States is succeeding or failing; to discover where freedom of expression is or is not limited, whether by government censorship, pressure from readers or advertisers or the unwisdom of its proprietors or the timidity of its management'. The Commission report broached, formally for the first time, the concept of *social responsibility* and listed criteria for the fulfilment of those critena.

1947–9   First UK Royal Commission on the Press – the Ross Commission.

1948   The Universal Declaration of Human Rights is adopted by the United Nations Assembly in Paris, 10 December.

NBC of America screens first TV western series, *Hopalong Cassidy*, starring Bill Boyd.

Bell Telephone Company scientists John Bardeen, Walter Brattain and William Shockley introduce the first transistor.

1949   Xerography invented by Chester Carlson, US, the same year as Peter Goldmark of the US introduces the first microgroove long-playing record.

          CBS launches first TV thriller series, *Suspense.*

1950   Yoshiro Nakamats of the Imperial University, Tokyo, develops the floppy disk.

1952   First video recorder demonstration conducted in the US by John Mullin and Wayne Johnson at the Bing Crosby Enterprise laboratories in Beverly Hills, California, 11 November. A colour video was demonstrated by the same company in September of the following year. Neither was developed commercially. Ampex was the first to go into production, its initial production model being acquired by CBS.

          In the UK the BBC's VERA came into operation in April 1958 with a recording of *Panorama.* Sony brought out a transistorized video recorder in 1961, while the first domestic video recorder, also from Sony, was launched in the US in July 1965. It was not until 1972 that Sony launched, in Japan, its first video cassette recorder.

          In Europe Philips introduced the first domestic video cassette recorder in 1974. The VHS format was introduced in 1976 by JVC of Japan; and in the same year JVC produced the first camcorders for amateur use.

1953   Inauguration of the British Press Council.

          BBC demonstrates colour TV. An outside broadcast of the Coronation procession was relayed by closed circuit at Great Ormond Street Hospital for Sick Children.

          The first movie in Cinemascope, 20th Century Fox's *The Robe*, is premiered at Grauman's Chinese Theater, Hollywood, and in the same month, September, *This is Cinerama* opened in New York.

1954   In the UK in July, the Television Bill is given royal assent, creating the Independent Television Authority. Commercial TV began broadcasting in Britain in September 1955.

          Eurovision is inaugurated on 6 June when TV services in eight European countries are linked together with a 4000-mile chain of relays. The first programme to be screened was the *Festival of Flowers* from Montreux, Switzerland.

1955–6   First daily TV soap broadcast in Britain – *Sixpenny Corner*, running for 15 minutes daily. It failed even though it was transferred by ITV to an evening slot.

1959   The *Manchester Guardian* becomes the *Guardian.*

1960   Bell Telephone's Touch-Tone telephone is successfully tested and becomes commercially available in 1963.

          ITV's *Coronation Street* opens its record-breaking run.

          The American Telephone & Telegraph Company makes the first transatlantic satellite transmission on 11 July, from Andover, Maine, to Goonhilly Downs, Cornwall, via Telstar.

          America launches first communications satellite, Echo 1.

          UK: death of the *News Chronicle*; first issue of the *Sunday Telegraph.*

1962 UK: Pilkington Committee Report on Broadcasting and the Shawcross Commission Report on the Press.

    First nights on UK TV for *Z-Cars*, *Steptoe and Son* and the satirical series *That Was The Week That Was*. In the following year, *Dr Who* and *World in Action*.

1963 Founding of International Publishing Corporation (IPC); following year, IPC launches the *Sun*, replacing the *Daily Herald*.

    UK: the BBC ends its ban on the mention of religion, politics, royalty or sex in comedy programmes.

    University of Michigan scientists Emmett Leith and Juris Upatnicks develop the first hologram.

1964 BBC launches new channel, BBC2, in April.

    UK starters: *Match of the Day* and *Crossroads*.

1965 Via the Early Bird satellite on 2 May, 300m viewers in nine countries sample the first transatlantic programme relay; 15 days later America's NBC was first with a colour transatlantic satellite programme transmission.

    Influential drama-documentary *Cathy Come Home*, about Britain's homeless, is broadcast by the BBC.

    Smoking advertisements are banned from UK television.

1966 Lord Thomson buys *The Times*.

    China: Chairman Mao launches the Cultural Revolution against 'reactionary bourgeois ideas in the sphere of academic work, education, art and theatre and publishing'.

1967 First colour TV broadcast in the UK, BBC2, 1 July.

    BBC Radio 1 is launched, 30 September.

    The Postmaster-General, Edward Short MP, opens Radio Leicester, the first local radio station in the UK.

1968 In UK first broadcast of comedy series *Dad's Army*.

1969 First commercially produced microprocessor developed by Edward Hoff of the Intel Corporation of California.

    Australian Rupert Murdoch buys the *Sun* and the *News of the World*.

    Denmark: film censorship is abolished.

    UK: York University launches first university radio station.

1972 US: first pre-recorded video tapes offered for hire by Sears, Roebuck. Pre-recorded tapes were not available in the UK until 1979, supplied initially by Intervision who acquired 200 film titles from United Artists for £250,000. By the end of the year they had franchised some 150 outlets.

Such was the immediate competition that Intervision soon went under despite the increase in the sales of VCRs and rental outlets.

The UK *Sunday Times* is banned on 17 November from publishing a series of articles on Thalidomide, a drug taken by expectant mothers and causing horrific deformities in babies.

Cable TV transmission starts in UK.

1973   London Broadcasting (LBC) is the first commercial radio station in mainland UK, on air 8 October.

1974   UK: BBC inaugurates Ceefax, the UK's first teletext service.

1975   Angela Rippon becomes first regular woman newsreader on British terrestrial television (BBC). ITN's *News at Ten* waited until 1978 before employing Anna Ford to front the news.

1977   UK: Annan Commission Report on Broadcasting and the McGregor Commission Report on the Press.

1978   UK: first series of the comprehensive school-set series *Grange Hill.*

         First video cassette recorder introduced in the UK.

         Japan: the Sony Walkman is launched.

1979   UK: Williams Committee Report on Obscenity and Film Censorship.

         First digital recording, by Decca, of a New Year's Day concert in Vienna; recorded live by the Vienna Philharmonic Orchestra and issued in April.

1980   The compact disc (CD), developed by Philips over several years, is demonstrated at the Salzburg Festival in April. By agreement with Philips, the Japanese firm Sony launched the first CD in 1982. With a playing time of 75 minutes, the CD used a grooveless miniature 12cm disc using a laser beam to read digitally encoded information.

         MacBride Commission Report for UNESCO.

         UK: ITV documentary *Death of a Princess* causes offence to the government of Saudi Arabia; millions of pounds in trade orders are lost as a result. The British government apologizes to the Saudis, 22 April.

1981   UK: Australian media baron Rupert Murdoch acquires the British newspapers, *The Times* and *The Sunday Times*, having been exempted from a monopolies enquiry by the Conservative government, led by Margaret Thatcher.

1982   UK: Hunt Committee on Cable Expansion and Broadcasting Policy.

         UK: Channel 4 television begins transmission.

1983   Breakfast TV starts on the BBC; the CD player, the pocket TV and the first cordless telephone are introduced to the UK.

1984   UK: first satellite TV channel – Rupert Murdoch's Sky – begins transmission, 16 January.

Civil servant Clive Ponting is acquitted by a jury of breaking the Official Secrets Act. His revelation to the press of details concerning the British sinking of the Argentine battleship *The Belgrano* were justified in court as being in the public interest. Later the Act was redrafted to exclude public interest as a defence. The advent of a Labour government has not led to the return of the public interest clause.

Robert Maxwell takes over the *Daily Mirror* group.

1985   Rupert Murdoch buys American film company 20th Century Fox.

Panasonic of Japan introduces to the UK the first VHS camcorder in January, and in May Sony launches the digital video recorder.

British Board of Film Censors issues age classification for videos, following the passing of the Video Recordings Act.

1986   Eddy Shah's *Today* newspaper, published in the UK, is the first to use on-the-run colour. Launched on 4 March, the 44-page paper carried 16 pages in colour.

Australian TV soap *Neighbours* is introduced to the UK on the BBC.

USSR: Mikhail Gorbachev announces new policy of Glasnost, 'openness'.

Wapping, London: thousands of print workers picket Murdoch's new premises, protesting about computerization and the loss of jobs.

Czechoslovakia: the Jazz Union is closed down for urging the freedom of the arts.

1987   Sydney, Australia, September: British government is rebuffed in its courtroom appeal against the decision to permit the publication of Peter Wright's *Spycatcher*.

1988   The first transatlantic optical-fibre cable is laid, costing £220m, between the US and UK/France, able to carry simultaneously 40,000 telephone calls.

1989   The Iron Curtain that divided eastern European nations – Poland, Hungary, Czechoslovakia and East Germany, etc. – from the West, is drawn aside. The trades union Solidarity is permitted to contest elections in Poland; in Hungary border troops tear down the barbed-wire frontier with Austria. Most significantly, the Berlin Wall is dismantled. However, in June, freedom protests in Beijing are crushed in Tiananmen Square. The rest of the world watches events on TV.

In Iran, the Ayatollah Khomeini condemns as blasphemous the novel *The Satanic Verses* by British writer Salman Rushdie and issues a *fatwa*, or edict, calling on all Muslims to strike down the offender. Despite worldwide protests, the death sentence remained active until September 1998 when the government of Iran distanced itself from, without rescinding, the Khomeini edict.

Tim Berners-Lee, British inventor of the Internet, first scrawls the following on a blackboard: w.w.w.

1990   UK: Broadcasting Act separates control of commercial television (ITC, Independent Television Commission) and radio (the Radio Authority).

The *Northern Echo*, edited in Darlington, becomes the first UK newspaper on CD-ROM.

The first tapeless answering machine, the ADAM (All-Digital Answering Machine), storing messages on a silicon chip, launched in the US by PhoneMate.

Iraq: Farzad Barzoft, journalist on the UK *Observer*, is executed in Baghdad after 'confessing' to spying.

UK: Calcutt Committee reports on its deliberations concerning 'a wide public aversion to newspaper intrusion', and recommends 'reform by self-regulation' and a Code of Practice. The Press Complaints Commission emerged from Calcutt recommendations.

1991   Robert Maxwell dies in a drowning accident.

1992   Los Angeles: street riots after screening of police beating up black motorist Rodney King.

UK: first land-based national commercial radio station – Classic FM – launched 7 September.

Canada: Government Bill C-128 bans the depiction of under-18s engaging in any form of 'explicit sexual activity', including kissing.

1993   UK: carried via London Interconnect cable network, the first black TV service – Identity TV – begins, 13 July, with estimated audience of 150,000, and on 1 September BSkyB launches first women's TV channel.

Transmitting from coaches driving round London, the BBC begins first experiments in DAB (Digital Audio Broadcasting).

1994   BBC converts generalist service, Radio 5, which featured programmes for young listeners, to Radio 5 Live, dedicated to sports, news and chat.

1998   UK: Sky TV launches digital television service, 1 October.

1999   A jury in Oregon, US, fines anti-abortionist campaigners for publishing on their website a 'wanted' list of abortion doctors, their clinics and addresses, seeing it as a thinly veiled death threat.

During the war for Kosovo, NATO bombers target TV stations in Serbia's capital, Belgrade.

UK: Greg Dyke is appointed new director-general of the BBC in succession to Sir John Birt.

2000   UK: Regulation of Investigatory Powers Act (RIPA), extending official surveillance to Internet communication.

US: merger of the world's biggest media giant, Time Warner, with AOL (America On Line).

Launch of Women's Enews, Internet news service.

Ukraine: campaigning journalist Georgi Gongadze abducted, murdered and beheaded, allegedly with the connivance of government authorities.

2001   11 September: TV viewers across the world witness the terrorist destruction of the Twin Towers of New York's World Trade Center.

Italy: Silvio Berlusconi, media magnate, becomes Italy's prime minister for the second time.

2002   Labour government issues Communications Bill proposing the loosening of broadcasting regulations and abandoning rules concerning cross-media ownership. With modifications, becomes Act of Parliament, 2003.

ITV Digital services go bust, but a consortium led by the BBC steps in to offer over 20 digital channels (Freeview). New digital services from the BBC: CBBC (for children, aged 6–13), CBeebies (for under-6s) BBC4 (art, history, current affairs), BBC3 (drama, entertainment, music). At the same time, BBC Radio goes digital (BBC Digital, Asian Network, 6Music, 1Xtra, 5 Live Sports Extra and BBC7 (comedy, drama and children's programmes)).

China: analysts estimate that the state employs 30,000 people to monitor and control information.

Gulf Cooperation Council, meeting in Oman, warns satellite TV station al-Jazeera to make programmes 'more respectful'.

Poland: Church-run Radio Maryja is shut down on the orders of the Catholic primate, Cardinal Josef Glemp.

US: Iranian film-maker Abbas Kiarostami is denied a visa permitting him to enter the country at the invitation of the New York Film Festival to lecture at Harvard University.

UK: David Shayler, former MI5 officer, is jailed for six months for breaking the Official Secrets Act by leaking documents concerning alleged malpractice in the UK secret service.

Announcement of plans for a £2.6bn merger between Granada (seven ITV licences) and Carlton Communications (five ITV licences), subject to approval by the UK Office of Fair Trading. The merger leaves only three independent UK franchises – Grampian, Scottish and Ulster TV.

Report on human rights in 50 countries by the Electronic Privacy Information Center and Privacy International declares that post-11 September 2001 'many new anti-terrorist laws adopted by national governments ... threaten political freedom'.

2003   Federal Communications Commission (US) initiates major shift towards loosening regulations concerning the delivery of TV and radio news, considering that many in-place rules are 'antiquated' – that is, standing in the way of further media mergers.

Global publics find their voice in protesting against war in Iraq, but million-strong marches do not prevent US and UK forces going into battle despite the failure to obtain a United Nations mandate for military action.

Natalie Maines, lead singer of the Dixie Chicks, tells fans in London that the prospect of the invasion of Iraq makes her ashamed to be from the same state as President Bush. Radio stations part of the conglomerate Clear Channel Communications (which had offered financial sponsorship and on-air promotion for pro-war 'Rallies for America') pull the Dixie Chicks from their playlists. Clear Channel suspends two DJs in Colorado Springs for defying the ban. Cumulus Media, owning 262 radio stations, bans the Dixie Chicks from all its country stations.

UK: merger between independent television broadcasters Carlton and Granada.

UK: 29 December, the responsibilities of the Broadcasting Standards Commission (BSC), the Independent Television Commission (ITC), the Office of Telecommunications (Oftel), the

Radio Authority and the Radiocommunications Agency pass to the new regulatory body, the Office of Communications (Ofcom).

During 2003, 42 journalists were killed worldwide, 766 arrested, 1460 physically attacked or threatened and 501 media censored, according to Reporters Without Borders (Reporters Sans Frontières).

2004   Hutton Report, UK, examines the circumstances surrounding the alleged suicide of government weapons expert Dr David Kelly, who was the source of an early-morning BBC radio report by Andrew Gilligan suggesting government claims that Iraq possessed weapons of mass destruction had been exaggerated. The report, exonerating the government of any blame in the 'outing' of Kelly, resulted in the resignation of the Chairman of the BBC, Gavyn Davies, the Director General, Greg Dyke, and Gilligan.

Rupert Murdoch's BSkyB wins contract, in face of competition from Independent Television News (ITN), to supply news to UK's Channel 5 (five).

Butler Report subjects government claims concerning weapons of mass destruction (WMD), and the performance of the security services in monitoring the true situation in Iraq, to highly critical scrutiny. However, finds no one intentionally to blame for claims that proved unfounded.

Phillis Review of Government Communications.

Russia: journalist Anna Politkovskaya is poisoned on her way to cover the school massacre in Beslan.

UK: Piers Morgan, editor of the tabloid newspaper the *Daily Mirror*, resigns following the publication of pictures – later declared fake – purporting to show British soldiers ill-treating Iraqi civilians.

US: the Disney company blocks distribution of Michael Moore's documentary, *Fahrenheit 9/11* exposing links between American President George W. Bush and prominent Saudi-Arabian families, including that of Osama bin Laden.

14th Press Freedom Day. Reporters Without Borders (Reporters Sans Frontières) announce that ten journalists and media assistants were killed between January and May, 431 journalists arrested worldwide, 366 physically attacked or threatened and 178 media censored. In 22 countries, 133 journalists are imprisoned, including 73 'cyber-dissidents', 61 in China.

Birmingham, UK: the depiction of a rape scene in a Sikh temple sparks a riot outside the city Repertory Theatre in protest at Gunpreet Kaur Bhatti's play, *Behzti* (Dishonour). Despite the play being written by a Sikh (or perhaps in a way *because* it was written by one of the faith) the action against the play – 400 protestors battling with riot police – leads to its closure. The playwright, Ms Bhatti, is believed to have received death threats.

Launch in the UK of Spinwatch, a collaborative venture between practising investigative journalists and academics with the aim of countering government and corporate 'spin'.

2005   Freedom of Information Act (UK) comes into force.

Somalia: BBC correspondent Kate Peyton is fatally wounded on her way to interview the speaker of the country's transitional parliament. According to Reporters Without Borders

(Reporters Sans Frontières), 38 of the 636 journalists killed since 1992 have been women. In the same month, journalist Raeda Mohammed Wageh Wassan was found dead in Mosul, northern Iraq, after being kidnapped by masked men.

In the run-up to the UK General Election in May, the Association of Gypsy Women releases a statement protesting at laws that 'are being used to target Gypsies and Travellers, with the open encouragement of the popular press': 'We categorically reject the terrifying image of Gypsies that is being promoted by the *Daily Mail*, *Sun* and *Daily Express*. We call on the British Press Council to intervene.'

UK: third reading of bill to ban incitement to religious hatred passes through the House of Commons.

New York Times journalist Judith Miller imprisoned for refusing to declare a source; spends 85 days behind bars for breach of a law forbidding the revealing of the names of secret service (CIA) agents.

Al-Jazeera journalist Taysir Alouni is jailed for seven years by a Spanish court after being found guilty of collaboration with the terrorist group, al-Qaeda.

Rania-al-Baz, a TV announcer with Saudi-Arabian TV, in order to publicize domestic violence in her country, publishes pictures of her disfigured face after being beaten up by her husband. To avoid reprisals, she flees to France.

UK: Channel 4 television launches new 'adult entertainment' channel, More4.

Frankfurt, Germany: first international Wikimania conference.

Six students at the University of Lancaster are charged by the University authorities with aggravated trespass after protesting against a 'corporate venturing' event in the University's George Fox building; press comments link the action with the New Labour government's anti-terrorism bill passing through Parliament.

The same unease concerning terrorism and legislation aimed at stifling it was highlighted during the annual Labour Party conference in Brighton in October: an elderly party member, Walter Wolfgang, once a refugee from Hitler's Germany, was forcibly ejected from the conference hall for shouting 'Rubbish!' during a speech by Foreign Secretary Jack Straw justifying the Iraq War. Mr Wolfgang, 57 years a party member, was held by the police under the Prevention of Terrorism Act and later released, the event forcing apologies from Labour ministers and causing a press furore.

The BBC announces plans to open new World Service broadcasting channel directed to the Arab region, and in competition with the 24-hour Arabic news channel, al-Jazeera.

China: 400m viewers – the largest TV audience in history – tune in to see 21-year-old Li Yuchun, without make-up, with spiky hair, singing songs aggressively, including songs written for men, win the Mongolian Cow Sour Yogurt Supergirl Concert award. Within days the shopping malls of Shanghai were heaving with Li Yuchun mugs, keyrings and T-shirts. A concert sponsored by the Better Posture Equipment Company in the city's largest, 39,000-seater stadium, was sold out in hours.

The number of UK households with digital TV has grown from 15.5 per cent in 2000 to 61.9 per cent in 2005.

Turkey: best-selling author Orhan Pamuk faces trial for 'denigrating the Turkish identity' for speaking out concerning the Armenian genocide of 1915, when almost 1m Armenians were killed in the Ottoman Empire.

British playwright, poet, actor, scriptwriter and political protester Harold Pinter (b. 1930), author of *The Birthday Party*, *The Caretaker*, *The Dumb Waiter* and *The Homecoming*, is awarded the Nobel Prize for Literature.

Following harassment by the authorities in Uzbekistan, the BBC closes its World Service operation.

2006   US search engine Google resists request by American Department of Justice to provide a list of every website address operating through Google for June and July 2005; but then announces net link with China, offering a service available to 110m online users. This agreement is subject to Google's willingness to operate as a filter – a censor – of information exchange. In short, Google subscribes to the Great Firewall of China, restricting access to many western websites and blocking words such as 'freedom' and names such as 'Tiananmen Square'.

In a US Congress House international relations committee meeting Yahoo!, Cisco Systems, Microsoft and Google are accused of collusion with a repressive regime (China).

Following publication in Danish and Norwegian newspapers of cartoons satirizing the prophet Mohammed, widespread Muslim protests occur across the Arab world, with the Danish and Norwegian embassies in Damascus being burnt to the ground. Crowds of protestors also burn Danish flags in several other countries. Violent demonstrations take place in Lebanon and Afghanistan. In Jordan, two newspaper editors who published the cartoons are charged with offences.

UK: House of Commons votes to reinstate the 'glorification of terrorism' clause in new anti-terrorism legislation; this shortly following on from Parliament's assent to New Labour plans to introduce ID cards for British citizens.

The Mexican government admits that it staged a kidnap and rescue operation as proof that it is winning the war on organized crime.

Australia: *Dateline*, current affairs programme of the Special Broadcasting Service, publishes images, previously unseen by the public, of abuse of Iraqi prisoners by American military personnel at the Abu Ghraib jail.

Al-Jazeera, the Arab news station, begins news service in English. British broadcaster Sir David Frost is contracted to front a one-hour daily programme.

UK: Government White Paper announces that the BBC licence will be extended to 2016. The governors will be replaced by a trust with sovereign control of the corporation, leaving responsibility for the day-to-day running of the BBC to an executive board. The White Paper urges that entertainment be placed at the heart of the Corporation's broadcasting mission.